MICROSOFT

WORD & EXCEL 2021

FOR BEGINNERS & POWER USERS

The Concise Microsoft Office Word and Excel 2021
A-Z Mastery Guide for All Users

Tech Demystified

ISBN: 9798749912647

CONTENTS

INTRODUCTION

Microsoft Office Suite is the "come to stay" version of Word processor that can be periodically updated without any threat of software crash or unauthorized version. Office 365 has evolved and transformed to stay relevant in today's business world but despite this, many businesses still use it exclusively for Microsoft Word and Excel only. If you find yourself looking at the other apps and features and wondering what they do, keep reading this guide to Office 365 till the end.

The most commonly used Office 365 apps include Word, Excel, PowerPoint, and Outlook. These applications are essential for creating documents, spreadsheets, presentations, and communicating both internally and externally but these are not all Office 365 entails, other apps like SharePoint, Access, etc. are also included in the Office 365 suite. This user guide has been specially prepared to teach you the in and out of these powerful programs in Office 365 with *Word and Excel* being the specificity. This is a guide that does not only explain "WHAT" (theoretical application), but also "HOW" (practical application). I am excited because you have just made the right choice.

OVERVIEW OF OFFICE 365

Introduction to Office 365

In the past, Microsoft Office was always sold as box software, so when you buy your new computer, you have the options of buying Office whether Microsoft Office 2007, 2010, 2013, 2016 or other subsequent versions. You could pay $300USD to $500USD depending on the version you request for, and you will get the software on your machine which would be installed into your PC as infinity software, meaning you will pay once and never pay again for the software, this is how Microsoft deals with its previous products for very long time.

In the past years, many companies have started switching over to a subscription model of selling software such as Adobe, Photoshop, and other subscription software; you can't just buy them completely anymore. You purchase a subscription and through that subscription, you always get the latest updated and upgraded version of any other program you subscribe for. So, with Microsoft, they sell box software which also leads to an upgrade in its service rendering for a quick solution to unexpected issues, flexible storage space, and secured information with other benefits only available to its subscribed users.

What is Office 365 Cloud Service?

Office 365 is a collection of different cloud applications which serve different purposes but similar in features. It is important to note that Office 365 has been synchronized as Microsoft 365 which comes with many packages such as:

- **Word:** It is a text editor specifically designed to process text, image, shapes & other features without the need to manually install it on your PC.
- **PowerPoint:** It is the software majorly constructed for presentation purposes.
- **Excel:** This is a calculation framed software used to solve the complexity of statistics, Mathematics, and plotting of graphs with other features in a flexible way.
- **Outlook:** Outlook is an email that is designed to receive incoming messages and also send outgoing messages.

- **OneDrive**: This is an online storage space specifically designed for all Microsoft users to store personal data which can be accessed anywhere around the world. It also comes with a link privilege to share files and other items stored on it.
- **OneNote:** OneNote is a note-taking software
- **To Do:** It is a task management utility that is designed to take your regular activities schedule.
- **Family Safety:** This is also another feature of Microsoft that gives the privilege to monitor your family activities such as setting screen time limits, filtering of content, activities report, and lots more to make sure family members are safe while using the internet with Microsoft.
- **Calendar:** It is used to schedule and share meetings and event times. One can automatically get reminders.
- **Skype:** This is a meeting software which is designed to make video and voice call, chat and share file or screen if need be.

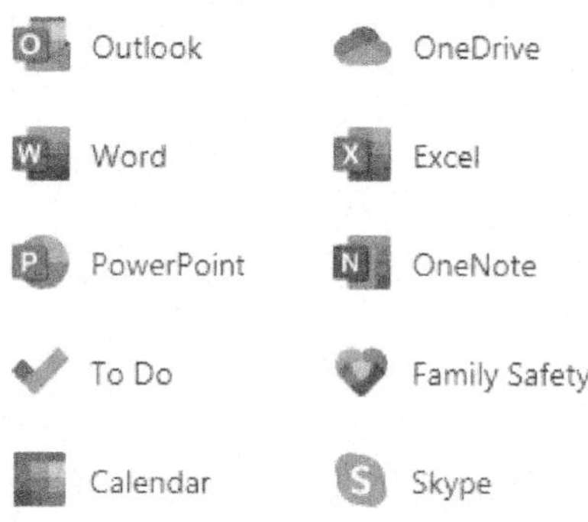

Difference between Office 365 & Microsoft 365

Office 365 is a cloud-based software collection of applications such as Word, Excel, PowerPoint, and more. Microsoft 365 is a bundle of existing services under one license that includes Office 365 with several other services including Windows 10 Enterprise plus Security tools. Sooner or later, Microsoft will be branding its cloud-based productivity suite, Office 365, as Microsoft 365. This amendment in the naming resolution reflects Microsoft's strategy to convert all its products & services under one common name to avoid any confusion among its users by bringing everything under one umbrella.

Types of Microsoft Office 365 Suite

For every Microsoft product and service, there is always an avenue for multiple choice for users. Microsoft Office 365 suite is divided into two categories:

Microsoft Office 365 Subscription Plans	Description
Home Plans Family Personal	Microsoft 365 **Family** costs $95USD to $100USD per year for 2 to 6 people with 1 Terabyte (TB) storage per person. Microsoft 365 **Personal** costs $60USD to $65USD. Only per year package is available for 1 person with 1 Terabyte (TB) storage Both plans give access to Microsoft Office applications such as Word, Excel, PowerPoint, OneDrive, 60mins Skype per month, and more.
Business Plans Business Basic Business Standard Business Premium Apps for business	Microsoft 365 **Business Basic** costs $5 per month with access to Office suite packages Microsoft 365 **Business Standard** costs $12.50 per month with access to Office suite packages Microsoft 365 **Business Premium** costs $20USD user per month with access to Office suite packages Microsoft 365 **Apps for Business** costs $8.25USD per month. It is best for businesses that need easy remote solutions, with Microsoft Teams, secured cloud storage, and Office Online. The business plan includes a 300-user limit. Packages are a little different from one another depending on your need.
Enterprise Plans Enterprise 3 Enterprise 5 Firstline 3	Microsoft 365 E3 costs $32USD per month Microsoft 365 E5 price is not fixed Microsoft 365 F3 costs $8USD per month

Apps for Enterprise	Enterprise plan includes unlimited user features. All these prices might vary depending on your country's currency and Microsoft update of other features which might affect the price.

Note

i. **Microsoft 365 for home plans:** are for family usage which gives room for monitoring of family members' activities for the sake of children.
ii. **Microsoft 365 for business plans:** are mainly for organizational usage. It is designed to suit office performances and is also used to secure remote work.
iii. **Microsoft 365 for enterprise plans:** This is similar to the business plan but different in some aspects, enterprise plan gives the privilege

Why should I use Office 365 over previous versions?

It is important to note that the world at large is moving fast beyond human imagination, just as we have our daily experience so also is the advancement of technology moving rapidly.

Over time, Microsoft has found it a bit difficult to release an update on the purchased version since all previous versions of Suite majorly work offline; auto-update will be difficult or impossible to occur to them all from Office 2007, Office 2010, Office 2013, Office 2016 to Office 2019. Microsoft users find it a waste of time to update since everything is working perfectly, which led to the latest version which is online-based known as Office 365. It's a cloud service that works directly from the Microsoft database for security and monitoring purposes. Very soon application installation won't relent any longer due to the rate of technology advancement daily.

Becoming a Microsoft User

Many people find it difficult to create an account with Microsoft, which without an account you can't enjoy the limitless benefits of Microsoft features. Below are steps on how to go about it

- Go to your browser search for **"Microsoft office 365",** make sure it is Microsoft link then click on **"Official Microsoft 365® Site - Formerly Office 365®"**

- You will be brought into the Microsoft website, below is a link to **"Sign in",** click on it or you can also locate an image icon at your top right-hand side, you can also click on it

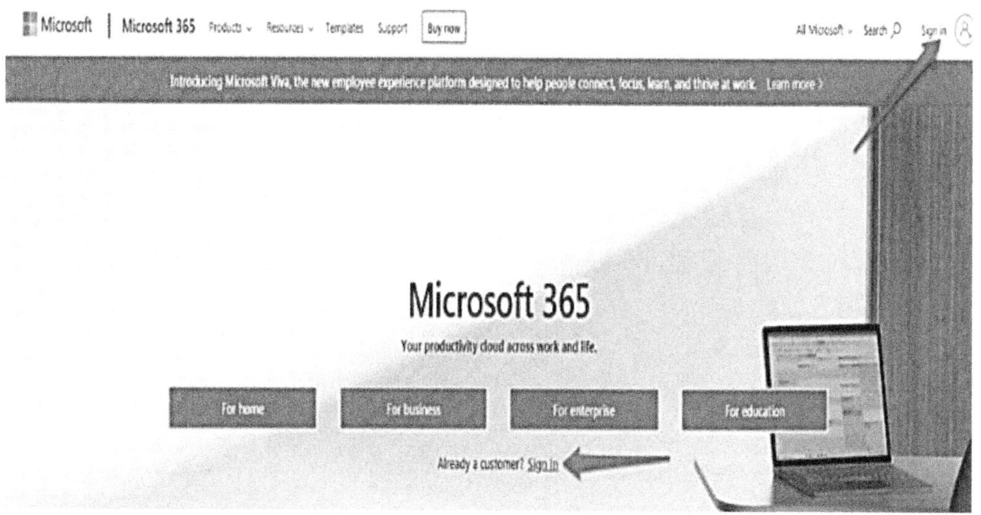

- Or you can directly type Microsoft website into your browser www.microsoft.com. Once the Microsoft website is done loading, look at your right-hand side you will see **an image icon,** click on it to create your user account

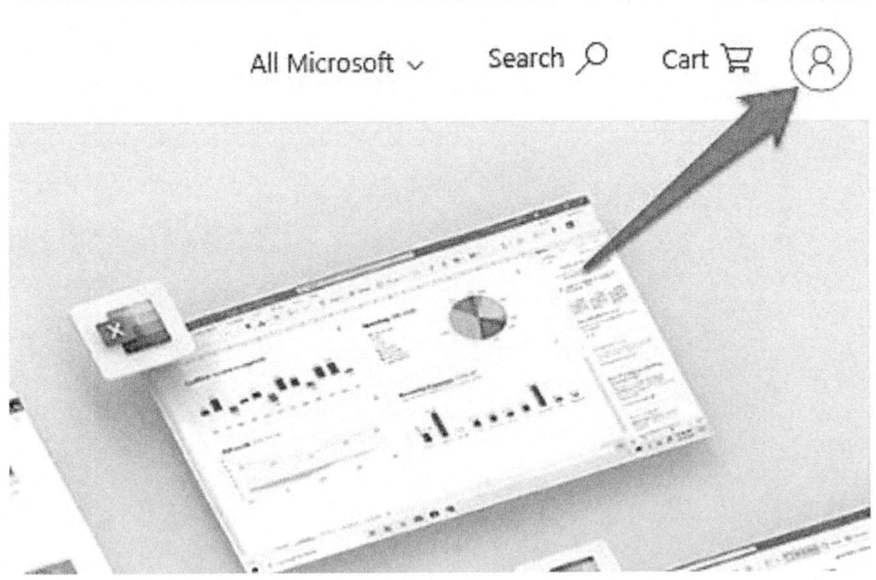

- You will be brought here, simply enter your existing Microsoft account. If you don't have one click on **"Create One".**

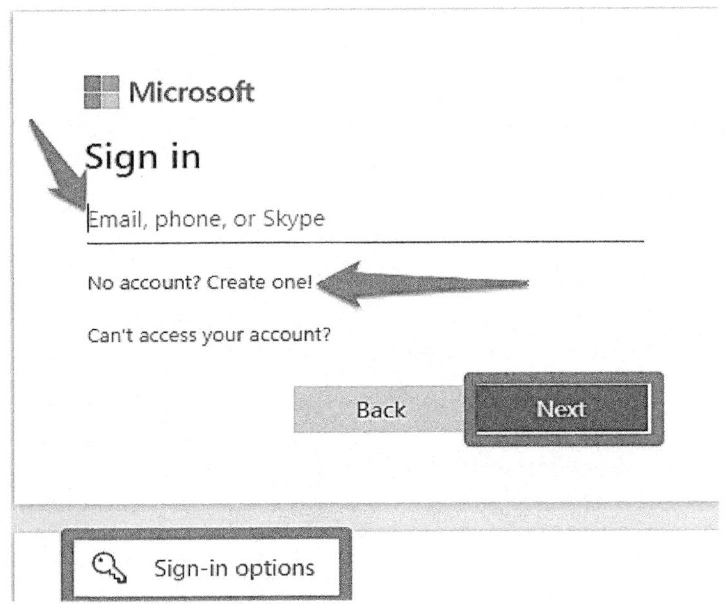

- In case you can't access your account, click on **"Can't access your account"** below create one, a dialog box will appear notifying you that your Windows 10 operating system will receive a security key that will give you access

Microsoft
← bamideleojo6@outlook.com
Sign in with a security key
Your PC will open a security window. Follow the instructions there to sign in.
Try again

- Or you want a sign-in option without you having to enter your password for reasons best known to you, simply click on **"Sign-in options"**

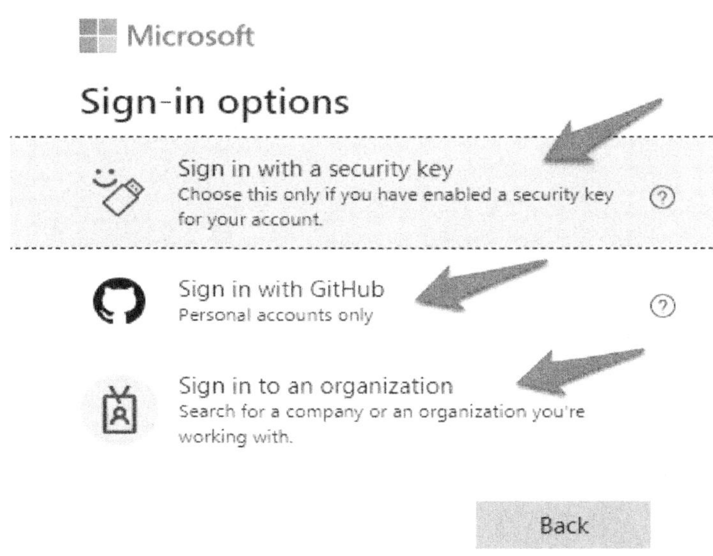
Microsoft
Sign-in options
Sign in with a security key
Choose this only if you have enabled a security key for your account.
Sign in with GitHub
Personal accounts only
Sign in to an organization
Search for a company or an organization you're working with.
Back

- If none of these is your case but want to create an account simply click on **"Create one"**

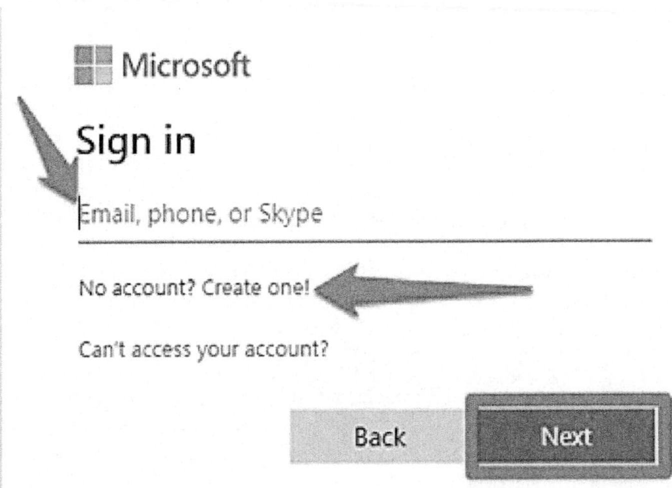

- Simply follow the instructions to get your Microsoft account opened, once done, you will be brought into Microsoft 365 environment

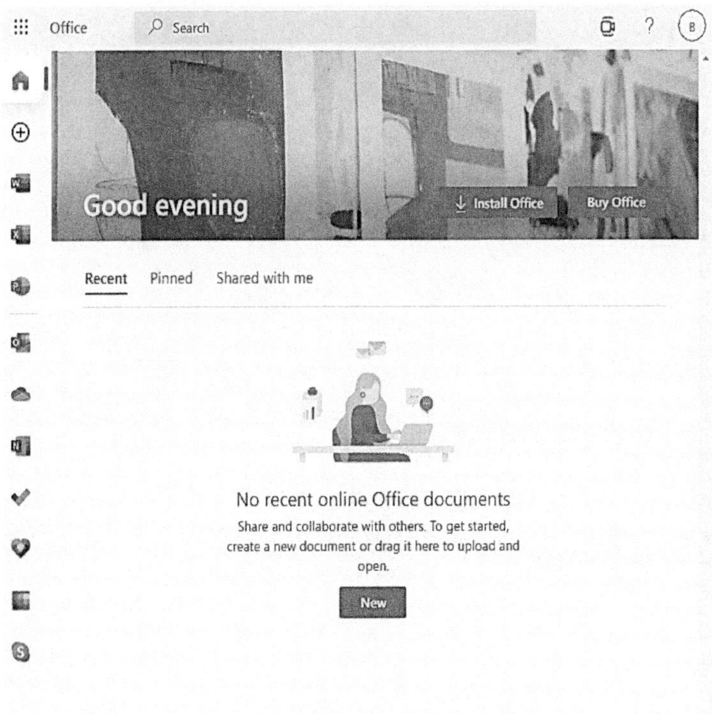

BOOK ONE

WORD 365

CHAPTER ONE

WELCOME TO WORD 365

Word 365 Installed License Environment

Word 365 Free Web based Environment

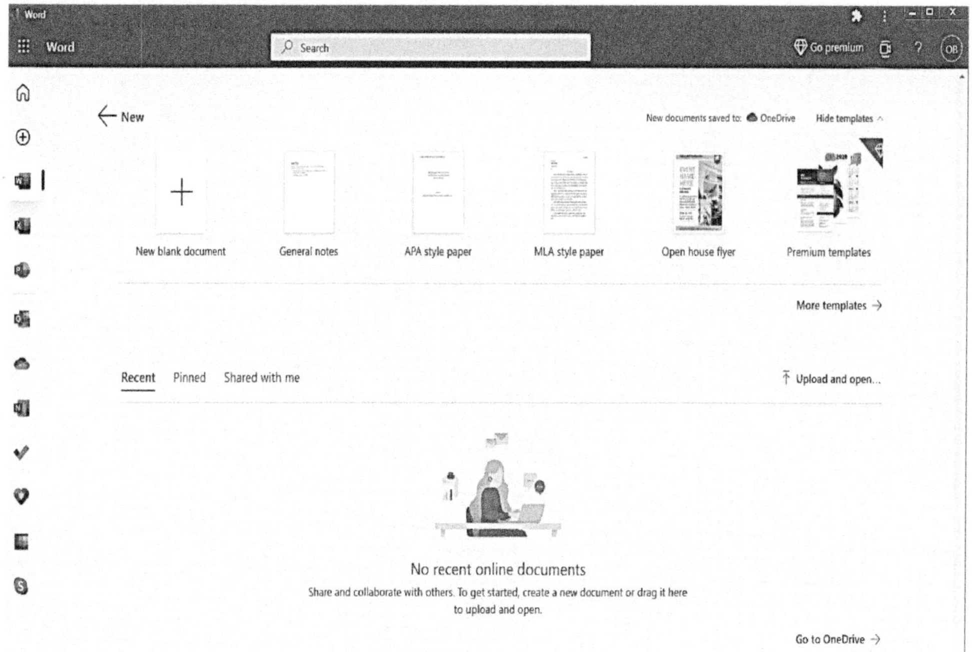

Word 365 interface is designed to perform similar tasks as previous versions with more added features such as online help, latest release, online sharing, and lots more.

Historical Background of Microsoft Word

- ***Microsoft Word DOS:*** The first version of Microsoft Word was released in 1983, it was named Microsoft Word DOS which stands for "Disk Operating System", with a 16bit system type capacity.
- ***Microsoft Word for Windows:*** Another version of Microsoft Word was released in 1989 with a different edition.
- ***Microsoft Word 95:*** After the release of Microsoft Word for Windows which had a lot of limitations, Microsoft Word 95 was released in 1995 to solve the problem of graphics and limited features.
- ***Microsoft Word 97:*** Microsoft Word 97 was released on November 19, 1996, to solve the limitation of Microsoft Word 95.
- ***Microsoft Word 2000:*** Microsoft Word 97 was replaced by Microsoft Word 2000 as a new release on July 7, 1999.
- ***Microsoft Word 2001/Word X:*** Word 2001 was packaged with the Macintosh features. Word 2001 was released in October 2000 and was also sold as an individual product. Word X was released in 2001 and was the first version to run natively
- ***Microsoft Word 2002/XP:*** Word 2002 was also released in 2001 to replace Microsoft Word 2001 & Word X. It had several of the same features as Word 2000, but a new feature was added called the "Task Panes", which gave quicker information and control to a lot of features.
- ***Microsoft Word 2003:*** Microsoft Word 2003 is an office suite developed by Microsoft for its Windows operating system. Office 2003 was released on October 21, 2003. It was the replacement of Word XP.
- ***Microsoft Word 2007:*** Word 2007 was introduced with a graphical user interface called the "Fluent User Interface", ribbons and an Office menu. It was released on January 30, 2007.
- ***Microsoft Word 2010:*** Microsoft Word 2010 is another version of the Microsoft Office suite for Microsoft Windows. Office 2010 was released on the 15th of April 2010. It is the successor to Word 2007.

- ***Microsoft Word 2013:*** Word 2013 was released on January 29, 2013, with more updated features and was later replaced by Word 2016
- ***Microsoft Word 2016:*** Word 2016 was launched on September 22, 2015, with a lot of built-in features such as auto-correct, spelling check, auto-save, and lots more. Word 2016 was later replaced with Word 2019.
- ***Microsoft Word 2019:*** Word 2019 was released on September 24, 2018, with similar yet upgraded features such as Sign in, share, and auto-resume with other friendly tools. It was later replaced with Word 365.
- ***Microsoft Word 365:*** Word 365 was released on June 28, 2011, with a similar interface yet different with newly added features such as speech dictation, resume assistant, sharing of documents online, OneDrive cloud storage, and lots more. Word 365 is the latest version of Microsoft Word which functions online; without having a Microsoft account you are not eligible to make use of it.

Exploring Word 365

For simplicity and comprehension, I will be using the free web version to explain Word 365 features for the sake of those who can't afford a license version yet, and for those that can, I will be using both to explain along the line to be able to cover both parts.

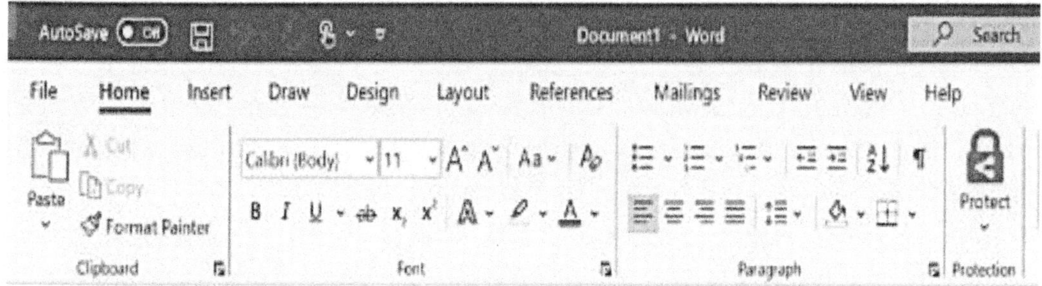

Word 365 comes with simple yet loaded features that autosave itself online into your OneDrive cloud storage

Title bar functionality

The title bar consists of your application name which is **"Word"** and beside it is your current working document which can be renamed, and also the location of your document storage which is OneDrive as seen above.

Exploring tab Functionality

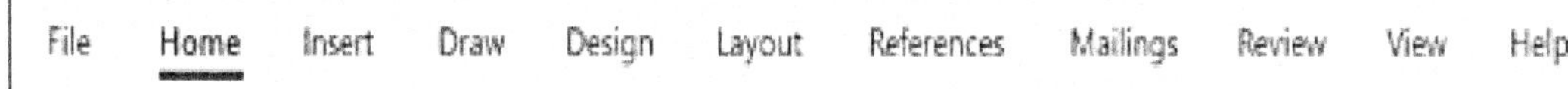

A menu bar is the anchor or entry point that leads to other features. The menu bar names details where you can access such features from:

File tab features

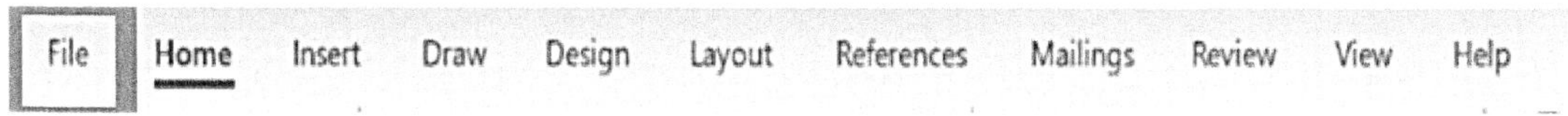

Once you click on "file", it'll display a dialog box that gives an overview of multiple features of what **"File menu"** represent.

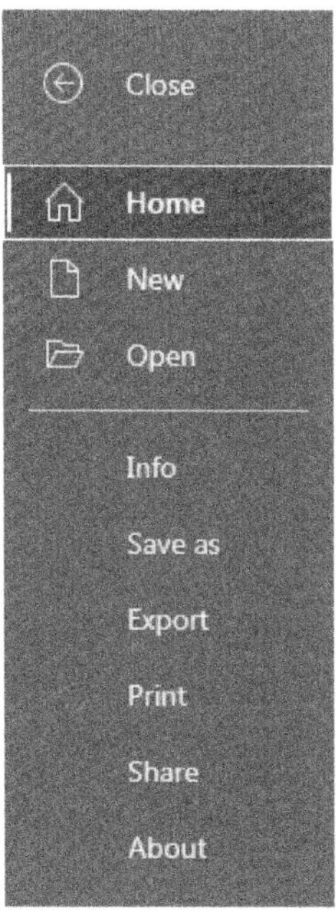

Home: Home under **"File menu"** also known as the **"backstage view"** takes you to Word 365 launching page where you can open a new document to work on, locate existing documents and also see your recent works.

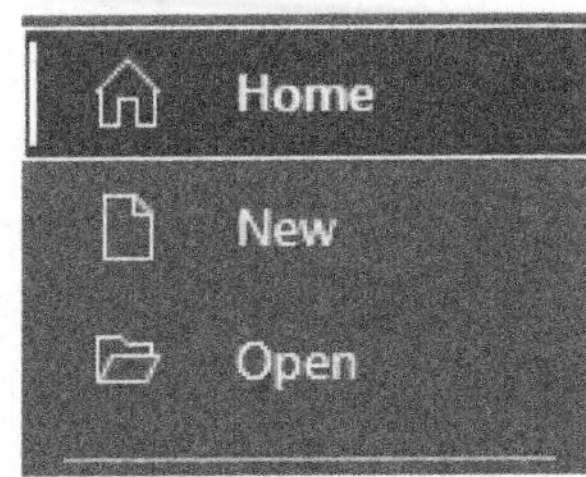

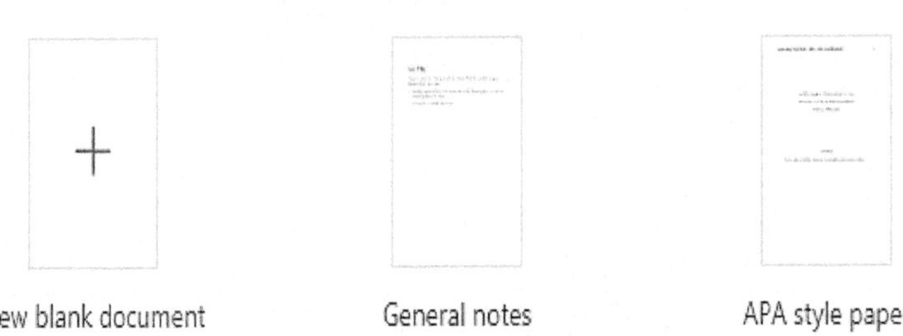

Info: Info gives the privilege to make use of previous Microsoft Word on your desktop or PC, Protection view and to view, restore or download previous versions of your document.

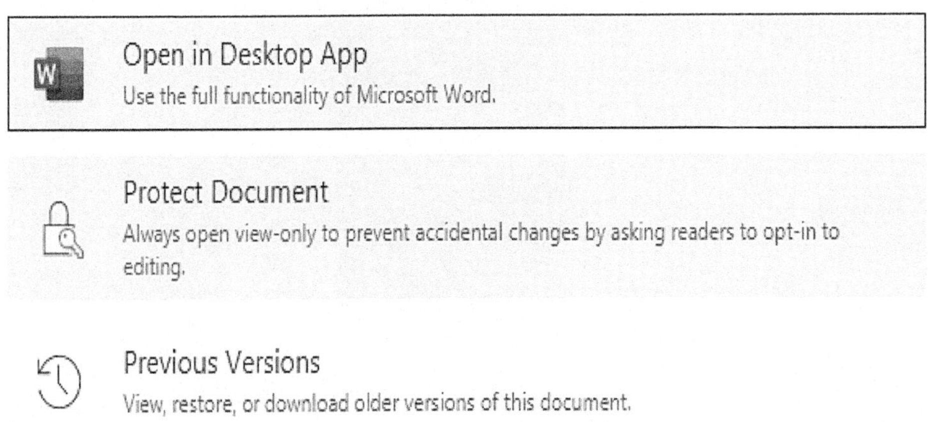

Save as: This is the feature that makes Microsoft Word 365 save & rename an active document because there is no save button, every work is automatically saved online. You can also click on **"Download a copy"** to download a duplicate copy into your PC, or **"Download as PDF"** directly into your PC, or **"Download as ODT"** to your PC.

Save as

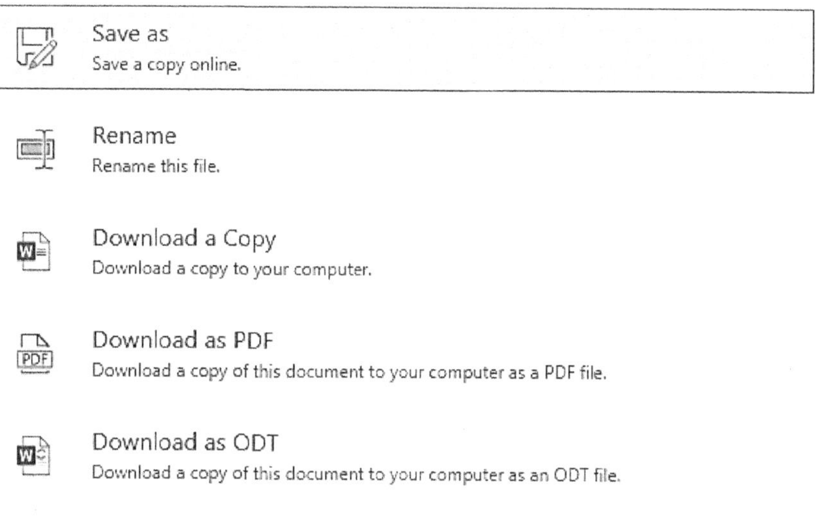
Save as
Save a copy online.
Rename
Rename this file.
Download a Copy
Download a copy to your computer.
Download as PDF
Download a copy of this document to your computer as a PDF file.
Download as ODT
Download a copy of this document to your computer as an ODT file.

Where's the Save Button?

There's no Save button because we're automatically saving your document.

Export: Export gives room for transferring a document into another Microsoft 365 Suite such as PowerPoint. As time goes on, more options will be added to the list.

Export

Export to PowerPoint presentation (preview)

Export your document into a multi-slide presentation with a design theme.

Print: The print option is designed to covert softcopy into hardcopy format, all that is needed is a connected printer to complete this process of printing.

Print

Print
Print this document.

Share: This is the feature that allows you to share your document with others by inviting them, and you can also embed this document in your blog or website

Share

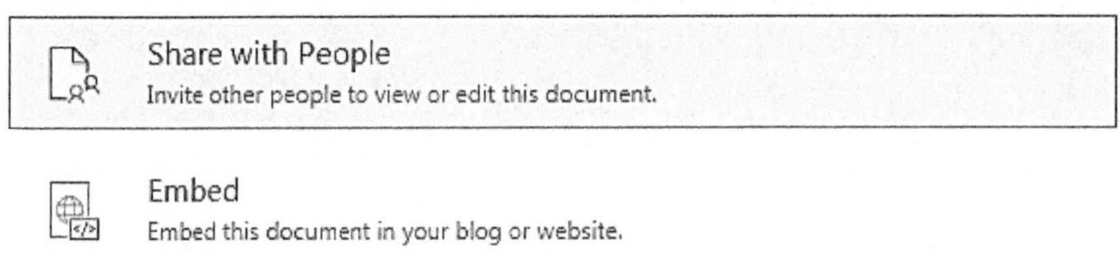
Share with People
Invite other people to view or edit this document.
Embed
Embed this document in your blog or website.

About: The about option gives the summary of terms and conditions of using Word 365 with third-party notice. Under the about option is where you get your product ID known as "Session ID", and "Build" for any technical support from Microsoft.

About

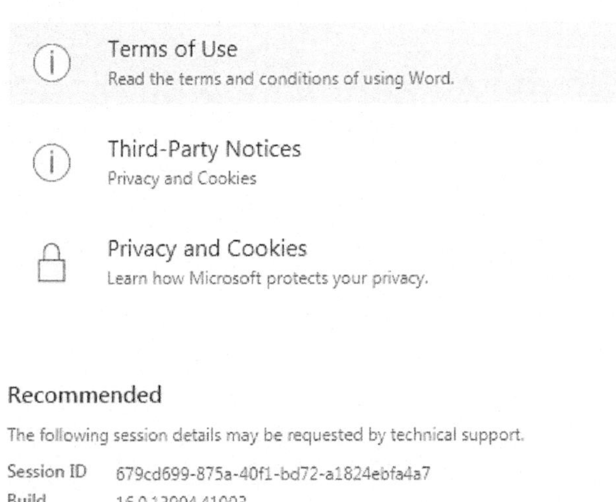
Terms of Use
Read the terms and conditions of using Word.
Third-Party Notices
Privacy and Cookies
Privacy and Cookies
Learn how Microsoft protects your privacy.
Recommended
The following session details may be requested by technical support.
Session ID 679cd699-875a-40f1-bd72-a1824ebfa4a7
Build 16.0.13904.41003

Home tab feature

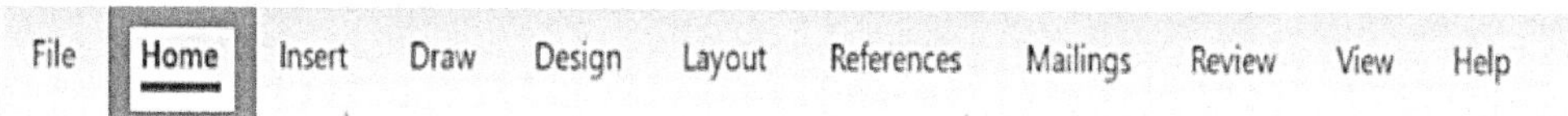

"Home" as its name implies, is the default displayed feature of the Word 365 interface which comes with ribbons that are grouped for your command, these can also be categorized as ***Standard toolbar*** for customizing your text and ***formatting toolbar*** for editing your text. Home comes with tools for beautifying text such as:

- **Clipboard ribbon tab:** Clipboard is one of Microsoft tool designed as part of Word 365 to cut, copy and paste an item

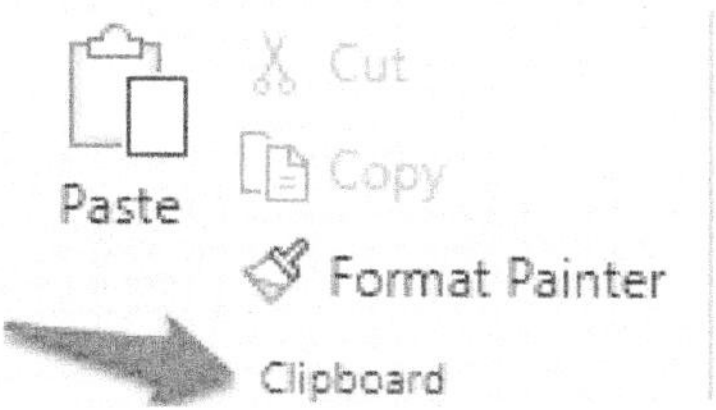

- ***Cut:*** Cut removes a selected portion and stores it directly into your clipboard.
- ***Copy:*** Copy duplicates item and stores it into your clipboard.
- ***Format Painter:*** This is a tool used to duplicate a text format into another text format.
- ***Paste:*** Paste displays all cut or copied items to any assigned destination.
- **Font ribbon tab:** Font is a Word 365 ribbon that consists of various tools for editing your text font style, font size, superscript, subscript, color, and lots more.

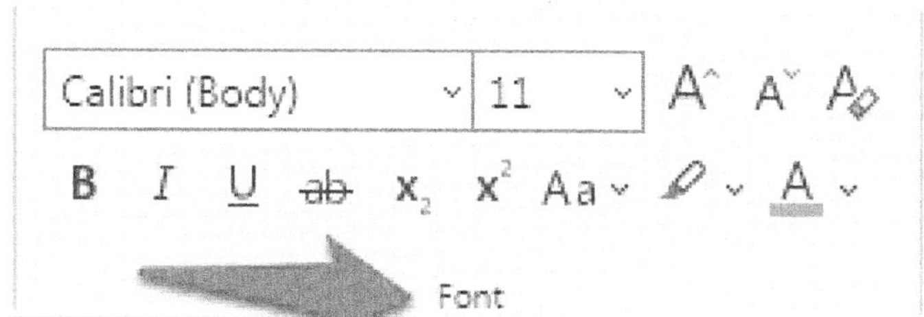

- ***Bold:*** It is a tool that makes your text appear in a bold form, it is recognized by a bold **B** icon

- ***Italic:*** It is a tool that slants or slopes your text, it is recognized by a slant "*I*" icon
- ***Underline:*** It is a tool that rules a line under a selected text, it is recognized by an underlined U icon
- ***Strikethrough:*** It is a tool used to cross through your text, it is recognized by a strikethrough ~~ab~~ icon

- ***Font style:*** It is designed to beautify text style into your preferred choice.

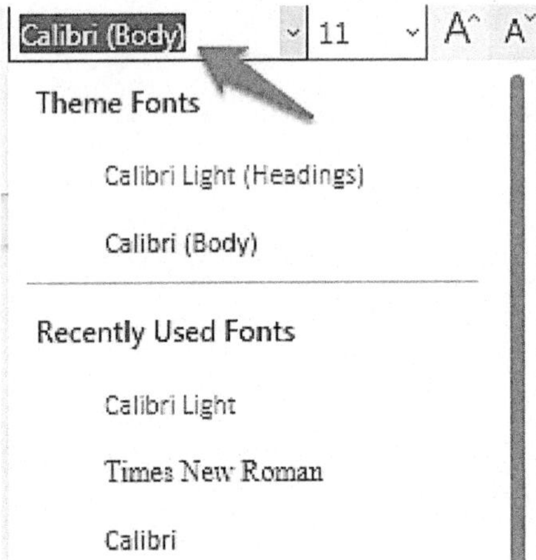

- ***Font size:*** This is another portion that gives increment and decrement to your text.

- ***Font Color:*** It is the tool that changes the color of your text into your preferred choice, it affects the selected text body. It is represented with a capital letter A underlined with red color.

- ***Text highlighted color:*** This is similar to font color. Text highlighted color affects highlighted text background areas. It is represented with a pen icon underlined with yellow color.

- ***Superscript & Subscript:*** This is the feature responsible for text positioning, superscript makes text above the text line, while subscript makes text below the text line.

- ***Change Case:*** It is a feature that gives the privilege to change text into lowercase, uppercase, sentence case, and other formats, it is represented with capital letter A and a small letter 'a' (Aa)

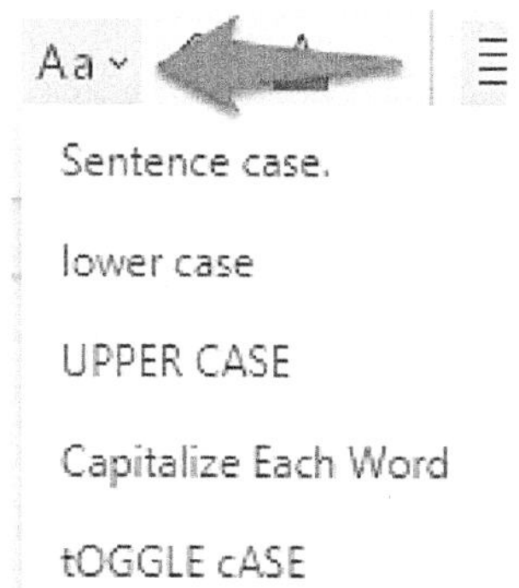

- ***Clear formatting:*** This helps to remove all formatting from the selection, leaving only the normal text unformatted. It is represented as seen in the illustration below

- **Paragraph ribbon tab:** "Paragraph" is a ribbon tab that other commands are grouped into for specialization. Paragraph features are also known as formatting toolbar for aligning text in an orderly approach. Part of paragraph features are:

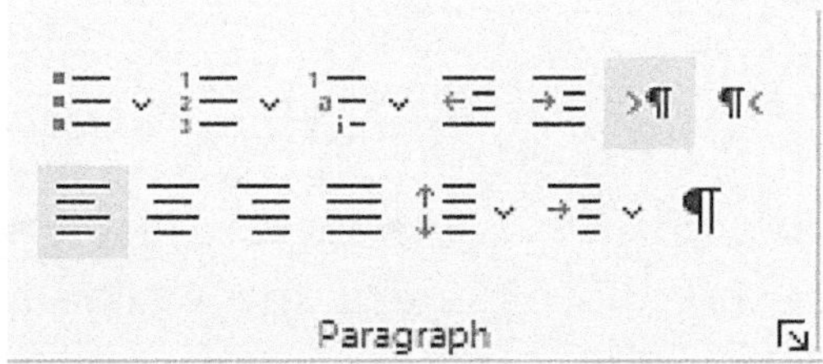

- ***Bullet's library:*** Bullets is a tagged icon that works in form of numerical numbering. In bullets, every symbol icon is the same in listing except there is a need to have sub-list items

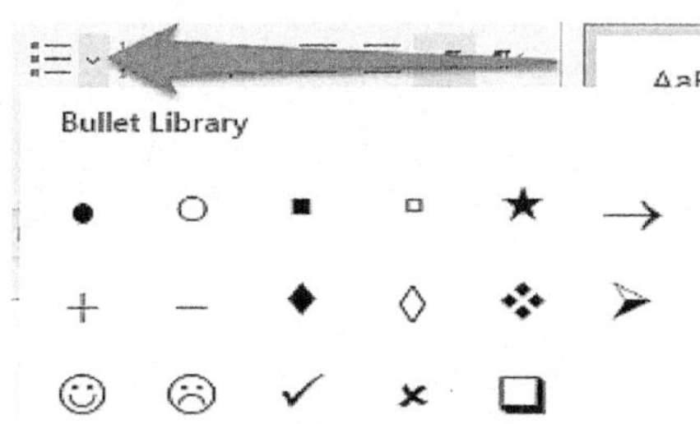

- ***Numbering library:*** Numbering is the opposite of bullets. Numbering comes in forms, numerical order, alphabetical order, and roman figure order

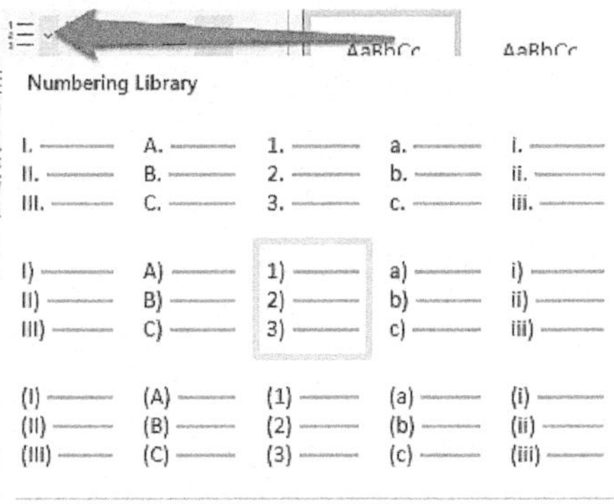

- ***Multilevel library:*** It is a sub-listing arrangement that consists of a mixture of bullets listing & numbering listing in sublevels.

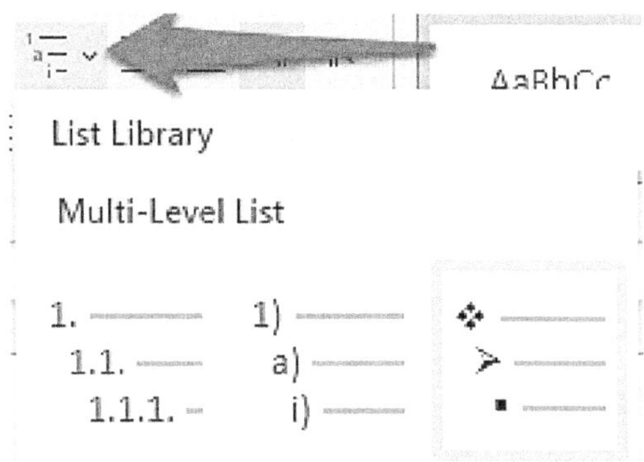

- ***Decrease & Increase Indent:*** It is designed to adjust the movement of text from a standpoint to another standpoint.

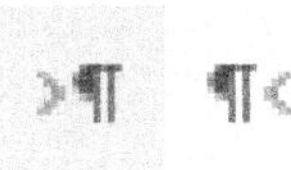

- ***Left-to-right text direction:*** This is an auto feature that moves an item from the left-hand side position to the right-hand side

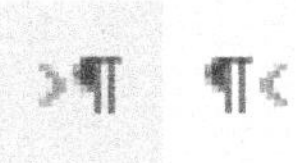

- ***Right-to-left text direction:*** It is the opposite of the left-to-right text direction. It automatically moves text from the right-hand side position to the left-hand side position

- ***Left alignment:*** It helps to align your content to the left margin

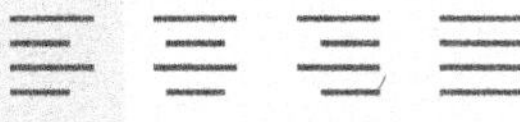

- ***Center alignment:*** It helps to centralize your content
- ***Right alignment:*** It helps to align your content to the right margin
- ***Justify alignment:*** It helps your content to look fit on right and left margin
- ***Line spacing:*** This is another feature of the paragraph ribbon tab. Line spacing determines the space between lines of text or between paragraphs.

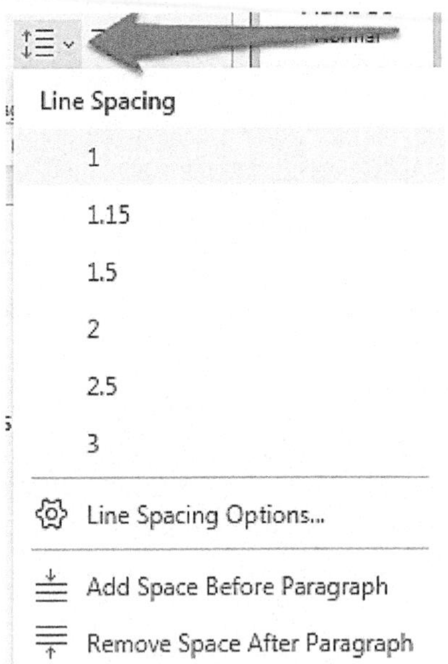

- **Styles:** Style gives your content a consistent polish look. It also comes with multiple options to choose from through the navigation pane

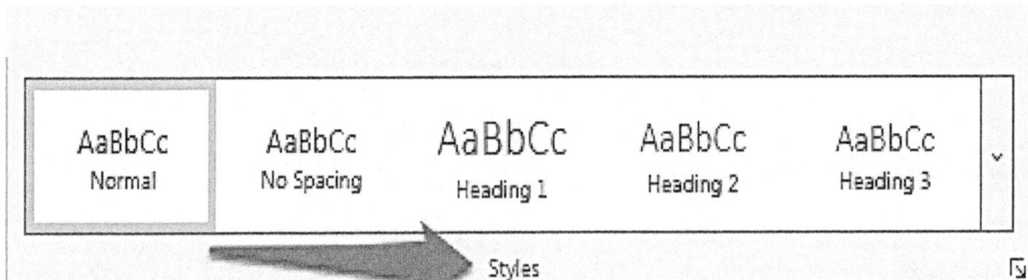

- **Editing:** Editing is a tool that is used to find text, replace text, and also to select text

- **Dictate:** Dictate is a new tool added into Word 365 that allows its users the privilege to use speech-to-text.

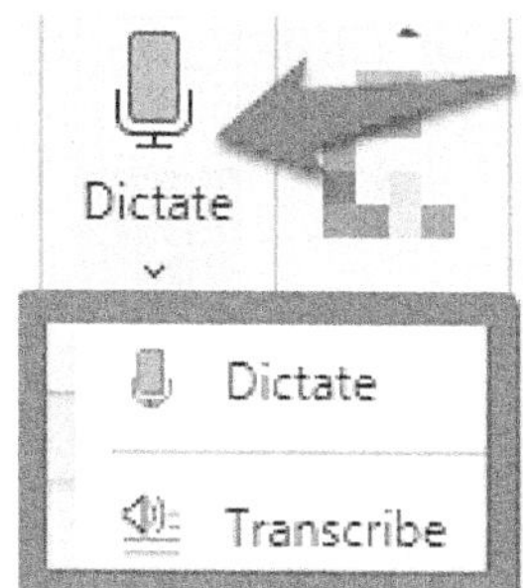

- **Editor:** Editor is a tool in Word 365 that offers auto spelling & grammar suggestions.

- **Designer:** Designer is a newly added tool that presents a list of potential features for fonts and headings that you can apply to your document to make it professionally presentable. It also gives users the privilege to professionally design complete templates

Insert tab feature

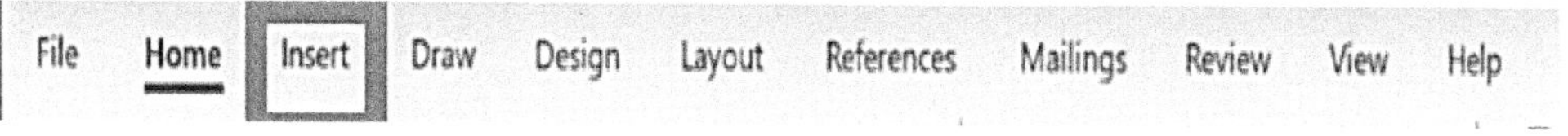

Insert menu bar feature is designed to add, import & customize your content in a lovely way. Insert menu bar has many tools such as:

- **Pages ribbon tab:** This is the controller of your contents, that involves page breaks. Subsequent updates from Microsoft will lead to additional features such as cover page and others.

- **Table ribbon tab:** The table ribbon tab is responsible for table creation based on your preferred choice

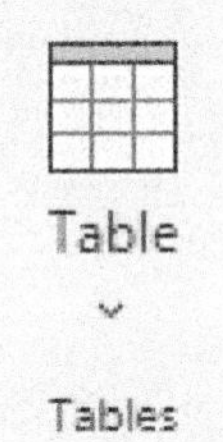

- **Picture ribbon tab:** It is a tool that grants access to images from external images on your PC into Word 365 environment.

- **Add-ins ribbon tab:** Add-in is a feature that allows Microsoft users to merge external application features with Word 365

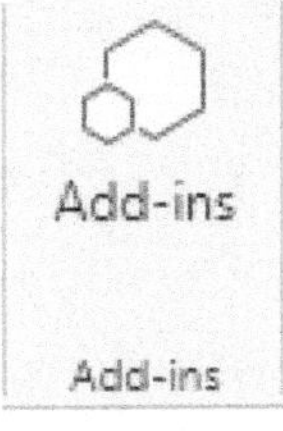

- **Link ribbon tab:** Link makes it possible for link creation into another file, webpage, and lots more.

- **Comments ribbon tab:** This is a feature that adds a note on a selected text, majorly for reference purpose.

- **Header & Footer:** "Header" helps you to repeat content at the top of every page while "footer" helps you to repeat content at the bottom of every page.

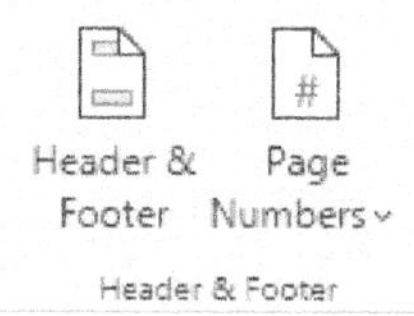

- **Symbols ribbon tab:** Symbol comes with various mathematical representations that can be used for different purposes based on the user's preferred choice.

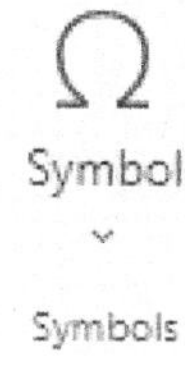

- **Emoji ribbon tab:** Emoji is a newly added feature that is still under development. Emoji is a little facial expression image that was first recognized on smartphones. Microsoft is bringing the possibility of Word 365 emoji.

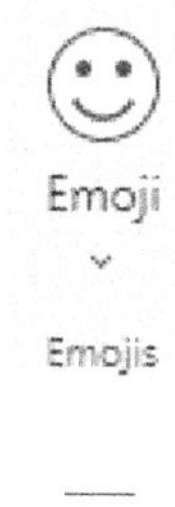

Note: More features are being updated daily with time, and there will be lesser usage of offline Word application once Microsoft stops it support from previous versions.

Design tab features

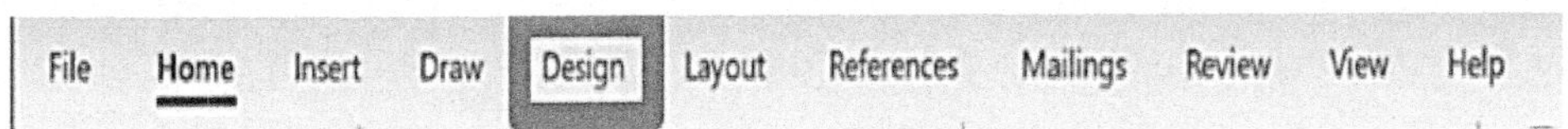

The design tab is an embodiment of document formatting tools and page background styling such as:

- **Document Formatting ribbon tab:** It is a group collection of tools for styling your document
- **Themes:** This is a feature that enables a predefined template format for styling your document content from a professional viewpoint.

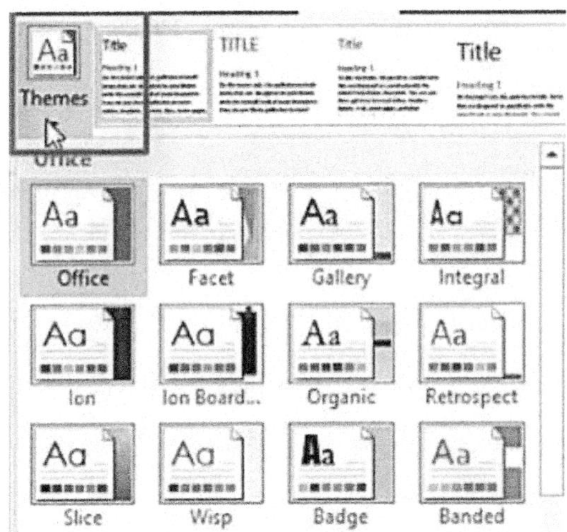

- **Colors:** Microsoft Word predefined templates also come with redefining colors for an individual preferred choice.

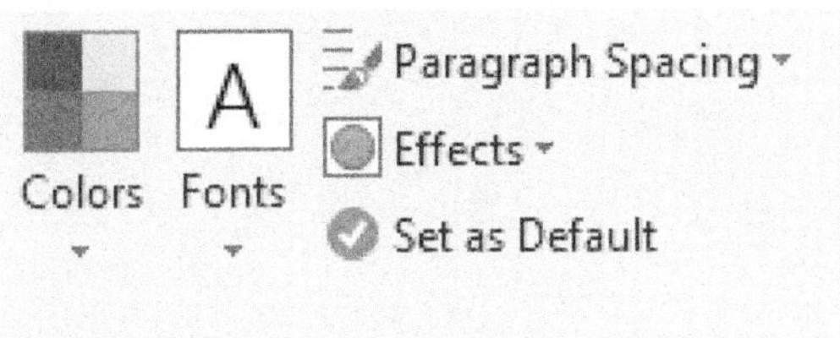

- **Fonts:** Microsoft also comes with a lot of fonts that can sort your preferred choice since individual taste varies. With this, you can redefine your theme font.

- **Page Background ribbon tab:** It is a group of collections used to edit your theme template and also to customize your pages.

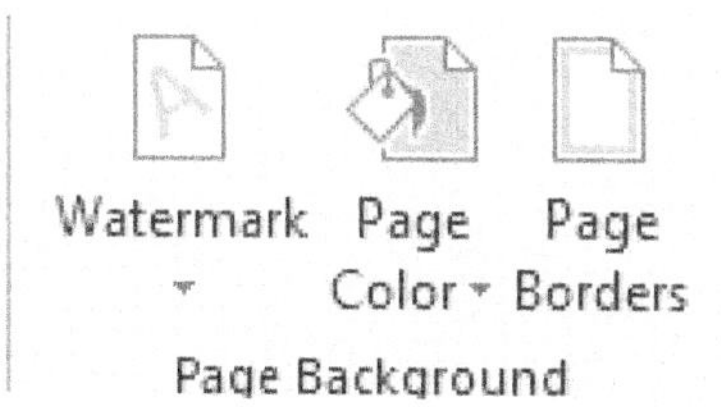

- **Watermark:** Watermark is a great tool used to design your background document with either a text or image depending on the individual preferred choice.

- **Page Color:** This helps you to customize your page document from the default white color to another color of your choice.

- **Page Borders:** It is used to create a variety of line styles, widths, and colors.

Layout tab feature

Layout is Word 365 menu bar that is responsible for page settings such as:

- **Page Setup ribbon tab:** This is the ribbon tab that groups other commands responsible for page configuration such as:

- **Margins:** It is used to set the right and left edge for all pages, it is a manual page setting.

- **Orientation:** Page orientation is divided into two categories, portrait & landscape; by default, your Word settings is on portrait, the landscape is used for different purposes such as tabulation of analysis.
- **Size:** Page size helps to make use of different paper sizes such as A4 (which is Word default paper size), A5, and many more. It is an auto page setting.
- **Paragraph ribbon tab:** This is a manual setup for paragraph settings, it is used to set indent and space.

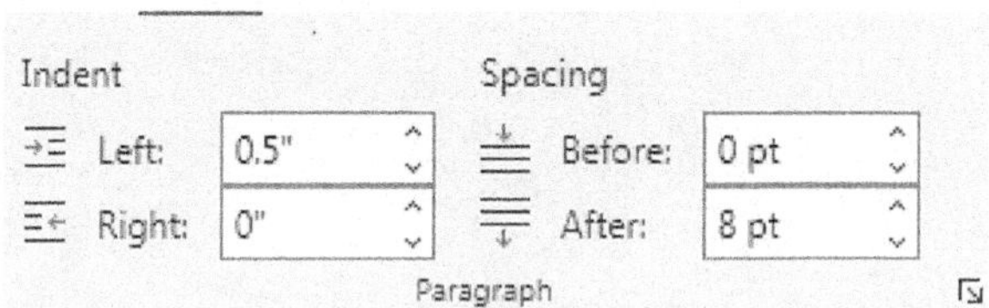

- **Left & Right Indent:** They both determine how far to move the paragraph away from the left margin and the right margin.
- **Before & After Spacing:** They both determine how much space appears above or below the selected paragraph.

References menu bar:

The references menu bar consists of different Word 365 tools such as Updating table of contents, Footnotes, and Insights

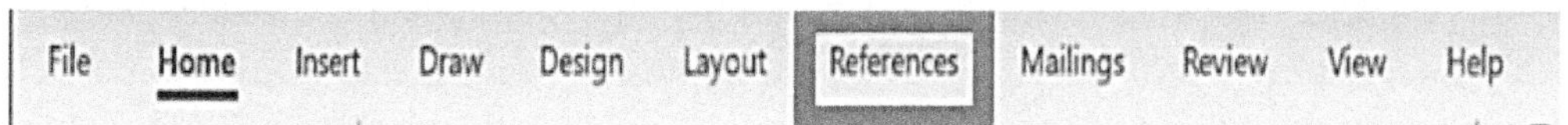

- **Table of Contents ribbon tab:** This is used for the arrangement of contents.
- **Footnote ribbon tab:** Is used to take note for citation of written words.
- **Update Table of Contents:** Word 365 provides an overview of your document by adding a table of content
- **Remove Table of Contents:** You can auto-remove your created table of contents at your wish
- **Footnotes ribbon tab:** Footnote is a written text on the bottom of Word 365 page to reference a sentence; it is majorly used for journals.
- **Insights ribbon tab:** This is a newly added feature that serves as a mini browser to get an insight into a word or statement.

Review tab:

The review menu bar is designed to give a comprehensive detail on your written document such as:

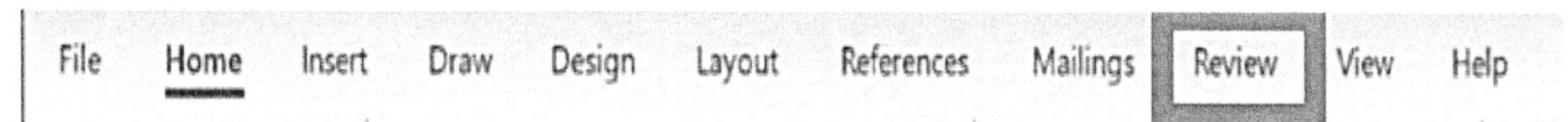

- **Editor ribbon tab:** It is a tool used to check spellings and correct words.

- **Word Count ribbon tab:** It is a tool designed to auto count words & pages.

- **Accessibility ribbon tab:** The Accessibility feature helps to verify your document against a set of instructions that detect possible issues for people who have disabilities. Depending on how severe the issue is, the Accessibility Checker classifies each issue as an error, warning, or tip.

- **Translate ribbon tab:** The Translate feature is a tool that helps you to interpret text into a different language. By using Word 365 you are already connected online to get your translated words.

- **Comments ribbon tab:** It helps to add a note about any selected part of your content and also, other tools reveal your comment items

- **Tracking ribbon tab:** Tracking helps you to keep in touch with your document in case of any changes made by you or other people you shared your document with. It is majorly used to note every single step of added and removed words.

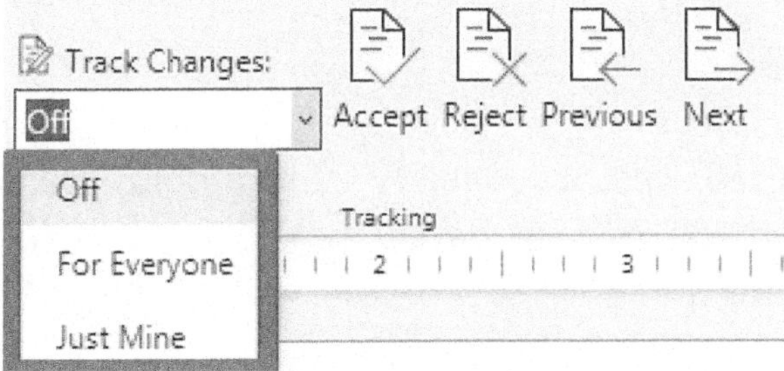

- **Resume Assistant:** It is a newly added feature from Microsoft Word 365 that enables its users to get different templates.

Mailing's tab

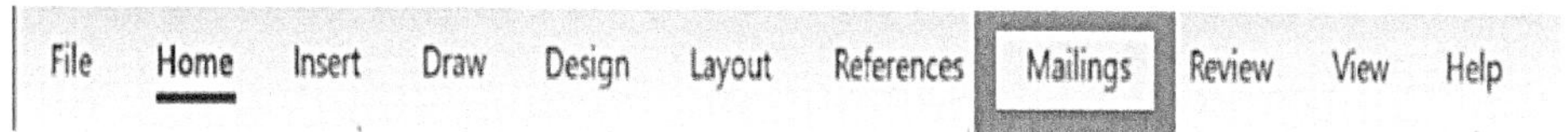

Mailing's tab is a feature used to forward, edit, and select emails.

View tab

The view menu bar is constructed to preview content, read content, zoom in & out, and lots more

- **Document Views ribbon tab:** This is a new feature added into Word 365 where you can view your content and also make your PC auto-read it
- **Zoom ribbon tab:** Zoom is a tool used for viewing your content into a level that is suitable for you
- **Show ribbon tab:** Show ribbon tab consists of ruler for margin measurement, navigation to search words from your content, header & footer to cite or number pages, with other features.

Help tab:

Help is a newly added feature that provides a solution, contact support, and feedback to Microsoft users.

Editing tab:

Editing is also a new feature from Microsoft; this makes you choose to edit your work, review it for additional touch, or view your document

without making any change depending on the users' choice (majorly seen at the top menu of Microsoft Word free web version also in licensed version but not placed above your menu)

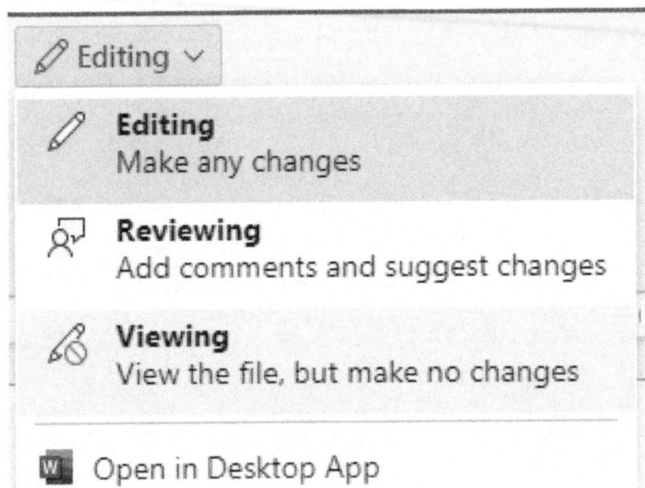
Editing
Editing
Make any changes
Reviewing
Add comments and suggest changes
Viewing
View the file, but make no changes
Open in Desktop App

CHAPTER TWO

WRESTLING WITH THE TEXT

Manipulating the text

Text manipulation is done in different ways; some of it which are:

Alignment of Text

Text alignment is achieved in four (4) different ways based on an individual purpose of usage:

- **Left Alignment:** By default, all texts are located at your left-hand side; for any reason it is not so, simply click on the arrow indication to return it to your left-hand side or you can highlight it for specialization in a situation where there is more than one line of text. It is also used for heading and footer.

Note: In left alignment, only the left-hand edge will be aligned on the same lines. You can also use ***Ctrl + L*** as the left alignment shortcut.

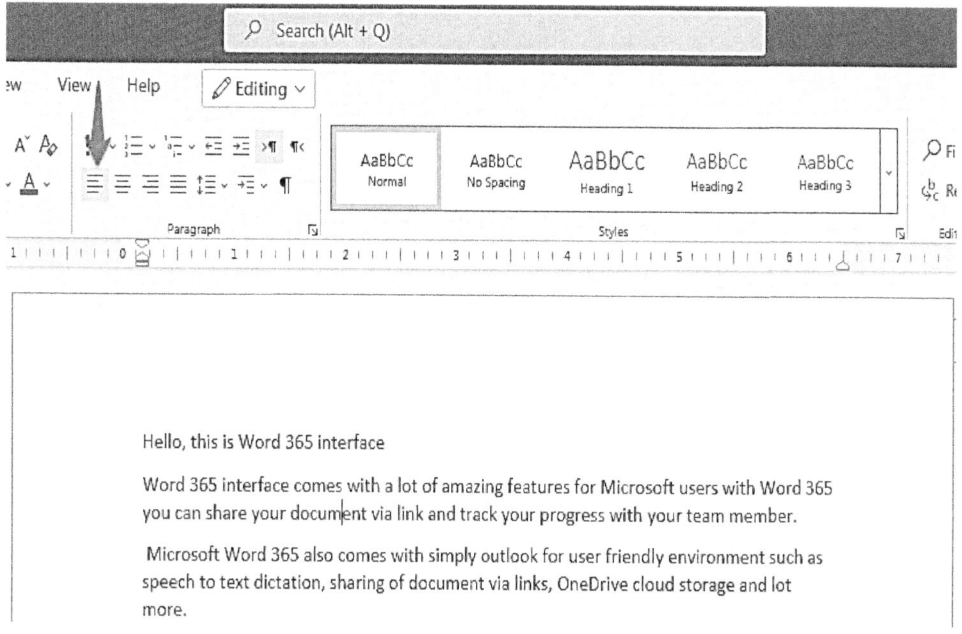

- **Right Alignment:** Right alignment is used majorly for special purposes such as addressing a letter. The arrow in the illustration below indicates the function command responsible for right alignment after you select your text.

Note: In right alignment, only the right-hand edge will be aligned on the same lines. You can also use ***Ctrl + R*** as the right alignment shortcut

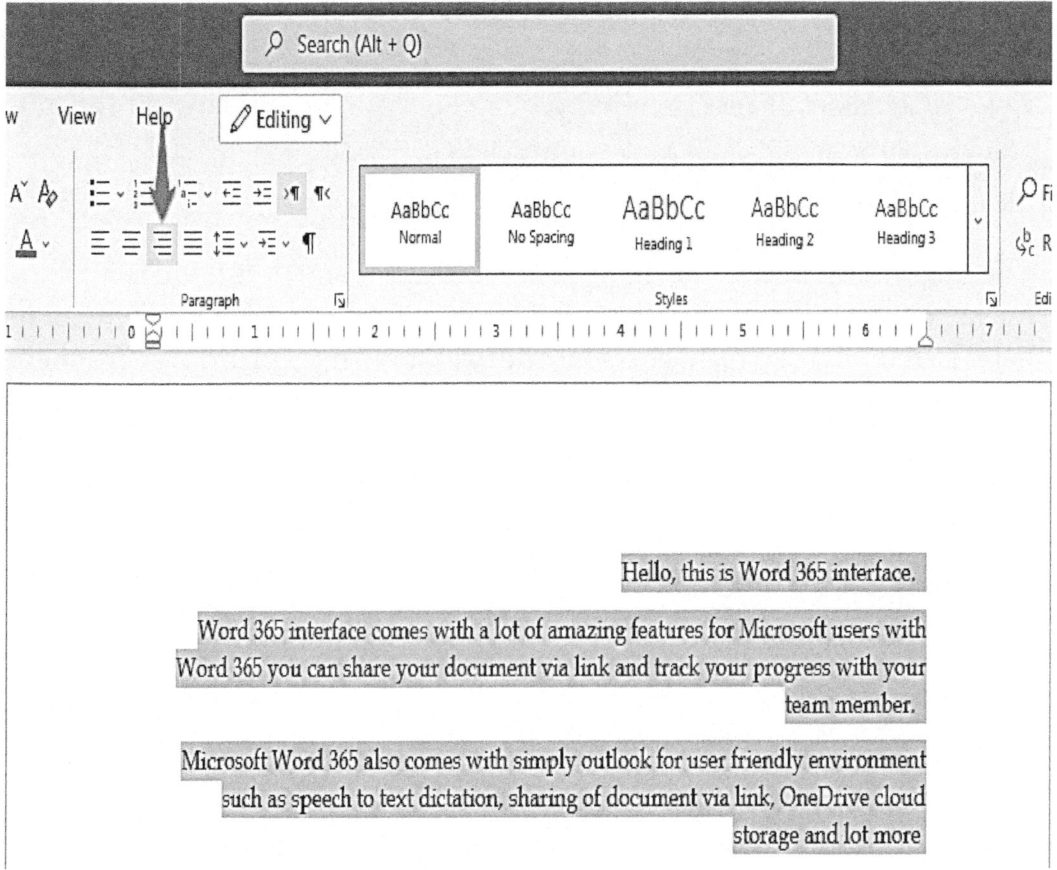

- **Center Alignment:** Center alignment positions your text at the middle of the Word interface; it's majorly used for headings. The pink arrow indicates the command function responsible for center alignment positioning; it is often used for a cover page, quotes, and sometimes headings.

Note: In center alignment, selected text will all be aligned in the middle altogether. You can also use ***Ctrl + E*** as the center alignment shortcut.

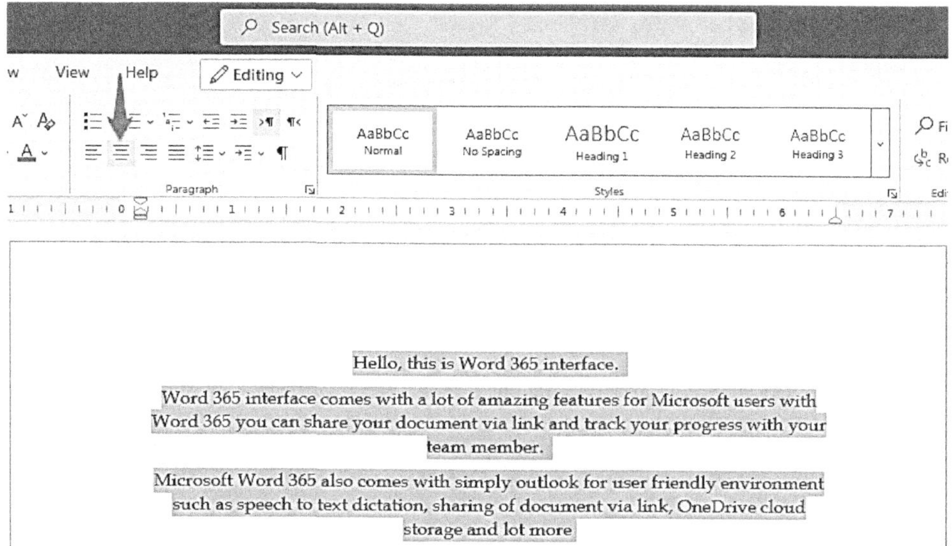

- **Justify Alignment:** Justified text gives your document clean and crisp edges so it looks well organized. Go to the home tab, select the **justify command** as illustrated below.

Note In justify alignment, all selected texts will be justified on the left and right-hand edges altogether. You can also use **Ctrl + J** as the "justify alignment" shortcut.

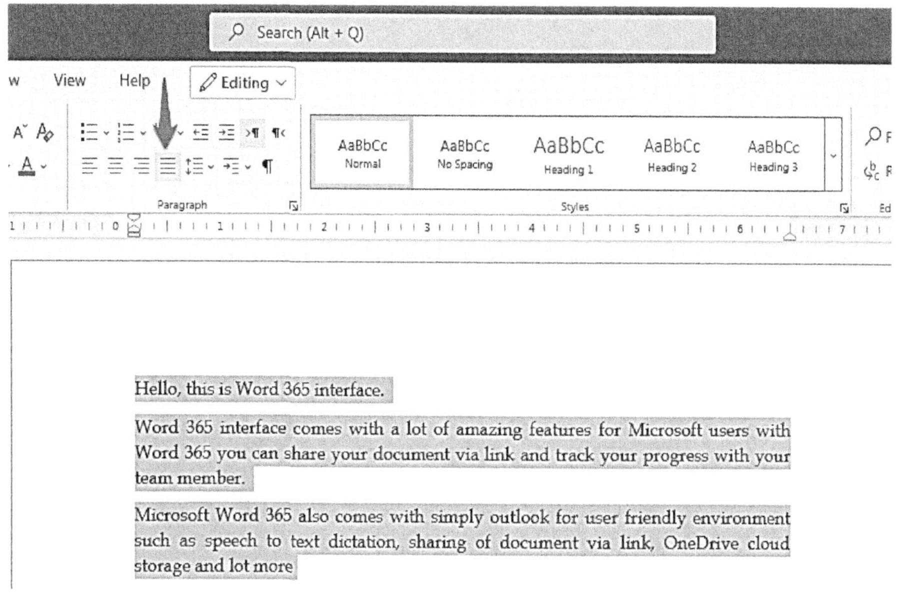

Bolding Text & Adjusting font size

To bold text, select the portion you want to bold, then go to the home tab, select the **B** icon which stands for bold, your text will be in bold format; make sure it is still highlighted then also go to font size as indicated below through the pink arrow, click on it or type the font size you want. You can use **Ctrl + B** as a shortcut to bold text.

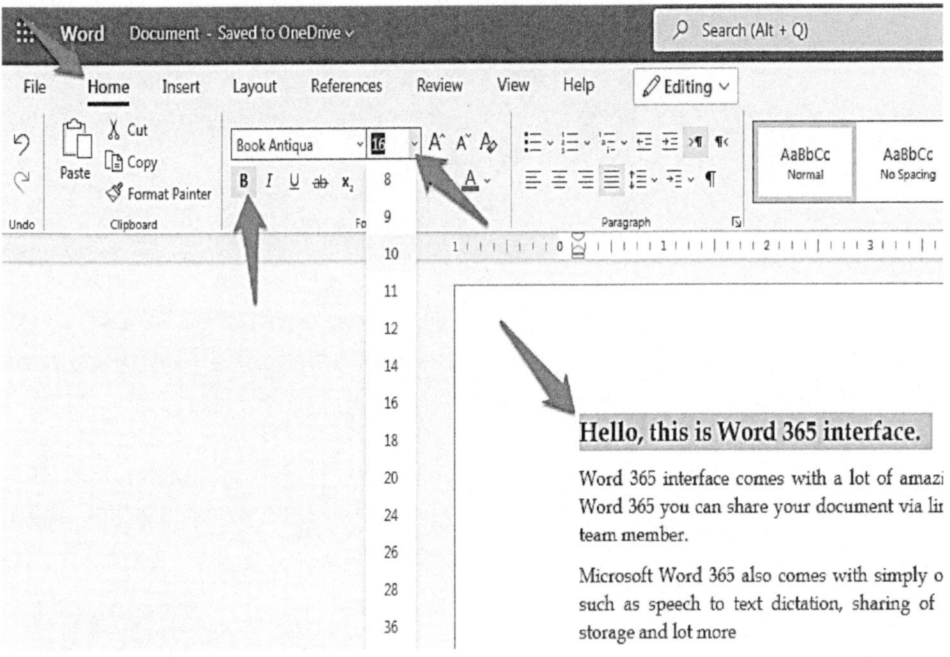

Underlining your text

Go to the home tab

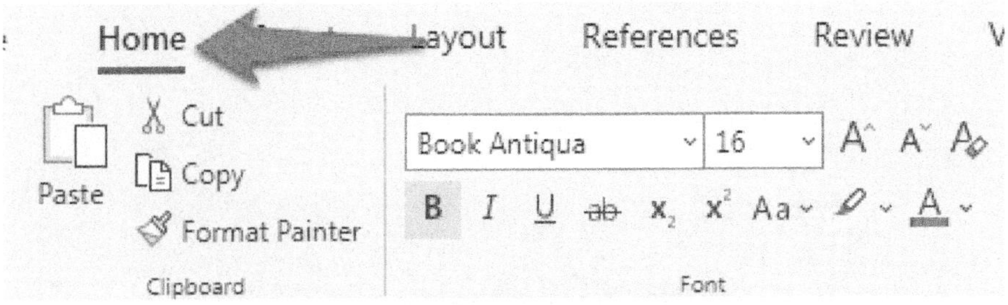

Make sure the text you want to underline is highlighted

Hello, this is Word 365 interface.

Word 365 interface comes with a lot of amazing features for Microsoft users with Word 365 you can share your document via link and track your progress with your team member.

Microsoft Word 365 also comes with simply outlook for user friendly environment such as speech to text dictation, sharing of document via link, OneDrive cloud storage and lot more

Select the **underlined icon (U)**

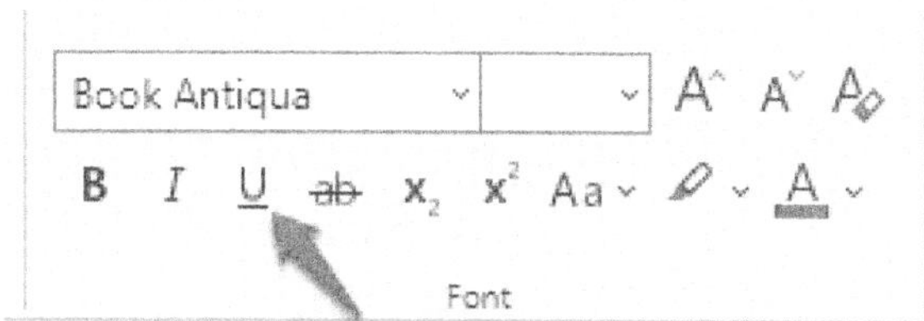

Your highlighted text will become underlined

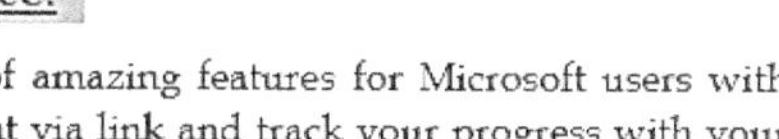

Hello, this is Word 365 interface.

Word 365 interface comes with a lot of amazing features for Microsoft users with Word 365 you can share your document via link and track your progress with your team member.

Microsoft Word 365 also comes with simply outlook for user friendly environment such as speech to text dictation, sharing of document via link, OneDrive cloud storage and lot more

Italicizing your text

Go to the "home tab", select the text to be italicized by highlighting it with your mouse

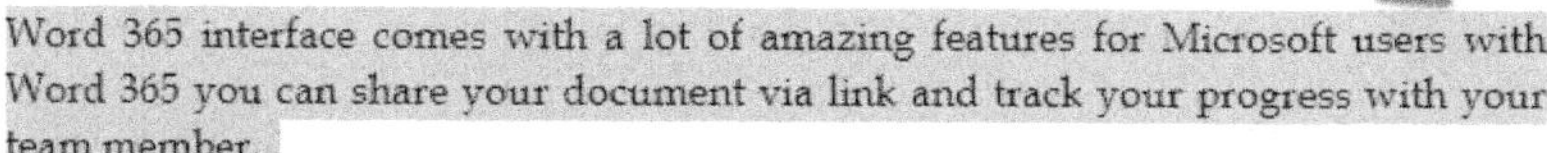

Hello, this is Word 365 interface.

Word 365 interface comes with a lot of amazing features for Microsoft users with Word 365 you can share your document via link and track your progress with your team member.

Microsoft Word 365 also comes with simply outlook for user friendly environment such as speech to text dictation, sharing of document via link, OneDrive cloud storage and lot more

- Go to the "Font ribbon tab" beside your bold icon (**B**), click on **the italic icon (*I*)**

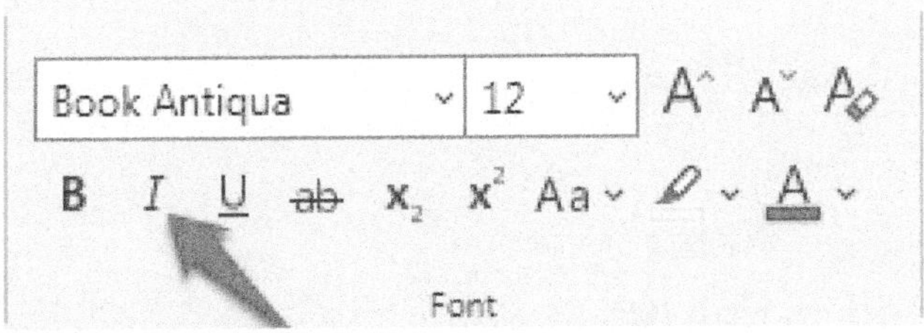

- Then, your highlighted text will become italicized

Hello, this is Word 365 interface.

Word 365 interface comes with a lot of amazing features for Microsoft users with Word 365 you can share your document via link and track your progress with your team member.

Microsoft Word 365 also comes with simply outlook for user friendly environment such as speech to text dictation, sharing of document via link, OneDrive cloud storage and lot more

Selecting Text

You can select text with your mouse by left-clicking and simultaneously dragging through the text you want to select. Your arrow keys can also perform the task by holding the shift key and pressing the arrow key in the direction you want (if it is forward highlighting you want, click on the forward arrow key without leaving your shift key).

Hello, this is Word 365 interf

Word 365 interface comes with a lot of ar
you can share your document via link and

Microsoft Word 365 also comes with sim
speech to text dictation, sharing of docume

Moving & Copying Text

Moving & copying of text, highlight on the text to be moved

Word 365 interface comes with a lot of amazing features for Microsoft users with Word 365 you can share your document via link and track your progress with your team member.

Microsoft Word 365 also comes with simply outlook for user friendly environment such as speech to text dictation, sharing of document via link, OneDrive cloud storage and lot more.

Left-click and hold, simultaneously drag your mouse on the highlighted text and drag it to anywhere you want it to be. In this illustration, drag beside the last line, then drop it.

Word 365 interface comes with a lot of amazing features for Microsoft users with Word 365 you can share your document via link and track your progress with your team member.

Microsoft Word 365 also comes with simply outlook for user friendly environment such as speech to text dictation, sharing of document via link, OneDrive cloud storage and lot more. Hello, this is Word 365 interface.

Changing the font color of your text

To change the look of your text, highlight your text

Hello, this is Word 365 interface.

If your Word 365 interface is not on the "home tab" as its default display, simply go to the "home tab" and click on it

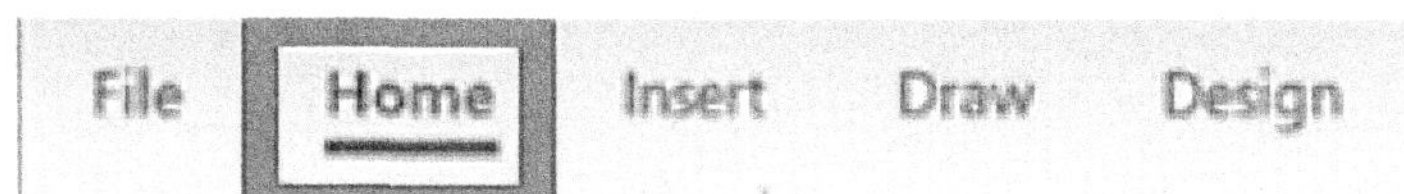

Below the "home tab", select "font color" which is identified by a capital letter A underlined with a red stroke as illustrated with an arrow sign below. Are we together? Right let us continue

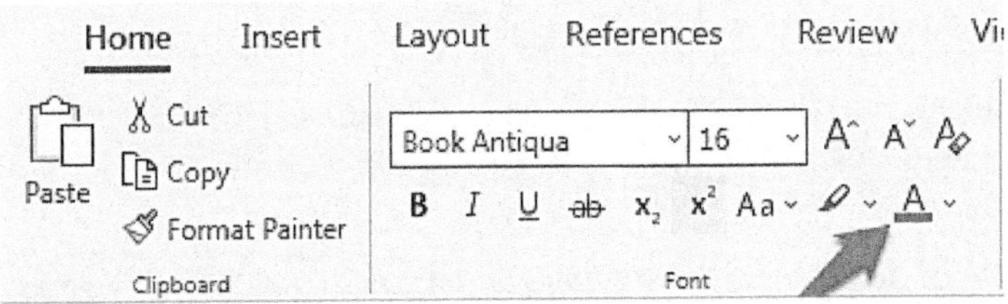

Remember that your text is still selected (highlighted), once you click on "font color", your highlighted text will change to red color.

Hello, this is Word 365 interface.

Choosing more color

You can also click the little arrow beside the "font color" to select your preferred choice, if not found check below for "more colors"

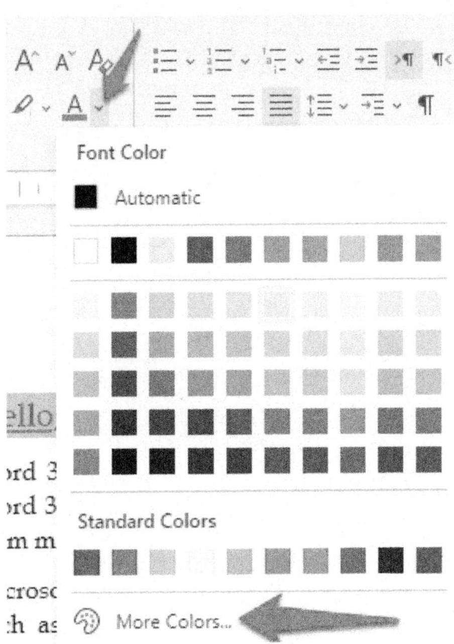

You can also decide to change the ***"font style"*** known as ***"font name"*** by selecting ***"home tab",*** check on the little arrow beside your current font, dropdown options will be displayed, you can select your preferred choice, but for similarity and understanding purpose select ***"Calibri Light (Headings)"***

Your highlighted text will take effect immediately

Before

Hello, this is Word 365 interface.

After

Hello, this is Word 365 interface.

Speaking, not Typing Words

Microsoft Word 365 comes with many added features, one of which is the "Dictate tool" which makes keyboard typing less needed due to time consumption and speaking more needed due to time utilization.

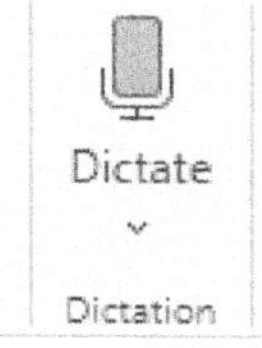

How to use Dictate tools

Go to the ***"Home tab"***

At your right-hand side, you will see ***"Dictate",*** click on it and two options will appear to you ***"Dictate"*** & ***"Transcribe",*** select ***"Dictate"***

Then, you can start your speech to text typing. Make sure you have an internet connection and the illustrated speaker is turned on from a white icon to a red icon

Hello, this is Word 365 interface.

Word 365 interface comes with a lot of amazing features for Microsoft users with Word 365 you can share your document via link and track your progress with your team member.

Microsoft Word 365 also comes with simply outlook for user friendly environment such as speech to text dictation, sharing of document via link, OneDrive cloud storage and lot more.

Applying Text Effects to Texts

- Highlight your text

Hello, this is Word 365 interface.

- In the "Home tab"

- Within your "Font ribbon", you will see "text effects", click on the drop-down arrow

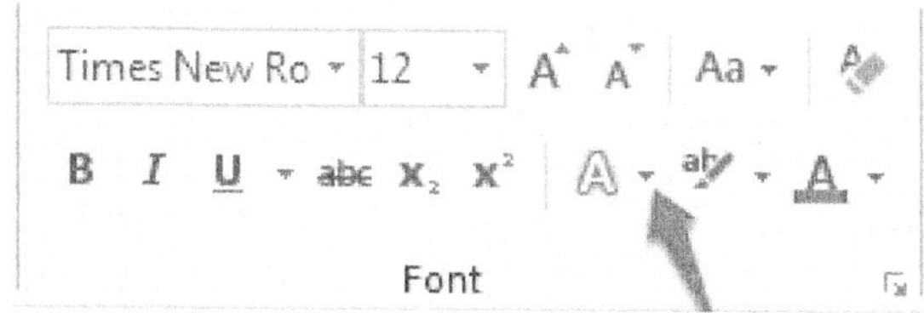

- Select your preferred text effect template and click on it, your text will have the same effect of the format immediately

Hello, this is Word 365 interface.

Quick Ways to Handle Case or Capitalization

Change case is a tool for transforming text from small letters to capital letters or a mixture of both with other preferred options. Cases are divided into five (5) segments which are:

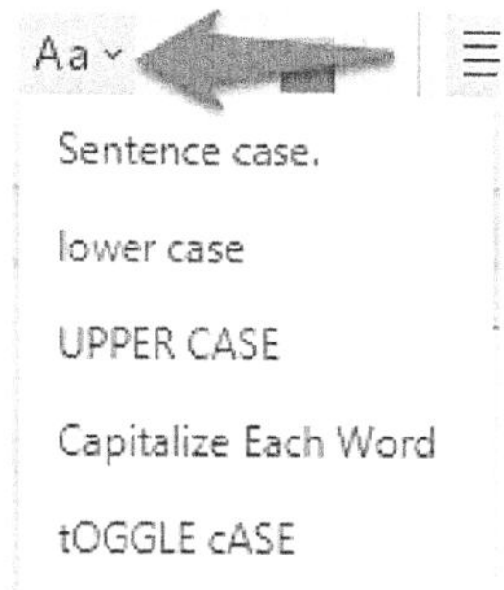

- **Sentence case:** Sentence case only capitalizes the first letter of every new paragraph, it is also applicable after a statement ends with a full stop, the next first letter only will be capitalized. To apply sentence case, highlight your text, under the "home tab"

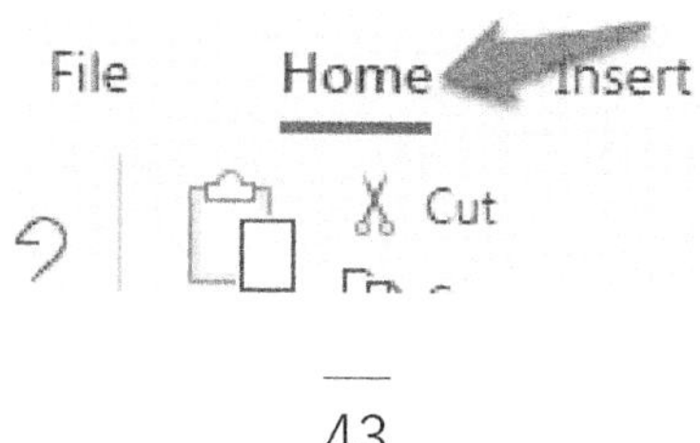

Locate “font ribbon” and select “change case” identified by a capital letter A and a small letter a. Pick “Sentence case”

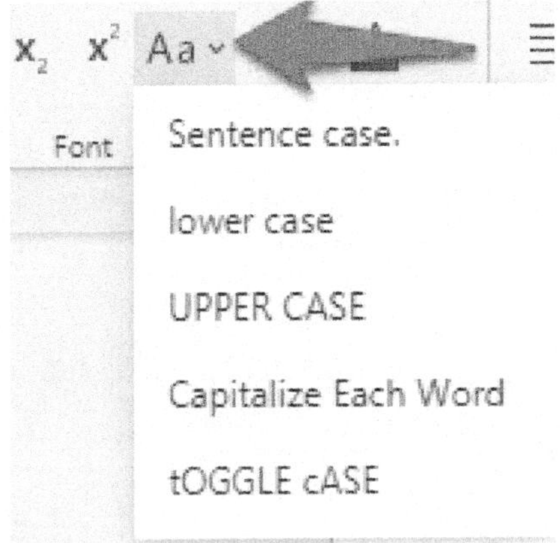

Then, your text will take effect immediately. Note that every first letter in every paragraph and a new sentence are all in capital letters only, which might affect other words in a statement that should start with a capital letter by default. For example, take a look at the illustration below.

In the first line second paragraph, “Microsoft” carries a small letter ‘m’ which should always be in capital, not a small letter; that is why it is underlined with a red line, indicating it has a mistake. Right-clicking on the word “Microsoft” will give you the right spelling.

Hello, this is word 365 interface.

Word 365 interface comes with a lot of amazing features for microsoft users with word 365 you can share your document via link and track your progress with your team member. I am a new sentence after a full stop

Microsoft word 365 also comes with simply outlook for user friendly environment such as speech to text dictation, sharing of document via link, onedrive cloud storage and lot more.

- **Lower case:** Lower case makes every word be in a small letter. To apply lower case, highlight the portion you want to effect lower case into, for this illustration, let’s highlight all the text

Hello, this is word 365 interface.

Word 365 interface comes with a lot of amazing features for Microsoft users with word 365 you can share your document via link and track your progress with your team member. I am a new sentence after a full stop

Microsoft word 365 also comes with simply outlook for user friendly environment such as speech to text dictation, sharing of document via link, onedrive cloud storage and lot more.

Go to the "Home tab"

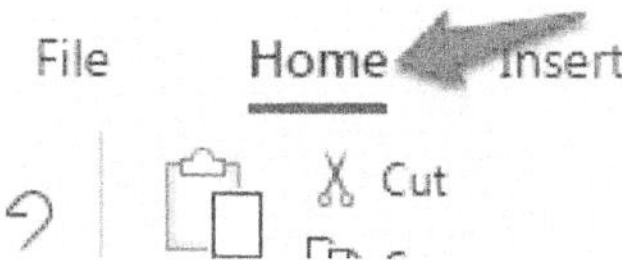

Locate "font ribbon" and select "change case". Pick "lower case"

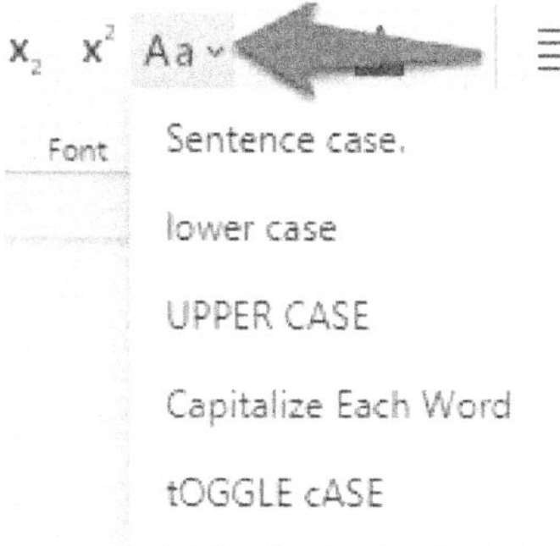

Then, it will take effect immediately on your text. Note that all the text including the first letter of every paragraph will reflect lower case by default

hello, this is word 365 interface.

word 365 interface comes with a lot of amazing features for microsoft users with word 365 you can share your document via link and track your progress with your team member. i am a new sentence after a full stop

microsoft word 365 also comes with simply outlook for user friendly environment such as speech to text dictation, sharing of document via link, onedrive cloud storage and lot more.

- **Upper case:** Upper case is used to capitalize words. This is majorly used for headings or a title that reflect what a bunch of words represent. To apply upper case, kindly highlight your text

hello, this is word 365 interface.

word 365 interface comes with a lot of amazing features for microsoft users with word 365 you can share your document via link and track your progress with your team member. i am a new sentence after a full stop

microsoft word 365 also comes with simply outlook for user friendly environment such as speech to text dictation, sharing of document via link, onedrive cloud storage and lot more.

Go to the "Home tab"

Locate "font ribbon" and select "change case". Pick "upper case"

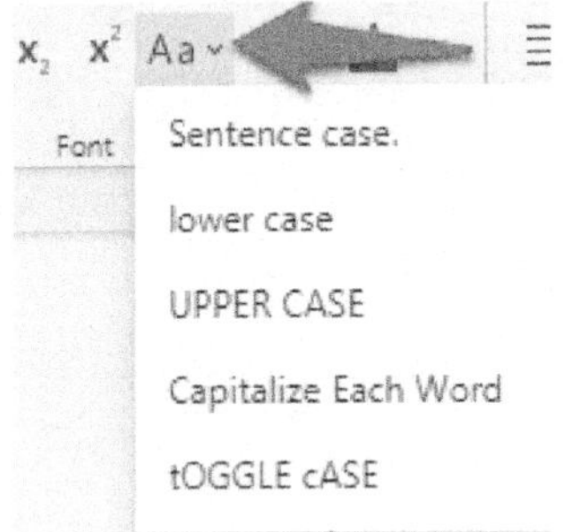

Then, it will take effect on your text immediately. Note all text will be capitalized by default

HELLO, THIS IS WORD 365 INTERFACE.

WORD 365 INTERFACE COMES WITH A LOT OF AMAZING FEATURES FOR MICROSOFT USERS WITH WORD 365 YOU CAN SHARE YOUR DOCUMENT VIA LINK AND TRACK YOUR PROGRESS WITH YOUR TEAM MEMBER. I AM A NEW SENTENCE AFTER A FULL STOP

MICROSOFT WORD 365 ALSO COMES WITH SIMPLY OUTLOOK FOR USER FRIENDLY ENVIRONMENT SUCH AS SPEECH TO TEXT DICTATION, SHARING OF DOCUMENT VIA LINK, ONEDRIVE CLOUD STORAGE AND LOT MORE.

- **Capitalize each word:** this is used to capitalize each word in a sentence. To apply this, highlight all your text or the specific one you want it to affect; based on this guide we will be highlighting all, after highlighting all

Hello, this is word 365 interface.

Word 365 interface comes with a lot of amazing features for Microsoft users with word 365 you can share your document via link and track your progress with your team member. I am a new sentence after a full stop

Microsoft word 365 also comes with simply outlook for user friendly environment such as speech to text dictation, sharing of document via link, onedrive cloud storage and lot more.

Go to the "Home tab"

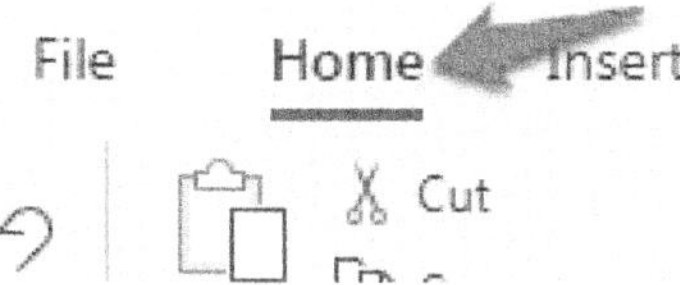

Locate "font ribbon" and select "change case", pick "Capitalize each word"

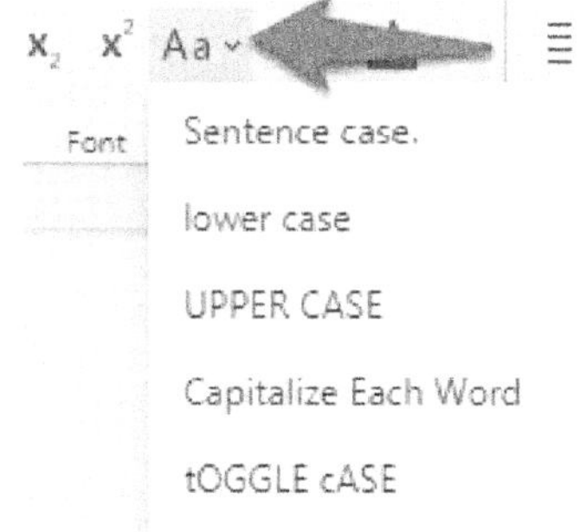

Then, it will take effect immediately on your text. Note all first words will be capitalized by default.

Hello, This Is Word 365 Interface.

Word 365 Interface Comes With A Lot Of Amazing Features For Microsoft Users With Word 365 You Can Share Your Document Via Link And Track Your Progress With Your Team Member. I Am A New Sentence After A Full Stop

Microsoft Word 365 Also Comes With Simply Outlook For User Friendly Environment Such As Speech To Text Dictation, Sharing Of Document Via Link, Onedrive Cloud Storage And Lot More.

- **Toggle word:** Toggle word is the opposite of "capitalize each word". In the toggle word, every first letter of a paragraph or a letter of a new sentence is in small letters while others are in capital letters. To apply toggle word, simply highlight all your text as usual

Hello, this is word 365 interface.

Word 365 interface comes with a lot of amazing features for Microsoft users with word 365 you can share your document via link and track your progress with your team member. I am a new sentence after a full stop

Microsoft word 365 also comes with simply outlook for user friendly environment such as speech to text dictation, sharing of document via link, onedrive cloud storage and lot more.

Go to the "Home tab"

Locate "font ribbon" and select "change case". Pick "toggle case"

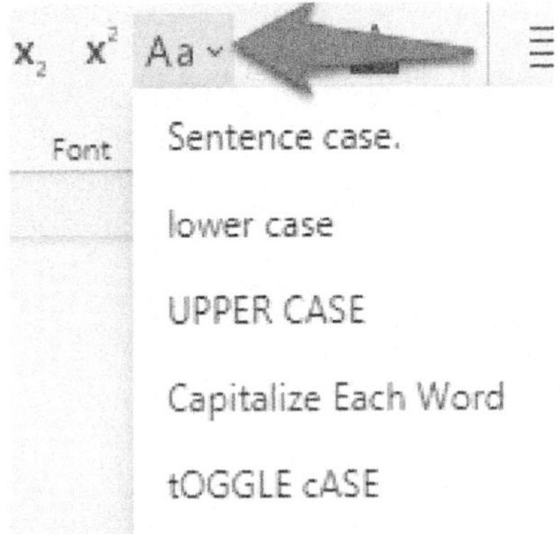

Then, it will take effect immediately on your text. Note that all first letters in each paragraph and a new text after a full stop will start with a small letter.

hELLO, THIS IS WORD 365 INTERFACE.

wORD 365 INTERFACE COMES WITH A LOT OF AMAZING FEATURES FOR mICROSOFT USERS WITH WORD 365 YOU CAN SHARE YOUR DOCUMENT VIA LINK AND TRACK YOUR PROGRESS WITH YOUR TEAM MEMBER. i AM A NEW SENTENCE AFTER A FULL STOP

mICROSOFT WORD 365 ALSO COMES WITH SIMPLY OUTLOOK FOR USER FRIENDLY ENVIRONMENT SUCH AS SPEECH TO TEXT DICTATION, SHARING OF DOCUMENT VIA LINK, ONEDRIVE CLOUD STORAGE AND LOT MORE.

Entering Symbols and Foreign Characters

Symbol as its name implies is a sign or a tag used to list and categorize text. Symbols include a variety of options such as mathematical symbols, currency symbols, copyright symbols, and lots more.

- How to apply it; assuming we want to create a fruit list and the first fruit on the list is orange, point your cursor to where orange is located at the beginning of the letter "O" of orange.

- Now, go to the "Insert" menu" bar

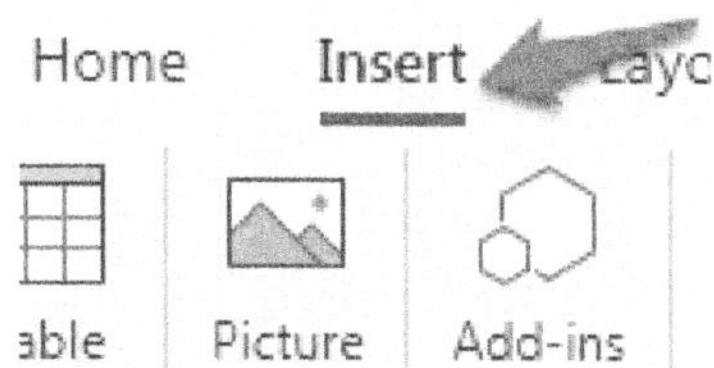

- You will locate your "symbols ribbon" at your right-hand side

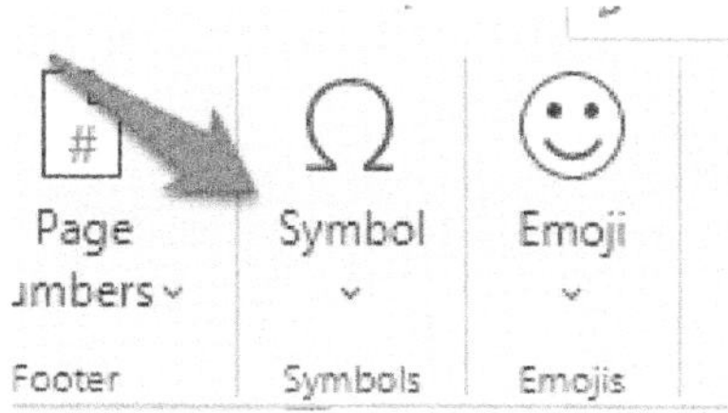

- Click on "Symbol's ribbon" to select your preferred choice

- Once selected, it will affect the cursor position, you can do the same to other items on the list

List of fruits

• Orange

Apple

Dragon Fruit

Blueberries

Melon

Raspberries

Creating Hyperlinks

Creating a hyperlink is a great feature of Microsoft Word that redirects you to the web for more info on the linked text. It is majorly used for references.

Linking a hyperlink to a web page

- First, select your text to be linked

Hello, this is word 365 interface.

- Secondly, go to "Insert menu bar"

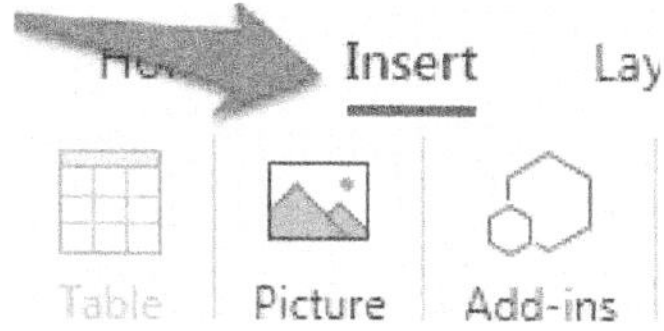

- By your right-hand side, you will see "link", click on it

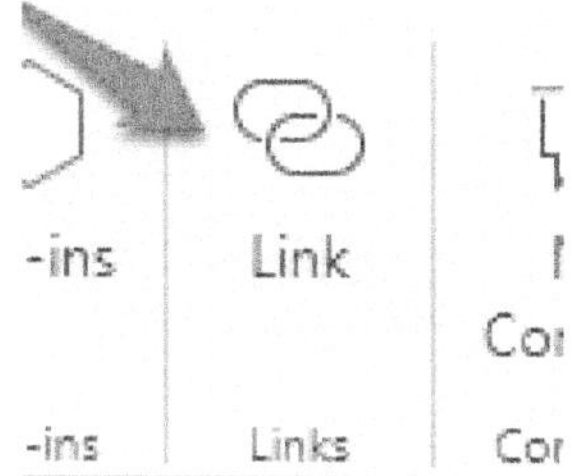

- Once you click on it, a dialog box will appear (still make sure your link text is highlighted), if your text is still highlighted, it will show automatically on the ***"Display text box".*** Let us assume we want our link to redirect us into Microsoft website, simply type the website, www.microsoft.com and click the ***"Insert option".*** This is your result for Microsoft Word 365 web users.

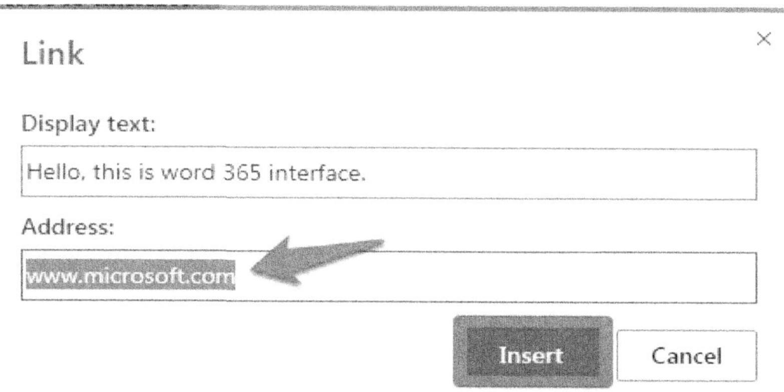

For Microsoft Word 365 license users, this is your result, locate ***"Existing file or web page"*** by your left-hand side which is titled ***"Link to",*** select the first option ***"Current folder"*** under ***"Look in",*** once selected, look down, you will see another titled bar named ***"Address"*** enter your redirected address and press ***"Ok".***

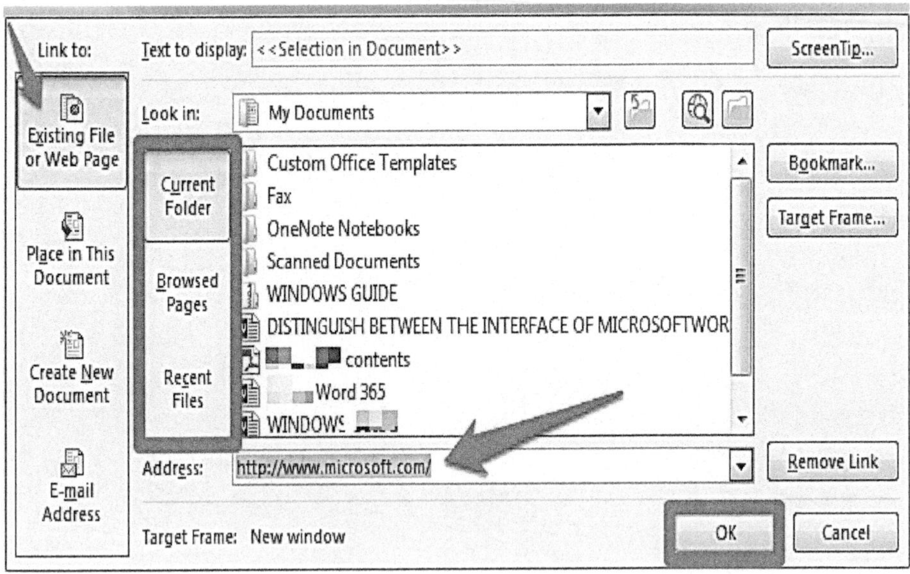

- Your highlighted text will be converted into a blue color with an underline

Hello, this is word 365 interface.

- To redirect into the Microsoft link, kindly press your "Ctrl key + Left-click". You will be redirected to the Microsoft website we inputted

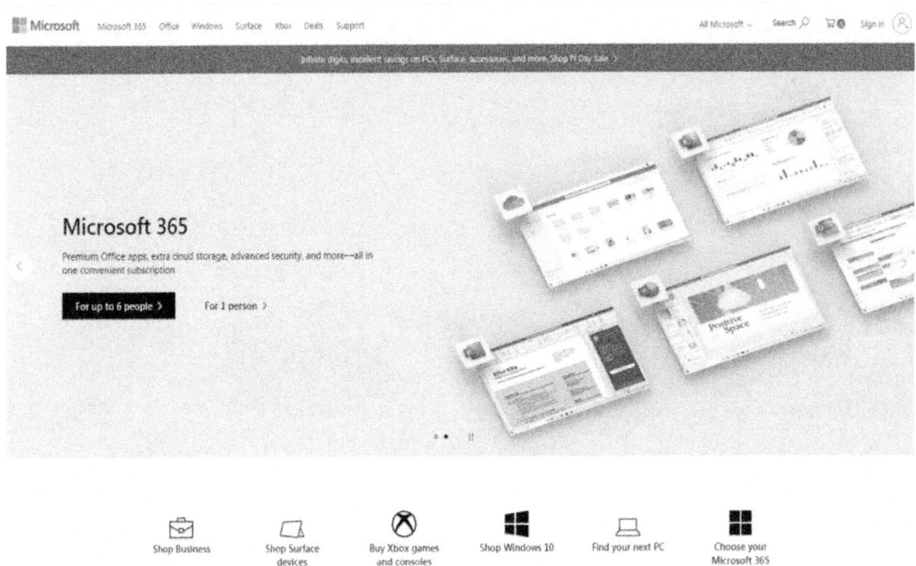

Note: this can be used on any other website of your choice.

Creating a hyperlink to another place in your file.

Note: By now, this feature of linking one file to another has not yet been included on Microsoft Word 365 Cloud version, it's still under improvement, and due to being a free version, some features are withdrawn and only available on Microsoft Word 365 installed application version which comes with a licensed product key that can be purchased from Microsoft official website (www.microsoft.com). So, this illustration is based on Microsoft Word 365 licensed version. Are we together? Alright, can we continue? Okay.

- Select the text you want to link into another file

Hello, this is word 365 interface.

- Go to ***"Insert"*** in the menu bar

- By your right-hand side, locate the ***"Link ribbon"*** click on it

- A dialog box will pop up, select ***"Existing file or web page",*** then click on ***"Current folder"*** or ***"Browsed pages"*** to locate your file, once seen, select it as illustrated in arrow three, it will be automatically selected in the "Address bar". Above is our highlighted text named ***"text to display"***, except you highlight it as explained above, it won't reflect on the above dialog box. Click "ok" to see the effect.

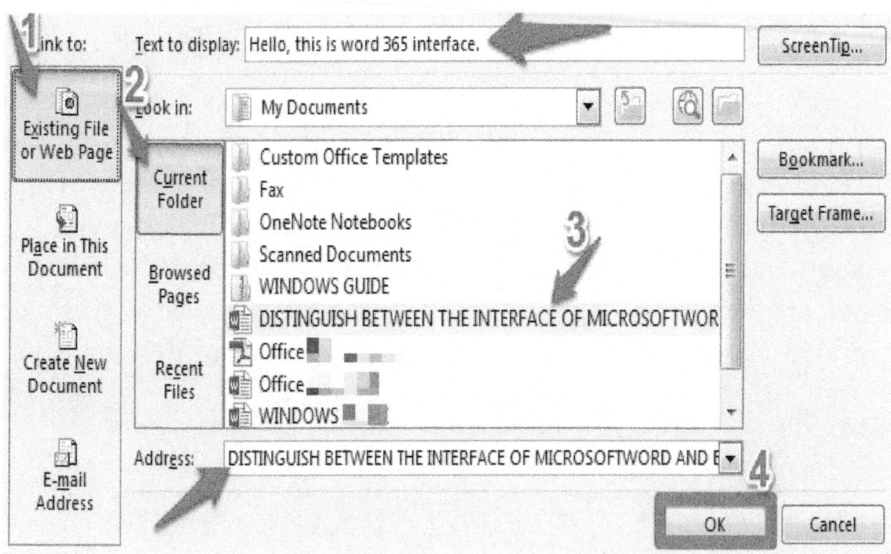

- Below must be your outcome, the highlighted text will change from its normal black color to blue or orange color, press Ctrl and simultaneously left-click on your mouse.

Hello, this is word 365 interface.

- A dialog box will be displayed warning you that hyperlinks might be harmful to your computer and data, that you should only click those hyperlinks you trusted such as the one you created yourself and other trusted ones. Click ***"Yes"*** to proceed

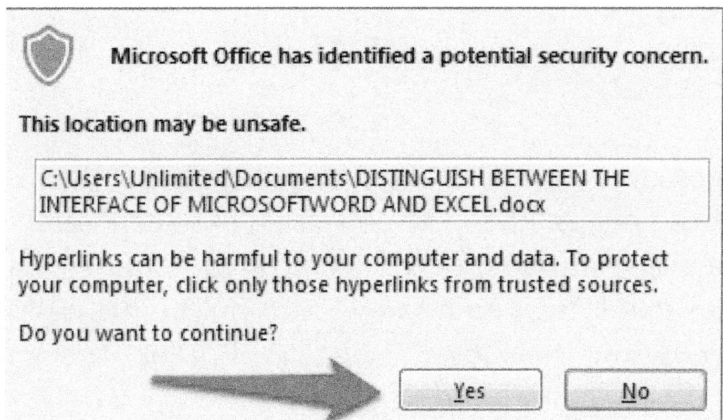

- Your linked file will be opened automatically

DISTINGUISH BETWEEN THE INTERFACE OF MICROSOFTWORD AND EXCEL

Word Handles Text Better

Word is made for text documents, including letters, books and academic papers. Text in Excel is usually a brief snippet used to describe the meaning of a number.

Word's for Printing

A Word document is formatted to fit on a specific size page with the text automatically flowing from one page to the next. Excel supports printing, but its page breaks are not obvious, and because it's printing area can extend multiple pages horizontally as well as vertically the page breaks can be difficult to manage.

Creating an email hyperlink

- Select the text you want to link into another file

Hello, this is word 365 interface.

- Go to "Insert menu bar"

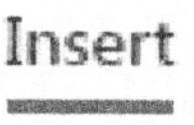

- By your right-hand side, locate ***"Link ribbon",*** click on it

- Link ribbon dialog box will pop up with multiple options, for this session we are going to create an email link. Don't let us forget our highlighted text at the top side that will still reflect itself as a means of reminding us that we highlighted a text before starting this process of creating an email link which is ***"Hello, this is Word 365 interface."***

Below at your left-hand side is your "Email Address", click on it, you will be brought here, enter your ***"Email address"*** & ***"Subject"*** and ***"Recently used email address"*** (This is optional except you have been using email linking before all your previous activities will be displayed here). Once you are done filling, click "Ok"

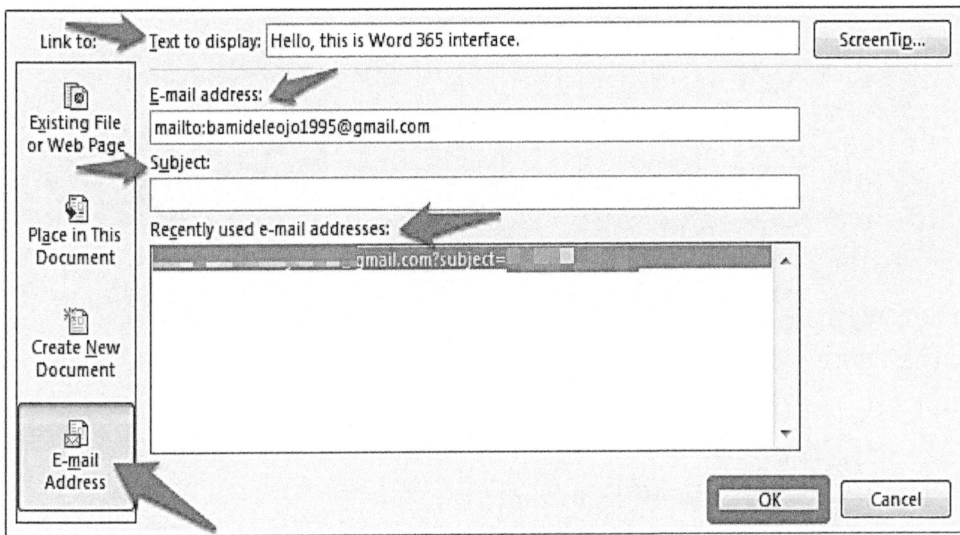

- Your highlighted text will automatically change from black to either blue or orange color as a sign that our process of creating a link via email is successful. To confirm, press Ctrl and simultaneously left-click, your cursor arrow pointer will change to the hand-click icon, then left-click to redirect you to your inserted details.

Hello, this is word 365 interface.

Removing hyperlink

No effect without remedy, every action on Microsoft Word has a way of maneuvering it. To remove the hyperlink on your affected text.

- Select your affected text that has a hyperlink effect

Hello, this is Word 365 interface.

- Go to "Insert menu bar"

Insert

- By your right-hand side, locate ***"Link ribbon"*** click on it

- The Link dialog box will appear, at your right-hand side as illustrated with the arrow below, click on ***"Remove Link"*** and hit ***"Ok"***

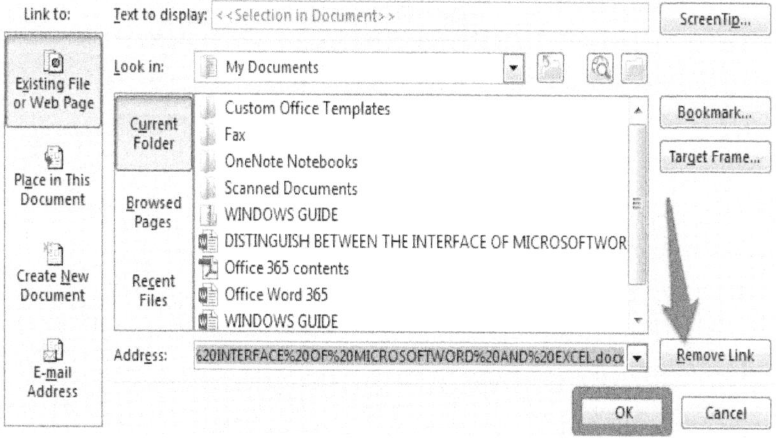

- Your highlighted linked text will automatically be removed from the hyperlink and it will become normal text with your default black color.

Hello, this is word 365 interface.

Notification

Notification gives more awareness about a newly added feature, which is one of the reasons software companies are all gradually moving online to reduce upgrading and different release.

How to rename your document

- Simply click on **"File"**

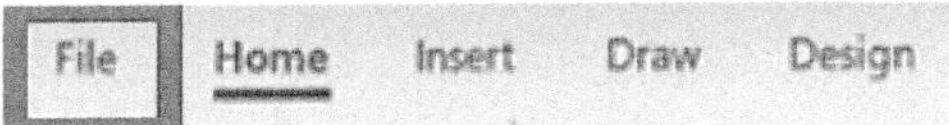

A dialog box will slide in by your left-hand side, look for **"save as"**, click on it

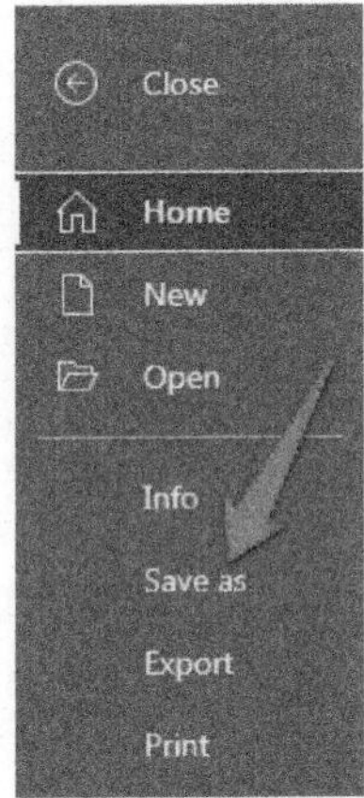

Note that there is no save button on Word 365 free online version, it AutoSaves itself online. Once you select **"Save as"**, a slide will appear beside the blue 'Save as' slide at your right, look for **"Rename"** and click on it**.**

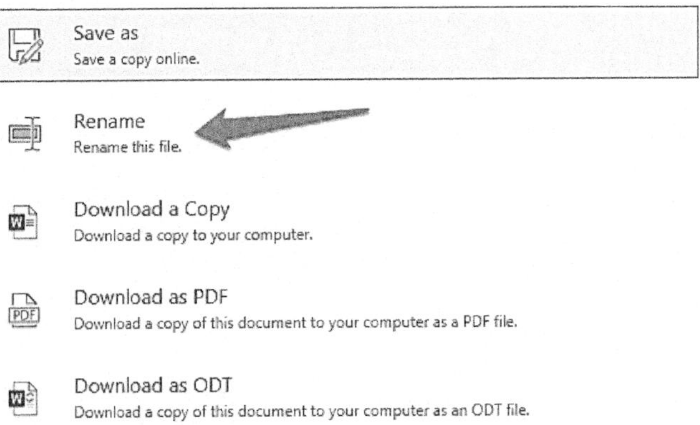

A dialog box will appear titled **"File Name"**, you can rename your document as you wish

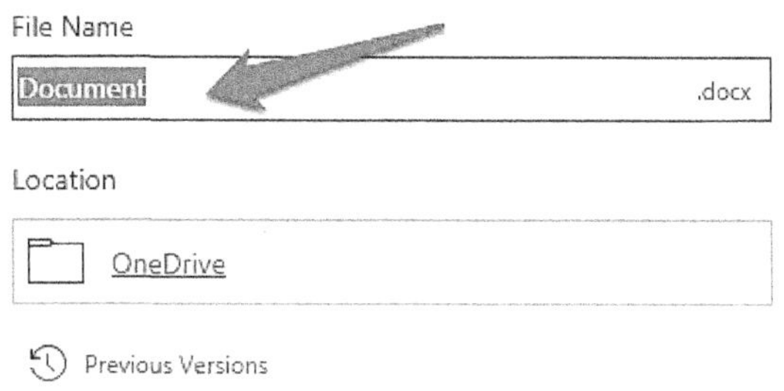

How to Save a document directly to your PC

- Go to "File menu"

- Select "Save option"

- A dialog box will appear, select the location you want to save, name your document on the "File name box" and click "Save".

Note: saving your document on your PC is only for licensed users, Microsoft Word online free version saves automatically online on OneDrive storage.

How to Save a document directly to your OneDrive cloud storage

- Go to "file menu"

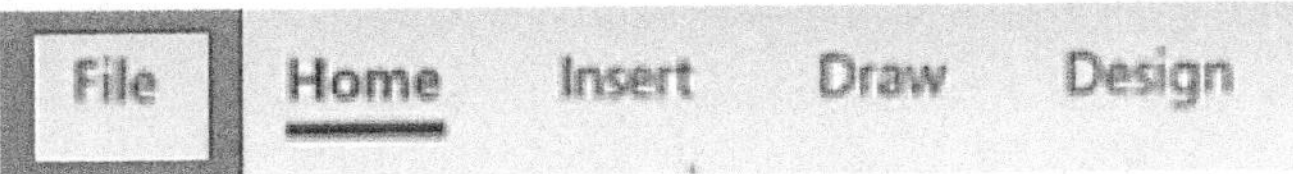

- You will see multiple options, select "Save as"

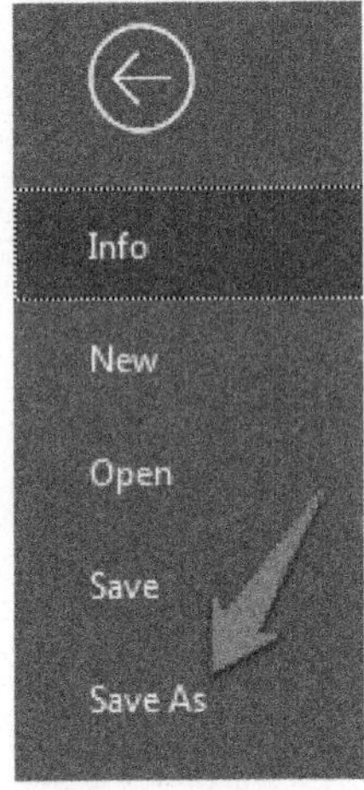

- A dialog box will appear, you will see the "OneDrive" option, once you click it, your document will be saved online. If you have many folders on your OneDrive storage, you will be asked to choose the destination you want your work to be saved in, once done, hit "Save".

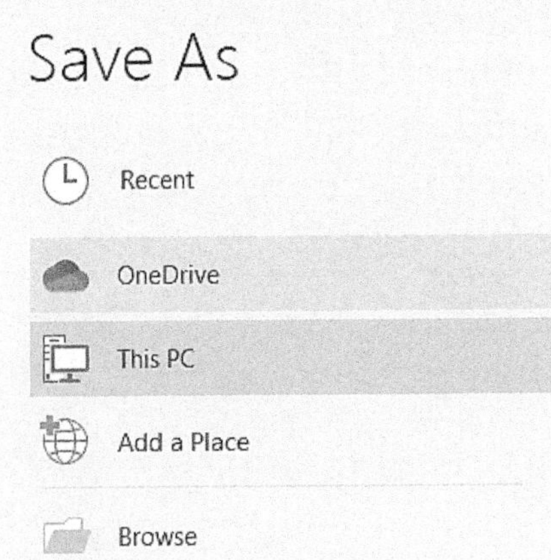

Where does my document go to?

Your document majorly comes to your PC storage or OneDrive cloud storage. OneDrive cloud storage serves as a physical hard disk drive, while PC storage is your system hard disk storage. When you put your files and photos in OneDrive, they are always at your fingertip, no matter where you are. It is important to note that your files are private until you decide to collaborate by sharing your documents with your team and edit together in real-time by sending them a link and authorization access to edit.

How to upgrade your Microsoft 365 web free version

Upgrading is only recommended for office usage or personal usage that has more files than the normal 1 Gigabyte free storage capacity can contain in the long run. Once you are among the license subscribers, you will be informed depending on your plan.

It is advisable to know what you want to achieve with an upgrade in order not to be charged unnecessarily.

CHAPTER THREE

SPEED TECHNIQUES WORTH KNOWING ABOUT

Undoing and Redoing Commands

Undoing and repeating commands are more of erasing and recalling words

To Undo Text

- After typing a bunch of text on Word 365

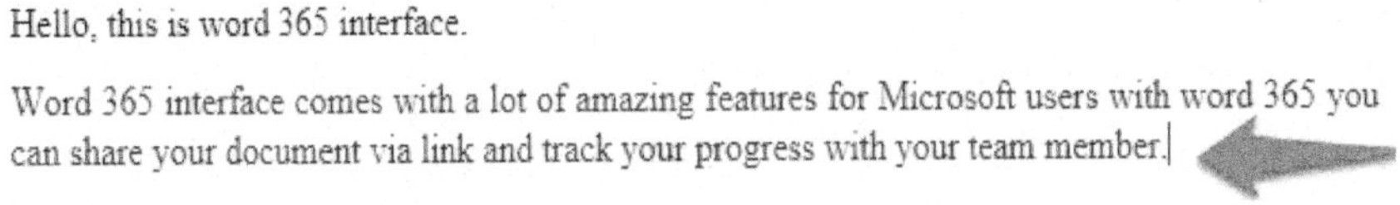

Hello, this is word 365 interface.

Word 365 interface comes with a lot of amazing features for Microsoft users with word 365 you can share your document via link and track your progress with your team member.

- You can press Ctrl + Z to undo your text, it will gradually backward your text

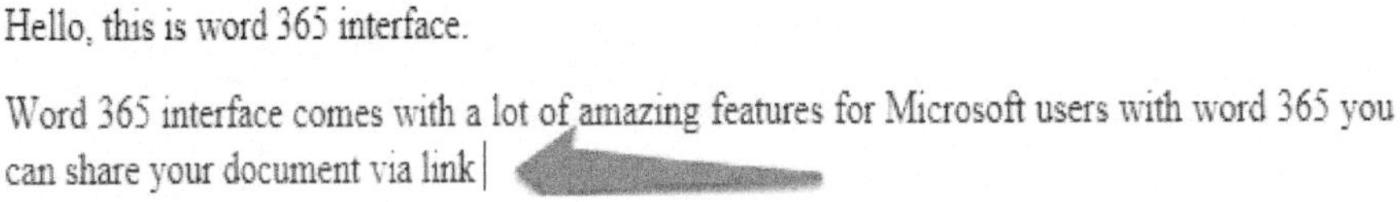

Hello, this is word 365 interface.

Word 365 interface comes with a lot of amazing features for Microsoft users with word 365 you can share your document via link

- Or you highlight the part to be removed and press ***"backspace"*** from your keyboard to remove it.

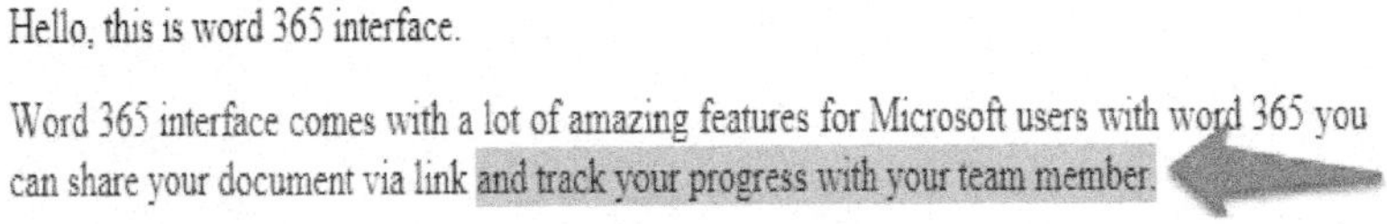

Hello, this is word 365 interface.

Word 365 interface comes with a lot of amazing features for Microsoft users with word 365 you can share your document via link and track your progress with your team member.

- You can also use Word 365 undo icon to backward your text, either way, your text will be undone. Simply go to the ***"home tab",*** which is your default display interface and by your left-hand side you will see your Undo icon. The first arrow is your undo icon facing backward while the second one is your redo icon facing forward.

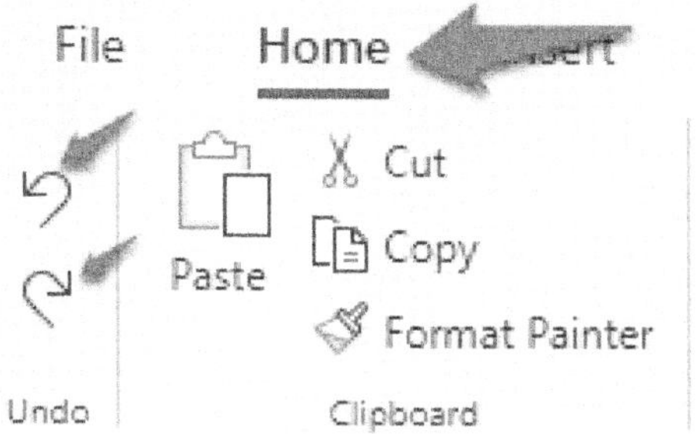

To Redo Text

- After typing a bunch of text on Word 365

Hello, this is word 365 interface.

Word 365 interface comes with a lot of amazing features for Microsoft users with word 365 you can share your document via link and track your progress with your team member.

- You can press Ctrl + Y to redo your text, it will redo what you earlier undo

Hello, this is word 365 interface.

Word 365 interface comes with a lot of amazing features for Microsoft users with word 365 you can share your document via link

- You can also use Word 365 redo icon to forward your text only if it had been earlier back-warded. Your text will redo when you mistakenly remove or delete some text. To use the redo icon, simply go to the ***"home tab"*** which is your default display interface, by your left-hand side, you will see your redo icon the first arrow is your undo facing backward while the second one is your redo facing forward.

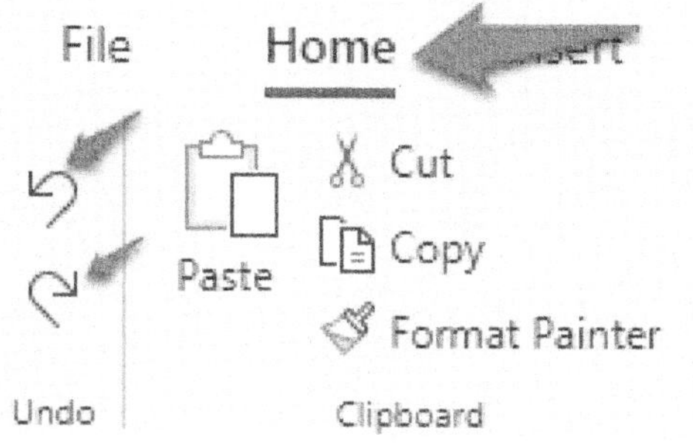

Zooming In and Zooming Out

Zooming In & Zooming Out is a feature of Microsoft Word that makes the Word interface clearer and more readable depending on the user's choice. You see that Microsoft Word is embedded with simplicity and flexibility.

How to Zoom In & Zoom Out

- Go to ***"View menu bar"***

- Under ***"View menu bar",*** select ***"Zoom percentage"***

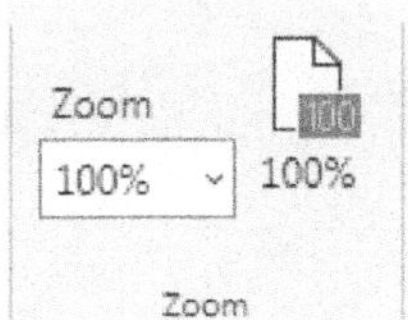

- Once you click on the little arrow beside the ***"100%"***, dropdown options of Zooming In & Zooming Out will pop up, select your preferred choice and it will affect the entire interface of your current working document.

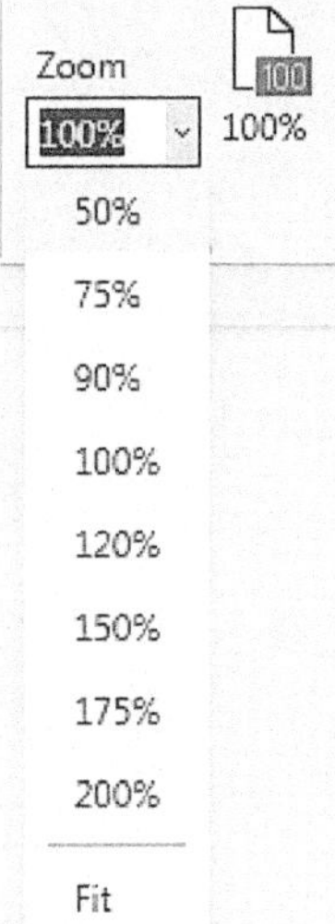

- The other ***"100%",*** will return your zooming in & out to 100% default displayed zooming settings

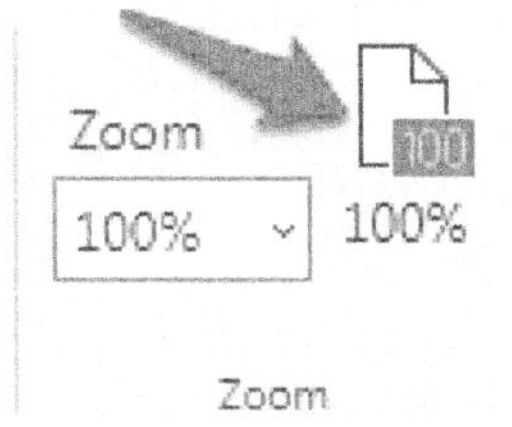

Viewing a File through More than One Window

Viewing of file through more than one Window creates the possibility to work in another Window and not affect your original Window.

Steps on how to apply it

- From your current opened document, go to "View menu bar" by your right-hand side

- It is advisable to purchase a license Microsoft Office installation software because the one online is still very much under progressive development; not all features are on Word 365 web base.

- Under the "view menu bar", click on "New Window" (which is known as document interface), your current document which is opened will be duplicated and named "document:1" by default, except you rename it. Another duplicated one will be named "document:2"

Document 1 - Saved to OneDrive

Document 2 - Saved to OneDrive

- Any changes in one will automatically lead to the same changes in the other.

Correcting Typos

Errors can be an omission in typing and as long as a human being is concerned, a computer can never use itself, but rather, human determines the behavior of a PC, this is the reason for misspelling and other mistakes made by PC users. Yet, Microsoft researcher team members look for a remedy to this issue, which leads to auto-correct in Microsoft packages.

Steps on how to enable auto-correct

Automatically, auto-correct is always activated on all Microsoft packages. Due to one reason or the other, if it is not, simply follow this simple process:

- Go to "Review menu bar"

Review

- At your left-hand side on "Proofing ribbon", click on "Spelling & Grammar"

- Once you click on "Spelling & Grammar", auto-correct for error detection are shown one at a time as they occur in your document. You must deal with them one after the other (serially).

Entering Text Quickly with the Auto-Correct

Entering text quickly with the auto-correct command is often used for frequently used words such as an address, greetings text format, letter text template, and other text purposes.

Steps on how to go about AutoCorrect Command

- First, select the text you do use often by highlighting it

1 The Street
The Town
The City
PO12 1AB

- Go to ***"Insert menu bar"***

Insert

- By your right-hand side, you will see "Quick Parts", click on it and select ***"Save Selection to Quick Part Gallery"***

- Make sure your selected text is still highlighted, if not ***"Save Selection to Quick Part Gallery"*** will not be visible

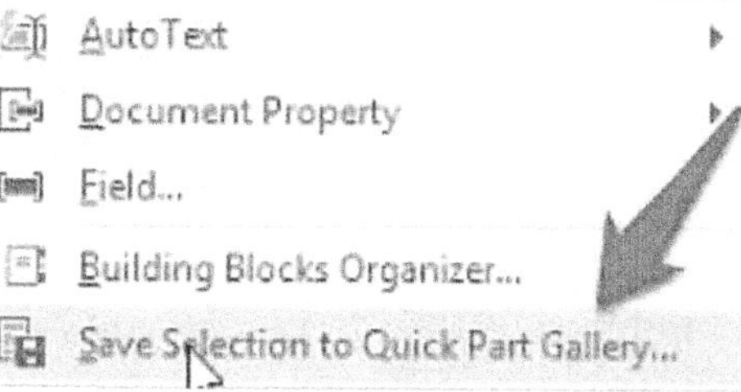

- After you select "Save Selection to Quick Part Gallery", a dialog box will appear with the name "Create New Building Block", there, you can rename the title of the highlighted text, and in the "Gallery" text box, select "Quick Part"

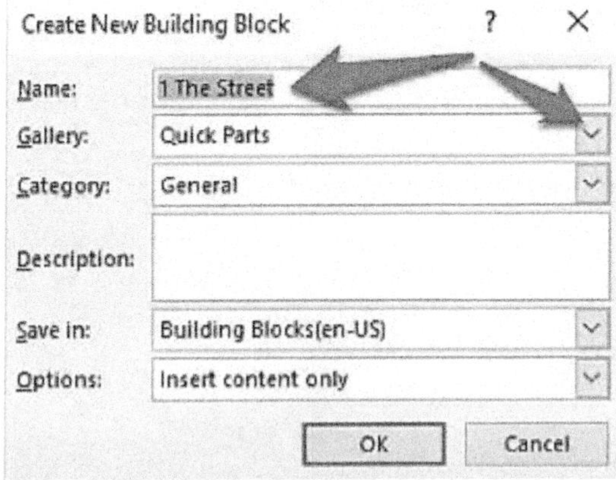

- Make sure this is what you inputted, if you followed and typed the highlighted text as instructed, for understanding purpose, leave the "Description", "Save in" & "Options" the way it is. Once done, press "Ok"

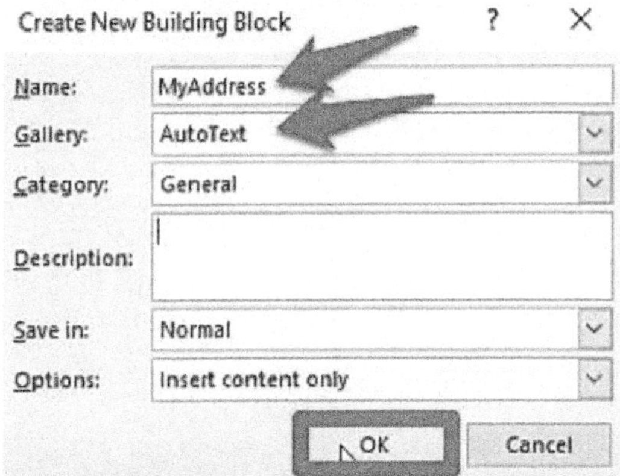

How do you assign a shortcut key to bring forth your auto text entry?

- Go to your "file menu bar" which is also known as "file menu"

File

- Under "file menu", select "Options"

- A dialog box will appear on your left-hand side, select "Customize Ribbon"

- By your right-hand side, "Customize Ribbon" features will appear, below it, you will see "Keyboard shortcuts", click on "Customize"

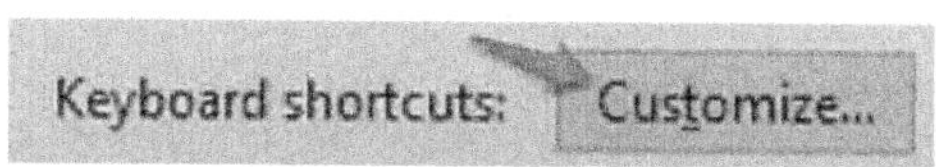

- Another dialog box will appear titled "Categories", search for "Building Blocks"

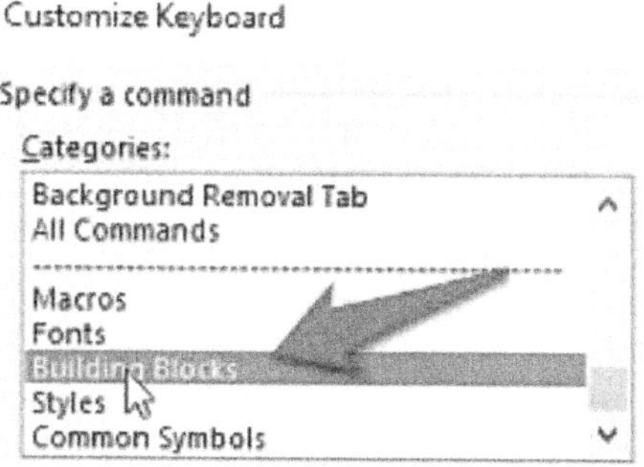

- Once you have located "Building Blocks", click on it, building blocks features will appear beside it at your right-hand side, locate "MyAddress"; based on my illustration on "Steps on how to go about AutoCorrect Command", I renamed the "Name" text box under "Create New Building Block" as "MyAddress" that is why I can locate it here. In case you name yours differently, search for it, or else, go back and follow how I did mine.

- Once selected, below it is a dialog box where you can assign a shortcut key to it, it is titled "Press new shortcut keys:"

- I will be inserting my preferred shortcut command which is "Ctrl+Shift+M". I will advise you do the same in order not to make any mistake, once you understand it you can repeat the process yourself.

- Once done, look at your left-hand side and click on "Assign"

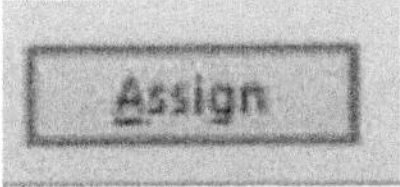

- Above the "Assign" option, your shortcut command will appear on a box titled "Current keys:" as against the previous title- "Press new shortcut keys:"

- Then, click on "Close"

- Also, click on "Ok" on the "Customize the Ribbon and keyboard shortcuts" dialog box that leads to "Keyboard shortcuts"

- Now delete your highlighted text or open a new document to confirm our newly added auto text shortcut key.

1 The Street
The Town
The City
PO12 1AB

- Once you press "Ctrl + Shift + M" from your keyboard, your auto-text will reappear back automatically.

Tips

Practice makes perfect, try doing something different by changing the address and shortcut to suit your taste and run your newly added shortcut to see if you will get it correctly without following my exact text & shortcut.

CHAPTER FOUR

LAYING OUT TEXT AND PAGES

Paragraphs and Formatting

It is important to note that paragraphs in a document cannot be ignored as far as typing is concerned. A Paragraph has different clicking methods: Single-click, double-click, triple-click, and click and drag

- ***Single-Click:*** Single-clicking on a paragraph only makes the cursor point on a particular text in the paragraph.

Single-Click single clicking
cursor point on a particular

- ***Double-Click:*** Double-clicking in a paragraph highlights a particular text

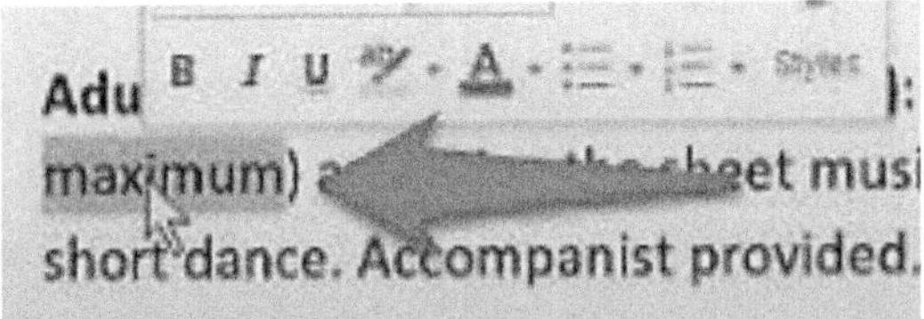

- ***Triple-Click:*** Triple-clicking highlights the whole text in a paragraph as illustrated below

It is important to note that paragraph in a document cannot be ignored as far as typing is concerned. Paragraph has different clicking methods: Single click, double click, triple click and click and drag

- ***Click and Drag:*** Click and drag selects within or beyond a paragraph depending on the user's preference.

Adult singers (18 years and older): Please prepare an upbeat song (other than one from the show) and bring the sheet music with you.

Adult dancers (18 years and older): Please prepare a short dance (2 minutes maximum) and bring the sheet music with you. Tap dancing is encouraged for the short dance. Accompanist provided.

Youth singers and dancers (9 to 14 years): You do not need to prepare a song.

Paragraph Settings

Paragraph Settings help to finetune the layout of the current paragraph, including spacing, indentation, alignment, outline level with other features.

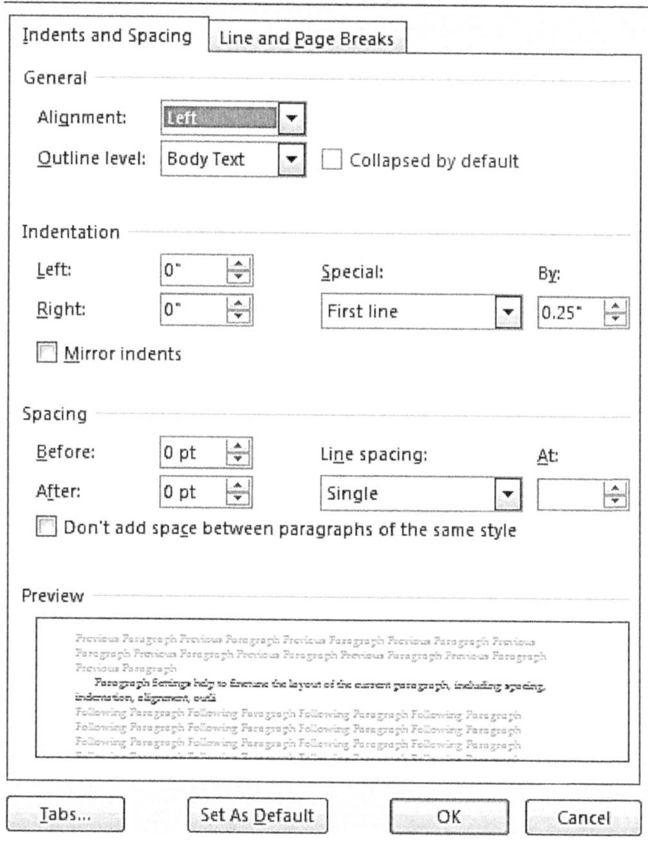

Page Formatting & Cover page

Page formatting is a tool that determines the outlook of your pages such as page margins, page orientation, page size, page columns, and lots more.

- **Page Margins:** Page margin is used to set the sizes for the entire document or the current section. Page Margins gives the privilege to choose from several commonly used margin formats or customize your own. Anyone you select will automatically affect your current working document.

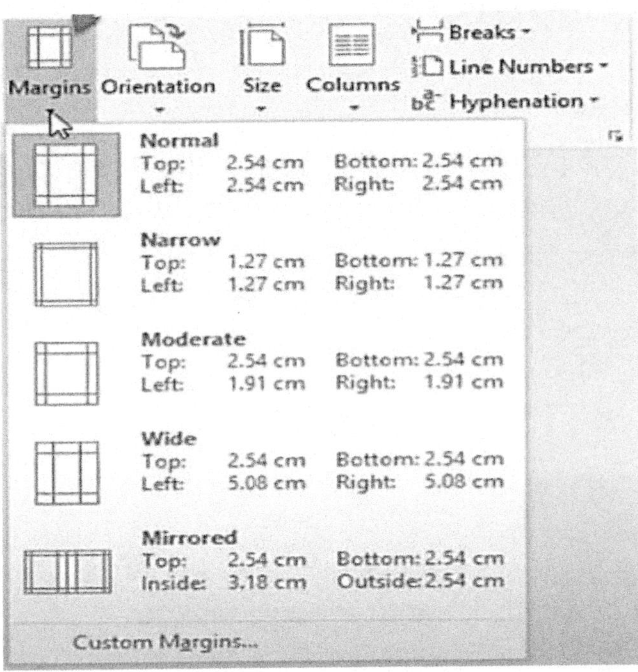

- **Page Orientation:** Page orientation determines the outlook of your page in portrait or landscape format. Anyone you select will automatically affect your current document.

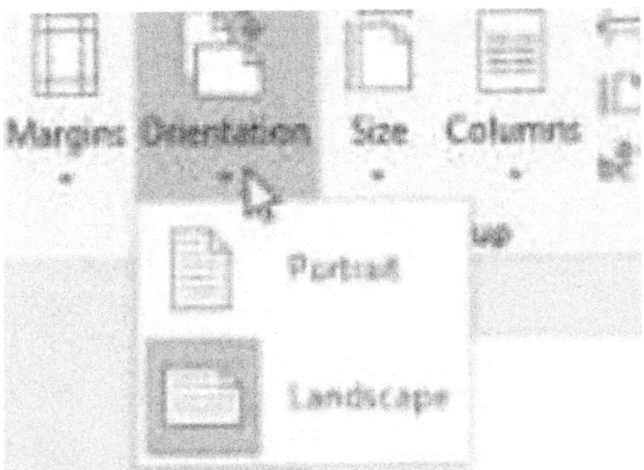

- **Page Size:** Page size comes in various forms but by default, A4 is the standard page size from Microsoft

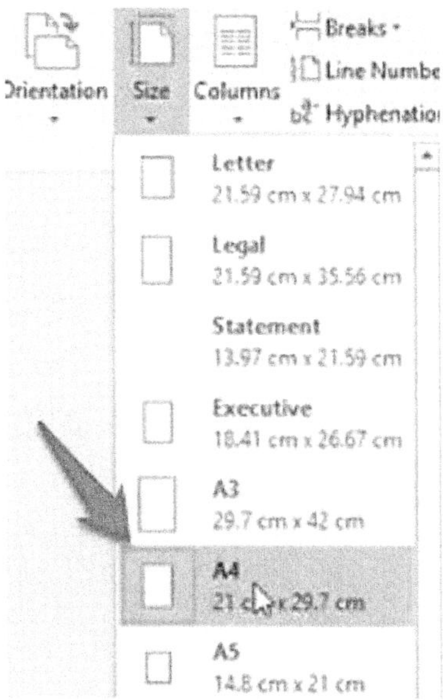

- **Page Columns:** Page columns give you the privilege to slit your text into two or more columns. You can also choose the width and spacing of your columns, or use one of the preset formats

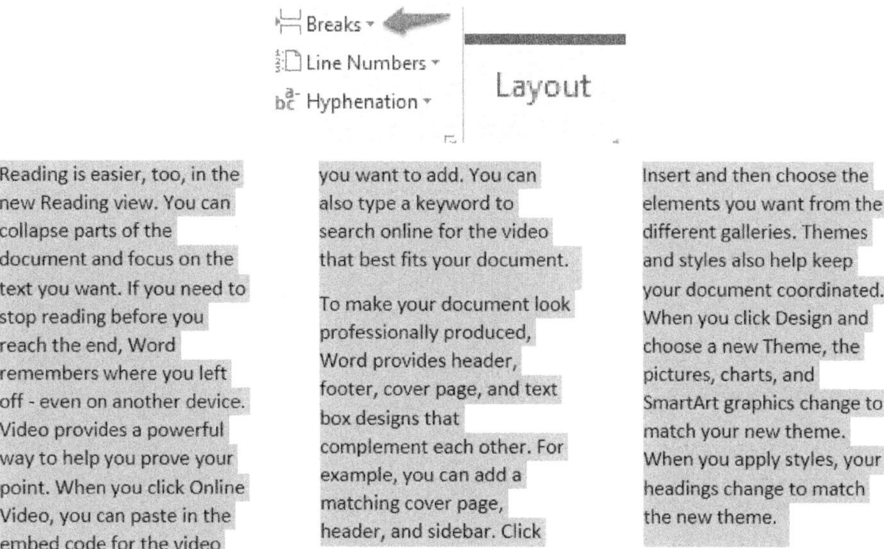

Above is an example of three columns, all you need to do is to highlight the area you want to make changes to, if you don't select it, the whole of your pages will be affected by the columns you choose.

Setting Up and Changing the Margins

Note: By default, Word document comes with default configurations, one of which is the normal margin.

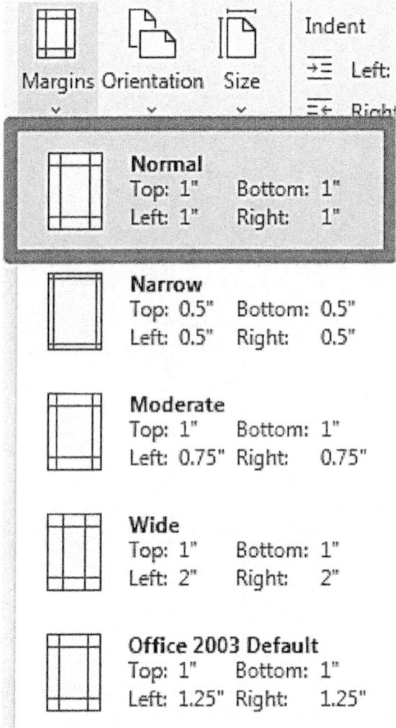

How to change your margins

- Go to "Layout tab"

- By your left-hand side, you will see "Margins"

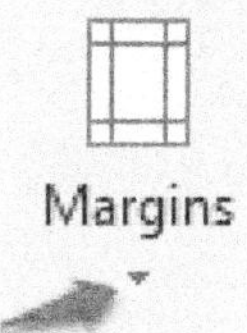

- Once you click in, your default "Margin" settings will be on "Normal".

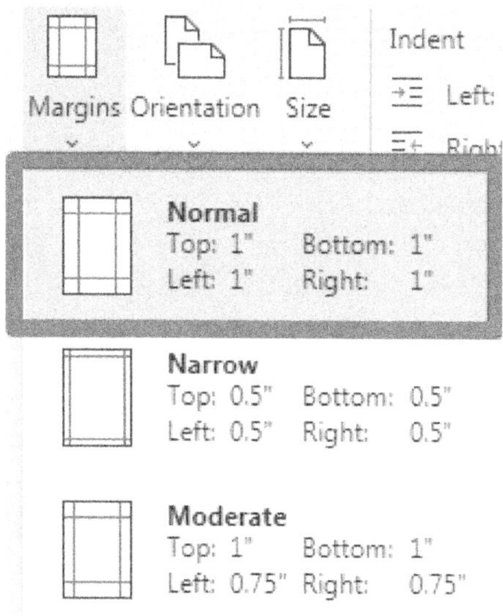

- Scroll through to select other desired options which will automatically affect your active opened document.

Note: Adjusting or changing of margin only affects your opened document, and it remains when you save the effect. For web users, you don't need to save, it automatically saves into your OneDrive cloud storage, while for offline users go to "file menu", and then you will see the save option. OneDrive storage is also available for offline users as long as you are connected to your Microsoft account.

Inserting a Section Break for Formatting Purposes

Before illustrating how to insert a section break format, it is important to know what "section break" is all about. Section break gives a separation between texts and sends the separated one into another page

- Point your cursor to where you want to set a section break

> Video provides a powerful way to help you prove your point. When you click Online Video, you can paste in the embed code for the video you want to add. You can also type a keyword to search online for the video that best fits your document. To make your document look professionally produced, Word provides header, footer, cover page, and text box designs that complement each other. For example, you can add a matching cover page, header, and sidebar. Click Insert and then choose the elements you want from the different galleries.
>
> Themes and styles also help keep your document coordinated. When you click Design and choose a new Theme, the pictures, charts, and SmartArt graphics change to match your new theme. When you apply

- Go to the "Layout tab"

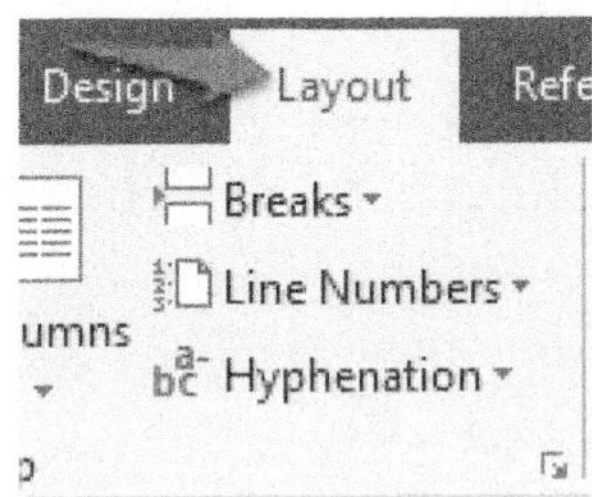

- Select "Breaks"

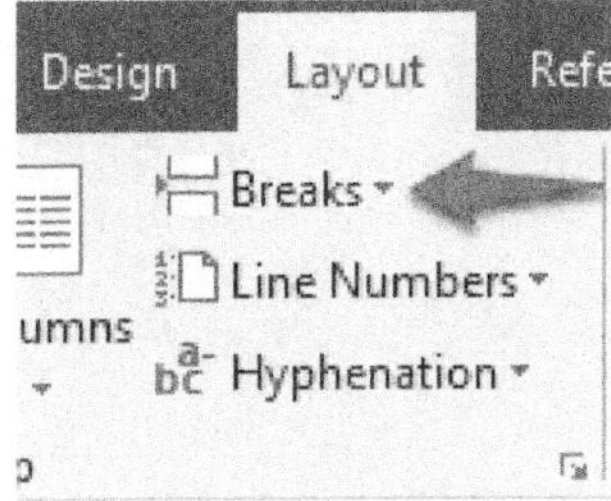

- Then, you can select "Page" to make your text have the section break effect

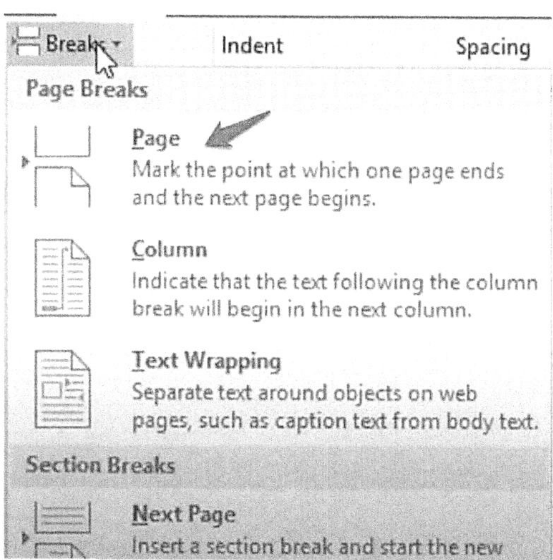

- Once you select "Page", the text where your cursor pointer is located will be automatically separated into a new page

Video provides a powerful way to help you prove your point. When you click Online Video, you can paste in the embed code for the video you want to add. You can also type a keyword to search online for the video that best fits your document. To make your document look professionally produced, Word provides header, footer, cover page, and text box designs that complement each other.

For example, you can add a matching cover page, header, and sidebar. Click Insert and then choose the elements you want from the different galleries.

Themes and styles also help keep your document coordinated. When you click Design and choose a new Theme, the pictures, charts, and SmartArt graphics change to match your new theme. When you apply styles, your headings change to match the new theme. Save time in Word with new buttons that show up where you need them. To change the way a picture fits in your document, click it and a button for layout options appears next to it. When you work on a table, click where you want to add a row or a column, and then click the plus sign.

There is also a shortcut to section break, once you set your cursor to the location you want to part, simply hold down your "Ctrl key" and hit "Enter key" from your keyboard. The point where your cursor is will automatically be parted into another page.

Cover Page

A Cover Page is a front guide of every documentation, project, brochure, and other documents which gives a summarization of what your content entails.

How to Insert a Cover Page on your Document

- Go to "Insert tab"

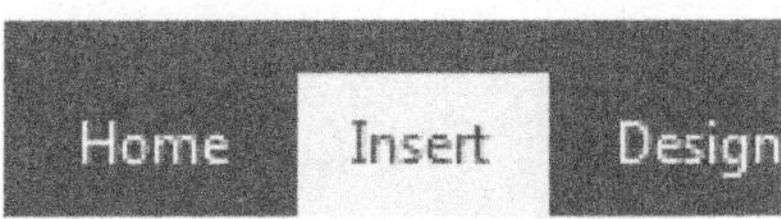

- At your left-hand side, you will see ***"Cover Page"***

- Click in to see multiple built-in "Cover Page" templates, select your preferred choice

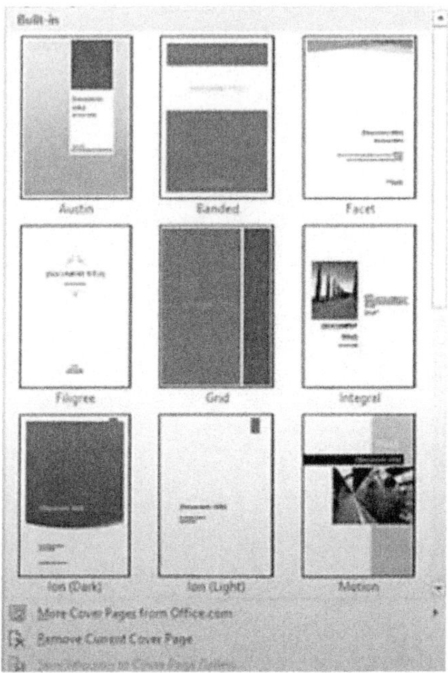

- Once you select your preferred choice, your selected cover page will occupy your front page

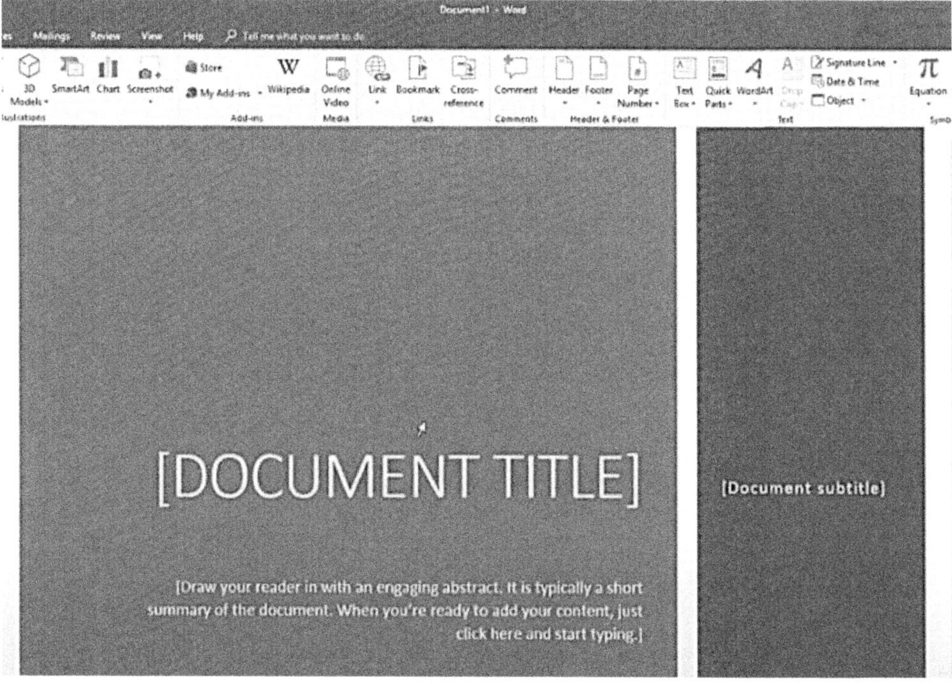

- Then, you can start editing the title page, the writeup below your title, subtitle, and other aspects depending on the template you selected

Indenting Paragraphs

- Go to the "Home tab" which is your default Word 365 interface

- At your right-hand side, locate the "Paragraph ribbon", you will see the decrease & increase indent

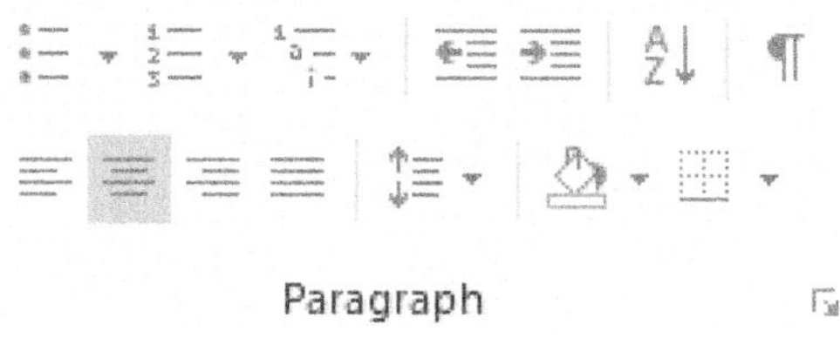

What is Decrease & Increase Indent?

Decrease Indent: Decrease indent moves your paragraph closer to your margin

Increase Indent: Increase indent moves your paragraph farther from your margin

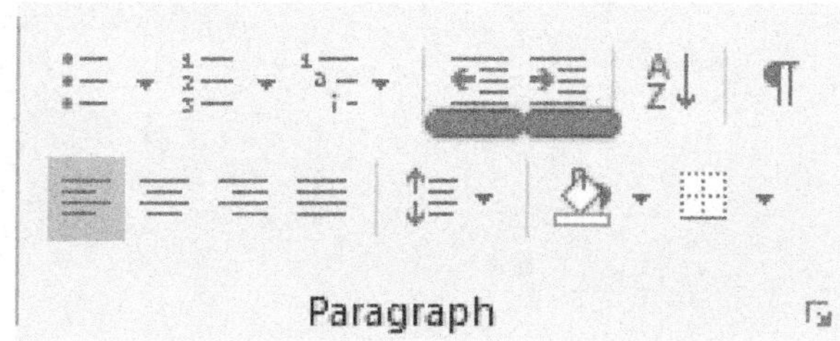

- Once you select increase indent, your paragraph moves to your right-hand side

Word Handles Text Better

Word is made for text documents, includir
Excel is usually a brief snippet used to desc

- And if you select decrease indent, your paragraph will move back to your left-hand side

Word Handles Text Better

Word is made for text documents, including
usually a brief snippet used to describe the n

- Decrease indent & Increase indent are both used depending on what is required or what the user wants to achieve

Numbering the Pages

Page Numbering is a way of making your content arranged serially for orderliness and reference purposes.

How to Insert Page Numbering

- Go to "Insert tab"

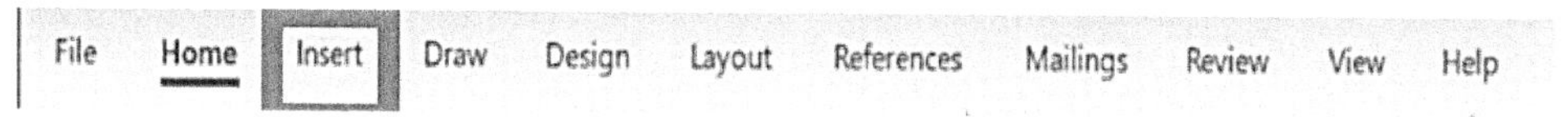

- At your right-hand side, you will see "Page Number" under "Header & Footer ribbon"

- Click on "Page Number", once you click on it, you will be given multiple options on where you want your page numbering to be positioned such as "Top of Page", "Bottom of Page", "Page Margins", "Current Position".

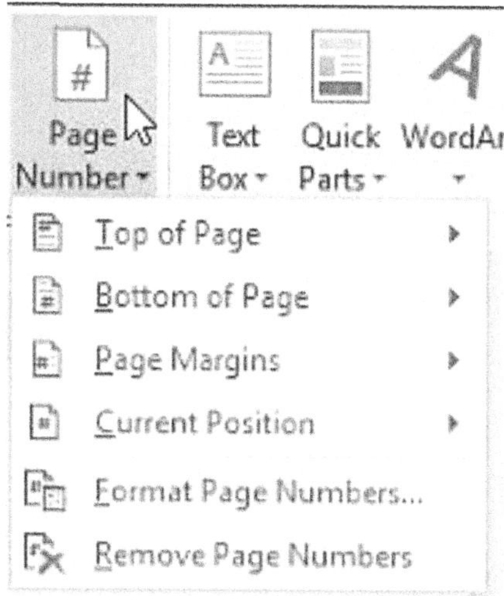

Or you can decide how you want your page numbering to look by clicking on "Format Page Numbers". A dialog box will appear for you to configure your Page Numberings such as "Number format", where you want to start effecting from, and lots more. Once you fill it, press "ok" to effect changes

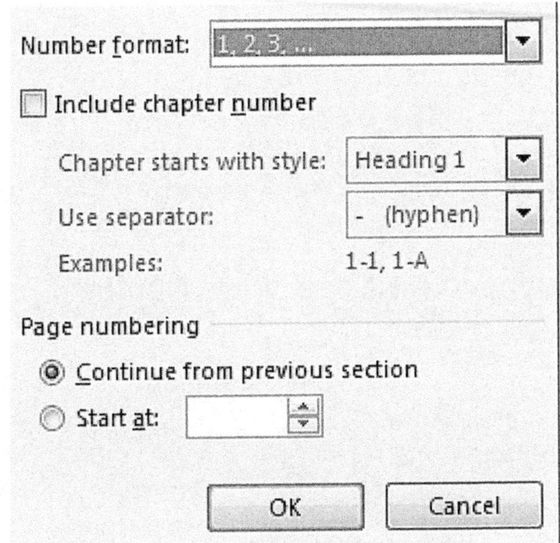

- Assuming you want the "Bottom of Page" option, click on "Bottom of Page" which is the normally used page numbering
- A dialog box will appear beside it, choose the middle numbering format

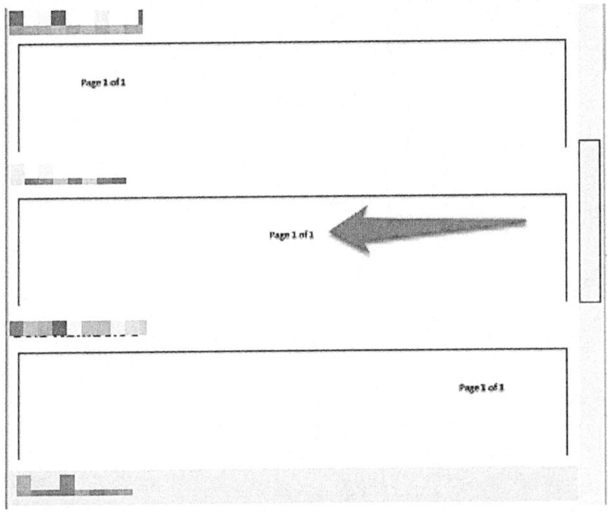

- By default, all your text will automatically be numbered serially

Remove Page Numbering

- Go to "Insert tab"

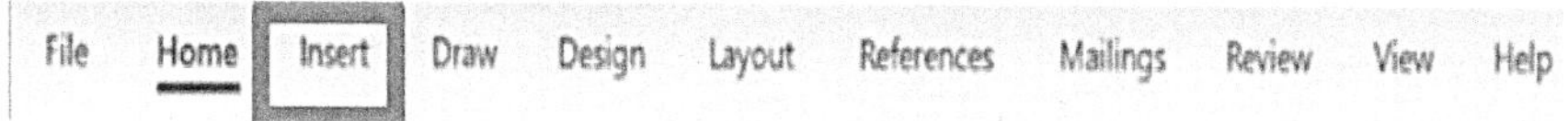

- At your right-hand side, you will see "Page Number" under "Header & Footer ribbon"

- Click on "Page Number", once you click on it, you will be given multiple options, look for "Remove Page Numbers", click on it, and every page numbering on your current opened document will be removed automatically

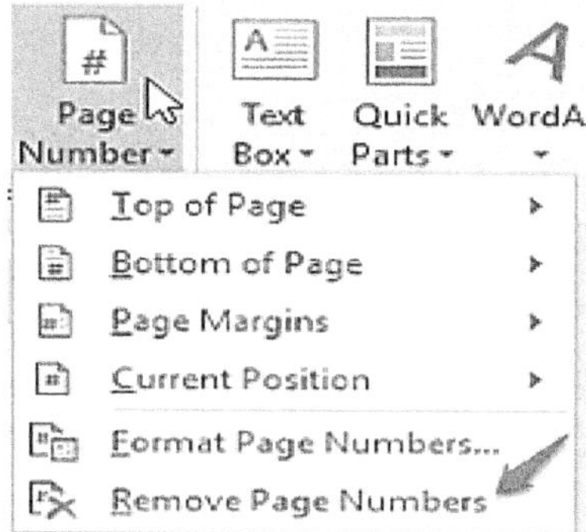

Putting Header on Pages

- Go to "Insert tab"

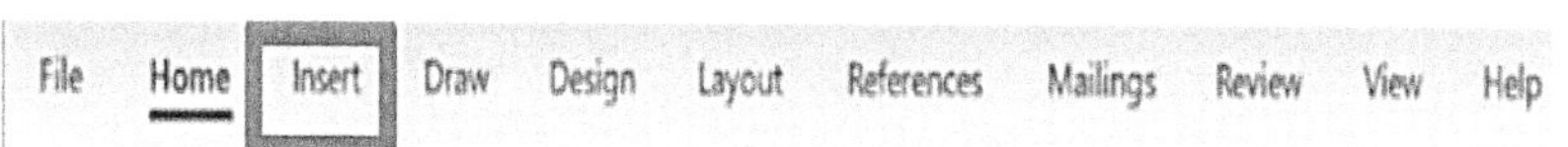

- At your right-hand side, look for "Header"

- A dialog box will appear, select your preferred alignment positioning

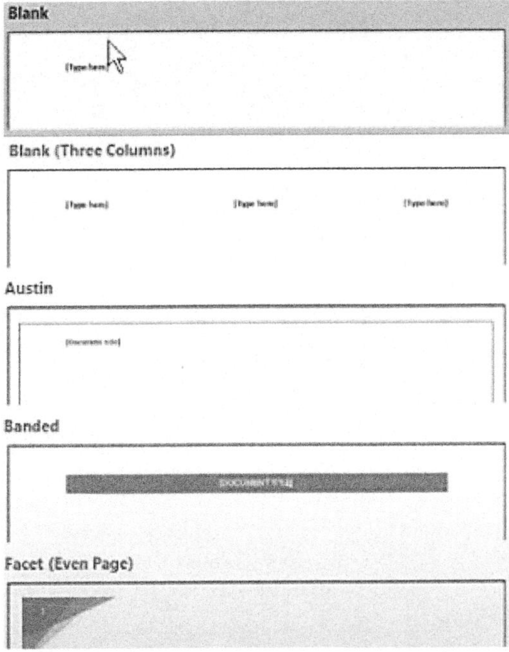

- Once done, you will be brought to your header editing edge to input your text

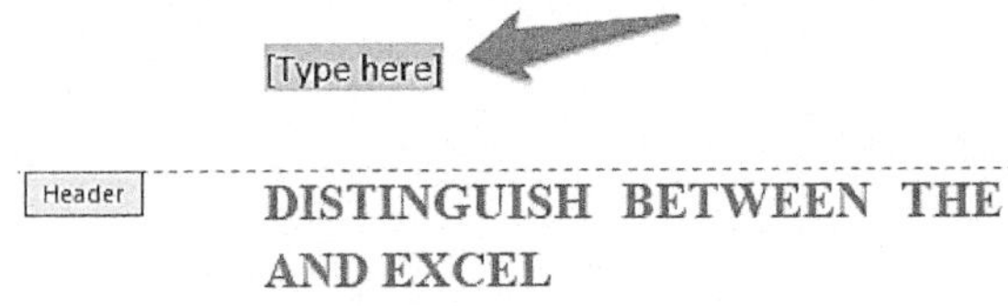

Word Handles Text Better

Note: You can also double-click on the top empty edge of your document to make use of the header format.

Removing Header from Pages

- Go to "Insert tab"

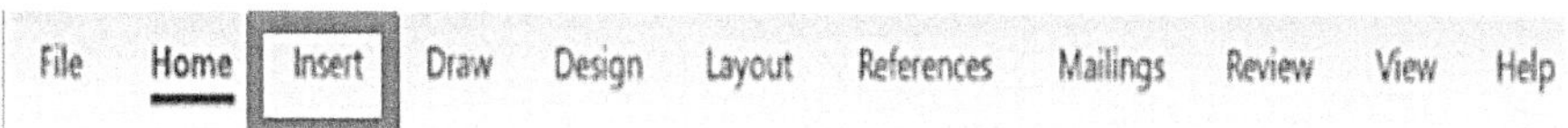

- At your right-hand side, locate "Header" and click on it

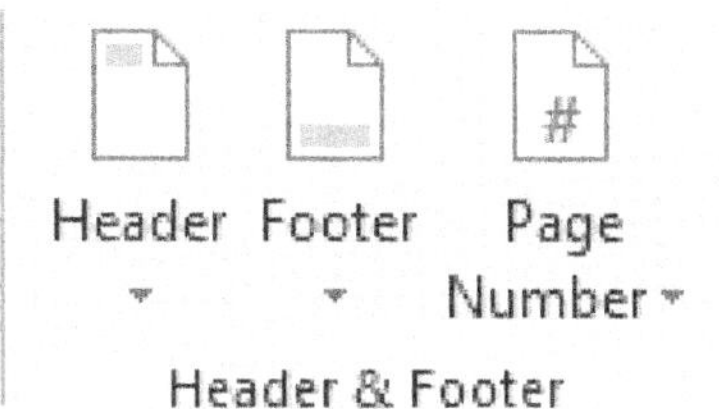

- A dialog box will appear below "Header" showing you header positioning, look down the list you will see "Remove Header". Once you click on it, your "Header" will be removed automatically

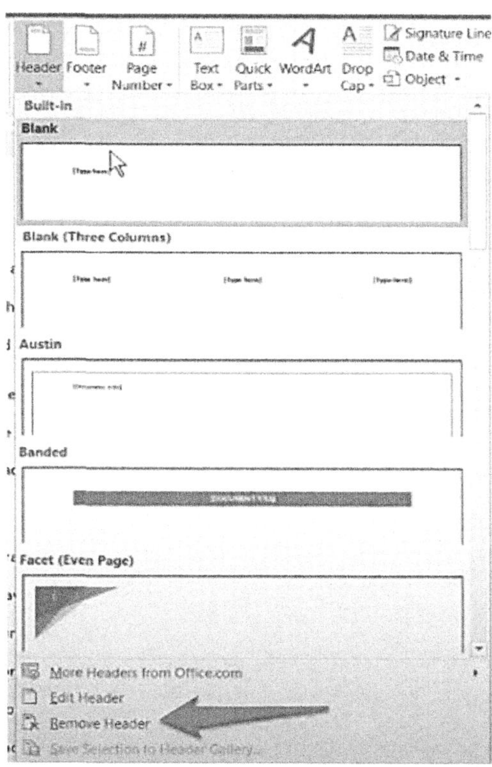

Putting Footer on Pages

- Go to "Insert tab"

- At your right-hand side, locate "Footer" and click on it

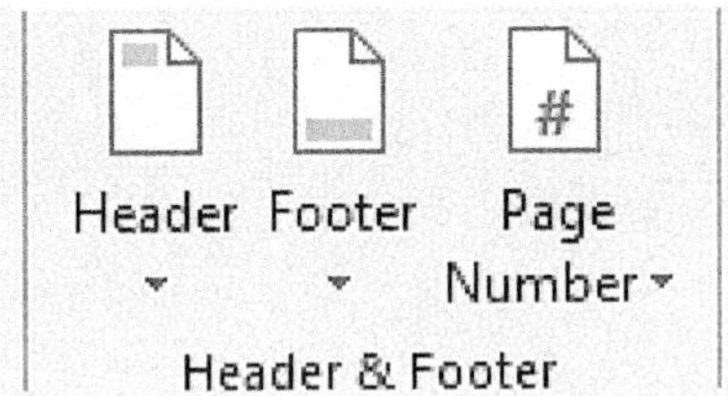

- A dialog box will appear, select your preferred alignment positioning

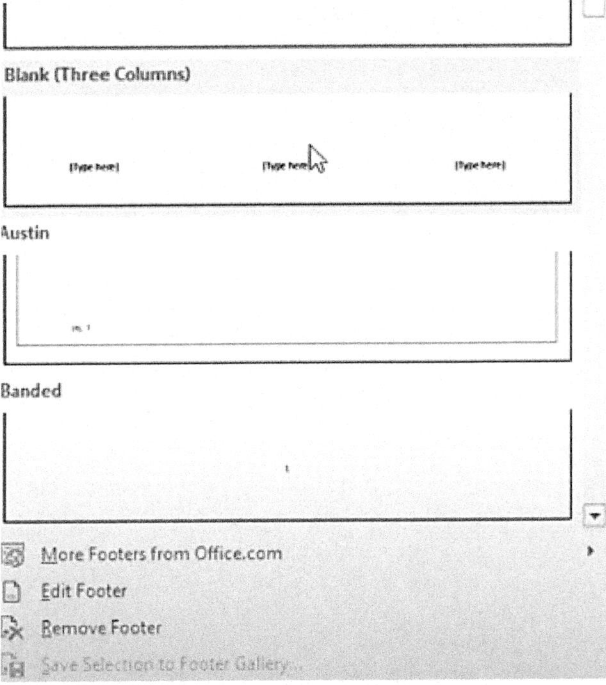

- Once done, you will be brought to your footer editing edge to input your text

and rows to huge tables with hundr
supports tables it cannot handle large t

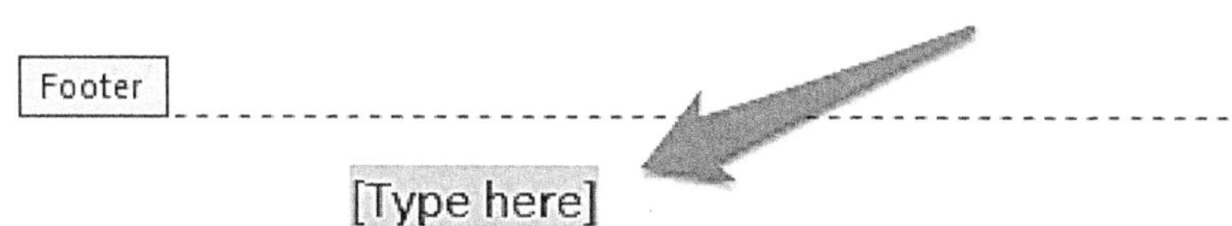

Note: You can also double-click below the page you want to insert the footer, you will be brought to an empty or footer format area where you can input your footer format.

Removing Footer from Pages

- Go to "Insert tab"

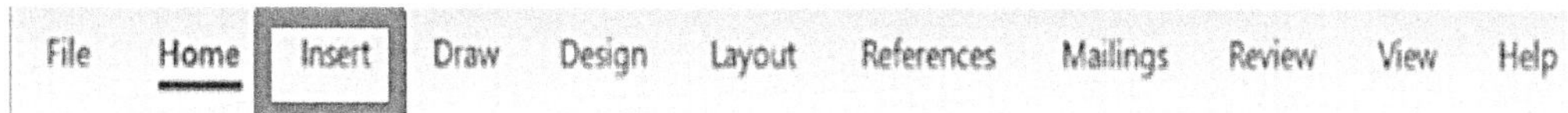

- At your right-hand side, locate "Header", click on it

- A dialog box will appear below "Footer" showing you footer positioning, look down the list, you will see "Remove Footer". Once you click on it, your "Footer" will be removed automatically

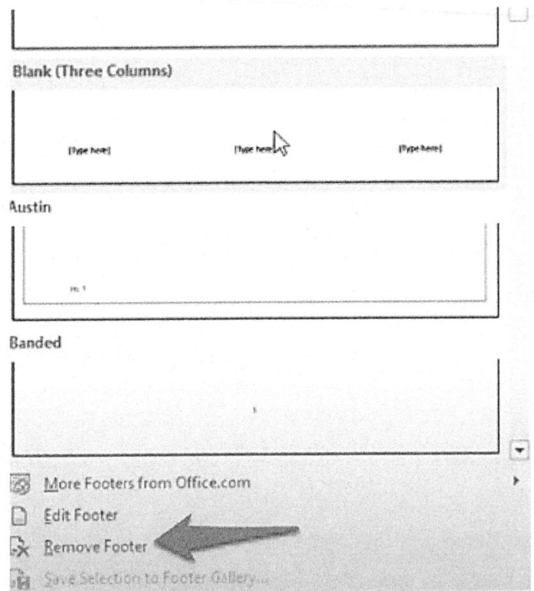

Line and Paragraph Spacing

Line and Paragraph determine how much space will be allocated between lines of text or between paragraphs. To apply the same spacing to your whole document, use the Paragraph spacing options on the "Design tab".

Adjusting the space between lines

- Go to "Home tab" which is Word 365 default displayed interface

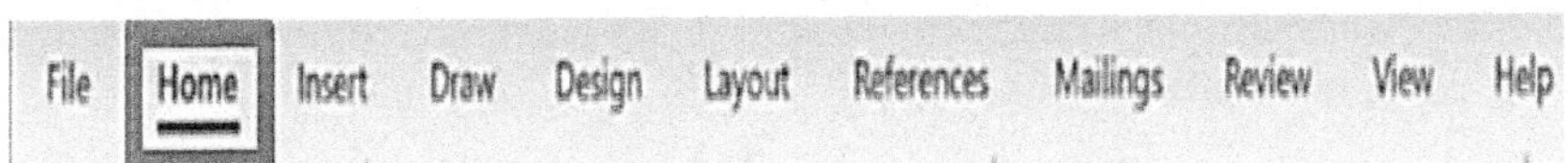

- At your right-hand side, locate "Paragraph ribbon", you will see the "line and paragraph spacing" icon

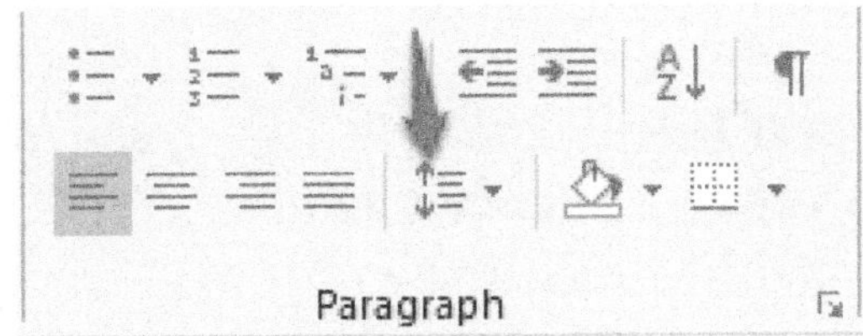

- Once you click in, you will be shown multiple options for line spacing between text or if your preferred choice is not in the list, click on "Line Spacing Options" to manually decide your choice

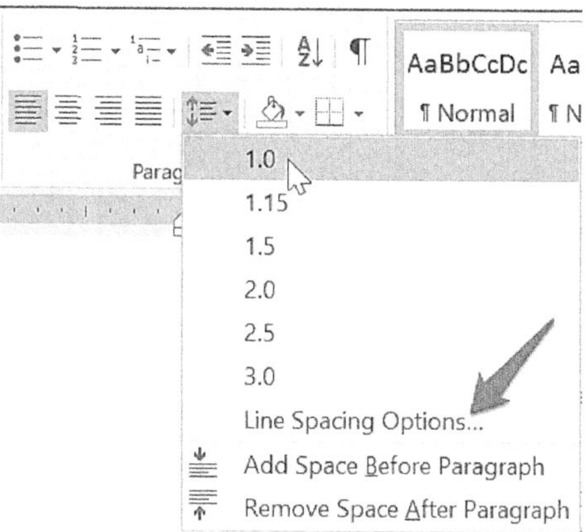

- If you click "Line Spacing Options", a dialog box will appear for you to decide your line spacing measurement "Before" & "After" once set to your preferred choice, hit the "Ok" button below

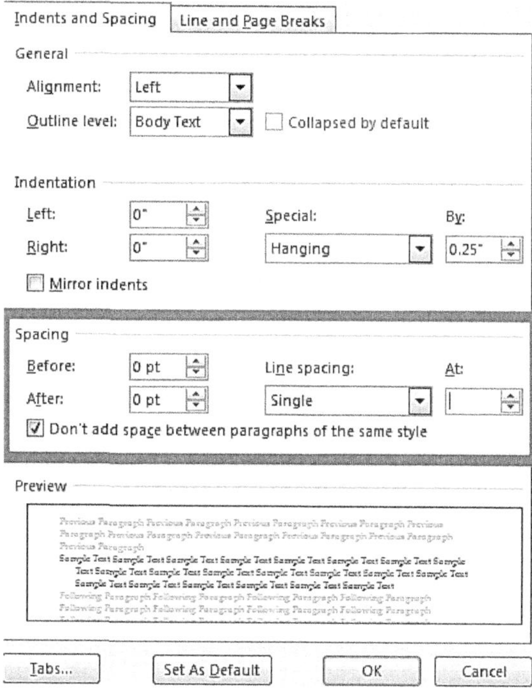

- It will automatically take effect on your opened document.

Adjusting the space between paragraphs

- Go to the "Design tab"

- Look at your right-hand side and select "Paragraph Spacing"

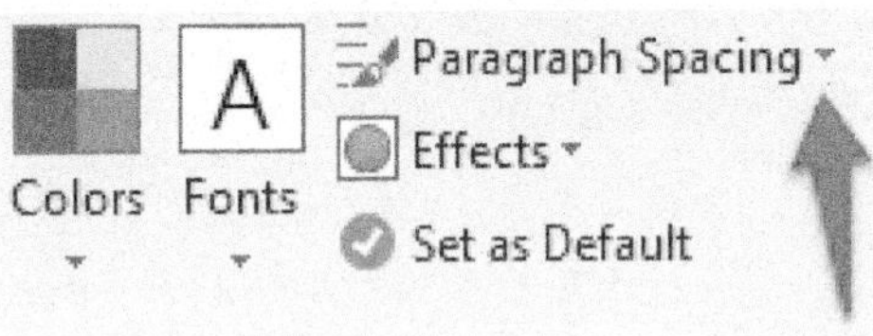

- A dialog box will appear displaying multiple options available for use

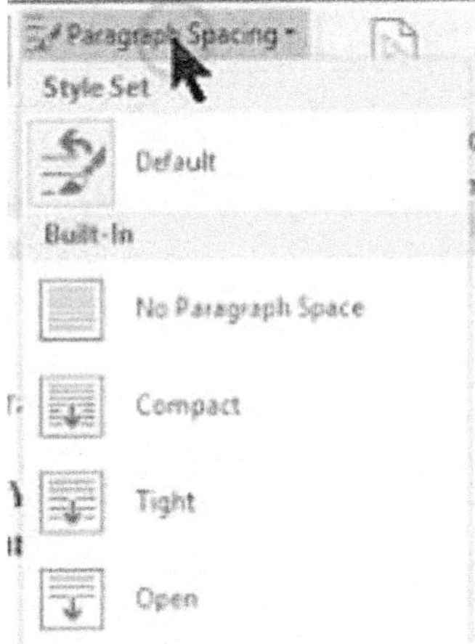

- Once you select your preferred choice, the effect will take place automatically on the entire document.

The difference between line spacing under "home tab" & paragraph spacing under "design tab"

Line and paragraph spacing under *"home tab"* adjust text manually, and it is done per paragraph, except you highlight the whole of your document.

Paragraph spacing under the *"design tab"* adjusts text automatically. This affects the whole of your document.

Creating Numbered and Bulleted Lists

Creating Bulleted Lists

- Highlight the portion of text that you want bullet list to take an effect on

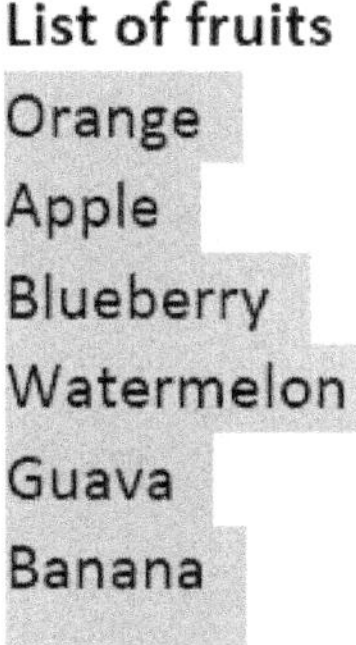

- Go to the "Home tab" which is your display settings interface

- At your left-hand side in the "Paragraph ribbon", the first tool you will see is the "Bullets list".

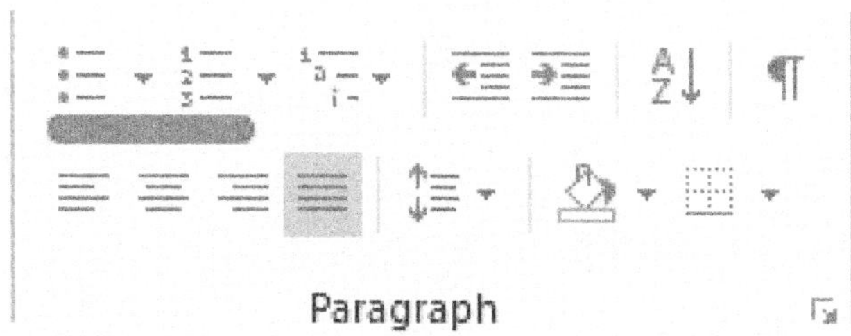

- In the "Bullet" list, select your preferred choice from your "bullet library" and click on it

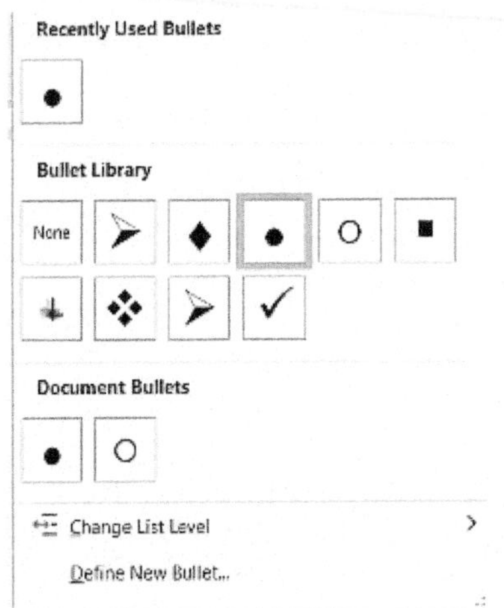

- It will automatically take an effect on your highlighted text

- Or you can click on "bullet list" and select your preferred choice on a free space in the document which also grants you access to be listing your item automatically.

- Once you enter an item and you click on "Enter key" from your keyboard, it will continue the bulleting automatically

Creating Numbered Lists

- Highlight the portion of text that you want the numbering list to affect

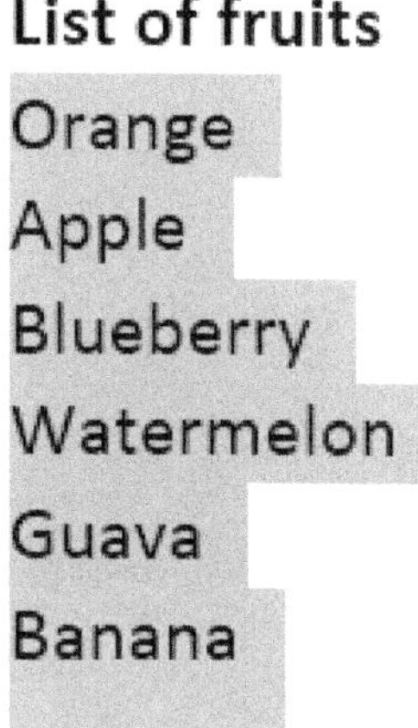

- Go to the "Home tab" which is your display settings interface

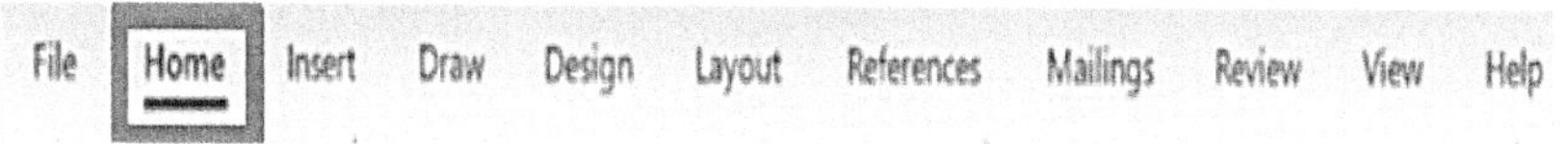

- On your left-hand side, locate the "Paragraph ribbon", the second tool you will see beside the bullet's icon is the "numbering list", click on it.

- You will be given many options to pick from, you can pick the numbering of your choice.

Note: The numbering library consists of number listing, alphabet listing, and roman figure listing, it's not designed for numbers alone.

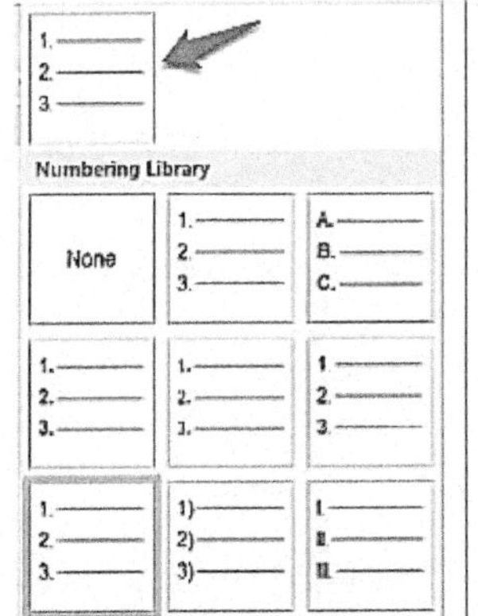

- Immediately you select the number list (you can pick your preferred choice), it will automatically take effect on your highlighted text.

List of fruits

1. Orange
2. Apple
3. Blueberry
4. Watermelon
5. Guava
6. Banana

- Or you can check "number list" and select your preferred choice on a free space in your document which also grants you access to be listing your item automatically.

List of fruits

1.

- Once you enter an item and you click your "Enter key" from your keyboard it will automatically continue the numbering.

List of fruits

1. Orange
2.

Constructing lists of your own

Either bullets list or numbering list, you can construct your own preferred choice of bullets list or numbering list

For bullets list

- Go to the "home tab" which is your default displayed interface

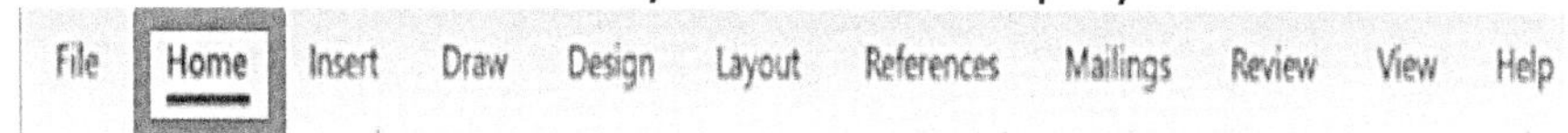

- At your right-hand side, you will see the "Paragraph ribbon", select bullets list

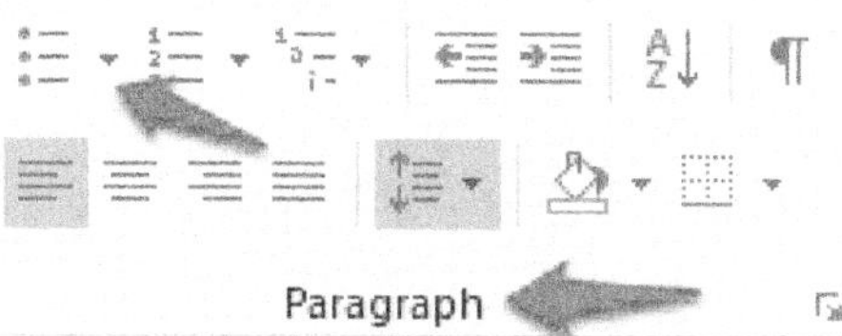

- Select "Define New Bullet"

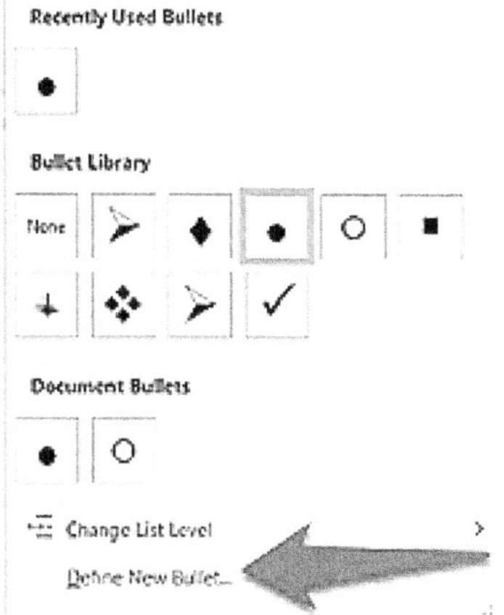

- A dialog box will appear titled "Bullet character" which comes with design tools for your configuration bullet list, you can make your list as an image format by browsing through your PC to select your preferred image, or mathematical symbols and also set the alignment positioning. Once done with the settings, hit the "Ok" option.

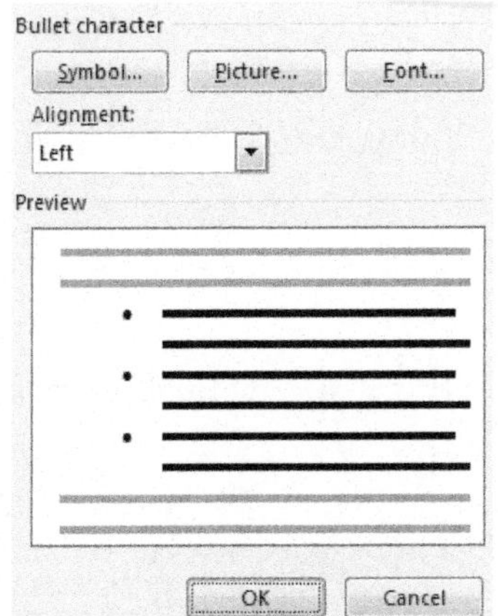

- Your selected image and other adjusted styles will take effect by default

List of fruits

- Orange
- Apple
- Blueberry
- Watermelon
- Guava
- Banana

For numbering list

- Go to the "home tab" which is your default displayed interface

- Around the middle area, you will see the "Paragraph ribbon", select the numbering list

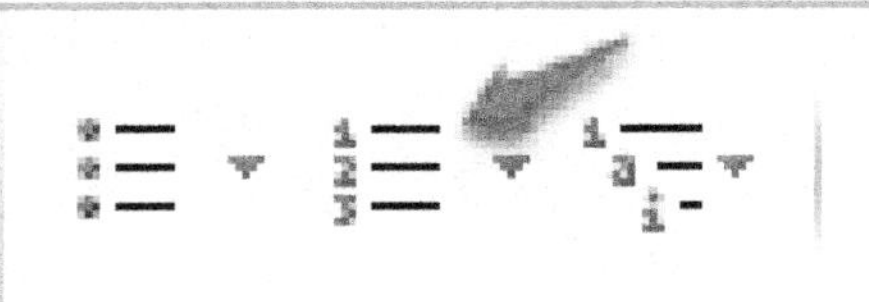

- Select "Define New Number Format"

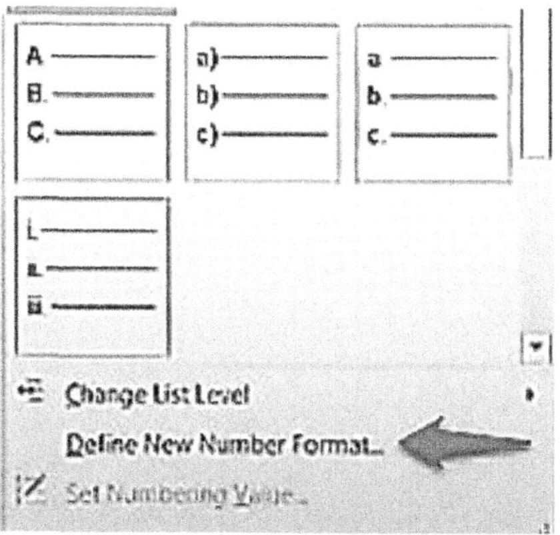

- A dialog box will appear titled "Number format", on the numbering list, you can't add an image or symbol, but you can determine your numbering format, be it alphabet format, roman figure format, or numbering format

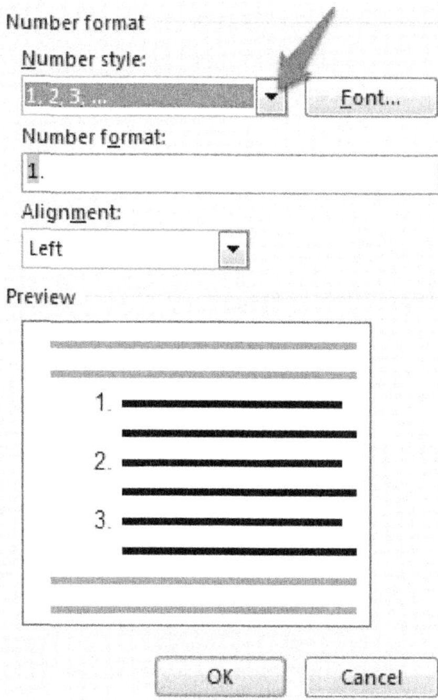

- Since the default numbering is numeric, let's choose the Roman figure to see the effect in a different way

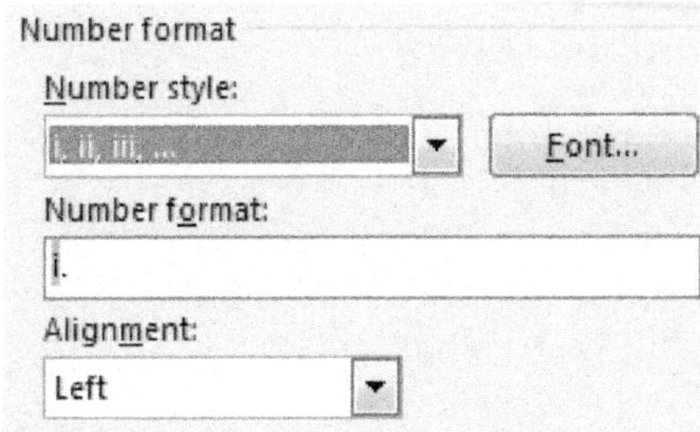

- Once selected, click "Ok"

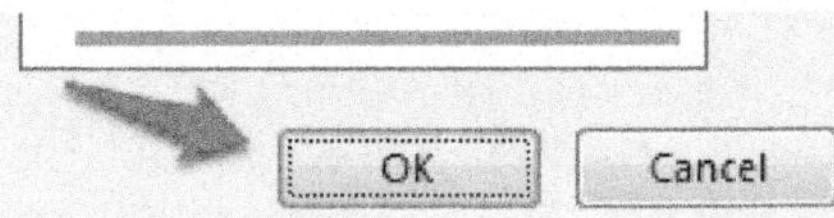

- By default, the selected roman figure will take effect immediately.

Note: There are other numbering formats available; you can choose something different after trying what we just accomplished.

List of fruits

i. Orange
ii. Apple
iii. Blueberry
iv. Watermelon
v. Guava
vi. Banana

Managing a multilevel list

- Highlight the portion of text that you want numbering list or bullet list to affect

List of fruits
Orange
Apple
Blueberry
Mango
Watermelon
Pineapple
Guava
Banana

- Go to the "Home tab" which is your display settings interface

- At your right-hand side in the paragraph ribbon, you will see "multilevel list", as indicated below with a pink straight line

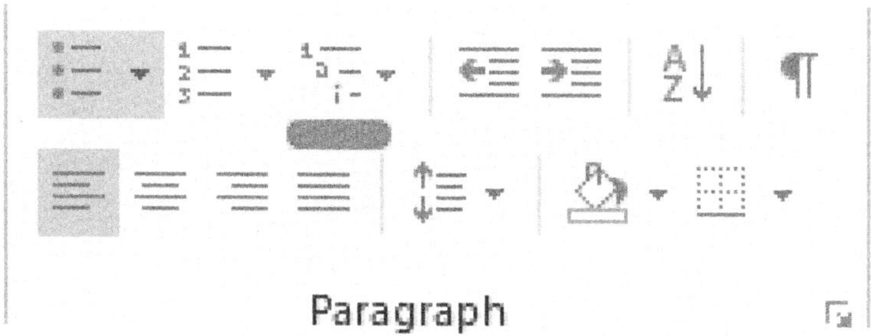

- Once you click on "Multilevel List", a dropdown of multilevel list options will appear

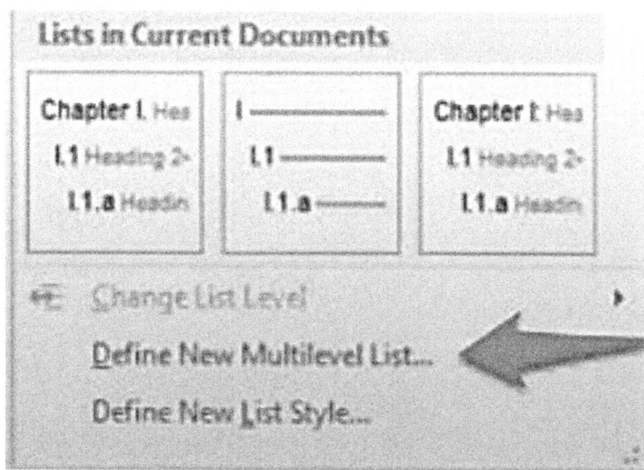

- Select "Define New Multilevel List" as illustrated above and a dialog box will appear named "Click level to modify", you will be instructed to set your multilevel list to your preferred taste.

The first numbering at your left is the first list item, the second is the second item till numbering 9 for the ninth item. Below is the "Enter formatting for number" option where you edit the dropdown (sub-list) item. Once done, click "ok".

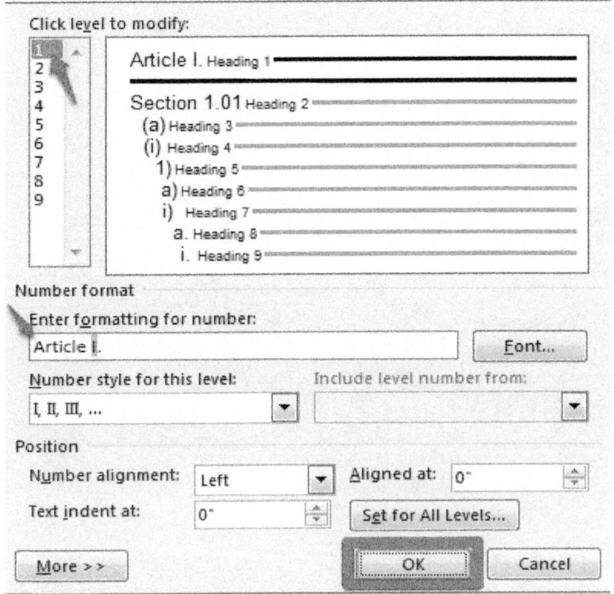

- Now back to our highlighted items

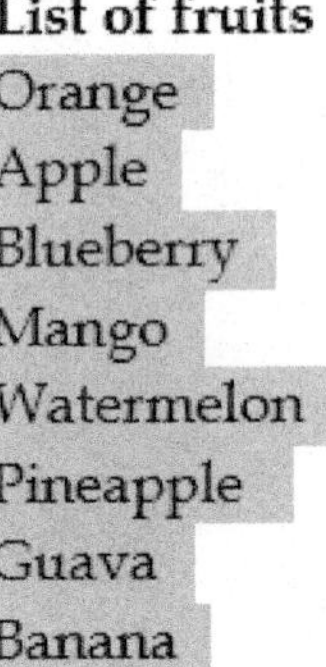
List of fruits
Orange
Apple
Blueberry
Mango
Watermelon
Pineapple
Guava
Banana

- Let make use of the "Numbering list"

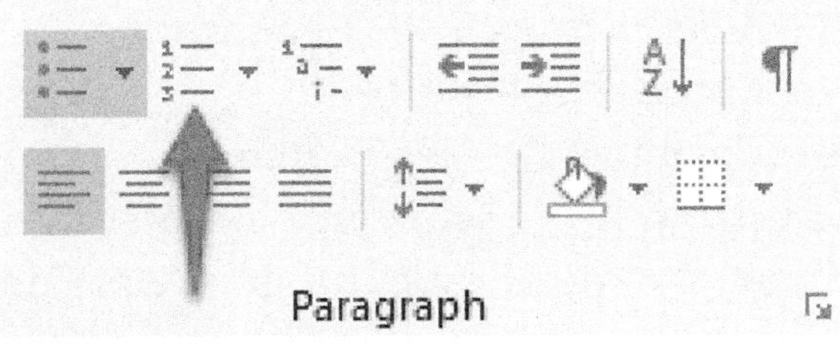

- Select numeric list, double-click on it

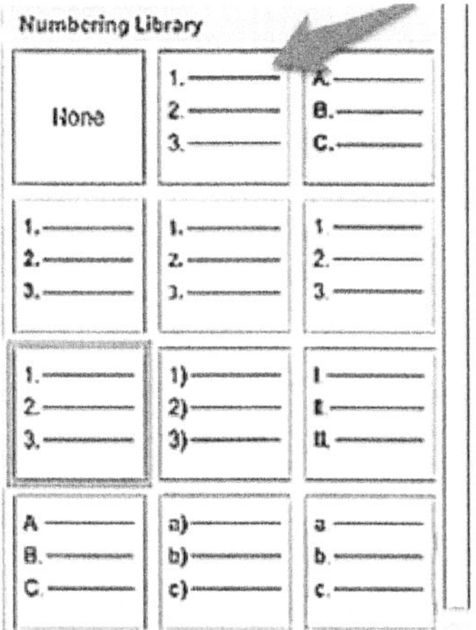

- Once it has been numbered, this will be the outcome of your highlighted items, but this is not what we still want to achieve

List of fruits

1. Orange
2. Apple
3. Blueberry
4. Mango
5. Watermelon
6. Pineapple
7. Guava
8. Banana

- Now, highlight only "Apple", "Blueberry", "Mango", "Watermelon", "Pineapple" (item 2 to 6 on the list).

List of fruits

1. Orange
2. Apple
3. Blueberry
4. Mango
5. Watermelon
6. Pineapple
7. Guava
8. Banana

- Then, press the "Tab" key on your keyboard located by your left-hand side, you will get this result; "orange" will have a sub-list below itself. We are getting closer but we can do beyond this, let's continue

List of fruits

1. Orange
    a. Apple
    b. Blueberry
    c. Mango
    d. Watermelon
    e. Pineapple
2. Guava
3. Banana

- Now, highlight only "Blueberry" & "Mango"

List of fruits

1. Orange
    a. Apple
    b. Blueberry
    c. Mango
    d. Watermelon
    e. Pineapple
2. Guava
3. Banana

- Then, press your "Tab" key located on your keyboard by your left-hand side, by default "Apple" will have a sub-list of items which are "Blueberry" & "Mango"

List of fruits

1. Orange
    a. Apple
        i. Blueberry
        ii. Mango
    b. Watermelon
    c. Pineapple
2. Guava
3. Banana

You can also play around it to achieve something different from my illustration. Now, you see how flexible working on Word 365 is.

Working with Tabs

Tab on your keyboard has been a wonderfully used key function, the beauty of it is that it can also be set to suit you.

- Go to your "Home tab"

- In the "Paragraph ribbon or group", choose Paragraph Settings.

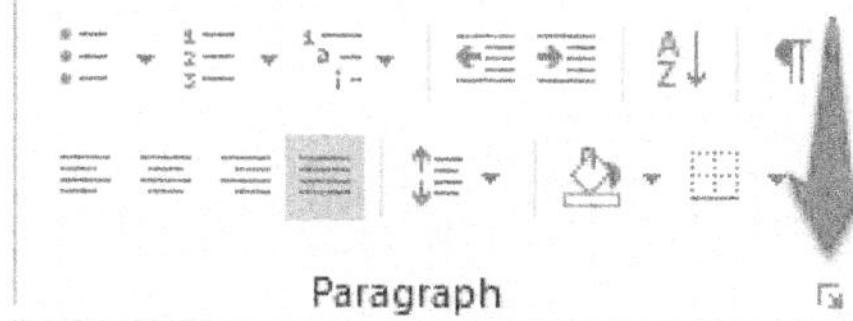

- Click the Tabs button.

- Set the Tab stop position, choose the Alignment and Leader options. By default, your tab stop is always on "0.5", you can also modify that and the positioning alignment with other aspects too, once done, click the "Ok" option and use your "Tab" key to test your text movement spacing.

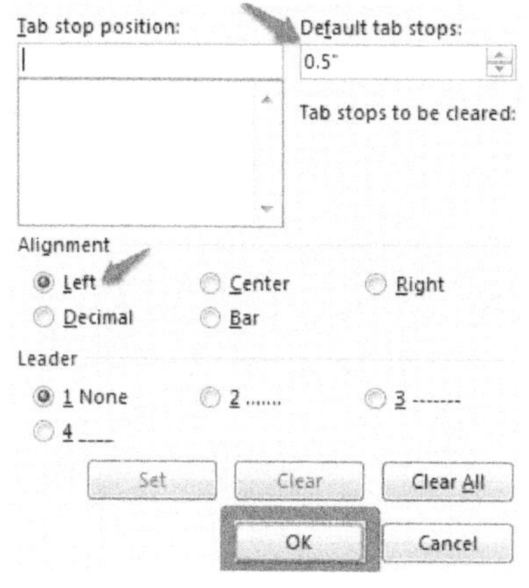

Hyphenating Text

Hyphenation is used when a text runs out of space on a line. With hyphenation, text will automatically move down to the next line. When you turn on hyphenation, the text will hyphenate itself by default when running out of space.

- Go to "Layout tab"

- Under the "Layout tab", below locate "Hyphenation"

- Once you select "Hyphenation", dropdown options will pop up such as "None", "Automatic", "Manual" and "Hyphenation options"

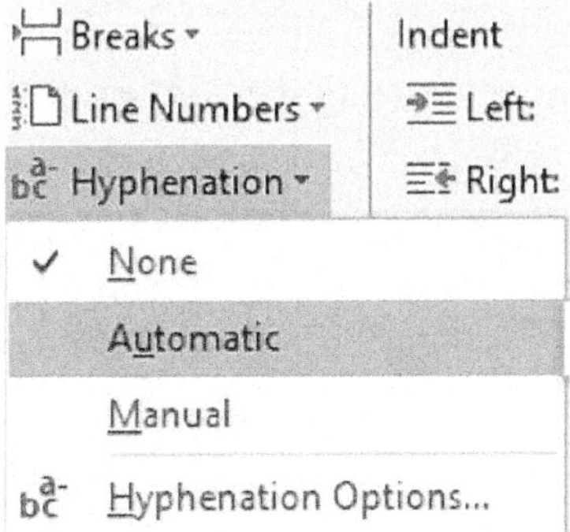

- Once you select "Automatic", it will take effect on your document

Excel allows you to perform complex calculations where changing one number causes many other calculated numbers to change as well. Excel includes an extensive library of built-in for-mulas to help you perform those calculations.

Automatically and manually hyphenating

Automatic hyphenating keeps all texts hyphenated, while manual hyphenating gives its user access to edit how text should be hyphenated.

CHAPTER FIVE

WORD STYLES

All About Styles

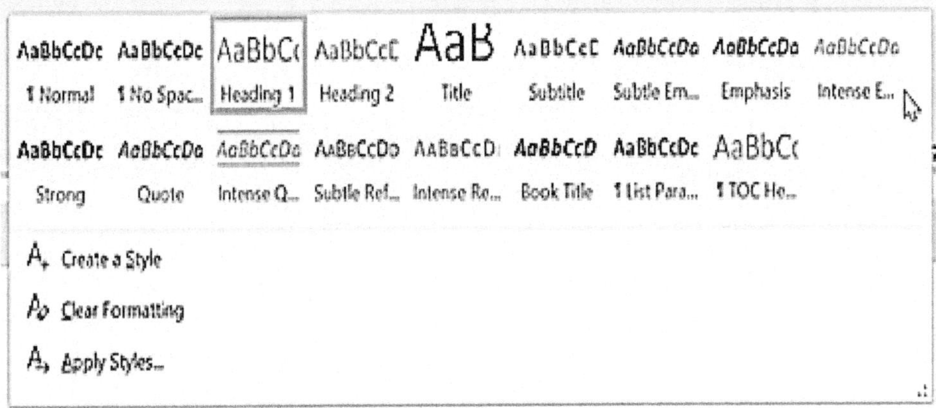

Style is a predefined template used to differentiate between texts such as heading text from body text. Style comes with other options for creating a new style, clearing an existing format, applying styles, and modifying styles.

Style and Templates

Style as said earlier is a predefined template that comes with auto-installed font style, size, and color which makes it a template to be used when the need arises. Note that style, as the name implies is not only for designing text, it can also be used for creating tables of content, headings, and lots more.

Types of Styles

It is important to note that one style is different totally from another with its unique name.

Paragraph styles

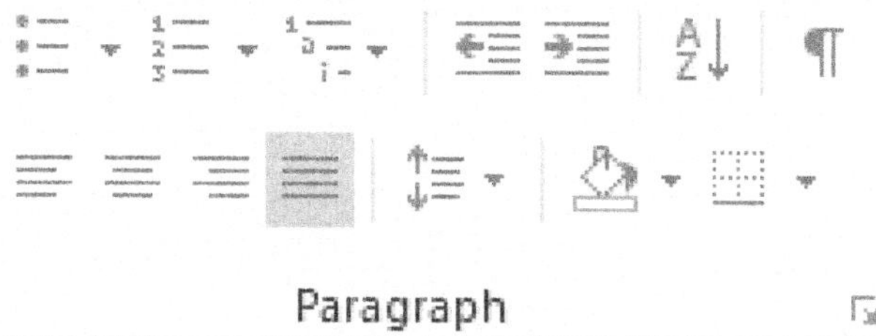

These styles control the appearance of a text in paragraph sections and allow you to edit large sections of text. A paragraph style may contain format settings for character style, it's also the overall design of a paragraph. The paragraph style Standard is usually preset for the entire text. Paragraph styles format Indents, and spacings, Line and page breaks, borders and shading, lists, tabs, all character attributes.

Character styles

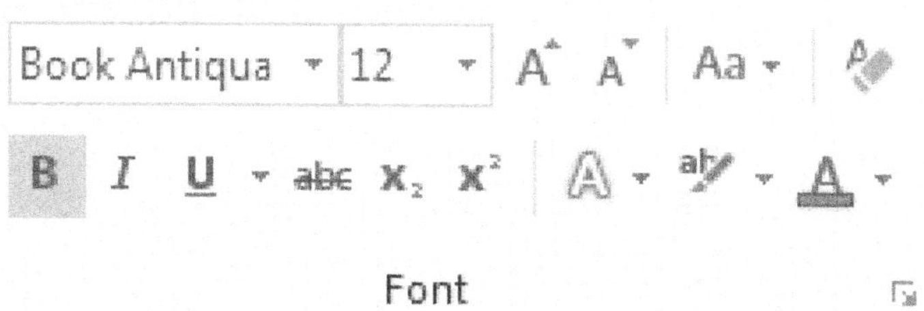

Character style is the appearance of text based on individual choice and is mostly used to format text sections such as highlighting words. Character styles do not format the entire paragraph, but rather, format font, font size, font color, bold, italic, or underlined markings, and so on.

Table styles

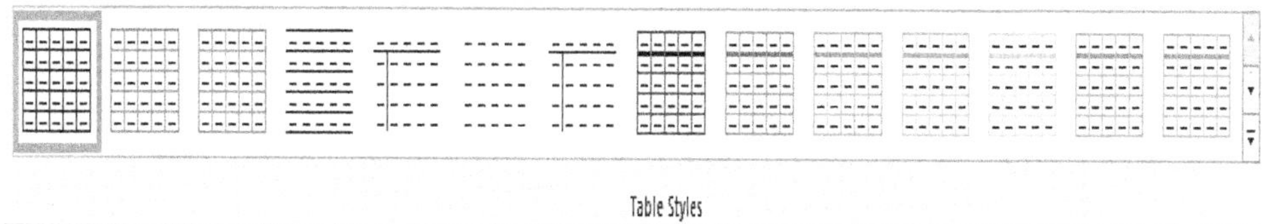

Table styles determine the formatting outlook of your table in terms of individual choice and the purpose of usage can be for creating a calendar, scoring list, items, and lots more.

List styles

List styles in Word format give the appearance that best suits the user, such as importing an image as 'list style', formatting of bulleted lists, formatting of numbered lists, indents, and lots more.

What are the advantages of Word styles when formatting a text?

Preset as well as custom styles make it easier to work on a text document with simplicity and flexibility. This is mostly visible while editing complex documents. Primarily, manual formatting seems easier and quicker, but for longer texts, it's more effective to use Word styles instead of frequently formatting text sections separately. The advantages of using styles in Word are:

- **Adaptability**
- **Simplicity**
- **Continuity**
- **Efficiency**
- **Navigation**
- **Outlining**

Applying Styles to Text and Paragraphs

- Highlight the text to be altered

Word's for Printing

A Word document is formatted to fit on a specific size page with the text automatically flowing from one page to the next. Excel supports printing, but its page breaks are not obvious, and because it's printing area can extend multiple pages horizontally as well as vertically the page breaks can be difficult to manage.

- Go to the "Home tab" which is your default displayed Word 365 interface

Home

- At your right-hand side, second to the last, you will see the "Styles" ribbon

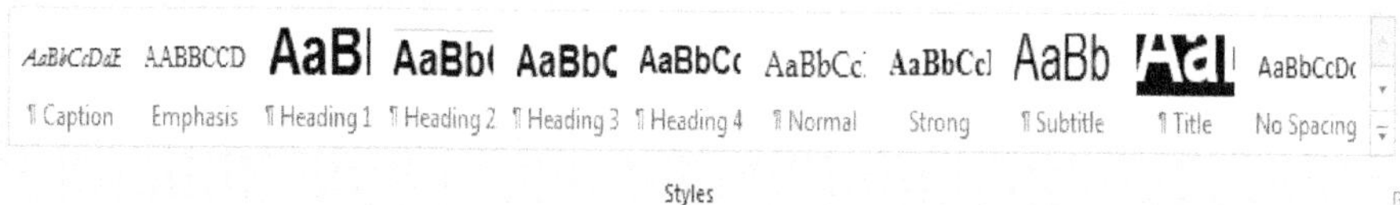

- Select one of the styles above, you can also click on the dropdown arrow to view other styles, let's assume we choose "Heading 1"

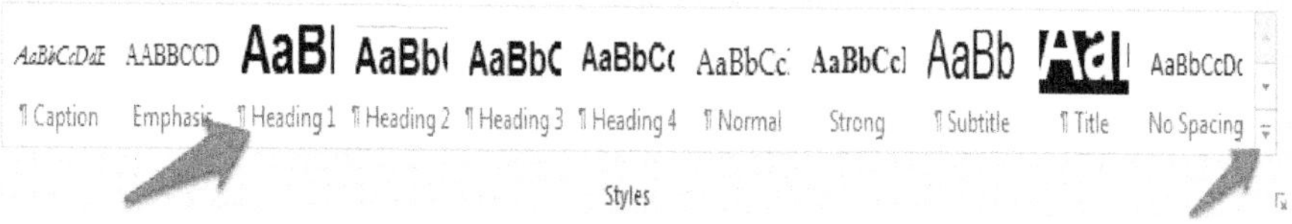

- Your highlighted text will be converted to the selected style which is "Heading 1"

Word's for Printing

A Word document is formatted to fit on a specific size page with the text automatically flowing from one page to the next. Excel supports printing, but its page breaks are not obvious, and because it's printing area can extend multiple pages horizontally as well as vertically the page breaks can be difficult to manage.

- You can also do something similar to your paragraph by also highlighting it

Word's for Printing

A Word document is formatted to fit on a specific size page with the text automatically flowing from one page to the next. Excel supports printing, but its page breaks are not obvious, and because it's printing area can extend multiple pages horizontally as well as vertically the page breaks can be difficult to manage.

- Go to the "Home tab" which is your default displayed Word 365 screen

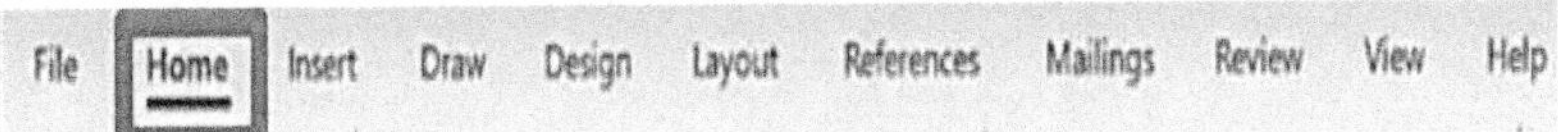

- At your right-hand side, locate the "Style" ribbon

- Now, let select the second heading which is "Heading 2"

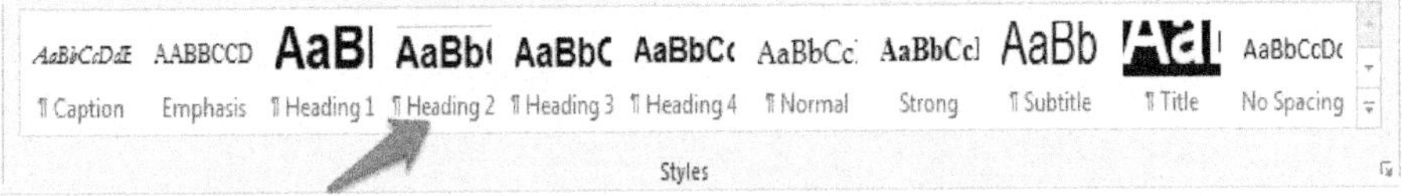

- Your paragraph text will change to "Heading 2" styling

Word's for Printing

A Word document is formatted to fit on a specific size page with the text automatically flowing from one page to the next. Excel supports printing, but its page breaks are not obvious, and because it's printing area can extend multiple pages horizontally as well as vertically the page breaks can be difficult to manage.

Experimenting with style sets

- Go to the "Home tab" which is your default displayed Word 365 screen

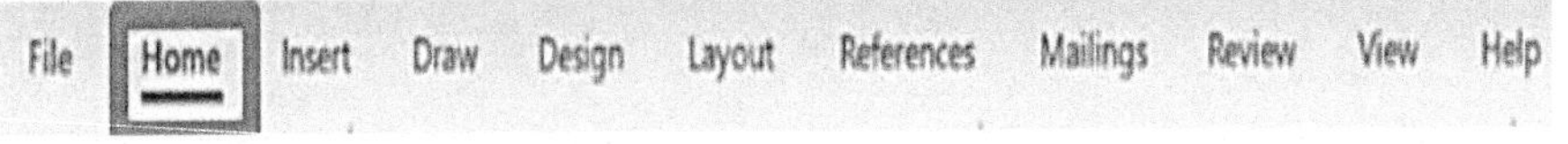

- At your right-hand side, locate the "Style" ribbon, click the dropdown arrow as illustrated below to see other options

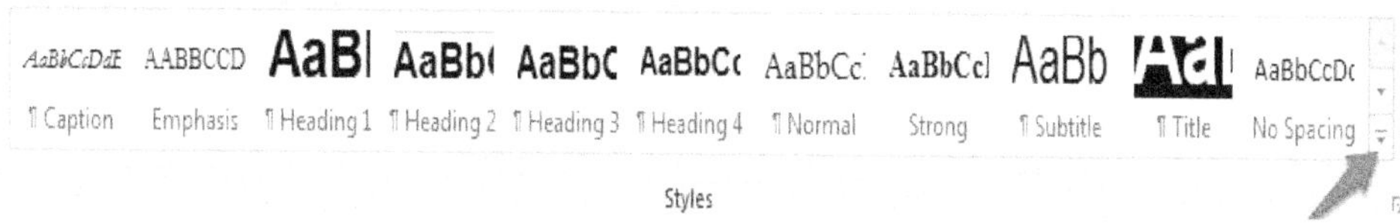

- Below is what you will be shown, you can select your preferred choice, or create your preferred choice; that is how style is applied to text.

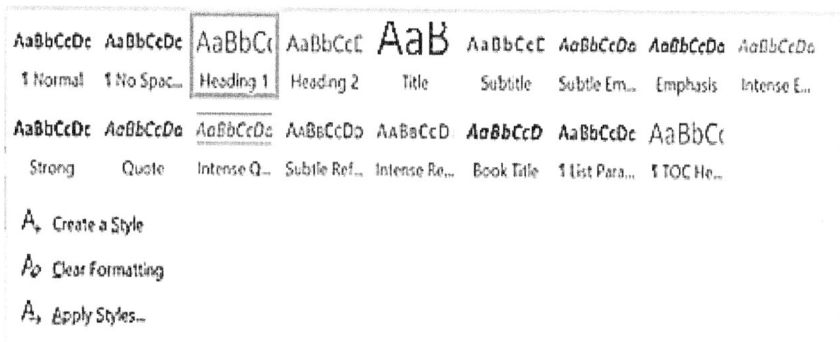

Creating a New Style

- Go to the "Home tab"

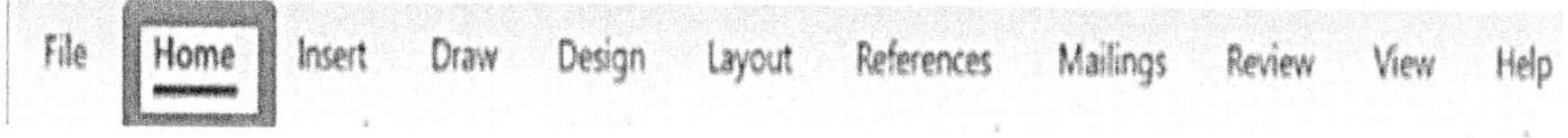

- At your right-hand side, second to the last ribbon, you will see "Styles", select the dropdown arrow as illustrated below

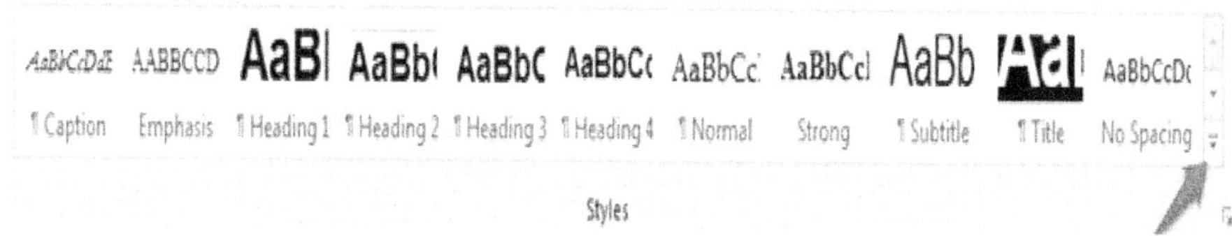

- Different options will be shown to you, among the options choose "Create a Style"

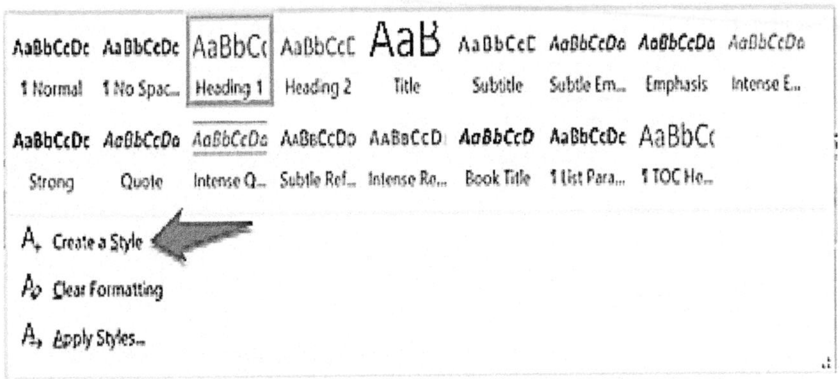

- Another dialog box will pop-up titled "Name", name it according to your choice

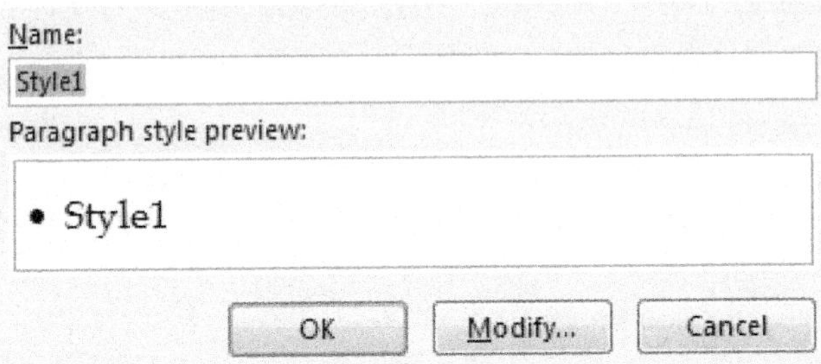

- Then, select "Modify" for more modification on your newly created style

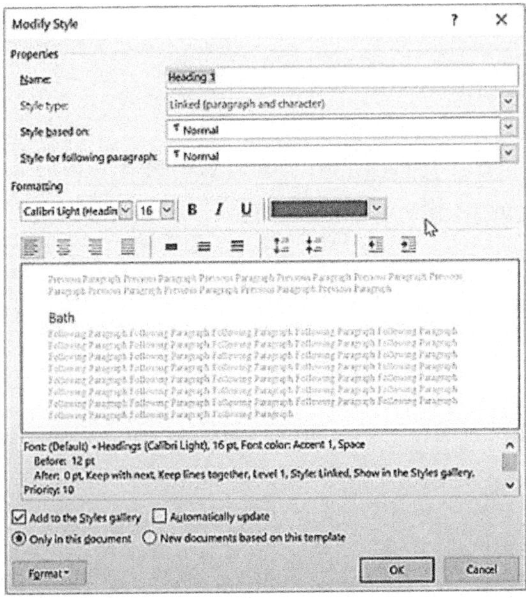

- Once done, click “Ok”, your newly created style will be added to the styles list

Modifying styles

Modification is majorly in two ways, you either modify your existing style or your just created style, I just explained ***“Creating a New Style”*** and I illustrated how to modify it. Here, I will be demonstrating how to modify existing styles

- Go to the “Home tab”

- On your right-hand side, you will see the “Styles” ribbon. Assuming we want to modify “Heading 1”, right-click on it, a dialog box will appear with many options, select “Modify”

- Here is where your “Heading 1” modification which is one of the existing styles on your list is. You can modify the font style, font size, boldness, color, and many more. For simplicity and illustration purpose, click on “color” and choose “red” color, then click “Ok”.

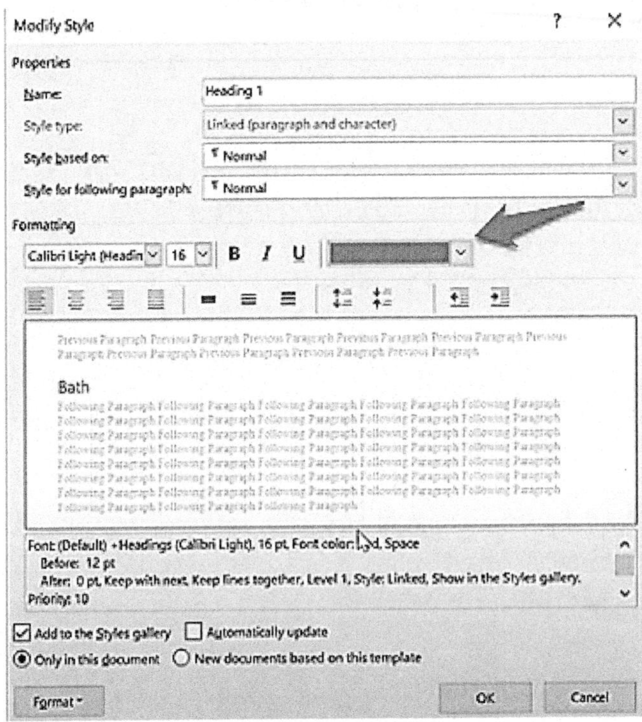

- Note the changes, "Heading 1" which is one of the existing styles will have the effect of color red which we modified it to

Renaming Styles

- Make sure your text that carries a style format is highlighted to recognize the specific style to be renamed

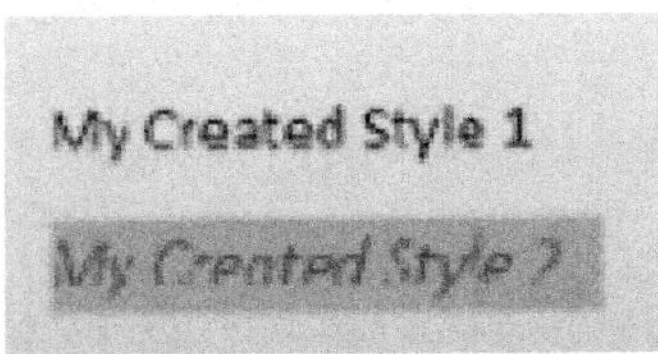

- Go to the "Home tab"

- At your right-hand side, you will see the "styles" ribbon

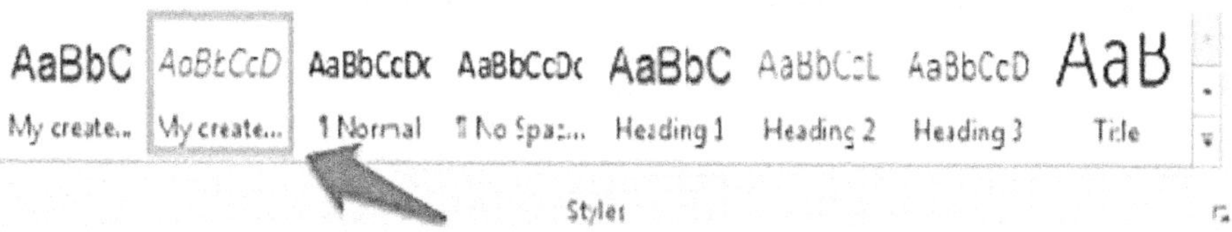

- Below the "styles" ribbon, click on the little arrow

- A dialog box will appear, indicating your selected or created style

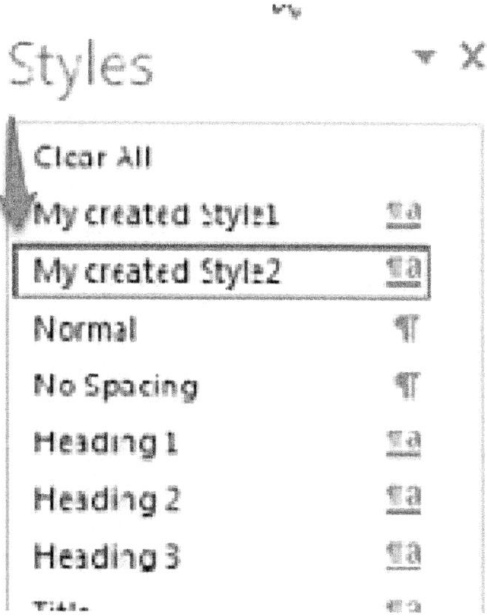

- Below the "Styles displayed box", select the last option titled "Manage Styles". Double-click on "Manage Styles"

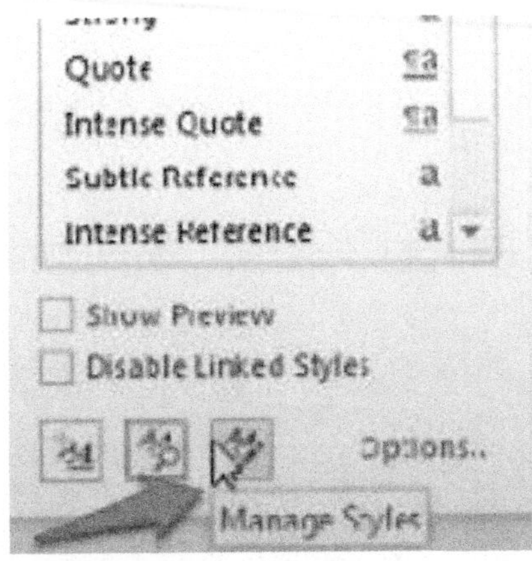

- Another dialog box will appear, make sure your style is highlighted as indicated in the illustration below, then click on "Modify"

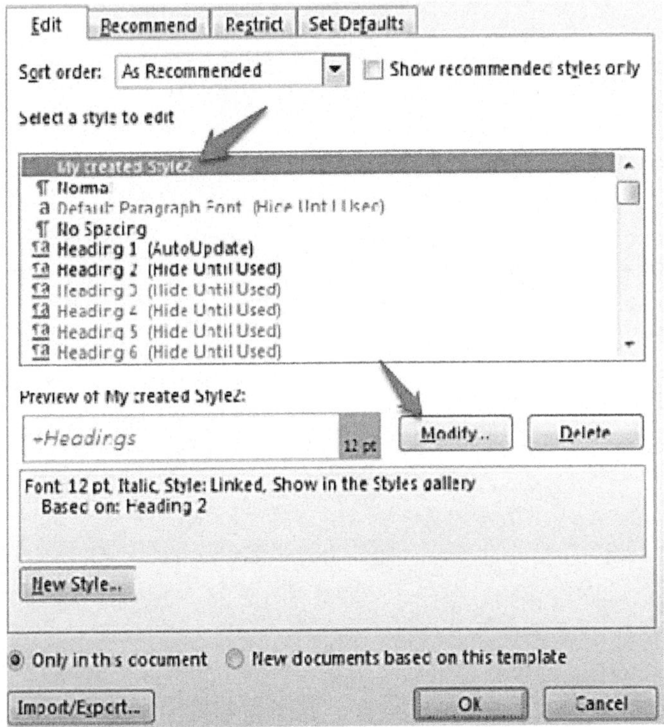

- You will be brought to the modification box named "Properties". This is where your selected style can be edited, renamed, and your font size, style, color, alignment, and the rest can be worked upon. Once done hit "ok"

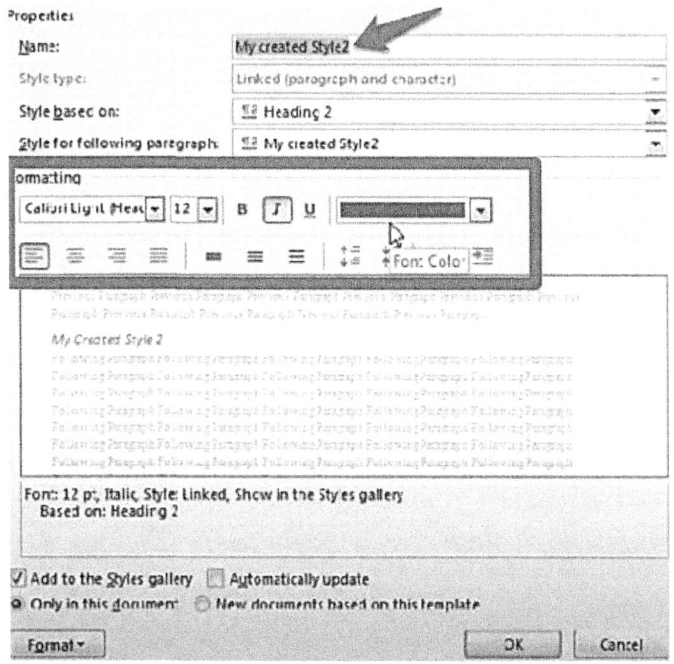

- Let's assume I only renamed my style from "My created Style 2" to "My 2"

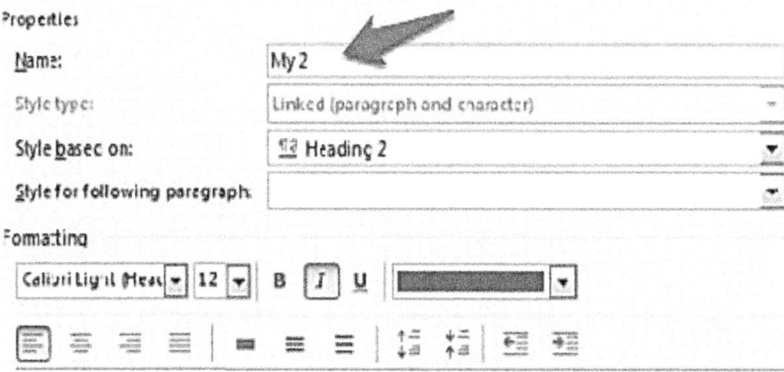

- Once done, click "ok"

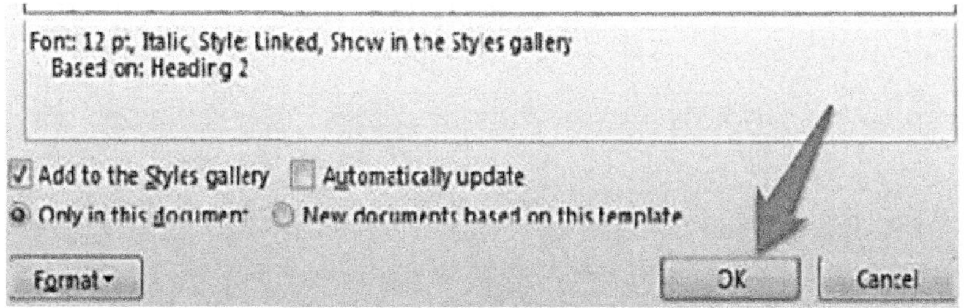

- Your previous displayed box titled "Manage styles" will also affect the new changes, also click "ok" to see your styles ribbon having the same effect

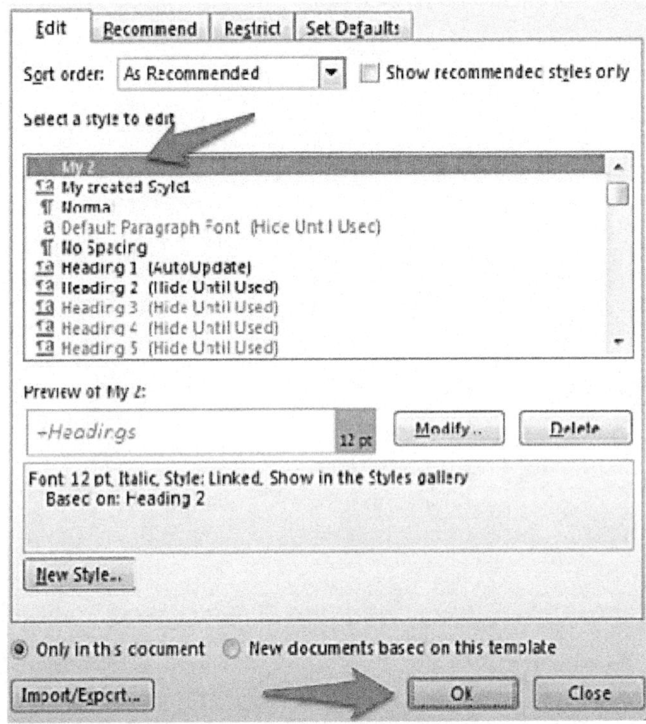

- Now, you will see the changes we made on renaming our style from "My created Style 2" to "My 2"

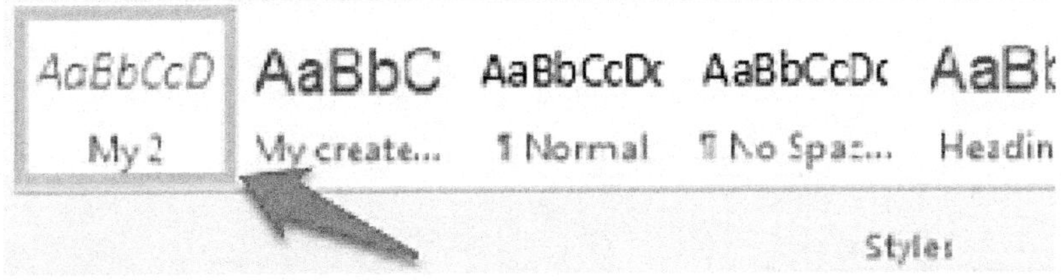

Applying Themes in Word 365

Themes is a multiple template design to suit individual preferred choice, its major purpose is to make Word interface stylish in a unique way. Themes, once selected, automatically changes the whole outlook of your content.

How to Apply Themes

- Go to the "Design" tab

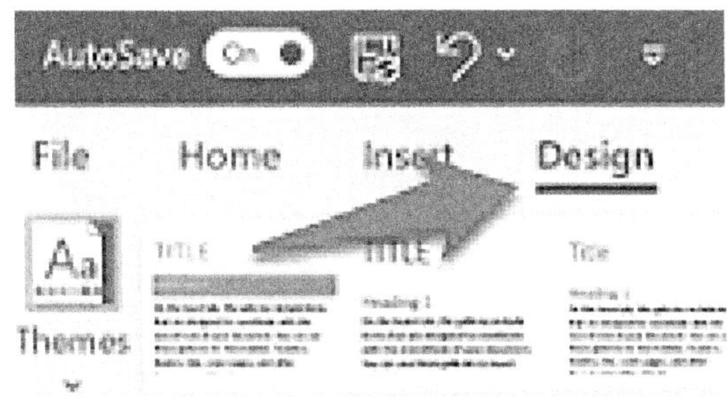

- At your left-hand side, select "Themes"

- Drop-down options of themes will be shown to you immediately

- Select your preferred choice. Each theme has its template style

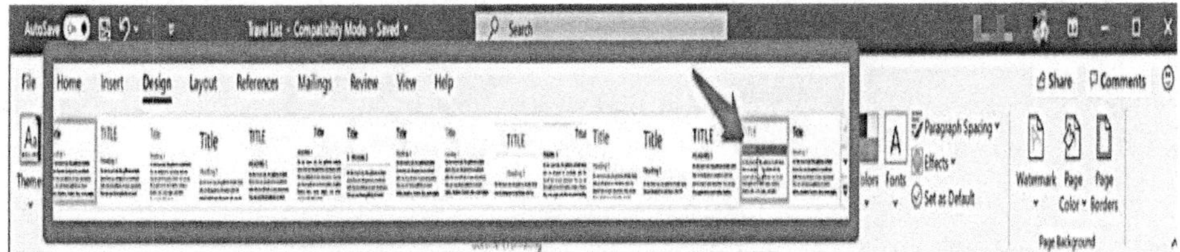

- Assuming we select the above theme where the arrow is pointed, all your headings will also be painted blue color, and any style that was there before will be changed.

CHAPTER SIX

CONSTRUCTING A PERFECT TABLE

Table Jargon

A table is a grid of cells arranged in vertical and horizontal order. It is also a great way to organize information within your document. Tables are useful for different activities such as the arrangement of description items, presenting text information and numerical data, text and image illustration, and lots more. In Word, you can create a blank table, convert text to a table, and apply a variety of styles and formats to existing tables.

Creating a Table

Creating a table has been for different purposes such as for grading, calculating, listing of names, items, and so on. To create a table, simply follow this procedure

- Go to the "Insert" tab

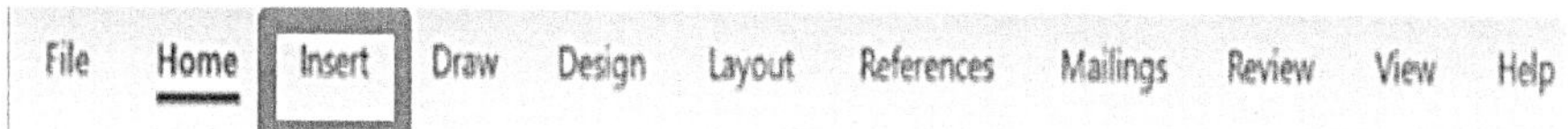

- Below the "Insert tab", you will see "Table", click the little arrow under to get the dropdown table options

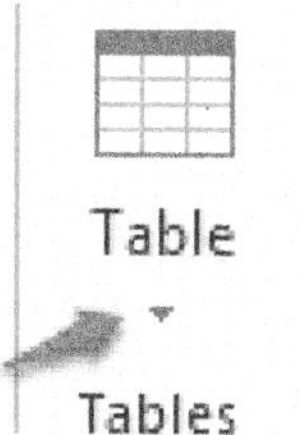

- Once you click on the arrow, you get the dropdown rows and columns which is known as "Table Grid". Select the numbers of rows and columns you want, then, click on the last selection of row and column to display it on your Word document

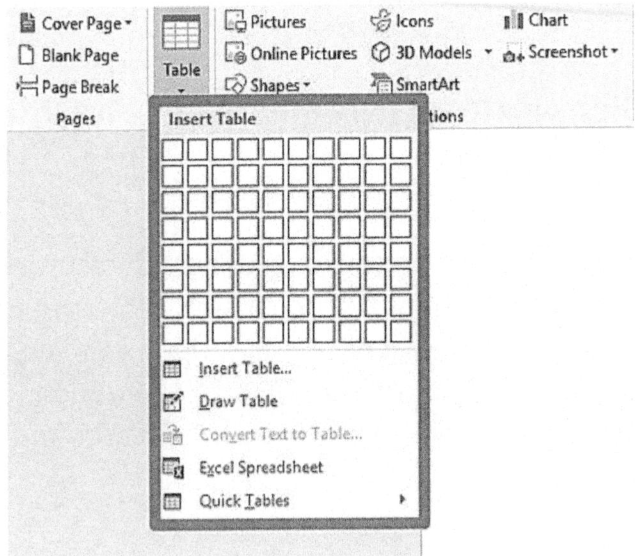

- Assuming we pick five rows and two columns, at the last selection, right-click on your mouse to effect it on your Word document

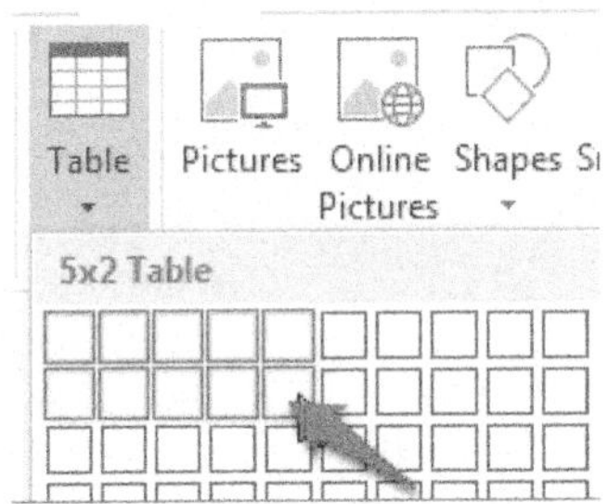

- Here is the result that you will have on your Word document

Styling your table

- Go to "Insert"

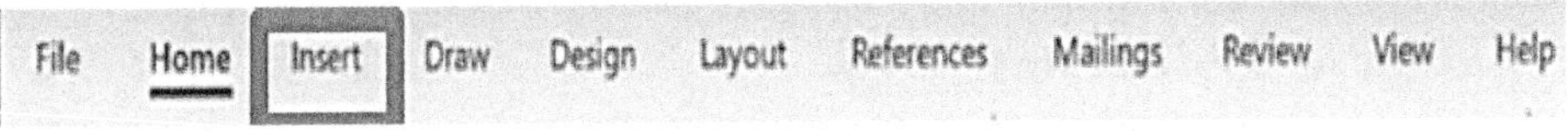

- Below the "Insert tab" you will see "Table", click the little arrow to get the dropdown table options

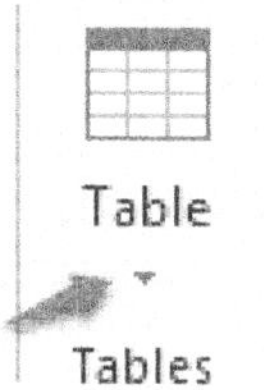

- Once you click on the arrow, you get the dropdown rows and columns which is known as "Table Grid". Select the numbers of rows and columns, then click on the last selection of row and column to display it on your Word document

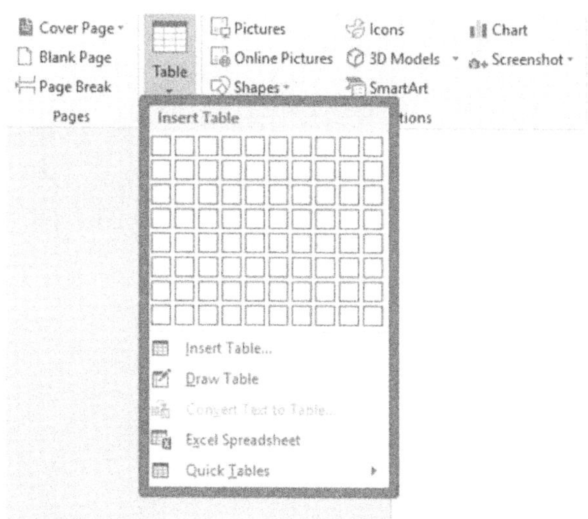

- Once you have selected the number of rows (horizontal) and columns (vertical), then your table will be displayed in your Word document, let's assume it is four rows and three columns

- Click inside one of the columns, once you do this, it becomes active to receive text

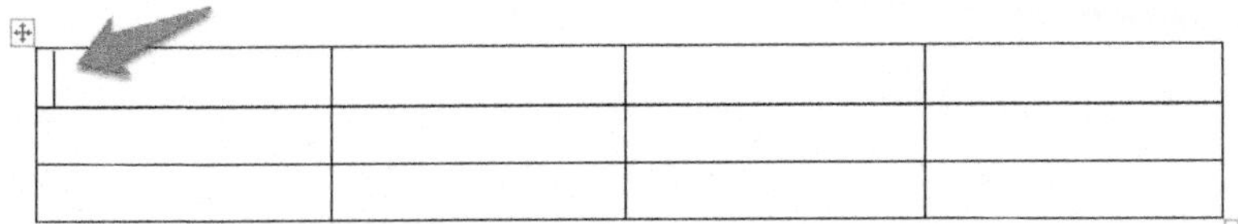

- Immediately, the menu bar will show "Table Tools" which are the "Design" table tab and "Layout" table tab, click on "Design table tab"

- Under "Design", you will see "table" styles which consist of predefined table styles to use, click on any colorful style to see its effect on your table

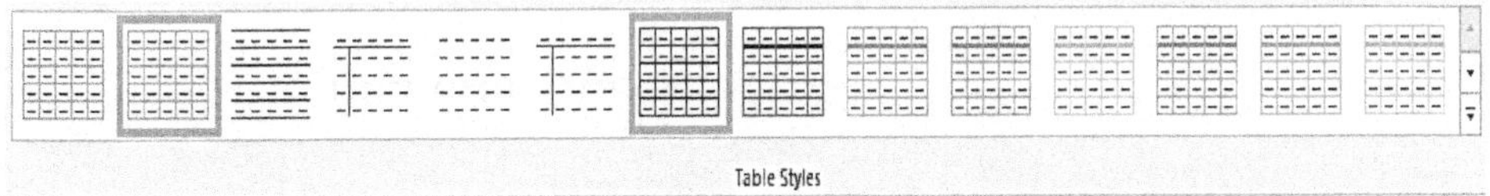

- You can also click on the dropdown arrow on your right-hand side to view other table options

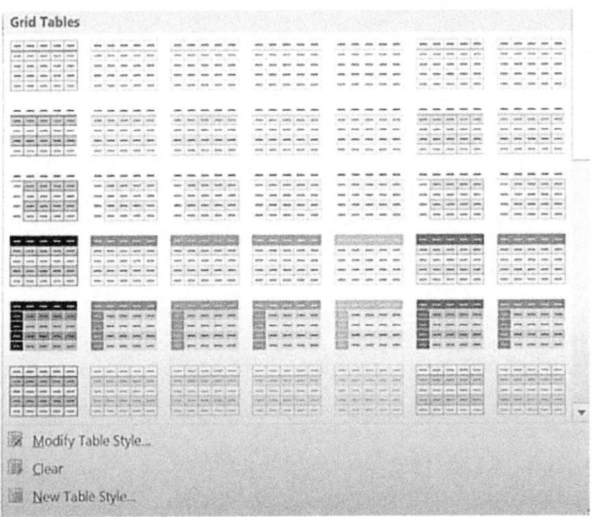

- Once selected, your created table will be transformed into the predefined template

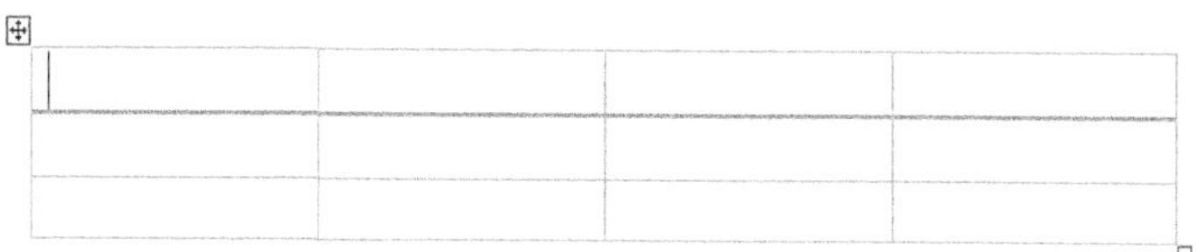

Note: "Table Tools" only show up whenever the table cell is active.

Entering Text and Numbers in your Table

- Go to the "Insert" tab

- Below the "Insert tab", you will see "Table", click the little arrow to get the dropdown table options

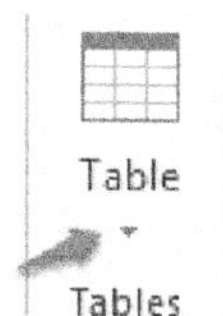

- Once you click on it, you get the "Table Grid", select the numbers of rows and columns you want, then click on the last selection of row and column to display it on your Word document

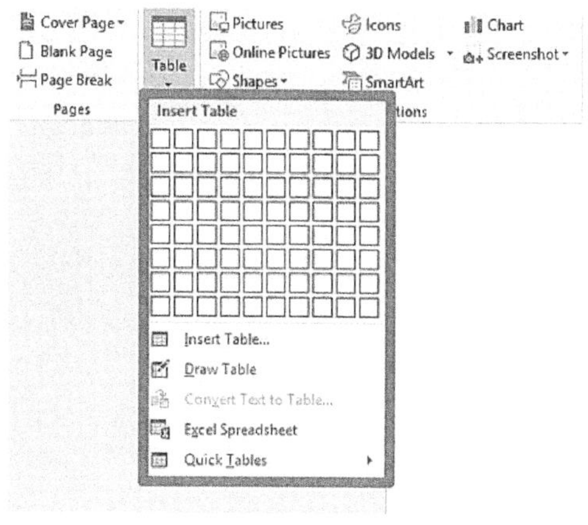

- Once you have selected the number of rows (horizontal) and columns (vertical), then your table will be displayed in your Word document. Assuming it is three rows and five columns, place your mouse cursor on the table to type your text and number

- Then, start typing your words inside

Number	Text	
1	One	
2	Two	
3	Three	
4	Four	

Adding additional rows and columns

- Go to "Insert tab"

- There, you will see "Table", click the little arrow to get the dropdown options

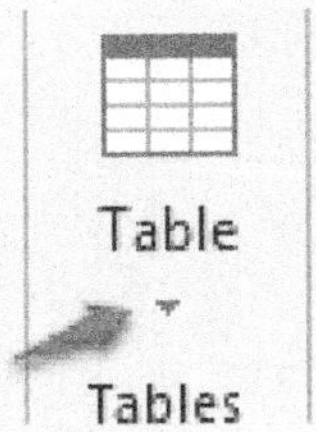

- Once you click on "Table", you get the "Table Grid", select the numbers of rows and columns you want, then click on the last selection of row and column to display it on your Word document

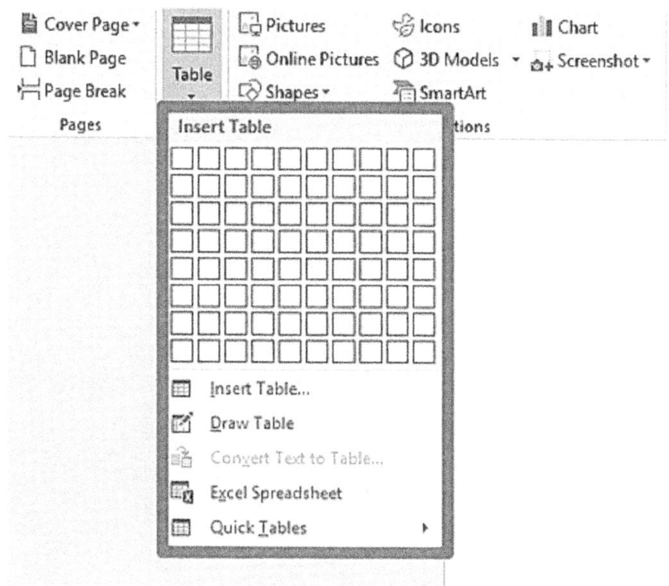

- Once you select the number of rows and columns and you have inputted your texts, there is a possibility of needing an additional table to continue your content, simply place your cursor at the edge of your table as illustrated below.

Position	Type	Location
Computer Engineer	Full-time, two months	Clearwater
Software Developer	Full-time, open-ended	Tampa
UI Designer	Part-time, two months	St. Petersburg

- Once you see the plus sign (+), click on it, another empty single row and column will be created

Position	Type	Location
Computer Engineer	Full-time, two months	Clearwater
Software Developer	Full-time, open-ended	Tampa
UI Designer	Part-time, two months	St. Petersburg

- You can then fill up the empty rows and columns with your desired text

Position	Type	Location
Computer Engineer	Full-time, two months	Clearwater
Project Assistant	Full-time, three months	Coral Springs
Software Developer	Full-time, open-ended	Tampa
UI Designer	Part-time, two months	St. Petersburg

How to use Autofit on Table

Before we go into how to use autofit, what is autofit all about? Autofit is a predefined feature that gives your table the privilege to fit automatically to the text length. How do we use autofit?

- Simply go to "Insert"

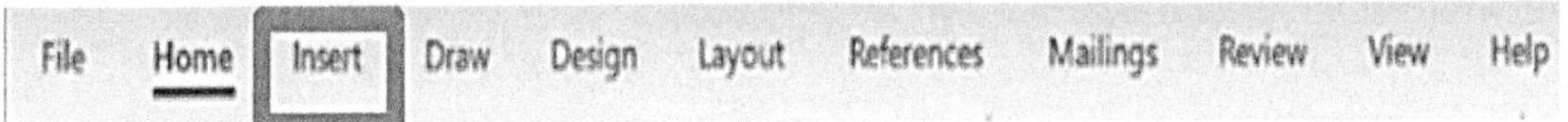

- Below "Insert", you will see "Table", click the little arrow to get the dropdown table options

- Once you click on "Table", you get the "Table Grid

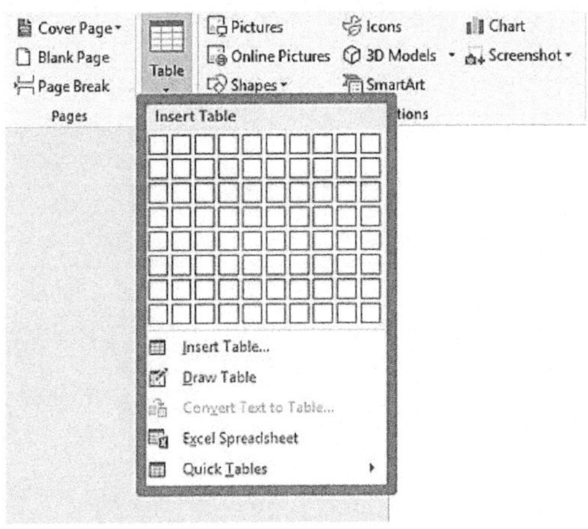

- Create the number of rows and columns for your table, then select it, once it appears on your Word document, you can type your text into it. For us to see how "Autofit" works, I will use my previous table to illustrate "Autofit"

Position	Type	Location
Computer Engineer	Full-time, two months	Clearwater
Project Assistant	Full-time, three months	Coral Springs
Software Developer	Full-time, open-ended	Tampa
UI Designer	Part-time, two months	St. Petersburg

- Once you click any part of your table, a little plus (+) sign will appear on your left-hand side, click on it

Position	Type	Location
Computer Engineer	Full-time, two months	Clearwater
Project Assistant	Full-time, three months	Coral Springs
Software Developer	Full-time, open-ended	Tampa
UI Designer	Part-time, two months	St. Petersburg

- Your table will be automatically highlighted

Position	Type	Location
Computer Engineer	Full-time, two months	Clearwater
Project Assistant	Full-time, three months	Coral Springs
Software Developer	Full-time, open-ended	Tampa
UI Designer	Part-time, two months	St. Petersburg

- Then, look above, you will see "Table Tools" appearing since your table is active. "Table Tools" comes with two options "Design" and "Layout"

- Select "Layout". Under "Layout", look for "Autofit"

- Click on “Autofit” and choose the first option which is “Autofit Contents”, once you click on “Autofit Contents”

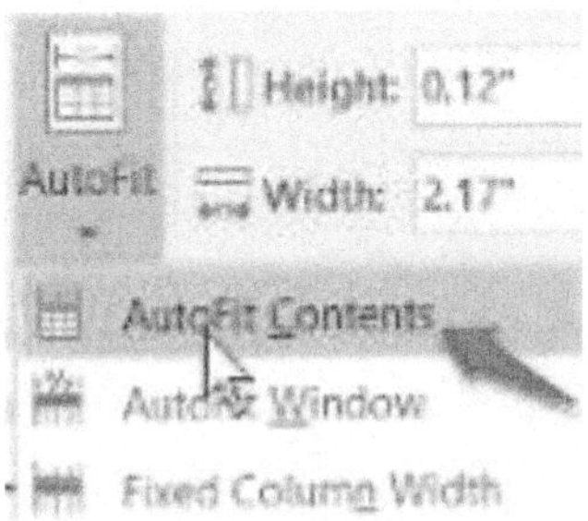

- Your table will automatically resize to your text contents size, you can compare the previous table and the recent “Autofit” to see the changes in size

Position	Type	Location
Computer Engineer	Full-time, two months	Clearwater
Project Assistant	Full-time, three months	Coral Springs
Software Developer	Full-time, open-ended	Tampa
UI Designer	Part-time, two months	St. Petersburg

Aligning your table positioning

- Simply go to “Insert tab”

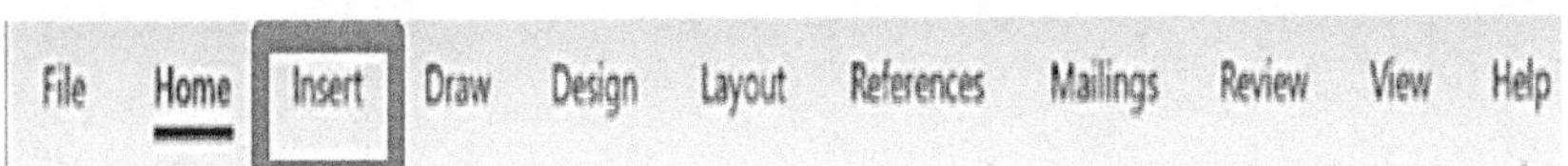

- Below “Insert”, you will see “Table”, click the little arrow to get the dropdown options

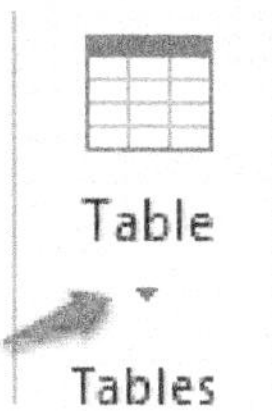

- Once you click on "Table", you get the "Table Grid", select the numbers of rows and columns you want to work with, then click on the last selection of rows and column to display it on your Word document

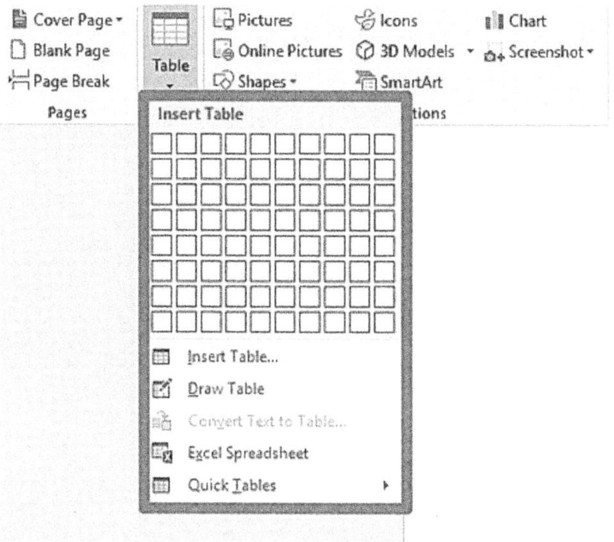

- Once it appears on your Word document, you can type your text into it. For us to see how to align a table, I will use my previous table to illustrate how to align your table

Position	Type	Location
Computer Engineer	Full-time, two months	Clearwater
Project Assistant	Full-time, three months	Coral Springs
Software Developer	Full-time, open-ended	Tampa
UI Designer	Part-time, two months	St. Petersburg

- Once you click any part of your table a little plus (+) sign will appear on your left-hand side, click on it

Position	Type	Location
Computer Engineer	Full-time, two months	Clearwater
Project Assistant	Full-time, three months	Coral Springs
Software Developer	Full-time, open-ended	Tampa
UI Designer	Part-time, two months	St. Petersburg

- All your table will be automatically highlighted

Position	Type	Location
Computer Engineer	Full-time, two months	Clearwater
Project Assistant	Full-time, three months	Coral Springs
Software Developer	Full-time, open-ended	Tampa
UI Designer	Part-time, two months	St. Petersburg

- Then, go to your "home" tab

- By your right-hand side under the "Paragraph" ribbon, there are four types of alignment; left alignment, center alignment, right alignment, and justify alignment. For understanding, we will be using center alignment to see the effect, because by default your table is on left alignment; simply click the "**center alignment**" which is the second alignment icon from your left

- You can press the shortcut, "Ctrl + E" on your keyboard, your table will be moved to the center point. Once you select center alignment as illustrated, here's what it will look like

For further information about any of these new jobs, or a complete listing of jobs that are available through the Career Center, please call Mary Walker-Huelsman at (727) 555-0030 or visit our website at www.fpcc.pro/careers.

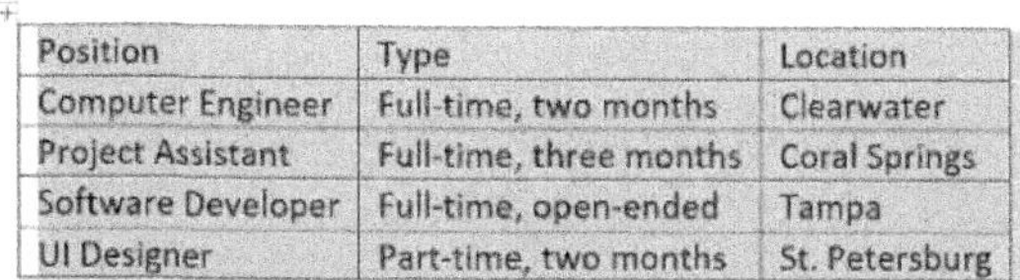

Position	Type	Location
Computer Engineer	Full-time, two months	Clearwater
Project Assistant	Full-time, three months	Coral Springs
Software Developer	Full-time, open-ended	Tampa
UI Designer	Part-time, two months	St. Petersburg

To help prepare yourself before applying for these jobs, we recommend that you review the following articles on our website at www.fpcc.pro/careers.

Manual Way of Inserting a Table

- Simply go to your "Insert tab"

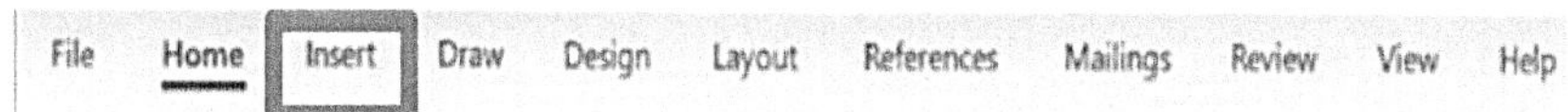

- Under "Insert", locate "Table" and click on it

- A dropdown option will be displayed choose "Insert Table"

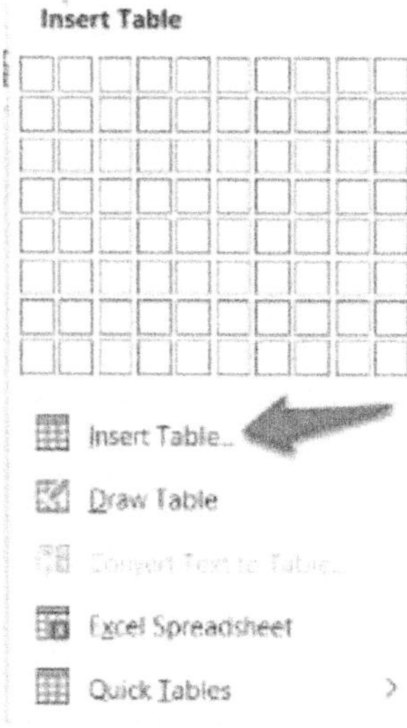

- Another dialog box will appear where you can insert the number of rows and columns to be displayed in your document. By default, manual insert for columns is five, while for rows is two, these can be adjusted at wish. You can also decide to choose "Autofit to contents", "Autofit to window" or "Fixed column width", then, hit "Ok" to effect your changes

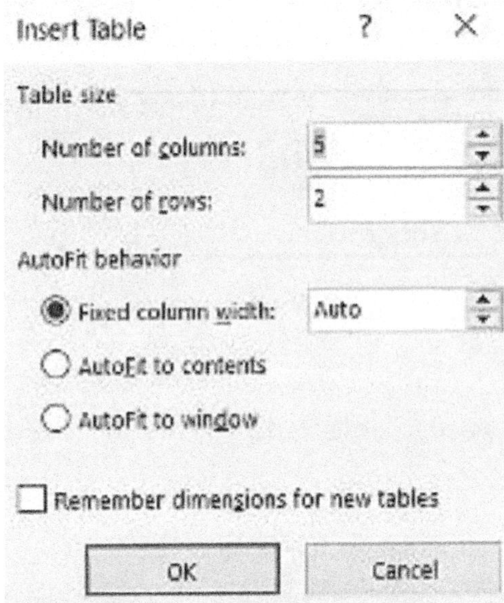

- If you did not edit the manual insert table, below is the result you will get

How to delete columns and rows

Since I have shown you how to insert tables, now let us look at how to delete or remove that which was inserted. Assuming we have five (5) rows and seven (7) columns, and all we need is only four (4) rows and six (6) columns, simply click on row 7 on the table as an indication of where we want to delete

1.				
2.				
3.				
4.				
5.				
6.				
7.				

- Look above, you will see “Table Design” and “Layout”, choose “Layout”

- Under “Layout” on your left-hand side, you will see multiple options on the “Rows & Columns” ribbon such as “Delete”, “Insert above”, “Insert below”, and other options. Click on “Delete”

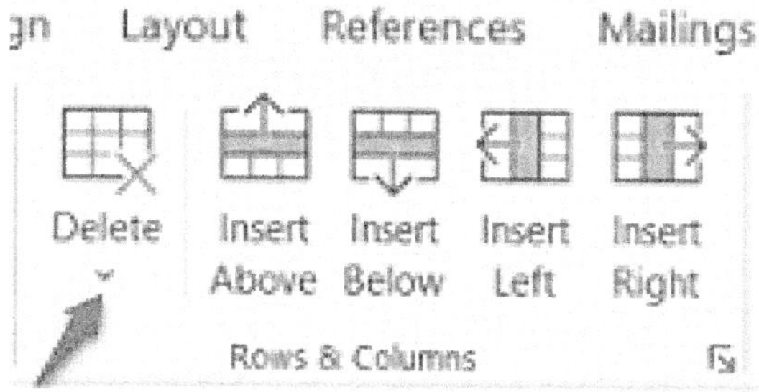

- A dropdown menu will be displayed, select “Delete Rows” from the options, your rows that was seven (7) in number will become six (6)

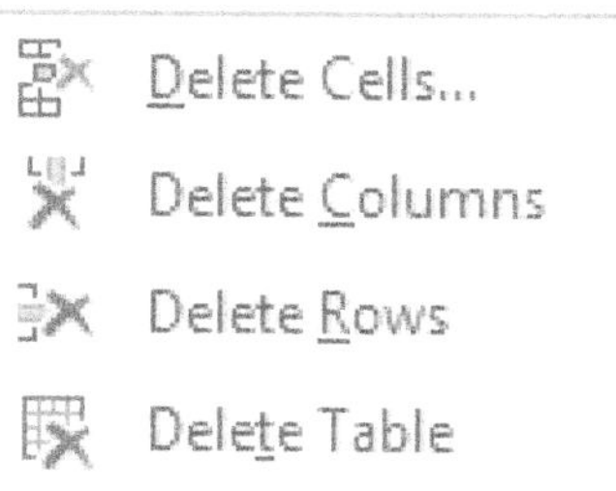

- This should be your result. **Note**, anywhere your cursor is within your table is where the delete will take effect from

1.				
2.				
3.				
4.				
5.				
6.				

How to Merge Cells in a table & Designing a table style

Beyond explanation, it is also important to understand the little element that the big element is made up of. “Cell” is the inputted part where your text and number are inserted into. So, why merge cells? Merging of cells is mostly needed for various reasons such as naming your table, constructing a calendar.

The month and year (for example, January 2022) need to occupy the first rows in a bold and large format to give a clear update on what the table is all about as seen in the image below

January 2022						
Sunday	Monday	Tuesday	Wednesday	Thursday	Friday	Saturday
						1
2	3	4	5	6	7	8
9	10	11	12	13	14	15
16	17	18	19	20	21	22
23	24	25	26	27	28	29
30	31					

Then, how do we merge cells?

- Since I have shown you how to insert tables, Let’s assume we want to create something similar to the calendar format above. For us to merge our table, if you count the rows, you will notice it is seven (7) in number, while the columns are eight (8) in number including the heading (January 2022). This is also an opportunity to create a calendar with Office Word document. After creating your table, input the text and number in its various location

January 2022						
Sunday	Monday	Tuesday	Wednesday	Thursday	Friday	Saturday
						1
2	3	4	5	6	7	8
9	10	11	12	13	14	15
16	17	18	19	20	21	22
23	24	25	26	27	28	29
30	31					

- Then, place your cursor at the beginning of "January 2022"

January 2022						
Sunday	Monday	Tuesday	Wednesday	Thursday	Friday	Saturday
						1
2	3	4	5	6	7	8
9	10	11	12	13	14	15
16	17	18	19	20	21	22
23	24	25	26	27	28	29
30	31					

- Once your cursor is blinking at the beginning of January 2022, simply hold down "Shift key" on your keyboard with the "forward Arrow" at the right-hand side of your keyboard. It will be highlighting your first row, once your highlighting gets to the last row, release your hand from the "Shift & "Arrow keys" on your keyboard, below is where the highlighting of your rows should stop

January 2022						
Sunday	Monday	Tuesday	Wednesday	Thursday	Friday	Saturday
						1
2	3	4	5	6	7	8
9	10	11	12	13	14	15
16	17	18	19	20	21	22
23	24	25	26	27	28	29
30	31					

- After highlighting it, go to the "menu bar", click on "Layout"

- Under "Layout" look at your left-hand side, you will see the "Merge" ribbon, click on "Merge cells"

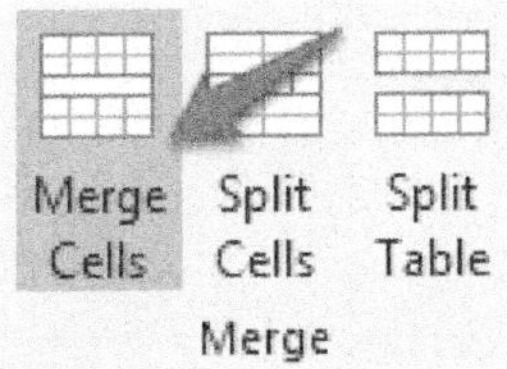

- By default, your highlighted row will be merged as one, you will also notice the column lines that separate the entire table is no longer applicable to the "January 2022" row

January 2022						
Sunday	Monday	Tuesday	Wednesday	Thursday	Friday	Saturday
						1
2	3	4	5	6	7	8
9	10	11	12	13	14	15
16	17	18	19	20	21	22
23	24	25	26	27	28	29
30	31					

Designing a table style

- Now, to make it look fashionable, simply click on "Design"

- Then select your built-in table template, you can click the little dropdown arrow for other options of your choice; remember we want it to look like the blue template shown earlier

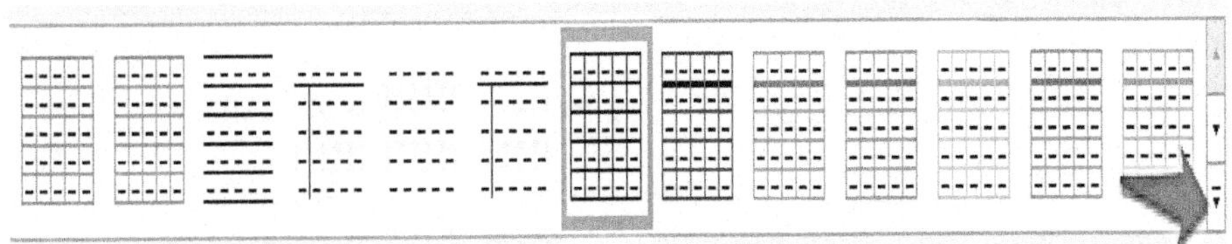

- You will be shown other table design options, the arrangement might be different but the table design remain the same, once you select it, your table will possess the template

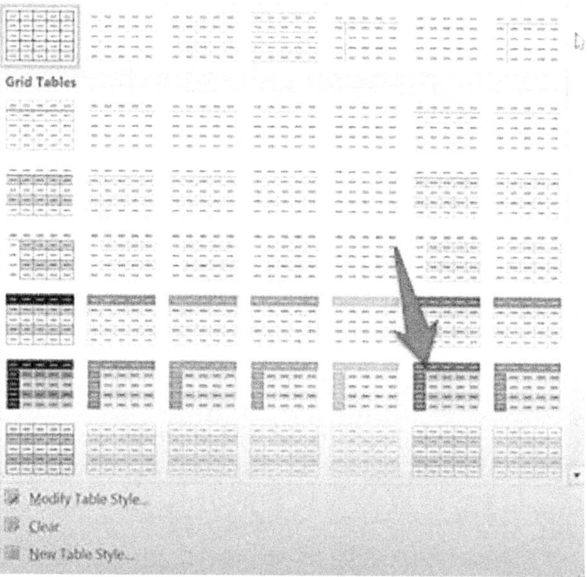

- Now, you see we are closer to what you saw earlier, don't forget to apply "Autofit Content" under "Layout" to make it look professional and similar to what I did, which I also applied into what you are seeing. You can revisit chapter seven to see how to apply "Autofit Content" to your created table

January 2022						
Sunday	Monday	Tuesday	Wednesday	Thursday	Friday	Saturday
						1
2	3	4	5	6	7	8
9	10	11	12	13	14	15
16	17	18	19	20	21	22
23	24	25	26	27	28	29
30	31					

- Now, let us do the final part, make sure your "January 2022" is highlighted. Simply to go your "Home tab" and under the "font" ribbon, select "**Bold**" if yours is not bolded. It is recognized with a **B** icon. Also, increase the "font-size" to "20" to get the same result

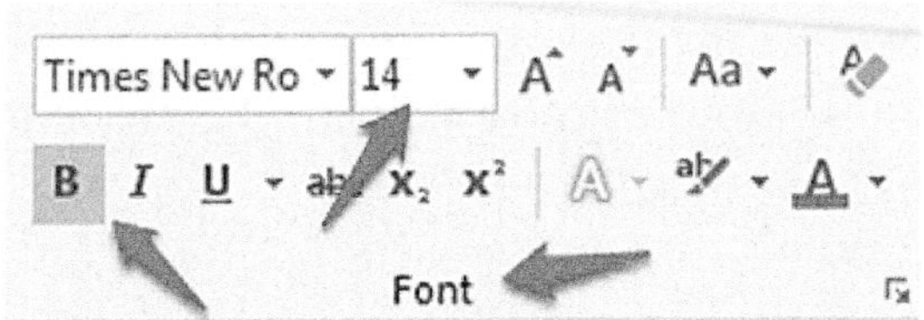

- Then, go to the next ribbon which is the "Paragraph" ribbon, select "center alignment" as illustrated below or you press the shortcut keys "Ctrl + E" from your keyboard to also get the same result

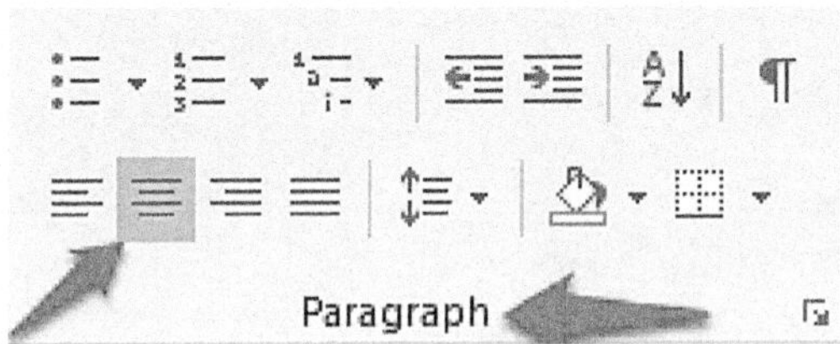

- Your highlighted text which is "January 2022" will move to the center, aligned to the middle, and also increase in size only if it is still highlighted

January 2022						
Sunday	Monday	Tuesday	Wednesday	Thursday	Friday	Saturday
						1
2	3	4	5	6	7	8
9	10	11	12	13	14	15
16	17	18	19	20	21	22
23	24	25	26	27	28	29
30	31					

How to Split Cells in a Table

Splitting of cells means dividing a Cell into multiple cells. Splitting cells is the opposite of merging cells. We will be using our calendar table to illustrate how to split a cell in a table by following these procedures:

- Assuming we are splitting back "January 2022" that was merged, simply highlight "January 2022", and click on "Design" in the menu bar to change its blue displayed design to black & white which is the default table color (black & white has nothing to do with splitting) just for us to be able to see the changes on the splitting of cells

January 2022						
Sunday	Monday	Tuesday	Wednesday	Thursday	Friday	Saturday
						1
2	3	4	5	6	7	8
9	10	11	12	13	14	15
16	17	18	19	20	21	22
23	24	25	26	27	28	29
30	31					

- Once you change your table template back to black & white, as long as you followed the illustration that led to me adding a table template, you get this as your result

January 2022						
Sunday	Monday	Tuesday	Wednesday	Thursday	Friday	Saturday
						1
2	3	4	5	6	7	8
9	10	11	12	13	14	15
16	17	18	19	20	21	22
23	24	25	26	27	28	29
30	31					

- Note that I still highlighted "January 2022" since it's what we merged before. Also, note that you can also split other areas of your table rows and columns which I will be illustrating soon. To proceed with the splitting, simply go to "Layout" on your menu bar

- Then, select "Split Cells"

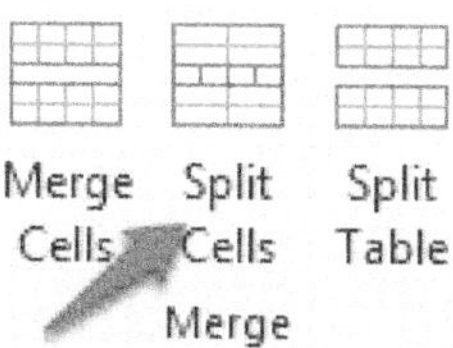

- A dialog box will appear, asking for how many rows and columns you want the highlighted area to multiply into. Note, your button might not be like the illustration below, depending on your operating system, therefore, don't be surprised by any changes you observe

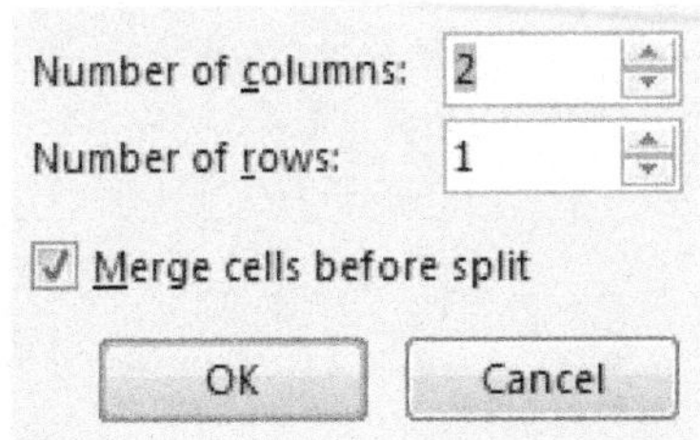

- Choose your preferred number, assuming we want to use the default numbering which is 2 columns and 1 row, your selection will reflect on your result and the highlighted "January 2022" will be moved to one cell since another cell has been created, but it will still maintain its alignment and other features format applied to it

January 2022						
Sunday	Monday	Tuesday	Wednesday	Thursday	Friday	Saturday
						1
2	3	4	5	6	7	8
9	10	11	12	13	14	15
16	17	18	19	20	21	22
23	24	25	26	27	28	29
30	31					

Moving columns and rows

It is possible to move your table around to any location on your document by simply following this simple step:

- For comprehensive understanding, let us use our created calendar table. As explained earlier, point your mouse cursor into your table in the next cell after number "31" as illustrated below, then, a plus (+) sign will appear at the top left corner, use your mouse cursor to hold it down and drag it to anywhere you want to place it within your document.

January 2022						
Sunday	Monday	Tuesday	Wednesday	Thursday	Friday	Saturday
						1
2	3	4	5	6	7	8
9	10	11	12	13	14	15
16	17	18	19	20	21	22
23	24	25	26	27	28	29
30	31					

Decorating your table with borders and colors

Borders are the lines that form table edges. With borders, you can decorate your table and design it to your preferred choice. How to decorate your table with borders and colors will be explained step by step below

- To save time because of the process of creating another table, we will be using our calendar table. Highlight your heading cell which is "January 2022" or you point your cursor into the "January 2022" row. Note you can use any cell, just for a well-ordered work, we will use the heading cell (January 2022)

January 2022						
Sunday	Monday	Tuesday	Wednesday	Thursday	Friday	Saturday
						1
2	3	4	5	6	7	8
9	10	11	12	13	14	15
16	17	18	19	20	21	22
23	24	25	26	27	28	29
30	31					

- Then, the table options will appear named "Table tools", under it is "Design" and "Layout", click on "Layout"

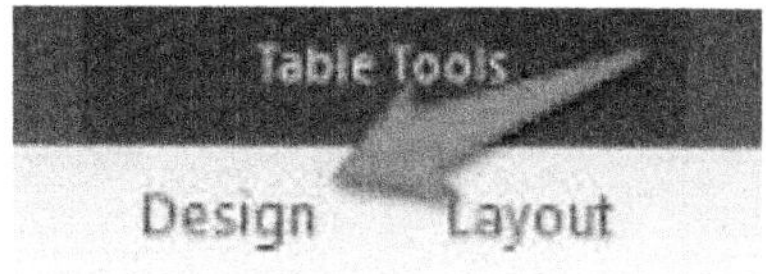

- At your right-hand side, locate "Borders"

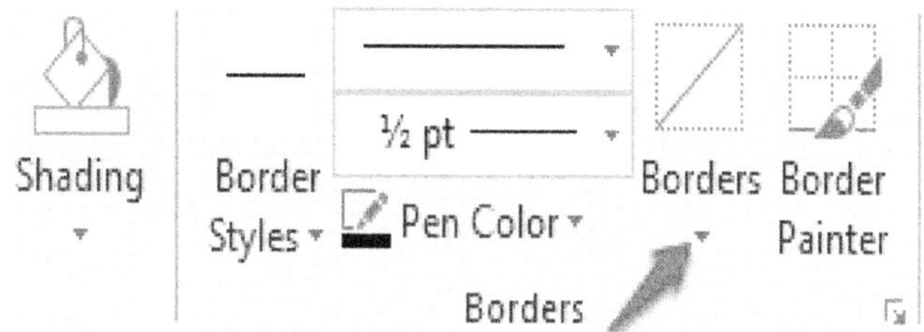

- Click on "Borders" to select a different line style format to replace the default borders. For example, we could choose a triple line border

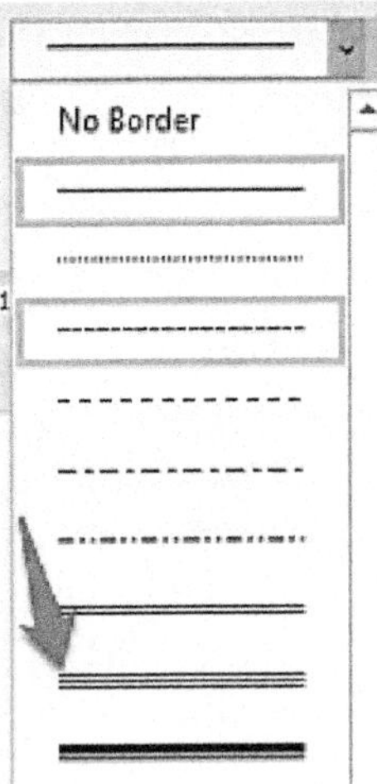

- We can also change the line weight to one and a half point ($1^{1}{}_{2}$ pt)

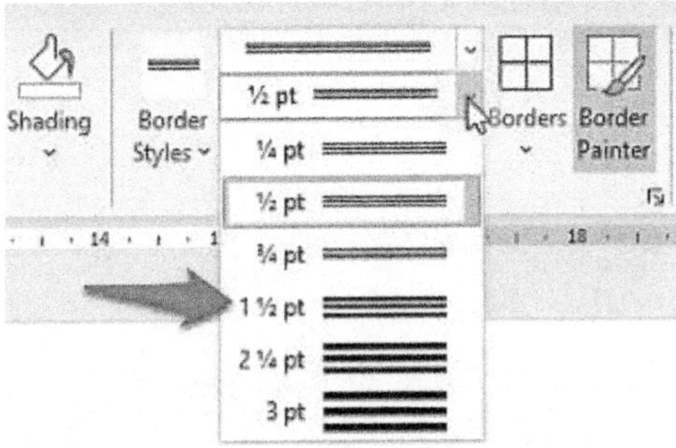

- We can also change the border color by picking the orange color

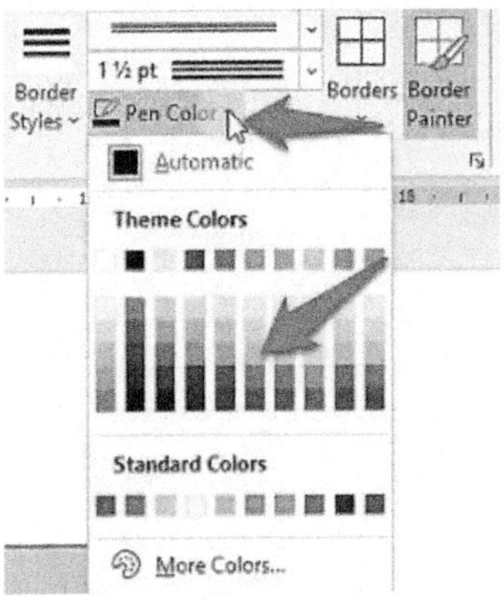

- Once your color has been selected, the "Border Styles", "Line Weight", "Line Styles" and "Pen Color" will have the effect of your chosen color. Note that your "Border Painter" is selected automatically

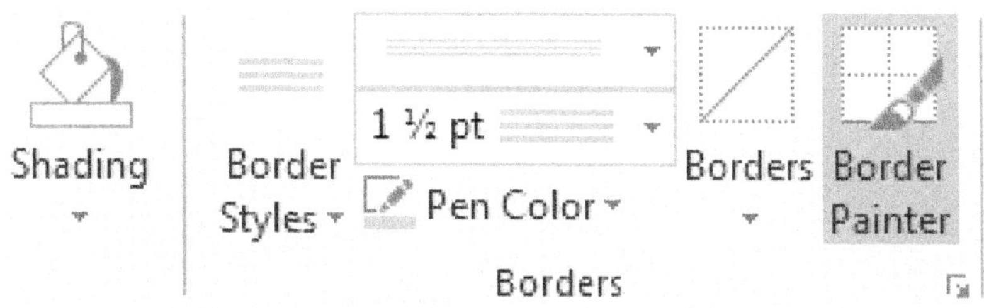

- Once your "Border Painter" is selected, your mouse cursor will change to pen cursor, simply place it on the line edge you want your triple line and color to affect. Note, if you place it wrongly, you will need to select "Border Painter" again

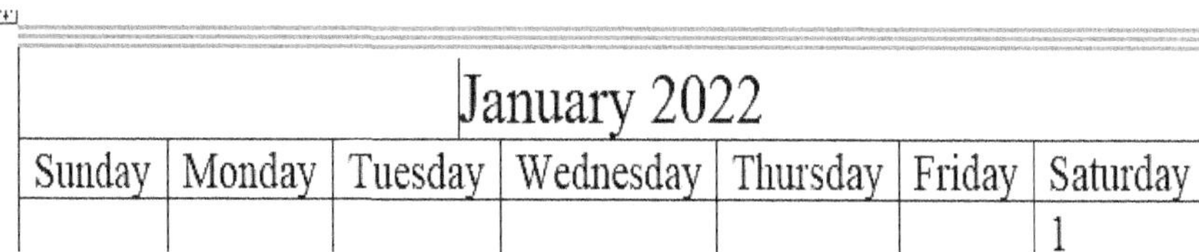

January 2022						
Sunday	Monday	Tuesday	Wednesday	Thursday	Friday	Saturday
						1

- But there is also another way out without having to click and wrongly place line edges; simply click on "Borders"

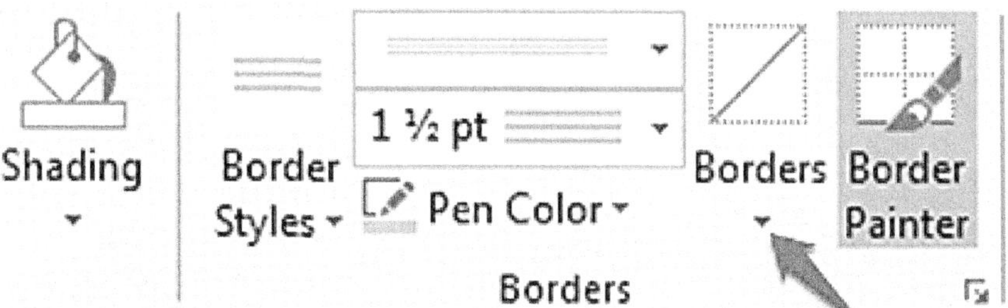

- Then, select what area you want your border to cover such as "Bottom Border", "Top Border", "Left Border", "Right Border" and so on. We will be clicking on "All Borders"

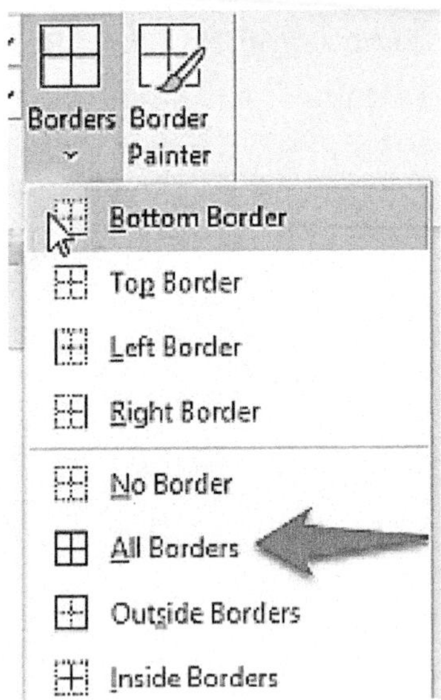

- Once "All Borders" has been selected, your created calendar table will be formatted on your active cell which is "January 2022" where your mouse cursor is pointing.

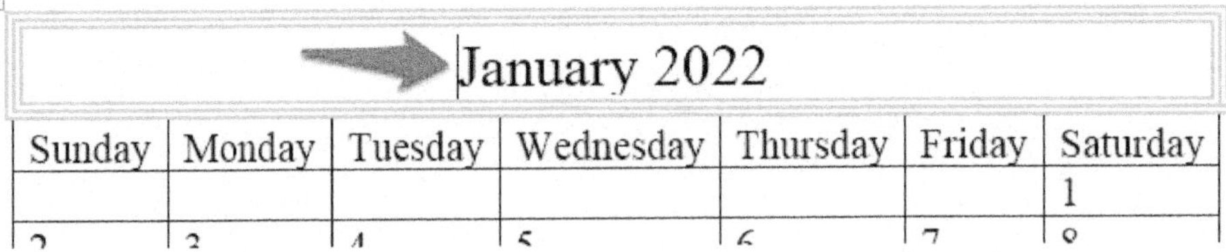

NOTE: If you want the remaining rows and columns to also be formatted, then, you need to highlight the entire table to perform such an operation.

- You can also add shade color on the background of "January 2022" by changing the white background. To do this, click on "Shading"

- Select your preferred color. For illustration, I will pick the gray color to achieve a color blend.

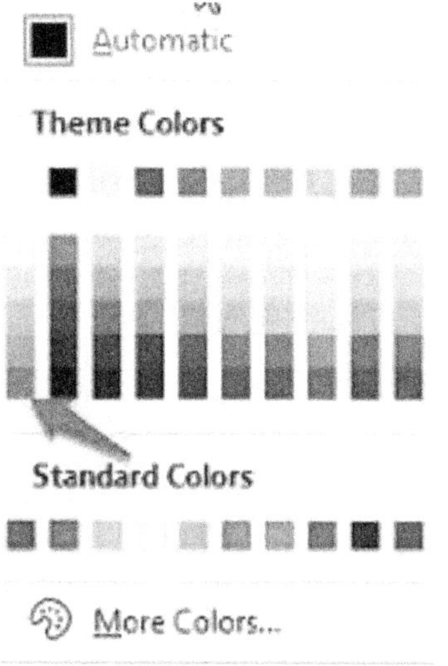

- Your outcome if you choose the same color with me, will be the illustration below

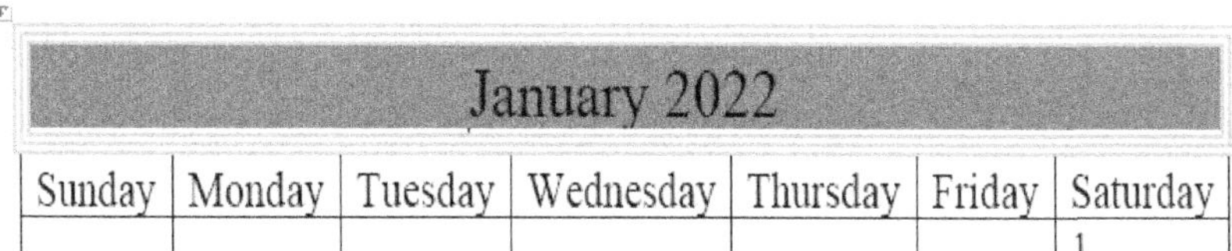

January 2022						
Sunday	Monday	Tuesday	Wednesday	Thursday	Friday	Saturday
						1

Exploring more on Borders

In continuation of ***"Decorating your table with borders and colors"***. It is important to note that there is also more to Border Style

- Still on our created calendar table illustration

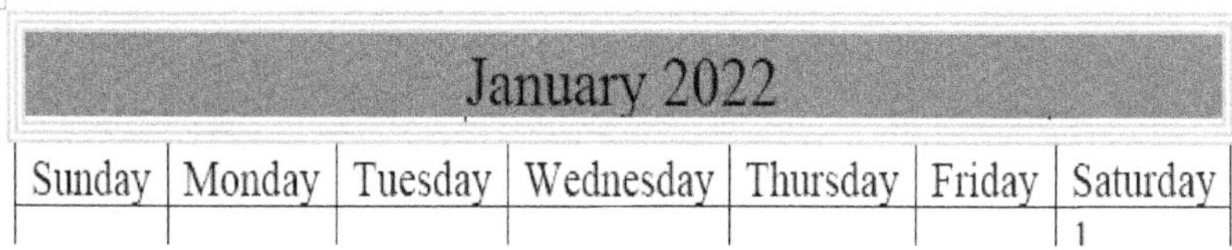

January 2022						
Sunday	Monday	Tuesday	Wednesday	Thursday	Friday	Saturday
						1

- Click on "Design" table tools

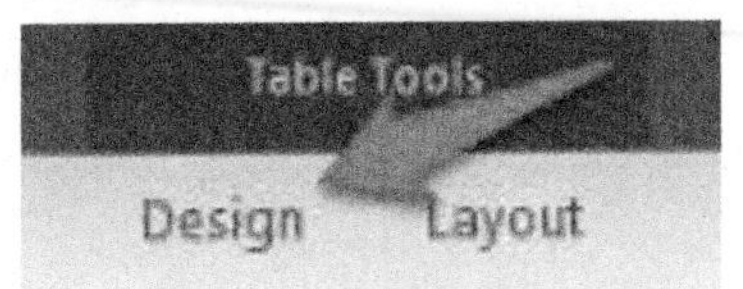

- At your left-hand side, you will see a dropdown arrow, click on it

- You will be brought here, where all our formatted styles are reviewed and edited. It consists of "Borders settings", "Page Border settings" and "Shading settings". If you remember, previously, we choose an orange color, that is why you are seeing orange color and one and half width. Click on the "Shading" option

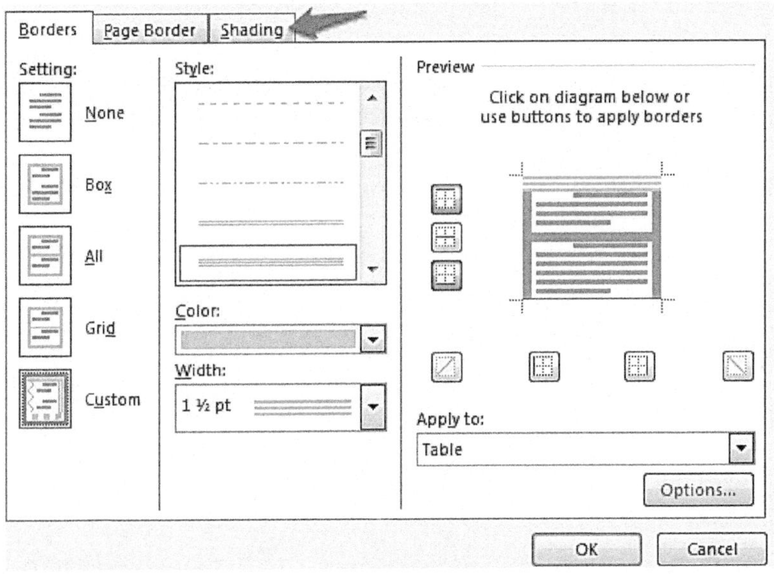

- Once you click on "Shading", you will be brought to this page, where you can set your "Shading Patterns", "Style", "Color" and "Apply to". Under "Apply to", select "Table", then click "Ok" to see the effect

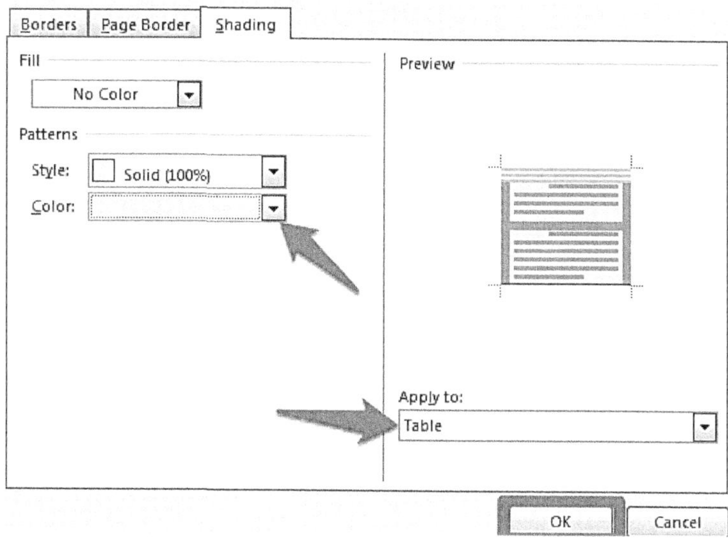

- Here is what your result will be if you do exactly as I did

January 2022						
Sunday	Monday	Tuesday	Wednesday	Thursday	Friday	Saturday
						1
2	3	4	5	6	7	8
9	10	11	12	13	14	15
16	17	18	19	20	21	22
23	24	25	26	27	28	29
30	31					

Using Math Formulas in Tables

This is the unbelievable part of Word; many thinks once you want to do any mathematical calculation you need to use other Microsoft products such as Excel to be able to do your calculation. Every Microsoft App has its uniqueness but can interchange some features within such other since all the applications are all Microsoft packages. Sooner or later, everything will come together uniquely, just as there is now "My Add-ins" that gives other apps the privilege to interact with the Word environment.

So, how do we use mathematical formulas in our table? Below is the step-by-step procedure on how to go about it:

- Create a table format as taught earlier, type the below information

Mick Scores	
Math	60
English	80
ICT	55
Physics	75
Total	

- Once done, click your mouse cursor directly to your empty cell which is where your total summation will be, make sure your mouse cursor is blinking on the empty cell for your summation

Mick Scores	
Math	60
English	80
ICT	55
Physics	75
Total	

- Now, go to "Layout" in your menu bar, click on it

- Look at the last tool on your right-hand side you will see "Formula" with an "fx" icon, click on it

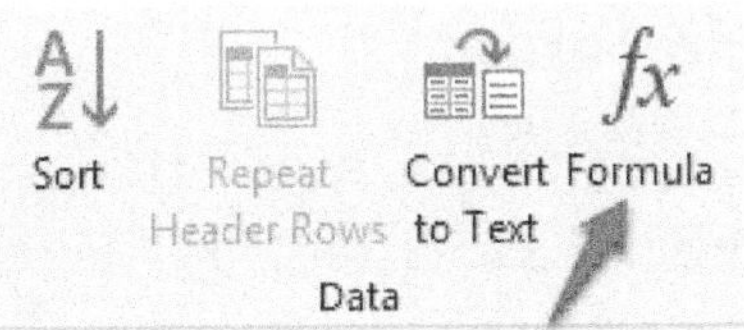

- A dialog box will appear, with a default formula "=SUM(ABOVE)"

=SUM, represent add up (+) your figures together. (ABOVE) represent add the numbers in the column above the cell you are in. (LEFT) represent add the numbers in the row to the left side of the cell you're in. (BELOW) represent add the numbers in the column below the cell you're in. (RIGHT) represent adds the numbers in the row to the right side of the cell you are in.

Your "Number format" represents your figure settings. For example, $100 can be $100.00 depending on how you want your number format to look.

Your "Paste function" is an added formula feature by Microsoft to perform more complex calculations by default. You can just click the "Ok" option to just perform your normal summing calculation.

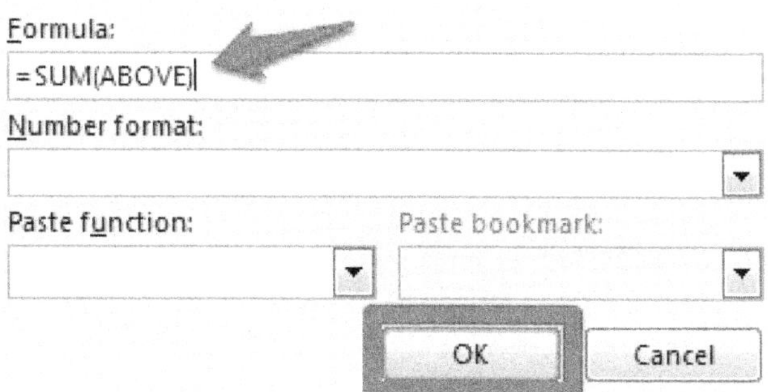

- Your "Mick Scores" will be summed up automatically

Mick Scores	
Math	60
English	80
ICT	55
Physics	75
Total	270

How to move or drag a table

- Assuming we are using the "Mick Scores" table,

Mick Scores	
Math	60
English	80
ICT	55
Physics	75
Total	270

- Place your mouse cursor on any cell, mine was placed on the "total score 270", a little plus (+) sign will appear at the left side, use your mouse cursor to pin it down then drag it to any position on your document

Mick Scores	
Math	60
English	80
ICT	55
Physics	75
Total	270

How to enlarge or reduce your table

- Assuming we want to enlarge the "Mick Scores" table

Mick Scores	
Math	60
English	80
ICT	55
Physics	75
Total	270

- Click on any cell in your table, for illustration, I will change my mouse cursor from "Total Scores" to "Mick Scores" which is the heading. Once your mouse cursor is blinking in any cell you choose, you will notice additional features joint together with your table, one is your top left cross arrow which has been discussed, while the other is a "little white box" below your table on the right-hand side as indicated with a pink arrow.

Mick Scores	
Math	60
English	80
ICT	55
Physics	75
Total	270

- Once you hold down the "little white box" with your mouse cursor, drag it down to enlarge it or upward to reduce it.

Enlarged

Mick Scores	
Math	60
English	80
ICT	55
Physics	75
Total	270

Reduced

Mick Scores	
Math	60
English	80
ICT	55
Physics	75
Total	270

Using a picture as the table background

- Let's create an empty table as you were taught earlier by checking on the "Insert" tab to locate your "Table" and create columns and rows

- Next, insert text inside your cells, type "Island", "Animal" and "Nature" on each cell by your left-hand side

Island	
Animal	
Nature	

- Now, place your mouse cursor in the first empty cell on the right side

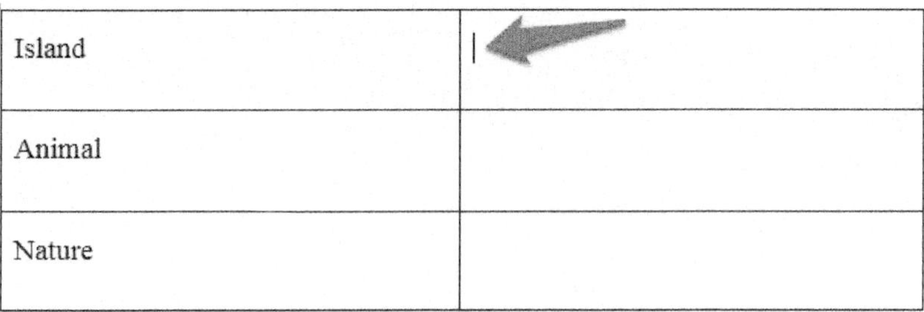

Island	
Animal	
Nature	

- Make sure your cursor is blinking, then go to your “Insert tab”

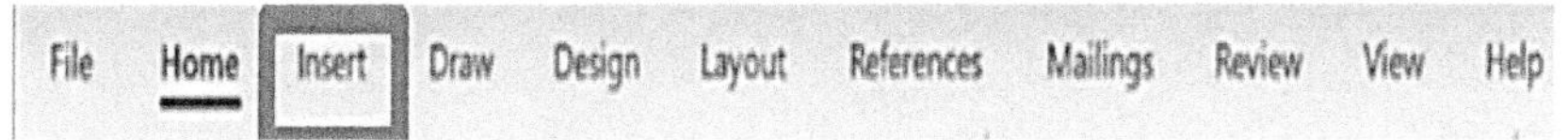

- In the “Insert tab”, you will see the “Illustrations” ribbon, select “Pictures” which is the first option

- You will be directed into your PC storage to locate the location of your picture manually, after getting it, then select it and click on the “Insert button” below. Note, you can also get the same image I used as long as you are running Microsoft operating system just go to your “Picture’s folder”

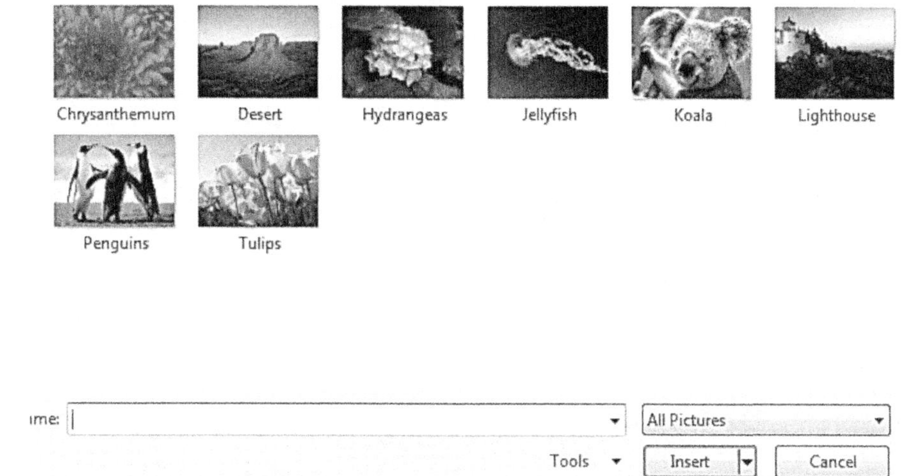

- Once your picture has been selected and inserted, the cell where your mouse cursor is blinking will display the picture. Note your picture might increase the table size, simply reduce it by 'reducing the little arrow dot', you can also rotate your picture by moving the curved arrow at the top of the picture

- Let's do the same to the other two empty cells

- Looking at it, you will notice it wasn't properly positioned, this is where additional adjustment is needed; simply click on any cell to make the little plus (+) arrow appear at the top left-hand side

- Once done, click on the plus (+) arrow above, all your table cells will be highlighted

- Then, in your menu bar, and click on "Layout"

- Make sure your table cell is still highlighted, then under "Layout" you will see the "Alignment" ribbon, select "Align Center" which is the middle icon, click on it

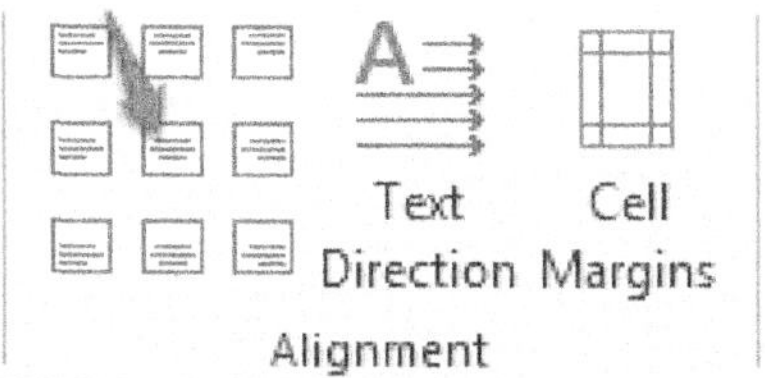

- All your entire table cells will automatically be centralized; you can compare the previous table with this adjusted table and see the difference

Drawing a table

- Go to "Insert tab"

- Under the "Insert tab", select "Table"

- It will display the “Table Grid”, under it, select “Draw Table”

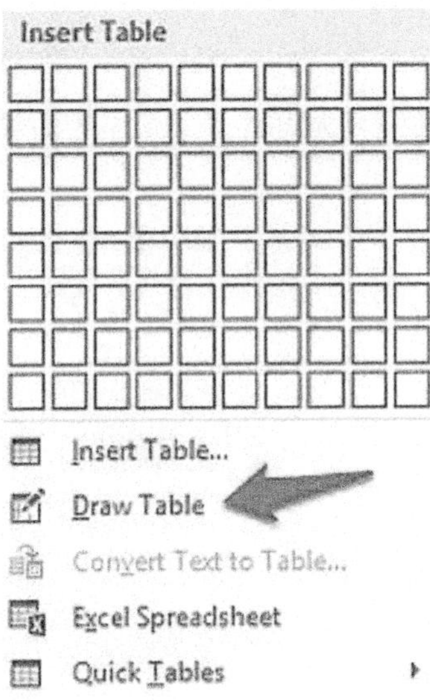

- You can design your table as desired as seen in the illustration below

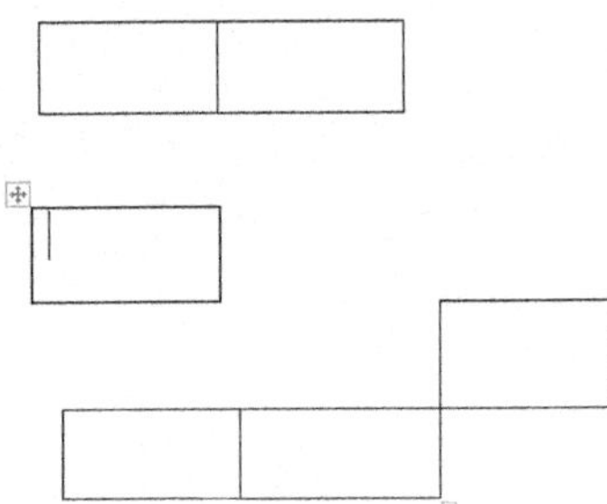

Drawing diagonal lines on tables

- You can draw any table of your choice and also add additional lines into your table as illustrated below. Note that your cursor will always change to a pen icon whenever you are working with the “Draw Table” Tool

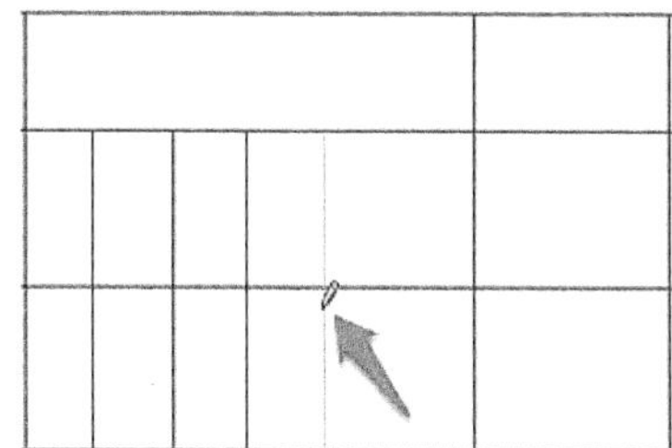

Wrapping text around a table

- Create a table of your choice as you were taught earlier, you can decide to replicate the one I'm using for illustration, two (2) rows, and three (3) columns. Make sure your cursor is blinking inside the one cell

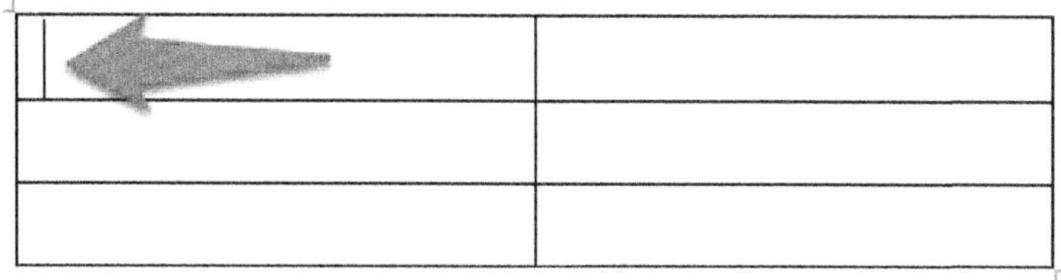

- Next, look above and locate "Table tools". Under "Table Tools", click on "Layout"

- Then, locate "Properties" and click on it

- Once you click on "Properties", a dialog box will be opened titled "Table" properties, under "Table", locate "Text wrapping", by default it is on "None", simply select "Around" and then press "Ok"

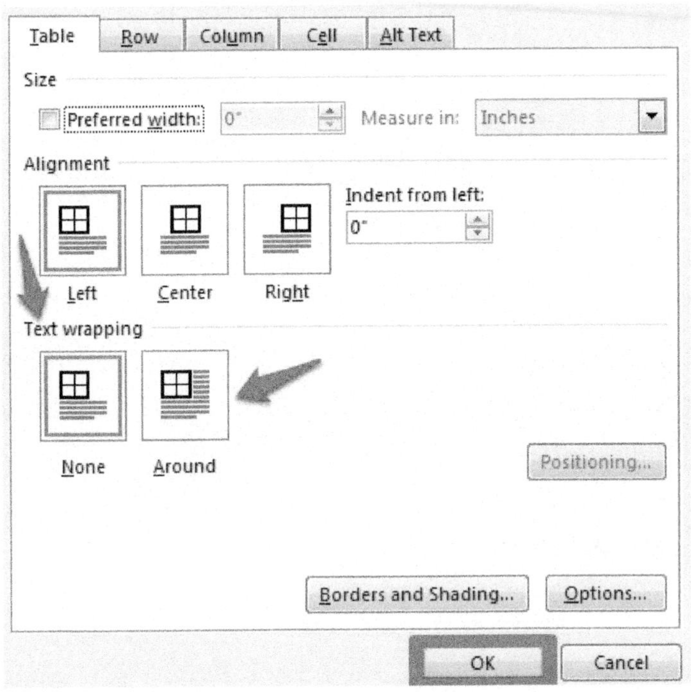

- Then, you can move your table to the center position and start typing or you can drag it into the middle of a text without having any issue with it, just as in the illustration below

A Word document is formatted to fit on a specific size page with the text automatically flowing from one page to the next. Excel supports printing, but its page breaks are not obvious, and because it's printing area can extend multiple pages horizontally as well as vertically the page breaks can be difficult to manage.

Tips

Now you see and understand how flexible and simplified Word 365 is. Simply do something different from what we have achieved, and let see how comprehensive you get what has been explained to you so far.

CHAPTER SEVEN

TAKING ADVANTAGE OF THE PROOFING TOOLS

Correcting Your Spelling Errors

Computer software such as Word processing has been a wonderful tool for effective means of simplifying human needs. While trying to construct words, typographical errors can occur, this led Microsoft corporation to look for a means to reduce the possibility of typographical errors while typing. Luckily, Word comes with several and different tools that can help you proofread your document and correct any mistake. Many don't know how helpful Word 365 is when it comes to autocorrect and spelling checking. To know how to autocorrect or scan your document against typographical errors, simply follow this step-by-step procedure below:

- Make sure you are currently on your document to be corrected

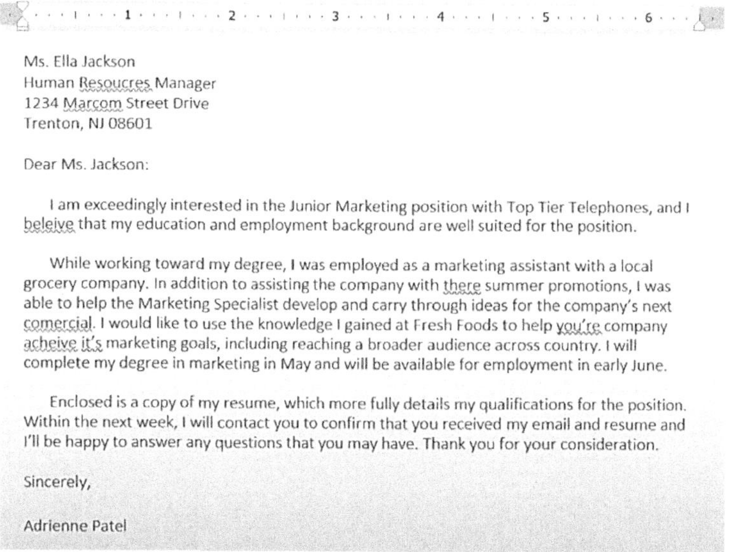

Ms. Ella Jackson
Human Resoucres Manager
1234 Marcom Street Drive
Trenton, NJ 08601

Dear Ms. Jackson:

I am exceedingly interested in the Junior Marketing position with Top Tier Telephones, and I beleive that my education and employment background are well suited for the position.

While working toward my degree, I was employed as a marketing assistant with a local grocery company. In addition to assisting the company with there summer promotions, I was able to help the Marketing Specialist develop and carry through ideas for the company's next comercial. I would like to use the knowledge I gained at Fresh Foods to help you're company acheive it's marketing goals, including reaching a broader audience across country. I will complete my degree in marketing in May and will be available for employment in early June.

Enclosed is a copy of my resume, which more fully details my qualifications for the position. Within the next week, I will contact you to confirm that you received my email and resume and I'll be happy to answer any questions that you may have. Thank you for your consideration.

Sincerely,

Adrienne Patel

- Go to the "Review" tab

- At your left-hand side, look for "Spelling & Grammar" and click on it

A dialog box will appear on your right-hand side which will start spelling check from the first error to the last, the first typographical error was "Resoucres" instead of "Resources", so if it was intentionally typed, you click on the "Ignore" option. If not, select the corrected word in the suggestion box, then click on the "Change" option to continue to autocorrect other words.

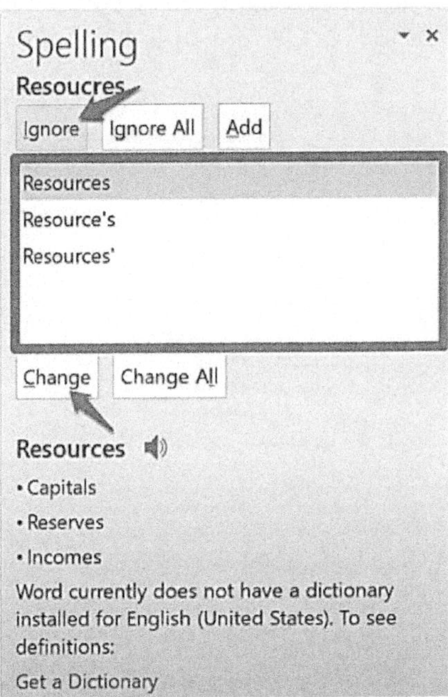

- Once you are done selecting the right suggested words, click on the "Change" option which will take you to the next misspelled text. In this illustration, the next is "Marcom", instead of "Marcum". Note that if the dictionary feature is installed on your Word 365 and it is a similar word in the dictionary, it will be explained below, if not, click on the "Get a Dictionary" option.

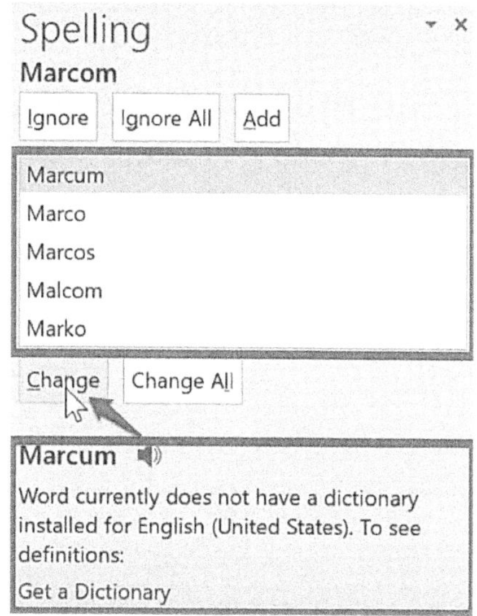

- It is important to note that the spell-checker is not perfect, sometimes it will say a word is spelled wrong when it is not, such as people's names, street names, and other unique proper nouns. If that happens, you have a couple of different options;
- The ***"Ignore"*** option will skip the word one time without changing it.
- The ***"Ignore All"*** option will skip the word every time it appears in your document.
- While the ***"Add"*** option will add the word to your inbuilt dictionary permanently, so it never comes up as an error again. Just make sure the word is spelled correctly before you go with any of these options.

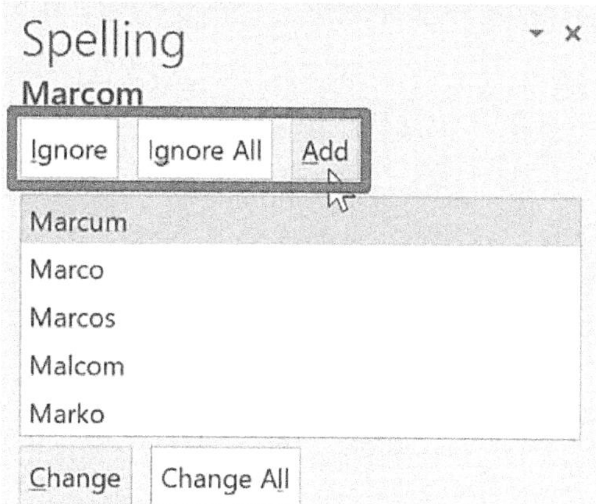

Correcting misspellings one at a time

- By default, Word is designed to mark spelling and grammar errors while you type, that is what the little red and blue wavy lines as seen in the illustration are for, so, you can check your document manually (like I have just shown you), or you can refer to the marks, and make corrections as you go.

Ms. Ella Jackson
Human Resources Manager
1234 Marcom Street Drive
Trenton, NJ 08601

Dear Ms. Jackson:

I am exceedingly interested in the Junior Marketing position with Top Tier Telephones, and I beleive that my education and employment background are well suited for the position.

While working toward my degree, I was employed as a marketing assistant with a local grocery company. In addition to assisting the company with there summer promotions, I was able to help the Marketing Specialist develop and carry through ideas for the company's next comercial. I would like to use the knowledge I gained at Fresh Foods to help you're company acheive it's marketing goals, including reaching a broader audience across country. I will complete my degree in marketing in May and will be available for employment in early June.

Enclosed is a copy of my resume, which more fully details my qualifications for the position. Within the next week, I will contact you to confirm that you received my email and resume and I'll be happy to answer any questions that you may have. Thank you for your consideration.

Sincerely,

Adrienne Patel

- Red means that there is a spelling error. To correct it, all you have to do is to right-click, then choose the proper spelling from the appeared menu after which the red curly line will be erased.

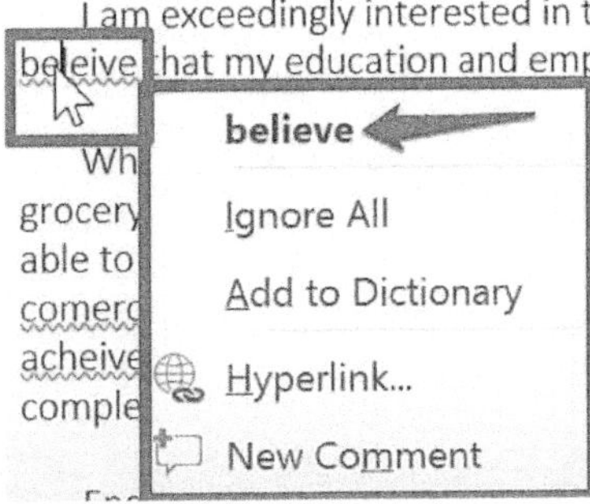

- Here is the corrected text "believe" instead of "beleive"

- Blue means that there is a kind of grammatical error. In this example, it looks like I used the wrong word in the context of the sentence. I should have used ***"their"*** instead of "there"

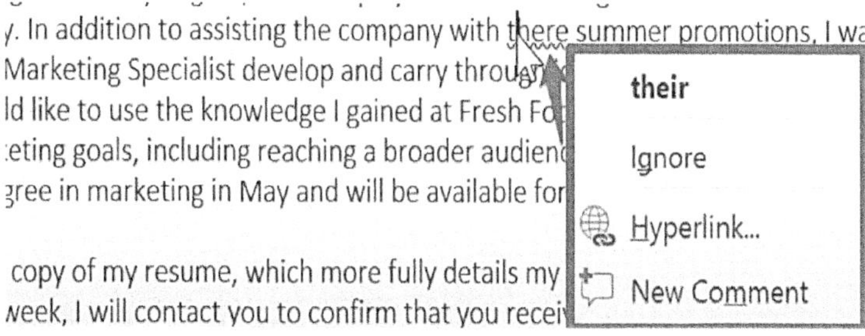

Customizing Spelling & Grammar Check

"Word" can be pretty good at picking up on errors like this, but there are certain things that it is set to ignore by default, including sentence fragments, poor sentence structure, and other common grammar mistakes. To include these things in your grammar check, you will need to adjust the default proofing settings. To do this,

- Go to the "Backstage view" which can be accessed through your "File menu"

- Click on "Options" in the left pane

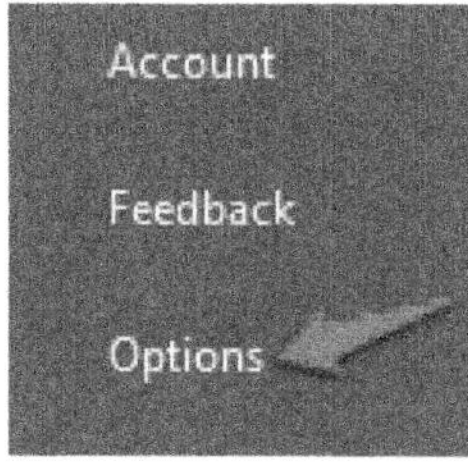

- Then, navigate to “Proofing” in the dialog box

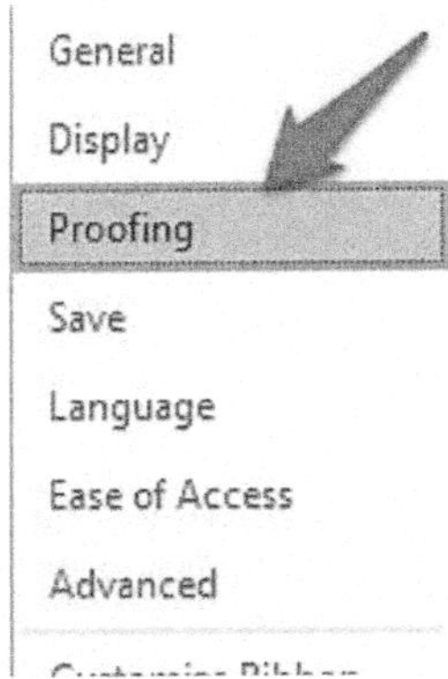

- To customize your grammar settings, look for “Writing Style” near the bottom of the Window. Then click the “settings” option located on the right side

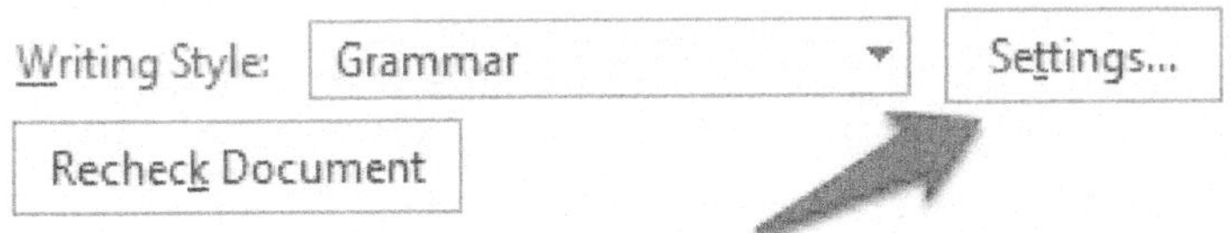

- And another dialog box will appear, here you can choose to set it to check Grammar Only, or Grammar & Style, which will cause Word to be strict about the style of your preferred choice. You can also turn specific items on or off to better suit your needs, for example, if you want Word to check for sentence fragments and run-ons, you can turn them on. Make sure you click the "Ok" button once you are through with the changes.

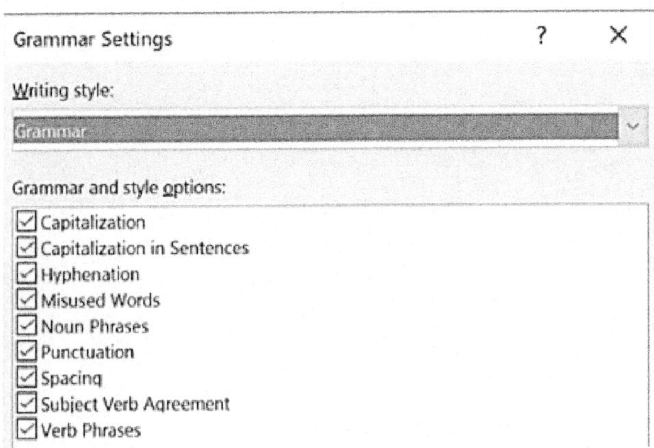

Preventing text from being spell-checked

- To do this, go to the "Backstage view" which can be accessed through your "File menu"

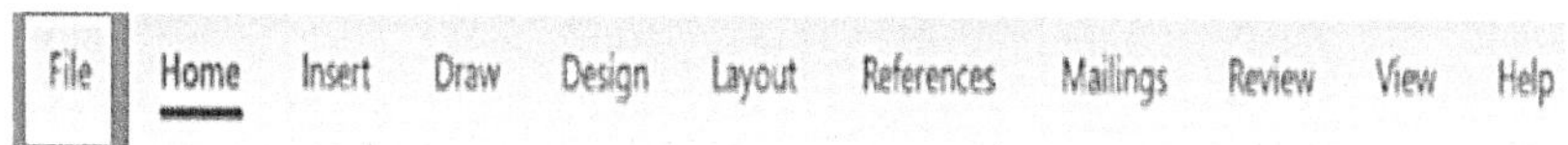

- Click on "Options" in the left pane

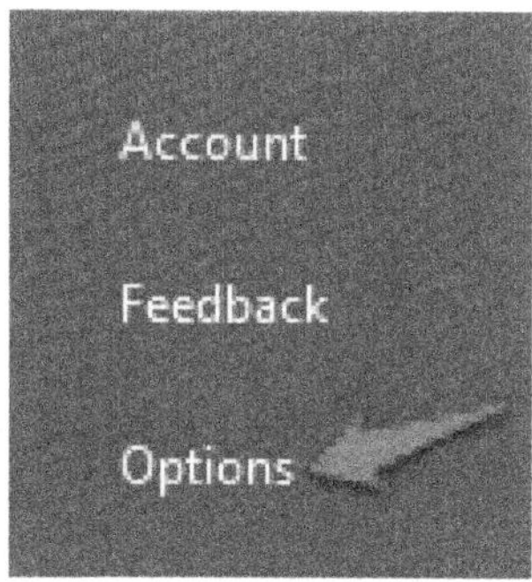

- Then, navigate to "Proofing" in the dialog box

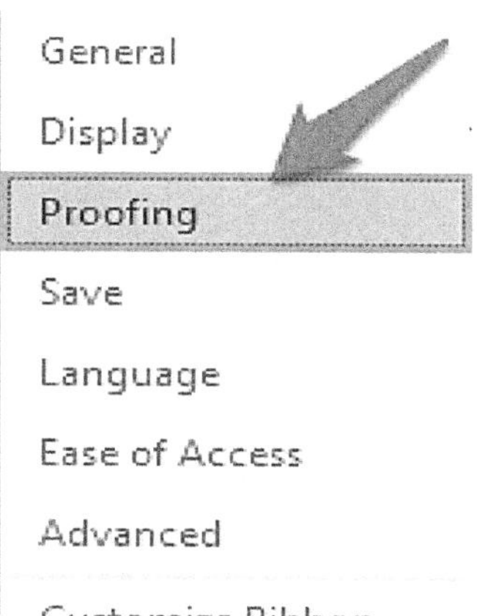

- There are still lots of other ways that you can use to customize your settings depending on your preference. For instance, you can stop Word from marking spelling and grammar errors while you type.

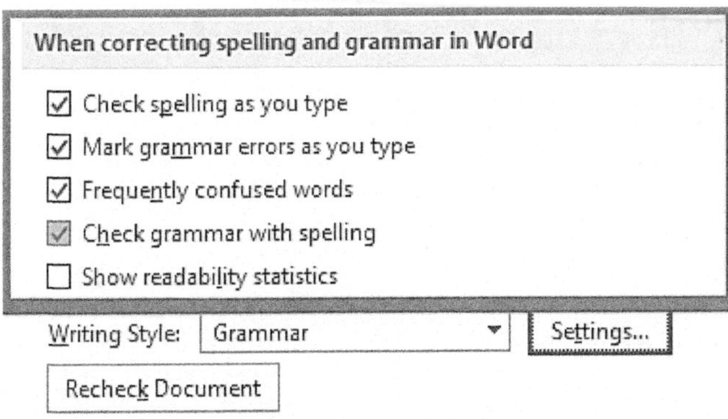

- You can also turn off frequently confused words, like *"**there** vs. **their**"*. Keep in mind, your spelling and grammar choices only apply to your copy of Word. So, if you ignore any error, or add a word to your dictionary (for example, your name), those wavy lines will reappear when you send the document to someone else. You can avoid this issue by hiding spelling and grammar errors in this particular document. Just check the two boxes near the bottom of the Window. When you are done, click "Ok" and now, the errors are hidden.

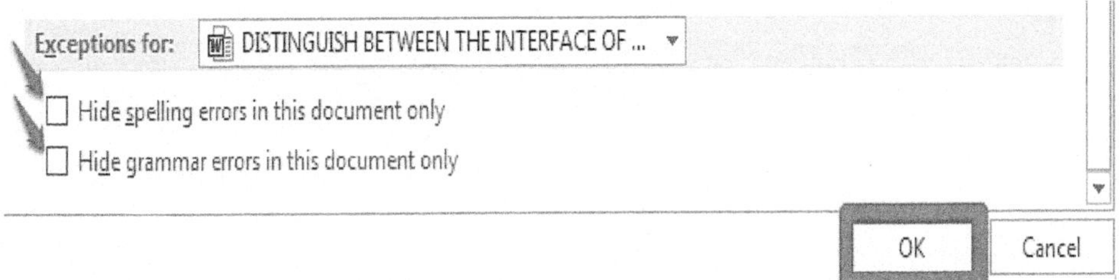

Finding and Replacing Text

Finding and replacing text is one of the Word features that give the privilege to replace text by finding it within a bunch of text without any complication, to know how to find and replace words, follow these simple procedures:

- Go to the ***"Home"*** tab

- Under the ***"Home"*** tab, kindly locate ***"Replace"*** click it or press ***"Ctrl + H"***

- A dialog box will appear, enter the word or phrase you want to locate in the ***"Find what"*** textbox. Also, in the ***"Replace with"*** textbox, enter the text or phrase you want what you found to be replaced with. For example, I can search for "Thank you" and replace it with "Thanks" on my document.

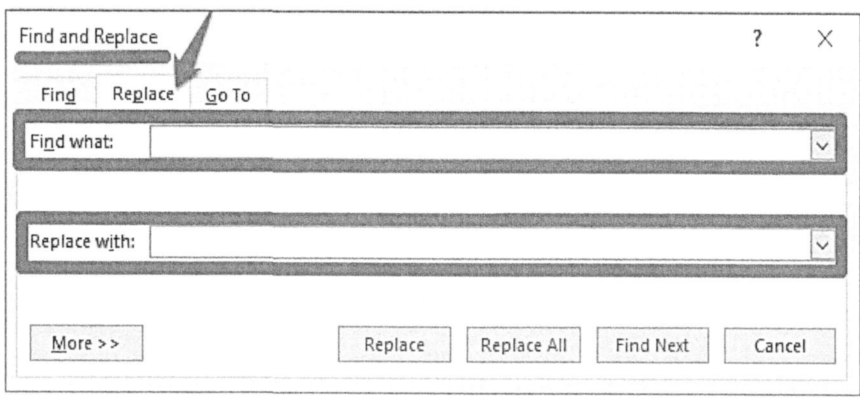

- To update all instances at once, choose "Replace All"

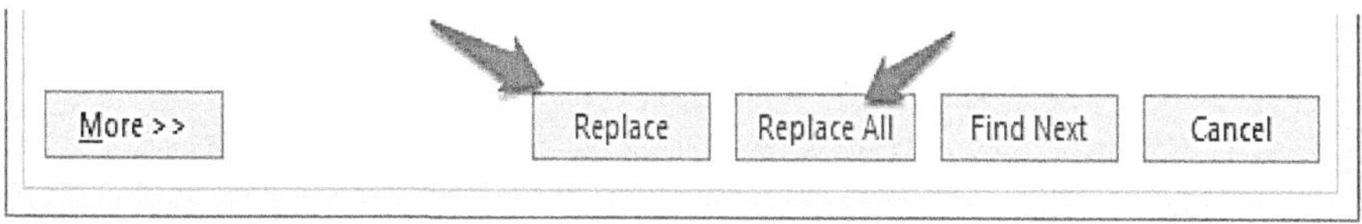

Finding the Right Word with the Thesaurus

Before I explain how to use "Thesaurus", it is important to know what "Thesaurus" is. Thesaurus is a tool that is specially designed into Word by Microsoft for getting the synonyms of whatsoever you are looking for by giving you a bunch of suggestions. For example, you can look for "benefit" and you will be given multiple suggestions of synonyms for "benefit" such as "advantage", "profit", with a classification of which part of speech such words fall under.

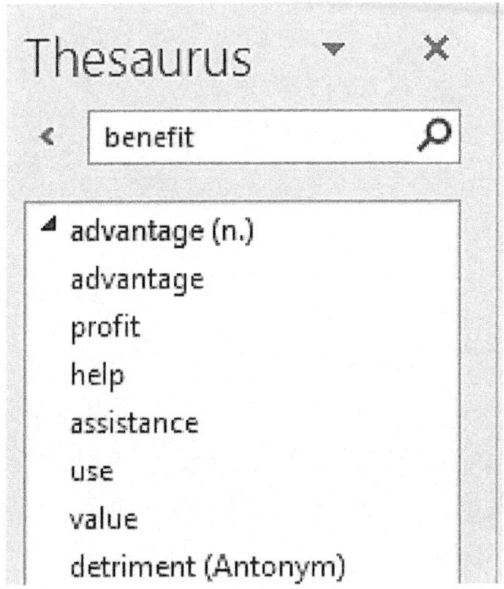

Now, how do we make use of Thesaurus? Simply follow these steps:

- Go to your "View" tab"

- Under the "View" tab, at your left-hand side, locate "Thesaurus" and double-click on it

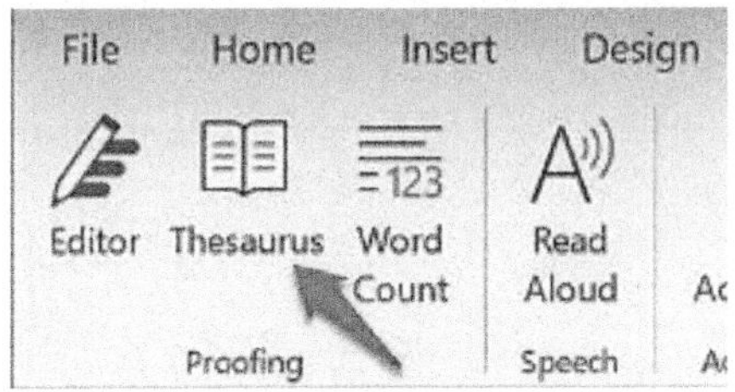

- A dialog box will appear at your right-hand side opposite your Navigation pane dialog box which is located at your left-hand side if activated

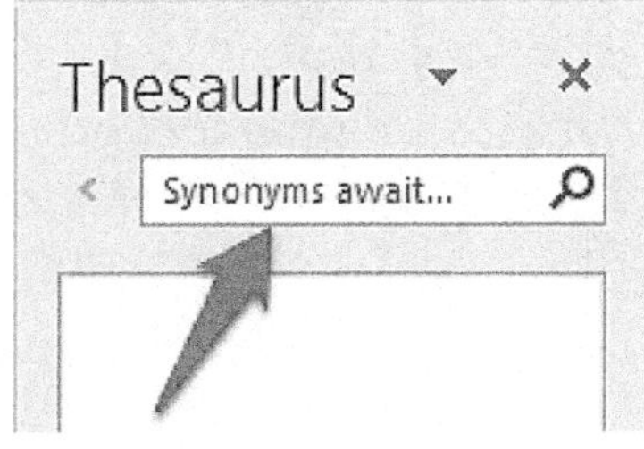

- Then, you can type your word or phrase into the "Search" bar. For example, we can look for "Environment" on our "Thesaurus pane" and see what our result will be. You can also type another word of your choice and also see what your result will be

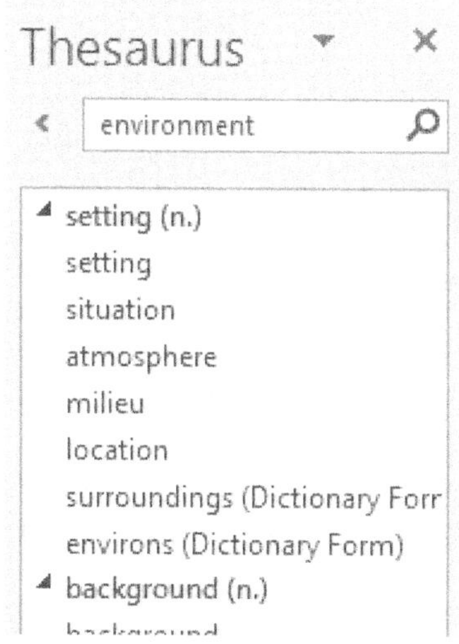

Proofing & Converting Text Written in a Foreign Language

- Go to your "Review" tab

- Under the "Review" tab, at your left-hand side, click on "Translate", this will allow you to translate your content into different languages of your choice

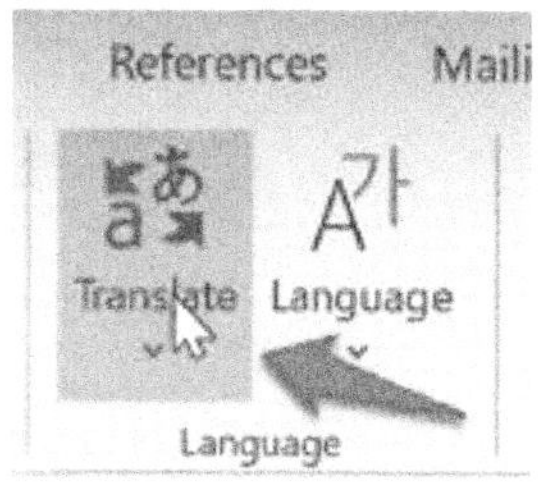

- Now, once you click on "Translate", you will be given two options, one is the "Translate Selection" which enables you to select the specific part of your document to be translated, while the other option is the "Translate Document" which creates a translated copy of your document with Microsoft Translator

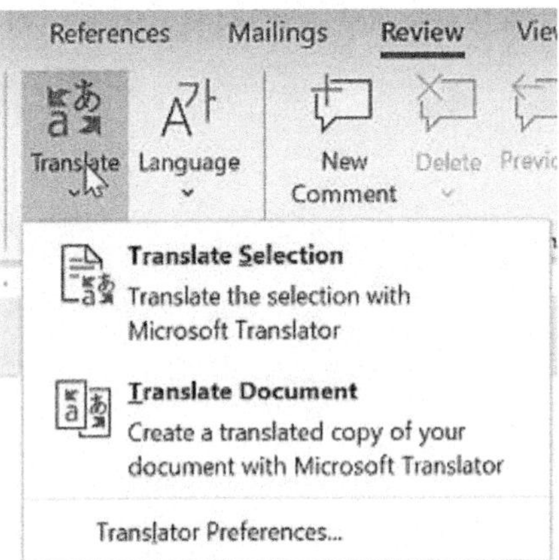

- Assuming you select "Translate Selection", a dialog box will appear at the right-hand side where you can select your text or type it inside in the provided textbox

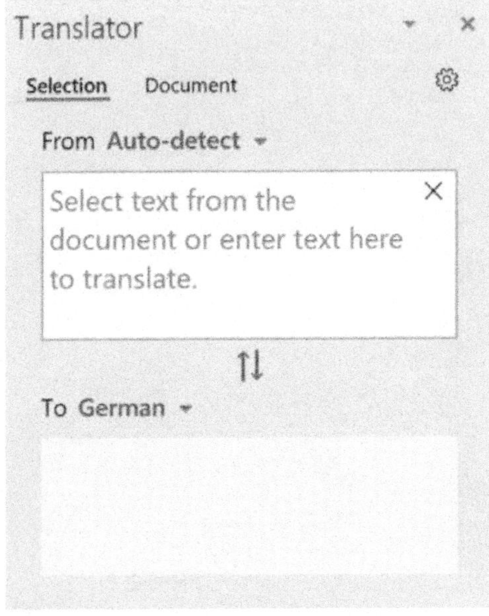

- Let also assume that I select a portion from my text

Hello Anna and Jacob,

Thanks so much for the wonderful book! It was very thoughtful of you two. We have been reading the book to Thomas every single night. He's a very sweet boy and we're very lucky that he's healthy. He'll turn 5 months old on the 14th of June. When we visit Germany, we'll introduce you to Thomas.

Best regards,
Kevin, Kerry, and Thomas

- It will automatically reflect on my translator pane. From English to German based on what I selected. To make use of other languages, click on the present language it will show you other language options

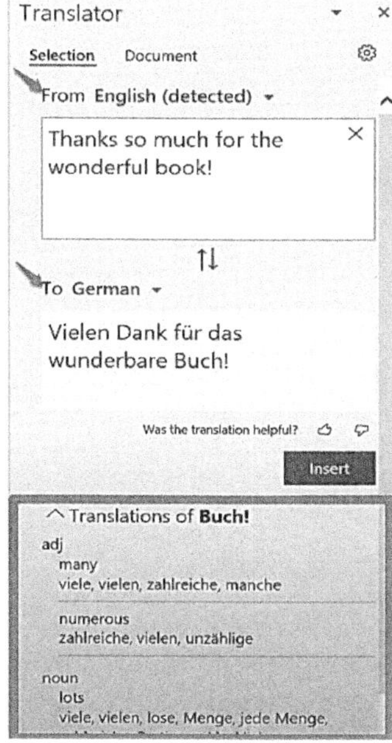

- You can also translate the whole paragraph

Hello Anna and Jacob,

Thanks so much for the wonderful book! It was very thoughtful of you two. We have been reading the book to Thomas every single night. He's a very sweet boy and we're very lucky that he's healthy. He'll turn 5 months old on the 14th of June. When we visit Germany, we'll introduce you to Thomas.

Best regards,
Kevin, Kerry, and Thomas

- Your text will also be interpreted

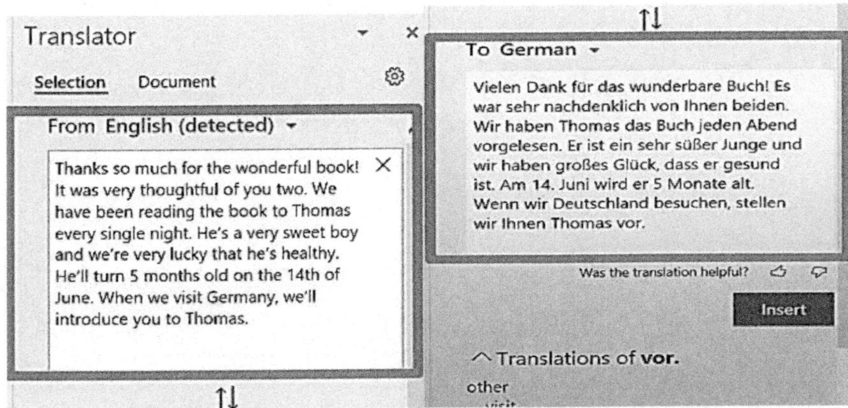

- Then, you can copy the translated copy by highlighting it, right-click, and pick the "copy" option.

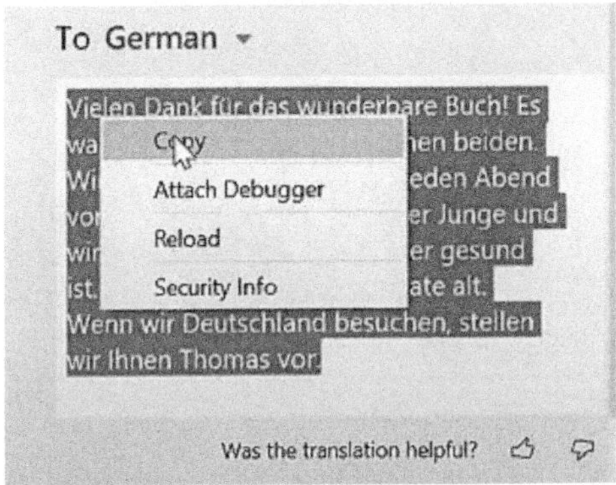

- This can also be pasted into your document.

Hello Anna and Jacob,

Thanks so much for the wonderful book! It was very thoughtful of you two. We have been reading the book to Thomas every single night. He's a very sweet boy and we're very lucky that he's healthy. He'll turn 5 months old on the 14th of June. When we visit Germany, we'll introduce you to Thomas.

Vielen Dank für das wunderbare Buch! Es war sehr nachdenklich von Ihnen beiden. Wir haben Thomas das Buch jeden Abend vorgelesen. Er ist ein sehr süßer Junge und wir haben großes Glück, dass er gesund ist. Am 14. Juni wird er 5 Monate alt. Wenn wir Deutschland besuchen, stellen wir Ihnen Thomas vor.

Best regards,
Kevin, Kerry, and Thomas

- Let's also see the other option which is "Translate Document". Just click on the other side of your "Translate pane" which is "Document", an instruction of what it is- "Create a translated copy of this document with the Microsoft Translator service" will be written below. Always note that you can change your language anytime you wish by clicking on the current language to select your choice.

- Once you click on "Translate", it will process the translation of your document. Note that you must be connected to the internet via modem, router, Wi-Fi or any means of connection for it to work effectively without bouncing back.

- It will be converted to "German" which is the selected language. Note, the translated document will be opened on a "New document" and your original document will be intact.

- Once completed, check the new document to see the translated document

Hallo Anna und Jakob,

Vielen Dank für das wunderbare Buch! Es war sehr nachdenklich von Ihnen beiden. Wir haben Thomas das Buch jeden Abend vorgelesen. Er ist ein sehr süßer Junge und wir haben großes Glück, dass er gesund ist. Am$^{14.}$ Juni wird er 5 Monate alt. Wenn wir Deutschland besuchen, stellen wir Ihnen Thomas vor.

Beste Grüße,
Kevin, Kerry und Thomas

- You can minimize one for the other to preview

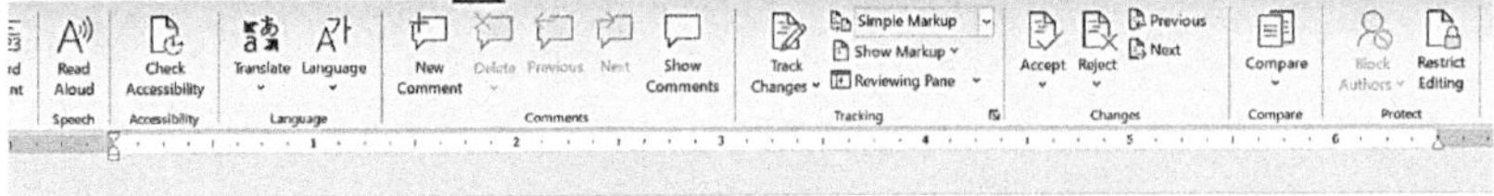

Hello Anna and Jacob,

Thanks so much for the wonderful book! It was very thoughtful of you two. We have been reading the book to Thomas every single night. He's a very sweet boy and we're very lucky that he's healthy. He'll turn 5 months old on the 14th of June. When we visit Germany, we'll introduce you to Thomas.

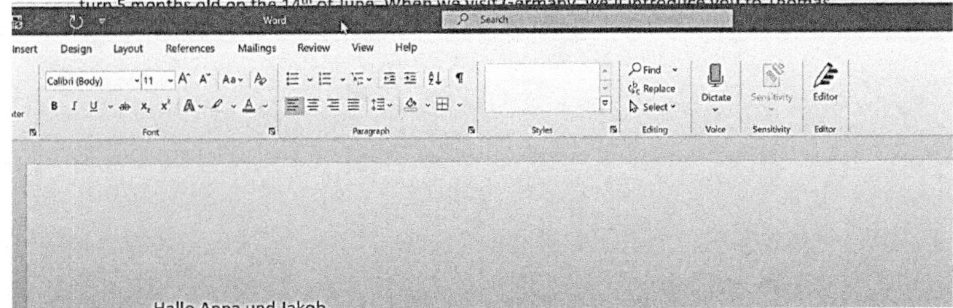

Making use of the Navigation Pane

For simplicity and flexibility, it is important to note that you can have your search bar pane through navigation pane side by side while typing in Word environment, simply follow these step-by-step procedures to achieve that:

- Go to the "View" tab

- Under the "View" tab, at your left-hand side look for "Navigation Pane" make sure it is ticked, if not, do so to see the effect on your document.

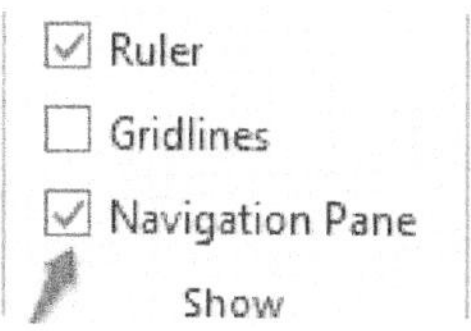

- Here is the result; the below "Navigation" dialog box will automatically appear on the left-hand side of your document permanently except you untick it from the "View" tab. It enables you to see your listed "Headings", slide "Pages", and search "Result" instantly.

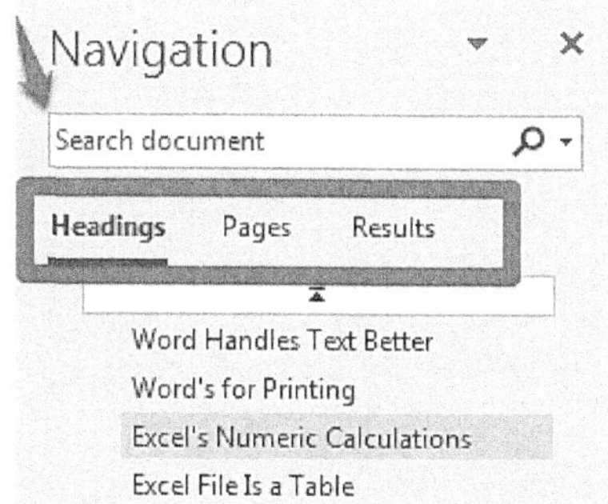

Choosing Language Option

- Go to the "File menu"

- At the displayed interface, click on "Options"

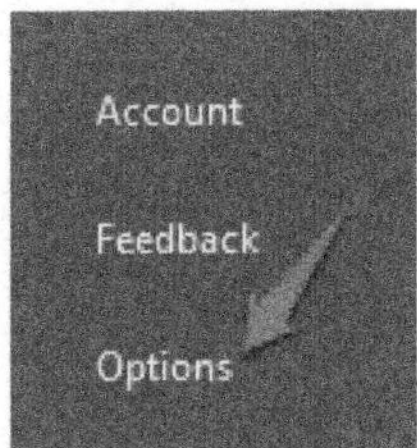

- A dialog box will appear on your left-hand side, select "Language"

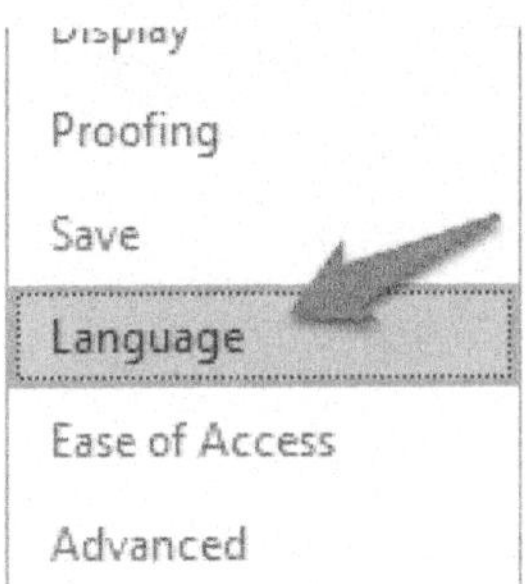

- Then, "Language" features will also appear on your right-hand side, below towards your left-hand side is the "Display Language" option, while at your right-hand side is the "Help Language" option. You can choose from the available languages by scrolling through to see other options.

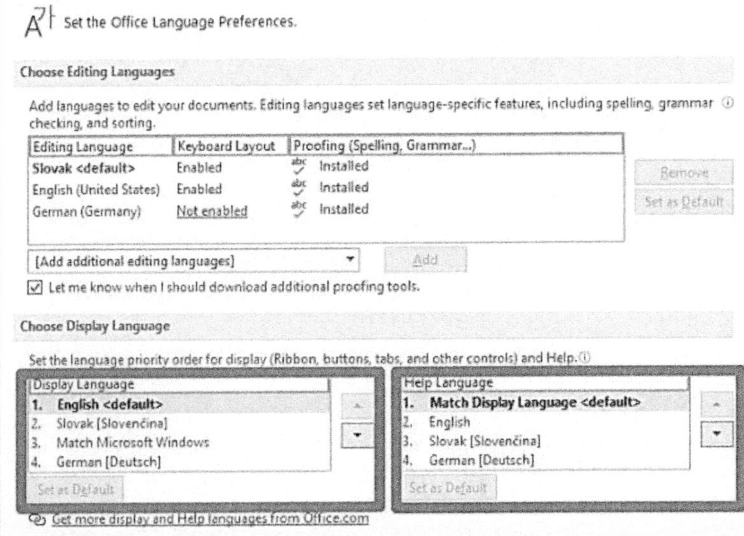

- Once done press, the "Ok" option

- Then, you will be instructed to restart Office so that your language changes can take effect.

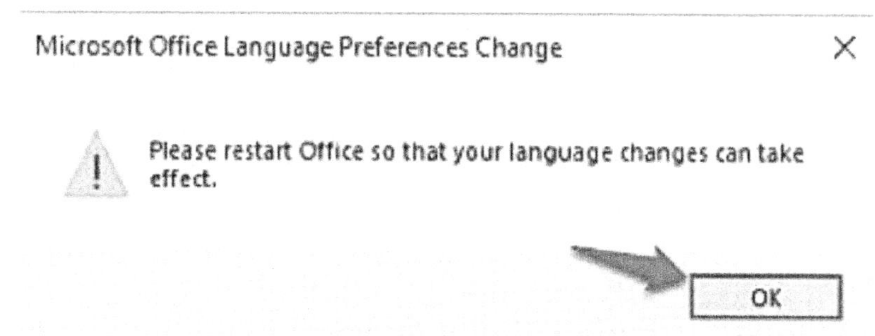

- Take note of your Word 365 interface before restarting your PC, it's by default in the English language

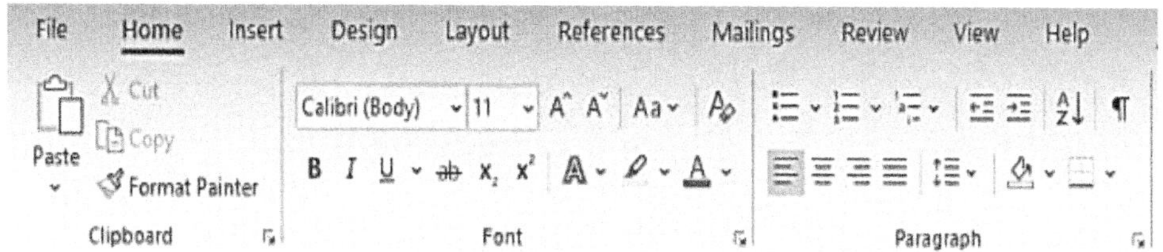

- And here will be the outcome after your PC has been restarted, everything will automatically be in the German language.

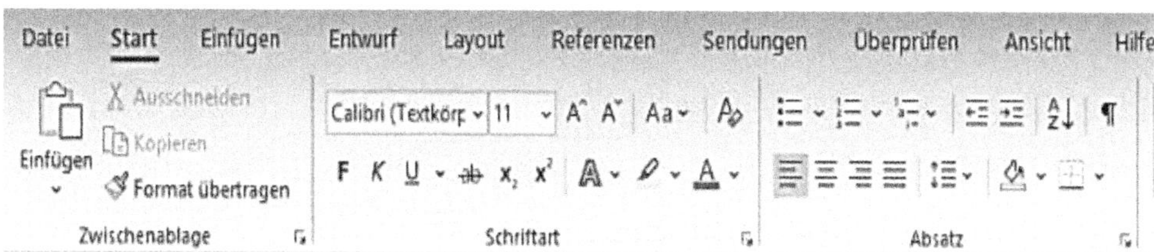

CHAPTER EIGHT

DESKTOP PUBLISHING WITH WORD

Experimenting with Theme

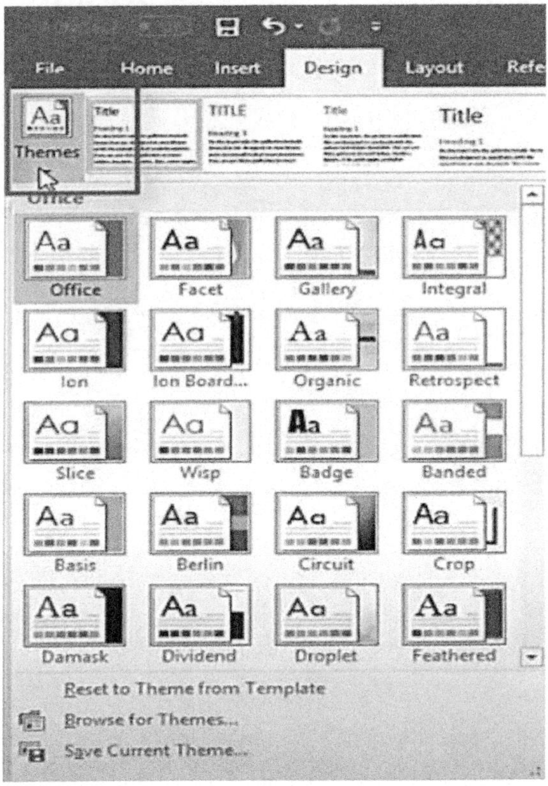

Themes are a predefined style template format that adds to your document content. Each theme uses a unique set of colors, fonts, and effects to create a consistent look. To access your various themes, all you have to do is to go to the "Design" tab, on your right-hand side you will see the word "Themes", click on it and you will be shown different unique themes interface to pick from and each theme as sub-template format.

Decorating a page with a border

- Go to the "Design" tab

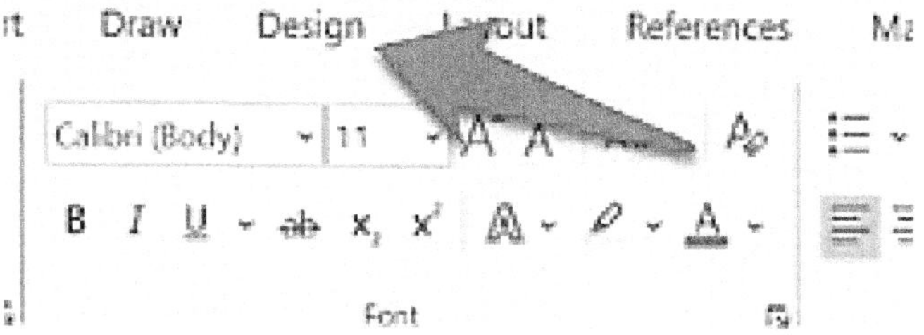

- Under "Design", at your right-hand side, you will see the "Page Background" ribbon, select "Page Borders"

- Once you click on "Page Borders", a dialog box will pop up which is your "Page Border" configuration. On the left-hand side is the "Setting" option for various page border templates. By the side of the "Setting" option is the "Style" option where you can choose the kind of lines you prefer. Below "Style" is the "Color" option where you can determine which color fits into your page document border.

Below the "Color" option is the "Width" option which is the only component that controls the border thickness. Below the "Width" option is the "Art" option that reflects different kinds of art designs to be used for your framework, while at your right-hand side is the "Preview" option which gives you what your outcome configuration will look like before you click on the "Ok" option.

The "Apply to" option is where you determine where your effect should take place such as "Whole document", "This section", "This section first page only", and "This section all except the first page." Your choice determines your outcome, once done hit the "Ok" button to see your changes.

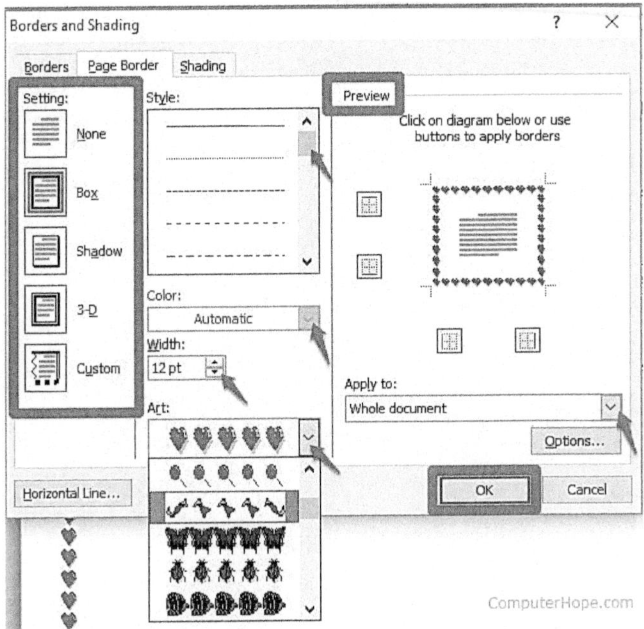

Putting a Background Color on Pages

- In the menu bar, click on "Design"

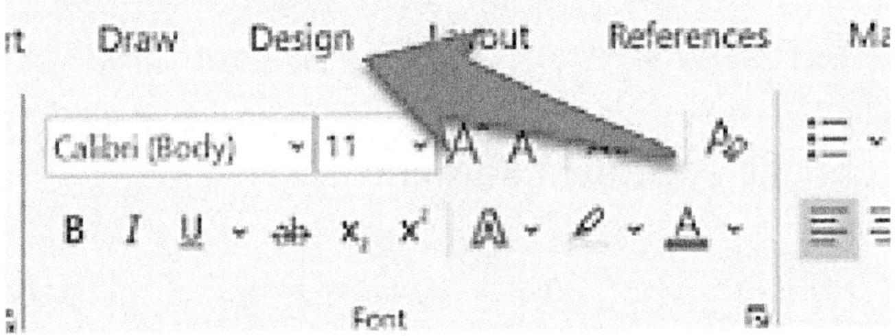

- Under "Design", at your right-hand side, you will see the "Page Background" ribbon, select "Page Color"

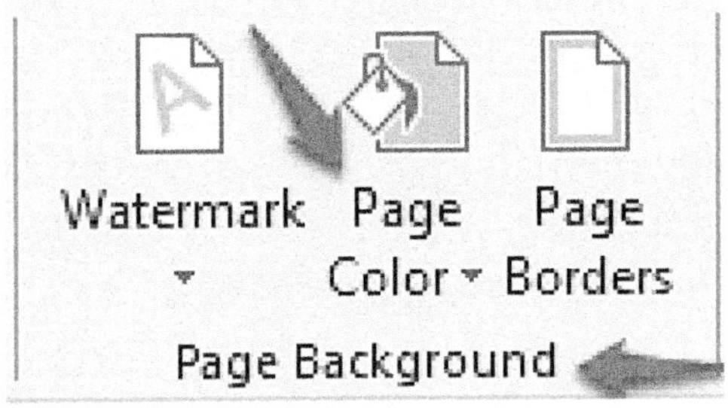

- Under "Page Color", a dropdown box will appear with different kinds of colors. If your preferred color was not found, there's a "More Colors" option below, click on it

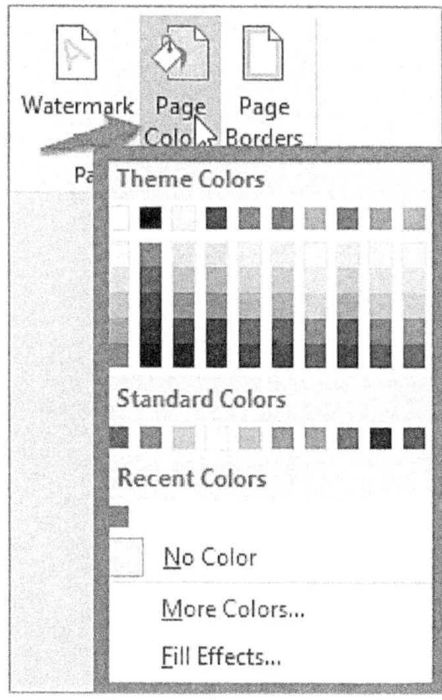

- After clicking the "More Colors" option, you will be brought here under "Standard" where you can randomly select your preferred color which was not found on the page displayed color. On your right-hand side is where your chosen color will be previewed. If you previously choose a color, it will be shown as "Current" with that color, while the newly selected will be shown as "New" with the color you selected as illustrated below.

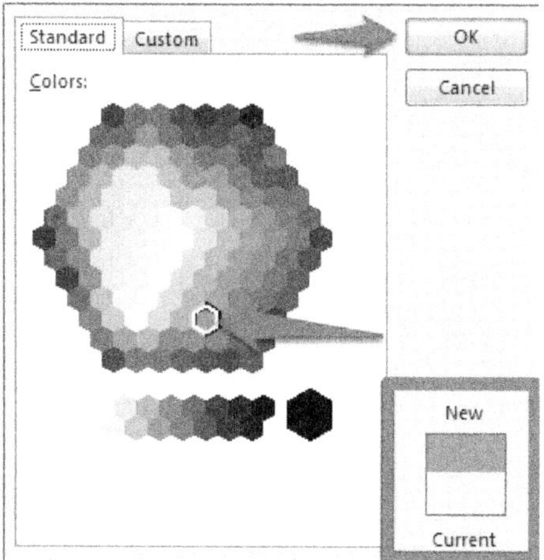

- You can also explore more colors on "Custom" which is an advanced color selection option where you can see the mixture of Colors Red, green, and Blue that was added together to make your preferred color. The illustration below shows that "Yellow color" was picked, and the mixture of it was calculated underneath as "Red: 221", "Green: 221", and "Blue: 35" which resulted in the color yellow.

Note also that beside the color picker, there is a black arrow (◄) which is used for adjustment of any preferred color, once done click the "Ok" button.

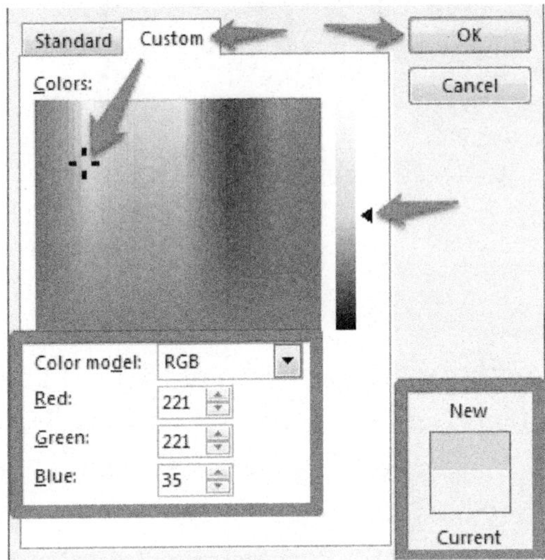

Getting Word 365 help with Resume Assistant

With Word 365, there are limitless possibilities to what you can access, that is why I am glad that you made the right choice for purchasing this valuable book which enables you to know some hidden features of Word 365. It is important to note that Word 365 has made it possible for third-party software to partner with them for flexibility and simplicity of technology advancement in our day-to-day life. To make Word 365 assist you with cover letters, simply follow these procedures

- Go to the "Review" tab

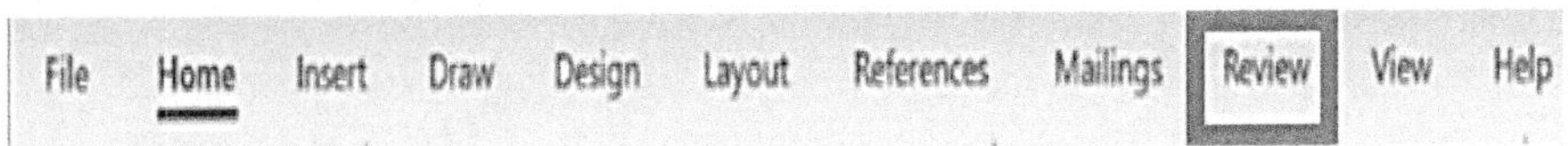

- Under the "Review" tab, look at your right-hand side, you will see "Resume Assistant", click on it

- A dialog box will appear on your right-hand side, click on "Get started" to proceed

- Another way to create a "Resume" is to go to your "file menu", click it

- Click on "New", then, you will be shown multiple template options to pick from, or you can also search online, this will require a data connection

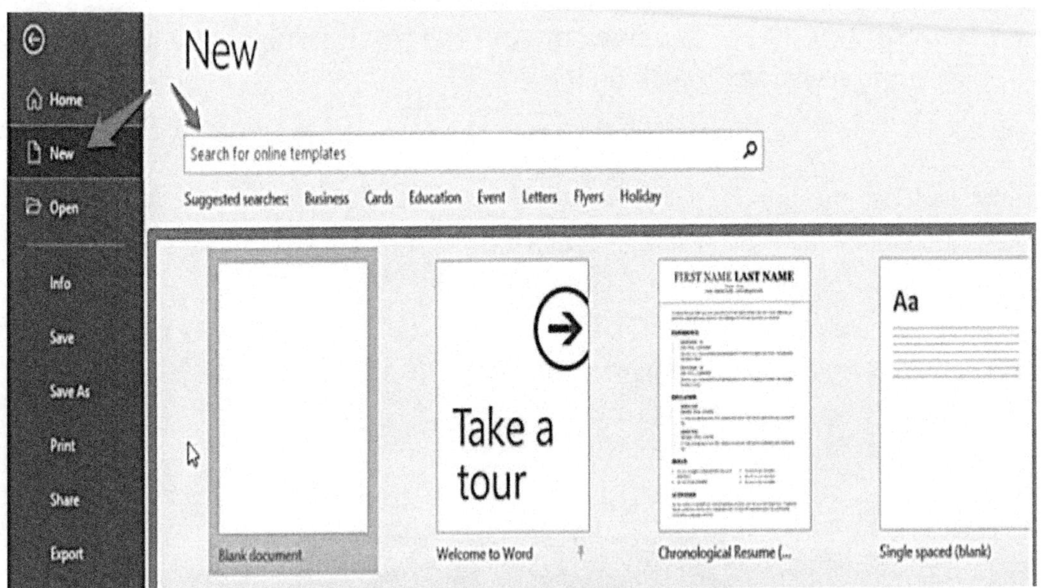

- You can also scroll down to see other "resume" options

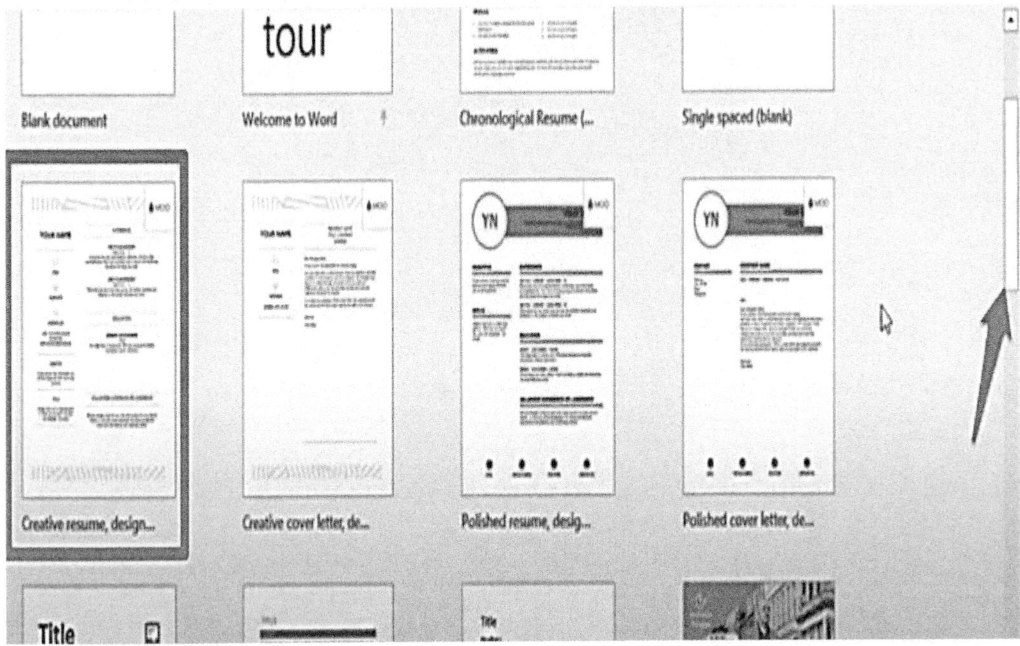

- Once you find your preferred choice, select it and see more information about it, then you can click on "Create"

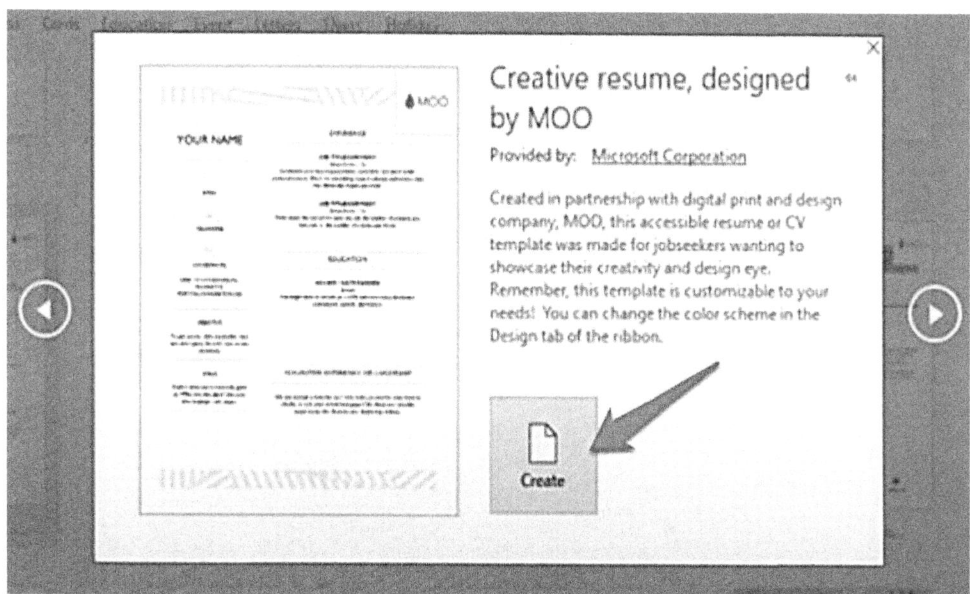

- Once you click on "Create" it will automatically create a template on your Word 365 for you to work on, and your "Resume Assistant" will also appear on your right-hand side for further assistance

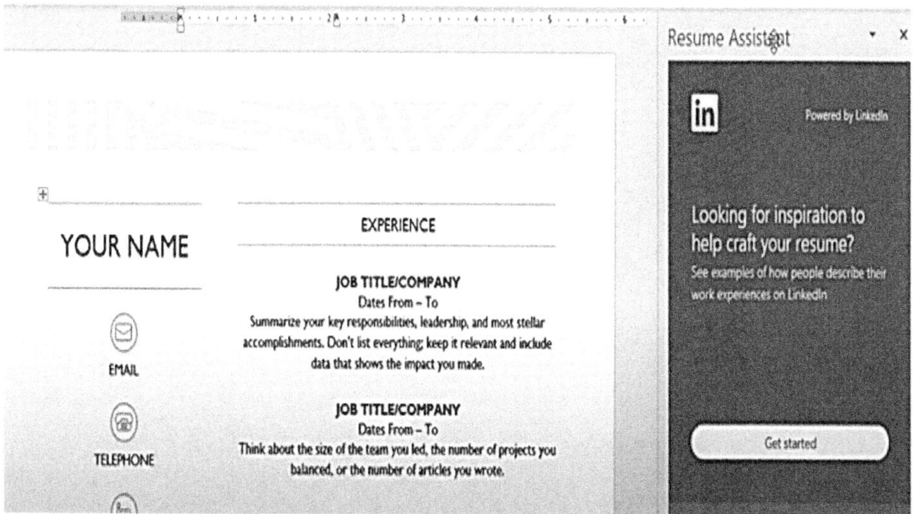

- At your right-hand side on your "Resume Assistant", you can click on "See examples" to see the role and industry format you are looking for

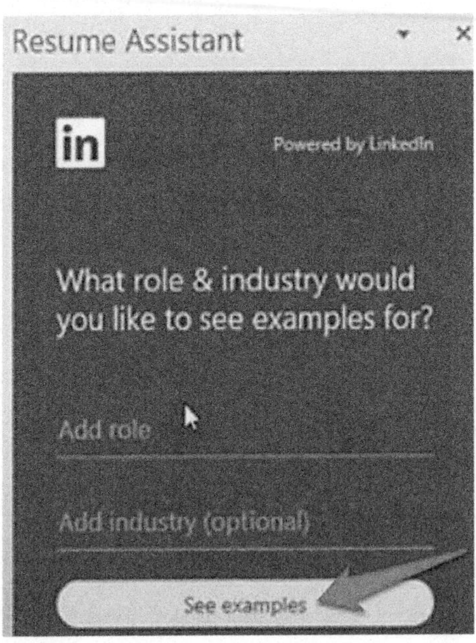

- Or you can go to https://www.linkedin.com/ (this is optional) which is a third-party affiliation to Microsoft. Once you get to the website, you either "Sign in" with your "Linkedin" account or you "Join now" to register afresh. Never enter your Microsoft account details, remember it is a third-party affiliation not owned by Microsoft.

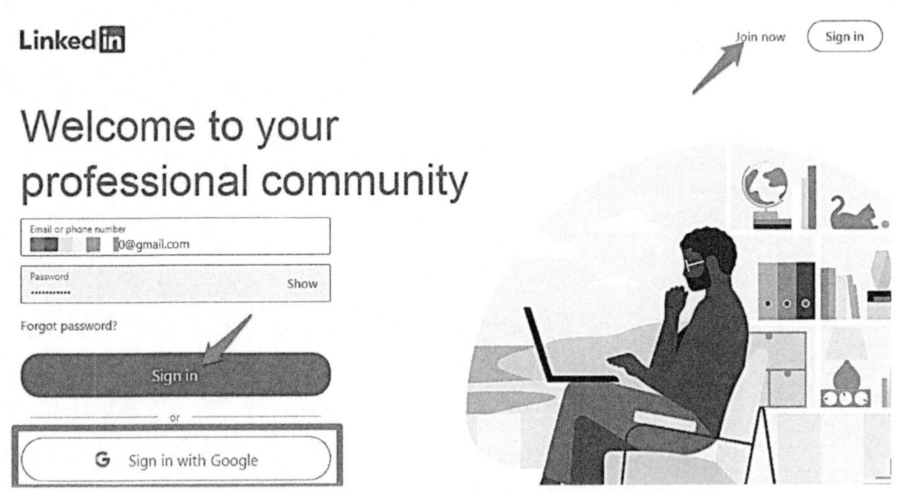

- To join, click on "Join now" at your top right-hand side as illustrated above, then a new page will be brought to you to fill up your registration form

Linkedin

Make the most of your professional life

Email or phone number

Password (6 or more characters)

By clicking Agree & Join, you agree to the LinkedIn User Agreement, Privacy Policy, and Cookie Policy.

Agree & Join

or

Join with Google

Already on LinkedIn? Sign in

- And if you already have an existing account with "Linkedin", enter it by clicking on the "Sign in" option to explore more on the third-party website, which is specifically designed for professional life where you can showcase what you are up to professionally, and it's also a way of meeting people around the world.

Getting Word 365 help with cover letters

- Go to your "file menu" click it

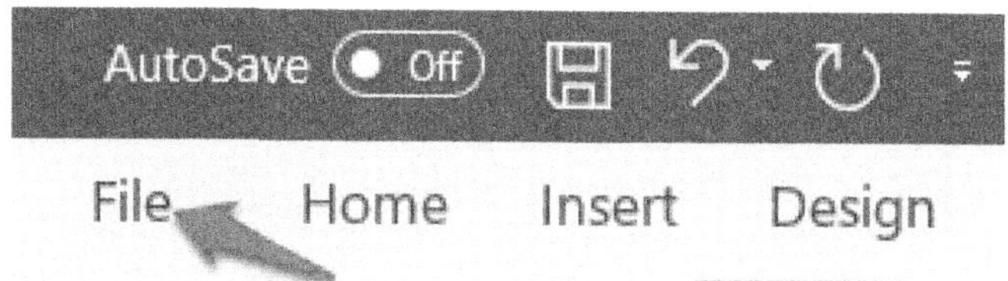

- Click on "New", then, you will be shown multiple template options to pick from or you can also search online, this will require a data connection

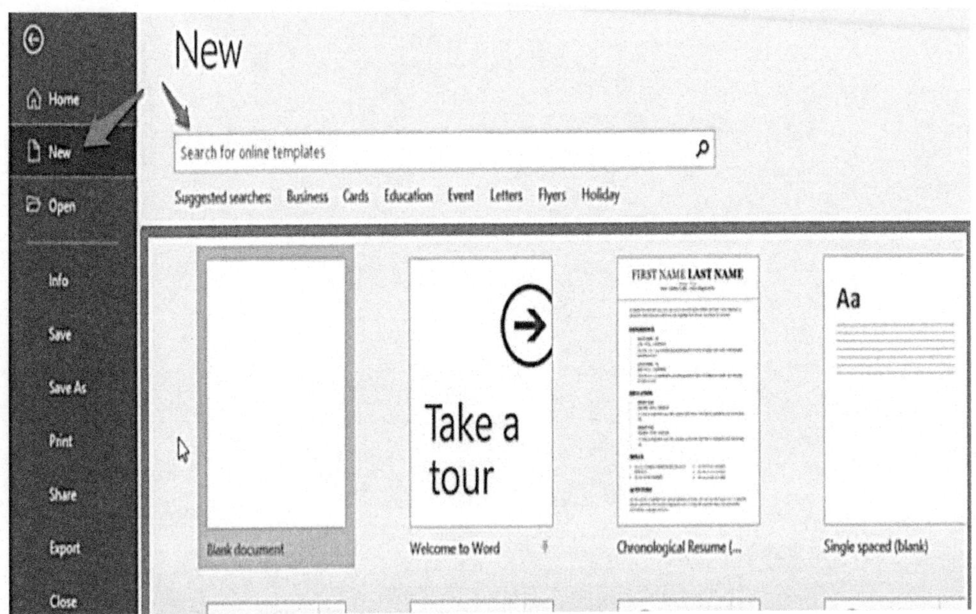

- You can also scroll down to see other "cover letter" options or type "cover letter"

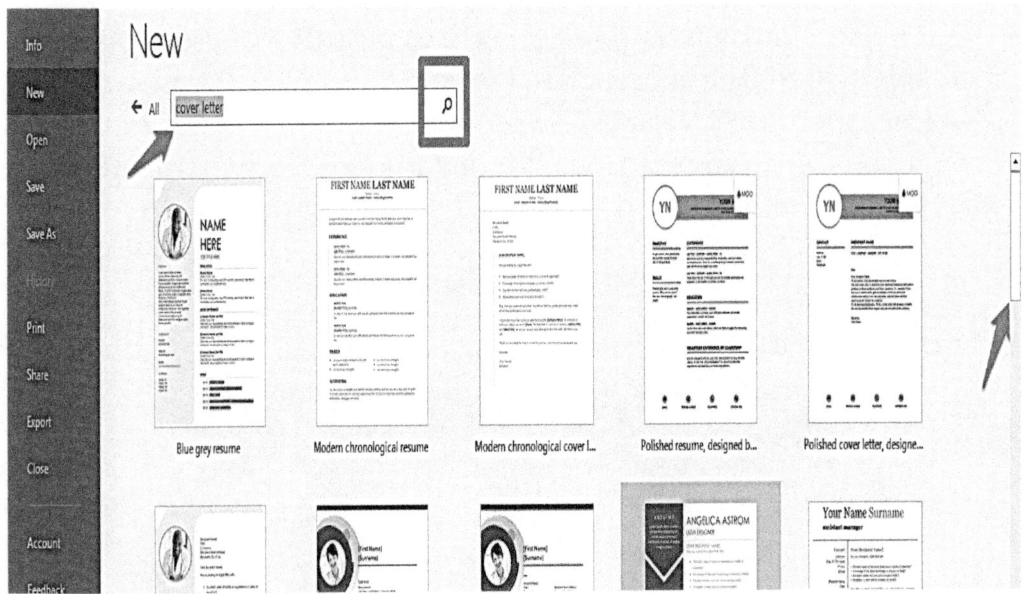

- Once you locate your preferred choice, select it, a pop-up box will appear where you can create it.

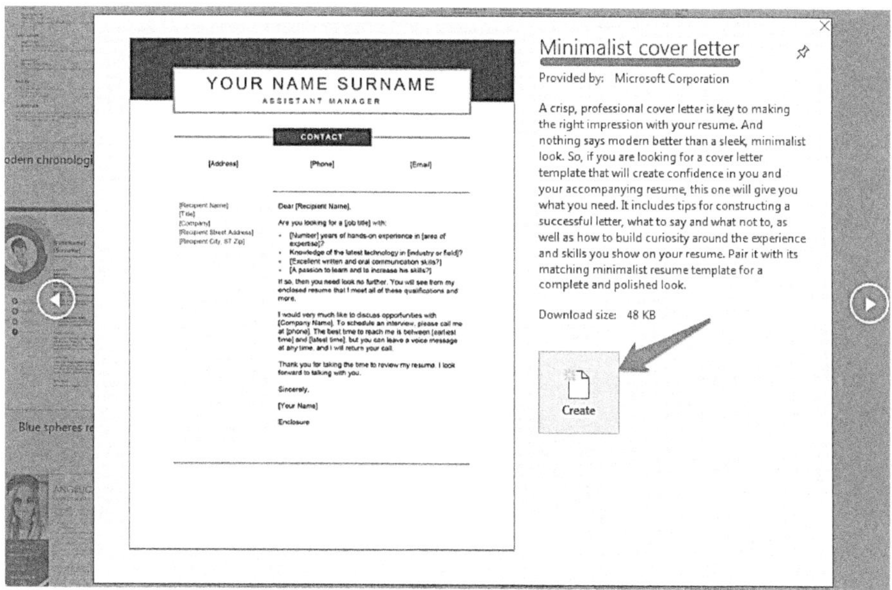

Making Use of Charts, Shapes, and Photos

- Go to your "Insert" tab

- Under the "Insert" tab, locate the "Illustrations" ribbon

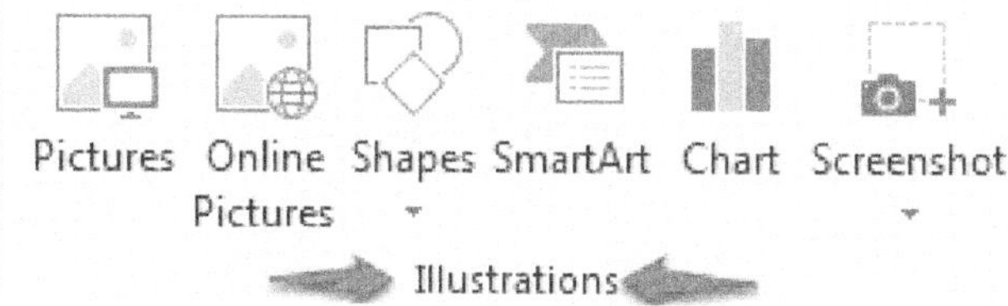

Before we proceed, let's begin by defining "Chart".

What is a Chart?

In a simple word, Chart is a spotted pattern and trend in data used to estimate the graphical scaling by inserting a bar, area, or line chart.

How to Insert "Chart"

- Select "Chart" in the "Illustrations" ribbon

- A dialog box will appear consisting of the "All Charts" features such as "Column", "Line", "Pie", "Bar", "Area", and other charts. It's majorly used to view the estimation of data after it has been concluded.

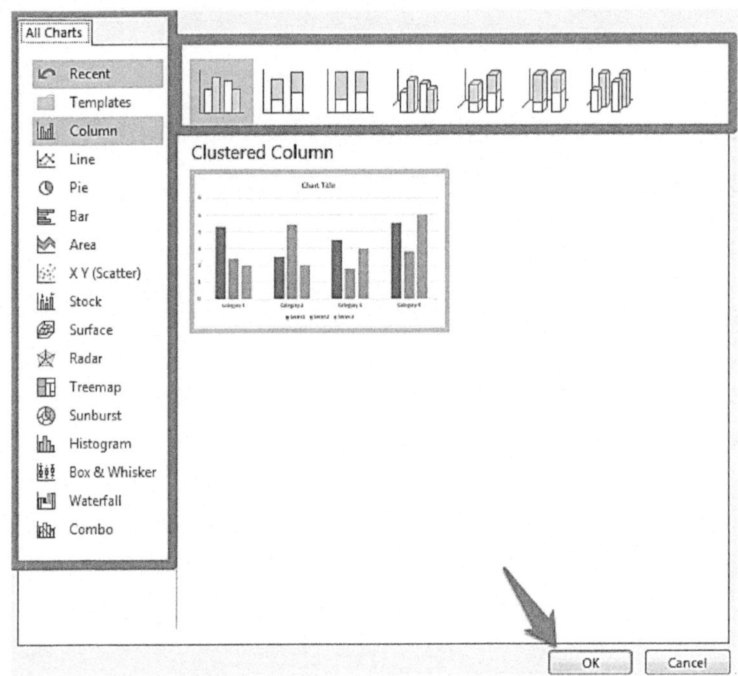

What is a Shape?

Shapes are predefined tools that are used for different purposes such as block arrows shapes, start and banner shapes, equation shapes, and others. To make use of "Shapes", follow these simple procedures below:

- Go to your "Insert tab"

- Under the "Insert" tab, locate "Illustrations", in the "Illustration" ribbon, you will see "Shapes", click on it

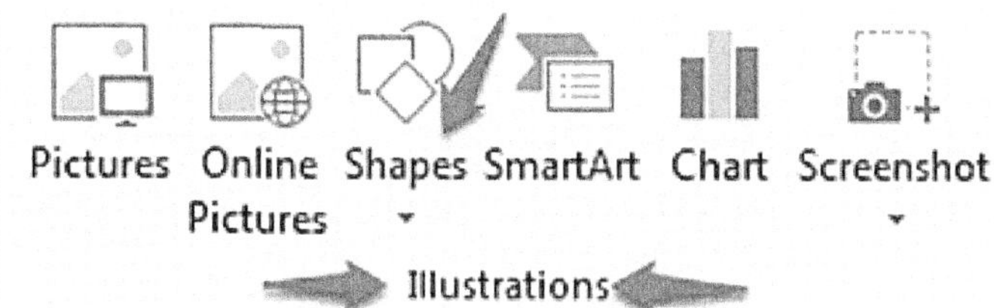

- "Shapes" will show its dropdown features where you can select from. Let's assume we select "love shape" under "Basic Shapes" where my mouse cursor is pointing.

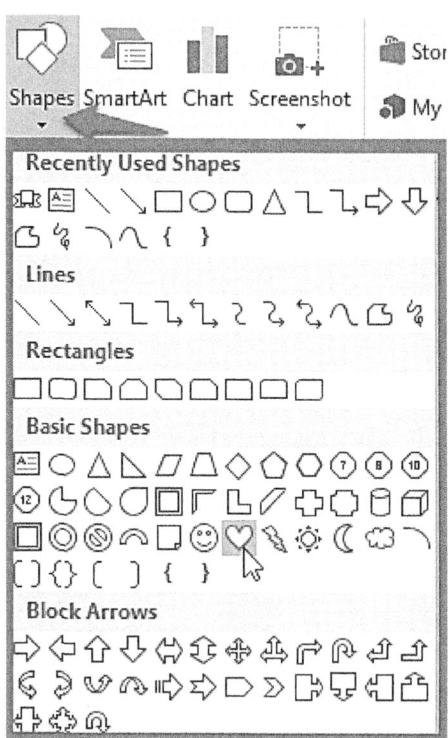

- Once the love shape has been selected, you can now double-click and drag your mouse cursor to make it more visible.

- You can also add more touch to your "love shape" by making sure your mouse cursor is placed on your "love shape", thereby, showing dots around it

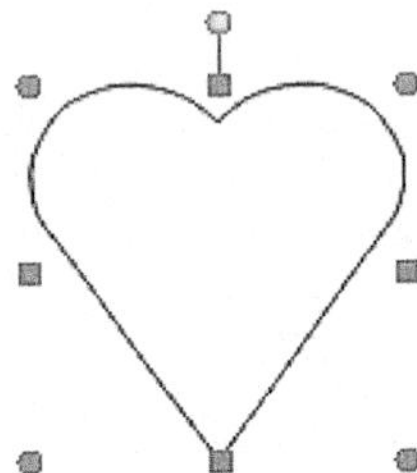

- Then, look above, you will see "Format", click on it

- And you will be shown different colors. You can also click on the dropdown arrow as indicated below to also see other options

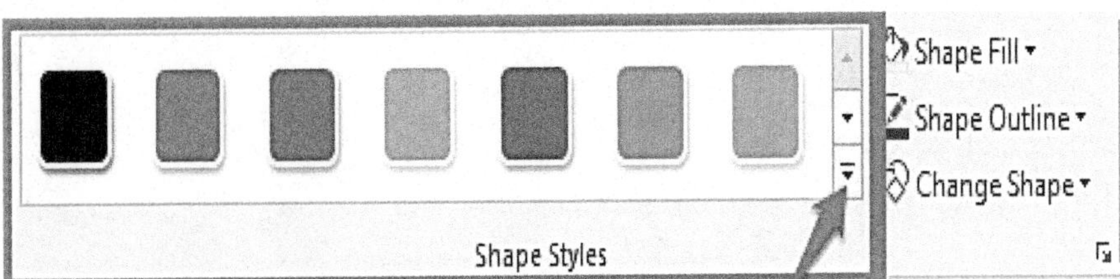

- Select your preferred choice and it will automatically take effect on your selected "love shape".

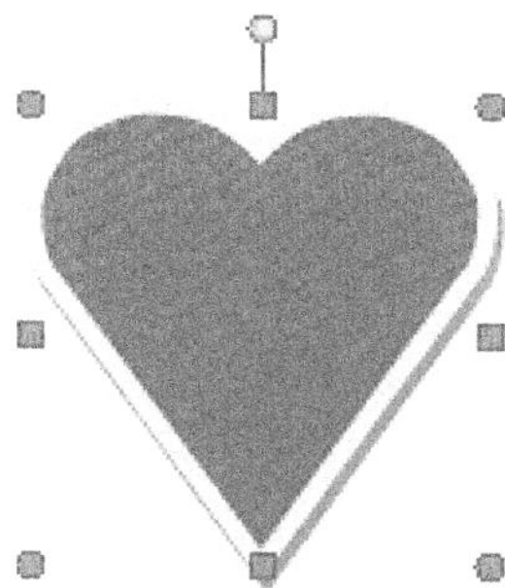

Now, let's discuss Photos which is also known as Pictures

What is a Picture?

A Picture is a static image used for different illustrations and purposes. Now, how do we insert pictures into our Word document?

- Go to "Insert" in your menu bar

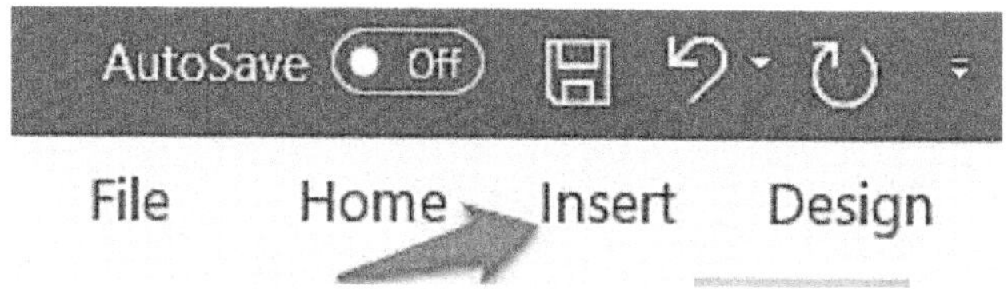

- Under the "Insert" tab, locate the "Illustrations" ribbon. In the "Illustrations" ribbon, select "Pictures"

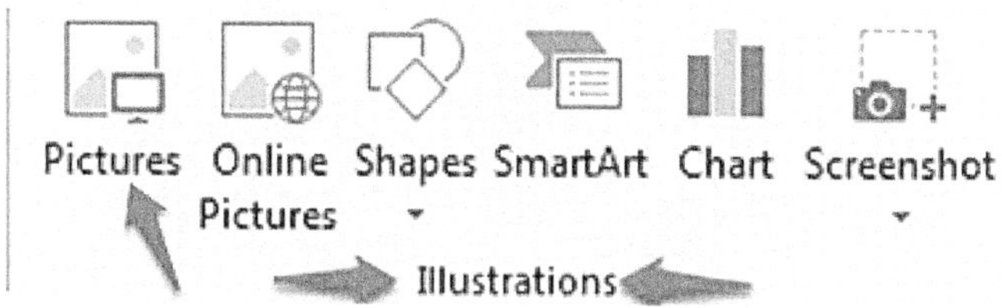

- Once you click on "Pictures", a dialog box will pop up and direct you to your PC storage, locate the folder where your pictures are stored and click on your preferred image, then click "Insert"

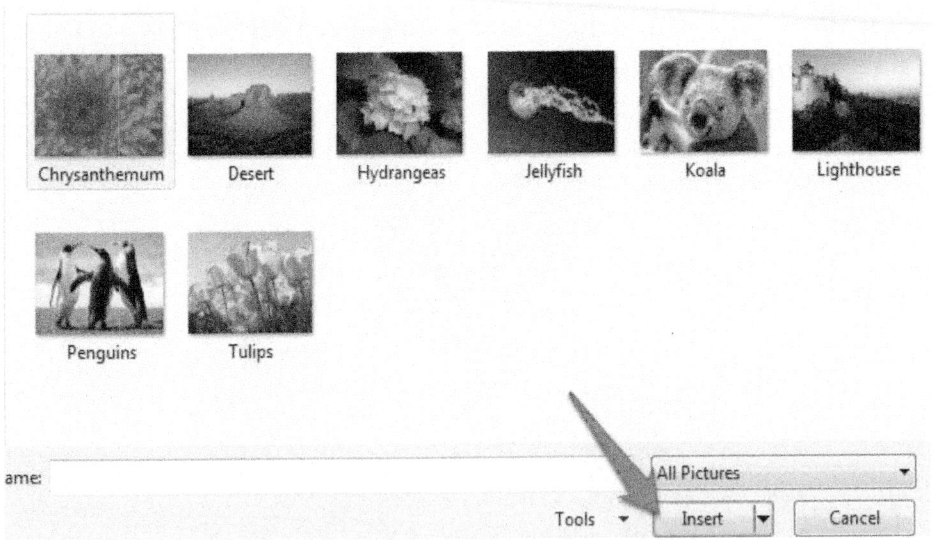

- Then, your image which is also the same as a picture will reflect on your Word document immediately. If you remember earlier when treating how to make use of "Table", I taught you how to resize your image at the dots areas and rotate it if need be, using the curved arrow icon as illustrated below

Positioning and Wrapping Objects Relative to the Page and Text

Positioning and wrapping objects to the page and text can be achieved with the help of "Text Box", which is another hidden feature. Many times, we come across some impossible mathematical images in students' textbooks and keep wondering how did this happen? It is simple, it happens with the help of Word unknown tools. With "Text Box", you can position your words in any area of your document by wrapping your content into it and place it wherever you want your text to be fixed. Then, how do we locate "Text Box"?

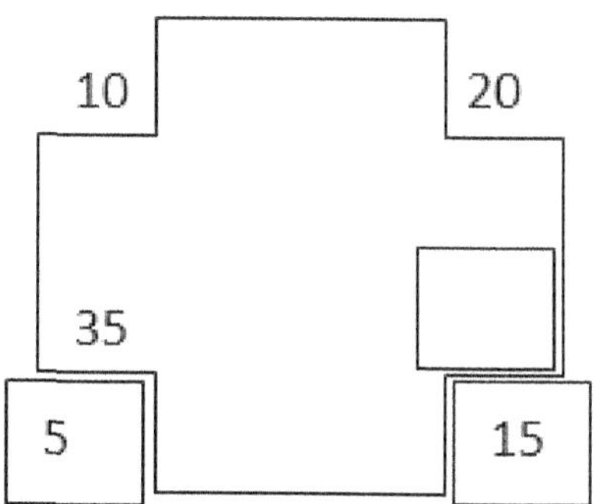

Working with Text Boxes

- Go to the menu bar, select the "Insert" tab

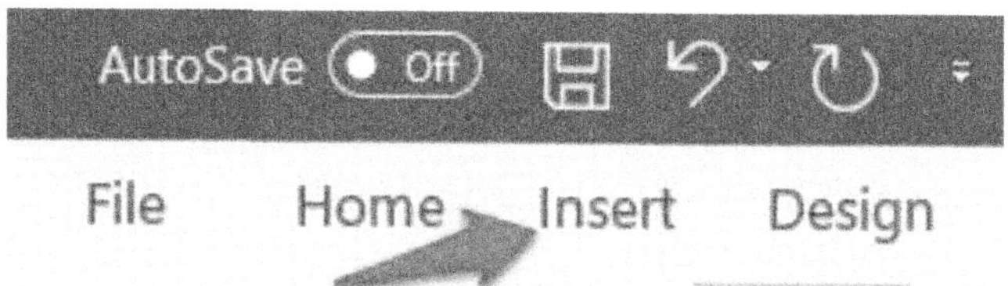

- Under the "Insert" tab, at your right-hand side, look for "Text Box"

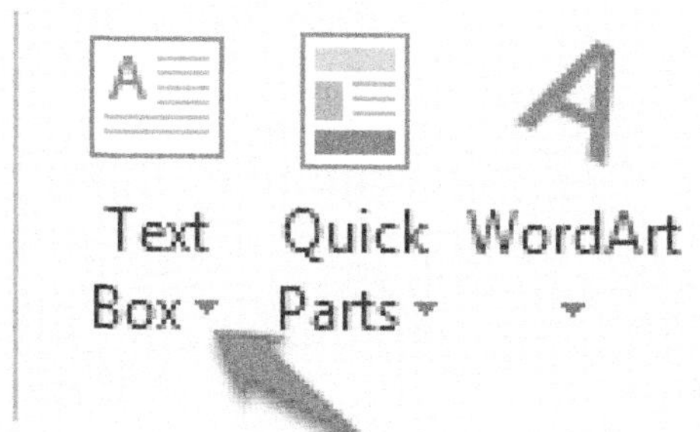

- Once you click on it, you will see "Text Box" options, just pick the first option which is "Simple Text Box"

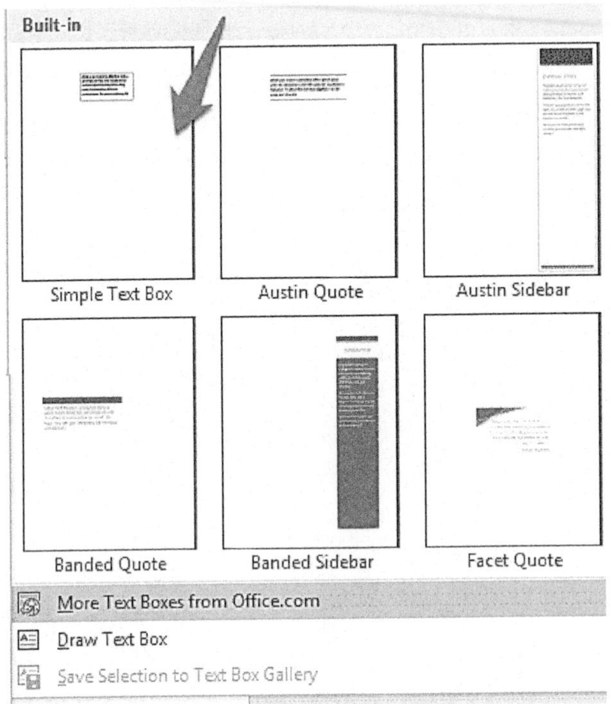

- Once selected, it will appear on your document with a bunch of texts telling you what "Text Box" is all about

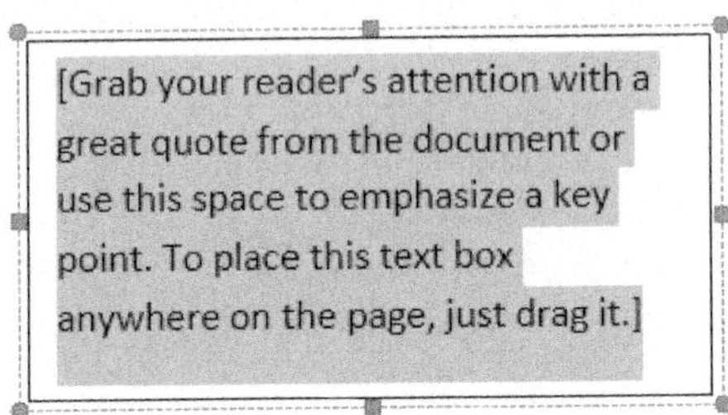

- Simply delete the highlighted instruction and insert your own words or number inside. Never forget that dots are used for resizing, it can be used to enlarge or reduce your "Text Box"

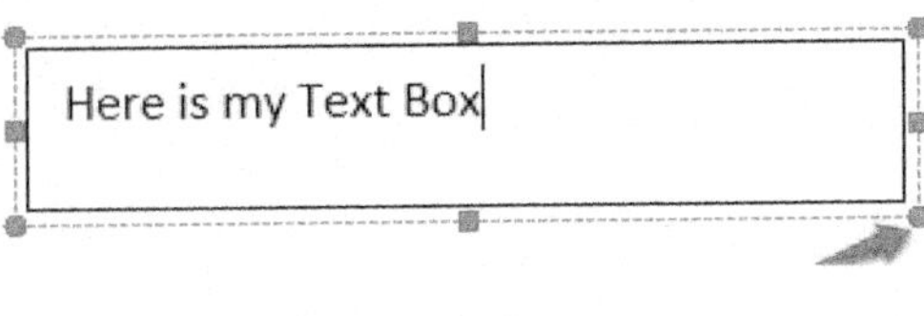

- You can also hide the lines in your "Text Box" by editing it, make sure your "Text Box" dots are still showing, look up, and select "Format". The "Format" tab only appears whenever any editable object is selected

Format

- Then, under "Format", click on "Shape Outline" and select "No Outline", by default, your "Text Box" outline will be hidden

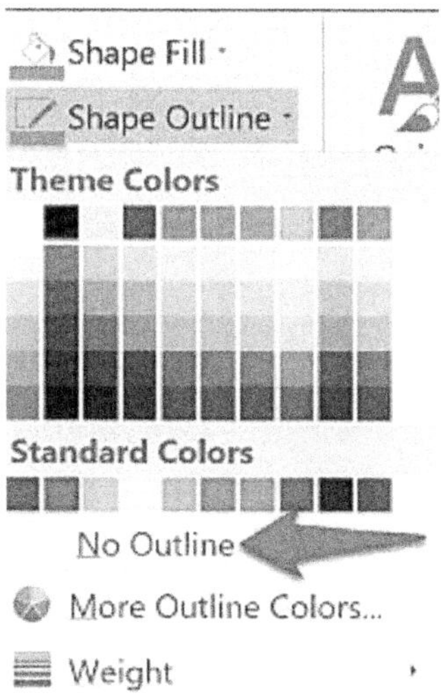

- Here is your result

- Then, click outside your "Text Box", you won't notice any line, as if the line never existed, whereas, it's still there but hidden. Whenever you click on the text, the dots will reflect that there is a "Text Box" on this text, you can also drag it as you were taught earlier by hovering on the dots at the edge, still, your mouse cursor shows plus (+) arrow, then you can drag and drop it in any area on your document.

Here is my Text Box

Drop Cap

Drop Cap is used to create a large format of text at the beginning of a paragraph

- To make use of "Drop Cap", simply highlight your text (a single letter)

A Word document is formatted to fit on a specific size page with the text automatically flowing om one page to the next. Excel supports printing, but its page breaks are not obvious, and because it's printing area can extend multiple pages horizontally as well as vertically the page breaks can be difficult to manage.

- Go to "Insert" in your menu bar

- Under the "Insert" tab, look for "Drop Cap" click on it

- Once you click on it, dropdown options will appear, select "Dropped" and your first letter at the beginning of your paragraph will receive the effect.

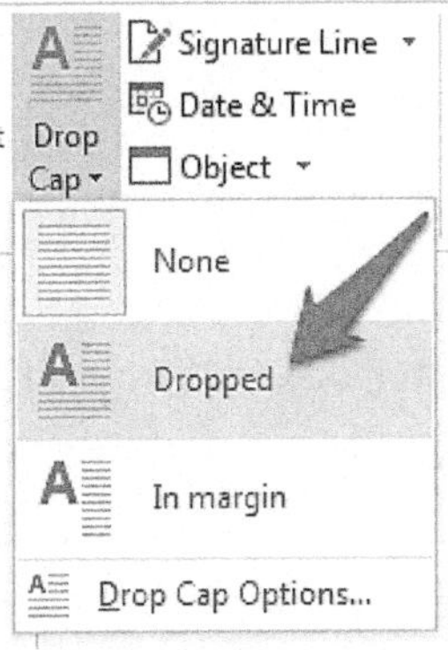

- **Note**: when it comes to "Drop Cap", if you highlight the first letter on the paragraph your mouse cursor is indicating, that is where your "Drop Cap" will take effect. Click outside the transformed text to make the dots and lines hidden.

A Word document is formatted to fit on a specific size page with the text automatically flowing from one page to the next. Excel supports printing, but its page breaks are not obvious, and because it's printing area can extend multiple pages horizontally as well as vertically the page breaks can be difficult to manage.

Watermarking for the Elegant Effect

Watermarking is a great way to show that a document requires special treatment without distracting from the content. How do we make use of Watermark? Simply follow these step-by-step procedures:

- Go to "Design"

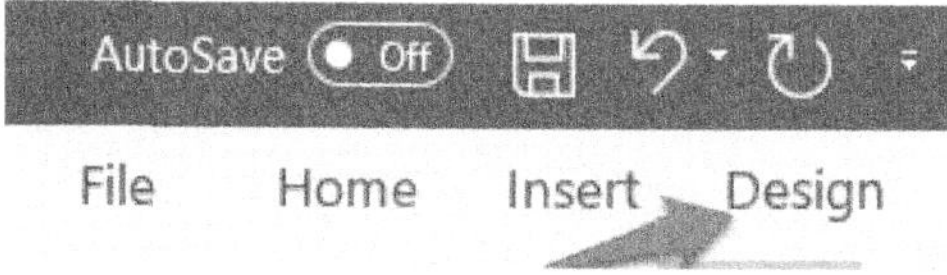

- Under the "Design" tab, look at your right-hand side, you will see the "Page Background" ribbon, above it, is the "Watermark" option, click on it.

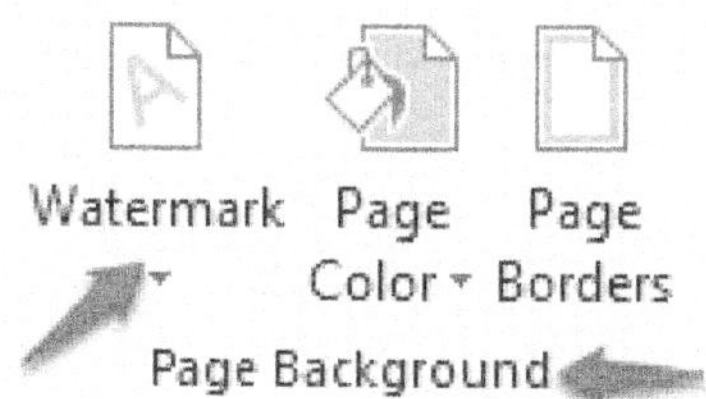

- Once you click on "Watermark", multiple options will be displayed, some are in diagonal format, and some are horizontal. Any template you click on will automatically reflect on your document. You can also customize your watermark. Select your preferred choice, or you choose "Custom Watermark" to customize your preferred choice

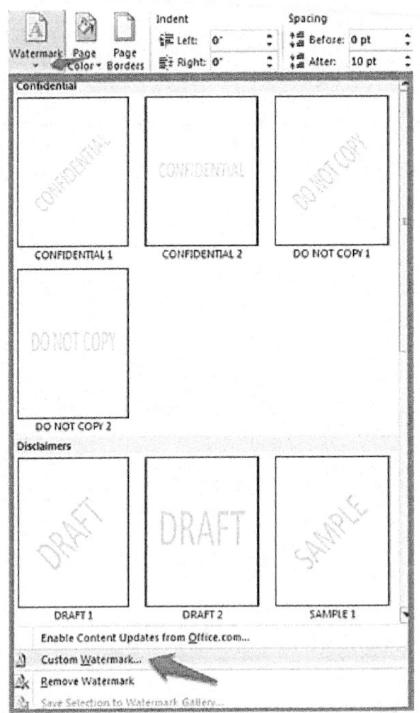

- Assuming we choose “Custom Watermark” by clicking on it, a dialog box will appear. There are three options to “Custom Watermark” which are: “No watermark”, for no effect, “Picture watermark” for image effect, and “Text watermark” for text effect. Choose the preferred “Text” and “Language” you want to insert as well as “Font” format, “Size”, “color” and “layout”, once done, click the “Ok” button.

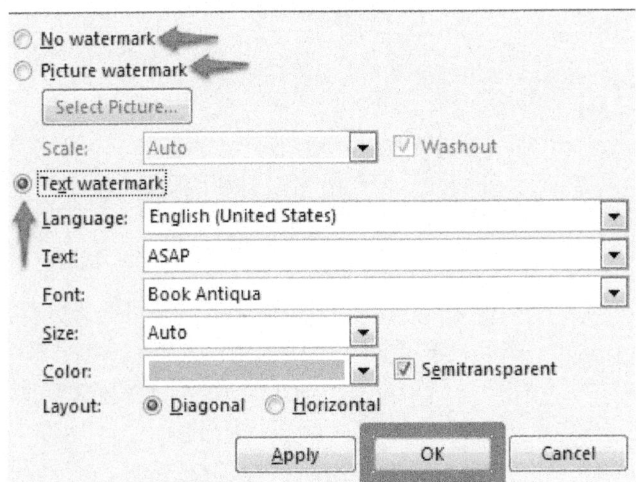

All the changes will automatically reflect on your document.

Putting Newspaper-Style Columns in a Document

- Go to the "Layout" tab

- Under the "Layout" tab, you will see the "Page setup" ribbon, within it you will also see your "Columns", click on it

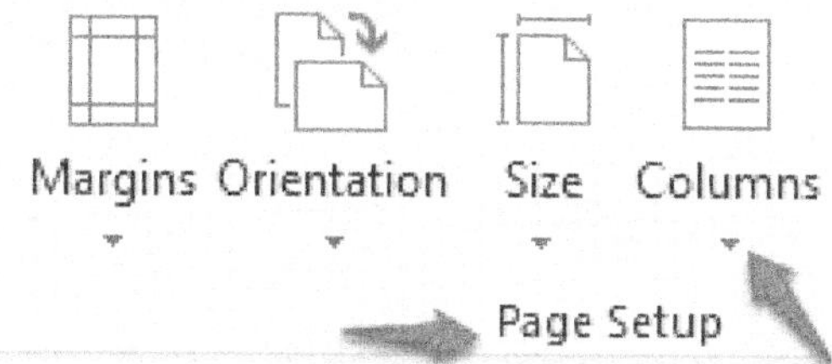

- You will see "Columns" dropdown options; let's pick "Three" because if you check any Newspaper, you will notice that on a page, the contents are normally divided into three columns.

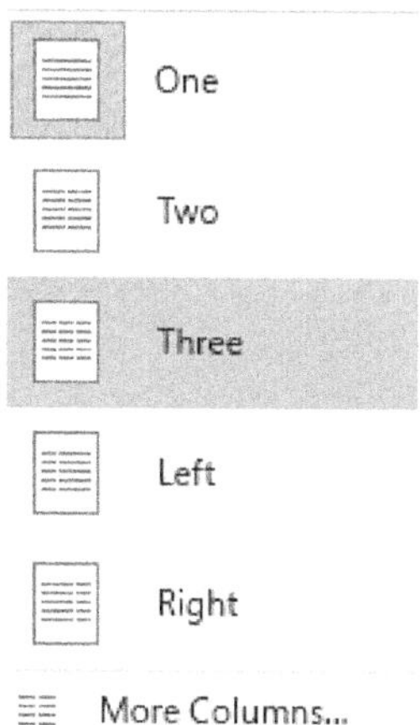

- Make sure you have content; else you won't see the effect of the "three" columns that you selected

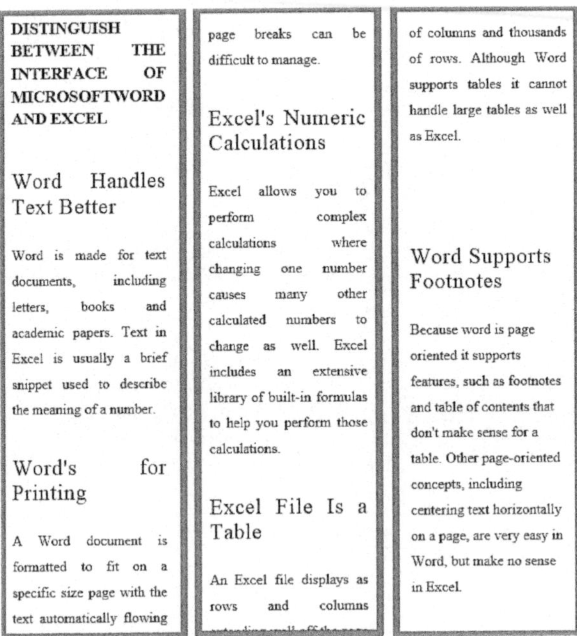

DISTINGUISH BETWEEN THE INTERFACE OF MICROSOFTWORD AND EXCEL

Word Handles Text Better

Word is made for text documents, including letters, books and academic papers. Text in Excel is usually a brief snippet used to describe the meaning of a number.

Word's for Printing

A Word document is formatted to fit on a specific size page with the text automatically flowing

page breaks can be difficult to manage.

Excel's Numeric Calculations

Excel allows you to perform complex calculations where changing one number causes many other calculated numbers to change as well. Excel includes an extensive library of built-in formulas to help you perform those calculations.

Excel File Is a Table

An Excel file displays as rows and columns

of columns and thousands of rows. Although Word supports tables it cannot handle large tables as well as Excel.

Word Supports Footnotes

Because word is page oriented it supports features, such as footnotes and table of contents that don't make sense for a table. Other page-oriented concepts, including centering text horizontally on a page, are very easy in Word, but make no sense in Excel.

Landscape Document

It is important to note that a Word document can be in two formats which are "Portrait" and "Landscape". By default, your Word document is in "Portrait" format. How do we now switch between Portrait & Landscape?

- Simply go to "Layout"

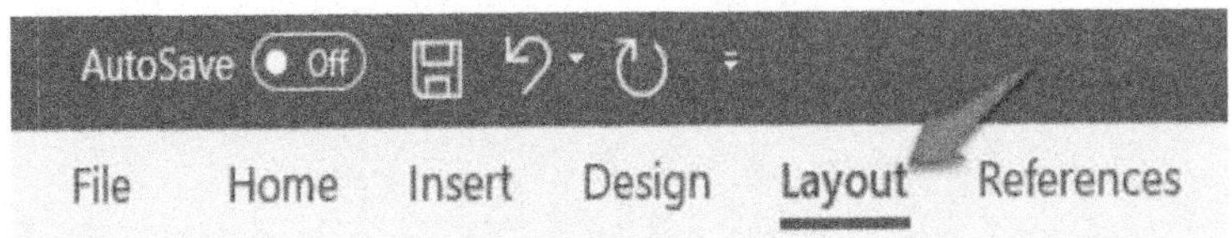

- Under "Layout", look for "Page Setup ribbon" select **Orientation**

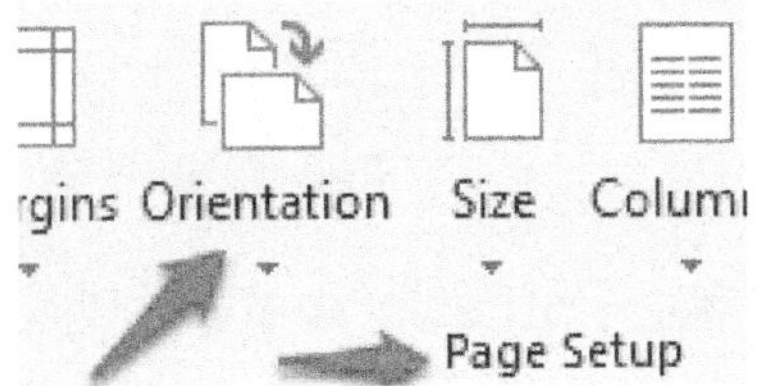

- You will see two options under "Orientation", which are "Portrait" & "Landscape". As I said earlier, a Word document by default is in "Portrait" (vertical format), once you switch it to "Landscape" as illustrated below, your presently opened Word document will be in horizontal shape.

Printing on Different Paper Size

To print on a different paper size,

- Simply go to "Layout"

- Under "Layout", look for "Page Setup" ribbon, select "Size"

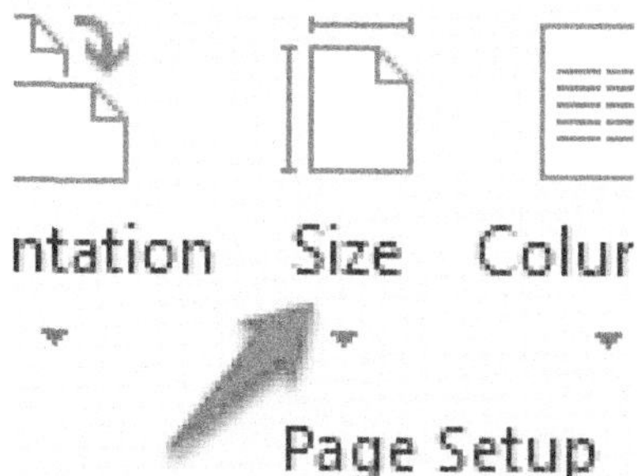

- Under "Size", multiple options will be displayed. By default, your Word document paper size is on "A4", you can choose other options or click on "More Paper Sizes"

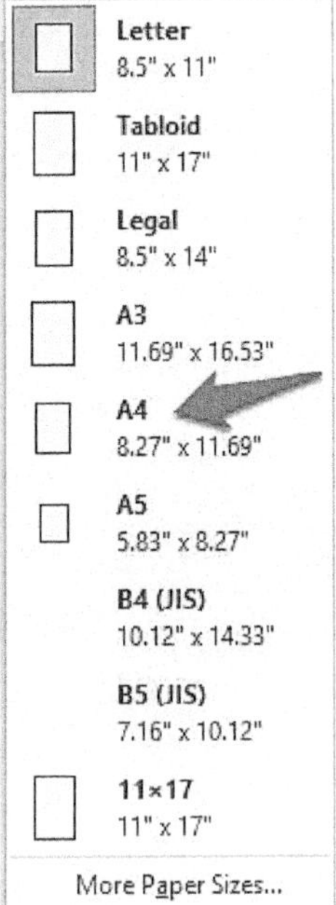

- Under "More Paper Sizes", you can set your paper "width" and "height" to your preferred taste, once you are done, press "Ok" to see the effect.

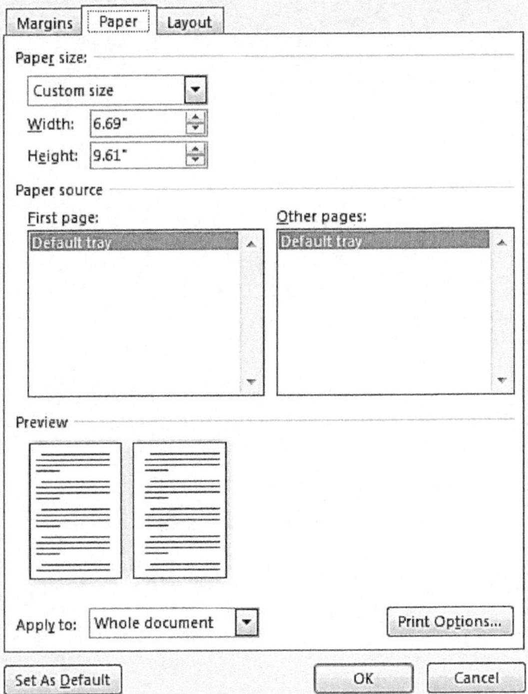

Showing Video in a Document

To show video in a document, follow these steps

- Go to "Insert"

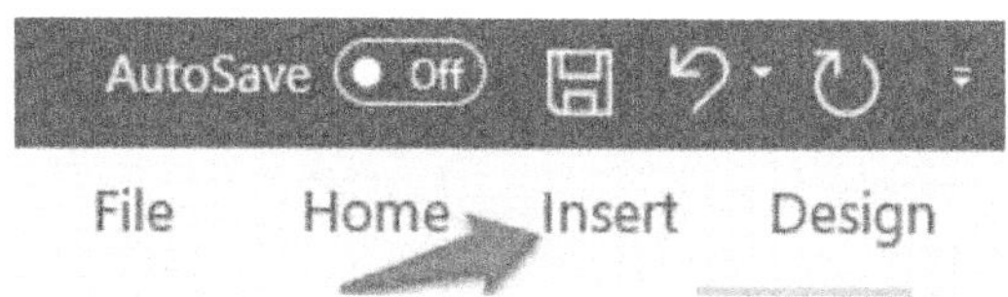

- Under the "Insert tab", on your right-hand side, you will see "Online Video Media", click on it

- A dropdown dialog box will appear with two options: "Online Video" which will refer you online (this requires your data connection) and "Video on My PC" (data connection not needed) which is the video from your PC storage. Once you choose your preferred choice you are good to go in watching your video through the Word environment

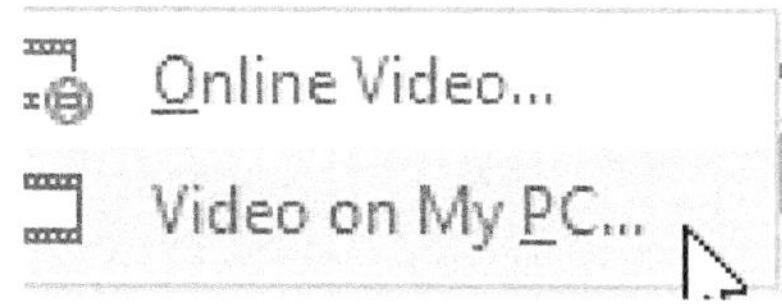

CHAPTER NINE

GETTING WORD'S HELP WITH OFFICE CHORES

Highlighting Parts of a Document

Highlighting parts of a document has been one of the quickest ways to perform your formatting tasks, such as bolding a text, increasing the font text size, changing text font, and other features. When it comes to effecting changes on some areas of your document content, the only option available is to highlight the parts of your document content.

How to Highlight a Text

There are only two ways of highlighting texts, which are: Mouse highlighting (click and drag) and Keyboard highlighting (Shift key + Navigation key).

Mouse highlighting (Click and drag)

- Place your mouse cursor at the beginning of your text area where you intend to start your highlighting from

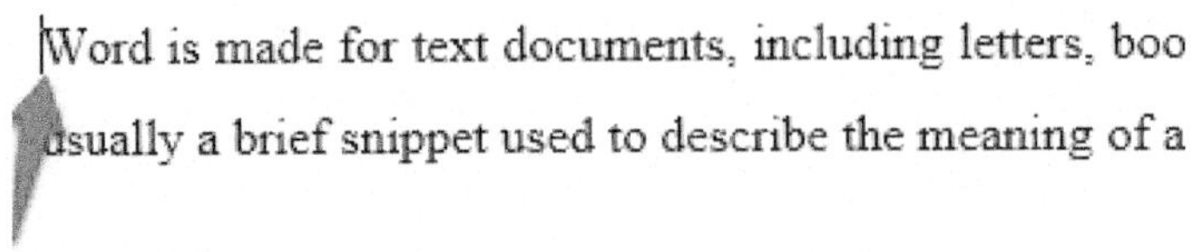

Word is made for text documents, including letters, boo
usually a brief snippet used to describe the meaning of a

- Once your pointer has been placed at the beginning of where you want to highlight, simply right-click on your mouse and hold down (if you are using a desktop, which has an external mouse) or left-click on your mouse and hold down (if you are using a laptop which has an internal mouse), then, start dragging it to the last edge where you want to stop.

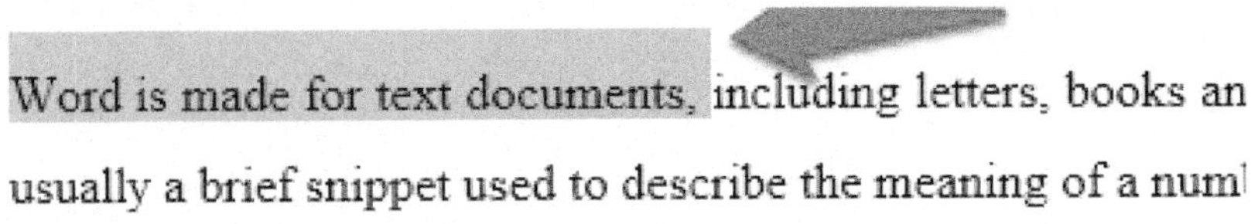

Word is made for text documents, including letters, books an
usually a brief snippet used to describe the meaning of a numl

Keyboard highlighting (Shift key + Navigation key)

- Place your mouse cursor at the beginning of your text area where you intend to start your highlighting from

Word is made for text documents, including letters, boo
usually a brief snippet used to describe the meaning of a

- Once it is rightly positioned, hold down the "Shift" key on your keyboard and simultaneously press the "Navigation key" depending on the direction you want to navigate it. There are four Navigation keys, "Upward navigation", facing up; "Downward navigation", facing down; "Backward navigation", facing the back direction, and "Forward navigation" facing front. Below is an illustration of the "Shift" key together with the "Forward" navigation key

Word is made for text documents, including letters, books an
usually a brief snippet used to describe the meaning of a num

Commenting on a Document

Commenting on a document is a great way of referring to it later and understanding your reason for particular tagged content.

Entering comments

- Select the content you want to comment on by highlighting it

A Word document is formatted to fit on a specific size page with the text automatically flowing from one page to the next. Excel supports printing, but its page breaks are not obvious, and because it's printing area can extend multiple pages horizontally as well as vertically the page breaks can be difficult to manage.

- Once your text has been selected, simply go to the "Review" tab

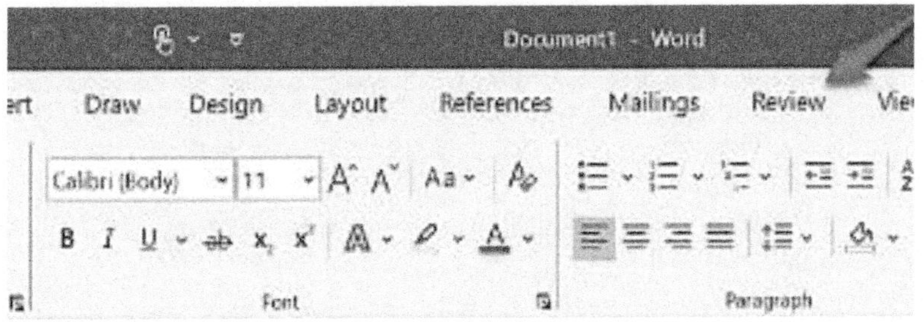

- Under the "Review" tab, you will see "New Comment" below it

- Enter "New Comment" by clicking on it, your highlighted text will be colored and another dialog box will appear on your right-hand side, the little "speech bubble rectangular shape" is a symbol or a referrer to your "comments box" at your left-hand side

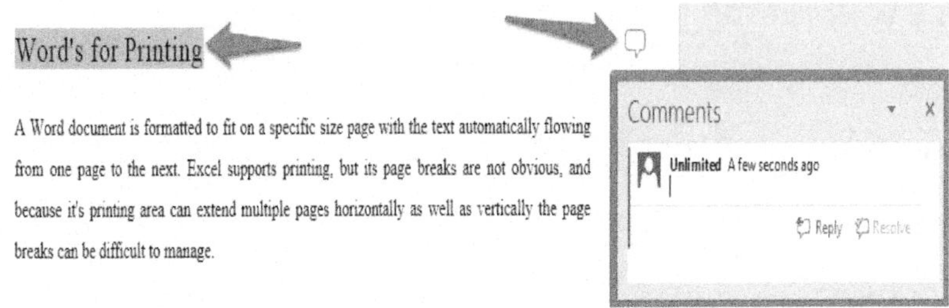

Replying to comments

- Input your text inside the "Comment box", since our text is centered on "Printing", I will be typing "Printing Instruction", note below is another session to also "Reply" on your comment, just like an online post.

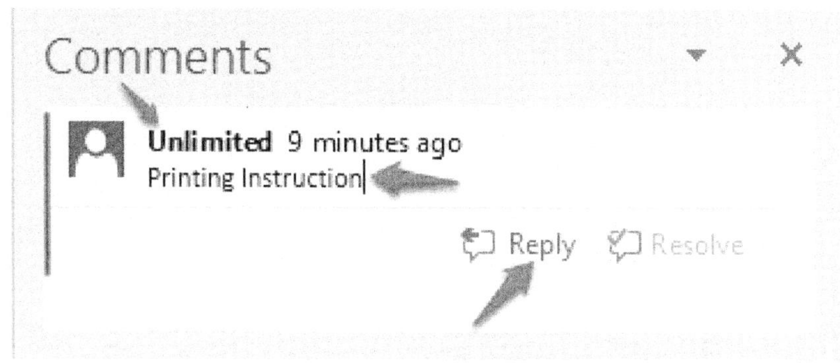

Note: don't be confused with the name "Unlimited" it is my PC name that I used, yours might not be "Unlimited", what your PC name is stored as is what will reflect on your comment session and your comment duration period after dropping your comment will be noted.

- You can reply on "Comment" with any word assuming I typed "More details on printing procedures" as my "Reply".

Note that on a single comment, your "Reply" does not have limits.

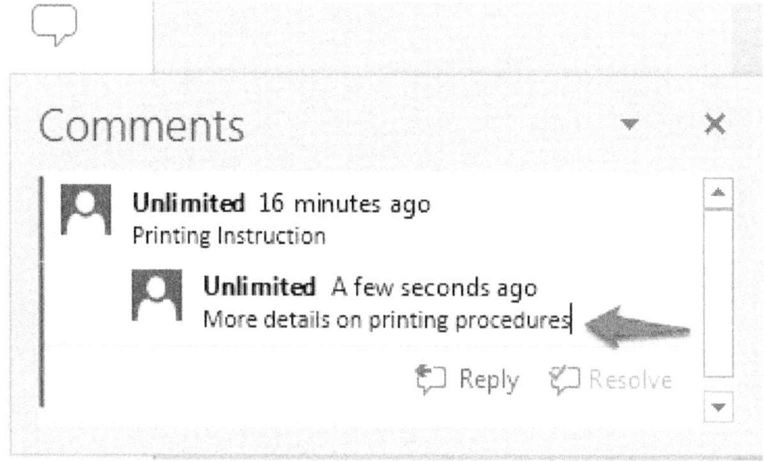

Resolving comments

- Highlight the comment or reply to be resolved or right-click on it to resolve it

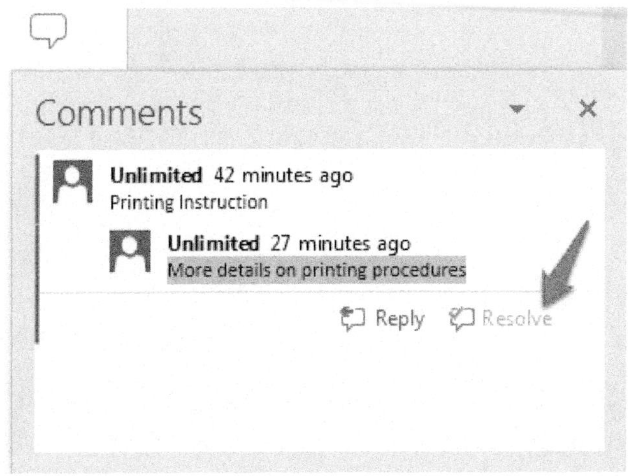

Viewing and Displaying Comments

- Go to the "Review" tab

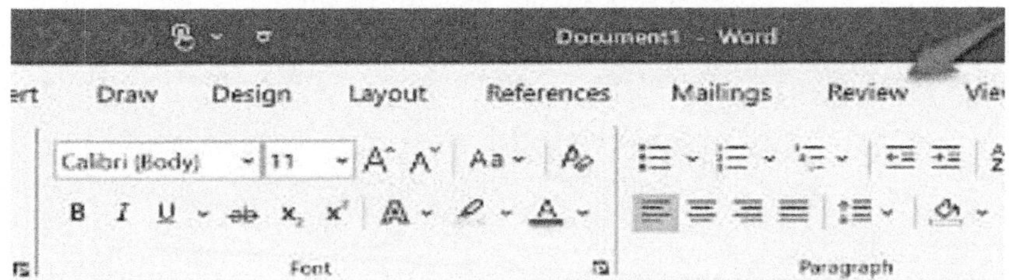

- You will see "Show Comments"

- Or on your document, you will notice a little speech rectangular icon, once you click on it, it will display your comments

- Your comment box will be displayed again for viewing or editing purpose

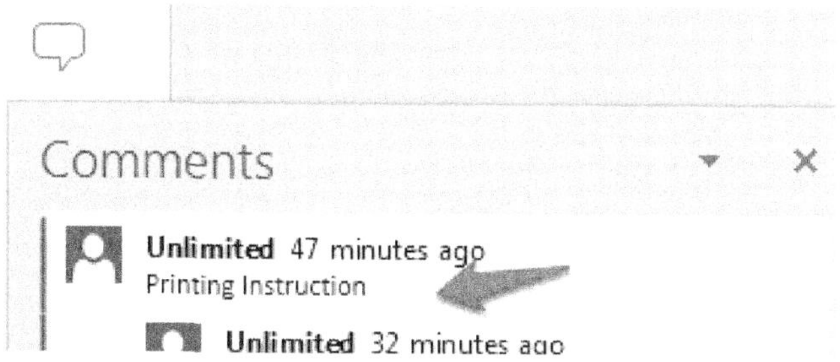

Tracking Changes to Documents

Keeping track of changes made to your documents is especially useful if the document is almost done, and you are working with others to make a revision or give feedback on your progress.

Working with Track Changes

- Simply go to "Review"

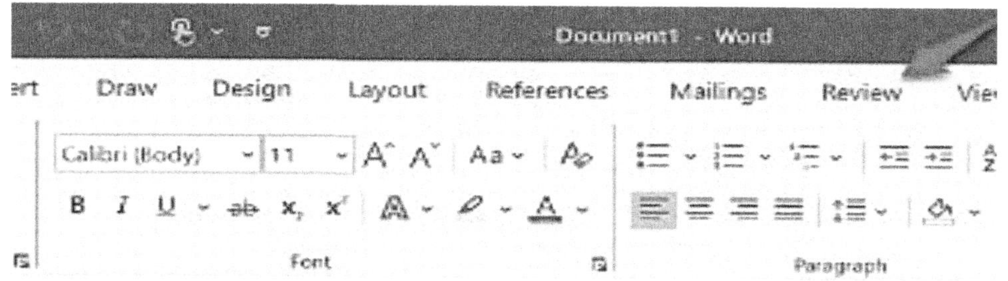

- Under "Review", at your right-hand side, you will see "Track Changes", click on it

- You will be given two options "Track Changes" & "Lock Tracking"

- Once you select "Track Changes", your content will be automatically monitored and tracked, and any changes made will be signaled with a red straight stroke as illustrated below with the additional words

A Word document is formatted to fit on a specific size page with the text automatically flowing from one page to the next. Excel supports printing, but its page breaks are not obvious, and because it's printing area can extend multiple pages horizontally as well as vertically the page breaks can be difficult to manage. Here is my additional input, kindly explain more further about printing

- You can also select "Lock Tracking" and a dialog box will appear requiring you to enter your "password" for prevention against unauthorized corrections which without the password, the other authors won't be able to add any changes.

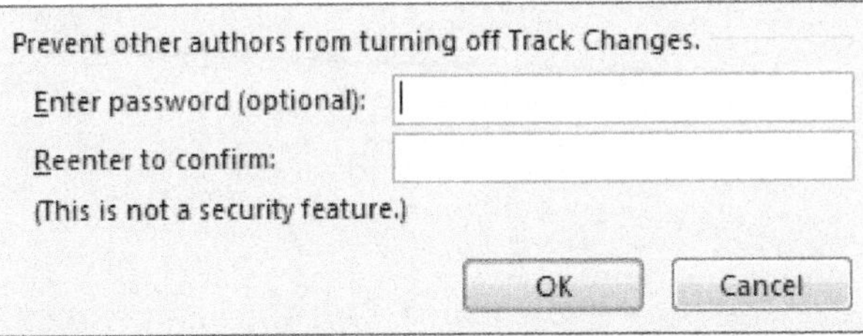

Reading and reviewing a document with revision marks

- Go to the "Review" tab

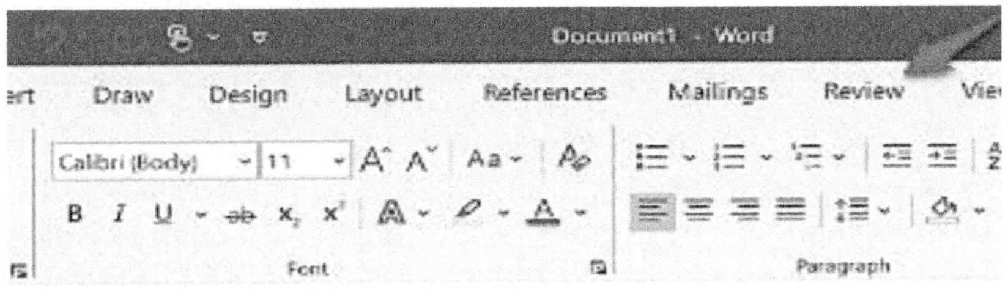

- Under the "Review" tab, at your right-hand side, you will see "Reviewing Pane", click on it

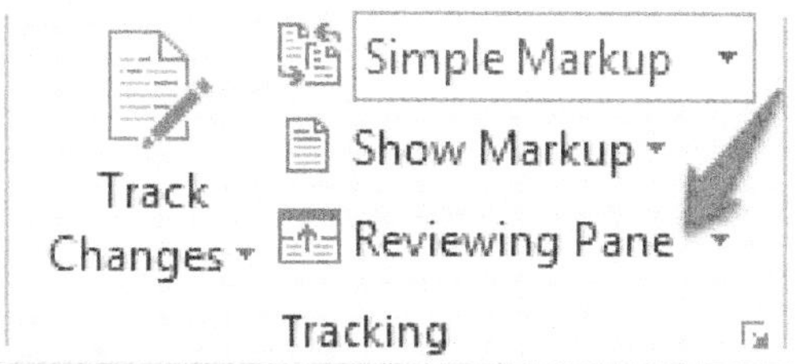

- Once you click on it, you will be given two options either to "Review Pane Vertically" or "Review Pane Horizontally". Assuming we choose "Review Pane Vertically", all your added words will be reviewed.

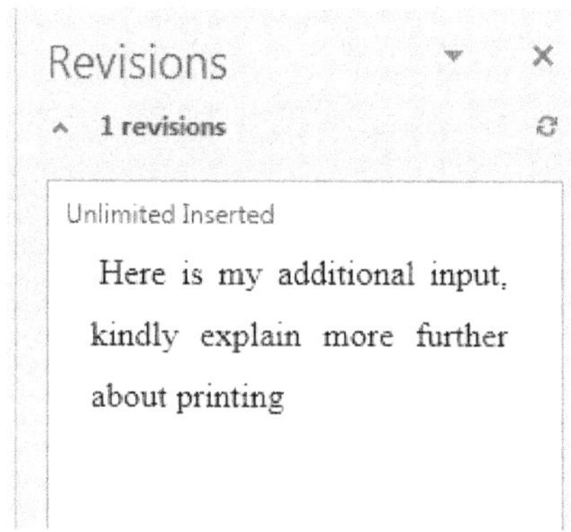

Marking changes when you forgot to turn on revision marks

- Go to "Review"

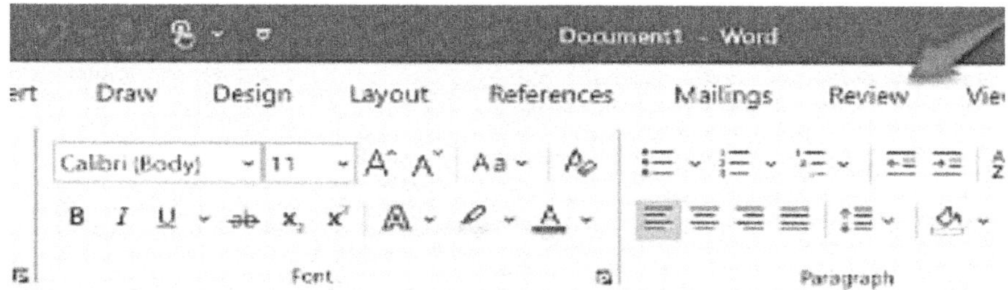

- Under the "Review" tab at your right-hand side, you will see "Sample Markup", click on it and select "All Markup"

- Then, all your added texts will be marked with a red color and also underlined, as a way to make one know the added content from the one that was previously there before adding additional words.

Word's for Printing

A Word document is formatted to fit on a specific size page with the text automatically flowing from one page to the next. Excel supports printing, but its page breaks are not obvious, and because it's printing area can extend multiple pages horizontally as well as vertically the page breaks can be difficult to manage. Here is my additional input, kindly explain more further about printing

Accepting and rejecting changes to a document

- Simply go to "Review"

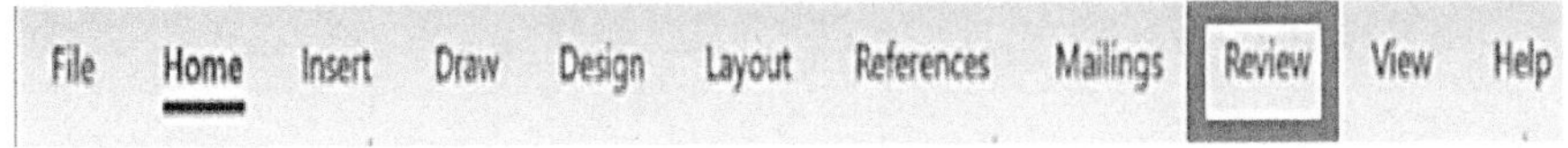

- Under "Review", at your right-hand side, you will see "Changes", above it is the "Accept" & "Reject" options

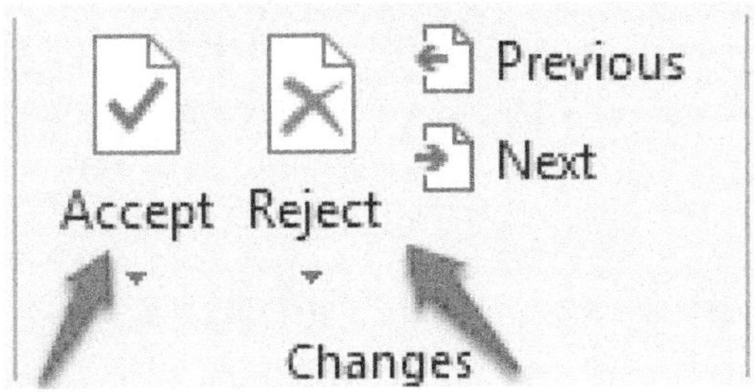

With the "Accept" option, you can move to the next track changes by selecting your preferred options under the "Accept" option

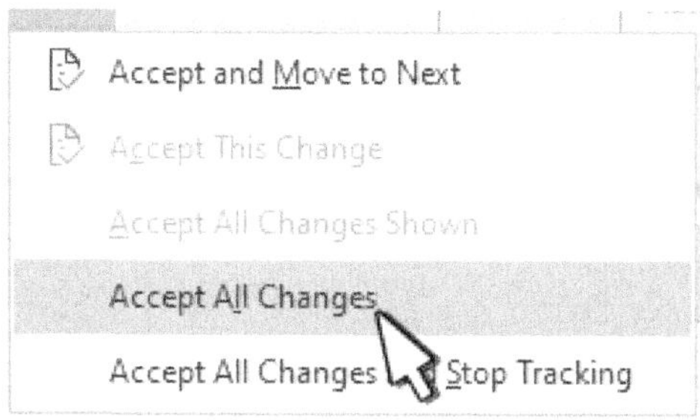

While the "Reject" option Undo changes and immediately moves to the next track changes. You can also select your preferred options under "Reject" just as in "Accept"

Printing an Address on an Envelope

- Go to "Mailings"

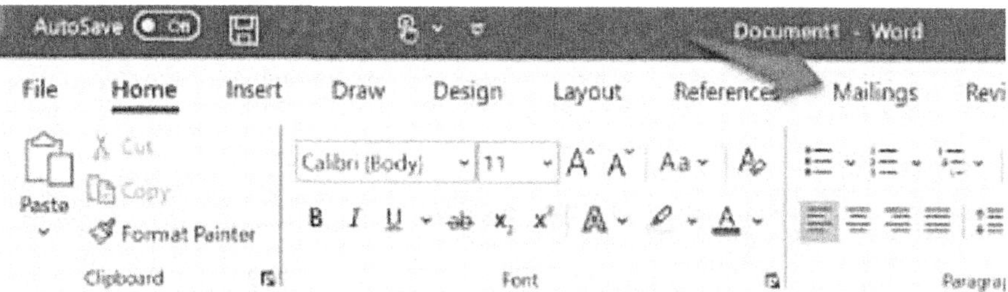

- Under the "Mailings" tab, at your left-hand side, you will see "Envelopes", click on it

- Simply fill in all the required details such as "Delivery address", "Return address", "Add to document" if need be. Once everything has been verified, click on "Print"

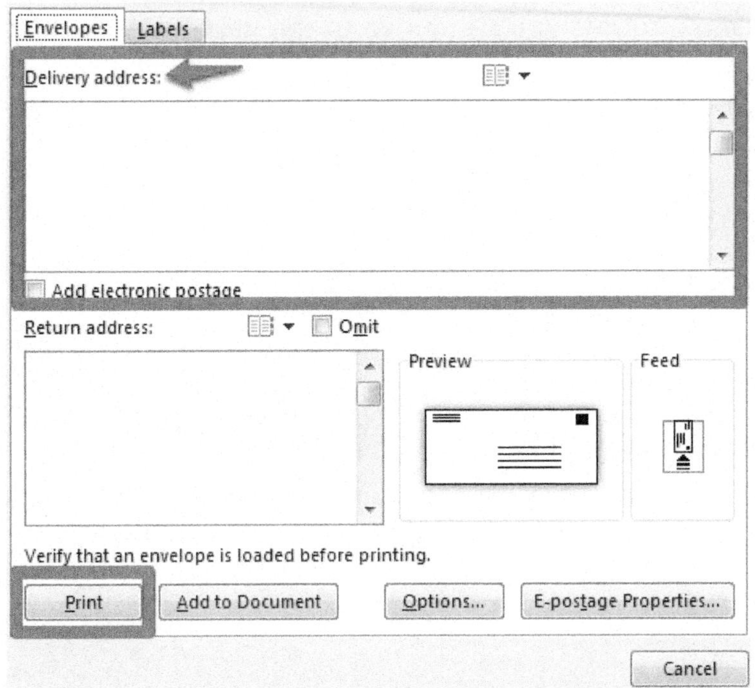

Printing a Single Address Label (or a Page of the Same Label)

- Go to "Mailings"

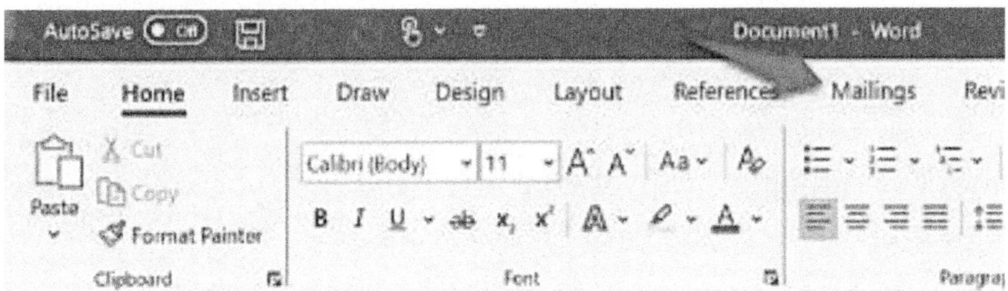

- Under "Mailings", on your left-hand side, you will see "Labels", click on it.

- Then, you can start filling the required input such as "Address", "Use return address" if need be (also select the amount of "Row" & "Column"), then click on your "Print" once you are done with labeling address.

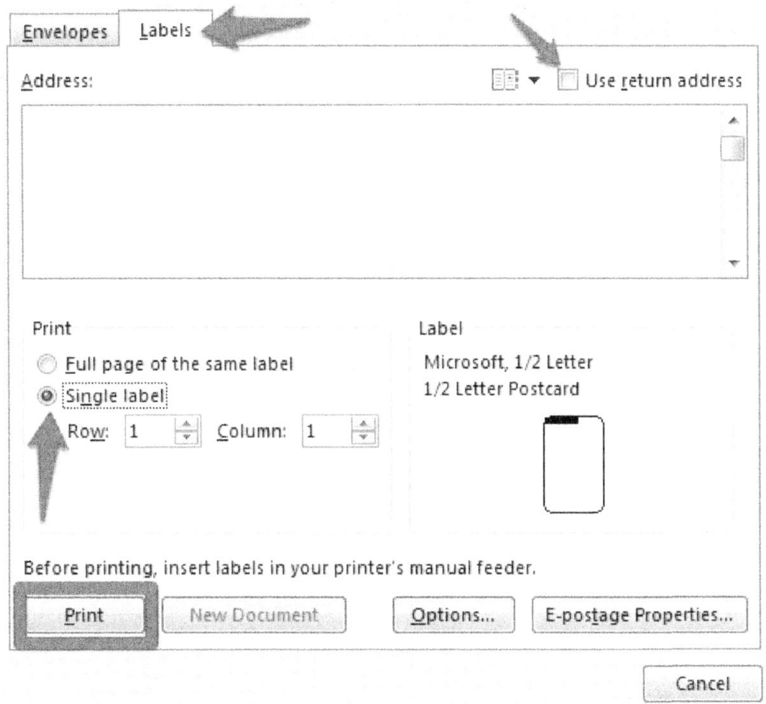

CHAPTER TEN

KEYBOARD SHORTCUTS

Frequently used shortcuts

Ctrl + A	Highlight all your content
Ctrl + B	Applying bold to selected text
Ctrl + C	Copy content into the Clipboard
Ctrl + D	Font dialog box
Ctrl + E	Centralized text
Ctrl + F	Navigation for searching
Ctrl + G	Go to a page, section, line number
Ctrl + H	To replace a text
Ctrl + I	Applying italic to selected text
Ctrl + J	To justify your text
Ctrl + K	Insert hyperlink to content
Ctrl + L	Align text to the left
Ctrl + M	Move paragraph
Ctrl + N	Create a new document
Ctrl + O	Open a document
Ctrl + P	Print out document
Ctrl + R	Align text to the right

Ctrl + S	Save document
Ctrl + U	Applying underline to selected text
Ctrl + V	Paste the copied contents from the Clipboard
Ctrl + W	Close current document
Ctrl + X	Cut the selected content
Ctrl + Y	Redo the previous action
Ctrl + Z	Undo the previous action
Ctrl + [	Decrease the font size
Ctrl +]	Increase the font size
Esc	Cancel a command
Ctrl + Alt + S	Split the document Window
Ctrl + Alt + S	Remove the document Window split

Access Keys for ribbon tabs

Alt + Q	Move to the "Tell me" or Search field on the Ribbon to search for assistance or Help content
Alt + F	Open the **File page** to use Backstage view.
Alt + H	Open the **Home tab** to use common formatting commands, paragraph styles, and the Find tool.
Alt + N	Open the **Insert tab** to insert tables, pictures and shapes, headers, and text boxes.

Alt + G	Open the **Design tab** to use themes, colors, and effects, such as page borders.
Alt + P	Open the **Layout tab** to work with page margins, page orientation, indentation, and spacing.
Alt + S	Open the **References tab** to add a table of contents, footnotes, or a table of citations.
Alt + M	Open the **Mailings tab** to manage Mail, Merge tasks and to work with envelopes and labels.
Alt + R	Open the **Review tab** to use Spell Check, set proofing languages, and to track and review changes to your document.
Alt + W	Open the **View tab** to choose a document view or mode, such as Read Mode or Outline view. You can also set the zoom magnification and manage multiple document Windows.
Alt or F10	Select the **active tab** on the ribbon, and activate the access keys
Shift + Tab	Move the focus to commands on the ribbon.
Ctrl + Right arrow	Move between command groupings on the ribbon
Arrow keys	Move among the items on the Ribbon
Spacebar or Enter	Activate the selected button.
Alt + Down arrow key	Open the menu for the selected button
Down arrow key	When a menu or submenu is open, it's to move to the next command
Ctrl + F1	Expand or collapse the ribbon

Shift+F10	Open the context menu
Left arrow key	Move to the submenu when the main menu is open or selected

Navigate the document

Ctrl + Left arrow key	Move the cursor pointer one space at a time to the left
Ctrl + Right arrow key	Move the cursor pointer one space at a time to the right
Ctrl + Up arrow key	Move the cursor pointer up by one paragraph
Ctrl + Down arrow key	Move the cursor pointer down by one Paragraph
End	Move the cursor pointer to the end of the current line
Home	Move the cursor to the beginning of the current Line
Ctrl + Alt+ Page up	Move the cursor pointer to the top
Page down	Move the cursor pointer by scrolling the document down
Ctrl + Page down	Move your cursor pointer to the next page
Ctrl + Page up	Move your cursor to the previous page
Ctrl + End	Move your cursor to the end of the document

CHAPTER ELEVEN

MICROSOFT WORD TIPS & TRICKS

Dark Mode

Do you know that you can turn on "dark mode" in Microsoft Word from the default background interface which is in white mode? The Dark mode is specifically designed for sight adjustment, majorly for the night users and other purposes.

To Enable Dark Mode

- Simply go to the top left-hand corner and click on your "File menu"

- Once you click on "File menu", scroll down, at the bottom left-hand corner, click on "Account"

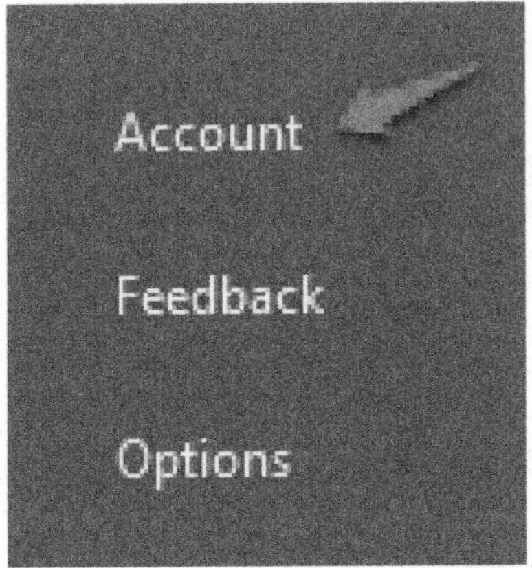

- Once you click on "Account", you will see your "User Information", below it is "Office Theme" by default, it is on "Colorful theme", click on the little dropdown arrow as illustrated below to see other options, next on the dropdown list is "Dark Gray", let's select it and see its effect.

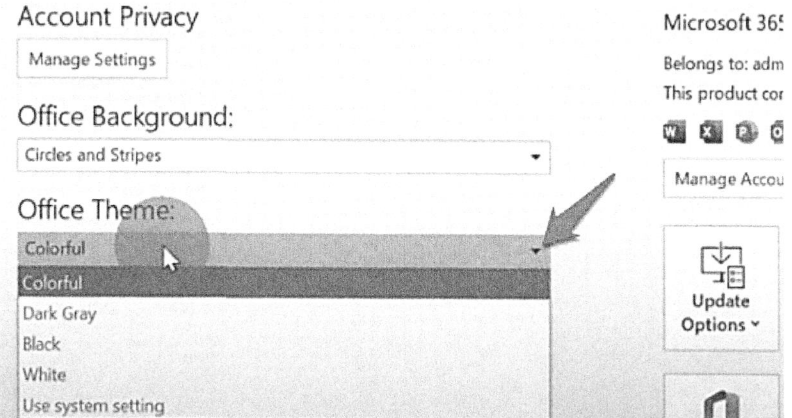

- "Dark Gray" makes your Word background interface a little bit dark

- You can select "Black" to get the "Dark mode" if you wish. Note that any change in your themes will also affect other Microsoft Suites such as Excel, PowerPoint, Outlook, and others.

- Here will be your Microsoft Word displayed interface

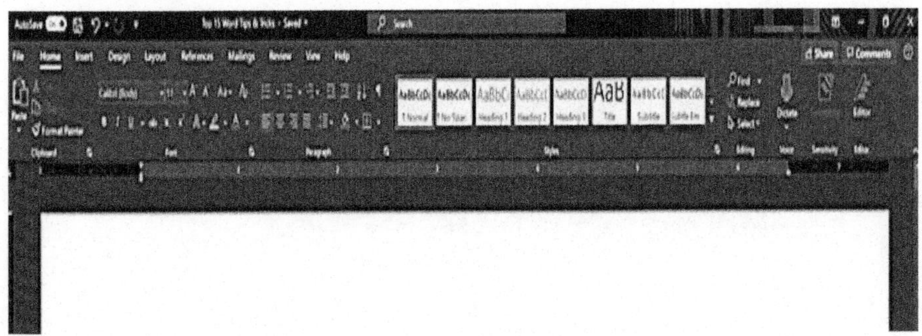

Changing the white document interface

Every of your theme settings or your customized theme settings can only affect the outlook, not the document content itself. To also change your white-board known as your document content area, simply follow these steps below:

- Go to your "Design tab"

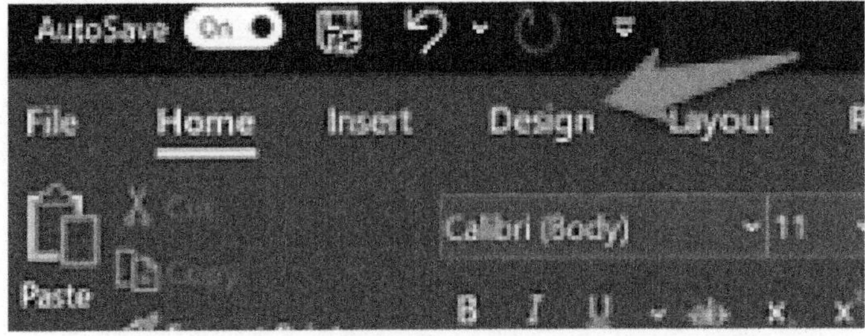

- Under "Design", at your right-hand side, locate "Page Color" and click on it

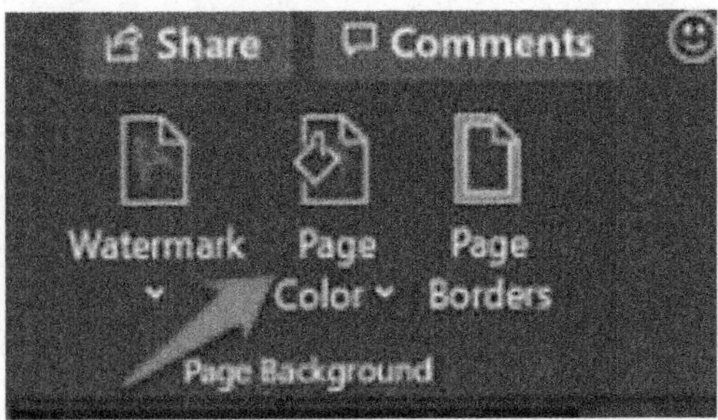

- Then, you can select "Theme Colors" to "Black"

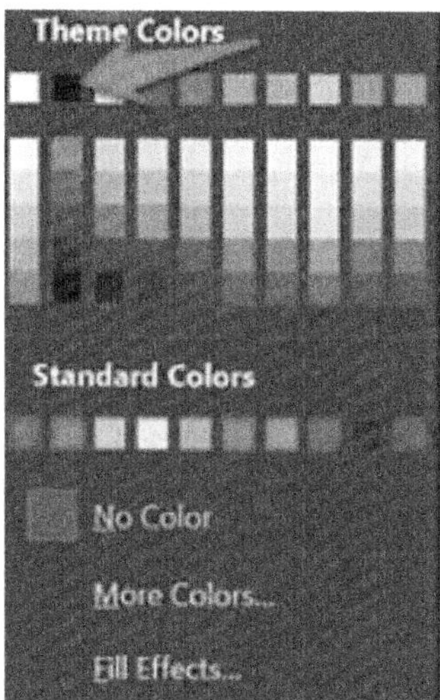

- Once you select "Color Black", your document content area will be on Black

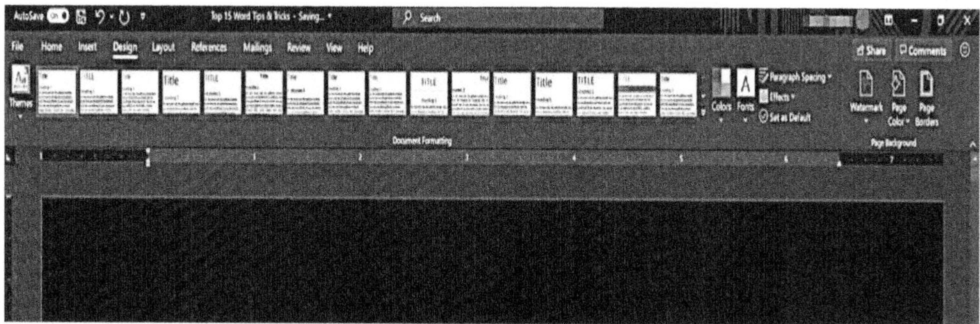

Note: Your dark document content area has nothing to do with your printing out the document, it will print out your standard white format and black texts, your themes selection, and design document content, it only affects your Word interface not with the copies to be printed.

Turn Word Document into Interactive Web Page

- Go to the menu bar, and click on "File"

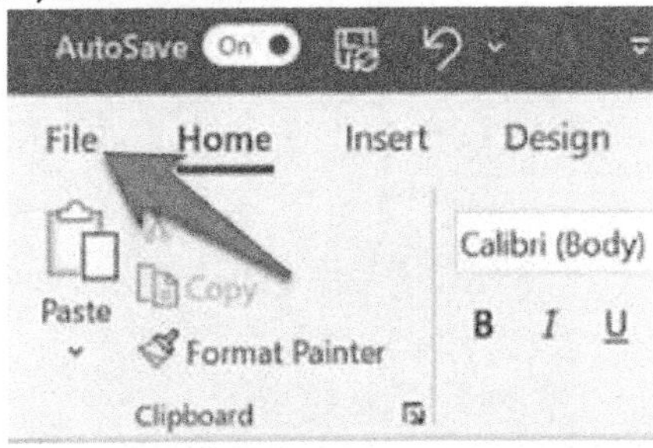

- Once you click on "File", scroll down and look for "Transform", once seen, click on it

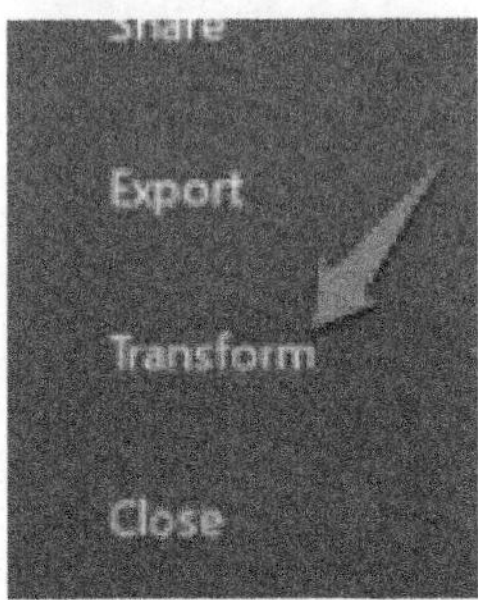

- This will automatically open a pane at your right-hand side in your document where you can select any "Web Page" template of your choice

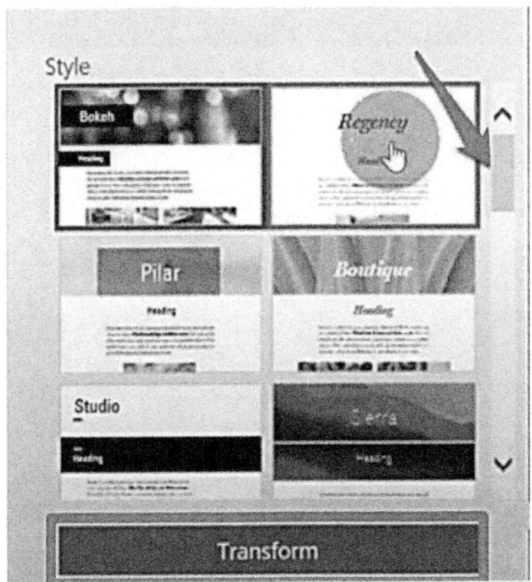

- Once you get your preferred choice, click on it and you will see the preview above

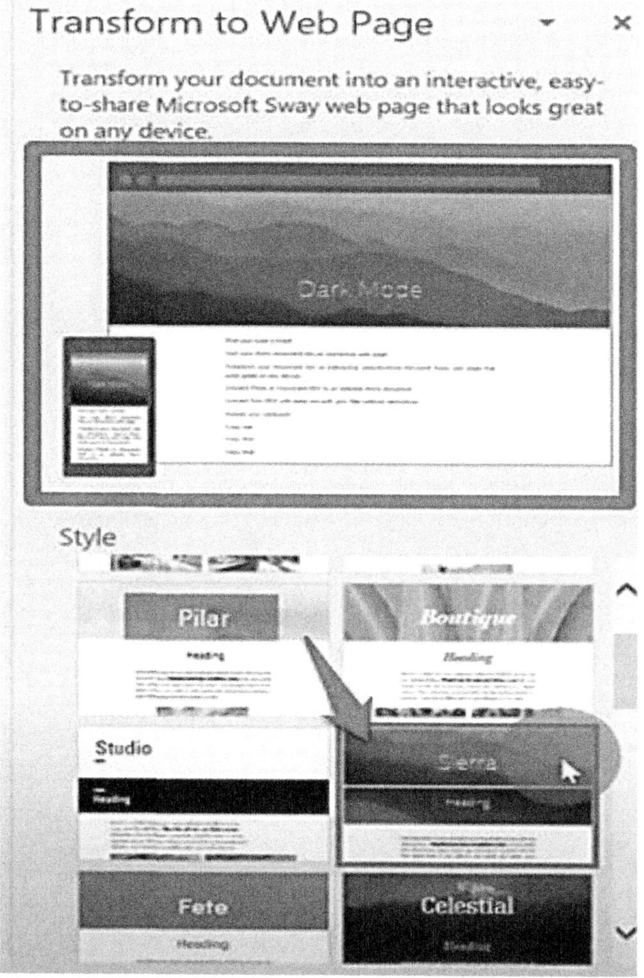

- Then, click on the "Transform" option to make changes

- You will be instructed about your preferred choice, that your document will be transformed to a Microsoft Sway web page. Once you are sure about your decision, simply click on "Transform" to proceed

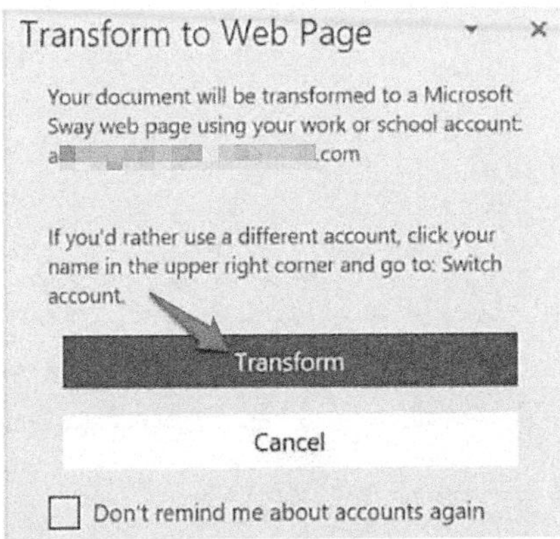

- Once done, your web page transforming template will automatically open on your web browser

- You can also edit your web page by clicking on "Edit" which gives you the privilege to modify your web page template.

- You can also review the "Navigation"

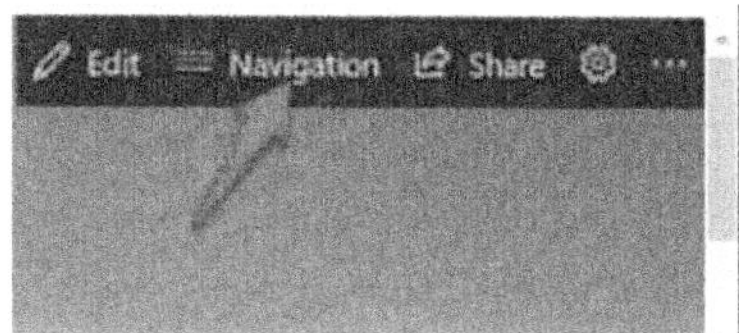

- And also "Share" the link with others

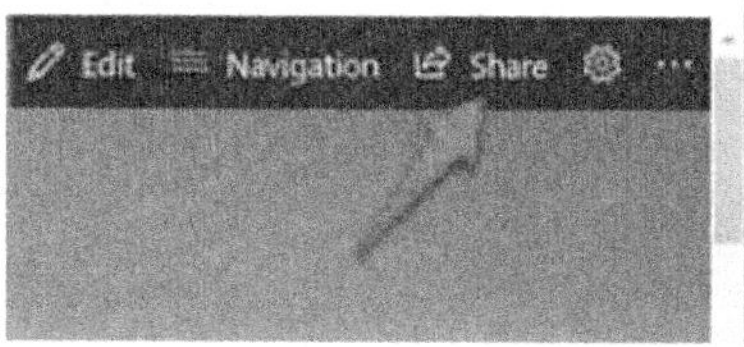

Converting Photo or Text PDF into Editable Word Document

Convert from PDF with ease and edit your files without any restrictions, you can also do the same to an image text with Word 365, you are limitless.

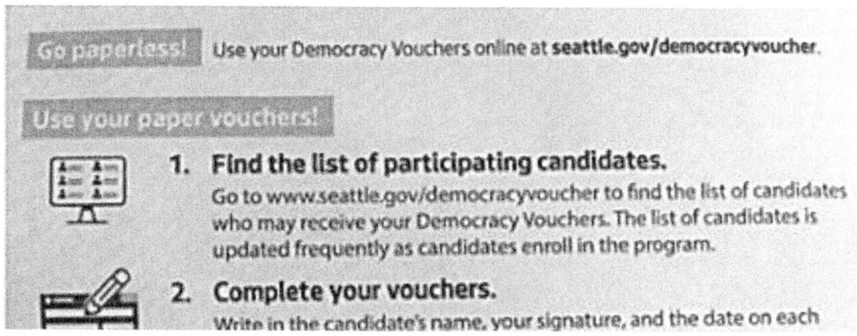

To see how this works;

- Simply go to the "File" menu

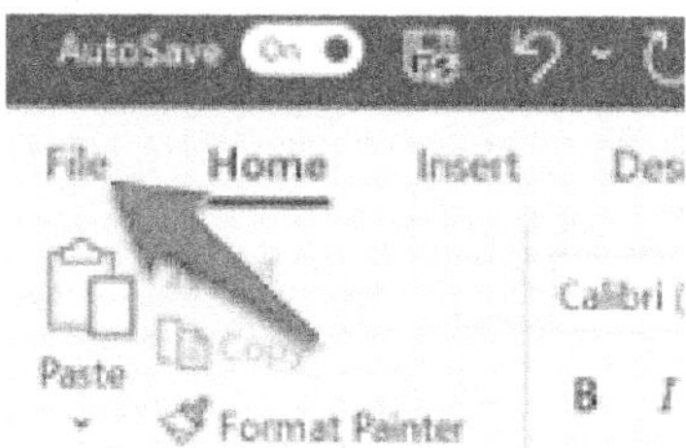

- In the "File" menu, a pane will appear by your left-hand side, click on "Open"

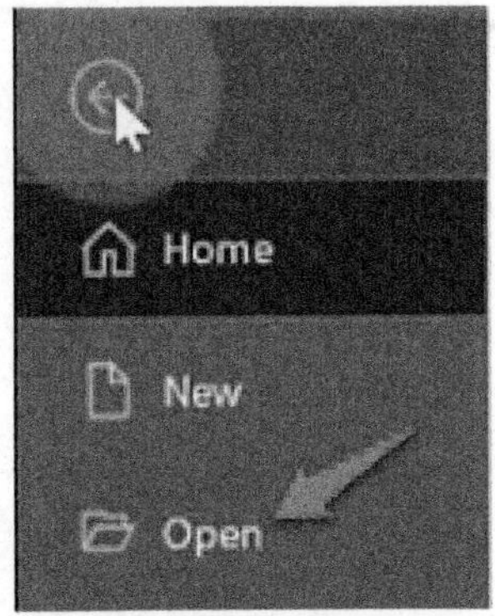

- At your right-hand side, “Open” features will appear, locate the document to be converted, whether an “Image text” or “PDF text”; if not found, navigate to where you have your file in your “Folders” to browse it or click and drag it into Word environment.

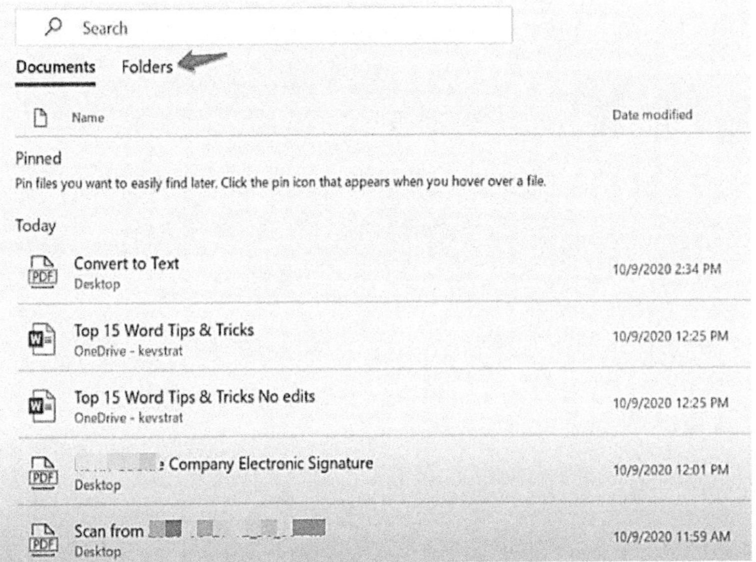

- You will get a “Microsoft Word Notification” that Word is about to convert your PDF to an editable Word document. The resulting Word document will be optimized to allow you to edit the text, so, it might not look exactly like the original PDF or Image-text especially if the original file contained lots of graphics. Note that for an effective result; make sure you have a data connection. Once you agree with the “Microsoft Word Notification” by pressing “Ok”, then your PDF or Image-text will be displayed as an editable Word document

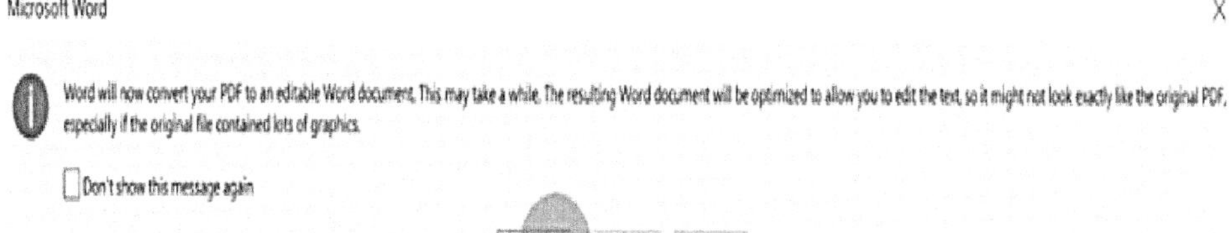

- Below will be your outcome, after the extraction of the text, which will be placed on your Word document for further self-editing.

Go paperless! Use your Democracy Vouchers online at seattle.gov/democracyvoucher.

Use your paper vouchers! 

1. Find the list of participating candidates.
   Go to www.seattle.gov/democracyvoucher to find the list of candidates who may receive your Democracy Vouchers. The list of candidates is updated frequently as candidates enroll in the program.
2. Complete your vouchers.
   Write in the candidate's name, your signature, and the date on each

Copy and Paste Multiple Items on Clipboard

Most of us are familiar with copy and paste but not aware of copying multiple texts differently and then see all your copied text while pasting it. Let me illustrate

- Assuming, I type “Copy me!”, “Copy this!”, and “Copy that!”

Access your clipboard

Copy me!

Copy this!

Copy that!

- Then, I copy it separately and I press “Ctrl + V” which is to paste, my result will only affect my last text which is “Copy that!”

Copy that!

- What if I want to paste the first text or the second text locally? Word will help with this by going to your "Home tab", below it, you will see your "Clipboard ribbon", there is a dropdown arrow indication, click on it to view all your different copied text

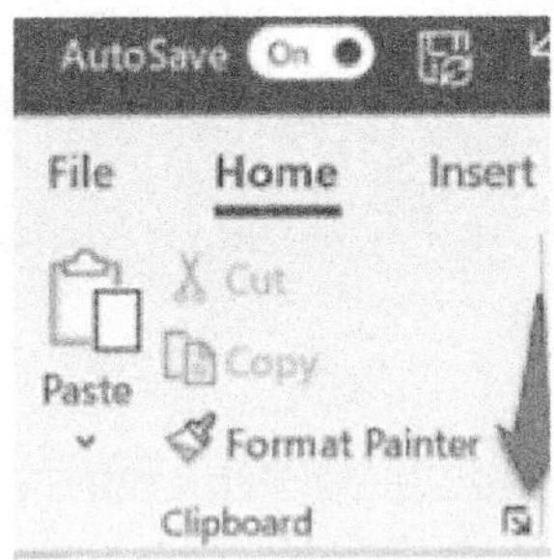

- Below is your outcome, where you can manually select the preferred text you want to paste by clicking on it, which in return will be pasted wherever your mouse cursor is pointing at (the blinking position).

Note: This is not limited to text, image also can be copied and pasted

Use formulas to calculate values

It is rarely known that Word performs mathematical calculations with different formulas like "Microsoft Excel", I will be showing you the possibilities

- Assuming, I have created my tabulated figures and all I need to do next is to sum it up without having to manually calculate it myself or with my PC calculator

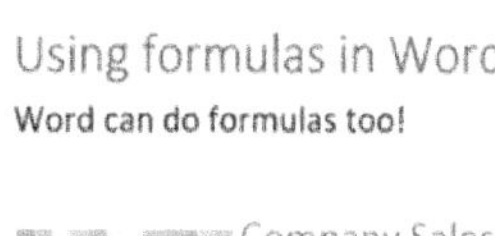

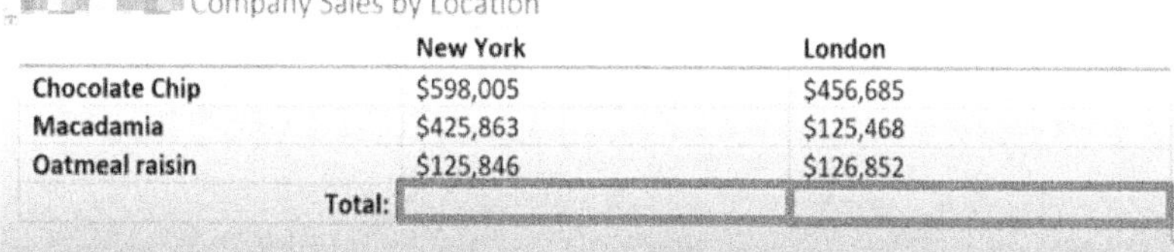

Company Sales by Location

	New York	London
Chocolate Chip	$598,005	$456,685
Macadamia	$425,863	$125,468
Oatmeal raisin	$125,846	$126,852
Total:		

- Look to the "menu bar" and select "Layout"

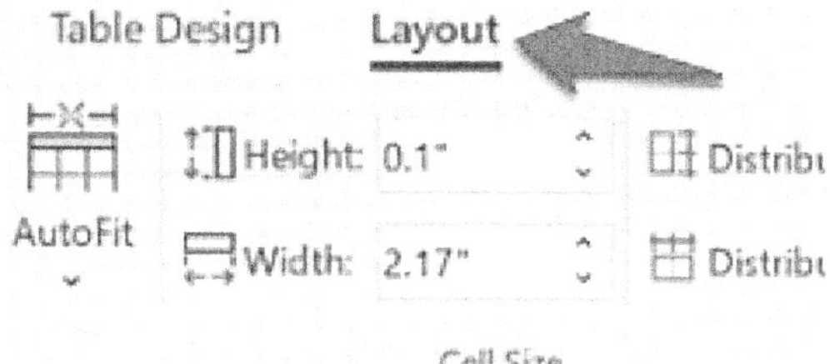

- Once selected, at your left-hand side, locate "Formula" and click on it

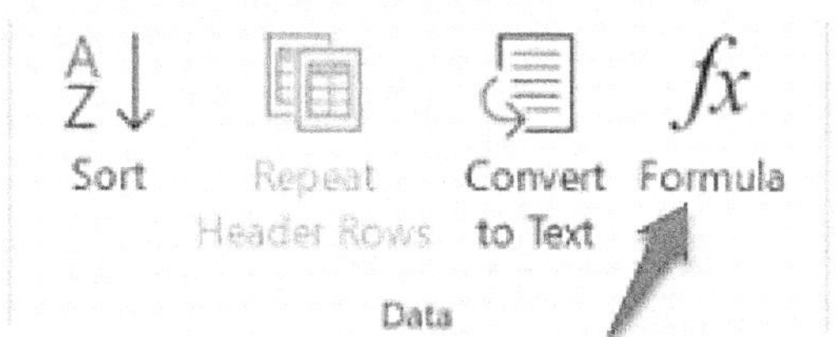

- Once you click it, a dialog box will appear where you can perform your arithmetic, this has been explained in "chapter seven", but for further understanding and the rareness of it. I have to show you more about it.

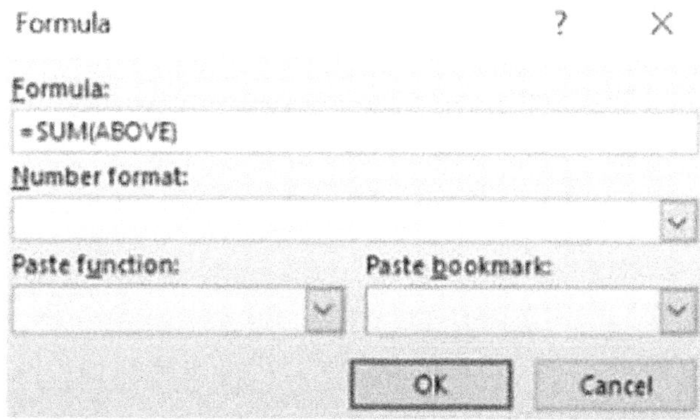

- Note, this is not only limited to summing up values, you can also click down below the illustrated apart and see all of the different formulas you can apply to your calculation. Calculating is not only about the summation of figures, other formulas can also perform other tasks such as getting your "Average" figure, "Max" for maximum figure, "Min" for minimum figure, and lots more, just scroll through the "scroll bar"

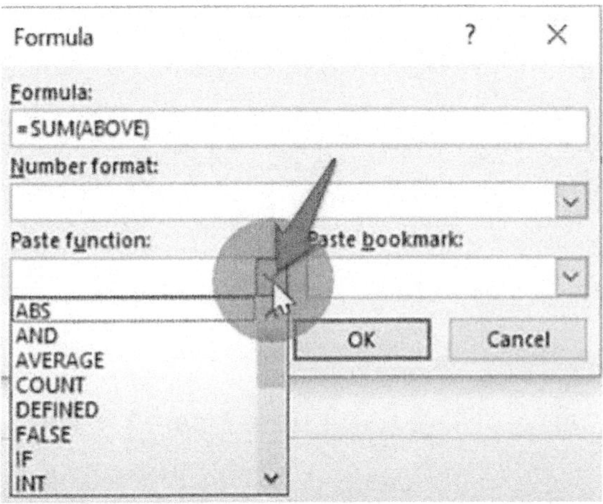

- I am going to stick to "=SUM(ABOVE)". To know more about what the symbols represent, kindly check back on "Chapter Seven" on the topic ***"Using Math Formulas in Tables".*** After you click on the formula you want, click "Ok" to see the effect

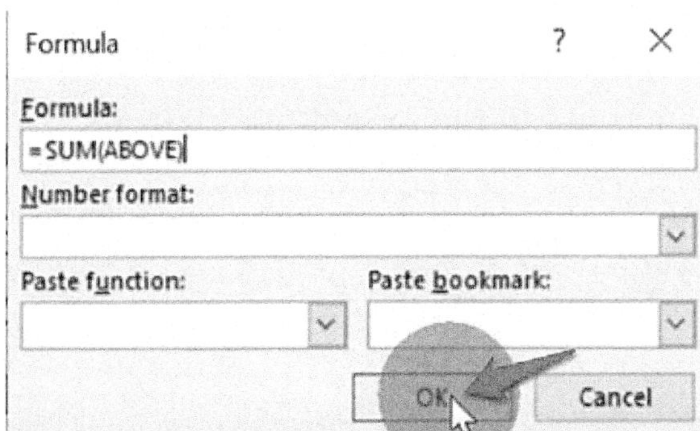

- Below is your total summation, make sure your cursor is on the cell where your total figure will be pasted, because if not you won't get your expected result

Sales by Location

	New York
	$598,005
	$425,863
	$125,846
Total:	$1,149,714.00

Assignment

From the table on pg. 241, calculate the total summation for "London" using the just explained procedure and do your manual calculation also for comparison.

Sort lists Alphabetically

- Do you know that you can sort lists in Microsoft Word and you can also sort lists in various ways? First of all, I will type some largest city in the World as illustrated below

Sort in Word

Tokyo
Lagos
Guangzhou
Istanbul
Karachi
Dhaka
Beijing
Mumbai
Shanghai
Delhi

- Secondly, the list will be automatically sorted out alphabetically. To do this, select (highlight) the list

Sort in Word

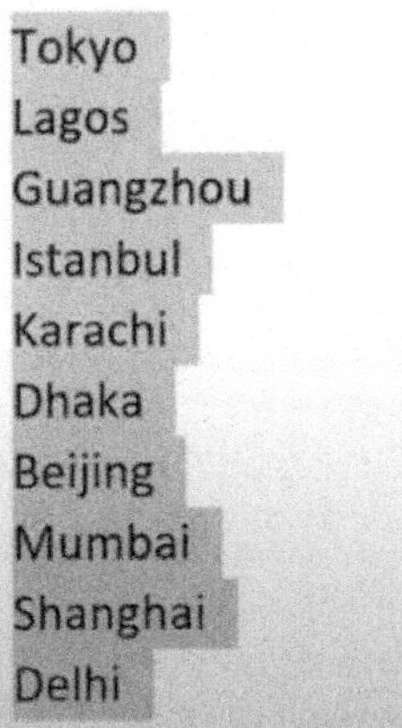

- And then, go to your "Home tab"

- At your right-hand side, click on the "Sort" icon which is represented with "upward A & downward Z with a downward arrow". After you click on it

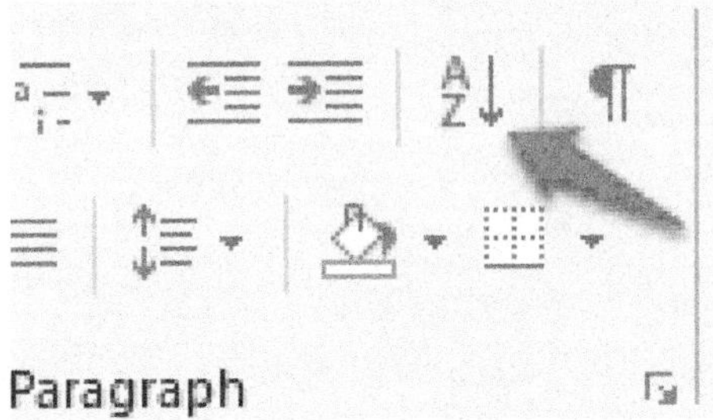

- A dialog box will appear titled "Sort Text"; make sure at your right-hand side you select "Paragraph", while at your left-hand side you select "Text", also click on the "Ascending" button for us to get our alphabetical order arrangement. Below it, you will see "My list has" which shows options, "Header row" and "No header row". For this illustration, I have no header row, which means I will click on "No header row". Once done, click on the "Ok" button.

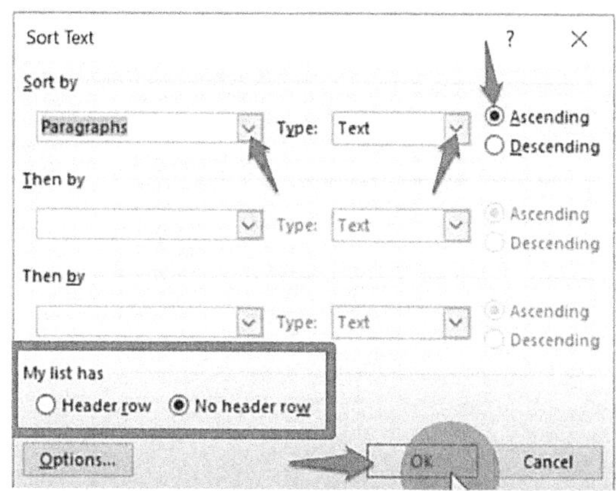

- You will notice your highlighted list will automatically rearrange itself alphabetically.

Sort in Word

Beijing
Delhi
Dhaka
Guangzhou
Istanbul
Karachi
Lagos
Mumbai
Shanghai
Tokyo

Sort lists Numerically

Sorting out lists is not only limited to alphabetical arrangement alone, but you can also sort out lists numerically by following these steps:

- Highlight your numbers to be sort

- Assuming, you want to rearrange the above numbers, simply go to your "Home tab"

- At your right-hand side, click on the "Sort" icon which is represented with "upward A & downward Z with a downward arrow". After clicking it

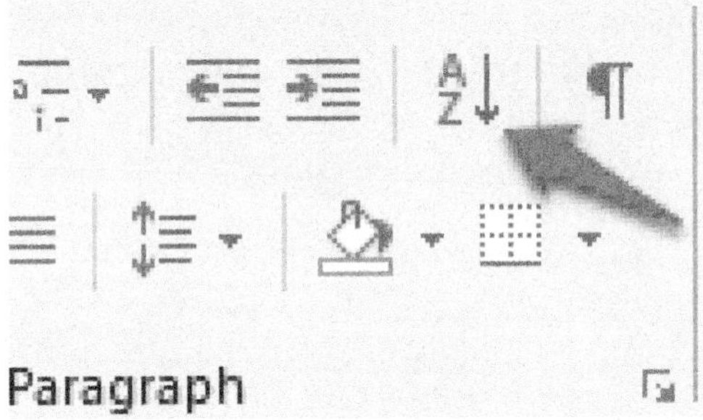

- A dialog box will appear titled "Sort Text", make sure at your right-hand side you select "Paragraph", while on your left-hand side you select "Number", also click on "Ascending" for us to get our numerical order arrangement. Below it, you will see "My list has" which shows options "Header row" and "No header row". For this illustration, I have no header row, which means I will click on "No header row", once done click "Ok".

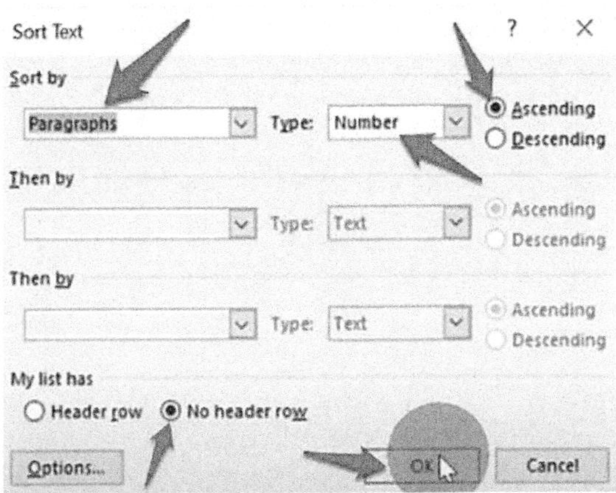

- You will notice your highlighted list will automatically rearrange itself numerically in ascending order.

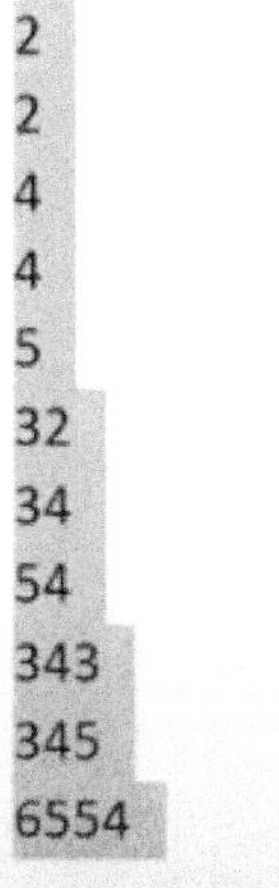

2
2
4
4
5
32
34
54
343
345
6554

Sort lists by Date

You can also sort out your listed dates in ascending order, without the use of Microsoft Excel. I know you are amazed by a lot of interesting Microsoft Word features. Now you understand, when I said, this is the right book you have purchased for your self-improvement. So, let us also see how sorting out dates works.

- Highlight your dates

2/15/1985
1/1/1929
5/4/1956

- To rearrange the above numbers, simply go to your "Home tab"

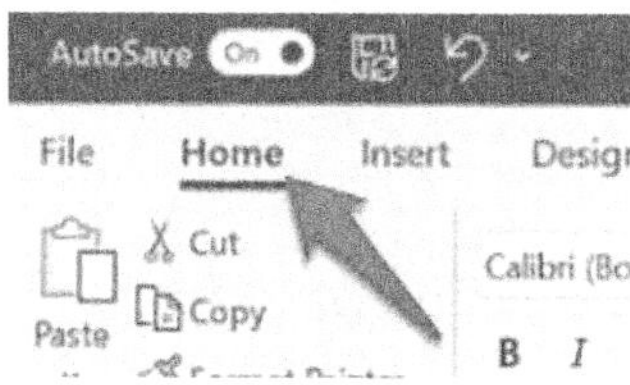

- At your right-hand side, click on the "Sort" icon which is represented with "upward A & downward Z with a downward arrow". After you click on it

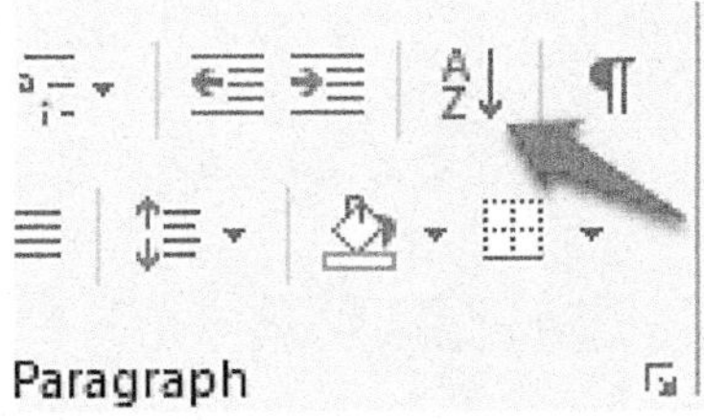

- A dialog box will appear titled "Sort Text", on your right-hand side, select "Paragraph", while on your left-hand side, select "Date". Also, click on "Ascending" for us to get our alphabetical order arrangement. Below, you will see "My list has", which shows options, "Header row" or "No header row". For this illustration, I have no header row, so, I will select "No header row". Once done, click on the "Ok" option.

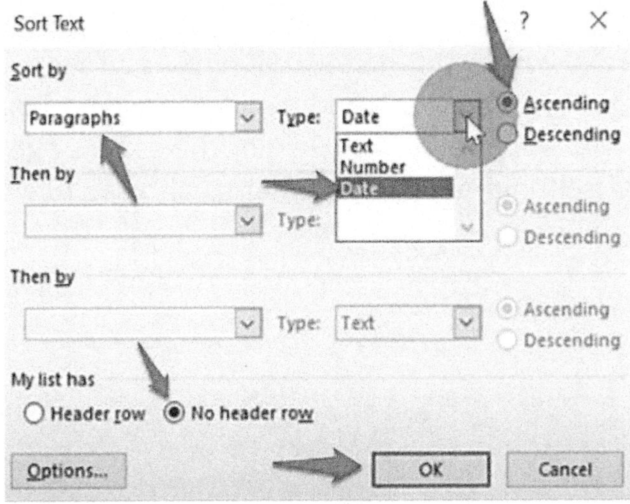

- You will notice that your highlighted date will automatically rearrange itself in an ascending way

1/1/1929
5/4/1956
2/15/1985

Collaborate with others via a link

Easily share your documents to work together with others as a team by using a link to send your document. In the past, if you wanted to work with others on a document, you have to email them by sending an attachment of your document for editing. They do the editing, send it back to you, and then, you have to merge all the edits which might consume a lot of time, especially when you are trying to see what has been added or removed; what a stressful process! Luckily, things have gotten a lot easier

- Simply look at the top right-hand corner of your Word 365, you will see a "Share" option, click on it

- This opens a "share" dialog box which gives the access to share your document via a link. By default, it is on "Anyone with the link can edit"

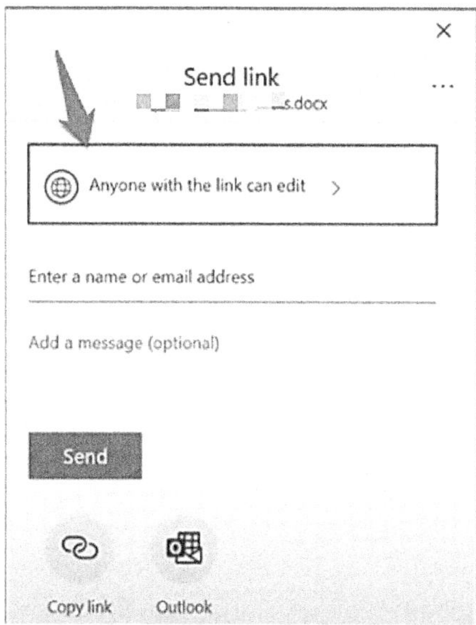

- You can click on the default settings which is "Anyone with the link can edit", you will be shown other options such as "People in your domain with the link", "People with existing access", and "Specific people". Below are other functions you can tick or untick; "Allow editing", "Set expiration date" for termination of your shared link, "Set password" against unauthorized co-authors, you can also set "Block download" at your wish. Once you are through with your configuration, click on "Apply"

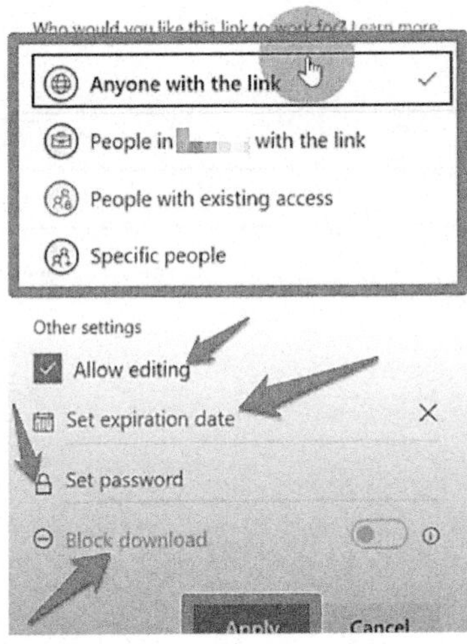

- If the above illustration is not what you need, press the "Cancel" option beside "Apply". After you click on apply, you will be brought here, type in the co-author email, you can also add some write-up with it, then send it, or you can also copy the link to your document depending on your preferred choice

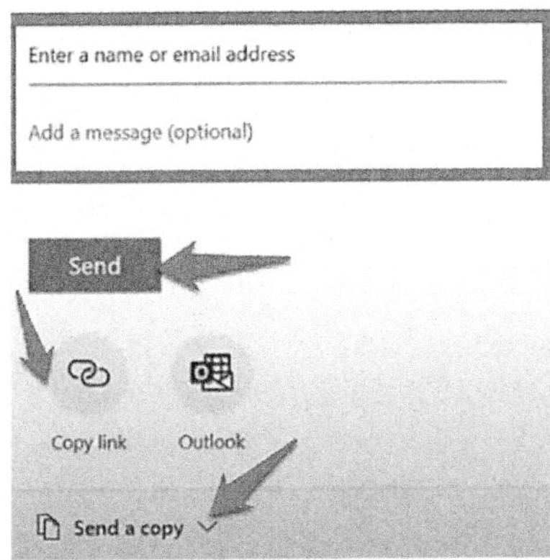

Collaborate with others via mentioning someone's name

Easily share your documents to work together as a team with others by using "@" mentioning others to get their attention in responding to you as it is on your Facebook, whenever your name is mentioned, you are notified about it. To see how this works,

- highlight any part of your text document you want to inform others about

Easily share your documents to work together with others. @ mention others to get their attention.

- Then at the top corner of your right-hand side, click on "Comments"

- You see a dropdown option, click on "New Comment"

- Once you click on "New Comment", your highlighted text will be colored and another dialog box will appear at your right-hand side with your PC name or your Microsoft account name at the top of the "comment box"

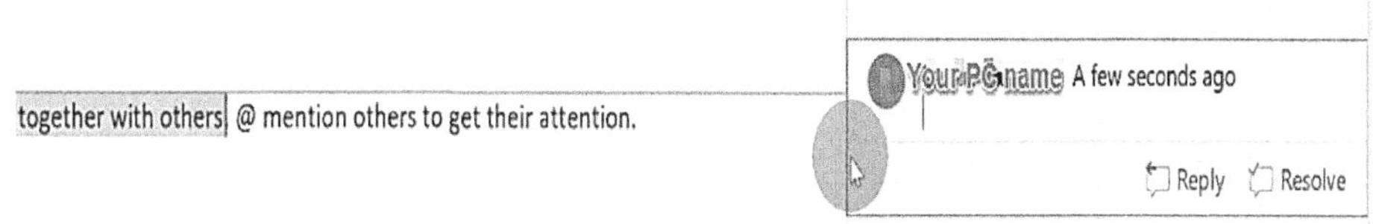

- If you want to get someone's attention, simply start with an at "@" symbol, then you will be shown people within your list to be mentioned on your comment, which they are also going to be notified about

- Once you type or select the name of the person you want to add to your comment, you are going to be informed on granting access into your commented document by selecting either you "Share and notify" or "Don't share" button

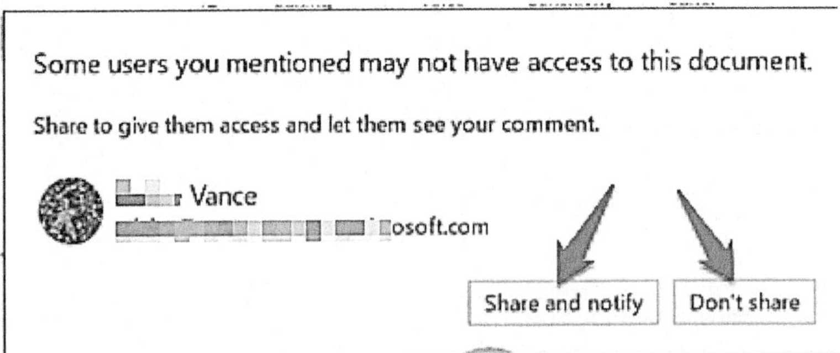

- Once you select "Share and notify", their names will appear at your comment session, then, you can now type what you want them to do about your comment when your notification reaches the other end

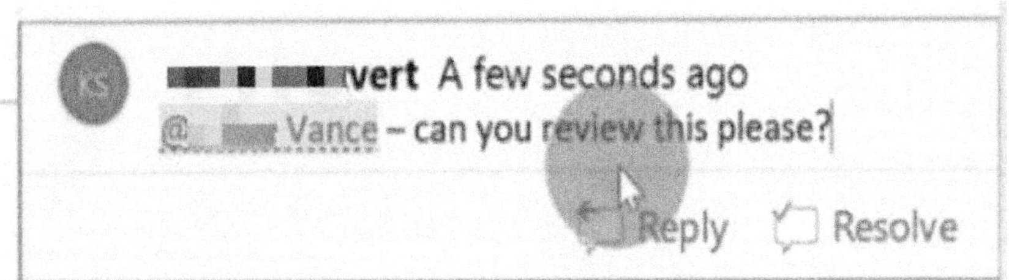

Pinning a Document

Another hidden feature on Word 365 is the "pin" feature that enables you to quickly pin down a document and get back to the content in the future.

- To pin a document, simply go to "File menu"

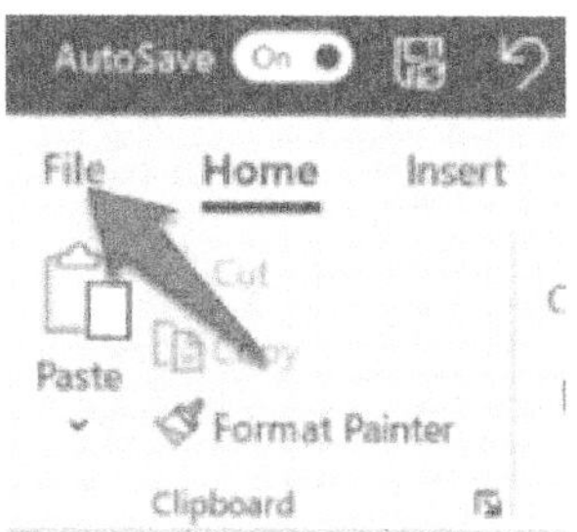

- This brings us to the backstage within your "Home view"

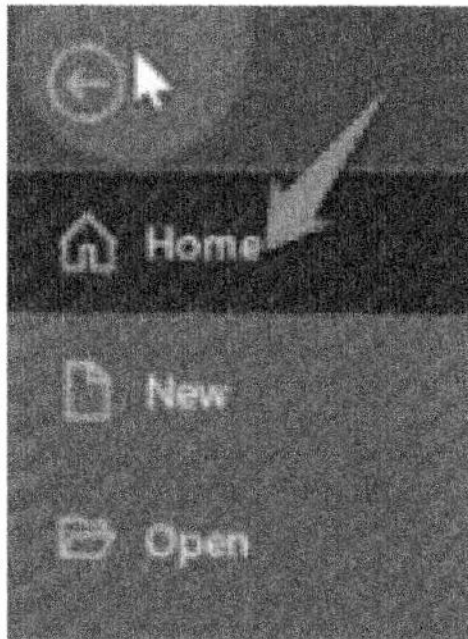

- Look at your right-hand side, you will notice all your recently opened documents

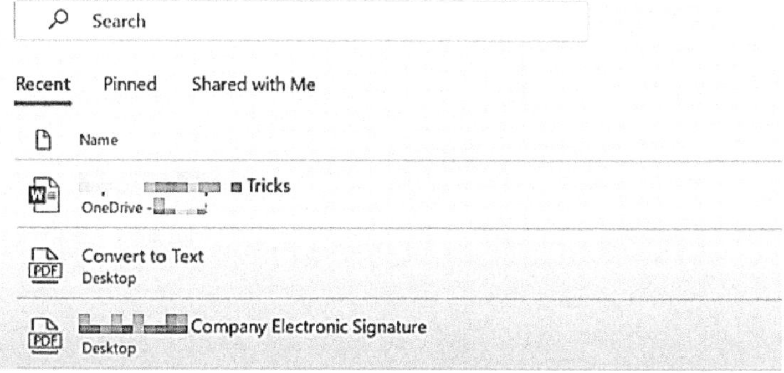

- When you click on any of the recently opened documents, on your right-hand side, you will see two icons, the first one is the "share" icon which I have explained earlier, while the second one is the "pin" icon. Click on the "pin" icon to pin your preferred document

- Once you have clicked on "pin" to pin down your preferred document, simply click on the title "Pinned" to see your pinned document.

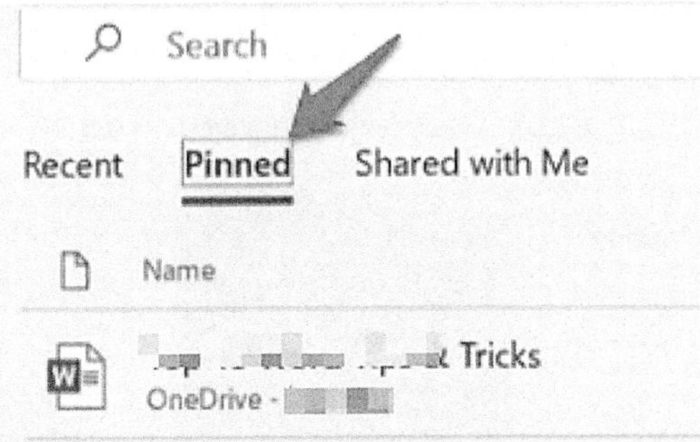

Rewrite suggestions

Another newly added feature of Microsoft Word 365 is the "Rewrite Suggestions" which gives its subscribers access to rephrase words. Let's see how it works

- Assuming I typed the below sentence

I'm **always working** to **continuously improve** my videos.

- Now, you highlight the area which you want to rephrase. Let's assume it is "always working" in the above illustration

I'm **always working** to **continuously improve** my videos.

- Right-click on the selected text, a dialog box will appear, locate and click on "Rewrite Suggestions"

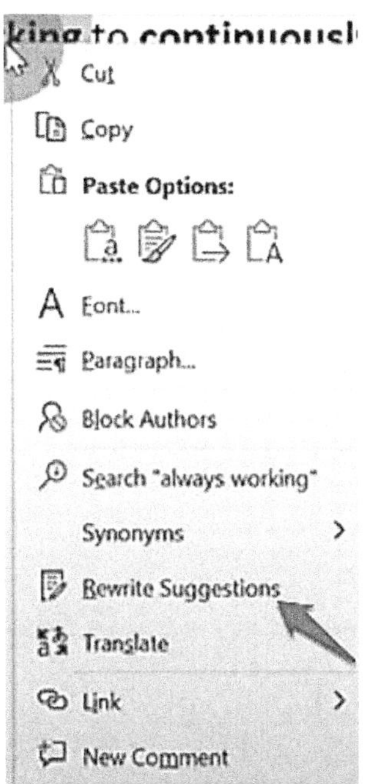

- Once you click on "Rewrite Suggestions", another dialog box will appear at your right-hand side with a suggestion of my highlighted text instead of "always working to" you can say "constantly working to" or "working all the time to"; I will click on "constantly working to"

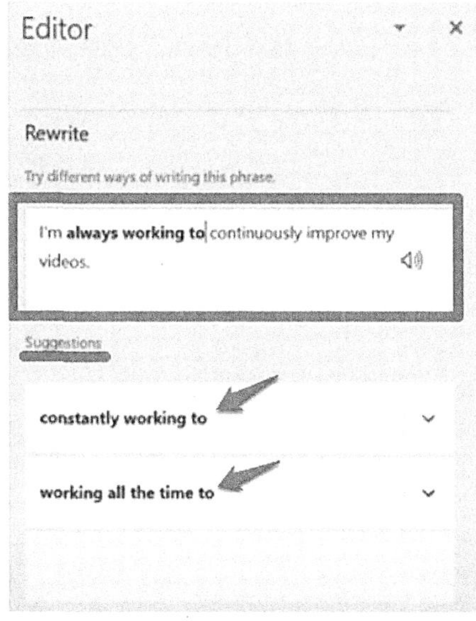

- Then my highlighted text will be replaced with “constantly working to”.

I’m constantly working to continuously improve my videos.

Assignment

Simply get another word replacement by using your “Rewrite suggestions” to rephrase “continuously improve” as illustrated below

I’m constantly working to continuously improve my videos.

Table of Contents

Microsoft Word has made it extremely easy to insert “table of contents”

- Simply go to the “References” tab

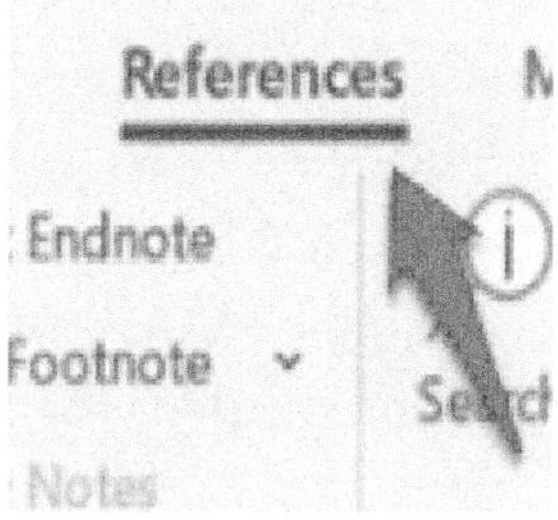

- Under “References”, at your left-hand side, you will see your “Table of Contents”, click on it

- Dropdown options of “Table of Contents” will appear where you can pick your preferred choice

Built-In

Automatic Table 1

Contents

Heading 1 1

Heading 2 1

Heading 3 1

Automatic Table 2

Table of Contents

Heading 1 1

Heading 2 1

Heading 3 1

Manual Table

Table of Contents

Type chapter title (level 1) 1

Type chapter title (level 2) 2

Type chapter title (level 3) 3

Type chapter title (level 1) 4

Type chapter title (level 2) 5

- To customize your own "Table of Contents", make sure you first highlight your headings then, go to the "Home" tab and select your "heading style" on all your headings or titles, once done, position your cursor in your document area where you want your "Table of Contents" to appear on

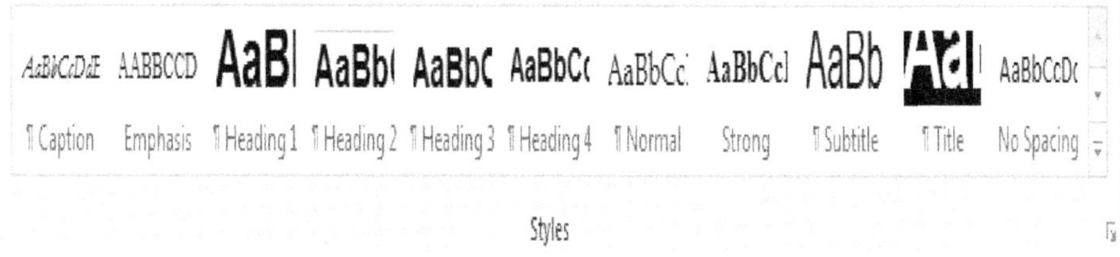

- Then, you can go back to your "References" tab to select your preferred "Table of Contents" as illustrated earlier

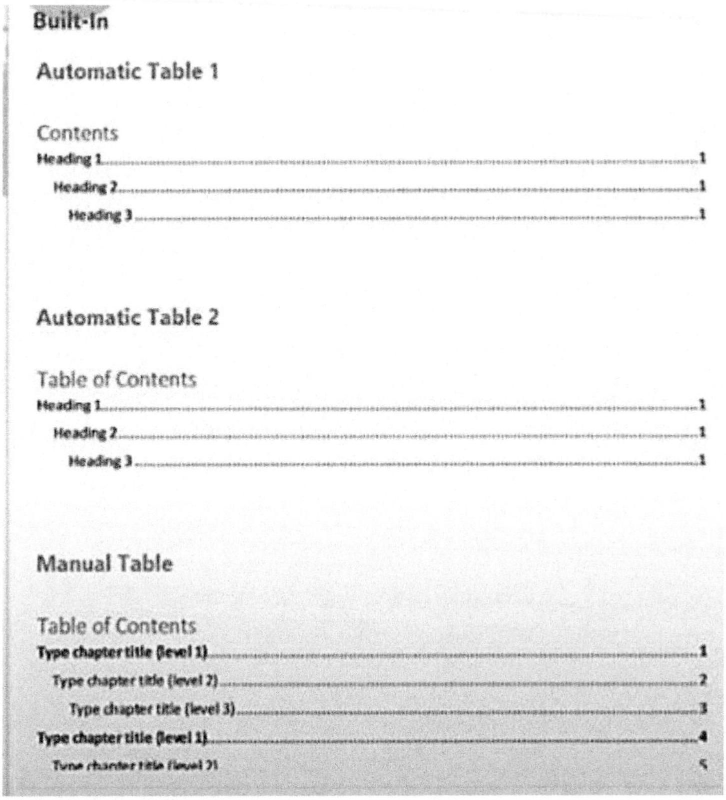

Built-In

Automatic Table 1

Contents

Heading 1 1

Heading 2 1

Heading 3 1

Automatic Table 2

Table of Contents

Heading 1 1

Heading 2 1

Heading 3 1

Manual Table

Table of Contents

Type chapter title (level 1) 1

Type chapter title (level 2) 2

Type chapter title (level 3) 3

Type chapter title (level 1) 4

Type chapter title (level 2) 5

- Then, your highlighted headings and selected heading style will enable your "table of contents" to display automatically. As you go through your document to add more words, some of your "Table of Contents" might change in numbering due to newly adjusted words

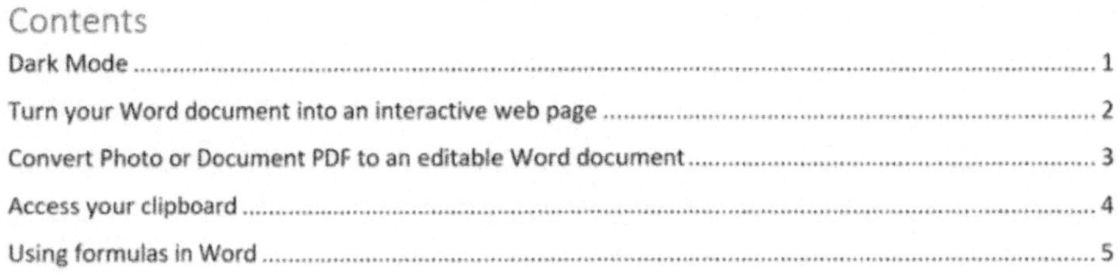

Contents

Dark Mode 1

Turn your Word document into an interactive web page 2

Convert Photo or Document PDF to an editable Word document 3

Access your clipboard 4

Using formulas in Word 5

- You can keep your "Table of Contents" updated by clicking inside the top left-hand corner of your created "Table of Contents". A little displayed dialog box will popup named "Update Table"

- When you click on "Update Table", a dialog box will appear titled "Update Table of Contents", requesting you to select one of your preferred options between "Update page numbers only" and "Update entire table"

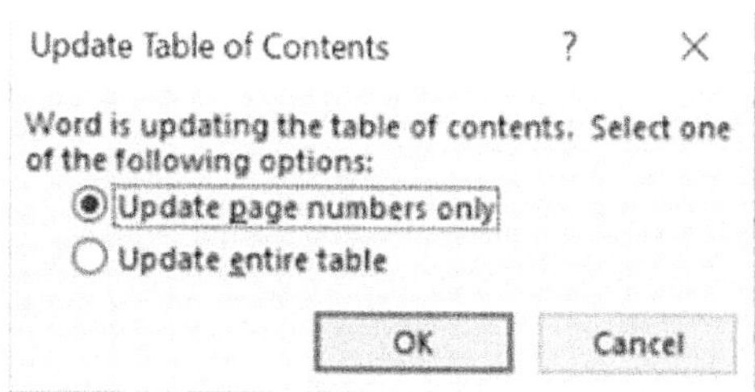

Citations and bibliography

Citation and bibliography on Microsoft Word are used to give credit to a source of information by citing the article, book, or other sources it comes from.

How to Insert Citation

To insert your citation, simply follow the steps below

- Firstly, construct a bunch of text to be cited

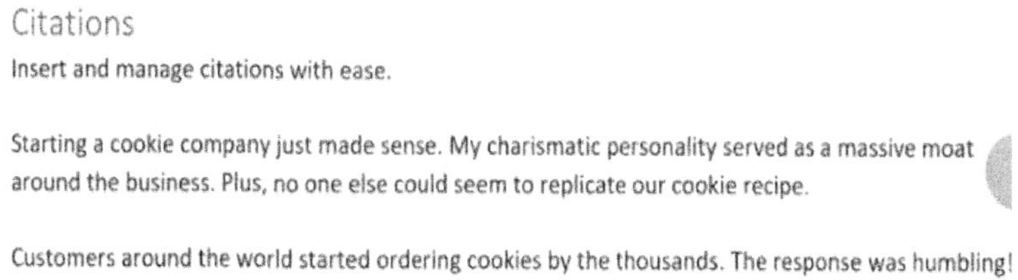

- Go to the "References" tab

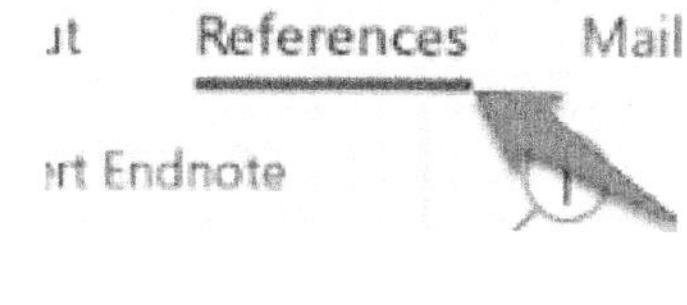

- At your right-hand side, locate "Insert Citation" and click on it

- Once you click on "Insert Citation", you will see dropdown options, choose "Add New Source" by also clicking on it

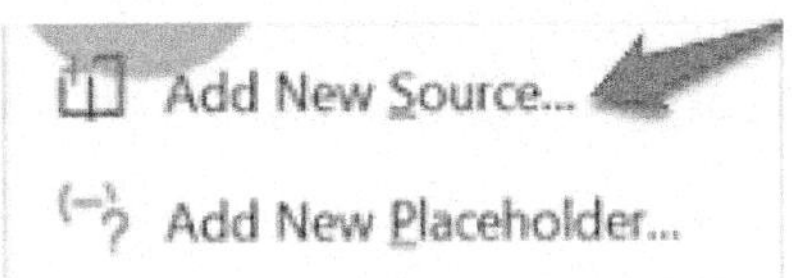

- Clicking on "Add New Source" will automatically open another dialog box titled "Create Source"

- Here, you can add all necessary information related to your source of information. For example, "Type of Source" will give you a dropdown of suggested lists to choose from about your citation, once you fill every required question, you can then click the "Ok" option

- Once you are done, your citation will automatically be added to your text

nality served as a massive moat
cookie recipe. (Williams, 2025)

How to Create Bibliography

- To also create your bibliography, you can first get your "Style" format. Assuming, we choose the first option which is APA style

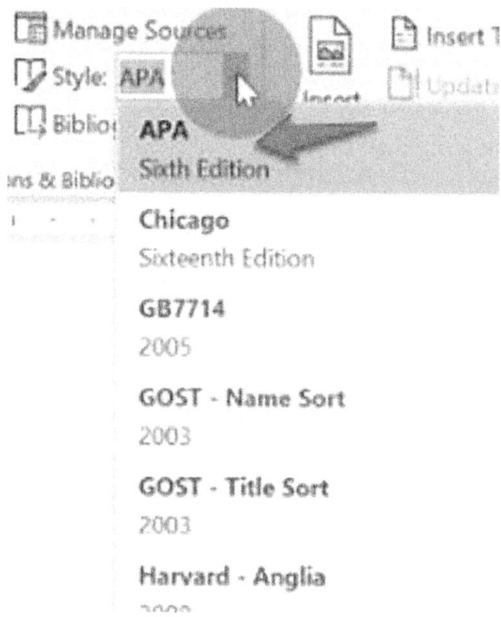

- Next, let also click on "Bibliography"

- A displayed dropdown list of “Bibliography” will appear, for understanding purpose, I will select “Works Cited”

- Then, your configured bibliography will appear below

Works Cited

Williams, J. (2025). *How the [illegible] Company took over the food industry.* New York: Stratvert Publishing.

- You can also update subsequent citation by clicking on the “Bibliography” table and at your top left-hand corner, you will see “Update Citations and Bibliography”

Conclusion on Word 365

Wow, am glad you were able to make it through this practical guide (Book 1) on Word 365. Now that you have gone through the process of learning, you can now see the power behind reading the right book. I believe you have no more worries about Word 365 again.

I encourage you to also use this knowledge to contribute towards the wellbeing of humanity in your unique way, which in turn, your value will be appreciated in a greater way than you can ever imagine, how do I know this? This is the foundation of how Bill Gate, the founder of Microsoft started his pathway in life.

Can you compare before you went through this guide, and now after going through this guide? Now you fully understand what I meant by practical guide for all, irrespective of your career path.

Kindly, share with us your experience of this guide, looking forward to hear from you soon.

BOOK TWO

EXCEL 365

INTRODUCTION

Excel Office 365 is a new update patching into an excel program and it uses a more powerful tool that can allow you to create a document in a better way and to work with others conveniently. Excel 365 permits you to put together a lot of information from various people and sectors into a single worksheet, above all, you will be permitted to work with two or more persons on a similar worksheet at the same time which in turn improves efficiency and leads to a new vision for an organization as information is shared with all relevant personalities within the organization. In the same vein, it introduces an Excel pivot that can let you convert Excel into a driving force that can combine considerable volumes of data from numerous sources and construct a connection between them.

It is the free version of Excel that allows you to use a web browser by signing up for a Microsoft account with a new email or an existing email address with monthly or yearly payment to have access to Excel 365 features as well as the privilege to update to the latest version and effective security updates and bug fixes.

Above all, it securely stores all your document into the cloud with 1 TB of one cloud storage, nevertheless, you can access this cloud anywhere.

Do not get it twisted, Online Excel remains Microsoft Excel with a few differences from the traditional Excel. For instance, you run Excel on your computer by navigating to the start menu, search for Excel and click on it to open it, while Excel Online runs on the cloud and it can only be accessed with your web browser over the Internet by using Outlook.com or Gmail.com.

Once you acquaint yourself with the traditional Excel, you will find Online Excel interface very easy to work with because they are very similar in major aspects, though with little but significant differences, and thus there won't be a problem using Excel 365.

This is a well-designed user guide for all levels of users that is produced to grant you the prerequisite skills and knowledge you need to produce an accurate worksheet be it from a blank document or template with the necessary formulas for all data and text values input.

CHAPTER ONE

OVERVIEW OF MICROSOFT EXCEL

Origin of Excel

Microsoft has been in existence since early 1980 but it began to come into the limelight in 1987/1988 when Excel version 2.0 was released. It started to gain significance during the release of Excel version 5.0 with the inclusion of VBA (Visual Basic for Application) which opened many opportunities for crunching data and present the result to offices and organizations for use.

The present version of Excel is the newest release of Excel version 2019 and Excel 365 which because of their capability and the change they bring to every business demand has helped them to gain popularity and be used in the universe. Using Excel with other Microsoft applications will do greater leveraging because there can only be little that will be unachievable when they come together.

Meaning of Excel

Excel is a spreadsheet application with the major purpose of organizing and carrying out calculations on data. It is a tool for recording, analyzing data, and representing such data on a graph or chart. It is the most potent electronic application for data analysis and documentation. It comprises several rows and columns, which in turn comprises data or pieces of fact through which you can build a formula or edit it.

Relevance of Excel

The relevance of Excel cannot be overemphasized, this makes it a preferable spreadsheet application over other spreadsheet programs, and this is the key reason why it always finds expression in both small and big offices. To say the fact, we can't talk about all Excel relevance, but we will touch the essential ones.

Among what makes Excel relevant are the following:

1. It is used in keeping track of expenditures you made and for monthly budget preparation.
2. Effective modeling and practically analyzing every data
3. It is used to create a formula and edit the formula.
4. Good for finance and accounting analysis.
5. It is used to create a check and balance of a report and checkbook.
6. Performing work easier and faster.
7. Performing better in making a concise and accurate prediction.
8. Virtually developing the new feature on every new release for proper calculation such as CONCATENATE and TEXTJOIN in Excel 2019.
9. It is used in storing and manipulating data.

What Is Excel 365?

Excel 365 is an online-based version of Excel with a monthly or yearly subscription which you can operate on the Web or Cloud and thereby grant you the privilege of getting new features anytime there is a new release of any kind. It permits you to save your document both on the Cloud and hard disc or storage device.

Differences Between Excel 365 And Traditional Excel Such As (2013, 2019 And Others)

Talking about Excel 365 and traditional Excel, there may be many similarities, nevertheless, there are few differences, they may be few, but significant. Let us delve into those differences in a jiffy:

PRICING METHODS (EXCEL 365)

It involves continuous monthly or yearly payments. It is just like leasing a house, immediately you stop paying, you stop enjoying the features, though it may be a continuous payment, yet, it is very little compared to an exorbitant one-time purchase.

	Monthly cost	Annualized cost	Number of users
Office 365 Personal	$7	$84	1
Office 365 Home	$10	$120	6
Office 365 Business	$8.25	$99	5 PCs/Macs for 1 user

TRADITIONAL EXCEL (2016, 2019, etc.)

It involves a one-time purchase and when you pay for it once, you enjoy it forever, nevertheless, you will not enjoy the new features unless you will have to pay for such. For instance, when new versions come, perhaps version 2022, 2025, etc. to enjoy any feature that comes with the newer version, you are going to pay an exorbitant price that comes with it.

UPDATED VERSIONS AND FEATURES (EXCEL 365)

It always stays updated whenever there is a release of newer versions or features including security updates and bug fixes. For instance, if there is a release of Excel 2022 or 2023 in the future, you will be informed when it is out and you will get the features of such version to your application with a single click on the **update** option and it will be downloaded to your system. In short, no need for any future payments aside from the monthly and yearly payments you have been paying.

TRADITIONAL EXCEL (2016, 2019, etc.)

It does not stay updated, when there is a release of a newer version, you will not even get to know, unless other users tell you. Besides that, you will have to pay another exorbitant amount before you can enjoy any newer features or versions including security update and bug fixes. In short, before you can enjoy a new feature, you will have to make a substantial payment again unless if your version will not be updated and you continue with the older version and features.

DOCUMENT SAVING TYPES (AUTOSAVING OR AUTO RECOVER)

EXCEL 365

It has an Autosaving format of saving a document, by saving automatically to OneDrive. When you are working with Excel 365, you do not have an issue with system crash or power breakdown and thus, you have nothing to lose, even if the system you are using gets destroyed or gets lost. In short, it has an ever-reliable saving format because you can access such documents anywhere in the world.

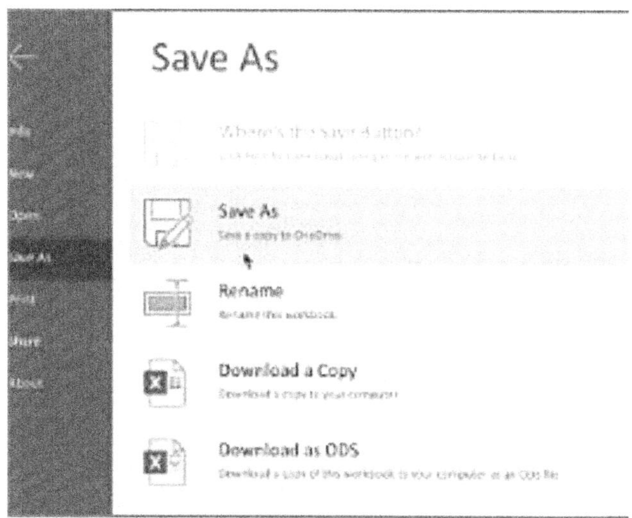

TRADITIONAL EXCEL (2016, 2019, etc.)

It has an Auto recover format of saving a document, by helping you recover the document you forgot to save maybe as a result of power breakdown or other things which may necessitate auto recovering of a document. Note that you have to meet the conditions of auto recovering before it can recover such a document. Nevertheless, it has a limitation, if the system crashes or gets lost; any document recovered or saved to that system has gone with it.

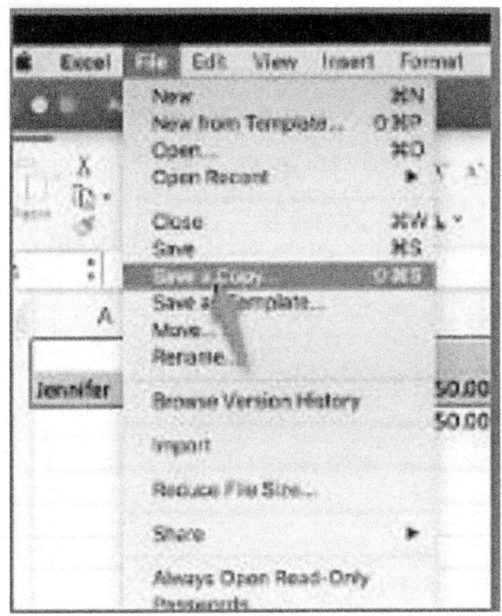

COLLABORATION (EXCEL 365)

You can collaborate and work with others through co-authoring feature which permits people to work together on a single document at the same time from anywhere in the world. This is done with an invitation via a link. To do this, single-click on “share” and enter their e-mail contact.

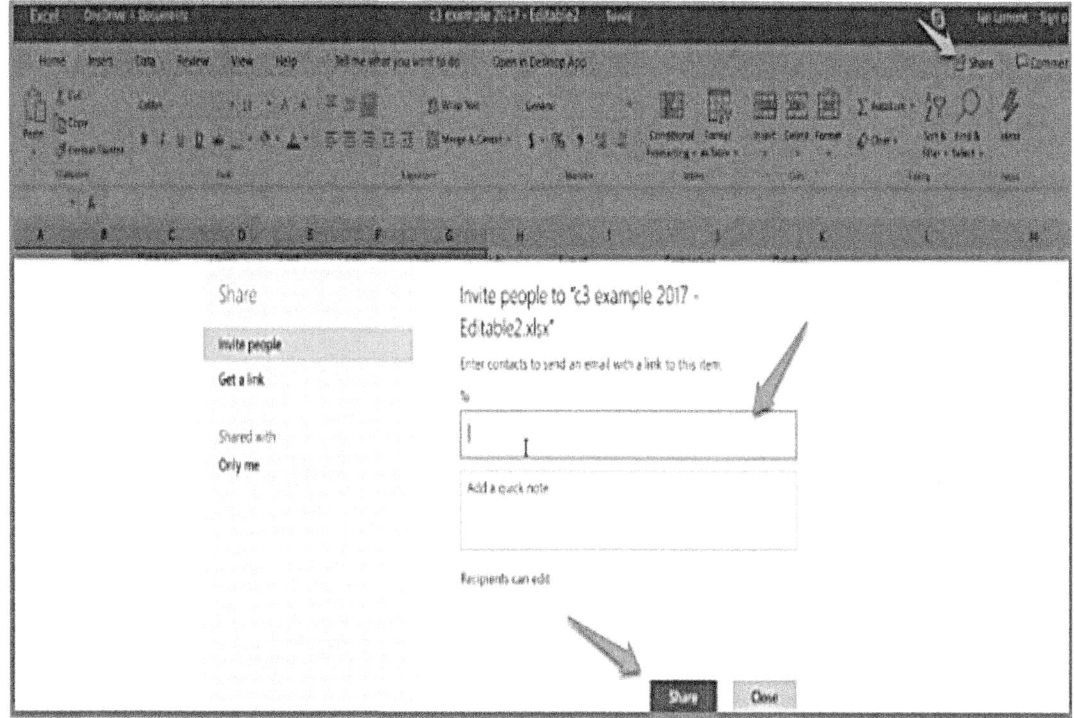

TRADITIONAL EXCEL (2016, 2019, etc.)

You can't collaborate with others, you are the only person that can work on the document unless you send the document to another email, and still, you can't work together on it at the same time with the person you sent it to.

SUB RIBBON MENU (EXCEL 365)

The sub ribbons of Excel 365 are not many; they involve basic tools for data analysis. They have a similar menu tab and you will notice they are the same but, immediately you click on each tab or ribbon, you will notice that they are little, each contains the basic tools.

TRADITIONAL EXCEL (2016, 2019, etc.)

It has full sub ribbons, it includes all the tools for data analysis and when you click on each tab or ribbon, you will observe it contains every tool you need for data analysis.

Similarities Between Excel 365 And Traditional Excel (Such As 2013, 2019 And Others)

Let us check the similarities between them, though we can't mention all, yet, we will mention the major ones.

1. Both are downloaded into the computer
2. Both are spreadsheets for recording and analyzing data.
3. The Window screen and menu tab are almost the same.

Importance of Excel 365

Excel 365 comes with a lot of benefits, but we will just make mention of the few essential ones which are:

1. Instant communication in and out of the organization: Excel 365 helps to forward instant messages to co-workers and invite them for online meetings to rub minds together on a particular document and work on it at the same time to reach a meaningful conclusion.
2. Security mindset priority: your Excel 365 document is scanned every minute, 24 hours a day to fight against malware of any type, and thus safeguard your document and information.
3. Cost-conscious and flexible: aside from pay as you go, that is, paying stipends for the service you are receiving from Excel 365, you can as well stop the payment when you do not need the service anymore, and also make payments again anytime you need the service again. This allows for immediate flexibility according to the trend.
4. 24 hours accessibility: having a consistent internet provider grants you access to the document, program, and other information on your Excel 365 program.

CHAPTER TWO

START YOUR EXPLOIT WITH EXCEL

Creating and Opening A New Excel Workbook

Before we go into creating a new excel workbook, what is a workbook? The workbook is an excel document that contains one or more worksheets that you can use to arrange your data. A workbook can be created from a blank document or an available template.

To create Excel workbook from a blank document, you have to:

- Navigate to the **start menu** and **scroll down or** you type **its name and** click on **Excel** to launch it**.**

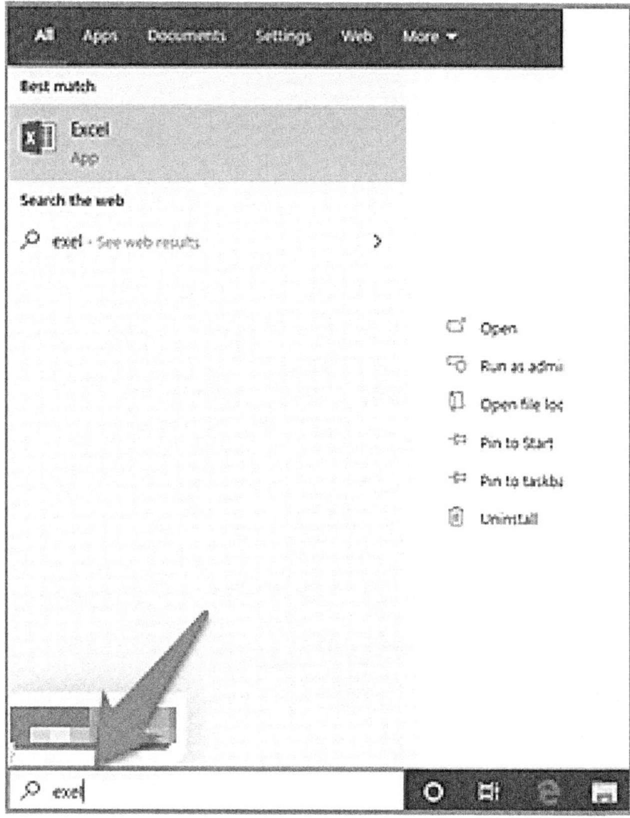

- Click on **New**, then click on **Blank Workbook**

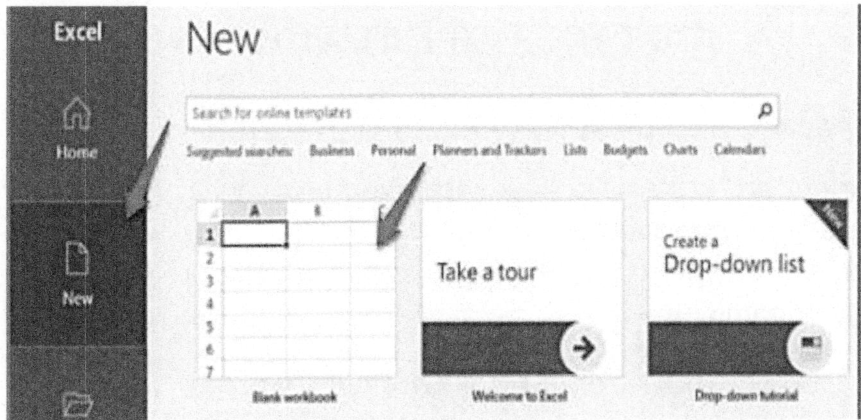

- Click on **each cell** and begin to **input data.**

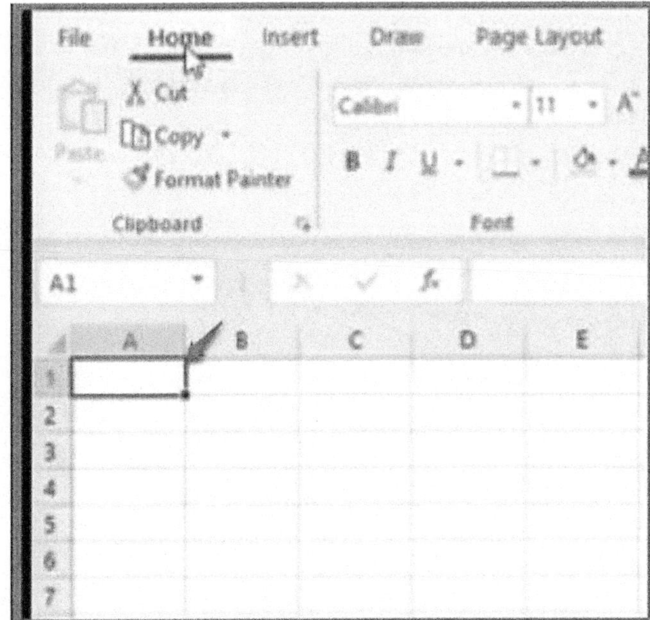

To create Excel workbook from a template, after you must have opened the Excel program, kindly:

- Search for the **desired template** by scrolling through the templates or type its name in the search box for the online template and then double-click on the desired one.

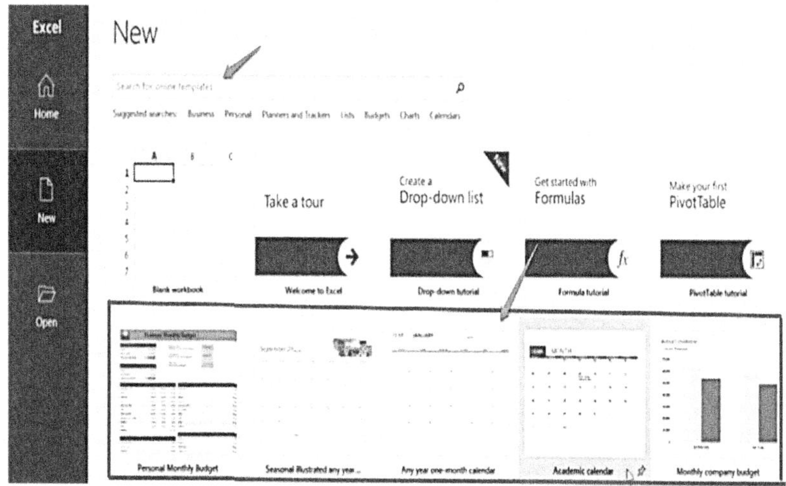

- Click on **each cell** and begin to input your data.

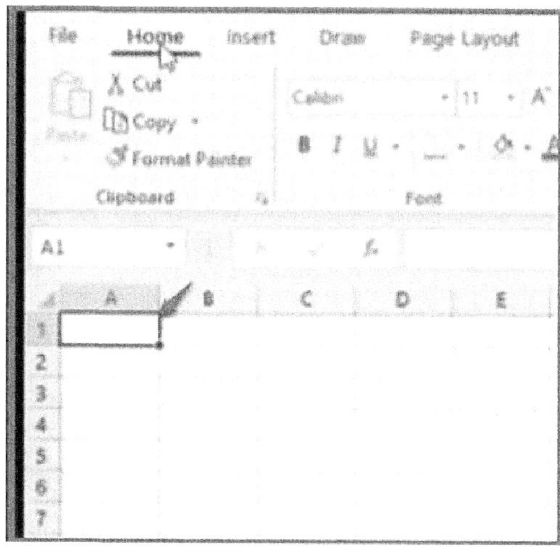

Note: Excel connects you to the online database with more than thousands of databases you can make use of.

Getting Familiar with The Excel Interface

Excel interface comprises of several keys which you can use together to produce a meaningful assignment, such as:

(1) **Excel document:** Excel document is called **a workbook**; the default name is **book 1**.

(2) **Excel ribbon:** it is broken into tabs, such as File, Home, Insert, and so on, they are used to perform specific commands. When you click on each tab, you will be able to see the various sub-grouping.

(3) Name and formula bar:

a. **The name box** is located at the upper left side above the Excel column and it usually displays the address of the current cell.

b. **The formula bar** is located after the **name box** to the right side and it is used to display the content of the current cell.

(4) Column, row, and cell:

a. **Columns** are the cells arranged vertically in the spreadsheet.

b. **Rows** are the cells arranged horizontally in the spreadsheet.

c. **A cell** is the intersection of row and column; it is represented by a rectangular box.

(5) **Worksheet navigation key**: this is a button that permits worksheet forward and backward movement within a workbook with a single click on each button.

(6) **Status bar:** it tells you the current mode of each worksheet such as:

a. **Ready mode:** it means you have not entered anything into the worksheet.

b. **Enter mode**: this means you are currently typing something into the worksheet.

c. **Edit mode**: it means you are correcting the current cell that has data inside. This is done by double-clicking on the cell to be corrected.

(7) **Plus icon**: this is a link to add more worksheets to your workbook. The more you click on it, the more worksheet you will be having within your workbook.

(8) **Worksheet:** this is the whole workspace where you can insert the numbers, letters, and formulas to carry out intended calculations.

(9) **Scroll bar**: it is the bar that navigates you to any other position within the worksheet and also an indicator of your current position.

(10) **Zoom Slider**: it is used to adjust the worksheet view by increasing or reducing the zoom ratio of the worksheet.

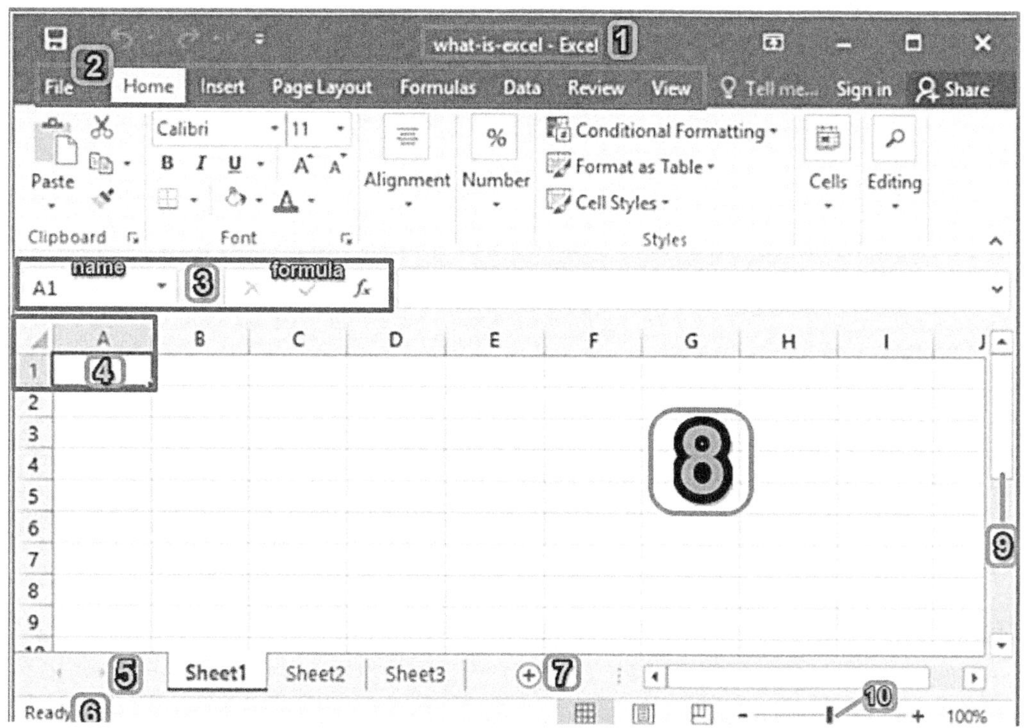

Understanding Rows, Columns, And Cell Addresses

Row carry headings with numbers, they are in the vertical level of the worksheet, and are identified with **numbers 1, 2, 3,** and so on. It ranges from 1 to 1048576.

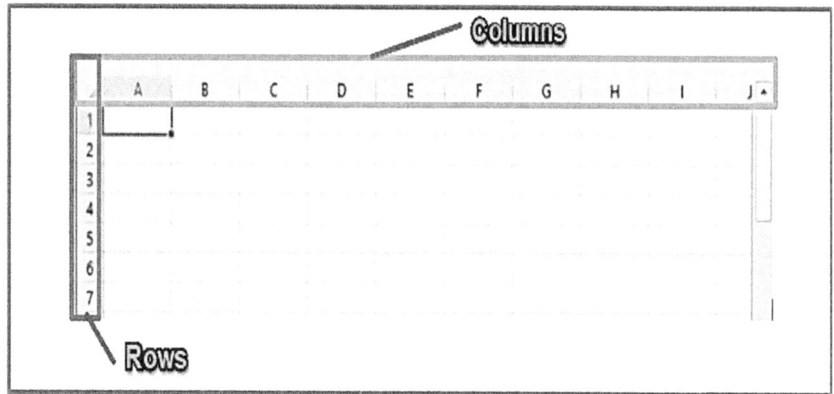

Column carry headings with letters, they are in the horizontal level of the worksheet, and are identified with **letters A, B, C,** and so on. It ranges from A to XFD.

A cell is a rectangular box that represents a point of intersection between columns and rows. This point of intersection is called cell reference, and it is used to address each cell. There are over thousands of rectangles (cell) inside a single spreadsheet.

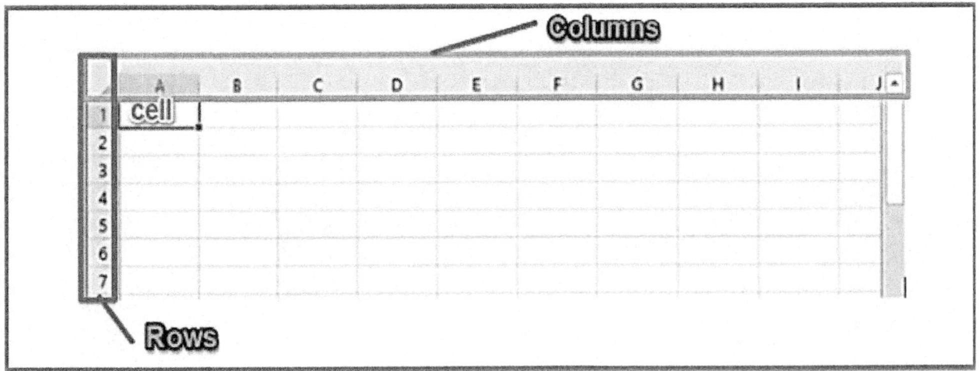

Cell range is the group of two or more cells. Cell range is addressed by **the first** and **last cell** in the cell range. For instance, the selected cell here is (A1:A8)

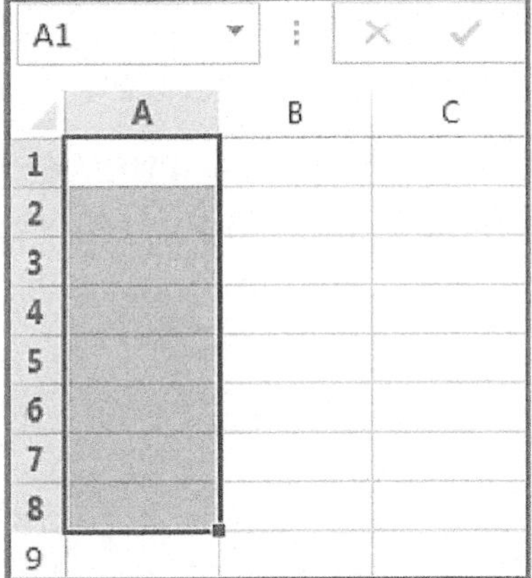

Workbooks And Worksheet

Excel Workbook is simply a file, or a document, or a book that consists of one or more worksheets with countless kinds of connected information. The workbook contains many worksheets with the drive to organize and arrange relevant data in a single place but in a different grouping which is known as a worksheet. Workbooks can hold unending amounts of worksheet depending on the size and magnitude of the data.

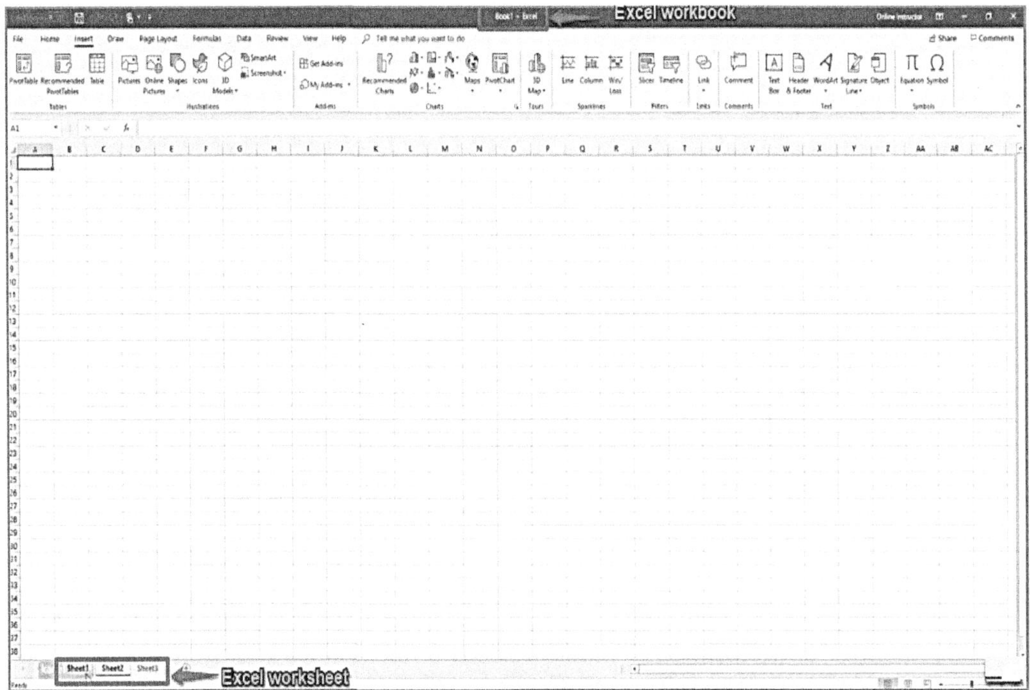

Excel worksheets can be likened to a single work page or spreadsheet in which Excel users can write, edit, and control data while the collection of such is what is referred to as a **workbook**. Though the worksheet is a single work page, it is a complete work page that contains a box of rectangular cells which is the intersection of rows and columns that you can use to reference each cell (Address). You can have as many as possible worksheets inside the workbook because there is no limit to the number of the worksheet that can be inside the workbook.

Entering Data in The Worksheet Cell

Data can be inserted in various ways in Excel. You can insert your data in a single cell, in many cells, or even more than a single worksheet at once. The data carries different forms such as texts, numbers, dates, or time.

Note: perhaps you cannot enter or edit data in a worksheet, such a worksheet might have been protected to avoid data being changed unintentionally either by you or another user. A locked/protected worksheet will allow you to view what is inside the cell but will not permit you to type or edit the cell.

To **unprotect the worksheet**:

- Go to the **Review tab.**
- Move to the **Changes** group and then to the **unprotect sheet** option and below, click **OK.** If it has a password, you will have to input the **password** before you can unprotect it.

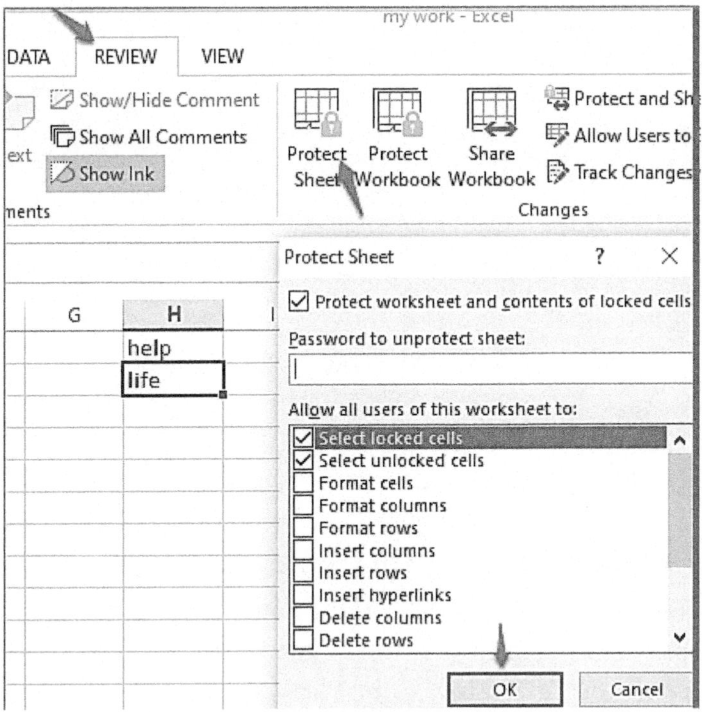

The Basic Knowledge of Entering Data

To enter data into an Excel worksheet, you have to understand what you have to avoid and what you have to practice to avoid frustration and difficulty later on and such basic knowledge will make using Excel tools, functions, and features very easy to use. The following are what you should put at the top of your mind as you begin entering data into the worksheet:

(1) **Do not leave an empty row or column as you are entering associated data:** any empty row or column inside a range of data or data table obstructs appropriate use of several Excel features such as charts, specific functions, pivot tables, and so on.

	A	B	C	D	E	F
1				Restaurant sales book		
2				April	may	june
3	Revenue from sales:					
4	pawpaw			$150	$180	$150
5	orange			$300	$250	$400
6	pearl			$100	$500	$180
7						

The nonexistence of empty spaces aid Excel to select related data when using a range of features such as sorting, filtering, or Auto sum.

(2) **Do not use figures as column headings and do not put units with the data:** simply use heading at the top of the column, not figures such as 200, 300, and 400, etc. when you use word heading such as equipment, advertising, etc. and not figures, it will make sorting easier

	A	B	C	D	E	F
1				Restaurant sales book		
2	Revenue from sales:					
3				2018	2019	2020
4	pawpaw			$150	$180	$150
5	orange			$300	$250	$400
6	pearl			$100	$500	$180
7	Total income			=SUM (D3:D6)		

If you use numbers as row and column headings, such may be mistakably included in the calculations, and also, using formula and function may not give adequate result when it includes all numbers in the calculation.

(3) **Keep unconnected data separately:** it is expedient to keep similar data together and at the same time it is very paramount to separate every unconnected data. Ensure to put a blank row or column between unalike data range on the worksheet so that excel will choose the correct connected ranges or tables of data.

(4) **Excel aligns texts to the left and numbers to the right:** this is the default alignment of the data which gives you the clue if you have input your data correctly and if it is formatted correctly in the worksheet.

(5) **Using cell references and named ranges in using formulas:** endeavor to use cell references and named ranges when you are using formulas so that the formulas and whole spreadsheet will be error-free and accurate.

E5 | fx | 250

	A	B	C	D	E	F
1				Restaurant sales book		
2	Revenue from sales:					
3				April	May	June
4	pawpaw			$150	$180	$150
5	orange			$300	$250	$400
6	pearl	cell reference		$100	$500	$180
7	Total income			550		

Tips: cell references recognize the position of the data by combining the row of numbers and column of letters (a single cell) while named ranges are used to recognize a range of cells in a worksheet (multiple cells combine).

(6) **Use of percent and Unit (currency, temperature, distance, and other units) symbols:** do not type percent and units' symbol along with numbers because Excel will recognize them as text, therefore, ensure you enter all your numbers to the worksheet then after the insertion of the numbers you can format the cell to display the accurate figures either as a percentage, currency or other units. Nevertheless, some Excel recognizes the British pound (£) and dollar ($) currency sign if you type them along with numbers in the cell, but every other currency symbols are not recognized and thus they will be interpreted as text, though, this is not the same for all Excel versions. To prevent such occurrence, enter the amount first then later format the cells to input currency instead of typing currency symbols along with the amount.

H6 | $260

	A	B	C	D	E	F	G	H	I
1				Restaurant sales book					
2	Revenue from sales:								
3				April	May	June			
4	pawpaw			$150	$180	$150		$200	
5	orange			$300	$250	$400		$180	
6	pearl			$100	$500	$180		$260	
7	Total income			550					
8									
9				formatting numbers				symbol with currency	

(7) **Pointing at the data:** pointing to the Excel data in a cell to enter the reference into the formulas minimizes the risk of error that may be caused by typing the wrong cell reference or address and range name misspelling.

(8) **Select the data to be sorted:** Excel has an interest in the exact range of cell data you need to sort and therefore identifies those related areas of data, even if there are:

a. Empty rows and columns between areas of related data.
b. No empty rows and columns between areas of related data.

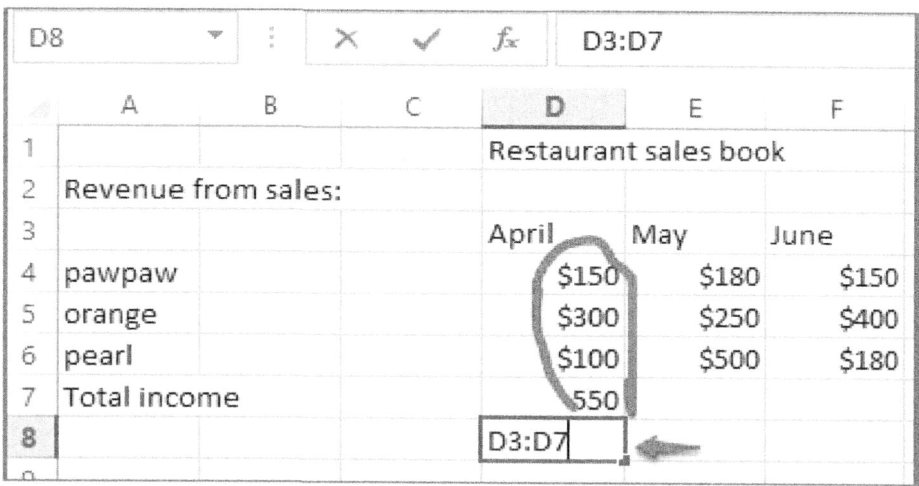

D8 | D3:D7

	A	B	C	D	E	F
1				Restaurant sales book		
2	Revenue from sales:					
3				April	May	June
4	pawpaw			$150	$180	$150
5	orange			$300	$250	$400
6	pearl			$100	$500	$180
7	Total income			550		
8				D3:D7		

Notes: Excel automatically excludes rows with field names from sorting. However, letting Excel choose the sorting area can be risky particularly when large data is involved.

Typing Your Text

The first assignment inside the worksheet is entering some headings into the rows and columns. Before you can make any data input into the worksheet, you have to make your preferred cell in which you want to input data an active cell by clicking on the cell first before typing. For instance, let us open a new blank workbook and enter some text:

1. Click **cell A2** to make it an active cell and type **Skateboarding**, press **"Enter"** to go down to another cell to make it an active cell. If you observe the text you just inserted, it seems like it stands in both A2 and B2 cells, but really, it is only in cell A2, B2 simply permits the rollover because there is no data in it. Believing the text is in cell B2 is a delusion.

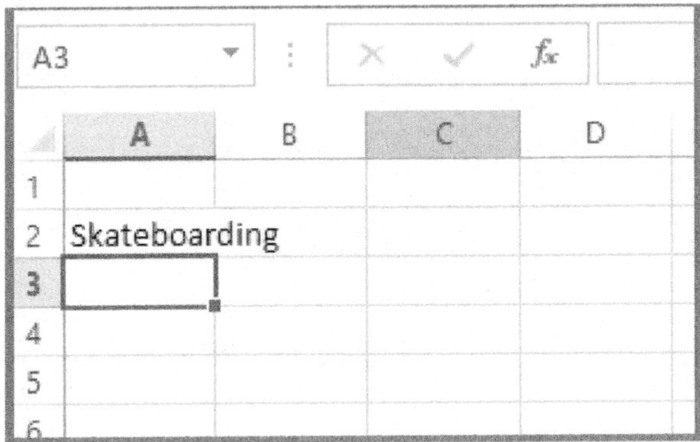

2. Let us continue and type Basketball, then press **"Enter"**.

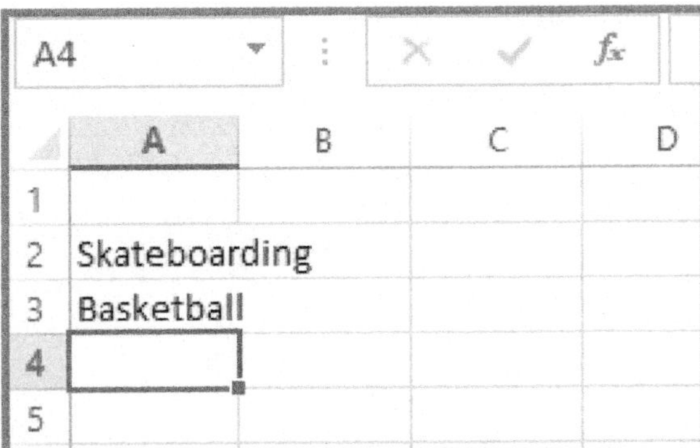

3. Repeat the above process to enter the remaining sport types in column A as shown below.

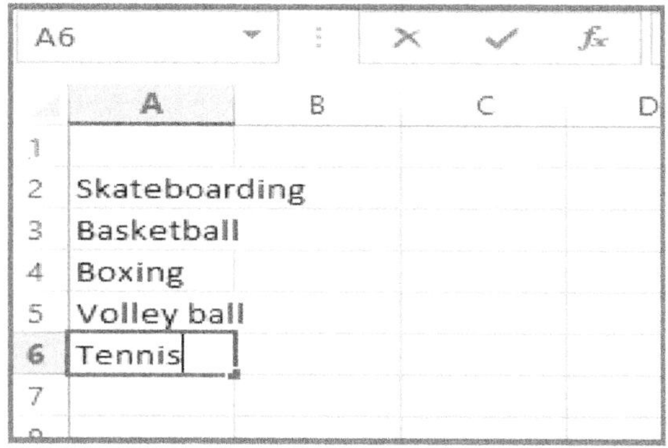

4. Click on **cell B1** and type **China**, then press **Tab** to navigate the cell to the right to make it an active cell.

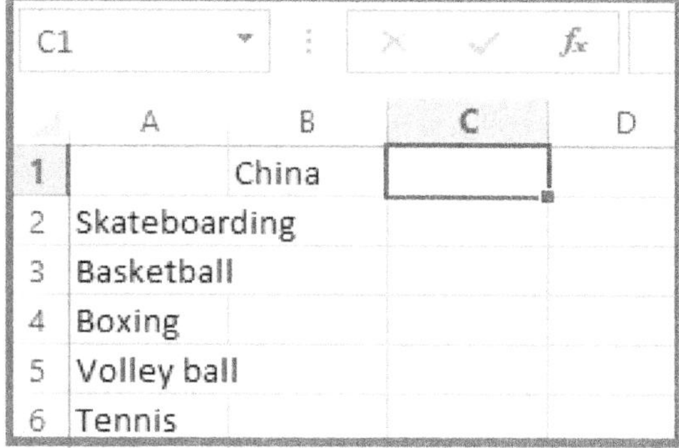

5. Enter the remaining country names in **row 1** as shown below.

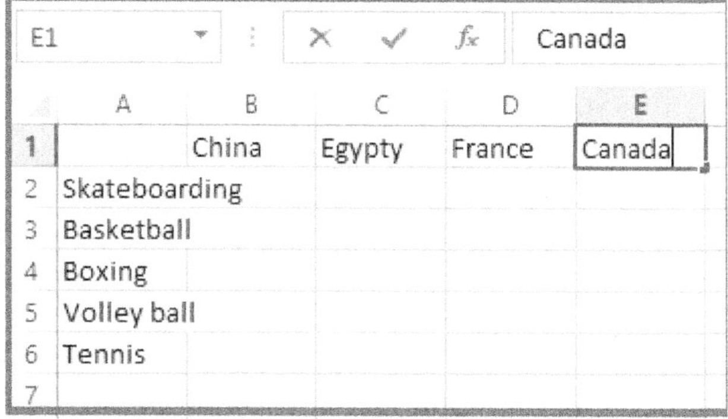

Tips: you are not restricted to use the enter or tab keys to make the cell active, you may use the arrow keys to click on each cell you want or in moving up, down, right, or left.

Typing Numeric Value

Typing number is the same way you type letters or text, by just clicking on the cell and make it active, then type the number inside. The only exception is that of the alignment, that is, the numbers will align themselves to the right side of the cell while letters align themselves to the left side of the cell, both alignments are by default. To examine how to type numbers, let us continue with the above text exercise by:

1. Clicking on **cell B2** to make it active, then type **15300,** and press **Enter** or the **down arrow**. If you observe very well, some of the texts in the left cell are not visible anymore, it is because cell B now has information inside and it has to show superiority of ownership over the texts that should not be in cell B, though some of the texts in cell A are still there.
2. Enter the remaining figures in the other cells to complete the illustration as shown below.

E6 | fx 24100

	A	B	C	D	E
1		China	Egypty	France	Canada
2	Skateboar	15300	10000	5800	12000
3	Basketbal	18500	15400	8000	6000
4	Boxing	15900	20000	24500	17000
5	Volley bal	53400	18000	16800	5000
6	Tennis	12000	6000	40000	24100

Note: to be sure of what is inside a cell (contents), click on such cell, and go to the **formula bar** at the uppermost of the worksheet to check the data contained in such active cell.

Typing Dates and Time Values

In Excel, dates are referred to a special data because immediately you insert those numbers into the cell inside the worksheet, Excel recognizes the format to which they come and instantly converts them to date. For example, 20-2, numbers like this will be converted to 20-February, from that henceforth, you can use such a date to carry out calculations.

Let us check the scenario by continuing with the previous worksheet by:

1. Clicking on **cell A8** to make it an active cell, then type **Sport at,** then tap **"Tab"** to move to the next cell.

B8

	A	B	C	D	E
1		China	Egypty	France	Canada
2	Skateboar	15300	10000	5800	12000
3	Basketbal	18500	15400	8000	6000
4	Boxing	15900	20000	24500	17000
5	Volley bal	53400	18000	16800	5000
6	Tennis	12000	6000	40000	24100
7					
8	Sport at:				

2. Type **20/03** to the active cell you have made above in (1), this number will be identified as a date and will be formatted as a date accordingly. Though you can change the format type at the latter period if you desire.

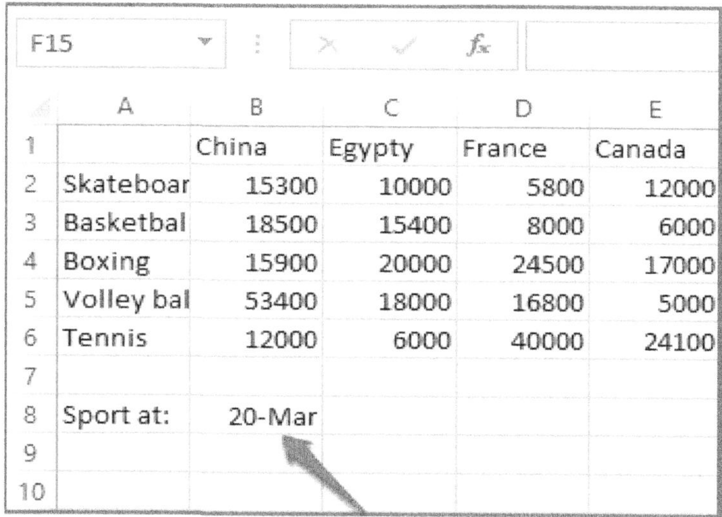

F15

	A	B	C	D	E
1		China	Egypty	France	Canada
2	Skateboar	15300	10000	5800	12000
3	Basketbal	18500	15400	8000	6000
4	Boxing	15900	20000	24500	17000
5	Volley bal	53400	18000	16800	5000
6	Tennis	12000	6000	40000	24100
7					
8	Sport at:	20-Mar			
9					
10					

3. Click on **cell A9,** and type **appraised,** then tap **"Tab"** to move to the next cell (B9).

	A	B	C	D	E
1		China	Egypty	France	Canada
2	Skateboar	15300	10000	5800	12000
3	Basketbal	18500	15400	8000	6000
4	Boxing	15900	20000	24500	17000
5	Volley bal	53400	18000	16800	5000
6	Tennis	12000	6000	40000	24100
7					
8	Sport at:	20-Mar			
9	Appraised:				

4. Go to the **formula box** and Type = **B8 + 5** and press **Enter**. **B8 + 5** is a **formula** that is referencing the date you typed above in cell B8. Formulas are used in the spreadsheet to carry out calculations just like the formula we used here by adding 5 to cell B8 (which signifies 5 days to the date).

B9 = SUM(B8 + 5)

	A	B	C	D	E
1		China	Egypty	France	Canada
2	Skateboar	15300	10000	5800	12000
3	Basketbal	18500	15400	8000	6000
4	Boxing	15900	20000	24500	17000
5	Volley bal	53400	18000	16800	5000
6	Tennis	12000	6000	40000	24100
7					
8	Sport at:	20-Mar			
9	Appraised	25-Mar			

Note: examine the alignment of your date, it should be to the right of the cell just like numbers. If the alignment is at the left, it means the date is invalid to Excel and it is not recognizing it as a date and thus, you have to take cognizance of how you enter your dates.

Taking Advantages of Flash Fill And Autofill Commands By Entering Specific Lists and Serial Data

Worksheet at times includes specific sequences of numbers drawn out of longer sequences. Entering and formatting these longer sequences will take a long time and therefore Excel has offered features like Flash Fill and Autofill to make such long tasks easier and faster. Let us quickly check how to use those features by starting with the Flash Fill.

A. **Combining data with Flash Fill:** let us begin the illustration by:

1. Opening the worksheet and input employer names; start with the First name, followed by the last name, and Establishment name in row 1 and other rows after you must have made those cells active.
2. We will assume all employers have the same format of email address which we will take as first name.last name@establishment.com.
3. We will now try to produce an automatic email address with Flash Fill by putting the first email manually. Simply click on **cell D2** and type Albert.dent@goldminers.com.

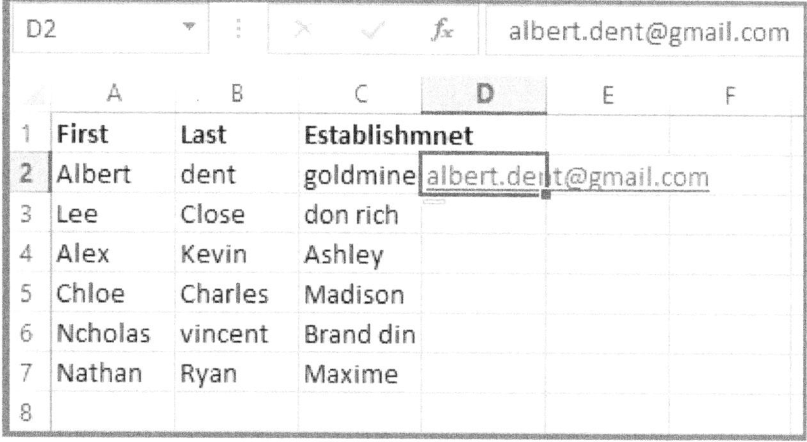

D2 | fx | albert.dent@gmail.com

	A	B	C	D	E	F
1	**First**	**Last**	**Establishmnet**			
2	Albert	dent	goldmine	albert.dent@gmail.com		
3	Lee	Close	don rich			
4	Alex	Kevin	Ashley			
5	Chloe	Charles	Madison			
6	Ncholas	vincent	Brand din			
7	Nathan	Ryan	Maxime			
8						

4. Now let us check the function of Flash Fill by navigating to the **Data tab** and click on the **Flash Fill** ribbon, Excel will operate it automatically, but ensure cell D2 remains cell active before you click on Flash Fill. Once you have done that, Excel will input the remaining employees' email by creating their email addresses based on the first email address's format.

FILE HOME INSERT PAGE LAYOUT FORMULAS DATA REVIEW VIEW

From Access | From Web | From Text | From Other Sources | Existing Connections | Refresh All | Connections | Properties | Edit Links | Sort | Filter | Clear | Reapply | Advanced | Text to Columns | Flash Fill

Get External Data | Connections | Sort & Filter

D2 | albert.dent@goldmine.com

	A	B	C	D
1	First	Last	Establishmnet	
2	Albert	dent	goldminers	albert.dent@goldmine.com
3	Lee	Close	don rich	lee.close@don rich.com
4	Alex	Kevin	Ashley	alex.kevin@ashley.com
5	Chloe	Charles	Madison	chloe.charles@madison.com
6	Ncholas	vincent	Ash cole	ncholas.vincent@ash cole.com
7	Nathan	Ryan	Maxime	nathan.ryan@maxime.com

5. If you observe row 3 and row 6 email addresses. You will notice that their establishment names have two words and spaces between them and thus those spaces were included in their respective email, let us get to correct the error.
6. Navigate to **column D** and click on **cell D3**, erase the email address inside it and type lee.close@donrich.com, the space between don and rich has been removed, now go to Flash Fill, and ensure you are still having D3 as the active cell, then click on Flash Fill to apply the same formulas to the remaining email address and you will perceive that no company name will have space in the email address again irrespective of whether there is space in their establishment name or not.

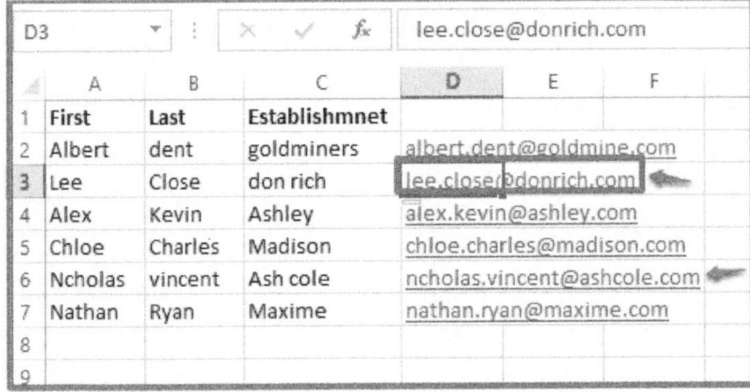

D3 | lee.close@donrich.com

	A	B	C	D
1	First	Last	Establishmnet	
2	Albert	dent	goldminers	albert.dent@goldmine.com
3	Lee	Close	don rich	lee.close@donrich.com
4	Alex	Kevin	Ashley	alex.kevin@ashley.com
5	Chloe	Charles	Madison	chloe.charles@madison.com
6	Ncholas	vincent	Ash cole	ncholas.vincent@ashcole.com
7	Nathan	Ryan	Maxime	nathan.ryan@maxime.com

Note: remember you have to enter one cell manually and use it as a formula, to let Excel know what you are trying to do.

B. **Extracting data with Flash Fill**: as you have combined data with Flash Fill, you can as well extract data with Flash Fill. How? Let us check the below illustration:

1. We are having a first name, last name, and security serial number (SSN), but the security number is not real and the actual SSN ought to be the first two (2) numbers and the last three (3) numbers of the initial SSN. Now we will be using Flash fill to extract the real SSN by clicking on **cell D2** and type **28/293** which represents the first two and last three digits of the first SSN to tell Excel what you are trying to do and what you want to do to the remaining ones.

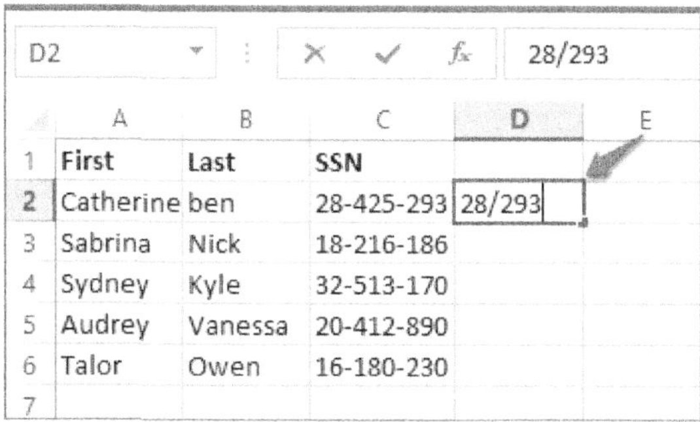

2. Ensure **cell D2** remains the active cell, now move to click the **Flash Fill** button, and you will notice Excel has grabbed the actual digits we want to extract and even add the Separator line to the digits, this is the power of Excel using Flash Fill.

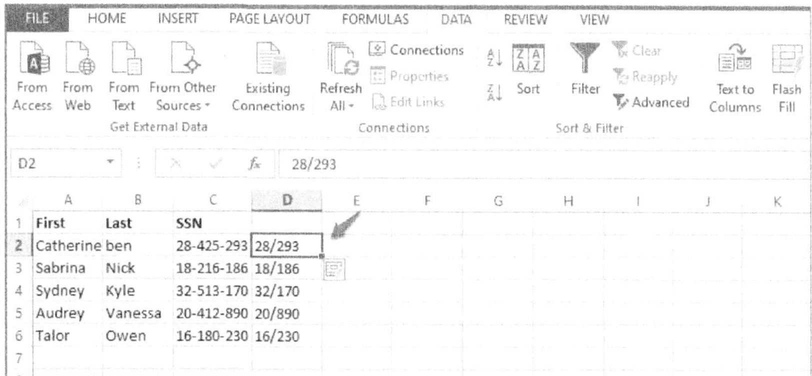

C. **Auto Fill command:** identifies a specific category of data such as consecutive numbers, dates, days of the weeks, and months of the year and therefore, instead of entering all these data manually, simply enter one or two pieces of such data and Excel will quickly fill the remaining data with the AutoFill command. To enjoy the AutoFill command, kindly observe the following processes:

1. Click **the cell** that will be the first in the sequences. For instance, list the month, and the day you want. For illustration, start with February, Wednesday, or a consecutive number such as 3.
2. Then enter the first item in sequence into the cell as stated above in (1).

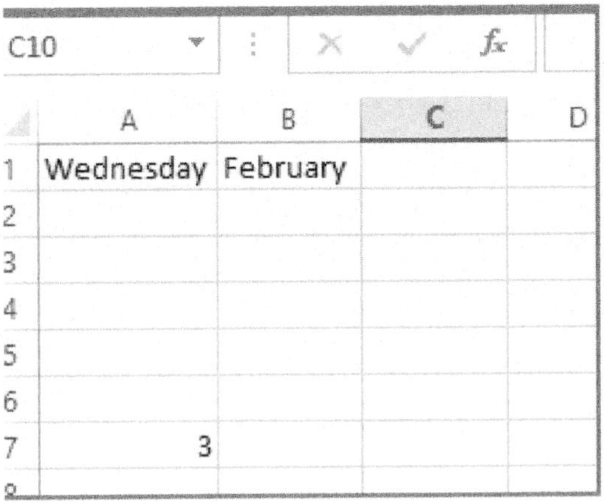

C10

	A	B	C	D
1	Wednesday	February		
2				
3				
4				
5				
6				
7	3			

3. Move to the **next cell** perhaps in row order or column order and enter the second item in the sequences such as March, Thursday, and 6, so that Excel can perfectly understand the flow of the sequences.

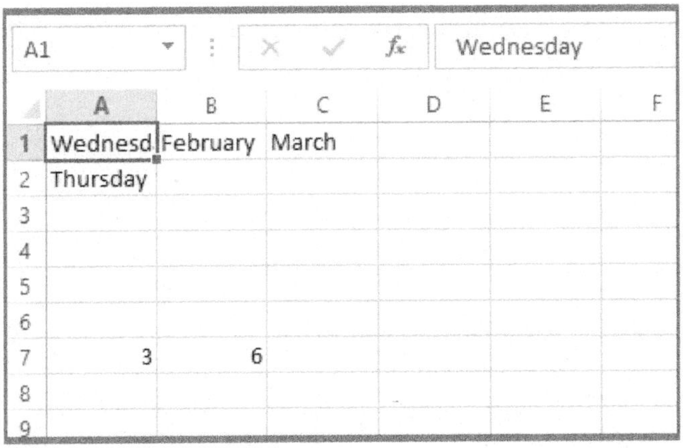

A1 Wednesday

	A	B	C	D	E	F
1	Wednesd	February	March			
2	Thursday					
3						
4						
5						
6						
7	3	6				
8						

4. You can now select the **cell or cells** you have inserted your data into, either you will select one of the two cells or both cells by a click on one cell or dragging over the two cells.
5. Then click on the **AutoFill** handle and double-click to begin dragging it to the direction you want those sequences to appear on the spreadsheet.

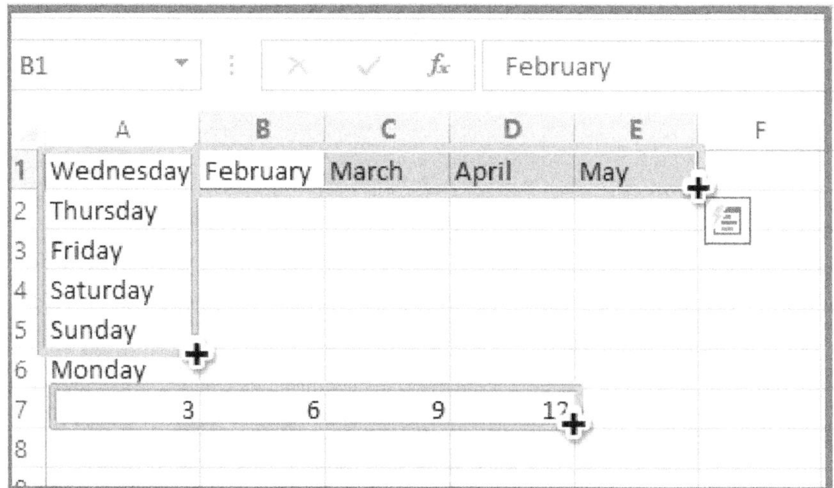

Note: **AutoFill** handle is the small green square located at the lower-right corner of the cells you selected. It is inactive until it changes to a black plus (+) sign, then you can drag it by double-clicking it. The more you drag the AutoFill handle, the more the serial data will be appearing in a pop-up box. AutoFill options appear immediately you start entering serial data, and it gives you the option to either copy or fill the cell without transferring the data along with the format.

Probably you want to enter the same item into many empty cells, drag over the cells to select those cells, then type the text or numbers you want to duplicate to other cells into the first cell in the sequence and press **Ctrl + Enter**. You can as well select those cells by holding down the Ctrl key and continue clicking on where you want the item to enter.

Applying Formatting to Numbers, Dates, Money, And Times Values

Formatting in Excel simply means changing the appearance of the numbers, dates, and times to your taste. For instance, if you type 23/3 in

a cell, Excel will change it to a date format and it will be displayed as 23-March in the cell, in the same vein you may type 11.15a, Excel will interpret it as time and show it as 11:15 AM. This format may not tally with your preference and thus you have to change it by formatting such data. To format numbers, times and dates kindly:

- Click **cell C2**, hold down the Shift key, and then click on **C7** to select a range of dates.

C2 | 15/05/2020

	A	B	C	D	E
1	First	Last	SSN		
2	Catherine	ben	15/05/2020	28/293	
3	Sabrina	Nick	23/07/2020	18/186	
4	Sydney	Kyle	13/08/2020	32/170	
5	Audrey	Vanessa	25/08/2020	20/890	
6	Talor	Owen	01/10/2020	16/230	
7	David	Henry	30/11/2020	13/153	

- Move to the **Menu bar** and click on the **Home tab,** then move to the **Number** group to see a number format.
- In the number group, click on the **Long date** option to change those selected short dates to a long and more explicit format.

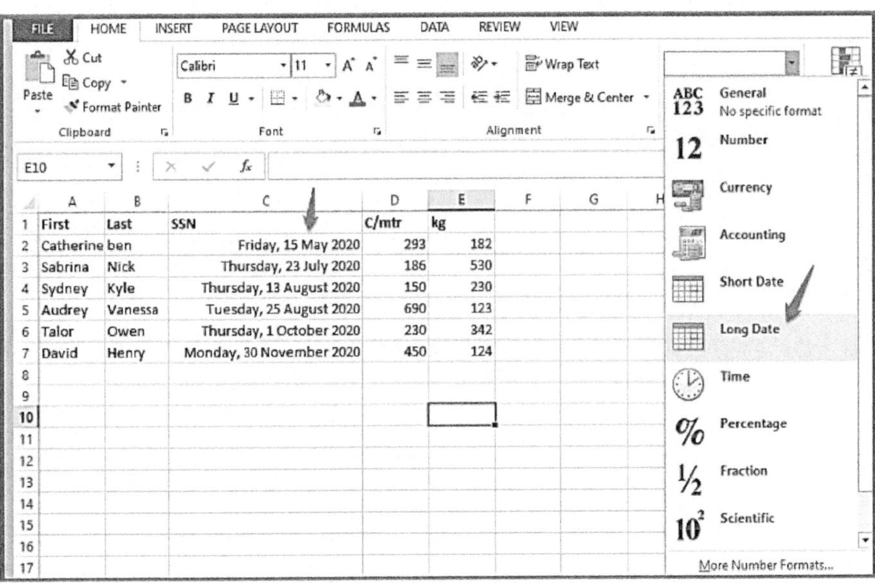

- For currency, select the range of cell D2 to cell D7, move to the **Number** group, then select **Currency**. The currency here is naira (#), you can check other currencies by moving to the "more number format" option to select your preferred currency.

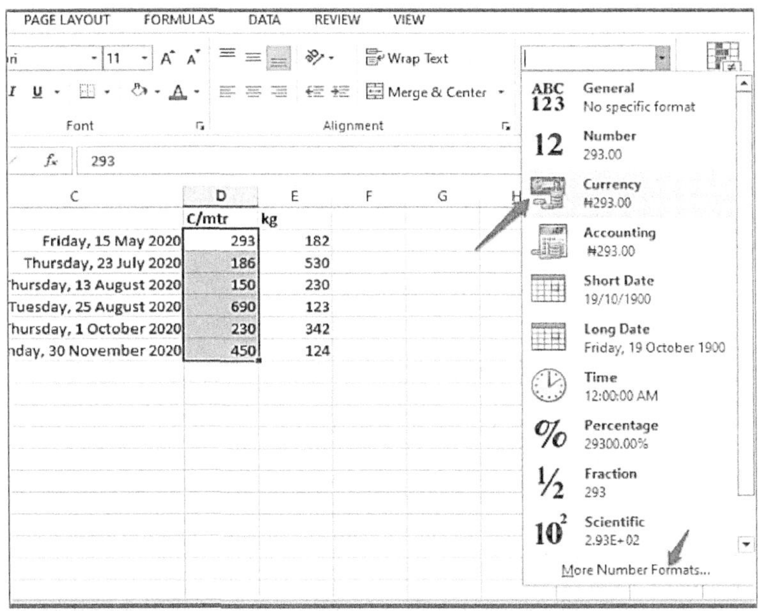

- On the Number bar, click on **Currency,** pick your preferred currency, and tap **Ok**.

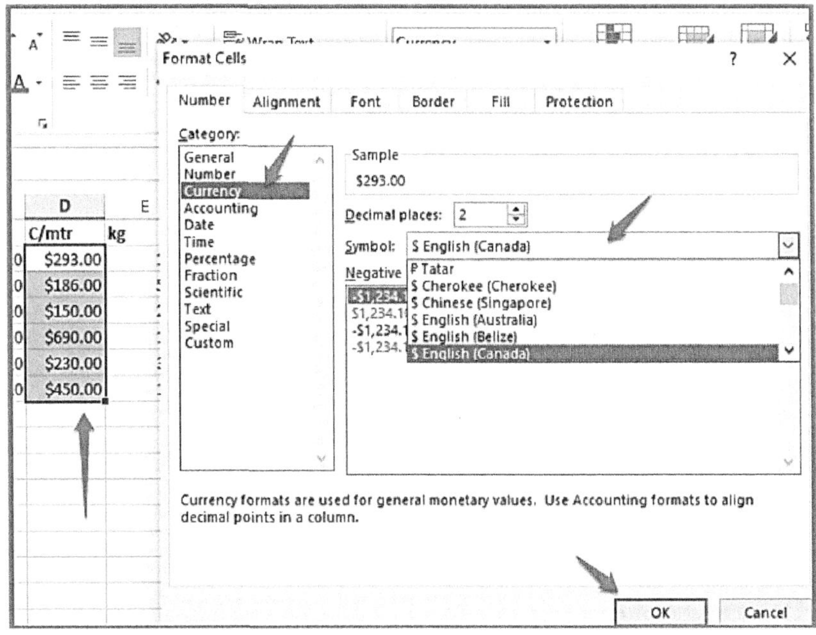

- Select a range of **Cell E2 to E7** and move to the **Number** group, then select **Number** to show numbers in two decimal places. You can still go to "More Number Format" for more options.

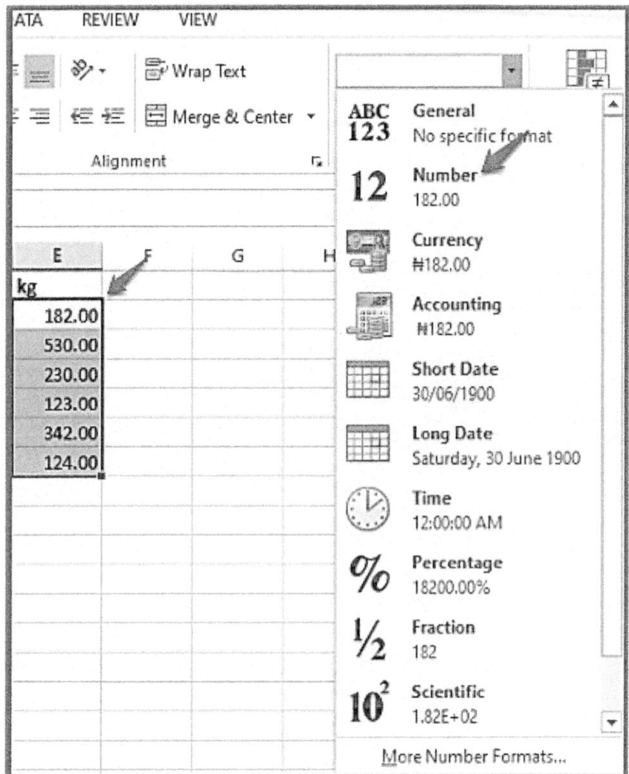

Note: you can press **Ctrl + 1** as a shortcut to access the "More Number Format" dialog box.

Essential Guide to Data Validation

Data validation is a special feature made by Excel that permits users to control what they enter into the cell. Data validation can help you to enter data in a preferred specified format, restrict the kind of data to be entered into the cell, and can be used to create a drop-down as well.

Let us now check types of data validation rule:

1. **Allowing whole numbers and decimal only:** to restrict the type of data that will enter into the cell such as whole numbers and decimal, you have to:

a. Pick **the cell** you want to restrict its data.
b. Move to the **Data tab** and select **data validation** to bring forth the data validation dialogue box.

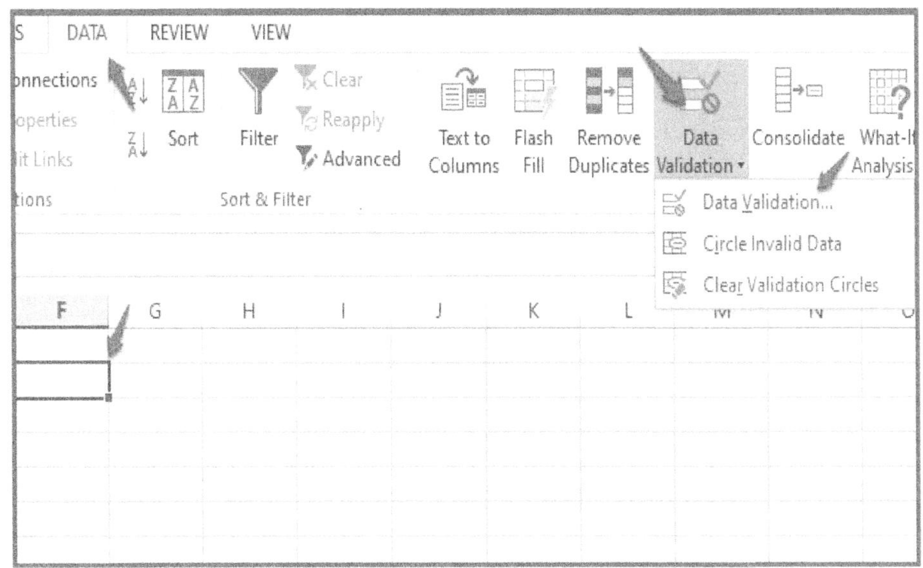

c. Pick the **Data type** under “Allow” such as whole numbers and decimal.

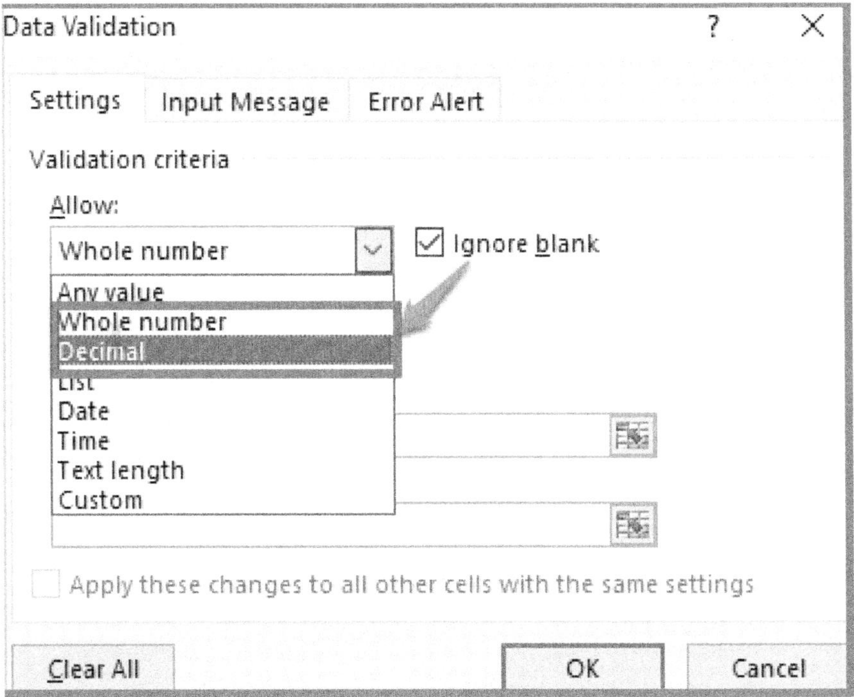

d. Then establish the measures by choosing under **“Data”** perhaps it is between, equal to, and so on.

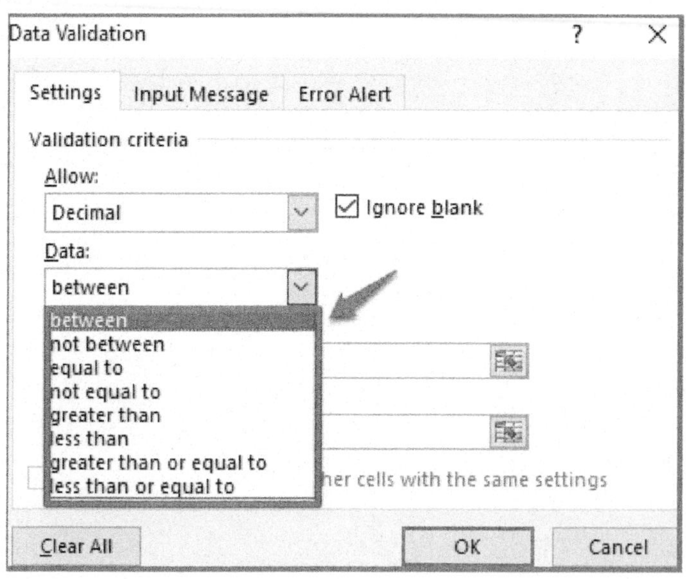

e. Supply further information that is required for restriction guidelines such as "Minimum" and "Maximum". For instance, a filling station attendant with a customer number between 5500 to 10000 will set the minimum as 5500 and maximum as 10000. After that, tap on **Ok.**

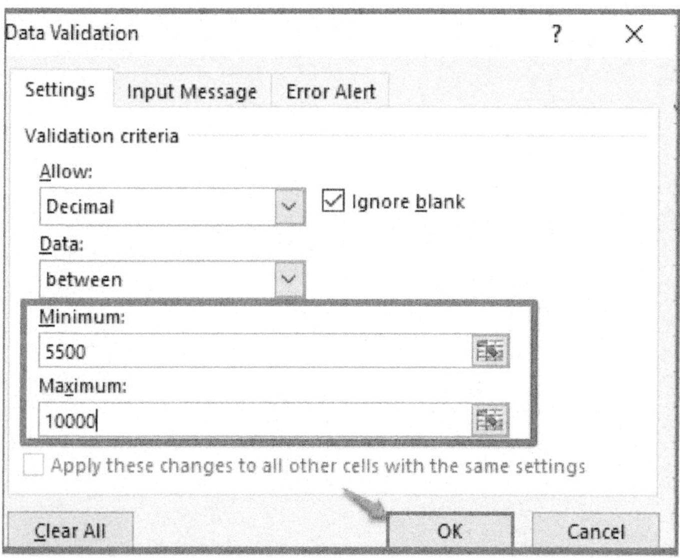

Note: immediately your data entry goes against the validation rule, there will be a prompt warning that the data doesn't match validation restrictions defined for the cell.

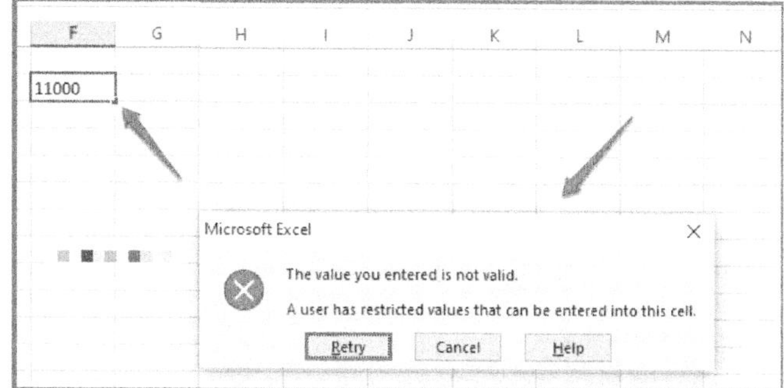

2. **Setting rules for text character length**: rules can be set for a particular text character length to limit the length of the text that can occupy the cell. To do that:
a. Select the cell or cells that will receive the restriction guideline.
b. Move to the **Data tab** and click on **Data Validation** to open the data validation dialogue box.

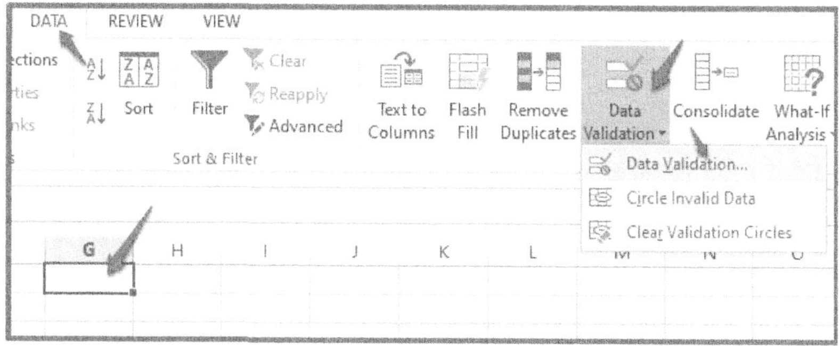

c. Pick **"Text length"** under "Allow".
d. Establish befitting measure under the **"Data"** option.

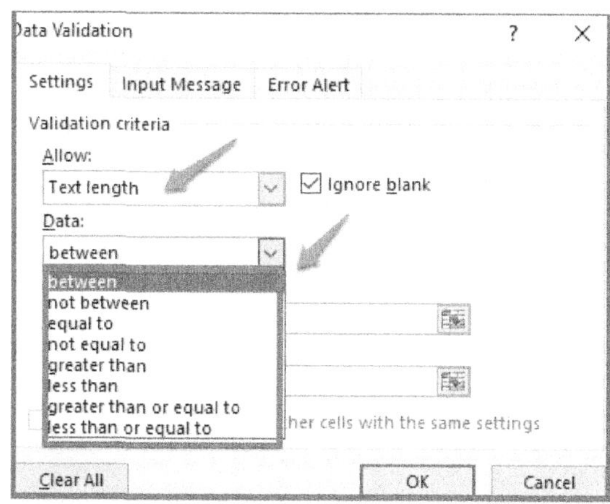

e. Supply further information which will stand as a restriction guide. For example, you might want the applicant's username to be within a range of 7 to 15 length in character. Input 7 in the minimum box space and 15 in the maximum box space.

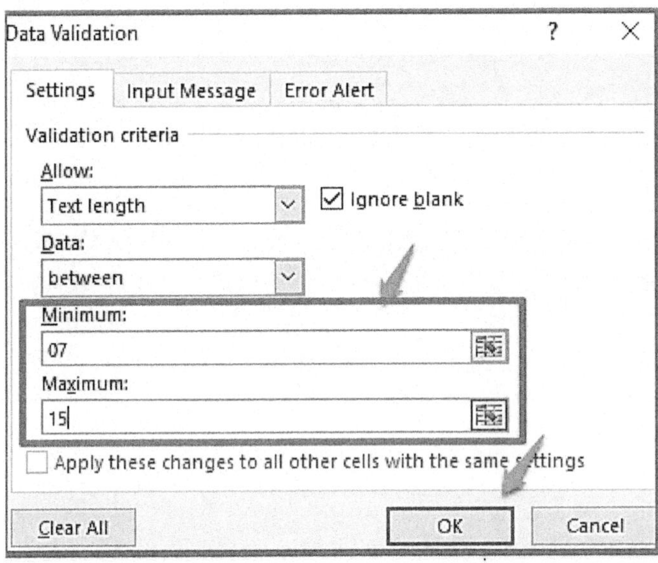

3. **Validating dates and times:** you may set a data validation rule to both the date and time to restrict specific entry into the cell. To achieve that, kindly:

a. Choose the cell or cells that will receive the validation rule.

b. Move to the **Data tab** and click on the **Data Validation** to open the Validation dialogue box.

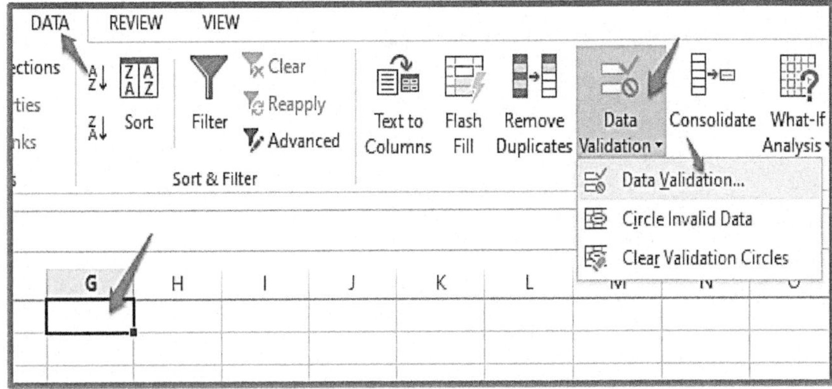

c. Pick the **"Date"** or **"Time"** option under **"Allow"** depending on the restriction item you want to incorporate first.

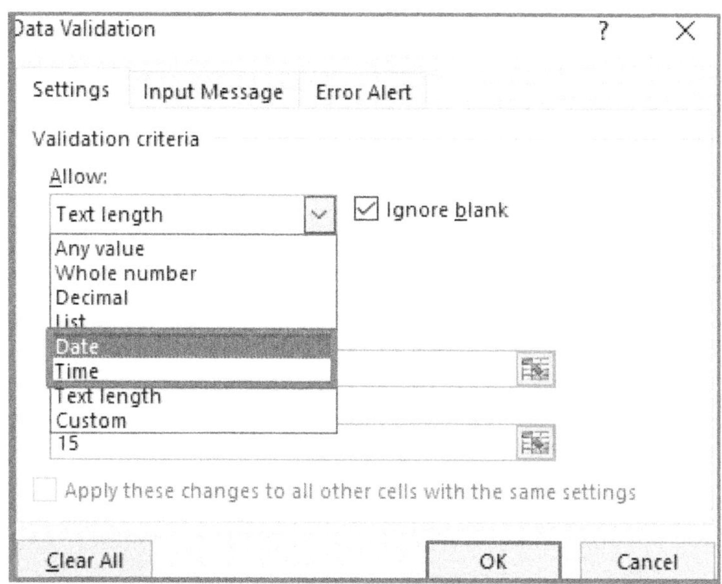

d. Pick the accurate measure that suits your preference under “Data” options.

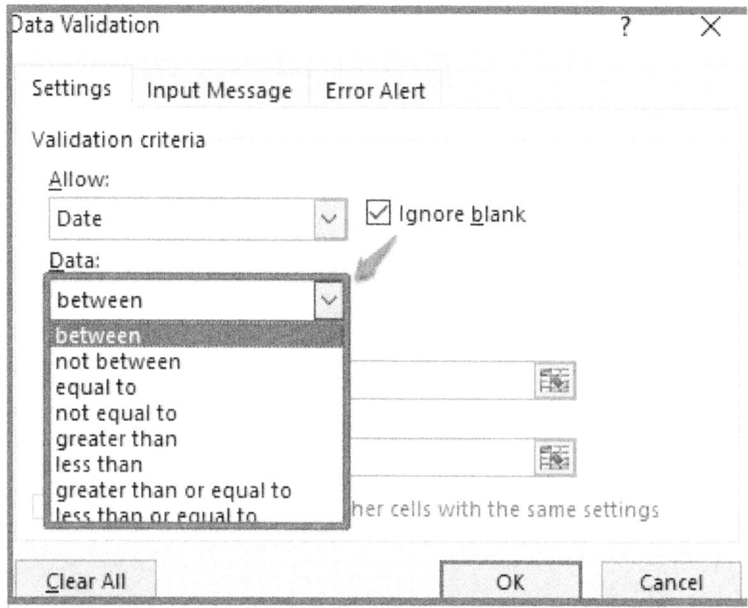

e. Supply further details needed for guideline restriction. For instance, you can choose to set employees’ leave periods within the limit of a specific week in a month (10th of June to 17 June). Set the **start date** as June 10 and the **end date** as June 17.

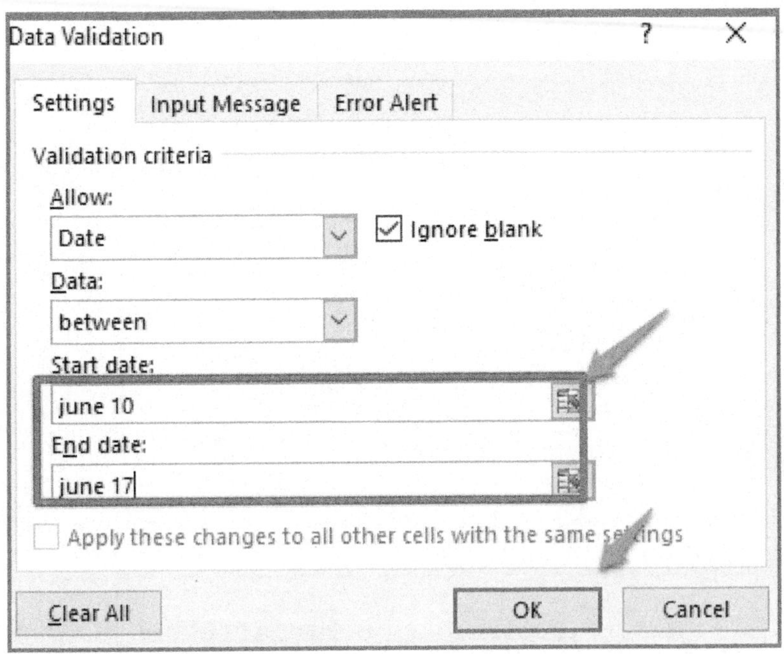

Note: Data validation guide helps Excel users to frame what they will enter within the restriction limit in such a way that it will not go beyond standard settings to avoid an error that may occur through data entry.

CHAPTER THREE

IMPROVING YOUR WORKSHEET

Editing Your Worksheet Data

Editing worksheet data simply means editing the contents of what is inside a cell either by clicking on each cell and editing it straightway or by typing data into the formula bar to edit what is inside the active cell. Any time you are editing your cell, Excel will be in editing mode.

How does Excel react in Edit mode? Some Excel users can't differentiate between Edit mode and Ready mode, Excel reacts in these two ways in Edit mode.

- In Edit mode, the "Arrow key" reacts differently, instead of moving the cursor from one cell to another cell, it will be moving from word to word within a cell.

- You can't apply special formatting or adjust the alignment of cell content in Edit mode.

How do I enter Edit mode?

To navigate into edit mode, use one of the following methods:

- Click the cell that contains the contents you want to edit, then proceed to click **the formula bar**.

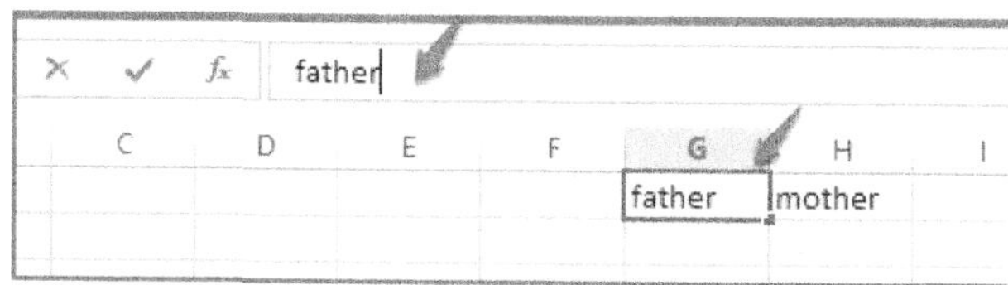

- Double-click on **the cell** that has the data you want to edit and press **"F2"** on the keyboard.

Navigating Around the Worksheet

To move around inside a worksheet, you have to make use of the cell cursor otherwise known as active cell indicator, which is the dark shape that surrounds the active cell. However, you can move round in the worksheet and alter the position of the active cell by:

1. Clicking on the cell you want to make active via the mouse.
2. Clicking on any of the four arrow keys on the keyboard to move the cell cursor in the direction of where the arrow is pointing till you get to your cell destination.

To navigate around the worksheet easily and speedily, you have to master the following shortcuts to fast-track your movement within the worksheet:

CODE	DIRECTION
Enter key	Moving to the next line near the left side.
Tab key	Moving from one cell to another in the right direction.
Shift + tab	Moving from one cell to another in the left direction.
Arrow keys	Moving cells in the direction of the arrow keys.
Home	Moving one cell to the beginning of the row that has the active cell.
Ctrl + Home	Moving one cell to the beginning of the worksheet
Ctrl + End	Moving one cell to the last cell in the worksheet.

Page down	Moving one screen down.
Ctrl + Page down	Moving to the next sheet in the workbook.
Page up	Moving one screen up
Ctrl + page up	Moving to the previous sheet in the workbook
Alt + Page up	Moving one screen to the left
Alt + Page down	Moving one screen to the right

Note: to scroll back to the active cell, perhaps you can't see it anymore on the screen, simply press **Ctrl + Backspace**.

Giving Your Worksheet A New Appearance

Programing your worksheet for a new and better look will even give you a vibe to work more on the worksheet. You have to structure your worksheet in such a way that you will be able to know which column and row you are inputting your data. The subsequent sub-topics under this chapter describe more on how to change the appearance of your worksheet for a better display such as rows and columns hiding, freezing and splitting of rows and columns, and so on.

Freezing and Splitting Columns and Rows

Freezing: Freezing is used to lock particular rows and columns while splitting helps to generate separate Windows for the same worksheet. Freezing and splitting are needed when you have navigated deeper into the worksheet to the extent that you can't see data tags on the first row and column which therefore makes it difficult for you to figure out where to input the data on the worksheet. For instance, if you have navigated deeper to W30 or C50, for you to make an area of the worksheet obvious as you have gone too far in the worksheet, you have to make use of Freezing and splitting.

Splitting: Splitting works better than freezing because you can drag the split line to another place whenever you split. Also, you can quickly get rid of both horizontal and vertical split by double-clicking on it, but all these do not apply to freezing (though it is only freezing that will make the top row and first column stand firm without moving, thereby, permitting you in return to view the row and column tag anywhere you are in the worksheet).

How do I freeze or split rows or columns on the screen? No qualms, follow the processes below:

1. Click **the row** that is exactly below the row you desire to freeze or split, or the column exactly at the right side of the column you desire to freeze or split.
2. Move to the **View tab**, click on **The Split Button** to split the row or column. You can take hold of the split bar, which has a small division marker that is exactly above the vertical scroll bar and exactly at the left side of the horizontal scroll bar. In splitting, you will be able to know the position of the split bar because the pointer arrow turns to two when the pointer is on the split bar.

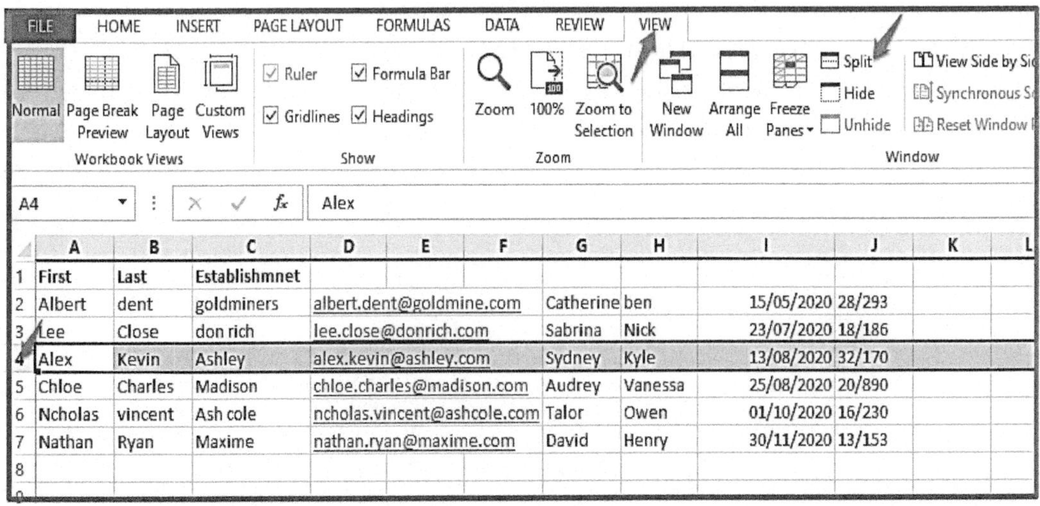

3. Click and drag **the split bar** when it turns to two arrow division to split the screen horizontally or vertically.

	A	B	C	D	E	F	G	H	I	J	K
1	**First**	**Last**	**Establishmnet**								
2	Albert	dent	goldminers	albert.dent@goldmine.com			Catherine	ben	15/05/2020	28/293	
3	Lee	Close	don rich	lee.close@donrich.com			Sabrina	Nick	23/07/2020	18/186	
4	Alex	Kevin	Ashley	alex.kevin@ashley.com			Sydney	Kyle	13/08/2020	32/170	
5	Chloe	Charles	Madison	chloe.charles@madison.com			Audrey	Vanessa	25/08/2020	20/890	
6	Ncholas	vincent	Ash cole	ncholas.vincent@ashcole.com			Talor	Owen	01/10/2020	16/230	
7	Nathan	Ryan	Maxime	nathan.ryan@maxime.com			David	Henry	30/11/2020	13/153	
8											
9											
10											
4	Alex	Kevin	Ashley	alex.kevin@ashley.com			Sydney	Kyle	13/08/2020	32/170	
5	Chloe	Charles	Madison	chloe.charles@madison.com			Audrey	Vanessa	25/08/2020	20/890	
6	Ncholas	vincent	Ash cole	ncholas.vincent@ashcole.com			Talor	Owen	01/10/2020	16/230	
7	Nathan	Ryan	Maxime	nathan.ryan@maxime.com			David	Henry	30/11/2020	13/153	
8											

4. For freezing, kindly click on **The Freeze Panes** button, then choose either **the top row or first column** which are the 2nd and 3rd options respectively. Immediately you are done freezing and splitting, there will be a line that will be displayed on the screen which signifies that rows and columns have been frozen and split.

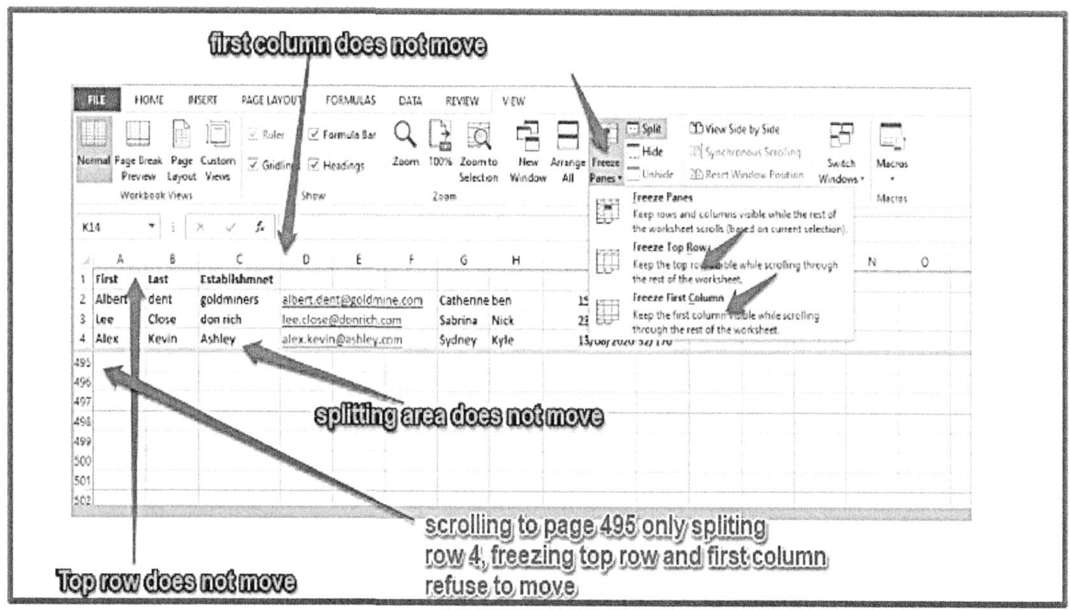

Note: Every other thing will move inside the worksheet except the frozen and split area.

Can I unfreeze and unsplit what had been frozen and split before? Yes, you can, by:

- Clicking on **the split button** once and then double-clicking either of the two bars to remove it. Drag the split bar to the top of the right or left side of the worksheet Window to unsplit rows and columns.
- Kindly click on **Freeze Panes** under the **View tab** and then proceed to pick **Unfreeze Panes** to unfreeze rows and columns.

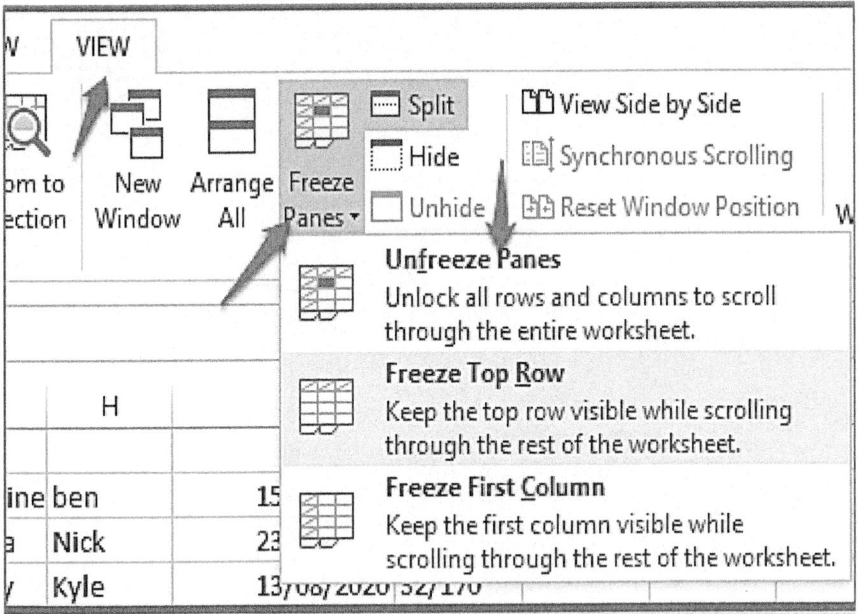

Hide and Unhide The Columns and Rows

Hiding rows and columns at times might be the best approach when you observe that you are having about thousands of rows and columns. It may be very disturbing to work in such a crowded environment, then, hiding such rows and columns will come forth as the only best option.

(1) **How can I hide a row?** This is the way:

a. Click on **the exact row (s)** you want to hide to select them.
b. Right-click on **the row(s)** after they have been selected and pick **hide** from the drop-down menu or you can press **Ctrl + 9** as the shortcut.

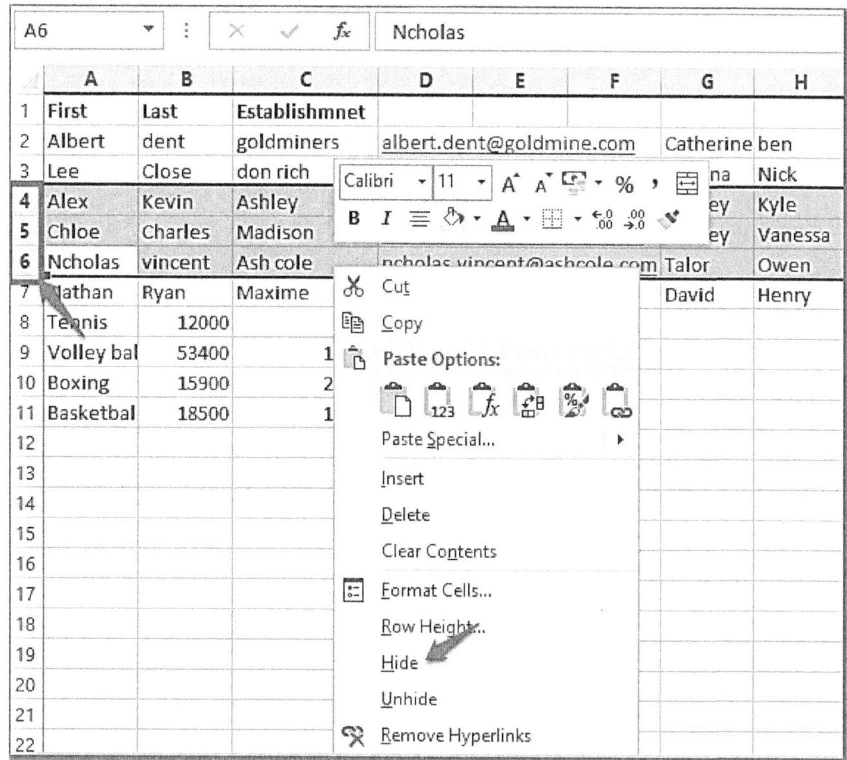

You will notice rows 4, 5, and 6 are not there anymore.

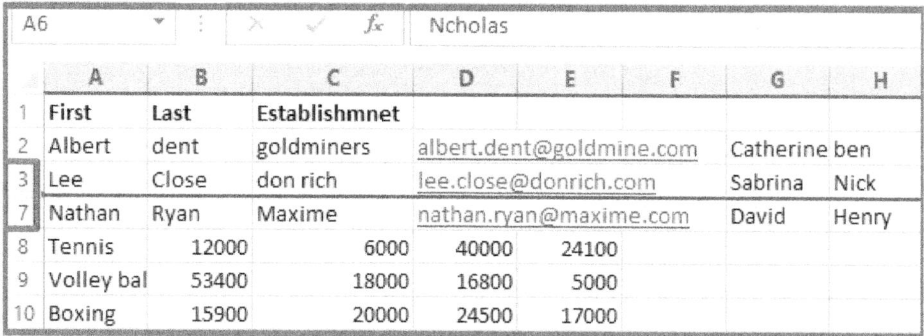

(2) Now, you have hidden rows, what if you want to unhide what you had hidden above? Let us dive into that:

a. Select **the rows** on both sides of the hidden rows (the row at the top and the row below the hidden rows).
b. Right-click on the selected rows and pick **unhide** from the drop-down menu or you can press **Ctrl + Shift + 9** on the keyboard as the shortcut.

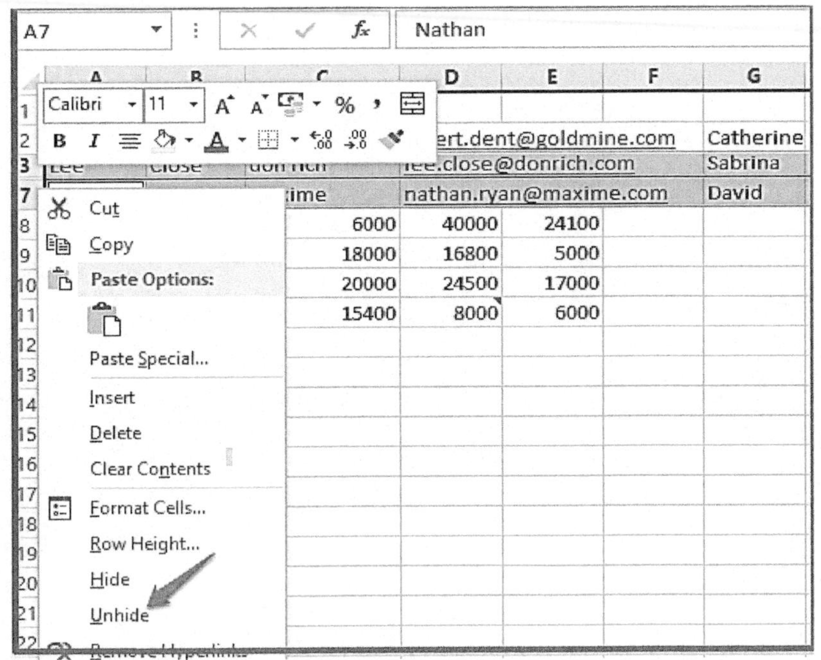

(3) However, this pattern to unhide rows can't work for the first row on the worksheet because it only has a row beneath and does not have any row above, as a result, to **unhide hidden row 1,** you have to use a different pattern:

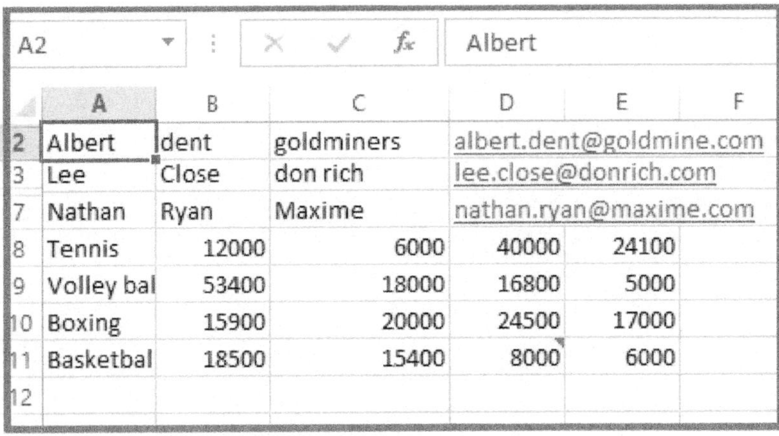

a. You will perceive row 1 of this spreadsheet has been hidden, now to unhide row 1, you will have to move to the cell selection box beside the formula bar at its left side, type A1, and press the **Enter key** so that Excel will understand you want to perform certain functions with A1.

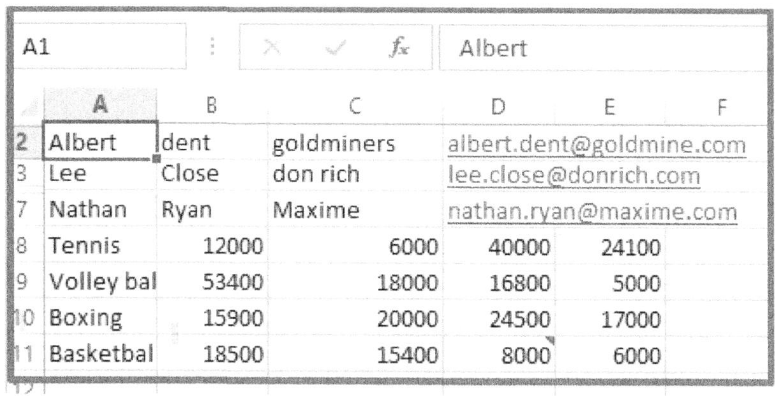

A1	Albert				
	A	B	C	D	E
2	Albert	dent	goldminers	albert.dent@goldmine.com	
3	Lee	Close	don rich	lee.close@donrich.com	
7	Nathan	Ryan	Maxime	nathan.ryan@maxime.com	
8	Tennis	12000	6000	40000	24100
9	Volley bal	53400	18000	16800	5000
10	Boxing	15900	20000	24500	17000
11	Basketbal	18500	15400	8000	6000

b. Go to **the Home tab,** click on **Format cell** ribbon, then pick **Hide & Unhide** from the Format cell drop-down, and lastly click **unhide rows** option from the drop-down list.

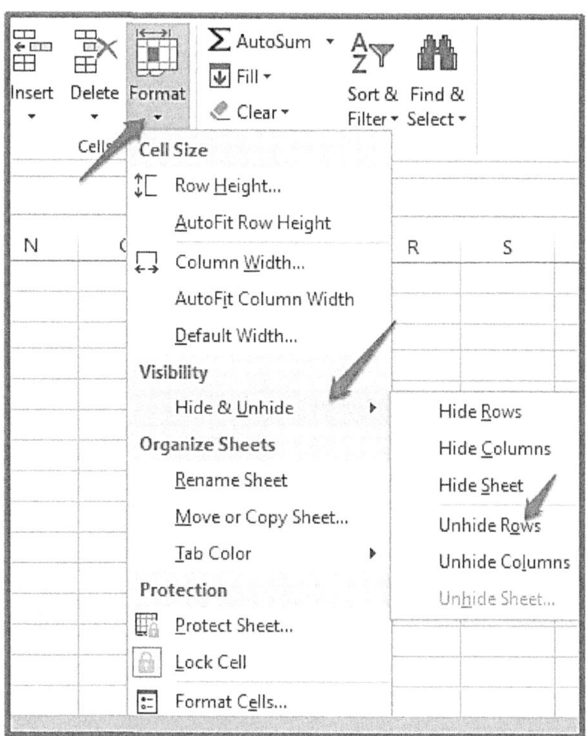

NOTE: You can simply press **Ctrl + Shift + 9** as the shortcut

(4) The Hide and Unhide Column is the next one. Though the patterns look similar, they are different. Let us quickly move to how to hide a column:

a. Let's attempt to hide **column D** as an example**.** Click on the **D identifier** which is above cell D1 to select the whole column as illustrated below.

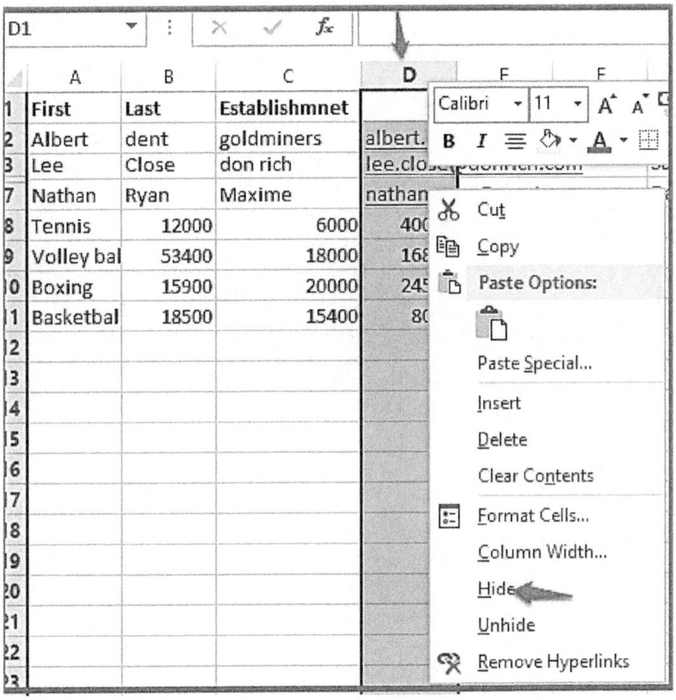

b. Right-click on it and pick **Hide** from the context menu or you can use shortcut **Ctrl + 0 (zero).** You will notice that column D has disappeared.

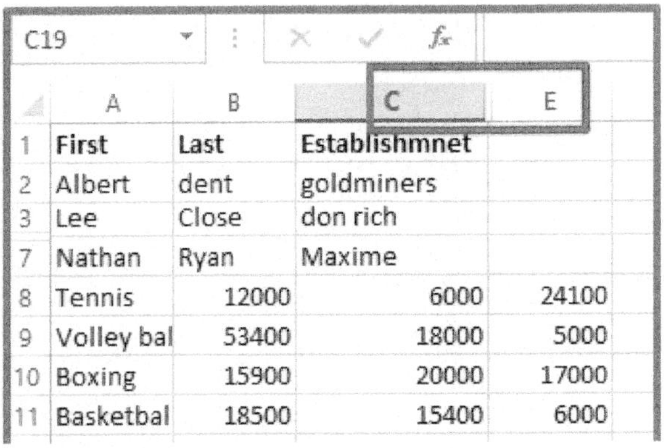

(5) To unhide the above-hidden column, you have to:

a. Select **the column** on both sides of the hidden column and then right-click on them.

b. Pick **unhide** from the drop-down menu or you can make use of the shortcut by pressing **Ctrl + Shift + 0 (zero).**

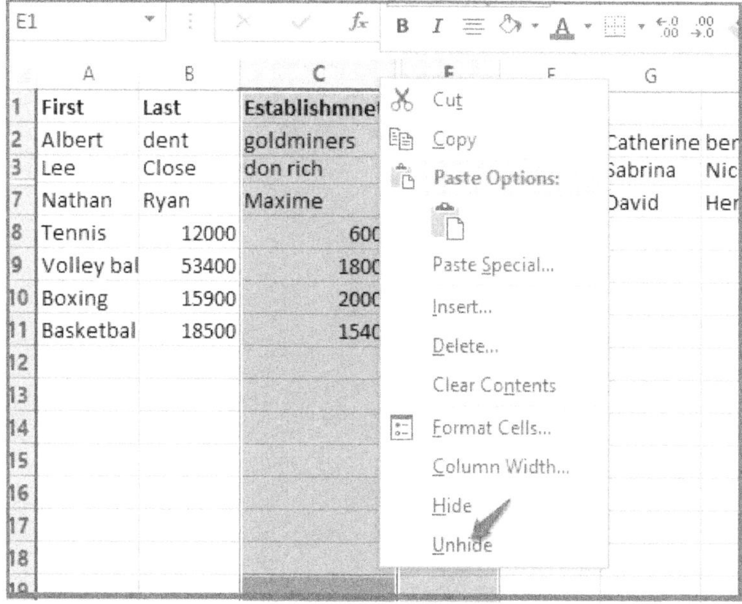

Note: probably you hide the first column, follow the same process we used in (3) above to unhide row 1 to unhide column A also;

a. Click into the **cell selection box** and input **A1.**

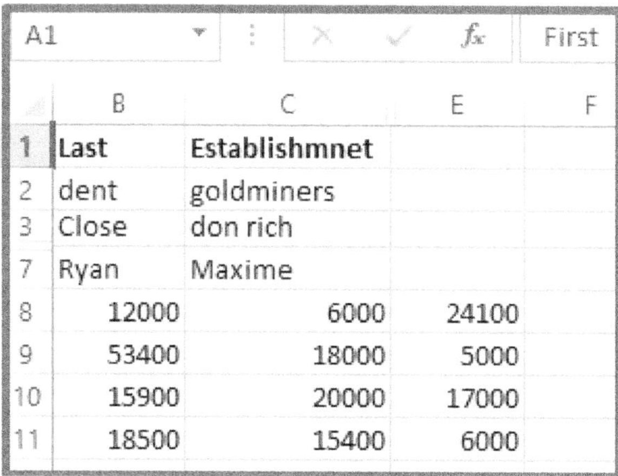

b. Navigate to the **Home tab,** and pick the **format** ribbon, and then choose **"unhide column"** from the drop-down menu.

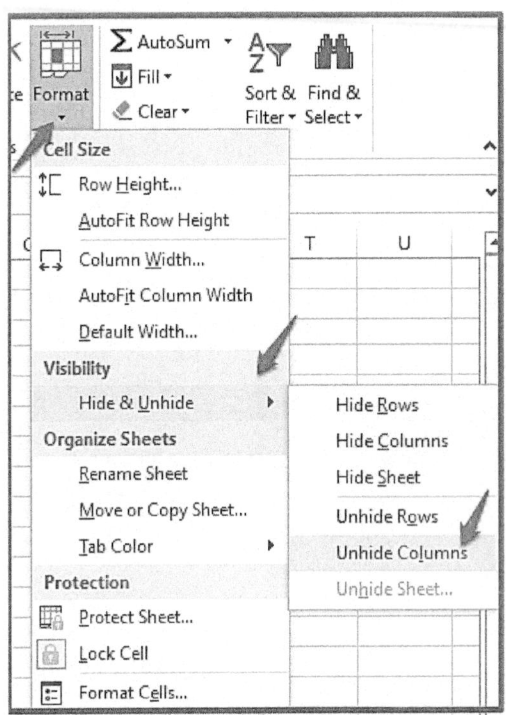

(6) **Unhide all rows and columns:** Let's assume you hid many numbers of rows and/or columns, it is not prudent to unhide them one after the other as such will take a lot of time and effort, unless you are not unhiding them all.

To unhide many rows and columns at once;

a. Highlight all the cells in the worksheet by pressing row and column identifiers or you press **Ctrl + A,** whichever you prefer.

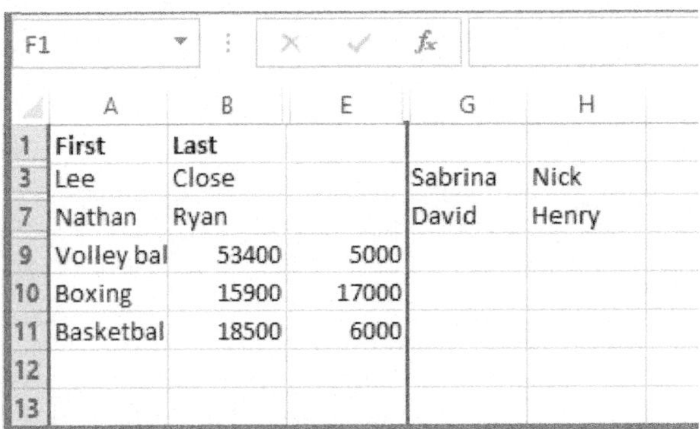

b. Right-click on **row and column identifiers** and pick **unhide** from the pop-up menu or you press **Ctrl + Shift + 9** to unhide all hidden rows and columns.

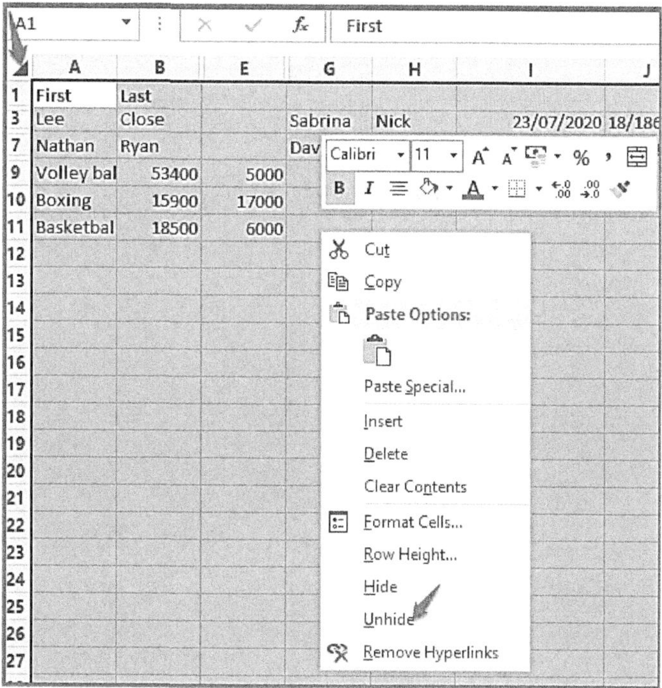

Note: perhaps you observe your worksheet is too crowded with contents, attempt to hide some rows columns to enjoy working with your worksheet.

Comments for Documenting Your Worksheet

Comments are the notes that are associated with a cell in the worksheet. They are used to give prescriptions to your worksheet. Those prescriptions give more details to the contents inside the cell, especially if it happens to be the cell with special numbers and formulas.

Comments are very easy to identify, they do have a little red triangular shape which will be displayed at the corners of each cell that has comment(s).

What do I have to know about comments? The following are the essential things you suppose to know about worksheet comments:

1. **Inserting a comment:** the first thing you can do when it comes to comment is inserting a comment. How can you do that?

a. Tap the cell you want to attach a comment to.
b. Move to the **Review** tab and click on the **"New comment"** option.

c. Insert your comment into the rectangle pop-up box that shows up after you click on the new comment option.

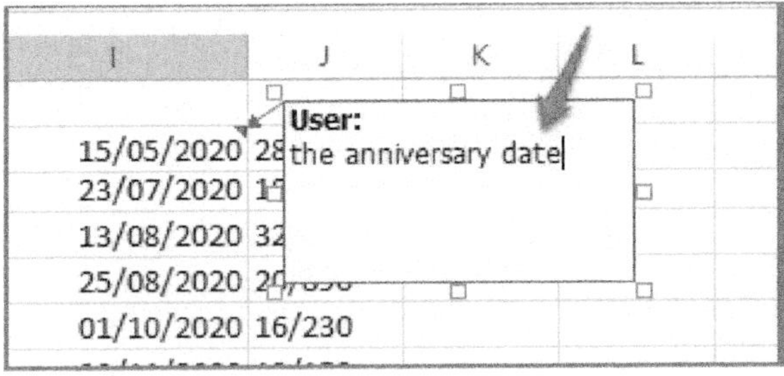

d. Click on **any cell** when you are done inserting your comment.

2. **Viewing a comment:** simply direct your mouse pointer to the little red triangle to view the comment in the pop-up box.

3. **Finding comment:** go to the **Review** tab, tap on the **previous or next** button to move from one comment to another comment to find the one you are looking for.

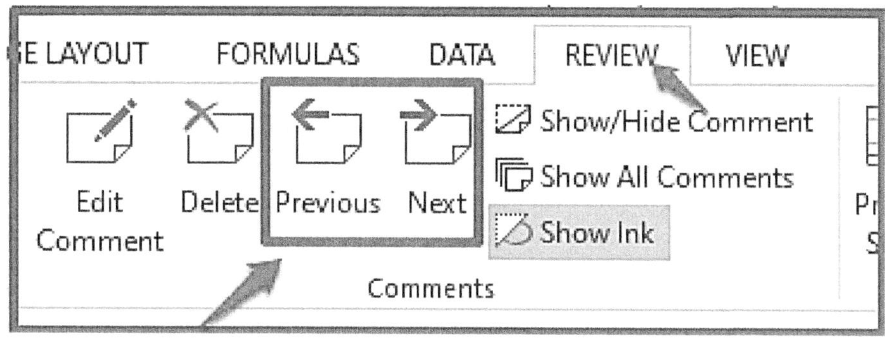

4. **Editing a comment:**
a. Select **the cell** with the comment.
b. Move to the **Review** tab and tap on the **Edit comment** button to edit the comment inside the pop-up box.

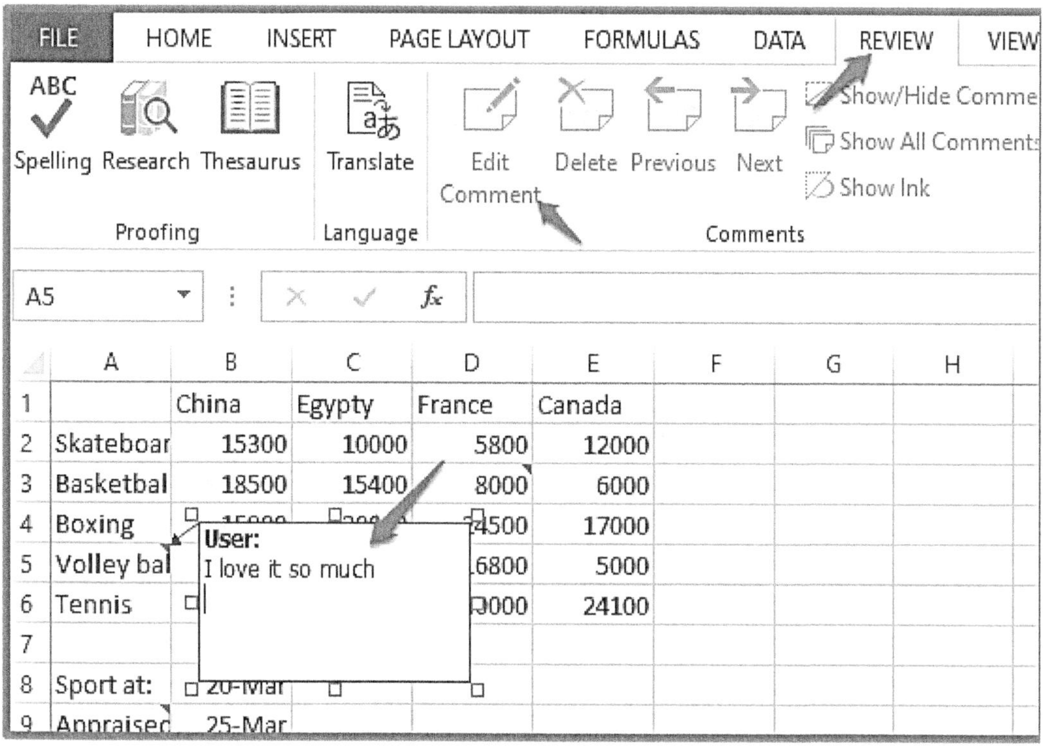

5. **Deleting all comments:** To delete comments, follow one of these methods:
a. Highlight all the cells with comments, go to the **Review** tab and tap on the **Delete** button.

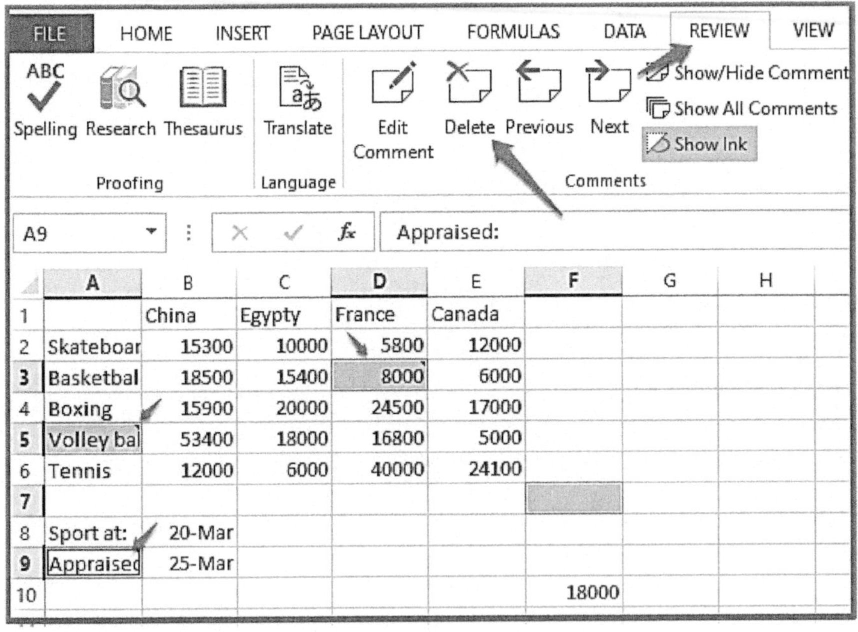

b. Alternatively, you can select all the cells with comments, go to the **"Home"** tab and then click on the **Find and Select** button.

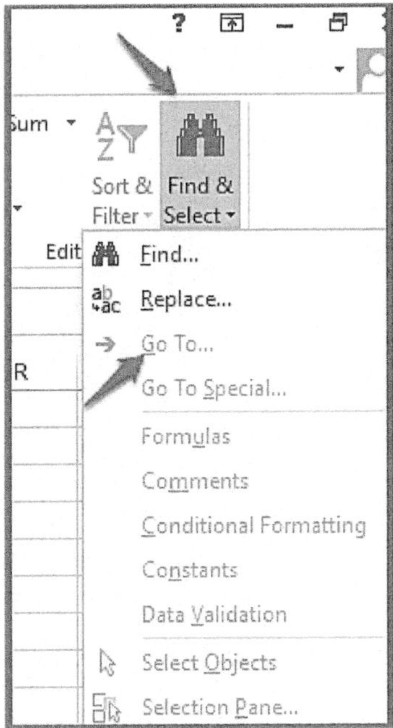

Under the **Find and Select** option, select **Go to** and tap the **Special** button.

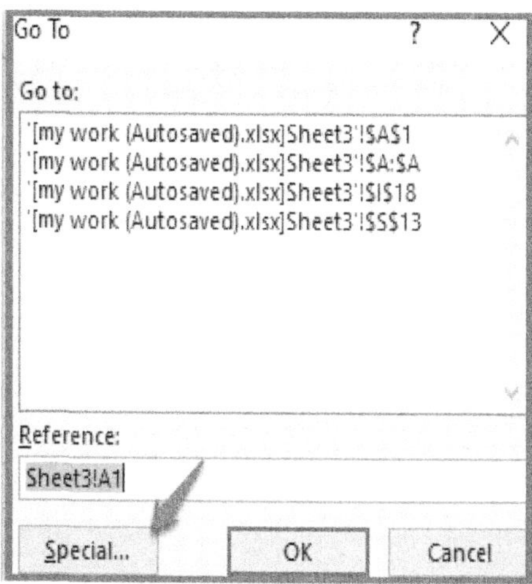

In the "Special dialog box", select **Comments** and tap **Ok**.

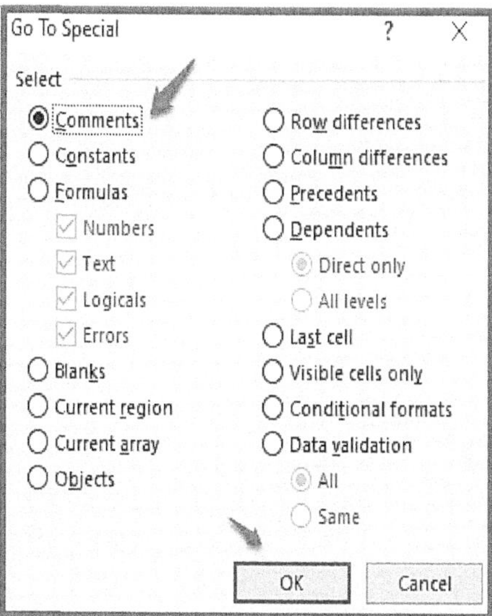

Tips: you can insert your name to the comment(s) you enter by clicking the **Office** button, select **Excel** options, and then proceed to pick a popular category from the Excel Options' dialog box where you will enter your name in the username text box.

Selecting Cells (S) In A Worksheet

You select cells most times in Excel to apply formatting effect to them or to perform a specific operation such as copy and the likes on the selected cell.

1. **How to select an individual cell:** you can select an individual cell by simply left-clicking on it. Immediately you do that, it will become an active cell, and the signal is that such cell will be surrounded by a thick box.

C2 | 10000

	A	B	C	D	E
		China	Egypty	France	Canada
	Skateboar	15300	10000	5800	12000
	Basketbal	18500	15400	8000	6000
	Boxing	15900	20000	24500	17000
	Volley bal	53400	18000	16800	5000

Alternatively, you can move arrow keys from one cell to another to select an individual cell. You can enter data in them immediately they become an active cell and you can as well edit the data you put in them by pressing F2 on the keyboard.

2. **How to select multiple individual cells:** multiple individual cells can be selected just by holding down the Ctrl key and then continue to click on the individual cells that you want to select.

C6 | 6000

	A	B	C	D	E
1		China	Egypty	France	Canada
2	Skateboar	15300	10000	5800	12000
3	Basketbal	18500	15400	8000	6000
4	Boxing	15900	20000	24500	17000
5	Volley bal	53400	18000	16800	5000
6	Tennis	12000	6000	40000	24100
7					

Note: as you continue to select them; those selected cells will be turning to a shaded cell to specify their selection. The last active cell is also part of the selected cell but it will not indicate immediately.

3. **How to select range of cells:** to select a range of cell, you have to:

a. Left-click via the mouse on the cell that will be the first in the range you want to select.

b. Press and hold down the Shift key.

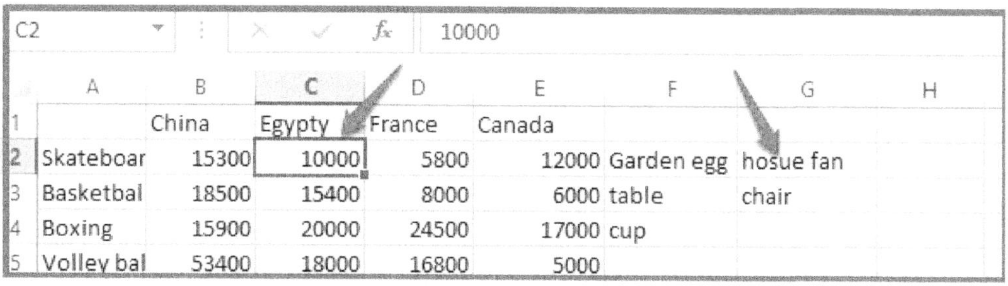

C2 | fx 10000

	A	B	C	D	E	F	G	H
1		China	Egypty	France	Canada			
2	Skateboar	15300	10000	5800	12000	Garden egg	hosue fan	
3	Basketbal	18500	15400	8000	6000	table	chair	
4	Boxing	15900	20000	24500	17000	cup		
5	Volley bal	53400	18000	16800	5000			

c. As you hold down the Shift key, move to the last cell in the range and left-click on it. For instance, you want to select cell C2 to cell G2, just left-click cell C2, then hold down the Shift key and move to cell G2 to left-click as well.

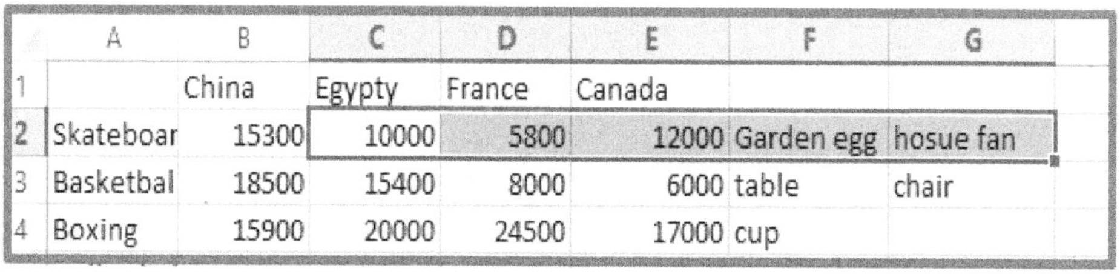

	A	B	C	D	E	F	G
1		China	Egypty	France	Canada		
2	Skateboar	15300	10000	5800	12000	Garden egg	hosue fan
3	Basketbal	18500	15400	8000	6000	table	chair
4	Boxing	15900	20000	24500	17000	cup	

Alternatively, left-click via the mouse on the first cell in the range of the cell you want to select, hold the left side of the mouse, do not release it, and then drag the mouse cursor to the last cell in the range. For instance, you want to select cell B2 through B6, left-click cell B2 and immediately without releasing the mouse, drag the mouse to cell B6.

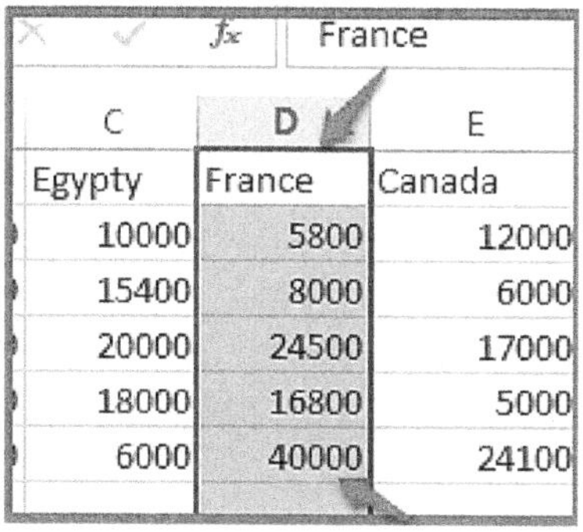

fx France

C	D	E
Egypty	France	Canada
10000	5800	12000
15400	8000	6000
20000	24500	17000
18000	16800	5000
6000	40000	24100

4. **How to select all cells:** you can select all the cells in the worksheet by:

a. Navigating to the uppermost of the row and leftmost of the column in the worksheet.

b. Tap on the square area that has a shaded triangle at the top of the first column and the left side of the row, instantly, all cells inside the worksheet will be highlighted.

A1

	A	B	C	D	E	F	G
1		China	Egypty	France	Canada		
2	Skateboar	15300	10000	5800	12000	Garden egg	hosue fan
3	Basketbal	18500	15400	8000	6000	table	chair
4	Boxing	15900	20000	24500	17000	cup	
5	Volley bal	53400	18000	16800	5000		
6	Tennis	12000	6000	40000	24100		
7							
8	Sport at:	20-Mar					
9	Appraisec	25-Mar					
10						18000	

Sheet1 | Sheet2 | Sheet3 | Sheet4 | Sheet5 | Sheet6

Alternatively, press **Ctrl + A** as a shortcut on the keyboard to select all the cells in the worksheet.

Deleting, Copying, And Moving Data

It is expedient at times to delete wrong input of data or incorrect data and in the same vein moving and copying data within and outside the worksheet can't be overemphasized.

1. Delete your cell contents by:

a. Highlighting the cells to be deleted, and then press the **Delete** Key on the keyboard.
   OR

b. Right-click the selected cells and pick the **clear contents** option or move to **the Home tab,** choose the **clear button** option, and lastly pick **clear contents.**

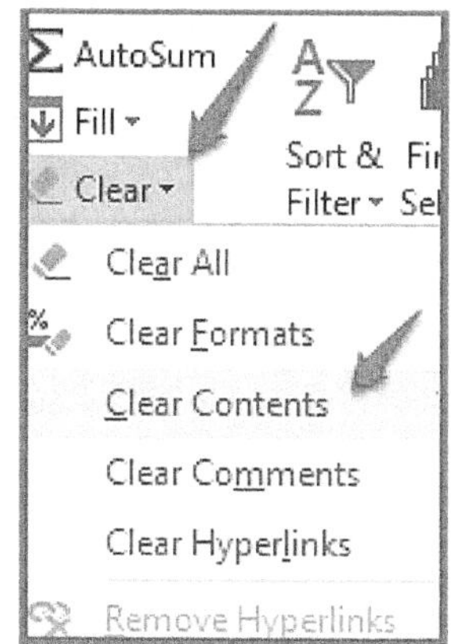

Note: Do not use the delete button on the home tab to delete cell contents because using it will delete cell contents and also the cell itself along with it.

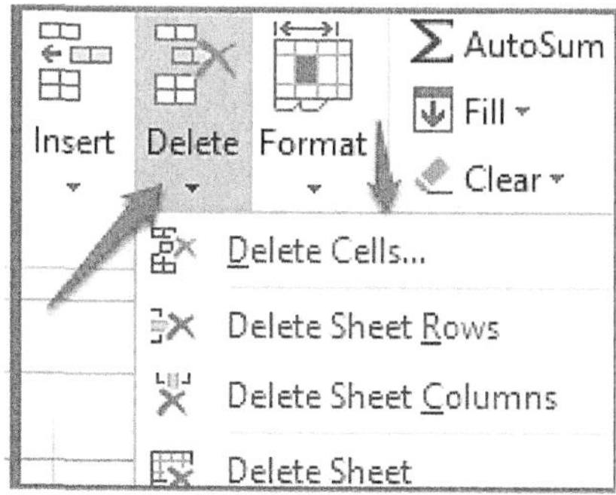

2. Moving and copying the cell contents are very similar, but has a little difference. To move and copy, kindly:
a. Select the cell you want to move or copy its content.
b. Right-click on the cell and pick **cut** or **copy** depending on which of it you want to do.

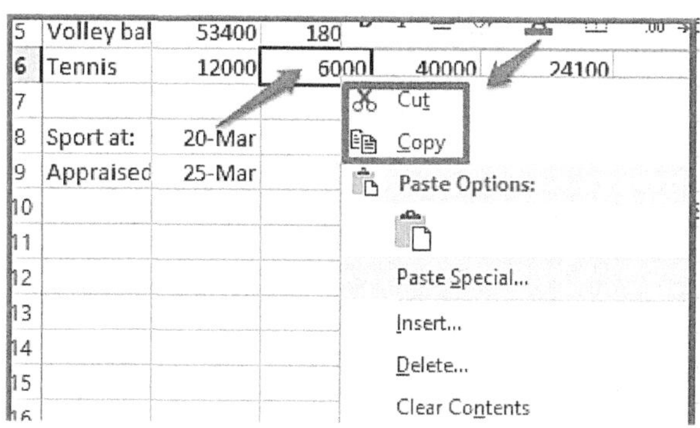

c. Go to the cell that will be the receiver of what you are moving or copying and right-click.
d. Pick **paste** from the pop-up menu, if you pick the **cut** option to cut the contents, the paste option will move the contents, and if you pick copy the content, the paste option will copy the contents.

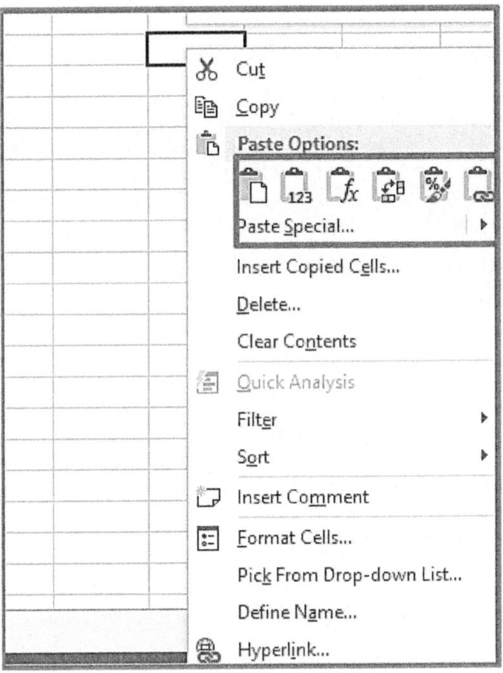

After you have selected the cell, and you are about to move or copy its content, then;

a. Move the pointer to the edge of the selected cell block (that is the cell that has the data inside), and wait till the pointer turns to a four-headed arrow.
b. Then double-click and start dragging to the receiver cell. You should hold the Ctrl key as you drag the four-headed arrow to the receiver cell to copy the contents, but if you want to move the contents, you should not hold the Ctrl key.

Managing the Worksheets in A Workbook

You can manage your worksheet inside the workbook by the way you handle the worksheet. Such management has to do with how to add, rename, delete and move amidst the worksheet inside the workbook.

Let us look at some ways of managing the worksheet:

1. **How to move a worksheet inside a workbook:** you can move from one sheet to another sheet in a workbook by clicking on each worksheet tab at the bottom of the screen.
   OR click on the navigation scroll button at the left side of the worksheet tabs.

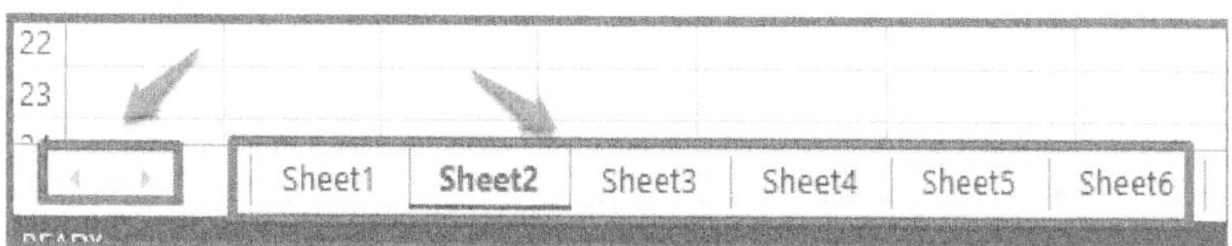

2. **How to rearrange worksheet:** worksheet can be rearranged with its tab by simply double-clicking to drag the worksheet tab to a new position. While you are dragging, you will see a little black arrow and a page icon that will appear to indicate the position of where your worksheet can be dropped to.

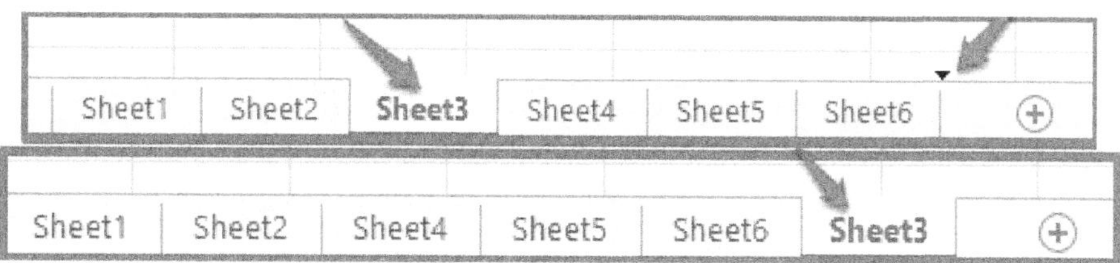

OR by:

a. Navigating to the **Home Tab**, go to the "Cells" ribbon and select **Format**.
b. Then choose **move** or **copy** from the drop-down menu, the dialog box will be displayed.
c. Tap the position of the sheet where you want to drop your worksheet and tap **Ok.**

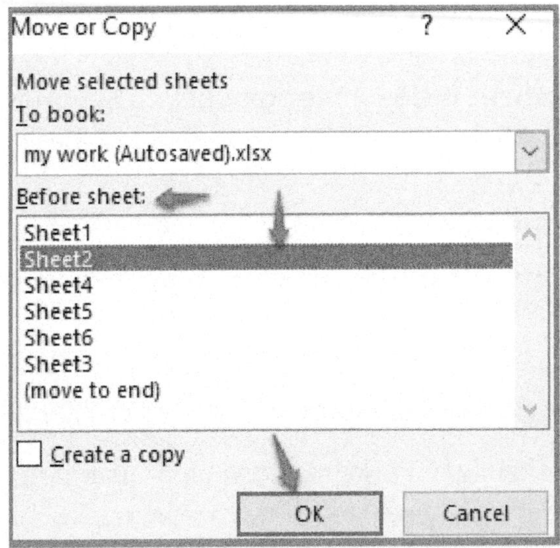

3. **How to select worksheet(s):** click on the worksheet tab to select a worksheet.

- You can as well select many worksheets at the same time by holding down the control key and continue clicking on the worksheet tabs to be selected.

- You may also select all the worksheets by right-clicking on the worksheet tab and pick "**Select All Sheets**" from the popup menu.

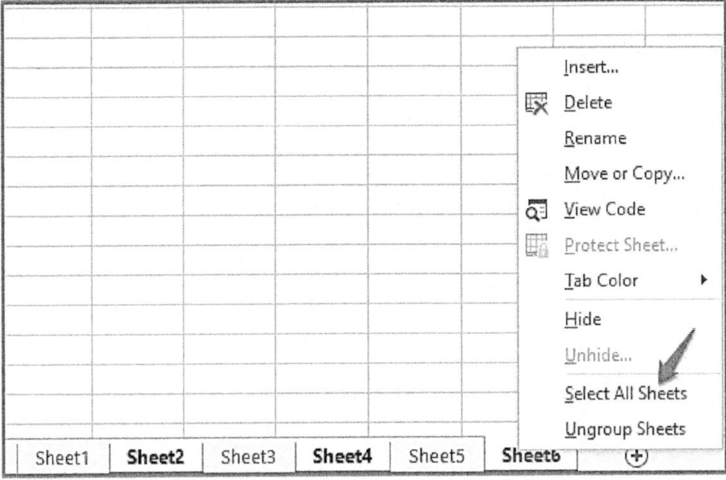

4. **How to rename a worksheet:** to rename a worksheet, you have to:
a. Go to the **Home** tab**,** move to the "Cells" ribbon and select **Format**.
b. Then select **rename** from the drop-down menu and insert a new name as desired.

Alternatively, simply right-click the **worksheet tab** and pick **rename** from the pop-up list.

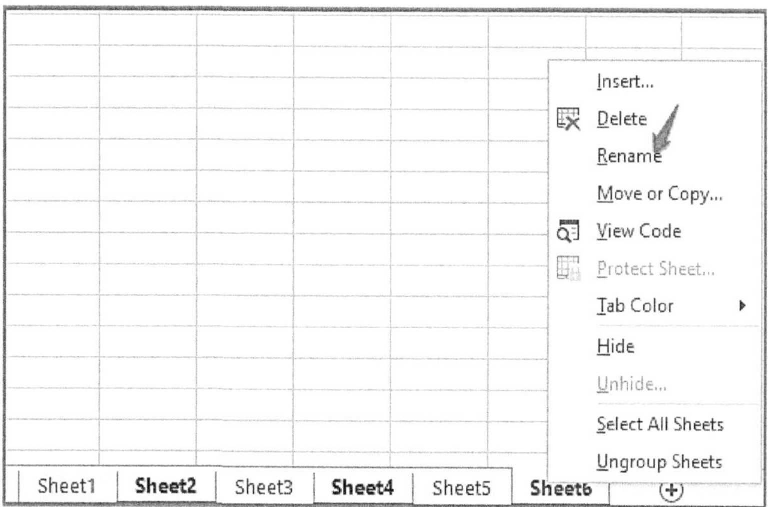

Then insert a new name and tap **Enter** to see its effect

5. **How to copy a worksheet:** copying a worksheet is very easy, just hold down the Ctrl key and double-click on the worksheet you want to copy and drag it to another position.

6. **How to add a new worksheet:** click on the **new worksheet icon (+)** that is located at the right side of the worksheet tabs, and a new worksheet will come forth.

7. **How to colorize your worksheet:** add color to your worksheet by following these steps

a. Highlight the worksheet and move to the **Home** tab, go to the "Cells" ribbon and select **Format**.

b. Select **tab color** from the drop-down menu and pick the color you want on the submenu.

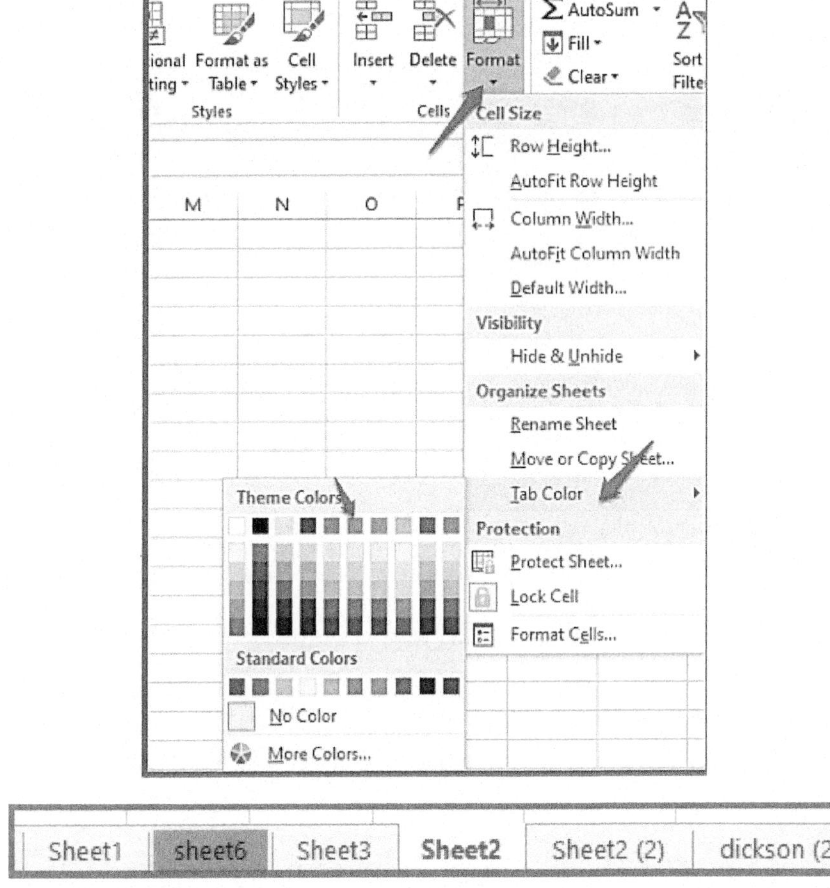

8. **How to delete a worksheet:** to get a worksheet deleted, kindly:

a. Select the worksheet you want to delete, go to the **Home** tab, locate the **delete** option under the "**Cells**" ribbon, and then select **Delete sheet** from the drop-down list.

   You can also delete a sheet by right-clicking on the **worksheet tab** and pick **Delete** from the options.

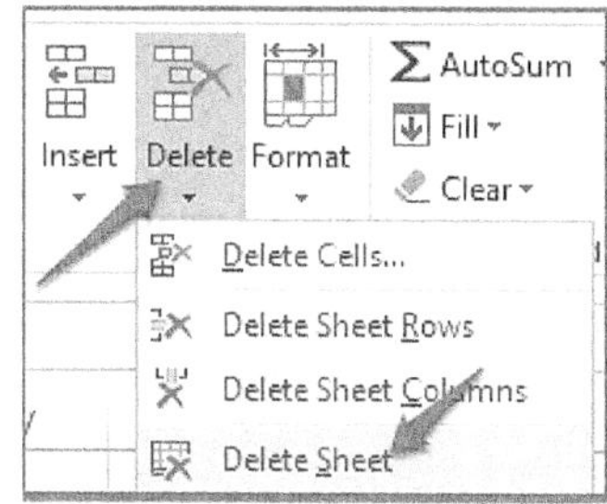

Restricting Others from Meddling with Your Worksheets

There are ways provided by Excel for a user to prevent others from meddling with their worksheet even if they access your PC. The two ways are worksheet hiding and protection.

Let us buttress more on these two ways. We'd start with hiding the worksheet, and then protecting the worksheet.

Hiding Your Worksheet

Observe the following steps to hide your worksheet so that others will not know it even exists except you

a. Select the **worksheet,** move to the **Home** tab, and locate the **Format** button under the "Cells" ribbon**.**
b. Select **Hide & Unhide** from the drop-down menu, and lastly, pick **Hide Sheet** from the drop-down list.

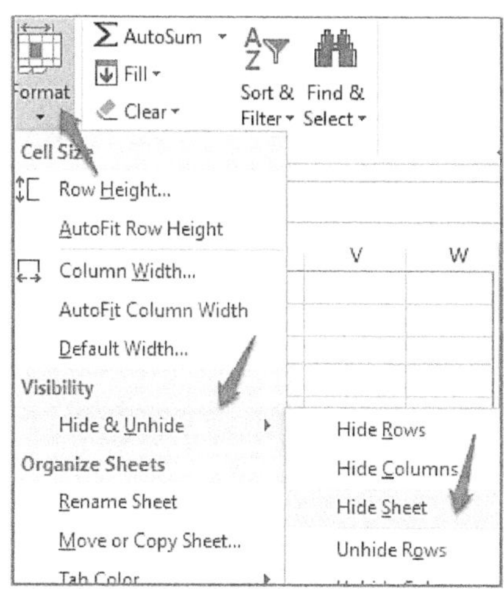

Shortcut: right-click the **worksheet tab** and pick **"Hide"** from the pop-up list.

You can as well unhide the sheet you have hidden previously by this method:

a. Move to the **Home** tab and tap on the **Format button.**
b. Then pick the **Hide & Unhide** option from the Format drop-down list and select **Unhide Sheet** from the list that pops up.

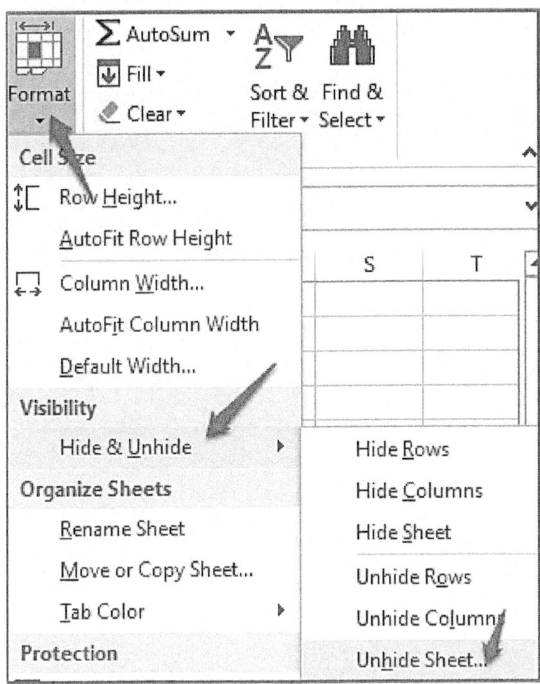

c. Immediately you click on **Unhide Sheet**, a dialog box will come up, kindly click on the **worksheet name** you want to unhide and tap **Ok.**

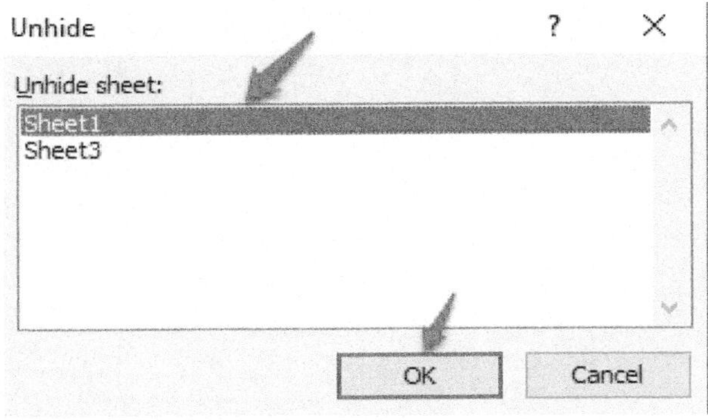

Protecting Your Worksheet

As I have said earlier, protecting one's worksheet means preventing it from any form of editing and formatting from unauthorized users. What are you preventing? They are your cell contents, rows, and columns of your worksheet, addition or removing of any row and column and so on.

Let us examine how to protect one's worksheet from an unauthorized editor:

a. Select the **worksheet** to be protected.
b. Move to the **Review** tab and tap on the **Protect sheet** button**,** and you will be provided with a sheet protector dialog box.

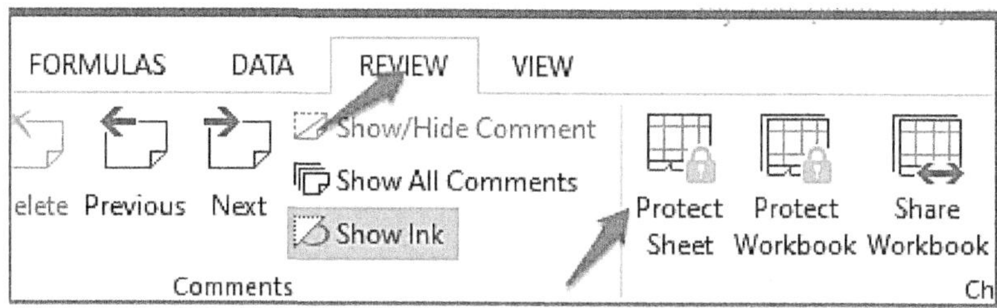

c. Input a **password** in the password space provided in the Protect Sheet box so that only those you authorize by giving them the password to unprotect it will have access to it.

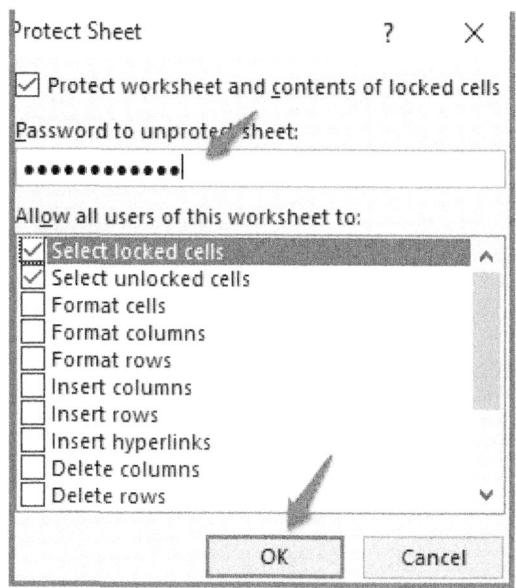

d. In the Protect Sheet box, go to **"Allow All Users of This Worksheet To:"** list, click what you want other users to do like **format cell** if you want them to format it. You only have to deselect **the "Selected locked cell"** to prevent anyone from adjusting anything on the worksheet because initially, by default, all the worksheet cells have been locked, and by deselecting the **"Selected locked Cell"**, you excellently prevent any cell from been edited.

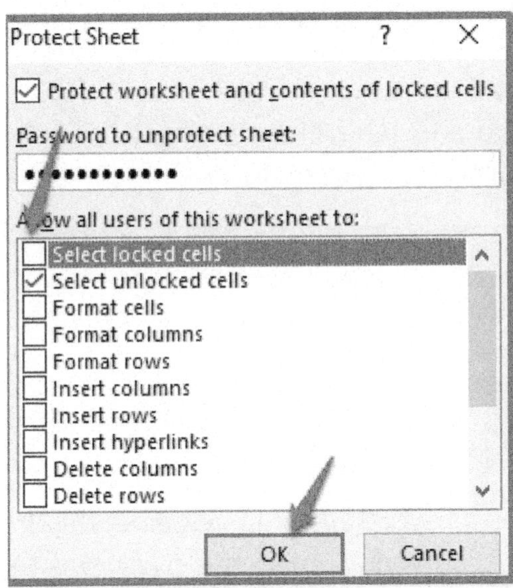

e. Tap **Ok** to effect the changes. Perhaps you entered the password in (c) above, you will have to enter it once requested for again, then you can tap **OK**.

Note: you can unprotect the sheet you have previously protected by following these simple steps:

a. Move to the **Review** tab and click on **Unprotect Sheet**.

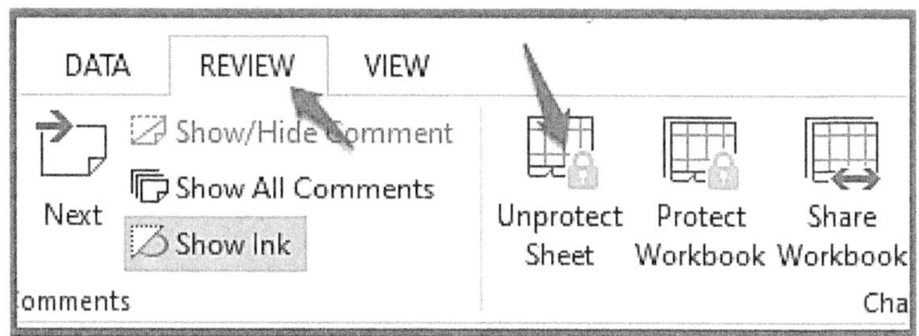

b. Input the **password** you have previously attached to it when you were protecting it.
c. Then tap **Ok**

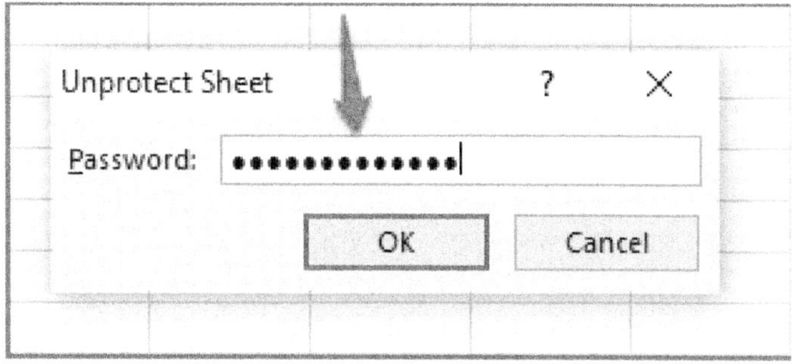

CHAPTER FOUR

COMPUTING DATA WITH FORMULAS AND FUNCTIONS

About Formulas

Excel formulas have been very helpful when it comes to numbers computation. There are certain things you will not be able to do with Excel unless you know how to structure formulas for such decisions. Excel formulas start with equal to (=), for instance, 8 + 4 = 12, that is, Excel formulas and the result. Yours is just to structure the formulas, Excel will do the computation and provide the result.

Referencing the Cells Via Formulas

Each formula you are using in Excel will be referring to some specific set of cells. Though Excel is referring to the cells, it is indirectly referring to the data or contents inside those cells to make use of them in the calculation. Let us quickly check the below illustration to get a glimpse of it:

Assuming cell C2 has 48 and cell C3 has 52, and a formula is structured in cell C4 in reference to cell C2 and C3, for example, C2 + C3, the result it will bring after you press **Enter** is 100 which is the addition of the contents that are inside cells C2 and C3. Though, Excel will not refer to the number in itself, but the cell number, therefore, if the number in cell C2 is changed to 30 and cell C3 is changed to 20, automatically, the result will be changed to 50 as well.

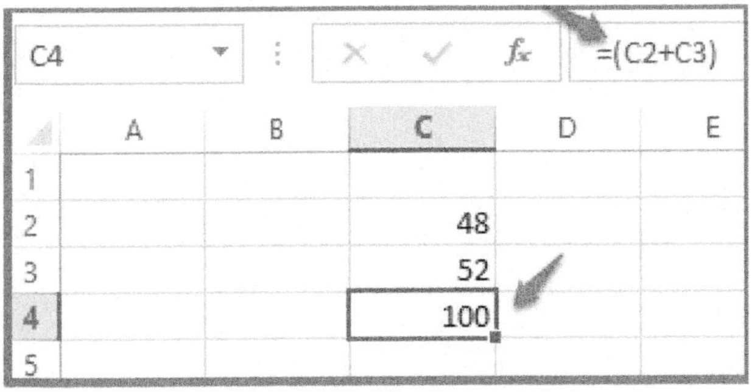

We need to study the illustration below to have the full understanding of how Excel goes in referring to cells and how it eventually makes use of the contents when it comes to formulas:

The example is about a small enterprise that forwarded its records to the worksheet with the agenda of checking the flow of income:

i. **Column B** is about the sales made and it shows all incomes from various sources.

ii. **Column C** is about the purchases made and it shows all expenses made to various sources.

iii. **Column D** is the actual profit, and it is derived by removing all the expenses from all the sales made.

D7 | =SUM(D3:D6)

	A	B	C	D	E
1					
2	Items	Sales	Purchases	Profit	
3	Toshiba	$4,500.00	$2,500.00	$2,000.00	
4	Lenovo	$3,800.00	$3,000.00	$800.00	
5	Hp	$6,000.00	$4,000.00	$2,000.00	
6	Dell	$3,000.00	$1,450.00	$1,550.00	
7	Total	$17,300.00	$10,950.00	$6,350.00	

The image below gives details of how the data in the worksheet is computed:

i. Column D shows the amount of profit from various sources calculated by subtracting the Column C (purchases amount) from Column A (sales amount).

ii. The **Total** derived in Row 7 is the SUM function of the amount in column 3 to column 6.

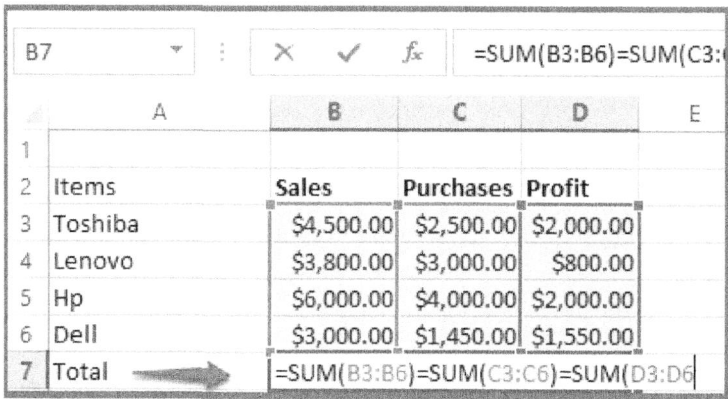

B7 | =SUM(B3:B6)=SUM(C3:

	A	B	C	D	E
1					
2	Items	Sales	Purchases	Profit	
3	Toshiba	$4,500.00	$2,500.00	$2,000.00	
4	Lenovo	$3,800.00	$3,000.00	$800.00	
5	Hp	$6,000.00	$4,000.00	$2,000.00	
6	Dell	$3,000.00	$1,450.00	$1,550.00	
7	Total	=SUM(B3:B6)=SUM(C3:C6)=SUM(D3:D6			

Referencing Formula Results in Subsequent Excel Formulas

Excel carries out its computation by referring to the previous formula results in the cells. Let us quickly examine the worksheet below which shows records of individual account types:

a. **Column E** displays the total aggregate savings of individuals.
b. **Column F** shows how much individual saved on average by using formula result of Total in Column E divided by 3 which stands for the total number of accounts opened by each individual.

F2 | =E2/3

	A	B	C	D	E	F
1	**individual**	**Savings**	**currents**	**fixed deposit**	**Total**	**Average**
2	Wayne lee	150	160	300	610	203.3333
3	Russell	200	180	430	810	270
4	Thompson	350	170	100	620	206.6667
5	Burns	400	120	190	710	236.6667
6		1100	630	1020	2750	916.6667
7						
8						

The average point in column F is derived from the formula of total calculation results divided by the average account type which is 3.

SUM | =SUM(B2:B5) =SUM(C2:C5) =SUM(D2:D5) =SUM(E2:E5) =E6/3

	A	B	C	D	E	F	G	H
1	individual	Savings	currents	fixed deposit	Total	Average		
2	Wayne lee	150	160	300	B2+C2+D2	=E2/3		
3	Russell	200	180	430	B3+C3+D3	=E3/3		
4	Thompson	350	170	100	B4+C4+D4	=E4/3		
5	Burns	400	120	190	B5+C5+D5	=E5/3		
6		=SUM(B2:B5)	=SUM(C2:C5)	=SUM(D2:D5)	=SUM(E2:E5)	=E6/3		
7								

Operators and Precedence of Excel Formulas

Excel users have to understand the use of operators in Excel as it indicates the kind of calculation you are about to carry out on the data as you begin to exploit the formula. There are four (4) types of Excel Operators. Let us buttress on each of them to get you acquainted with them.

1. **Arithmetic type:** This is the kind of operator that carries out basic math functions such as multiplication, subtraction, division, and many more.

Arithmetic Operators

Symbols	Meanings	Illustrations
***(asterisk sign)**	Multiplication	=6*2 or = A1 * 3
+ (plus sign)	Addition	=4+6 or = B2 + 4
- (minus sign)	Negative Subtraction	=-5 = 10-4 or = E3-2
/ (right slash)	Division	=10/2 or = D7/5
% (percentage)	Percent of	=20%
^ (caret)	Exponentiation	=10^2

2. **Text concatenation type:** this is an operator that joins one or more values together to produce a single piece of text.

Concatenation Operator

Symbol	Meaning	Illustration
& (connector)	Connecting two value together	= Total no & B3

3. **Reference type:** this is the operator that gathers a range of cells and refers them for calculation.

Reference Operator

Symbols	Meaning	Illustration
: (column)	It is called range operator. It is used to show the range of two or more cells by referencing those cells for computation	=SUM(D5:D8)
‘ (comma)	It merges multiple cell range and computes their value together to give one value	=SUM(C5:C6, G3:G7)
#	It is used to signify inadequate space, and once the cell is stretched, it will show the actual data inside	###### =SUM(D2##)
@	It indicates the indirect intersection of data items or cells in a formula	=@G1:G8 =SUM (Wednesday selling: Saturday selling)
() space	It is used in combining the intersection of two blocks of cells, those two blocks of the cell will overlap, if not there will be an error message.	(A1:D4 B2:C3)

4. **Comparison type:** this is the type of operator that compares one value with another and establishes reasonable outcomes, either True or False.

Comparison operator

Symbols	Meanings	Illustrations
= (Equal sign)	Equal to	= C1 = F1
< (less than sign)	Less than	= D4 < B2
>(greater than sign)	Greater than	= B2 > D4

Symbols	Details
:	Colon is used in separating all the cells you are referencing into two and gives them one reference for formulas.
‘	The comma is used to collect numerous cell references into one reference.
-	Negation like -4.
%	Percentage.
^	Exponentiation or raise to the power of.
*& /	Multiplication and division.
+ & -	Addition and subtraction.
&	Two values connectors or text joint
= < > <= >= <>	Comparison.

<=(less than or equal sign)	Less than or equal to	= E8 <= A7
>= (greater than or equal sign)	Greater than or equal to	= A7 >= E8
<>	Not equal to, it only gives returns of either True or False	= D3 <> 8

The Order of Operator Precedence in Excel Formulas

There are specific orders to which Excel performs its operation, which is why you have to order your data correctly to get an accurate result for your computation. Note that Excel starts its operation from left to right.

Changing Excel Order with Parenthesis

Excel grants you the right to adjust the order by which it calculates by enclosing part of the values or formula you want to calculate into the parentheses. Let us take this scenario for example:

= 8+2*3, you should know Excel will multiply 2 by 3 before adding it with 8 in accordance to its operator order. However, if you want the addition to be done first, you can dictate to Excel your order by structuring the formula like this =(8+2)*3, this structure will cause Excel to attend to the values inside the parentheses before multiplying the result by 3.

Let us consider the example of the table in the next page, Excel will have to add D3+1000 first, after then it will divide the result with the sum of B2 through to B4, but without the parentheses, Excel will take 1000 and divide it by the sum of B2 to B4. That is the power of parentheses.

=(D3+1000)/(B2:B4).

D4 | fx =(D3+1000)/(B2:B4)

	A	B	C	D
1	individual	Savings	currents	fixed deposit
2	Wayne lee	200	160	300
3	Russell	200	180	5000
4	Thompson	600	70	10
5	Burns	400	120	190

Foreknowledge of Entering A Formula

Getting yourself familiar with the basic understanding that involves entering a formula will help you to discover other Excel formulas and make the best exploits through it. The following are the steps you should acquaint yourself with before jumping to the pool of formula entering:

1. Select an empty cell where you will put the formula so that the value inside the cell before will not be erased.
2. Double-click the cell to write inside it.

B7 | × ✓ f_x

	A	B	C	D
1				
2	Items	Sales	Purchases	Profit
3	Toshiba	$4,500.00	$2,500.00	$2,000.00
4	Lenovo	$3,800.00	$3,000.00	$800.00
5	Hp	$6,000.00	$4,000.00	$2,000.00
6	Dell	$3,000.00	$1,450.00	$1,550.00
7	Total			

3. You may decide either to write directly into the cell or you move to the formula box above and write the formula there, whichever option you take you will later arrive at the same result.
4. Before you start typing, you have to start with the **equal sign (=)** always, to tell Excel you want to perform a specific function, otherwise, everything you type into the cell will be recognized as values and not a formula.

SUM | × ✓ f_x | =

	A	B	C	D
1				
2	Items	Sales	Purchases	Profit
3	Toshiba	$4,500.00	$2,500.00	$2,000.00
4	Lenovo	$3,800.00	$3,000.00	$800.00
5	Hp	$6,000.00	$4,000.00	$2,000.00
6	Dell	$3,000.00	$1,450.00	$1,550.00
7	Total	=		
8				

5. The accepted format of entering a formula is as **=(B3*5).** It simply means Excel should find the product of the value inside cell B3 and 5.

B7 | fx =(B3*5)

	A	B	C	D
1				
2	Items	Sales	Purchases	Profit
3	Toshiba	$4,500.00	$2,500.00	$2,000.00
4	Lenovo	$3,800.00	$3,000.00	$800.00
5	Hp	$6,000.00	$4,000.00	$2,000.00
6	Dell	$3,000.00	$1,450.00	$1,550.00
7	Total	$22,500.00		

Note: perhaps you want to use the same formula for every other cell in the same row, simply drag down the plus icon (auto command) and the formula will be assigned to other items in the cells based on the formula concerning their column.

D7 | fx =(D3*5)

	A	B	C	D
1				
2	Items	Sales	Purchases	Profit
3	Toshiba	$4,500.00	$2,500.00	$2,000.00
4	Lenovo	$3,800.00	$3,000.00	$800.00
5	Hp	$6,000.00	$4,000.00	$2,000.00
6	Dell	$3,000.00	$1,450.00	$1,550.00
7	Total	$22,500.00	$12,500.00	$10,000.00
8				

The Fast-Track Method to Observe in Entering A Formula

Excel is capable of calculating mass formulas at once if you get it right with its pattern and method. If you can observe the following patterns of entering a formula, you will never have any problem in getting a speedy result from the Excel formulas you enter:

1. **Make all your system processors available for Excel computation**: Setting all your processors for the task will increase the speed with which Excel works because it will have sufficient processor to handle all the data. You can set up your processor by:

a. Moving to the **File menu** to click on it and then tap on "**options"** from the drop-down list.

b. Click on **Advanced** from the Options drop-down menu and scroll down to where you can locate "**formulas".**

c. Then pick the "**Use all processors on this computer"** option, such will make your Excel calculation work faster than using the partial processor.

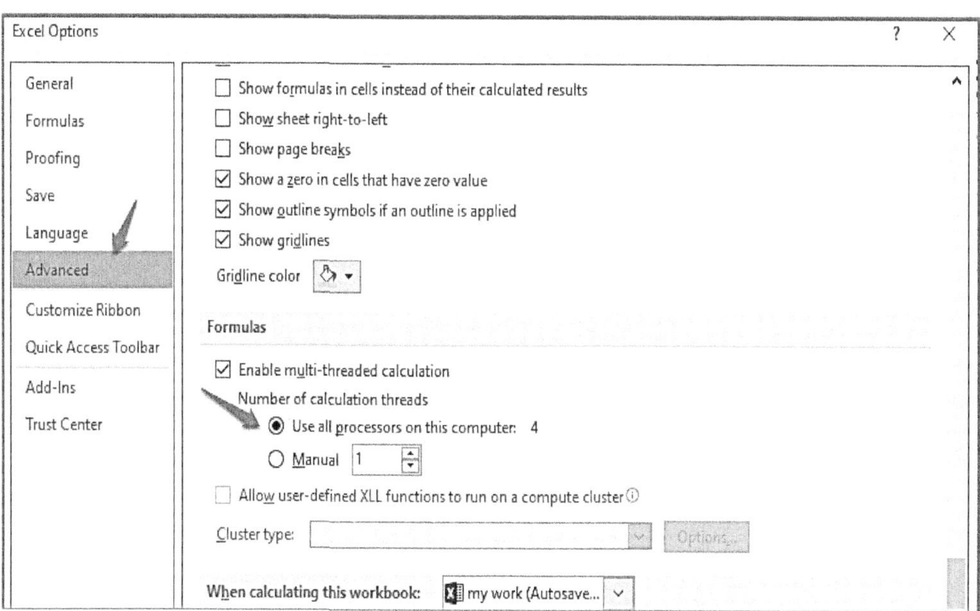

2. **Do not put the final parentheses to a function:** you should not waste time in putting a close parenthesis to your formula; Excel will do that for you automatically. For instance, **= SUM (D3+D4) or =SUM (D3+D4)*5,** just press **Enter,** Excel will add the parentheses and give out the result.

D7 | =SUM(D3+D4)*5

	A	B	C	D
1				
2	Items	Sales	Purchases	Profit
3	Toshiba	$4,500.00	$2,500.00	$2,000.00
4	Lenovo	$3,800.00	$3,000.00	$800.00
5	Hp	$6,000.00	$4,000.00	$2,000.00
6	Dell	$3,000.00	$1,450.00	$1,550.00
7	Total	$22,500.00	$12,500.00	$14,000.00

Though this tip will not work if you have more than one set of parentheses (it may be more than one parenthesis, but must not be than one set of parentheses) inside a formula, nevertheless, it will still guess the structure of what you want to type, you only need to press **Yes** if that's what you wanted to type.

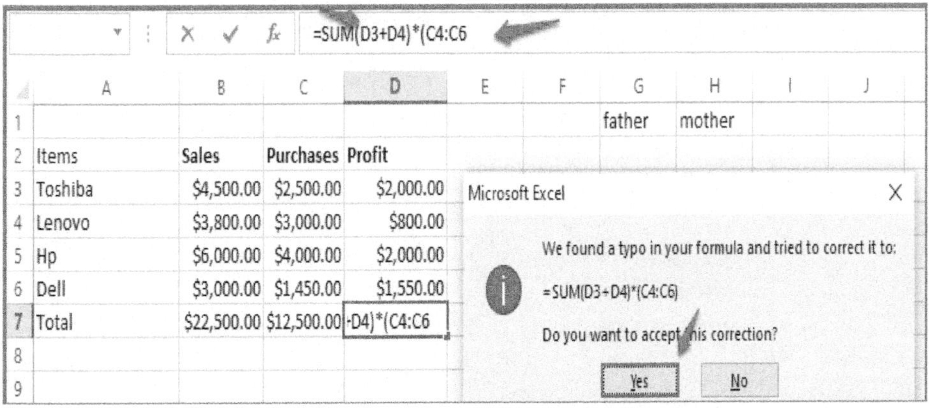

3. **Double click on the Fill handle to copy down the formulas:** when you add formulas together perhaps on the same column or inside the table, you may copy the formula used in the first row to the last row of the same column or table. Simply tap on the **Fill handle** located at the lower right corner of all your selections in Excel, immediately it turns to a plus sign **(+).** Provided the formula in the row sits next to the other row in the same column with a complete set of data

in other cells, just double-click the **Fill handle** and drag it over to copy the formula down to the bottom of the last column or table.

D3 =SUM(B3+C3)

	A	B	C	D
1				
2	Items	Sales	Purchases	Profit
3	Toshiba	$4,500.00	$2,500.00	$7,000.00
4	Lenovo	$3,800.00	$3,000.00	$6,800.00
5	Hp	$6,000.00	$4,000.00	$10,000.00
6	Dell	$3,000.00	$1,450.00	$4,450.00
7	Total	$22,500.00	$12,500.00	$35,000.00

4. **Move the "formula prediction box" out of your way:** at times during insertion of formula, the formula hint may be blocking your view or blocking other data that you may want to include into the formula. When you perceive such, just recall you can move the hint box to any other place inside the worksheet by moving the cursor to the edge of the box till there is a four-headed arrow.

=AVERAGEIF(

	D	E	F	G	H	I
	fixed deposit	Total	Average			
160	300	660	=AVERAGEIF(			
180	5000	5380	AVERAGEIF(range, criteria, [average_range])			
170	10	780				
120	190	710				

Then click and drag to any other position in the worksheet and continue to input your formula. Note that the hint box will still be predicting formulas for you wherever it is in the worksheet.

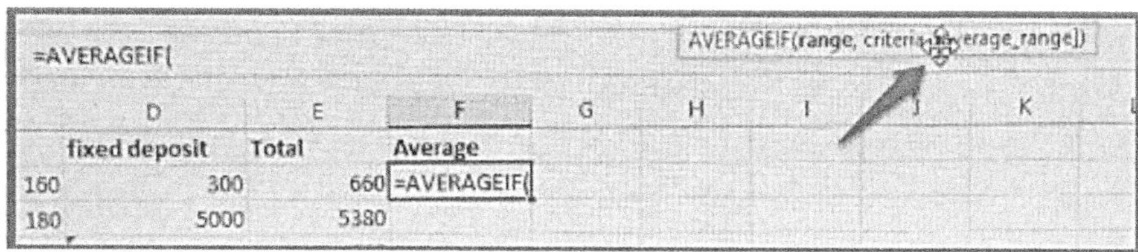

5. **Enter a formula automatically by creating a table:** when you create an Excel table, you can enter a formula faster than if you are using normal worksheet cells.

Immediately you convert your data to a table, any formula you insert into the first row will be copied down to the extreme bottom of the table automatically. Excel table makes work faster and averts errors as well. To create an Excel table, simply follow this procedure:

a. Select all the cells that involved.
b. Then press **Ctrl + T** to draw the table over the selected cells.

SUM | =SUM(D2+E2)

	A	B	C	D	E	F
1	Sport	China	Egypty	France	Canada	Column1
2	Skateboar	15300	10000	5800	12000	=SUM(D2+E2)
3	Basketbal	18500	15400	8000	6000	
4	Boxing	15900	20000	24500	17000	
5	Volley bal	53400	18000	16800	5000	
6	Tennis	12000	6000	40000	24100	
7						

- Excel will update every cell formula of that same column like that of the first column automatically without applying any command.

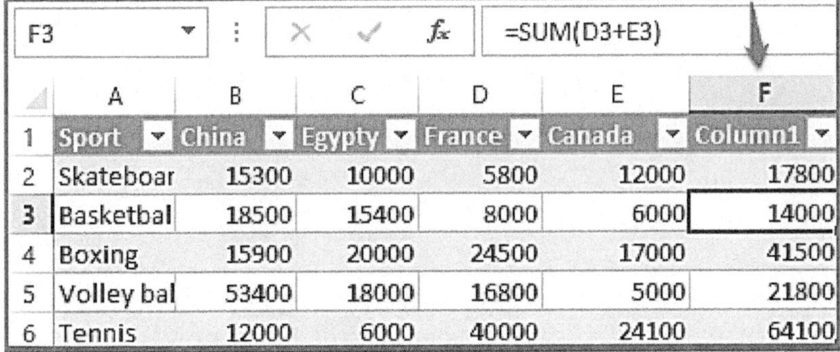

F3 | =SUM(D3+E3)

	A	B	C	D	E	F
1	Sport	China	Egypty	France	Canada	Column1
2	Skateboar	15300	10000	5800	12000	17800
3	Basketbal	18500	15400	8000	6000	14000
4	Boxing	15900	20000	24500	17000	41500
5	Volley bal	53400	18000	16800	5000	21800
6	Tennis	12000	6000	40000	24100	64100

6. **Take advantage of Auto commands, arrow key, and the tab key to enter a function:** As you are about to enter a formula,

a. Insert **an equal (=) sign** and start typing, Excel will begin to pair the text you are entering against the huge list of the functions which is accessible in Excel. The list will correspond with the first letter you type.
b. Scroll down with the arrow key and check the function you want. Immediately you sight the function you want, just make the arrow key remain on it and then press the **tab** key, immediately, such function will be selected.

Av

D	E	F
fixed deposit	Total	Average
300	660	=Av
5000	5380	AVEDEV
10	780	AVERAGE
190	710	AVERAGEA
		AVERAG[illegible] Finds average(arithmetic mean) for the cells
		AVERAGEI[illegible]

7. **Move a formula and retain its references:** know that you can copy a formula to another position and such formula address will be adjusted to the new position, but at times, the situation may demand that you will have to retain the formula's address for an essential reason. To do that, kindly drag and drop the value to another position, its address will remain untouched and unchanged.

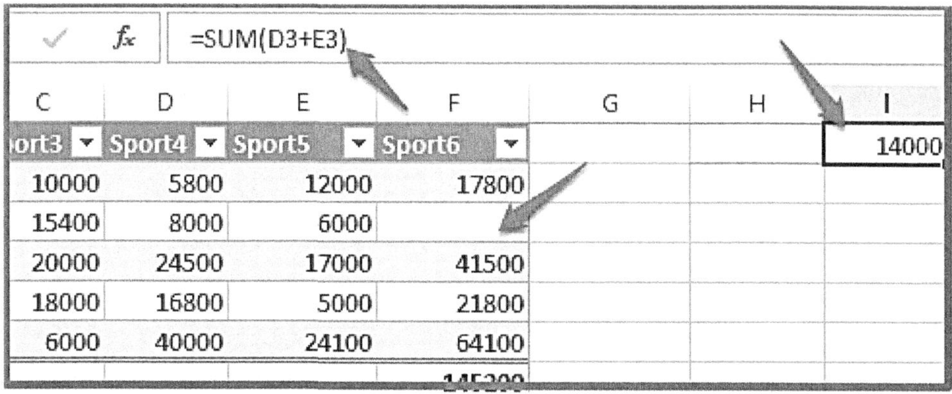

=SUM(D3+E3)

C	D	E	F	G	H	I
ort3	Sport4	Sport5	Sport6			14000
10000	5800	12000	17800			
15400	8000	6000				
20000	24500	17000	41500			
18000	16800	5000	21800			
6000	40000	24100	64100			

8. **Making use of named range makes formulas convenient and clear:** With named range, formula is easy to use, for instance using pounds or dollars always make cells' addresses more complicated. Making use of name range saves a lot of time and thereby makes formulas work faster. Creating a named range is as simple as ABC. Kindly:

a. Select the cells you wish to name
b. Move to the **Name box** beside the formula bar and type the name you want to use, and then press **Enter**, automatically, the cell range will name them. Hence, you can make use of it in the formula by pointing on the name range as you are structuring a formula.

Sales | fx 4500

	A	B	C
1			
2	Items		
3	Toshiba	4500	2500
4	Lenovo	3800	3000
5	Hp	6000	4000
6	Dell	3000	5000
7	Total	22500	12500
8			

Note: you may also move to the **Name box** and click on the drop-down arrow to pick the name from the name box and apply it to the cell you selected.

Reference Cells in The Worksheet by Clicking on The Cells

You can click on the cells inside the worksheet to enter their references instead of typing them into the box. Let us examine the steps that are involved:

1. Click **the cell** that will be the receiver of the cells you want to reference.
2. Input an **equal (=) sign** to the cell above in (1).
3. Click **the cell** or drag it over to the groups of cells you want to make reference to, then, the names or references of those cells will enter into the receiver cell instantly after the equal sign.

fx =D3:D7

	C	D	E	F	G	H
00	10000	5800	12000	17800		=D3:D7
00	15400	8000	6000	14000		
00	20000	24500	17000	41500		
00	18000	16800	5000	21800		
00	6000	40000	24100	64100		

4. Press **ENTER** to create cell references.

Inserting A Cell Range

A cell is referred to by the intersection of the column letter and its corresponding row number e.g., B2. Cell range or range of cell is called a group of adjacent cells because they are arranged next to each other, and they are separated with the use of column.

There two ways of inserting a cell range, these are:

1. Typing a cell range into the formula box.

SUM × ✓ fx =B3:B7

	A	B	C
1			
2	Items		
3	Toshiba	4500	2500
4	Lenovo	3800	3000
5	Hp	6000	4000
6	Dell	3000	5000
7	Total	22500	12500

2. Dragging the cursor across the cells to be included within the range of cells.

   Note: There are also two cell ranges, they are:

a. An adjacent range of cell (e.g. A3:A6), and
b. Non-adjacent cell range (e.g. C2:D6).

Creating Cell Range Name for Formulas' Use

Cell range name is the easiest way of entering data for formulas. Entering cell addresses one after the other is a very strenuous task (such as C3 + C4 + C5 + C6 + C7) and also, it may not be accurate as D4:D6. It is the cell range name that is very dependable and convenient for formulas' use. To create a cell range name, check the below guides for guidance:

1. Select the range of cells you want to name.
2. Click the **formula bar** and pick the **Define Name** button to command for the New Name dialog box.

FORMULAS DATA REVIEW VIEW

Date & Time ▾ | Lookup & Reference ▾ | Math & Trig ▾ | More Functions ▾ | Name Manager | Define Name ▾ | Use in Formula ▾ | Create from Selection

Defined Names

D	E	F	G	H	I
		4500	2500	7000	
		3800	3000	6800	
		6000	4000	3500000	
		3000	5000	8000	
		22500	12500	35000	

3. Insert a brief and concise name in the provided box.
4. Move to the **Scope** drop-down list, select the **worksheet name** if the use of the range name will not go beyond the worksheet to which it is created from, but, select W**orkboo**k if you have the intention of using the name range you have just created in another worksheet.
5. Then click **OK** for confirmation.

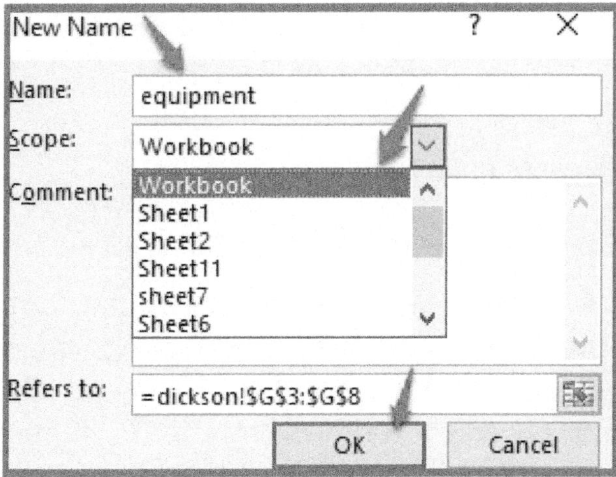

Note: range name reference does not change when you copy a formula with range name address from one cell to the other. A range name consistently refers to the same set of cells, and that is one of its merits.

To make use of the name range created above in a formula, simply:

a. Tap on the **Formula** bar at the place where you want to make use of the cell range name and pick the "**Use in Formula"** button.
b. Then choose **a cell range name** from the drop-down menu.

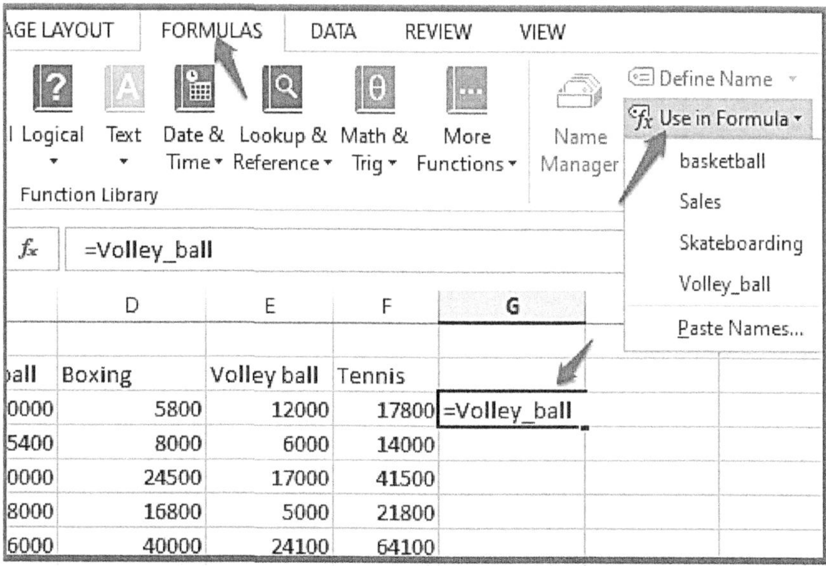

Alternatively, you can also do this:

a. Move to the **formula** button and click on it, then tap on the **"Use in Formula"** option.

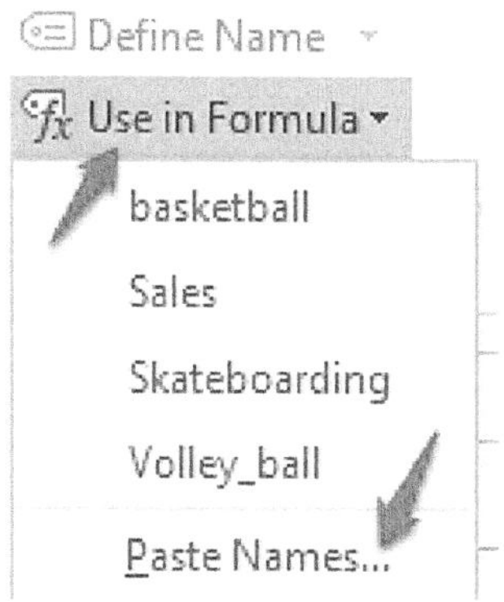

b. From the "**Use in Formula"** option drop-down, pick **Paste Names,** and a paste Names dialog box will come forth.

c. Choose a cell range name and tap **Ok**.

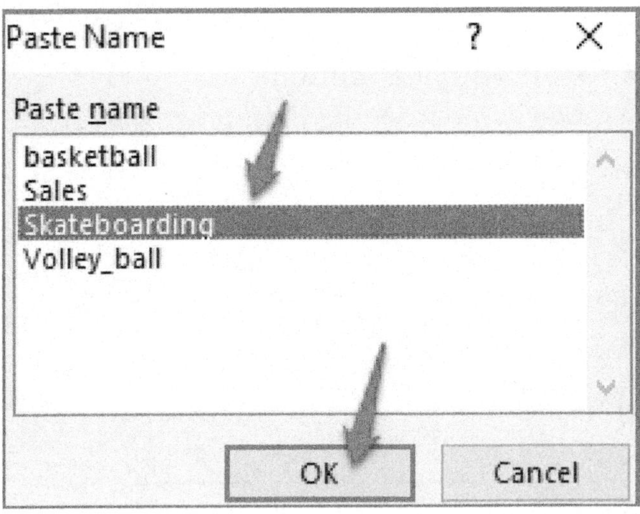

Handling the cell range name: the cell range name belongs to you; you have all the chance to adjust it to your taste whether you want to rename or delete it. To rename or delete a cell range name, follow these processes:

a. Tap on the **Formulas** bar and click on the **"Name Manager"** button**,** then, the Name Manager Dialog box with a list of cell range names shows up.

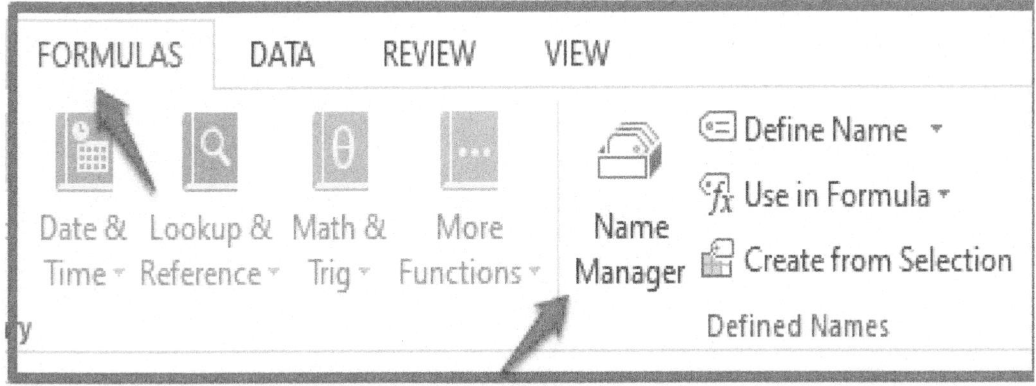

b. Simply click on the cell range name you want to adjust.
c. **To delete**, move to the top where the **Delete** button is and tap on it to delete the range name you want to delete, and then tap on **Ok** to effect the changes.

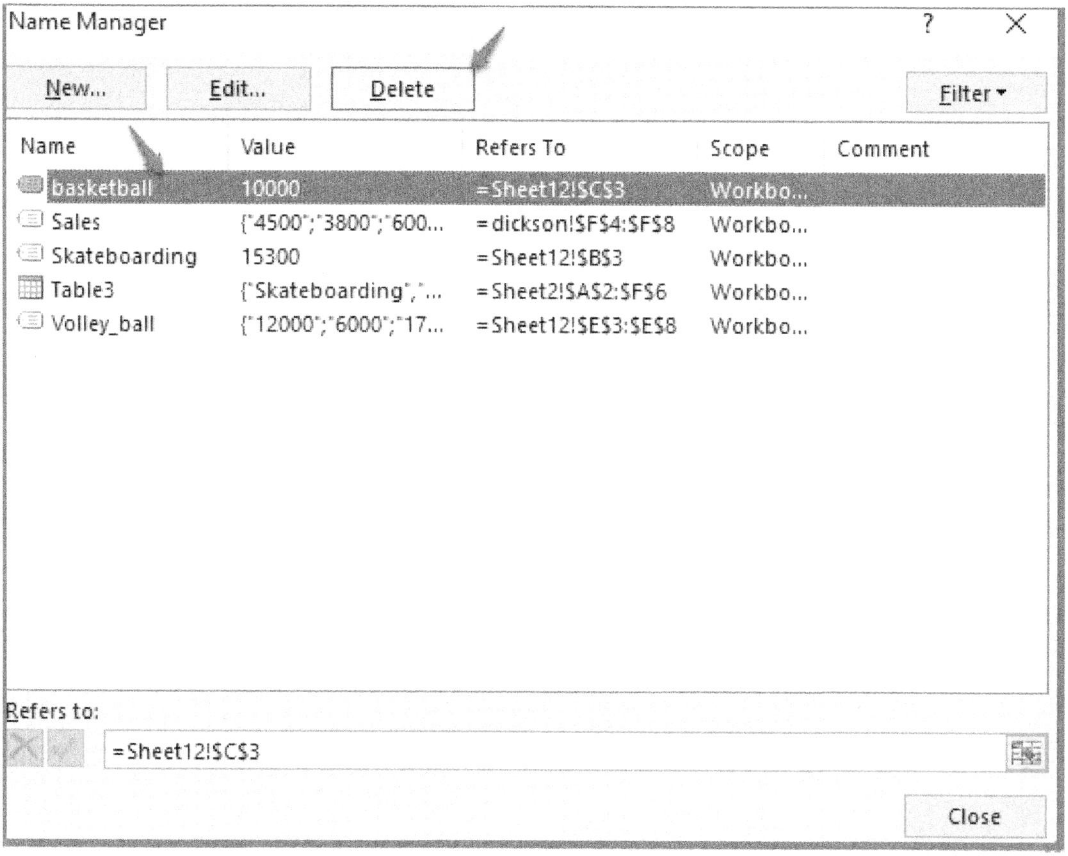

Name Manager
New...
Edit...
Delete
Filter
Name
Value
Refers To
Scope
Comment
basketball
10000
=Sheet12!$C$3
Workbo...
Sales
{"4500";"3800";"600...
=dickson!$F$4:$F$8
Workbo...
Skateboarding
15300
=Sheet12!$B$3
Workbo...
Table3
{"Skateboarding","...
=Sheet2!$A$2:$F$6
Workbo...
Volley_ball
{"12000";"6000";"17...
=Sheet12!$E$3:$E$8
Workbo...
Refers to:
=Sheet12!$C$3
Close

d. **To rename**, click on the **Edit** button at the top and insert the name of your choice in the Edit Name dialog box, then tap **Ok**.

Edit Name
Name:
basketball
Scope:
Workbook
Comment:
Refers to:
=Sheet12!$C$3
OK
Cancel

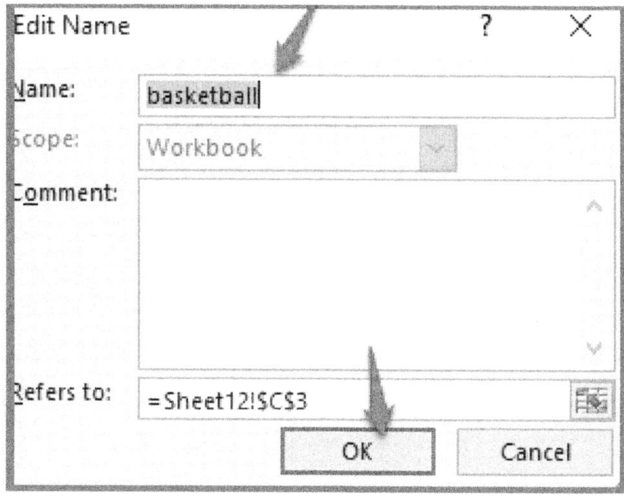

Pointing to Cells in A Worksheet for Formula Purpose in A Different Worksheet

You are permitted to use the cell content of another worksheet of the same workbook for your formulas since the worksheet contains the data and the contents you need for formulas computation. For example, Worksheet 1 has expenditure items for the whole month with the total aggregate amount; likewise, worksheet 2 has all income items with the total aggregate amount. If it happens that the profit establishment will take place in worksheet 2 with a formula, definitely you will need some figures in worksheet 1 before you can arrive at an exact profit figure and thus, you have to point to those cells in worksheet 1 for calculation. Let us check the below example for more comprehension of how to point to cells for the use of formulas in other worksheets.

a. Inside **Worksheet 2** where you want to use a formula, structure it as if you want to enter a formula by starting with **=SUM(D3+D6)-AVERAGE(**

SUM | =SUM(D3+D6)-AVERAGE(

	A	B	C	D	E	F	G	H
1								
2		Skateboard	Basketball	Boxing	Volley ball	Tennis		
3		15300	10000	5800	12000		=SUM(D3+D6)-AVERAGE(	
4		18500	15400	8000	6000	14000		
5		15900	20000	24500	17000	41500		
6		53400	18000	16800	5000	21800		Sheet2
7		12000	6000	40000	24100	64100		

b. When you need to enter contents of worksheet 1, click on **worksheet 1** tab to move into worksheet 1, immediately you move to sheet 1, you will see sheet1 with an Exclamation mark (sheet1!) in front of the formulas which you are typing in sheet 2

c. Click on the **cell or group of cells** that has the contents you want to make use of by dragging over them or by typing the range in front of (sheet1!) without going back to worksheet 2 where you started the formula. For this illustration, type (E4:E6).

d. Immediately you select the cell(s), it will reflect on the formula box as a continuation of worksheet 2 formula inside sheet 1.

Clipboard | Font | Alignment

A3 | × ✓ f_x | =SUM(D3+D6)-AVERAGE(Sheet1!E4:E6)

	A	B	C	D	E	F	G	H
3	Revenue from sales:			April	May	June		
4	pawpaw			150	180	150		$200
5	orange			300	250	400		$180
6	pearl			100	500	180		$260
7	Total income			550				
8				D3:D7				

sheet1

e. After the selection, close the parentheses and press **Enter**. Immediately you tap the enter key, you will be moved from sheet 1 to sheet 2 where you will see the result of the formulas you completed in sheet 1. Nothing will show again in sheet 1.

G3 | × ✓ f_x | =SUM(D3+D6)-AVERAGE(Sheet1!E4:E6)

	A	B	C	D	E	F	G
1							
2		Skateboard	Basketball	Boxing	Volley ball	Tennis	
3		15300	10000	5800	12000		22290
4		18500	15400	8000	6000	14000	
5		15900	20000	24500	17000	41500	
6		53400	18000	16800	5000	21800	
7		12000	6000	40000	24100	64100	

sheet2

Ways of Copying Formulas from One Cell to Other Cell

Excel provides a means of copying formulas from one cell to other cells instead of typing formulas again. Since the formula is of the same pattern, Excel will only amend the cell reference but will still be the same pattern of the formulas. Copying formulas from one cell to another is the easiest and fastest means.

To copy Excel formulas from cell to cell, kindly:

a. Choose **the cell** that has the formula you want to pass across to others.

G3 | f_x =SUM(B3:F3)

	A	B	C	D	E	F	G
1							
2		Skateboard	Basketball	Boxing	Volley ball	Tennis	Total
3		15300	10000	5800	12000	5000	48100
4		18500	15400	8000	6000	14000	
5		15900	20000	24500	17000	41500	
6		53400	18000	16800	5000	21800	
7		12000	6000	40000	24100	64100	
8							

b. Place the cursor to the lower part at the right side and wait till it turns to a black plus sign (+) so as to make use of it in **Autofill handle by dragging it** over the cell you want to copy the formulas to.

c. Release the mouse button to finish the process, and then go back to the cell that you copied it to, click on it and check if the formula pattern is correlated with what you want, because at times, you might have missed something in the formula and it will reflect on the subsequent result.

Discovering and Adjusting Formulas Error

Making an error in Excel formulas can't be overemphasized. One mistake inside Excel formulas can pollute all the calculations inside the worksheet. When a formula error occurs in Excel, you will discover by the presence of a small green triangle at the upper left side of the cell. Once you discover an error, the next action is an amendment. There are various errors that users can make in Excel formulas; let us quickly check those frequent errors that can occur during Excel formulas:

Frequent Message Error for Entering Wrong Formulas

Error symbols	The actual mistake
#NAME	Using a range name that is not well defined such as adding certain symbols to the range name. check the name and restructure it.
#NULL	Referring to a cell range that is not entered correctly.
#DIV/0!	Wrongly divide the number by something that does not exist, like zero.
#REF	Referring to a range name that does not exist
#VALUE	This occurs a lot, it occurs when formulas are being miswritten or you used incorrect functions.
#NUM	Using unacceptable and incorrect argument.

To amend any formula blunder you committed in Excel, there are ways of adjusting errors; we will look at them one after the other:

Discover More About the Error and Adjusting It

a. Select the **cell with signal error** (small green triangle at the upper left corner of the cell).
b. Then click the **Error Checking button** to know more about the error and a means of correcting it.

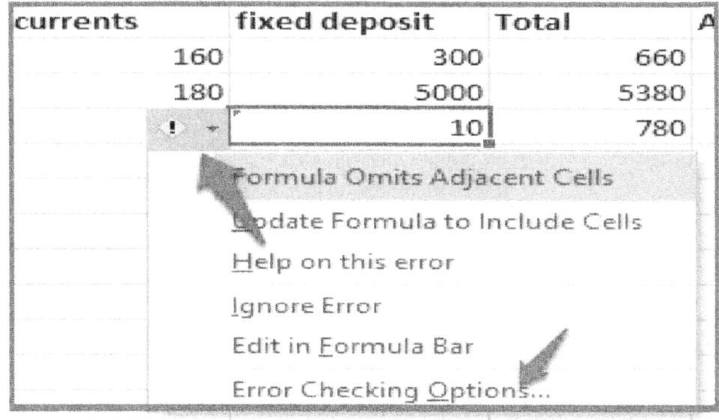

Tracing Cell References

This is meant for a crowded worksheet that is loaded with a lot of formulas even formulas from the neighbor worksheet. Tracing the cell reference will give you a hint of how the formulas are structured, and the error contains also a means of restricting the formulas. To trace cell reference, Excel has two types of cell tracer. Both show a connection about the cell you used in carrying out the formulas. A cell tracer shows a blue arrow in tracing the connection that exists between the formulas. Let us quickly run a quick check on the two cell tracers that are available in Excel:

1. **Tracing Precedent:** tracing a precedent helps Excel Users to discover those cells you used in arriving at the result of the formula. It points an arrow to all the cells that contain the data used in arriving at the result of the formula. To make use of Trace precedents, simply:

a. Select the **cell(s)** that has the formula inside and move to the **Formulas** tab.
b. Inside the formulas tab, click on the "**Trace Precedent"** button to check the cells that contribute to the formula and check if there should be a necessary adjustment to the data inside those cells.

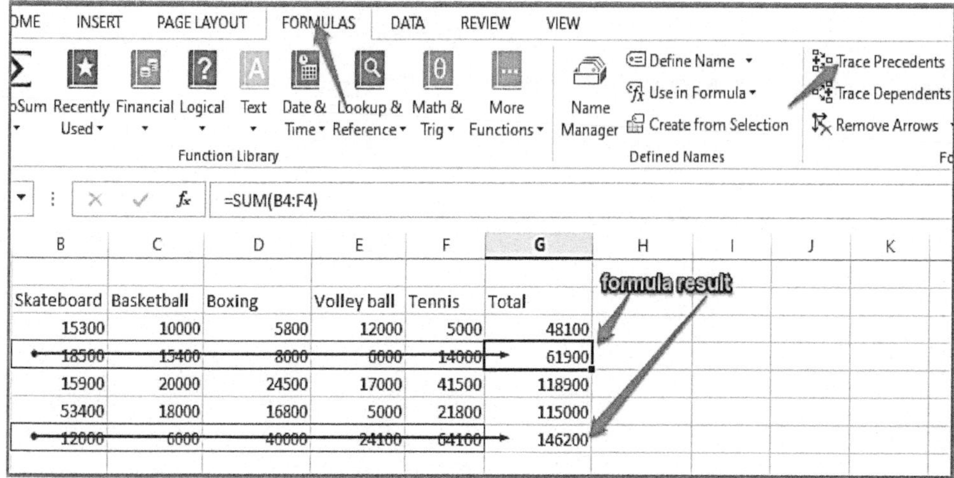

2. **Tracing dependents:** this is just the exact opposite of tracing precedent. Here the cell may have a formula or value inside, but its value or formula is used in producing formula result in another cell. And thus, cell tracer will trace from the cell selected (that is the cell that contributes to another cell formula result) to the

cell where its formula or value is used (the cell with the total formula result). To make use of the Trace dependents, you have to:

a. Select **the cell** you want to trace its dependence.
b. Maneuver to the **formulas** bar and pick the **"Trace dependent"** button, check the relationship and amend any necessary item that needs amendment.

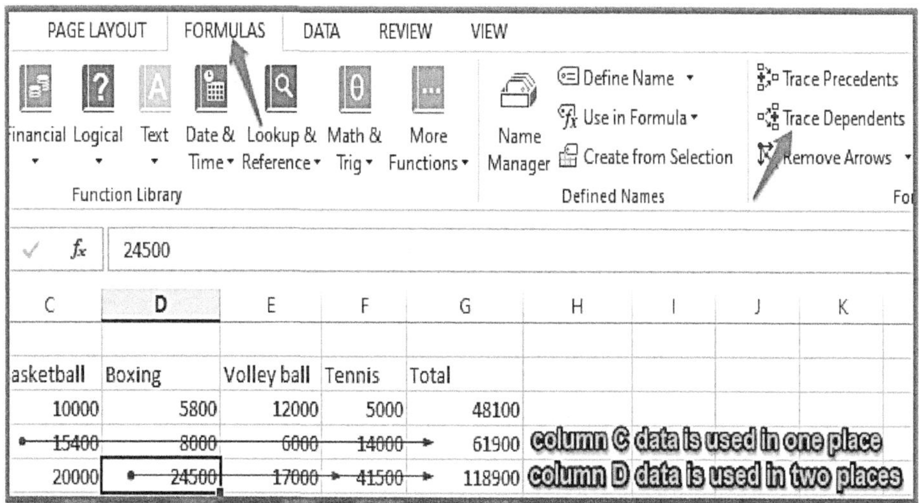

Immediately you are done tracing the cells in either option (precedent or dependent), and you are also done establishing the connection you want to establish, you can proceed to remove the cell tracer so you can have a real worksheet back by: following these steps:

a. Move to the **formulas** bar and tap on the "**Remove Arrows"** button below the precedent and dependent arrow.
b. Select either **Remove Precedent or Dependent** depending on the one you want to remove.

Making Use of Error Checkers Button

Error checker will move to the worksheet and check for any available error, once it detects the error, it will pass the details to you inside the dialog box, and then you can make the necessary adjustment.

How do I run the Error Checker? By:

a. Maneuver to the **formulas** tab and tap on **Error Checker** Button.

b. You will see the state of the error and the causative factor. Tap on **"Edit in Formula Bar"** inside the dialog box and adjust it there.

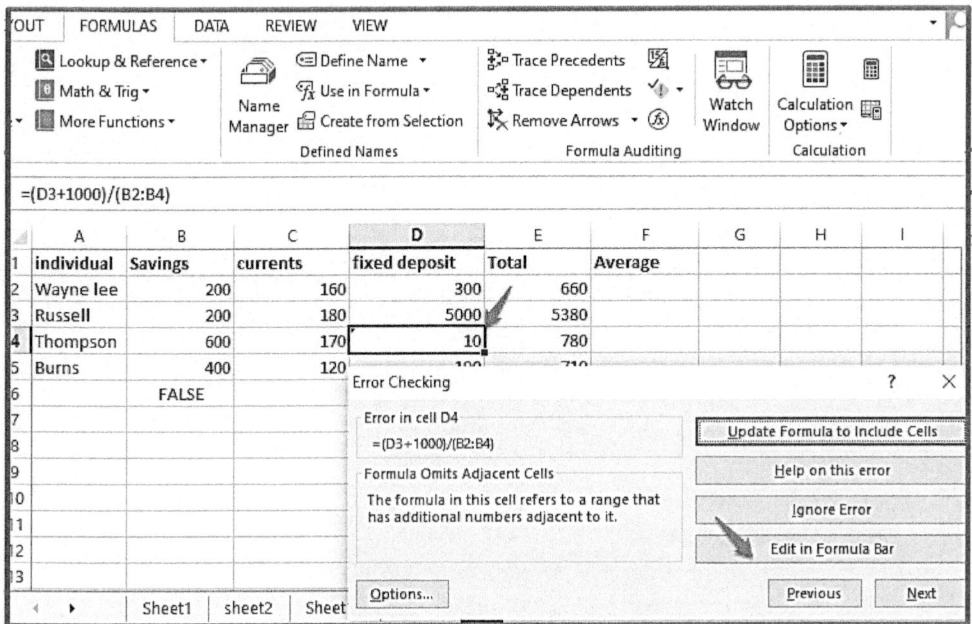

c. Then click on **Resume** when you are done adjusting.

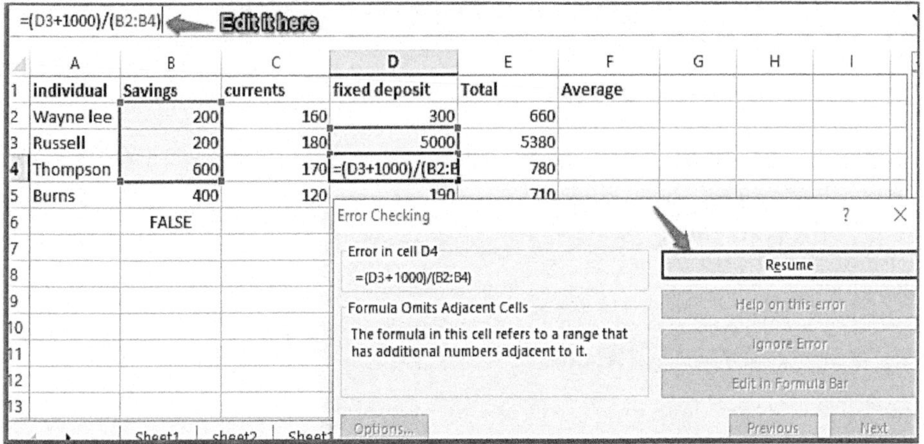

Note: immediately you done adjusting one error, you have to click on the **Resume** option so that every other key will be active again, then click on the **"Next"** button to check the worksheet's next error, but if the error needs no adjustment, tap on the **Ignore** button and you will be moved to the next error.

Stepping into A Function

A function is an embodiment of a formula that you can use in Excel. Excel has a lot of Functions, though areas of their use depend on the Excel user's discipline, nevertheless, there are general functions that cross all disciplines such as **AVERAGE, SUM, PRODUCT,** and other most used functions. They are all located in the formulas tab. This guide will explain more on the general workable functions and how to make them find expressions in formulas to Excel users.

Understand the Use of Argument in Function

Argument is any information you supply after the insertion of a function for instance, let us use SUM function and give it a correct argument, =SUM(B3:B7); (B3:B7) is an argument, though some function does not require an argument, for example**, =TODAY() and =NOW(),** these two functions require no argument, both of them are used to get actual date and time, that is why the parenthesis is empty.

=NOW()

B	C	D	E	F	G
gs	currents	fixed deposit	Total	Average	
200	160	300	660		24/03/2021
200	180	5000	5380		24/03/2021 13:03
600	170	10	780		
400	120	190	710		

Note: using more than one argument for a function needs a comma, for example, =LARGE(B2:B4, 3).

Checking Out the Necessary Argument for A Given Function

At a time, you may not know the specific argument for the function you are about to use, no qualms, for any function you want to insert, simply:

a. Click on a cell and input the equal (=) sign.
b. Insert the **function** and get the parentheses opened like =AVERAGE (double click on the Function replica in the guessing box.

× ✓ fx =AVERAGE(

B	C	D	E	F	G
gs	currents	fixed deposit	Total	Average	
200	160	300	660	=AVERAGE(	24/03/2021
200	180	5000	5380	AVERAGE(**number1**, [number2], ...)	
600	170	10	780		
400	120	190	710		

c. Immediately, Excel will activate a hint of all the arguments that are available for the function you have entered, follow it to explore any Function that you do not know its argument.

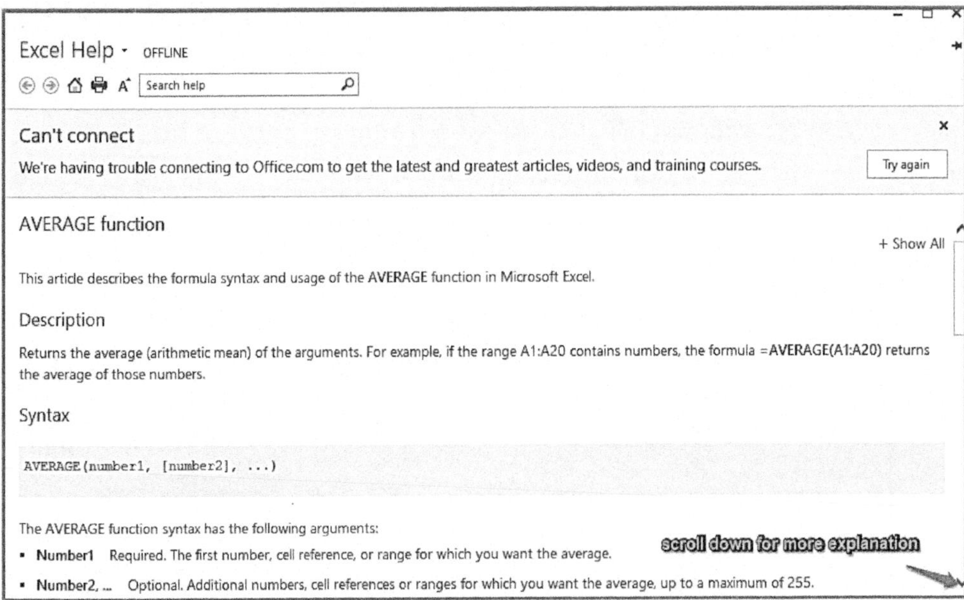
Excel Help · OFFLINE

Search help

Can't connect

We're having trouble connecting to Office.com to get the latest and greatest articles, videos, and training courses. Try again

AVERAGE function

+ Show All

This article describes the formula syntax and usage of the **AVERAGE** function in Microsoft Excel.

Description

Returns the average (arithmetic mean) of the arguments. For example, if the range A1:A20 contains numbers, the formula =**AVERAGE(A1:A20)** returns the average of those numbers.

Syntax

```
AVERAGE(number1, [number2], ...)
```

The AVERAGE function syntax has the following arguments:

- **Number1** Required. The first number, cell reference, or range for which you want the average.
- **Number2, ...** Optional. Additional numbers, cell references or ranges for which you want the average, up to a maximum of 255.

Note: those arguments in the bracket are optional, while those that are not in the bracket are required arguments for example = **NETWORKDAY(2/4/2021-4/6/2021, [today]).**

ENTERING A FUNCTION FOR BUILDING A FORMULA

You can either insert a function either by typing it in the formula bar or inviting Excel to guide you through, let us quickly examine the two ways:

1. **Typing into the formula bar or directly into the selected cell:**

a. Select **the cell** where you want the formula to be created.

b. Type the equal (=) sign directly into the cell after the selection of the cell or in the formula bar
c. Type the **function,** open parentheses and insert your argument, then close the parentheses and press **Enter.**

=AVERAGE(G3:G6)

D	E	F	G	H
Boxing	Volley ball	Tennis	Total	
5800	12000	5000	48100	85975
8000	6000	14000	61900	
24500	17000	41500	118900	
16800	5000	21800	115000	
40000	24100	64100	146200	

Note: you may enter the function in small letters to fast-track your speed, Excel will change it to upper case automatically.

2. Invite Excel to guide you in inserting the function:

a. Select **the cell** where you want the formula to reflect.
b. Maneuver to the **formulas** tab and select the **Insert Function** to open the Insert function dialog box.

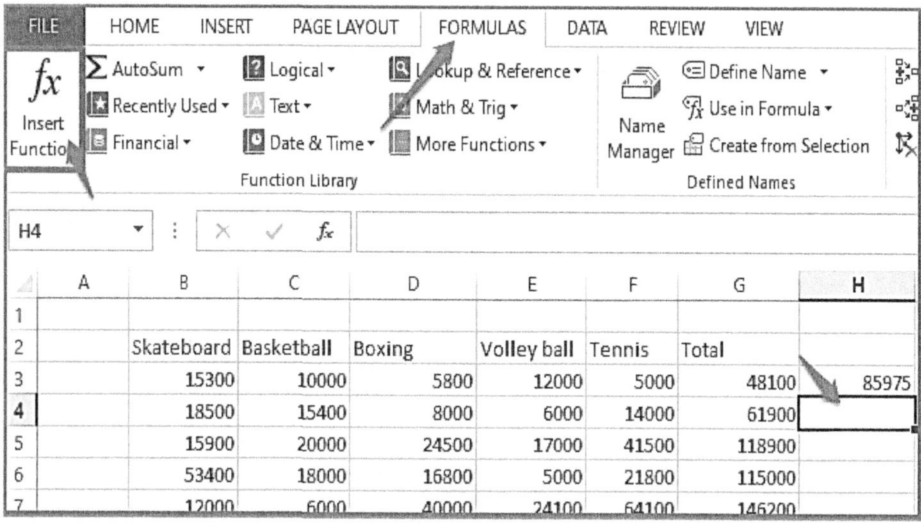

	A	B	C	D	E	F	G	H
1								
2		Skateboard	Basketball	Boxing	Volley ball	Tennis	Total	
3		15300	10000	5800	12000	5000	48100	85975
4		18500	15400	8000	6000	14000	61900	
5		15900	20000	24500	17000	41500	118900	
6		53400	18000	16800	5000	21800	115000	
7		12000	6000	40000	24100	64100	146200	

c. Choose a category from the **"select a category"** option which includes the most recently used, show all, and other categories.

d. Then choose a function from the **"Select a function"** list and tap **Ok**, another dialog box will appear where you will select the cells to be included in the formula.

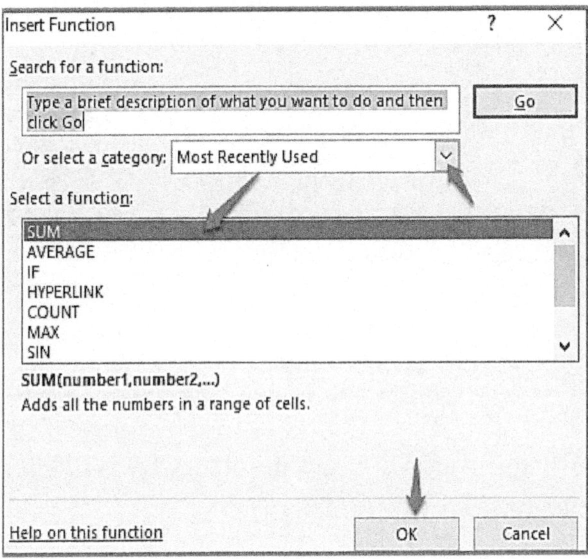

e. Select **the cells** you want to include by typing the cell address into the provided box or by clicking the first cell then drag it over the cell you want to include in the formula

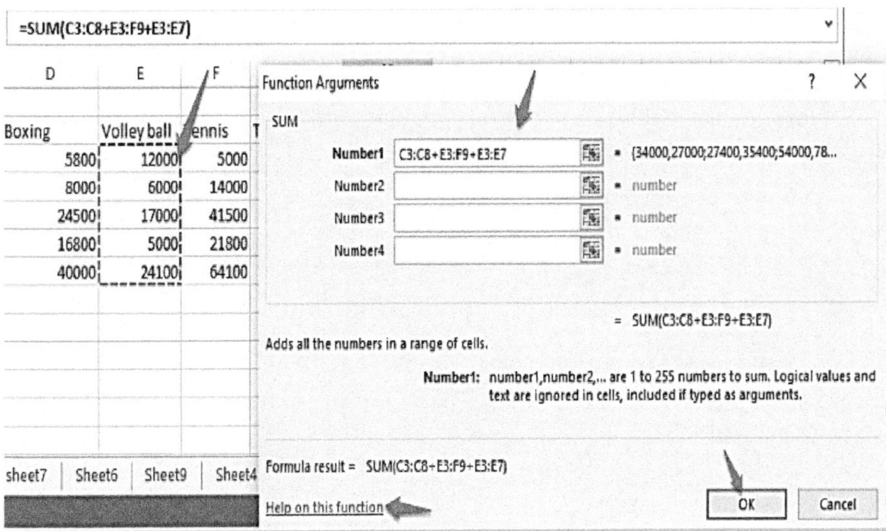

Note: each function has a separate box for the second Window dialog box. If you do not have an understanding of a specific function, call on Excel to help you out by clicking on the "Help on this function" located at the bottom left of the "Insert Function Dialog Box" and Excel will proffer a way out.

Glancing Through Generally Used Function

GENERALLY USED FUNCTION	DESCRIPTION
SUM	Addition of total cells listed in the argument.
AVERAGE	The average value of the cells recommended in the argument.
PRODUCT	The product or multiplication of the listed cell in the argument.
MAX	The largest value out of the listed cell in the argument.
MIN	The smallest value out of the listed cell in the argument.
COUNT	It represents the total number of cells listed in the argument
STDEV	Computation of a standard deviation per the sample of the cells listed in the argument.
STDEVP	Computation of a standard deviation per all the cells in the argument.

Using COUNT and COUNTIF To Count Data Item in A Cell Range

The **COUNT** function is used in counting the number of the data item you have in a selected range of cells, take for instance, =COUNT(B3:B7)

A9 | =COUNT(B3:B7)

	A	B	C	D
1				
2		Mass(Kilogram)	Classification of food	
3	Rice	500	Food	
4	Orange	320	Fruit	
5	Apple	400	Fruit	
6	Noodles	350	Food	
7	Banana	600	Fruit	
8				
9	5			

While COUNTIF function works very close to the COUNT function with the exception that the COUNTIF function adds A CRITERION to the argument. It counts how many cells are in the range of selected cells and how many have a particular value, and therefore to use the COUNTIF function you will be having two arguments (Cell range, and the Criterion). The criterion will be enclosed with quotation marks. Take for example, to know how many fruits are in the classification of food, the formula will be structured like this, =**COUNTIF(B3:B7, "Fruit").**

A10 | =COUNTIF(C3:C7, "Fruit")

	A	B	C	D	E
1					
2		Mass(Kilogram)	Classification of food		
3	Rice	500	Food		
4	Orange	320	Fruit		
5	Apple	400	Fruit		
6	Noodles	350	Food		
7	Banana	600	Fruit		
8					
9	5				
10	3				

Joining Text with Value with Concatenate

Concatenate Function is about value combination from different cells and merging such into a single cell for a particular purpose, take, for instance, having a three-column name joined together to produce a single full name. The structure of the Concatenate function is like this: **=CONCATENATE(text1, text2,text3,.......).** In combining texts, you have to include space that will be between the quotation marks as an argument for the below example; this is a formula for three (3) names that will combine to be the full name=**CONCATENATE(A3," ", B3," "," ", C3).**

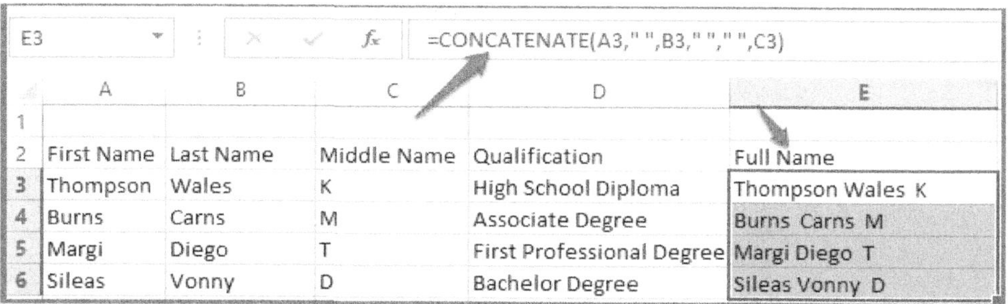

E3 | =CONCATENATE(A3," ",B3," "," ",C3)

	A	B	C	D	E
1					
2	First Name	Last Name	Middle Name	Qualification	Full Name
3	Thompson	Wales	K	High School Diploma	Thompson Wales K
4	Burns	Carns	M	Associate Degree	Burns Carns M
5	Margi	Diego	T	First Professional Degree	Margi Diego T
6	Sileas	Vonny	D	Bachelor Degree	Sileas Vonny D

Using Average for Averaging Point Value

The **AVERAGE** function is used in determining the average point of a given data of a selected cell or a cell range. Let us take the below table as an instance by using the AVERAGE to estimate the average point score of the four students in three subjects. This is the structure of the AVERAGE function, =**AVERAGE(cell range).**

E4 | =AVERAGE(B4:D4)

	A	B	C	D	E	F
2						
3		English	Maths	French	Average	
4	Alpha	80	50	60	63.33333	
5	Burney	70	50	40	53.33333	
6	Daves	40	80	90	70	
7	Hart	60	38	65	54.33333	

Excel exempts empty cells in the cell range during counting, but it regards zero (0) as part of the range and therefore computes for zero (0).

PMT For Estimating Periodic Payment of Loan

Have you borrowed a specific amount of money or you are about to take a loan but you are confused about the time it will take to repay the loan or how much can even borrow, no qualms, that is what PMT caters for, it describes the particular amount you can borrow at various interest rates and how much you will be paying on such loan yearly or monthly by dividing the yearly rate by 12 months to get the amount to be paid on monthly basis. To make use of the PMT function for calculating periodic payment, kindly observe this formula structure: =PMT(Interest rate, number of payment, amount of loan), let us check the structure worksheet for how PMT looks like:

D4 =PMT(A4,B4,C4)

	A	B	C	D	E
1					
2	Interest rate	No. of Payment	Amount of loan	Yearly Payment	Monthly payment
3	3.00%	120	$5,000	-$154.45	-$12.87
4	3.00%	120	$8,000	-$247.12	-$20.59
5	3.00%	120	$4,000	-$123.56	-$10.30
6	3.00%	120	$6,000	-$185.34	-$15.44

Explicit explanation:

a. **Interest rate**: do not put a percentage to the interest rate for it to be accepted as a number. After you are done typing the interest rate, move to the **Home** tab under number and go to percentage to format the column. That is, column (A).
b. **No of payment:** The no of time to redeem the loan is 10 years, long time loan payment ought to be paid every month, for the case of the loan in this illustration, it is 10 years, multiply it by 12 months in a calendar year, it equals 120 times in 10 years. That is column B.
c. **Amount of the loan:** insert the loan amount directly to column C, which is the amount you are calculating for what you want to borrow.
d. **Yearly payment of the loan:** this one will be having a formula in this structure: =PMT(A3, B3, C3), it is in column D.

e. **Monthly payment of the loan:** to get the amount to be paid every month, you have to divide the yearly payment with a 12-month calendar in formula (=D3/12) for cell E3.

Project Time Measuring with NETWORKDAY and TODAY

Networkday and Today measures the period of days to come, probably for a specific program, assignment, budget planning, etc. It is mainly concerned with workdays only and thus, excludes weekend (Saturday and Sunday), and therefore, the result of NETWORKDAY is for workdays alone. To make use of NETWORKDAY, structure its formula like this: =NETWORKDAY(Start date-End date).

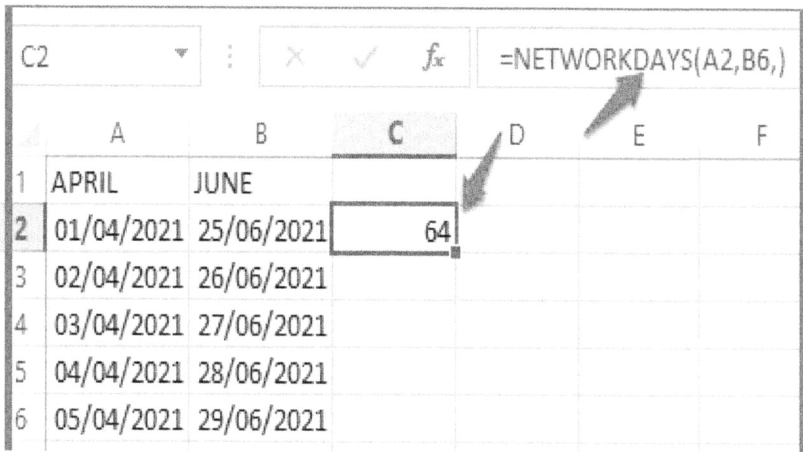

C2 | =NETWORKDAYS(A2,B6,)

	A	B	C	D	E	F
1	APRIL	JUNE				
2	01/04/2021	25/06/2021	64			
3	02/04/2021	26/06/2021				
4	03/04/2021	27/06/2021				
5	04/04/2021	28/06/2021				
6	05/04/2021	29/06/2021				

TODAY's function structure is like this: =**TODAY()** because it does not argue.

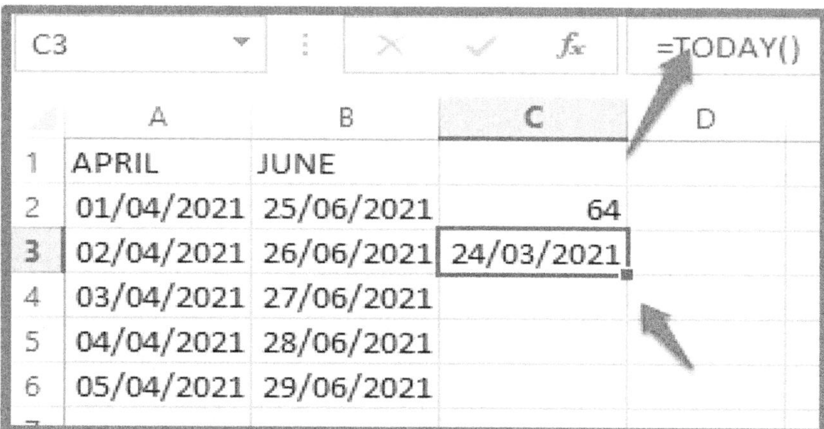

C3 | =TODAY()

	A	B	C	D
1	APRIL	JUNE		
2	01/04/2021	25/06/2021	64	
3	02/04/2021	26/06/2021	24/03/2021	
4	03/04/2021	27/06/2021		
5	04/04/2021	28/06/2021		
6	05/04/2021	29/06/2021		

Note: to get the number of days between two dates, simply remove the latest date from the earlier date by using the minus sign. It will give you a total of the days between the selected dates without removing Saturday and Sunday, =”30/6/2021”-“1/4/2021”. The enclosed quotation is for date identification to Excel.

C5 =("30/06/2021"-"1/04/2021")

	A	B	C	D	E	F	G
1	APRIL	JUNE					
2	01/04/2021	25/06/2021	64				
3	02/04/2021	26/06/2021	24/03/2021				
4	03/04/2021	27/06/2021					
5	04/04/2021	28/06/2021	90				
6	05/04/2021	29/06/2021					
7							

LEN For Counting Text Character

LEN function in Excel is referred to as the length Excel function as long as it is used to ascertain the length or character of a given word, cell numbers, and many more. To get an in-depth understanding of this function, let us make use of it with the SUM function. =SUM(LEN(A2),LEN(B2)).

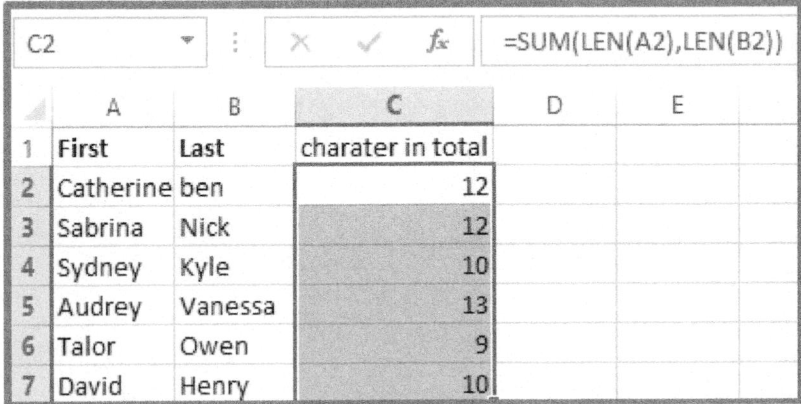

C2 =SUM(LEN(A2),LEN(B2))

	A	B	C	D	E
1	First	Last	charater in total		
2	Catherine	ben	12		
3	Sabrina	Nick	12		
4	Sydney	Kyle	10		
5	Audrey	Vanessa	13		
6	Talor	Owen	9		
7	David	Henry	10		

Note: LEN A2= 9 and B2= 3, the total is equal to 12, you will now use the auto-fill handle to copy the pattern of the formulas down.

Compares the Range of Values with LARGE And SMALL

LARGE and SMALL is used to compare which value is largest and which one is smallest within a given range, let us take for instance, the total number of the bag sold in the market.

- 100: maximum bag sold in one month in the market (**MAX).**
- 8: the least bag sold in one month in the market **(MIN).**
- 93: the second maximum bag sold in one month in the market (**LARGE).**
- 10: the second least bag sold in one month in the market **(SMALL).**

D8 =LARGE(B3:E6, 2)

	A	B	C	D	E	F	G
1							
2	Market	February	March	April	May	Total	Rank
3	Lhasa	50	100	40	70	260	1
4	Slovalaa	10	60	88	80	238	3
5	Moorish	90	50	75	30	245	2
6	Qatar	8	30	93	20	151	4
7		MAX	MIN	LARGE	SMALL		
8		100	8	93	10		

While you are having LARGE and SMALL, you may still at times have to use MAX and MIN. Let us check the use of the four functions in a jiffy with the above worksheet as an example:

1. **MIN:** it gives you the least number or value of the bags sold in the market throughout the whole four months with a given range of **=MIN(B3:E6).**

2. MAX: it gives the largest number or the values of the bags sold in the market throughout the four months with a given range of: =MAX(B3:E6).

3. **SMALL**: it gives you the nth position of the smallest value in the list. It will have two arguments, the first argument is the cell range and the second argument is the position of the nth lower value, which maybe 2nd or 3rd position, and the formula will be in a structure like this =**SMALL(B3:E6, 2) or =SMALL(B3:E6, 3)** depending on the nth position.

4. **LARGE**: it will give you the nth position of the largest value in the list. It will have two arguments as well, which are the cell range and nth position either 2nd or 3rd and the formula will be structured like this: **=LARGE(B3:E6, 2) or =LARGE(B3:E6, 3).**

5. RANK: it ranks the list of the data; the RANK function has three-arguments which are as follows:

G5 =RANK(F5,F3:F6,0)

	A	B	C	D	E	F	G
1							
2	Market	February	March	April	May	Total	Rank
3	Lhasa	50	100	40	70	260	1
4	Slovalaa	10	60	88	80	238	3
5	Moorish	90	50	75	30	245	2
6	Qatar	8	30	93	20	151	4
7		MAX	MIN	LARGE	SMALL		
8		100	8	93	10		

Using cell G5, second-ranking

a. The cell address with the value you are using for ranking. F5=245

b. The cell range with which you will match the value in deciding the ranking, F3:F6

c. The order of ranking, 0 for descending order, up to down, while 1 is for ascending order, down to up). 0

Text Capitalizing with PROPER Function

The **Proper** function is used to change editing text to upper, lower, or proper case. Excel does not have to confirm change case like MS word, though Excel's change case is not automatic like MS word but at the same time it is not difficult, it just requires some little processes. To change the case of the text you have used before, kindly:

a. Create a momentary new column to the right of the column that has the text you want to change its case, which you will later delete when it completes its mission. To create the column:

i. Select **the column** to the right where you want the new column to be situated.

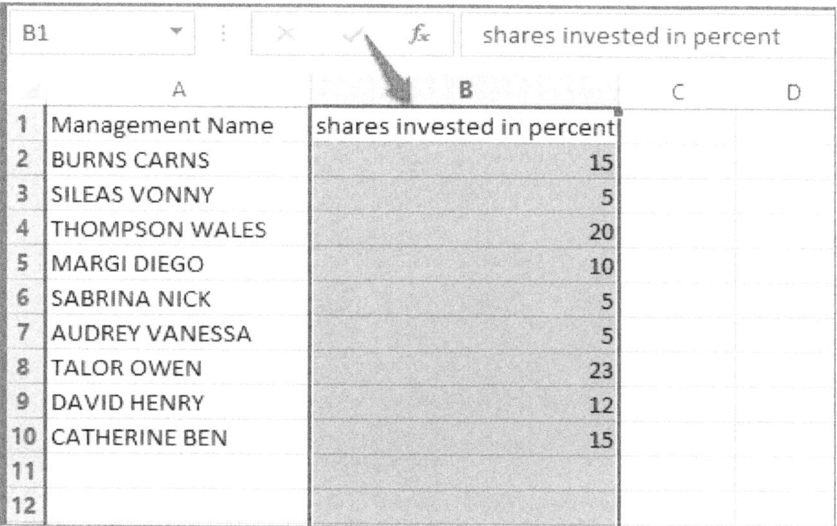

ii. Right-click on the **selected column** and pick **Insert**.

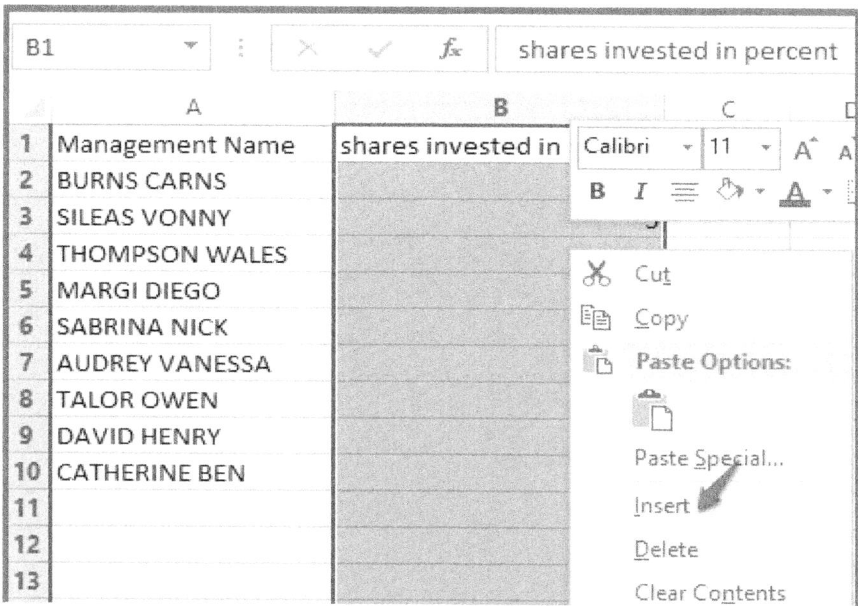

b. Immediately you are done with the insertion of the new column, tap on the **first column** on the column you have just created which is direct to the right side of the text you want to change its case.

SUM | =PROPER(B2)

	A	B	C
1	Management Name		shares invested in percent
2	BURNS CARNS	=PROPER(B2)	15
3	SILEAS VONNY		5
4	THOMPSON WALES		20
5	MARGI DIEGO		10
6	SABRINA NICK		5
7	AUDREY VANESSA		5
8	TALOR OWEN		23
9	DAVID HENRY		12
10	CATHERINE BEN		15
11			
12			

c. The column we want to change is in the upper case, but we want to change it to proper case. Now in the column, tap above in (b), insert a formula of this structure there: **=PROPER(B2)**. Perhaps we want to change it to a lower case, we would have replaced the **Proper** with **Lower** because we can only have upper, proper and lower. Immediately after the insertion of the formula, tap on the **Enter** key on the keyboard to initiate the process.

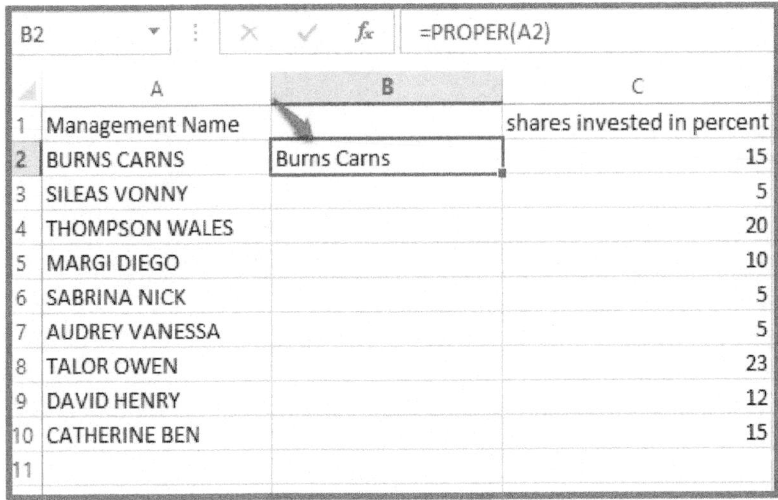

B2 | =PROPER(A2)

	A	B	C
1	Management Name		shares invested in percent
2	BURNS CARNS	Burns Carns	15
3	SILEAS VONNY		5
4	THOMPSON WALES		20
5	MARGI DIEGO		10
6	SABRINA NICK		5
7	AUDREY VANESSA		5
8	TALOR OWEN		23
9	DAVID HENRY		12
10	CATHERINE BEN		15
11			

d. If you observe, you will notice the text from the first cell A has been copied into the first cell of the new column (B) we created but in the proper case we desire.

e. Then use the auto-fill handle to copy down the process for the other names by dragging down the black arrow to the last name on the list.

B2 =PROPER(A2)

	A	B	C
1	Management Name		shares invested in percent
2	BURNS CARNS	Burns Carns	15
3	SILEAS VONNY	Sileas Vonny	5
4	THOMPSON WALES	Thompson Wales	20
5	MARGI DIEGO	Margi Diego	10
6	SABRINA NICK	Sabrina Nick	5
7	AUDREY VANESSA	Audrey Vanessa	5
8	TALOR OWEN	Talor Owen	23
9	DAVID HENRY	David Henry	12
10	CATHERINE BEN	Catherine Ben	15

f. At this moment, we have gotten the proper case in column B, all we have to do now is to copy the contents in the new column by selecting the names in the new column and press **Ctrl + C** to copy it.

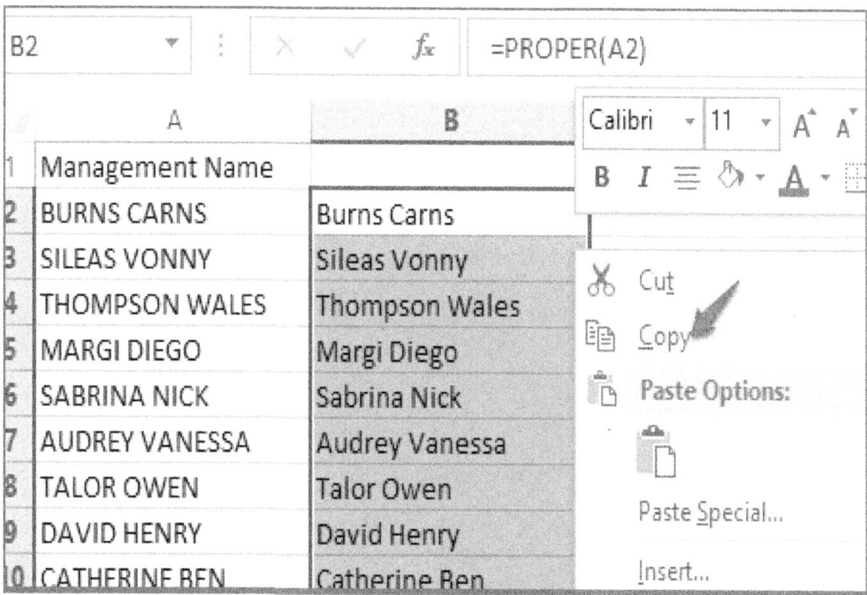

B2 =PROPER(A2)

	A	B
1	Management Name	
2	BURNS CARNS	Burns Carns
3	SILEAS VONNY	Sileas Vonny
4	THOMPSON WALES	Thompson Wales
5	MARGI DIEGO	Margi Diego
6	SABRINA NICK	Sabrina Nick
7	AUDREY VANESSA	Audrey Vanessa
8	TALOR OWEN	Talor Owen
9	DAVID HENRY	David Henry
10	CATHERINE BEN	Catherine Ben

g. Then right-click **the beginning of the column** that you want to change, here, we have it as cell A2, tap on the **Paste** special menu for the values you copied.

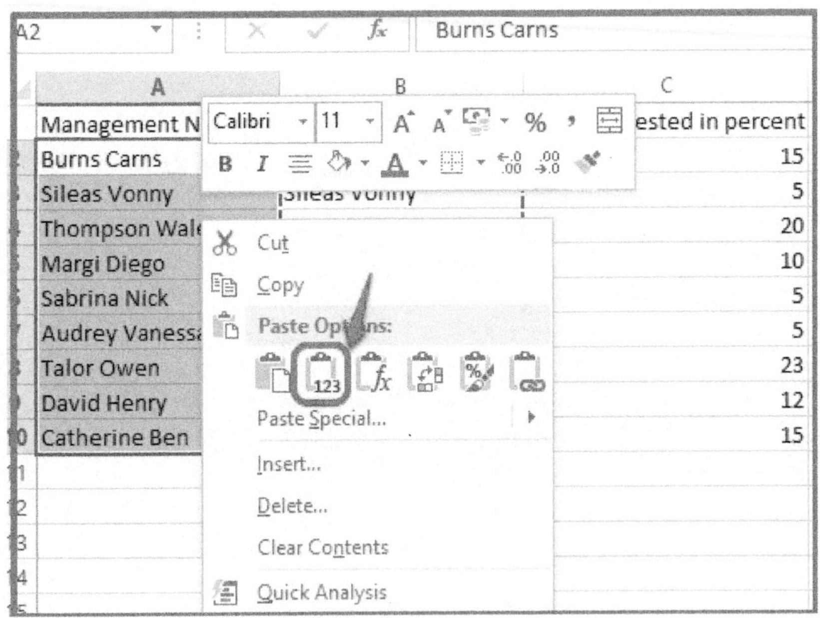

h. Now it is time to delete the momentary column that you used to format column A. this is done by selecting the column and right-click it, then pick the **Delete** option.

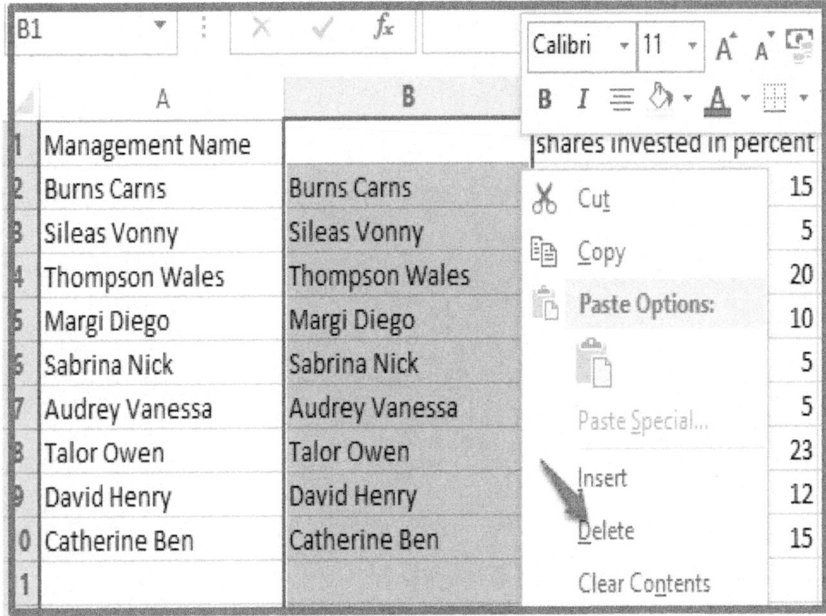

i. Column A is now having a set of **Proper cases** you want.

A	B
Management Name	shares invested in percent
Burns Carns	15
Sileas Vonny	5
Thompson Wales	20
Margi Diego	10
Sabrina Nick	5
Audrey Vanessa	5
Talor Owen	23
David Henry	12
Catherine Ben	15

LEFT, MID, AND RIGHT for Data Extraction

LEFT, MID, AND RIGHT are called text functions because they are made purposely to extract certain parts from a word or a group of words. As a means of explanation, you may need to extract the first two letters of a word, the last four letters, or the 6 letters from the middle of the sentence in LEFT, LAST, AND MID functions respectively.

- The **LEFT** function is used for middle extraction; let us put it to practice by starting with the left function.

=LEFT(text, num-chars) or =LEFT(cell address, num-chars)

Text: this is the word or group of words you type or the cell reference where you want to extract your sub word.

Num-chars: These are the numbers of characters you choose to extract from the left part. For instance, let us draw out 4 characters in the text "reference", the outcome is "Refe".

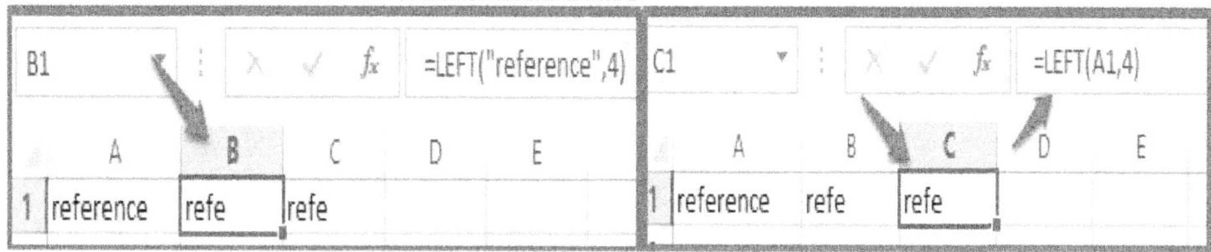

- Over to the **RIGHT** function, it is the exact opposite of the LEFT function, its structure is like this:

  =RIGHT(text, num-chars) or =RIGHT(cell address, num-chars)

  The explanation with the **LEFT** function is the same, except that you will extract from the right part. For instance, =**RIGHT("right choice", 3**). This will give us the word "ice", which occurs to be the first three letter from the right.

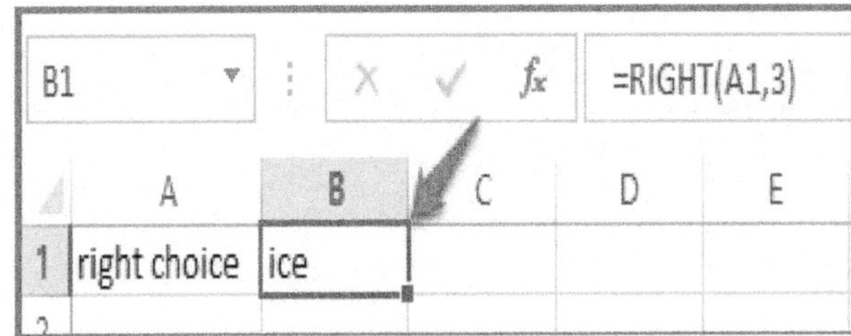

- The third function is the MID function and it is used in drawing out part of the middle letters from the text. It is will be in a structure like this:
  =MID(text, start-num, num chars) or =MID(cell address, start-num, num chars)
  Text: the text within where you wish to draw out words from.
  Start num: this is the number position where to start the extraction from.
  Num-chars: this is the number of characters it will be from the start-num.

  Let us take for instance; we want to draw out the word **"key"** from the text **"the key of diligence"**. The formula will be structured like this = **MID("the key to diligence",5,3)**

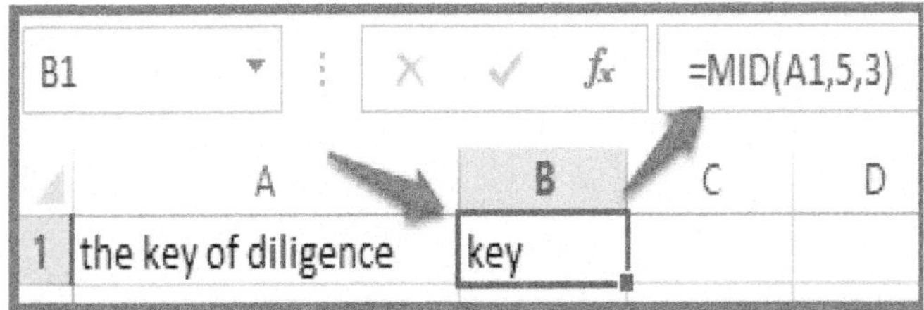

a. **5: start-num** which happen to be the position of the starting point, we will count five (5) characters ("the" is 3 characters, space is recognized in MID function making it four-characters, from the beginning, in short, the 5th number start from K).

b. **3: num chars**, the total character to draw out from the text is 3 from the starting point which is K, and counting 3 characters from K will be the word "key".

IF For Analytical Identification

The IF function is the most recognized used function for analytical comparison between a particular value and your expectation. True return means your expectation is right and if it is otherwise, then your expectation is wrong.

For instance, =IF(D1=8, "True", "False"), It means IF D1=8, then it's True, but if otherwise, return False.

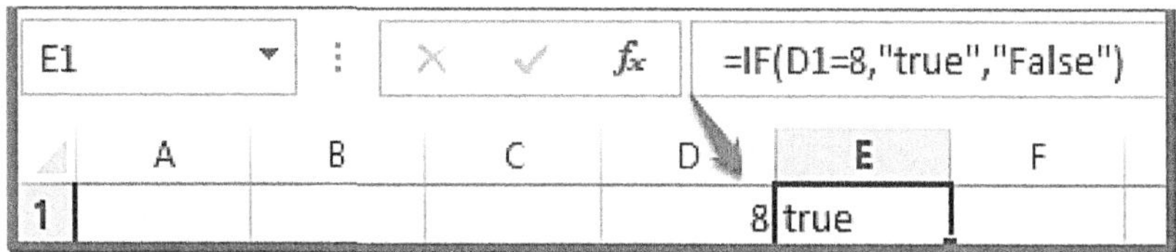

You can use the IF function to estimate text and values, it is called nest IFfunction, let us buttress more on the illustration below. IF(A4>B4," surplus" ", deficit").

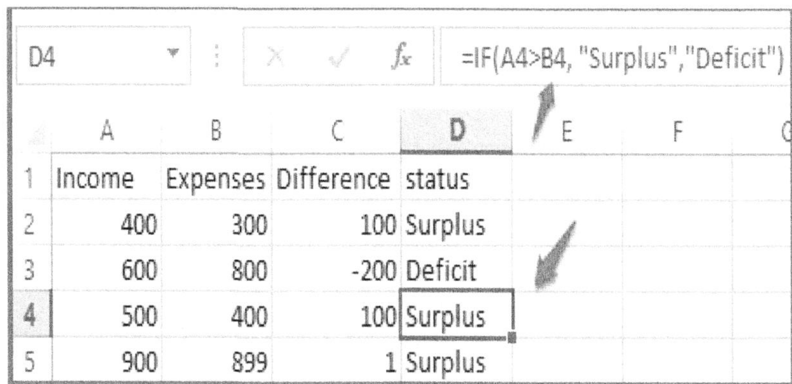
D4 =IF(A4>B4, "Surplus","Deficit")

	A	B	C	D
1	Income	Expenses	Difference	status
2	400	300	100	Surplus
3	600	800	-200	Deficit
4	500	400	100	Surplus
5	900	899	1	Surplus

The above illustration is saying IF(A4>B4, then return surplus, IF otherwise return deficit).

CHAPTER FIVE

CONSTRUCT WORKSHEET FOR EASY COMPREHENSION

Spreading Out Worksheet in An Orderly Manner

As you lay your bed, you shall lie on it, so they say. The same principle applies to the worksheet, if you learn how to manage the worksheet effectively, you will enjoy the result, even before and after you print it out, it will be wonderful and more comprehensive.

Managing a worksheet has a lot to do with how you arrange your worksheet and its contents, such as number formatting probably with percentage or dollars will make the reader understand the actual value of what you put inside the worksheet. Other worksheet management are change character, decorating with color and others that we will be discussing in length in this chapter.

Numbers and Text Alignment in Rows and Columns

The default alignment of the text in the worksheet is to the left, while that of the number is to the right; both default alignments can be adjusted if the need arises. The data inside the cell can be adjusted to the left, right, or middle or from bottom to center, top, and vice versa. You may as well justify cell data. At the time you have to change the alignment of the subject heading so that its look within the cell will be outstanding and that of the worksheet at large.

To change the alignment of the text and number, kindly do the following:

A. **For horizontal alignment** (left to right or side to side alignment.).
a. Select **the cells** that need alignment.
b. Move to the **Home tab** and click on **the respective button** (left align, center align and middle align button).

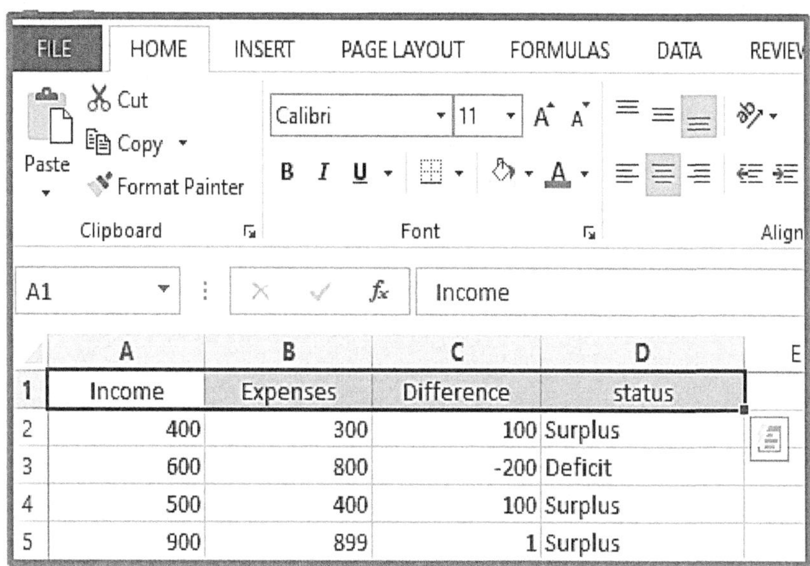

ALTERNATIVELY,

a. Tap on the **Alignment** group button and pick the **Format Cell Alignment** option from the drop-down list.

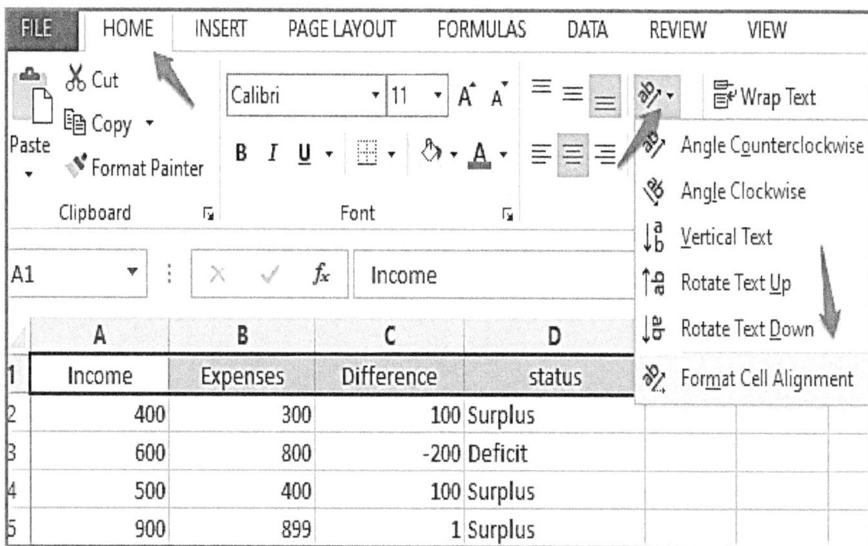

b. Tap on the **Alignment** tab inside the format cell dialog box.
c. Click on the **Horizontal section** and pick your desired alignment including justify that will fit your letter to the cell.

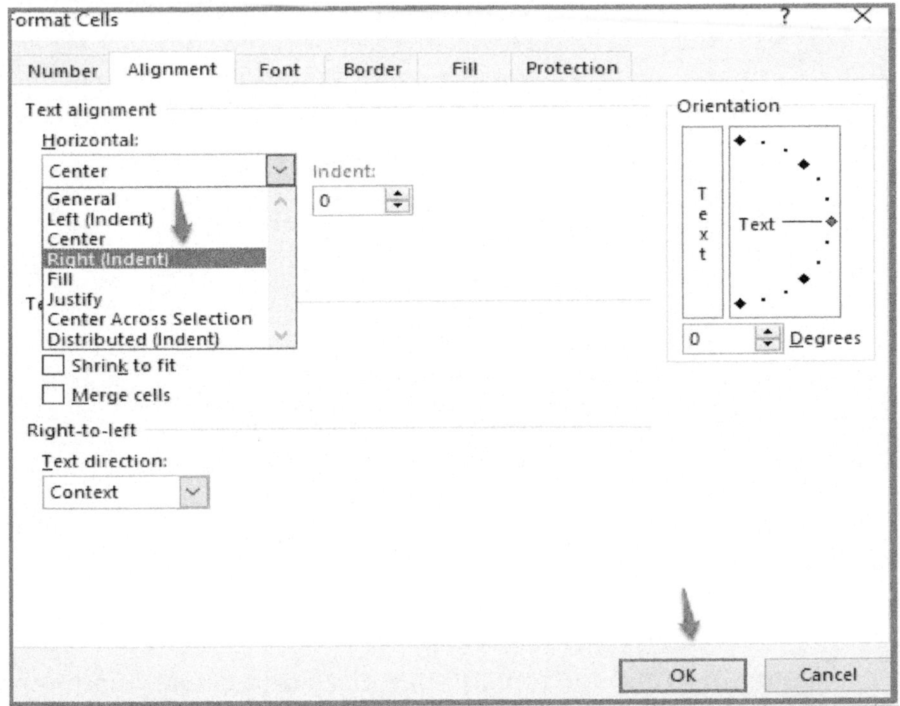

B. **For vertical alignment** (top to bottom or bottom to top):

a. Select the **cells** that need alignment.

b. Move to the **Home tab** and click on **respective alignment** (top align, middle align, and bottom align).

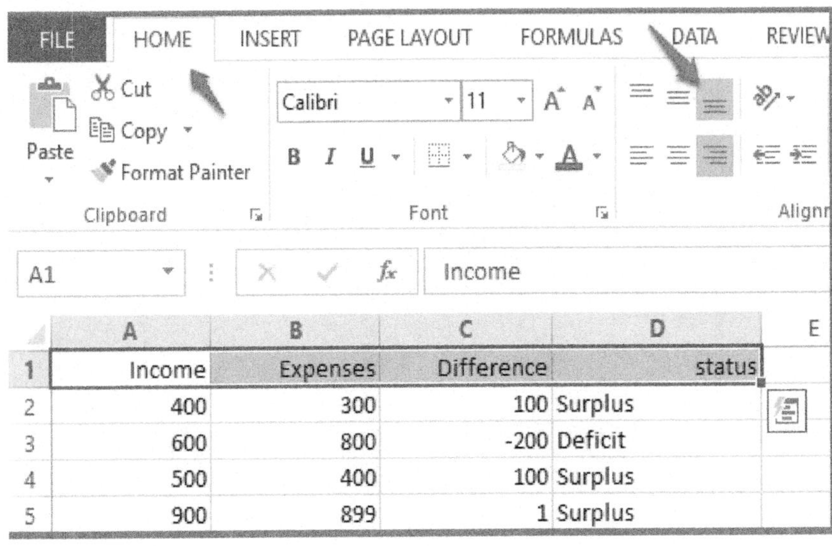

	A	B	C	D
1	Income	Expenses	Difference	status
2	400	300	100	Surplus
3	600	800	-200	Deficit
4	500	400	100	Surplus
5	900	899	1	Surplus

ALTERNATIVELY,

a. Tap on the **alignment group button** and pick the **format cell** button from the drop-down list.

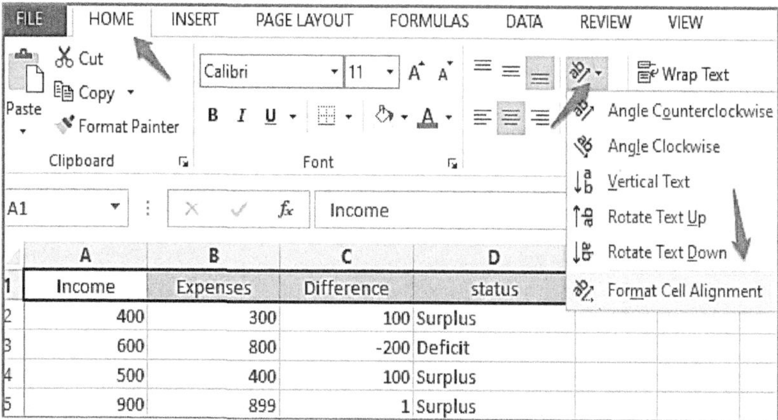

b. Tap on the **Alignment** tab inside the format cell dialog box.

c. Click on the **vertical section** and pick your desired **alignment** including justify that will fit your letter to the cell.

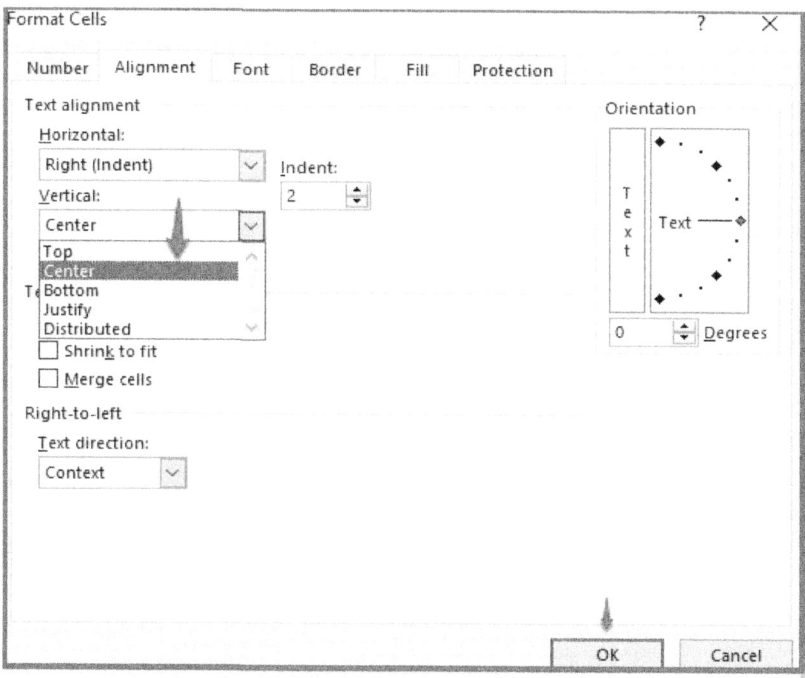

Text Merging and Centering Over Multiple Cells

Text is centered at times to show the information contained in the cell outstandingly or to create a sense of beautification. It helps you to present pieces of text over multiple columns. For example, the words "Local Government Chairman" is centered over five separate cells. To center and merge cells, do the following:

1. Drag your mouse over those cells to select them.

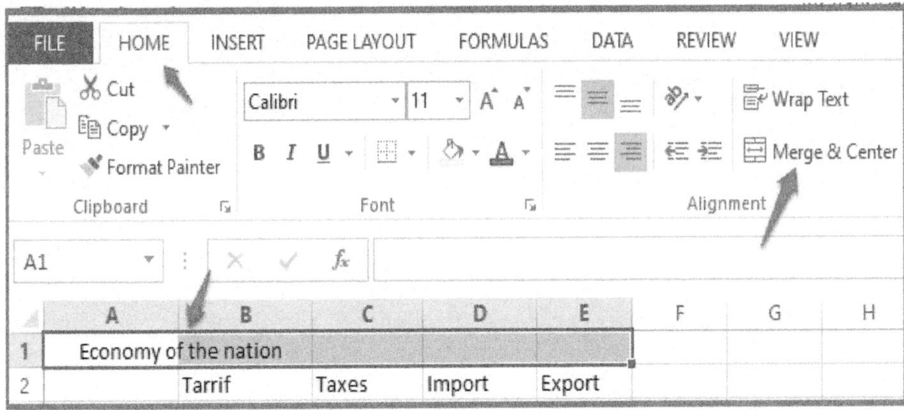

2. Maneuver to the **Home** tab, and then choose the **Merge and Center** button.

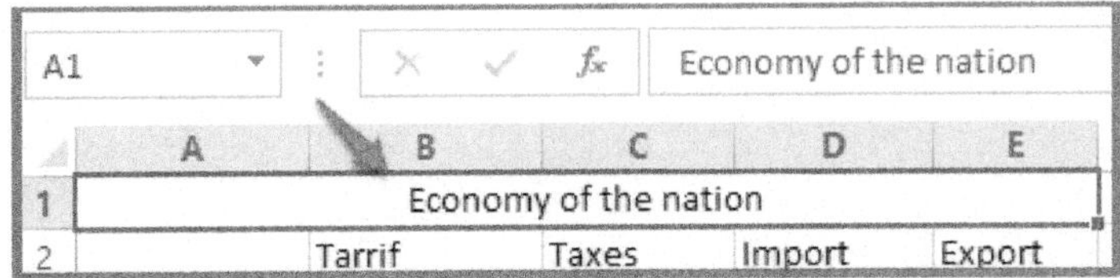

Note: when merging and centering, you will write the text to be merged in one cell, make sure the cell to its left and right side are empty; otherwise, it will be showing you that it's an error.

How do I "unmerge and uncenter" the cells that have been previously merged and centered? You can do that by following these simple steps:

a. Click on the "**Merge & Center"** option from the **Home tab**.
b. Pick **unmerge cells** from the "Merge & Center" drop-down list.

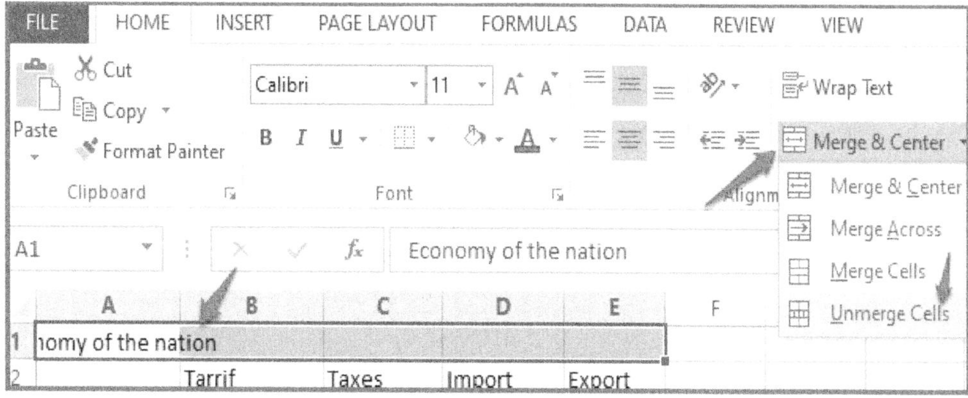

Delete and Insert Rows and Columns

There is always a motive behind deleting or inserting rows or columns, you have to insert a new row or column when you have skipped a particular heading or subject. Rows and columns are mainly deleted when they are not needed anymore.

To insert a new row, kindly do these:

a. Select **the row** that will be below the new row you are about to create.
b. Click on the **Home tab** and tap on the **Insert** button.

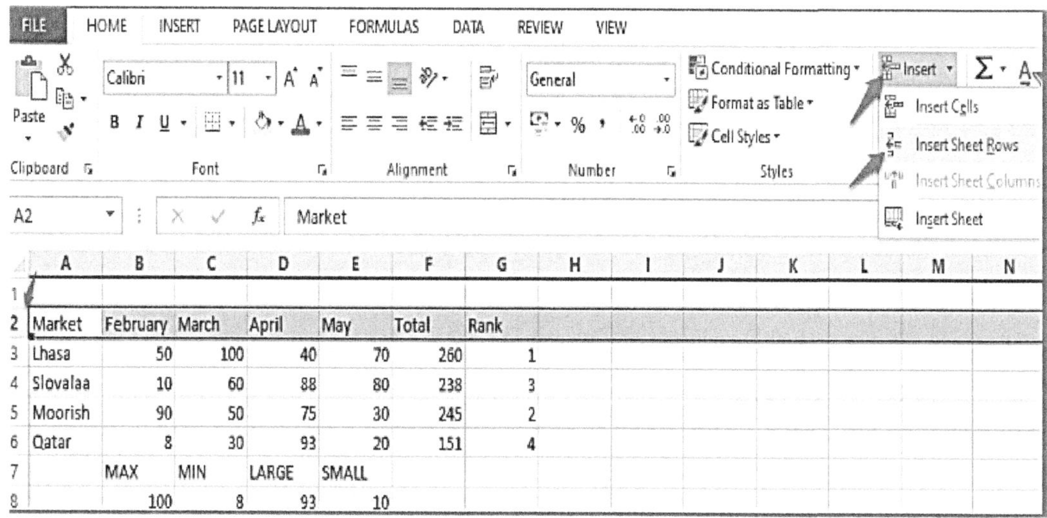

c. Then pick the **Insert Sheet Rows** option from the insert button drop-down menu as seen above.

	A	B	C	D	E	F	G
1							
2							
3	Market	February	March	April	May	Total	Rank
4	Lhasa	50	100	40	70	260	1
5	Slovalaa	10	60	88	80	238	3
6	Moorish	90	50	75	30	245	2
7	Qatar	8	30	93	20	151	4
8		MAX	MIN	LARGE	SMALL		
9		100	8	93	10		

ALTERNATIVELY,

a. Right-click on **the row** which will be below the new row you want to create.
b. Pick **Insert** from the drop-down menu.

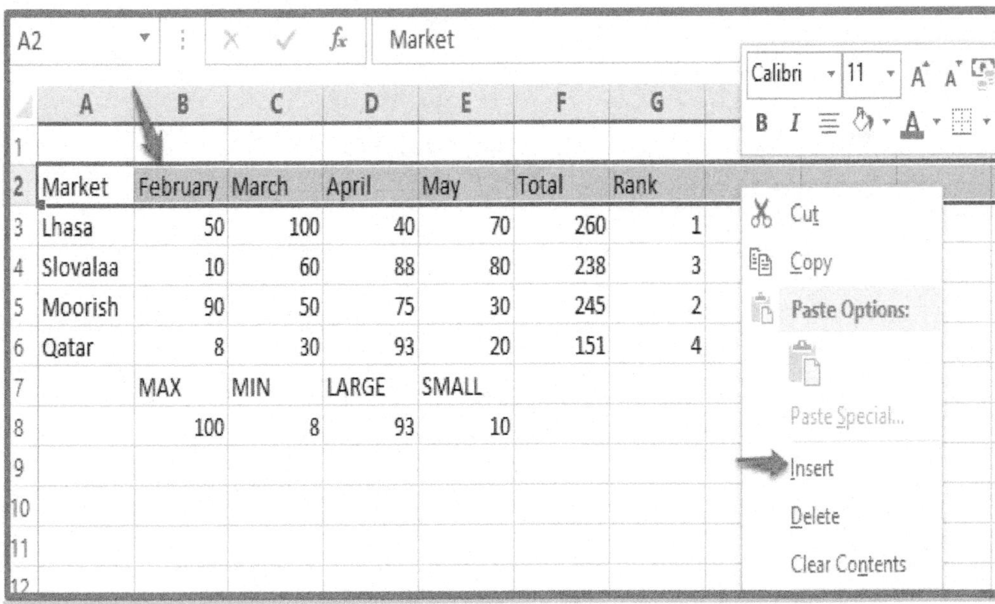

How do I insert a column? By simply:

a. Selecting **the column** that will be to the right of the new column you want to create.

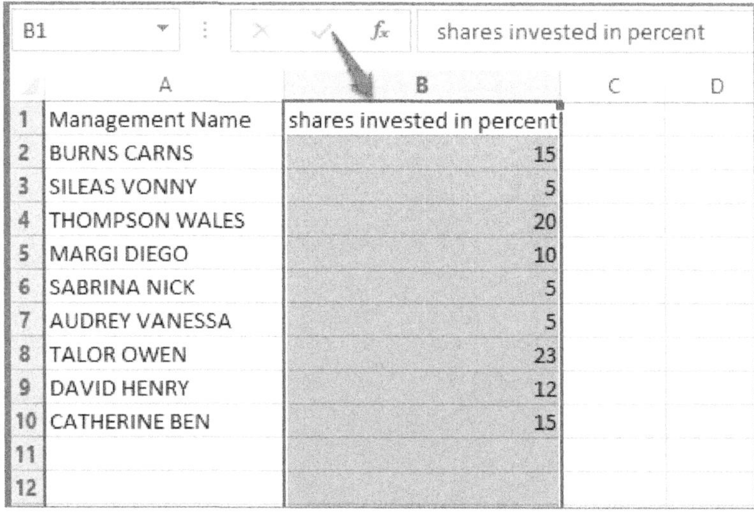

b. Click on the **Home** tab and tap on the **Insert** button.
c. Then pick the **Insert Sheet Column** option from the insert button drop-down menu.

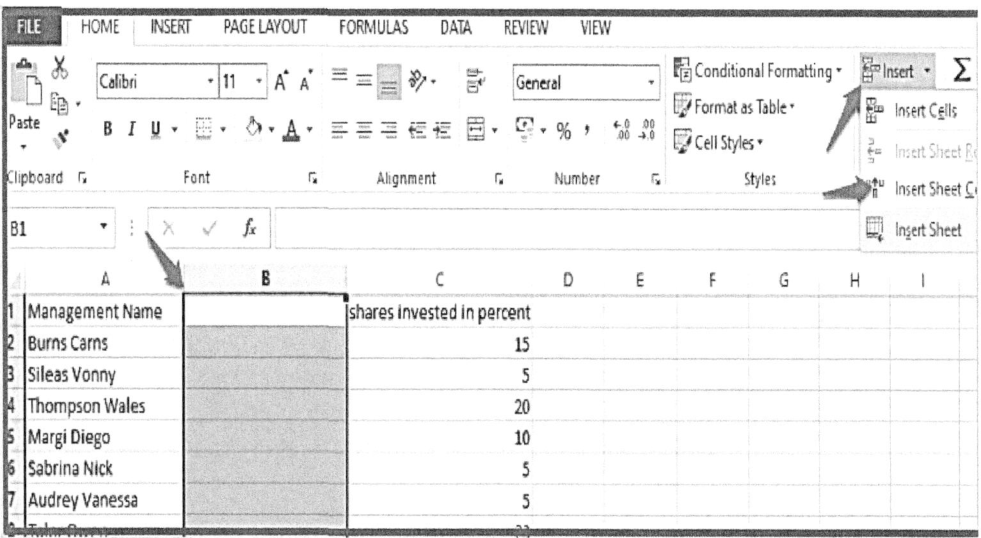

ALTERNATIVELY,

a. Right-click on **the column** which will be to the right of the new column you want to create.
b. Click on I**nsert** from the drop-down menu.

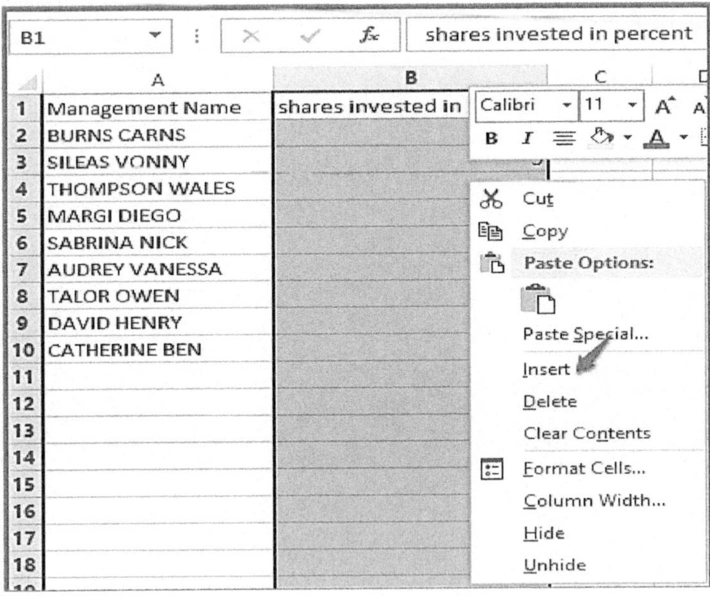

Deleting rows or columns

To delete rows or columns, you have to:

a. Select the **row** or **column** you want to delete or you can drag over the rows and columns and then right-click over them.
b. Pick **delete** from the drop-down list.

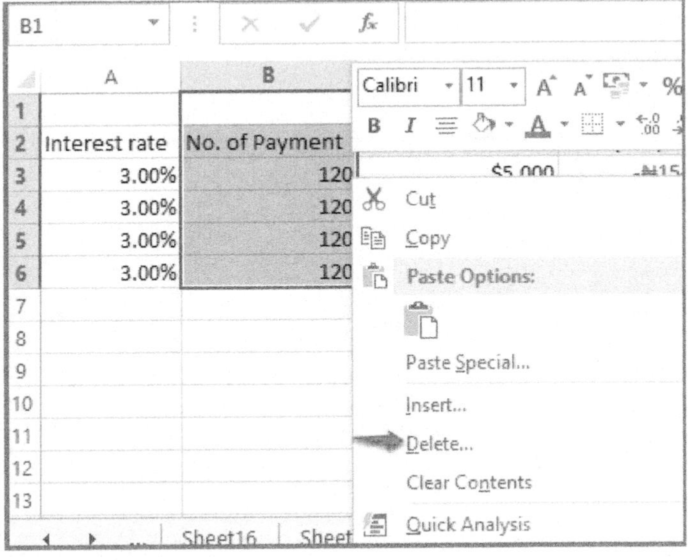

ALTERNATIVELY,

After the selection of the rows or columns to be deleted:

a. Move to the **Home** tab and tap on the **Delete** button.
b. Click on the **Delete Sheet Columns** or **Delete Sheet Rows** from the drop-down list.

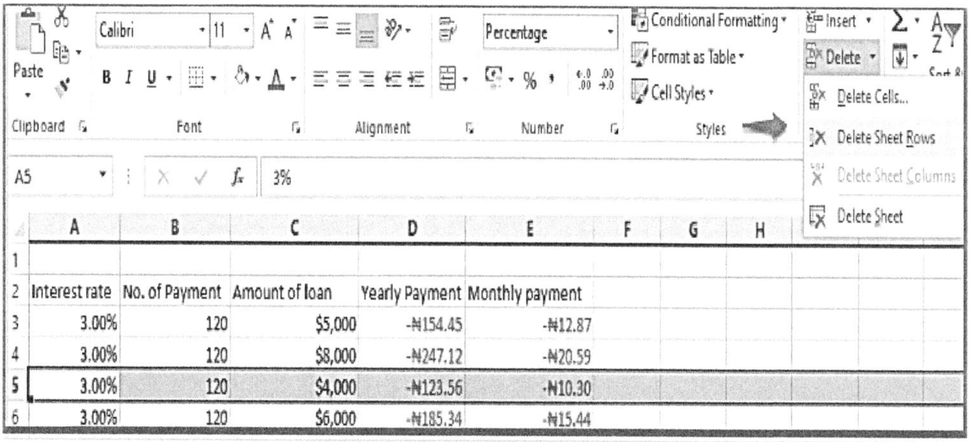

Note: you will see the Insert row and column options when are done inserting rows and columns, tap on it and pick the same format or different ones to the new columns and rows you have created from the pop-up menu.

Be careful not to delete a row that you will still later need because Immediately You Delete It, It Is Gone Forever.

Adjusting Rows and Columns Size

Excel programs the cell box (rectangular column and row box) to be 8.4 characters wide and 15 points high to column and row respectively. But at some point, Excel programming may not work when it comes to entering certain data which are wider than 8.4 in character and higher than 15points in height, as a result, Excel has made diverse preparations as a way of adjusting the sizes of columns and rows depending on what each user has to insert in the cell.

Adjusting the Height of The Rows

The following are the things to note in adjusting the height of the rows:

1. **Adjusting a single row**

a. Click over the **row** number to select the row that needs adjustment.

b. Place the mouse pointer into the boundary between two rows number with which the selected cell should share a boundary with.

c. Shift the pointer a little to change the pointer to a black plus (+) sign, then double-click and drag the boundary between the rows up and down to the measurement you are looking for.

A5 | f_x 3%

	A	B	C	D
1				
2	Interest rate	No. of Payment	Amount of loan	Yearly Payment
3	3.00%	120	$5,000	-₦154.45
4	[illegible]	120	$8,000	-₦247.12
5	3.00%	120	$4,000	-₦123.56
6	3.00%	120	$6,000	-₦185.34
7				

Height: 18.75 (25 pixels)

d. As you are shifting the boundary, there will be a prompt pop-up note giving you a hint about the row height measurement you have just reached and to guide you to the measurement you are aiming to reach.

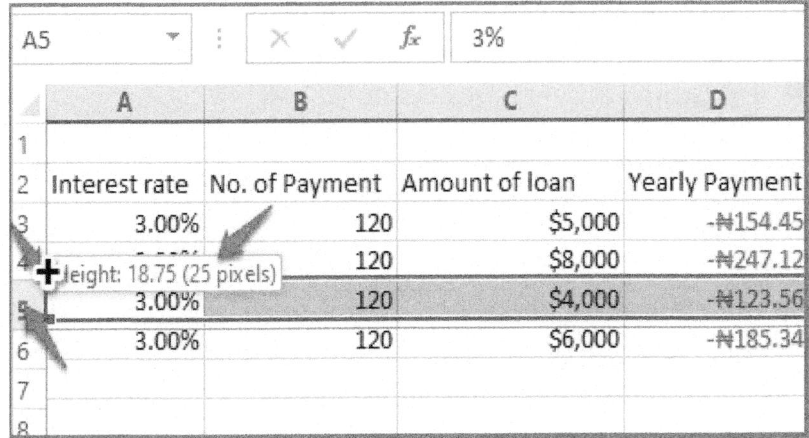

A5 | f_x 3%

	A	B	C	D
1				
2	Interest rate	No. of Payment	Amount of loan	Yearly Payment
3	3.00%	120	$5,000	-₦154.45
4	[illegible]	120	$8,000	-₦247.12
5	3.00%	120	$4,000	-₦123.56
6	3.00%	120	$6,000	-₦185.34
7				

Height: 18.75 (25 pixels)

e. Then release the mouse button after you double-click to complete the process.

2. **Adjusting Multiple rows height at once:**

a. Click on the **multiple rows** you want to adjust or drag over them for selection.

	A	B	C	D	E
1					
2	Interest rate	No. of Payment	Amount of loan	Yearly Payment	Monthly payment
3	3.00%	120	$5,000	-₦154.45	-₦12.87
4		120	$8,000	-₦247.12	-₦20.59
5	3.00%	120	$4,000	-₦123.56	-₦10.30
6	3.00%	120	$6,000	-₦185.34	-₦15.44

b. Then double-click and drag the boundary between one of the selected cells and all the other rows selected with it will be adjusted to the new measurement. Immediately, release the mouse after the double-clicking.

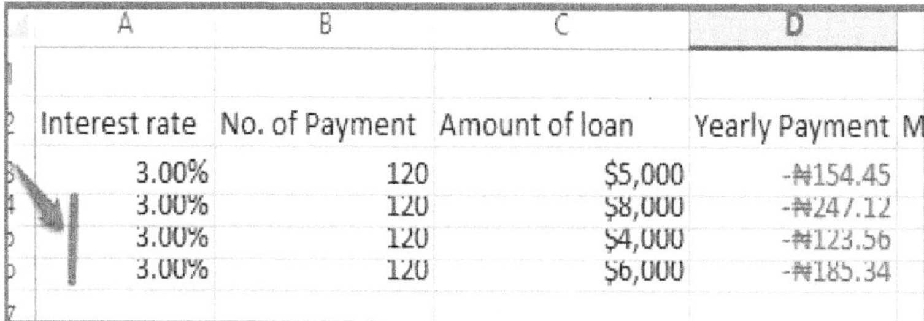

ALTERNATIVELY,

a. Maneuver to the **Home** tab and tap on the **Format** button.

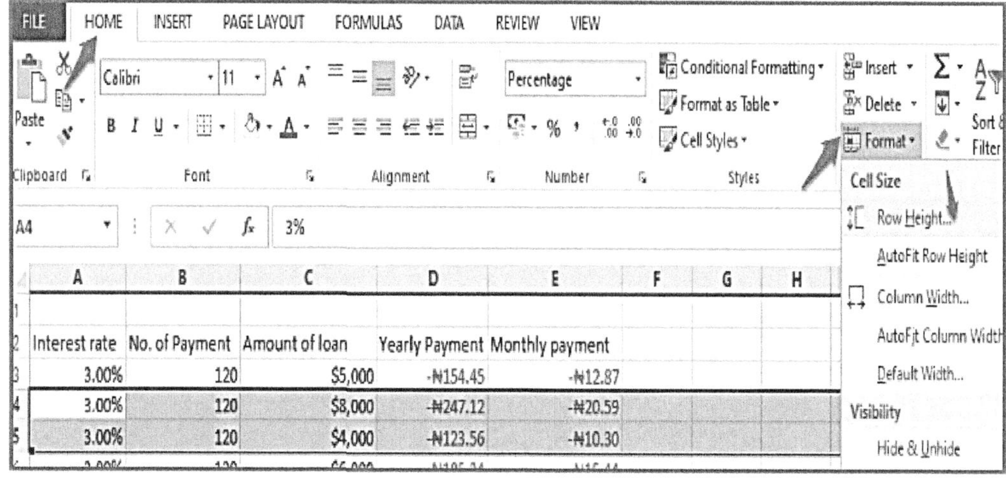

b. Select the **Row Height** option, and then insert the **row height** you prefer in the Row Height dialog box.

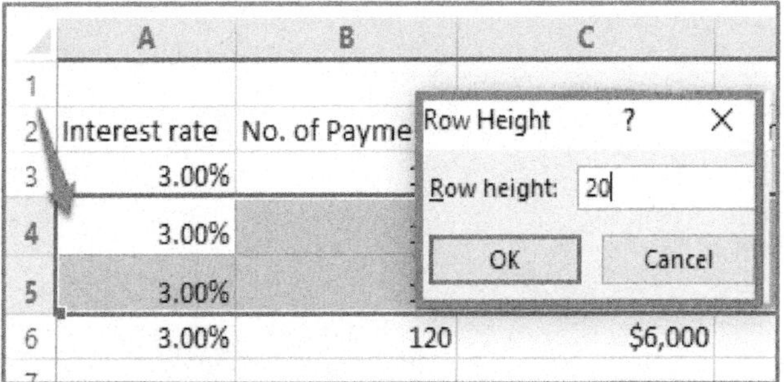

3. Adjusting cell entry to Autofit the row height:

You can adjust your row height automatically to make the data entry fit inside the cell accurately and so that row size will contain the data entry appropriately. Adjust your row height to fit in your data entry by:

a. Moving to the **Home** tab and tap on the **Format** button.

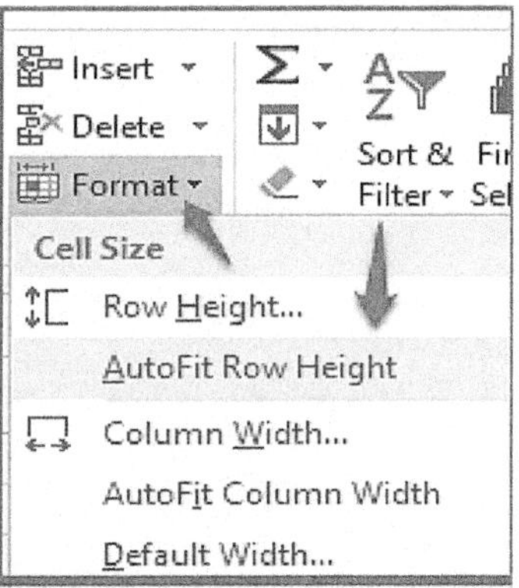

b. Then choose **AutoFit Row Height.**

Adjusting the Column Width

To adjust the column width, below are the steps.

1. Adjusting a single column:

a. Select **the column** to be adjusted.

b. Place the mouse pointer into the boundary between two column letters with which the selected cell shares a boundary with.

c. Shift the pointer a little to change the pointer to a black plus (+) sign, then double-click and drag the boundary between the columns up and down to the measurement you are looking for.

Width: 17.86 (130 pixels)

	A	B	C	D
1				
2	Interest rate	No. of Payment	Amount of loan	Yearly Payment
3	3.00%	120	$5,000	-₦154.45
4	3.00%	120	$8,000	-₦247.12
5	3.00%	120	$4,000	-₦123.56
6	3.00%	120	$6,000	-₦185.34
7				

d. As you are shifting the boundary, there will be a prompt pop-up note giving you a hint about the column width measurement you have just reached and to guide you to the measurement you are aiming to reach.

e. Then release the mouse after double-clicking to complete the process.

2. Adjusting multiple columns:

a. Click on the **multiple columns** you want to adjust or drag over them for selection.

b. Then double-click and drag the boundary between one of the selected cells and all other columns selected with it will be adjusted to the new measurement immediately you release the mouse after double-clicking it also.

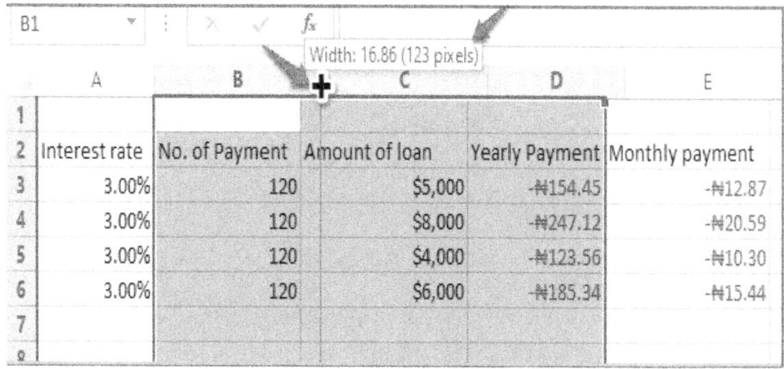

Width: 16.86 (123 pixels)

	A	B	C	D	E
1					
2	Interest rate	No. of Payment	Amount of loan	Yearly Payment	Monthly payment
3	3.00%	120	$5,000	-₦154.45	-₦12.87
4	3.00%	120	$8,000	-₦247.12	-₦20.59
5	3.00%	120	$4,000	-₦123.56	-₦10.30
6	3.00%	120	$6,000	-₦185.34	-₦15.44
7					

ALTERNATIVELY,

a. Maneuver to the **Home** tab, and tap on the **Format** button.

b. Select the **Column Width** button, and then insert the column width you prefer in the Column dialog box.

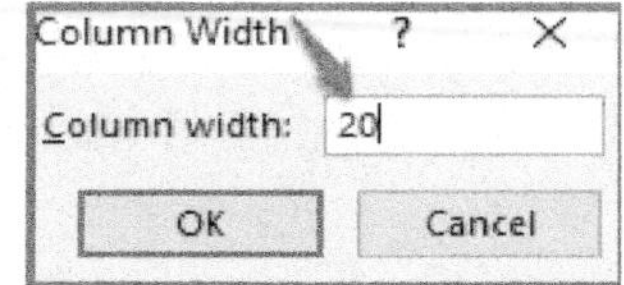

3. **Adjusting cell entry to Autofit the column width:**
   You can adjust the width of your columns automatically to make the data entry fit inside the column accurately and so that the column size will contain data entries appropriately. Adjust your column width to make data entry fit into it, by:

- Moving to the **Home** tab and tap on the **Format** button.

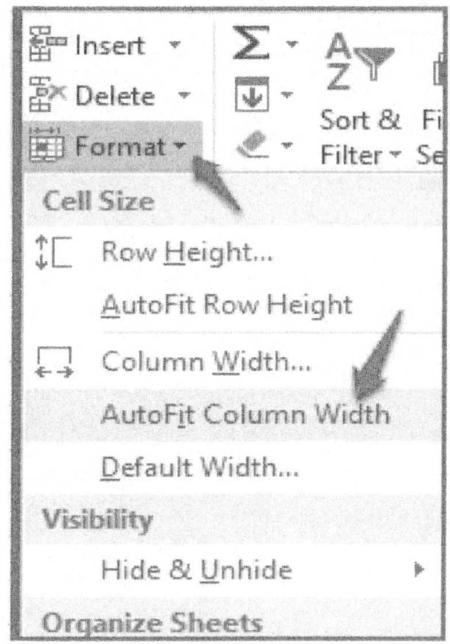

- Then choose the **AutoFit Column Width.**

Furnishing A Worksheet with Borders and Colors

Worksheet cell is arranged in a gridline format. The gridline is mainly for proper arrangement of your Excel work and thus, when you print Excel work, the grid background will not reflect. Nevertheless, if you prefer that your Excel work should look more presentable and meaningful, you must create something creative within the area of your Excel work, particularly an area that catches the reader's attention such as column heading, aggregate heading, and other essential parts. At the same time, it is of utmost importance to use color to decorate the background of your Excel work to add more life to your work.

Quick Way of Formatting Worksheet with Cell Style

Formatting simply means the appearance of things to make it better. For instance, formatting a worksheet is a way of changing its appearance for better improvement such as text, color, and drawing a table to surround your cells. The most pressing thing about formatting is that the look and

appearances you desire can come out in a jiffy with a little process. It does not take much time, and indeed it is a quick way of formatting a worksheet. There are two ways to format the worksheet either by choosing from thousands of built-in cell styles that comes with Excel or by customizing your cell style to suit your taste.

Making Use of Excel Built-In Cell Style

With Excel built-in cell style, you have limitless access to the collection of cell styles which you can apply to your subject headings or title to capture the attention of the reader. To pick from Excel cell style collection, simply:

a. Choose the **cells** to be formatted.
b. Move to the **Home** tab and tap on the **Cell style** button, to make the cell style collection open.
c. Pick a preferred cell style from the available collection of cell styles to add value to your Excel work.

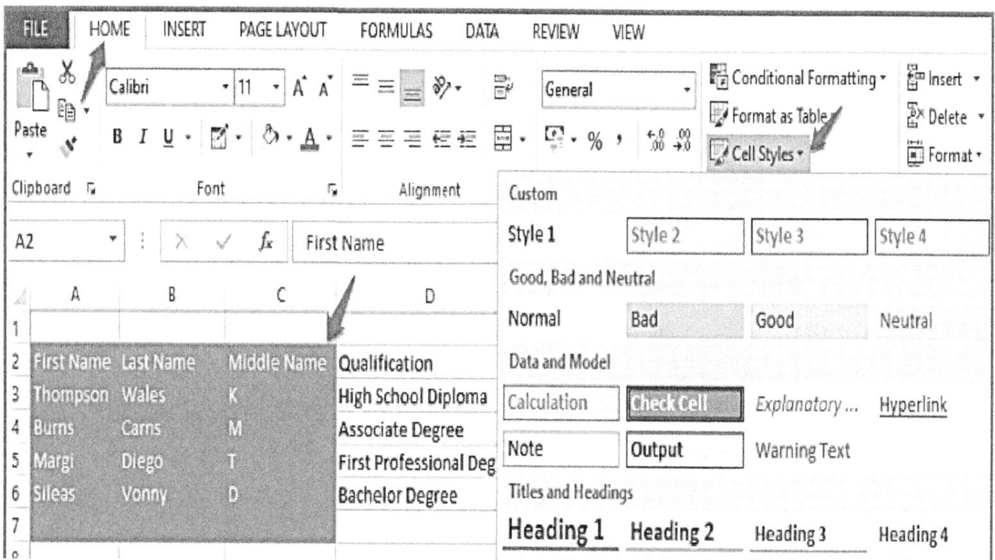

How can I remove cell style from the cell? By:

a. Selecting the cells with the formatting effect and move to the **Home** tab and tap on the **Cell style** button to make the cell style collection open.
b. Pick the **Normal** style from the available collection (the Normal style is under the group of good, bad, neutral, and normal).

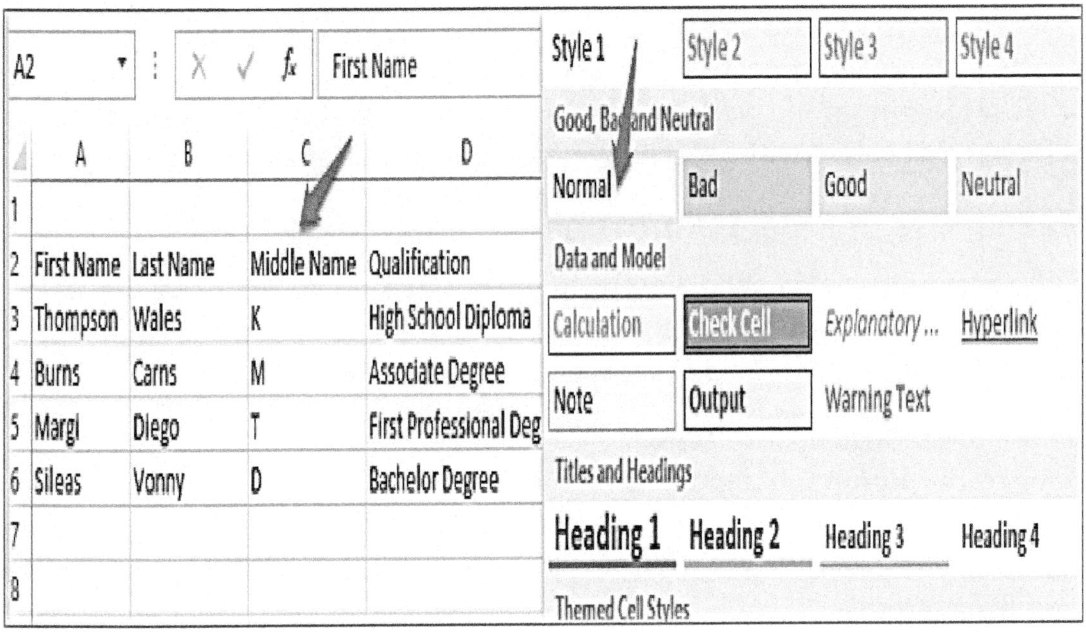

	A	B	C	D
1				
2	First Name	Last Name	Middle Name	Qualification
3	Thompson	Wales	K	High School Diploma
4	Burns	Carns	M	Associate Degree
5	Margi	Diego	T	First Professional Deg
6	Sileas	Vonny	D	Bachelor Degree
7				
8				

Customizing Your Cell Style

Excel allows for skill development and thus, it grants every user who is innovative an opportunity of building their cell style to suit their personalities. The cell style name you created will be on top of the cell collection under a customized heading for easy identification. To create your style, do the following:

a. Choose the formatting type you prefer for your style in a single cell, such as change case, change font, center alignment or middle alignment, and so on.
b. Move to the **Home** tab and click on the **Cell style** button, then choose the **New Cell Style** option as seen below from the drop-down of **Cell Styles** collection.

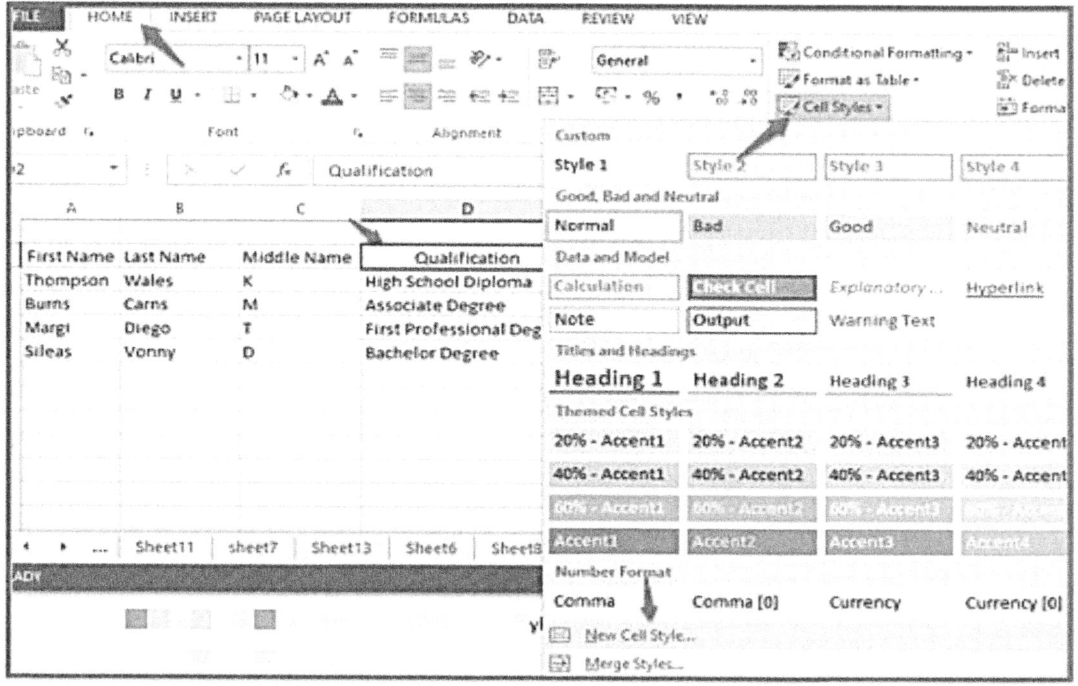

c. The Style dialog box will come forth with the style specification you entered at (a) above, if you wish to change that specification again, you can click on the **format** button to restructure the format at the upper right side of the dialog box.
d. Insert a brief and meaningful name to the style in the Name text box above for your style and tap **Ok**.

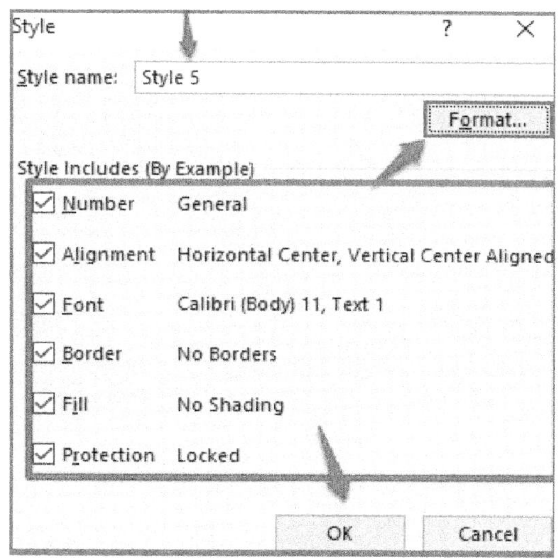

Note: you can remove the manual cell style you created by right-clicking on the name in the cell style collection box and choose the **Delete** option from the drop-down list.

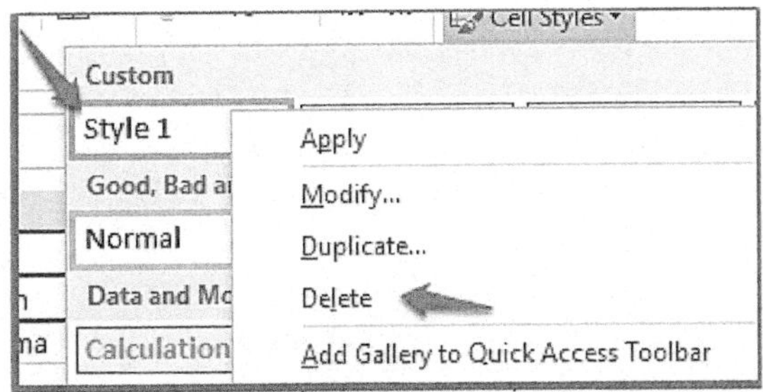

Using Table Style to Format A Cell

Table styles are used to add more decoration to the worksheet data; it gives more neatness and value to the contents inside the cells by creating a wall around them. Check the below steps to explore table style in Excels:

a. Choose the **cells** you want to add table style to.
b. Move to the **Home** tab and click on the **"Format as Table"** button.
c. Then navigate to pick a **table style** from the collection of table styles from the "Format as table" drop-down options.

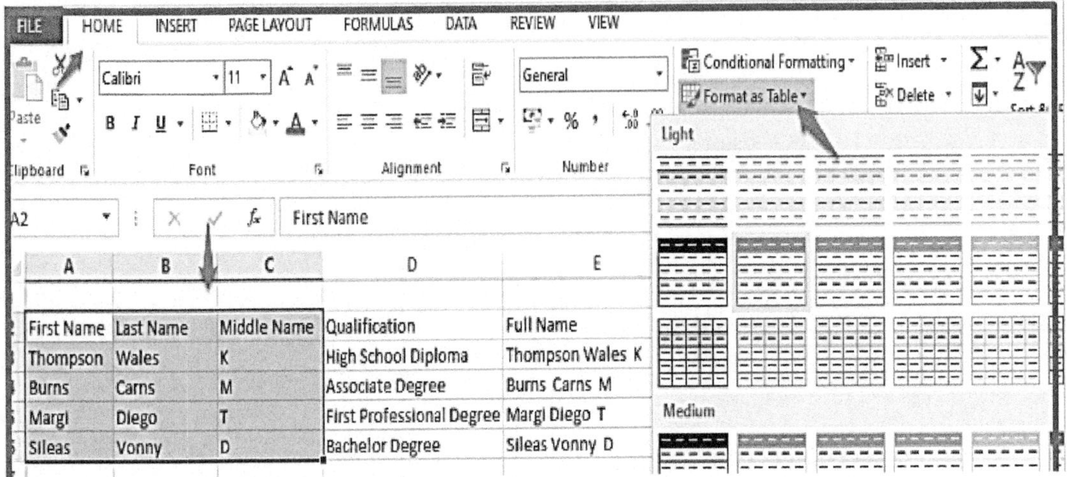

d. Immediately you pick one, you will see a small table style dialog box, tick **"My table headers"** if you have header, label, or title at the top of the column.

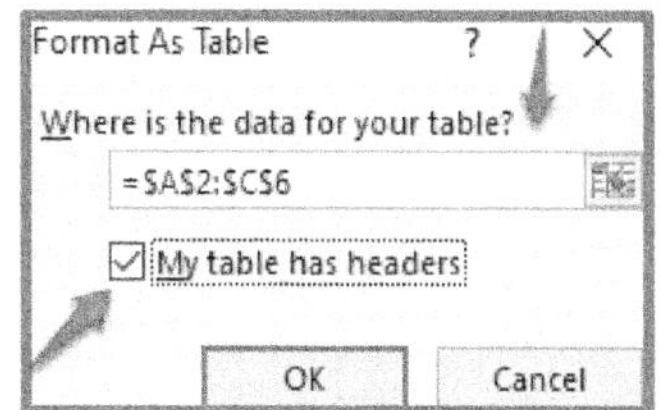

e. Tap **Ok** in the “Format as table” dialog box.

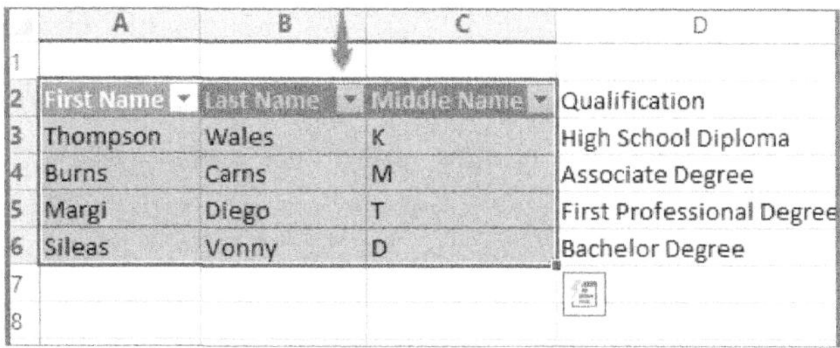

	A	B	C	D
1				
2	First Name	Last Name	Middle Name	Qualification
3	Thompson	Wales	K	High School Diploma
4	Burns	Carns	M	Associate Degree
5	Margi	Diego	T	First Professional Degree
6	Sileas	Vonny	D	Bachelor Degree
7				
8				

Note: you can improve the design of the table by:

a. Clicking on the **quick style** option or the **table tool** from the Table design.
b. Then select “**More Designs”** to improve the table from the table tool drop-down styles.

You can as well get the table removed from the quick style or table tool as well by moving to the bottom of the table tool and choose “**Clear”** in the table style collection.

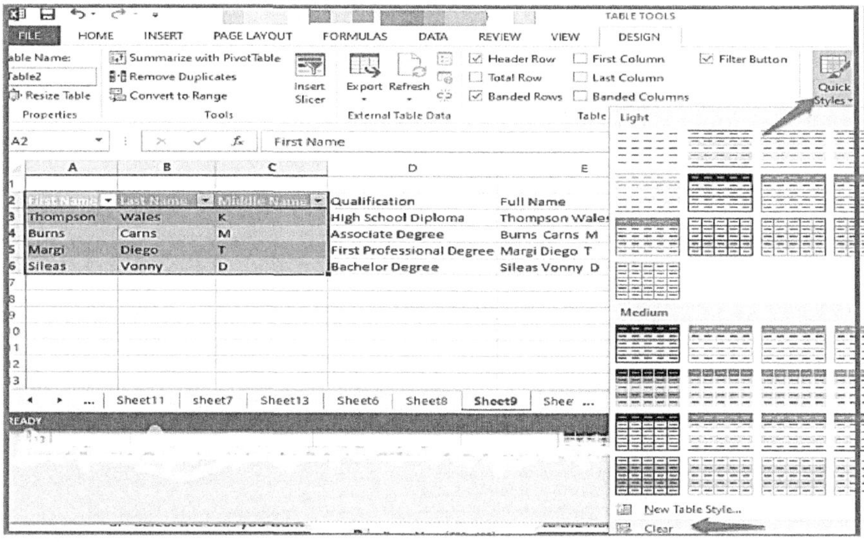

Creating Border on The Worksheet Cells

Borders are the lines that you can use to create a distinct zone between worksheet data and a specific area of worksheet that calls for special attention than the other data. Borders are used to give those items special attention, so that decision can be made with those values rather than glancing through the whole worksheet data. For instance, putting a borderline below the column data for totaling the data item gives the

reader and user a hint of the peculiarities of that area because decision can be made quickly with those distinct zones. Are you confused on how to draw the border on your worksheet, okay, no problem; we have you covered with this one-on-one process:

Create the border using the Format cell dialog box:

a. Select the **cells** you want to draw a border around and move to the **Home** tab to select the **Format** button.
b. Then select the **Format Cells** options from the Format button drop-down list to open the Format cell dialog box.

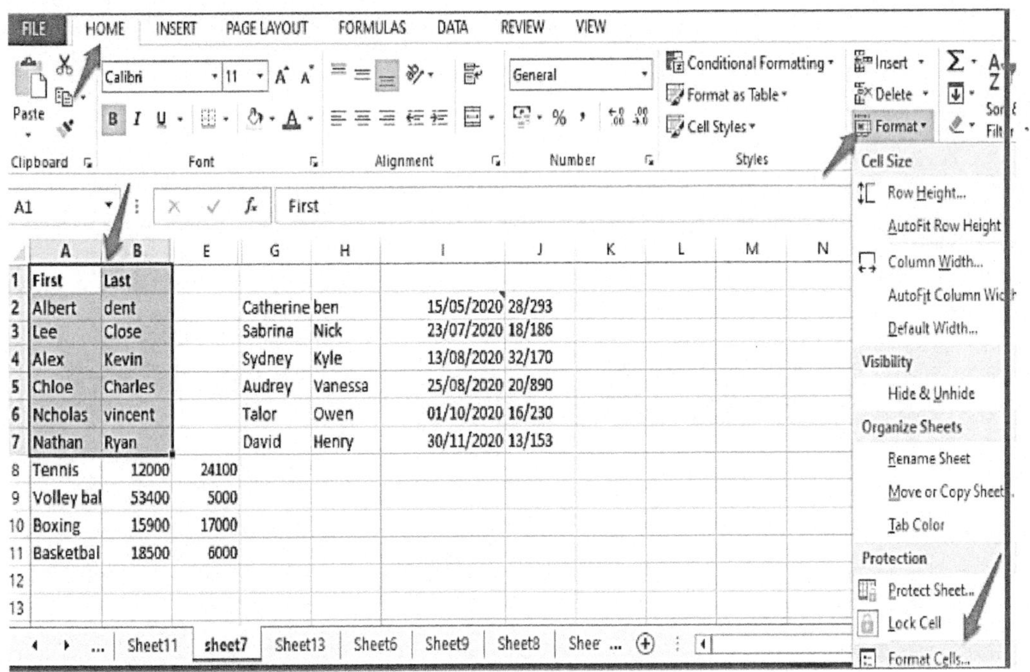

c. Tap on the **borders** tab inside the Format cell dialog box and select a border style for the cells you have selected in (a) above.
d. Click on the "**Preset"** button to show the preview of the border you chose and for the border to be reflected in the worksheet.

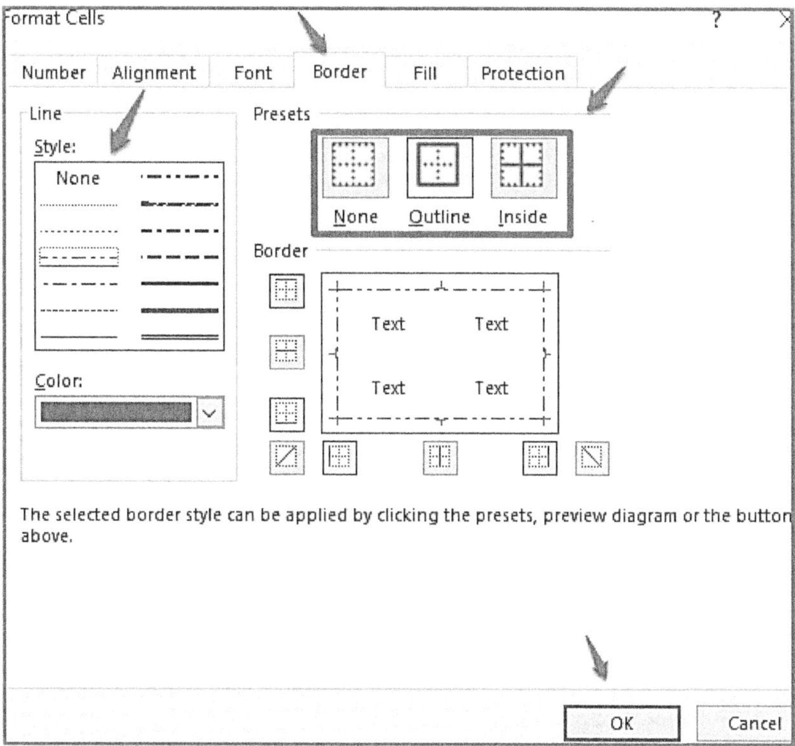

Note: border gives you the chance to use varieties of lines and colors for border, which makes it worthwhile.

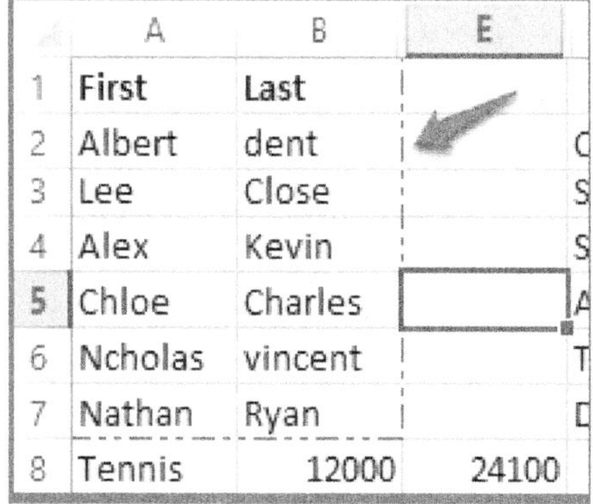

Using drawing to add a border to the worksheet:

a. Moving to the **Home** tab and click on the **Border** button.
b. You can either choose **Border or Border Grid** from the border button drop-down list.

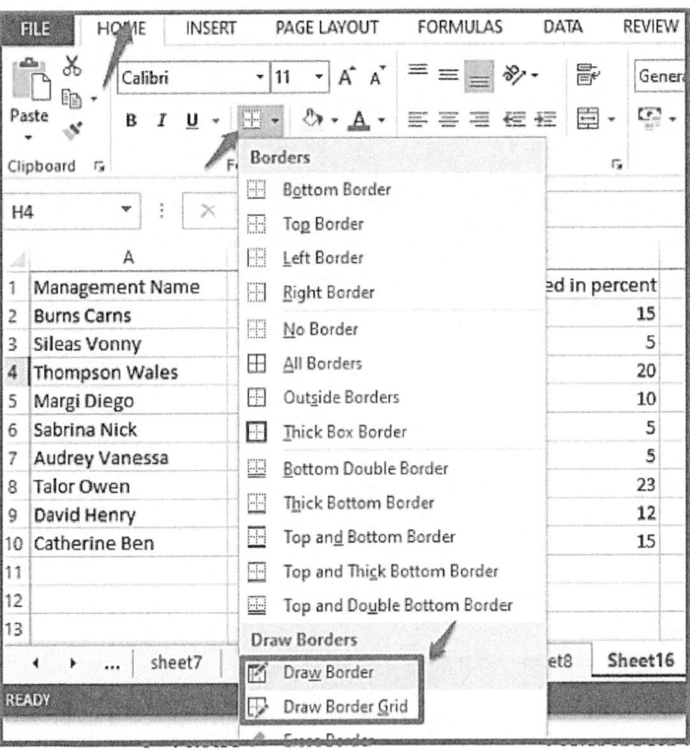

c. Before you draw the border, you can pick the **border style and color** from the border button drop-down list.

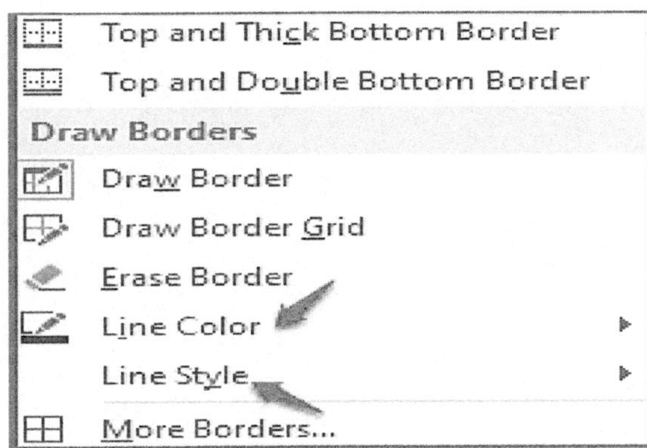

d. Then drag over to the position where you want to see your border. As soon as you are done with the border, tap on **Esc** to release the border pen.

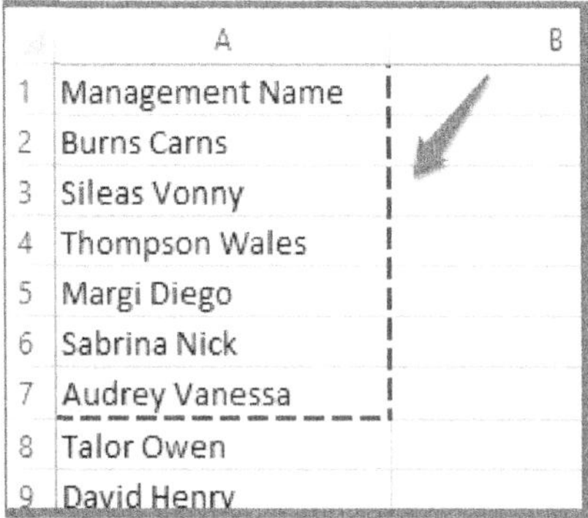

Note: You can remove the border from the cells. This can be done by:

a. Selecting the cells with border, from the **Home** tab, tap on **Border**
b. Then choose the **No Border** option from the border button drop-down list.

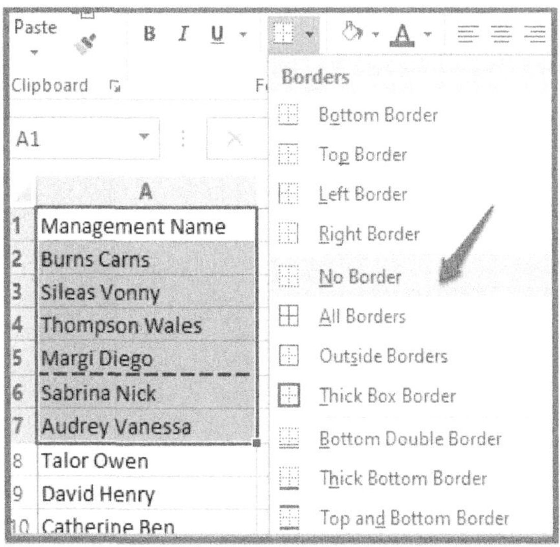

Colorize Your Worksheet

Colors add value and life to an object. Excel color is used to improve the Excel background to entice the interest of the reader to review it. When you are adding color to the worksheet, you have to pick a nice color, some colors are too harsh, do not pick such. To add color to Excel background, do the following:

a. Select **the cells** where you want to put the color and tap on the **Format** button.
b. Choose **Format cell** from the format button drop-down list and the format cell dialog box will come forth.

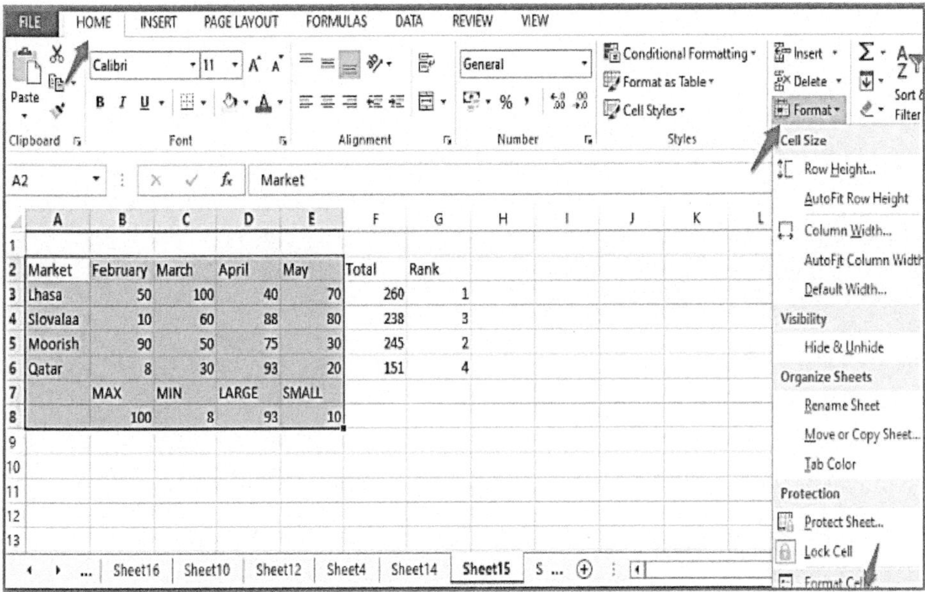

c. Select the **Fill** bar from the Format cell dialog box and choose an appropriate color from the collection, then click on **Ok**.

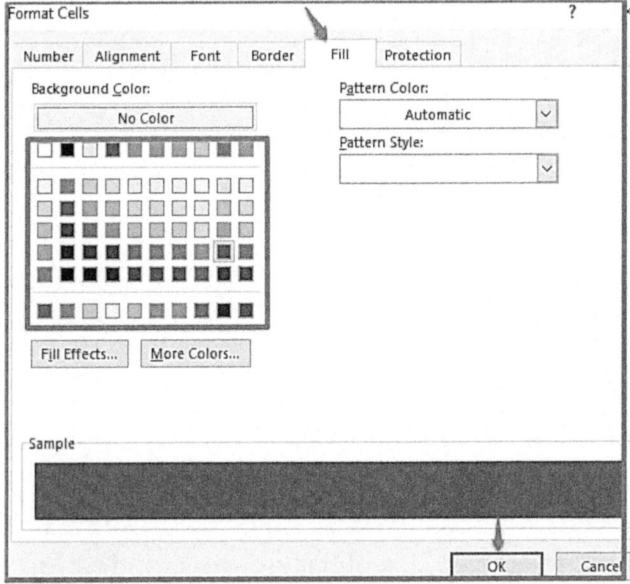

Be Prepared to Print A Worksheet

You have to prepare yourself ahead of printing a worksheet, don't just press Ctrl + P to print anyhow, there are certain steps to follow before you eventually print so that you will not end up printing what you do not want to print. The first process of printing is to check if the worksheet is rightly arranged on a single page so that you will not have a page break and end up printing a half page. To do that, you have to check these two sides of the worksheet (the bottom and right side of the worksheet) to confirm if the contents you are about to print is rightfully set very well.

Setting Up A Worksheet to Fit the Page

Setting up a worksheet to fit the page for printing is very expedient so that you will not end up printing what you do not expect. Excel starts its printing from the first column and first row (A1) to the last cell with data to the right side. To avoid page break of any kind and printing the actual document without wasting paper resources, you have to take worksheet page set-up with seriousness.

Note: before you click on print, check the **page layout** of your worksheet by clicking on the **View** button and tap on both **page layout** and **page break preview** to see the glance of what you are about to print.

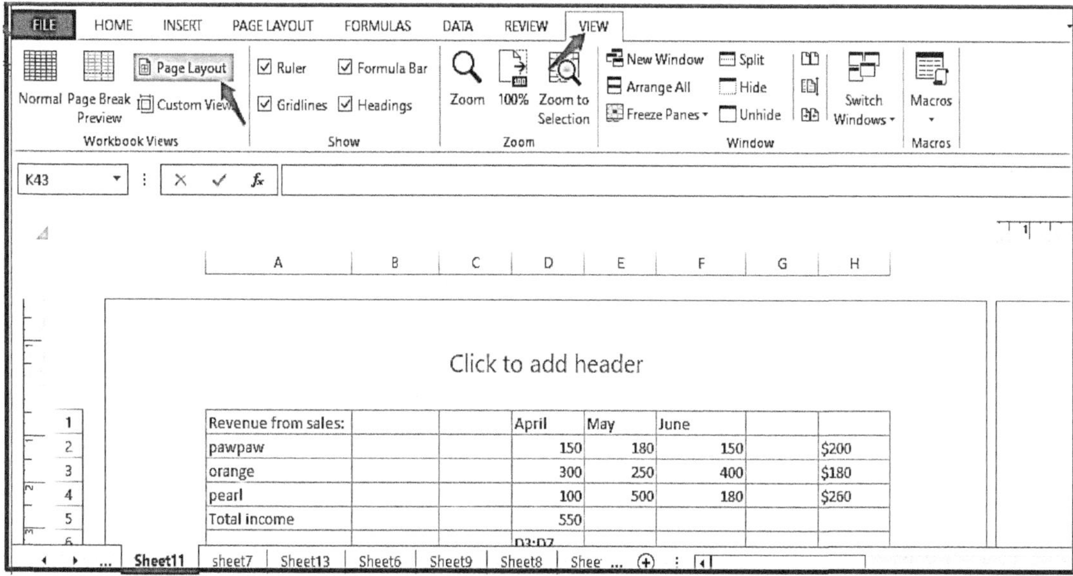

Printing section of the worksheet: you do not have to print the whole worksheet; you only have to print the useful part with contents that you need. To print a section of the worksheet, kindly:

a. Select **the cells** you want to print and move to the **Page Layout** tab.
b. Click on the **"Print Area"** button and select "**Set Print Area"** from the drop-down menu, and Excel will be authorized to print the only selected area.

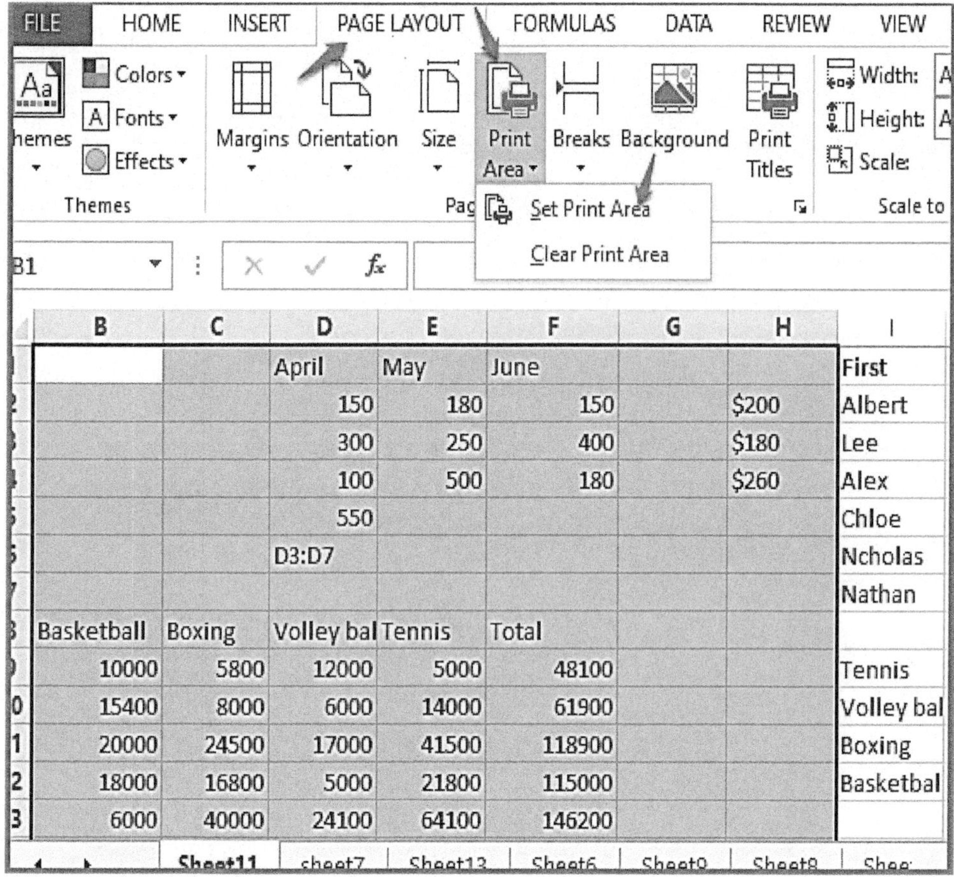

c. If you check your worksheet, you will notice an appearance of the box around the area you have selected for printing giving you an indication of the area you want to print.

Note: if you do not like to print the cells you have selected again, you can remove it by choosing "**Clear Print Area"** from the **"Print Area Button"** drop-down list.

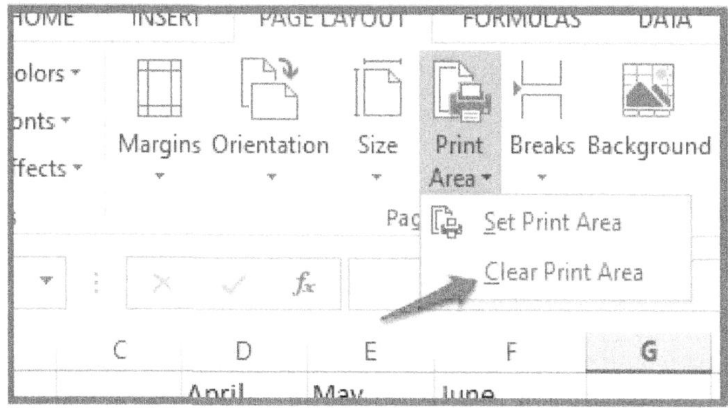

Printing a landscape worksheet:

The landscape is a horizontal printing, Excel users switch to landscape any time they perceive that the worksheet is too wide more than what portrait can accommodate. The beauty of landscape printing is that it permits Excel users to print a worksheet with a wider coverage which is not feasible with portrait printing. Print in a landscape format by simply doing these:

a. Move to the **page layout** tab and tap on the **Orientation button.**
b. Then, select **landscape** from the drop-down menu.

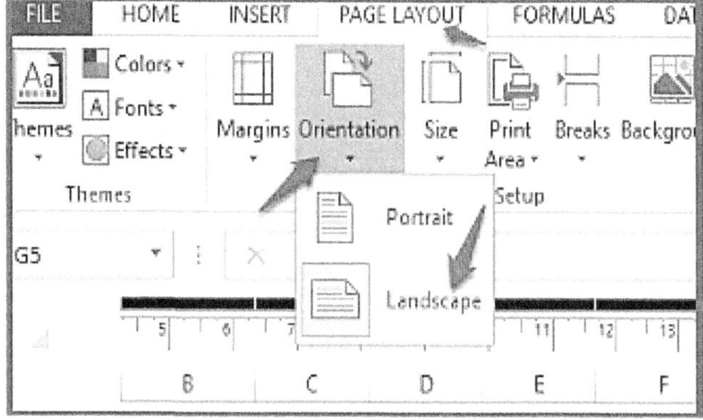

Dealing appropriately with the page break:

Page break is simply the same spot of the start point of one area and the endpoint of another area. There are ways to handle page breaks so that you will not want to have page breaks on page 10 and you will be having it on page 8. Let us quickly check how to manage page break:

1. **Viewing the actual position of the page break by:**

a. Navigating to the **View** bar and tap on the **Page Break Preview** button.

b. Inside the **Page Break Preview** view, under **"In this view",** you will see all the worksheet page numbers and their respective dashed lines which signify the point where each page break will occur.

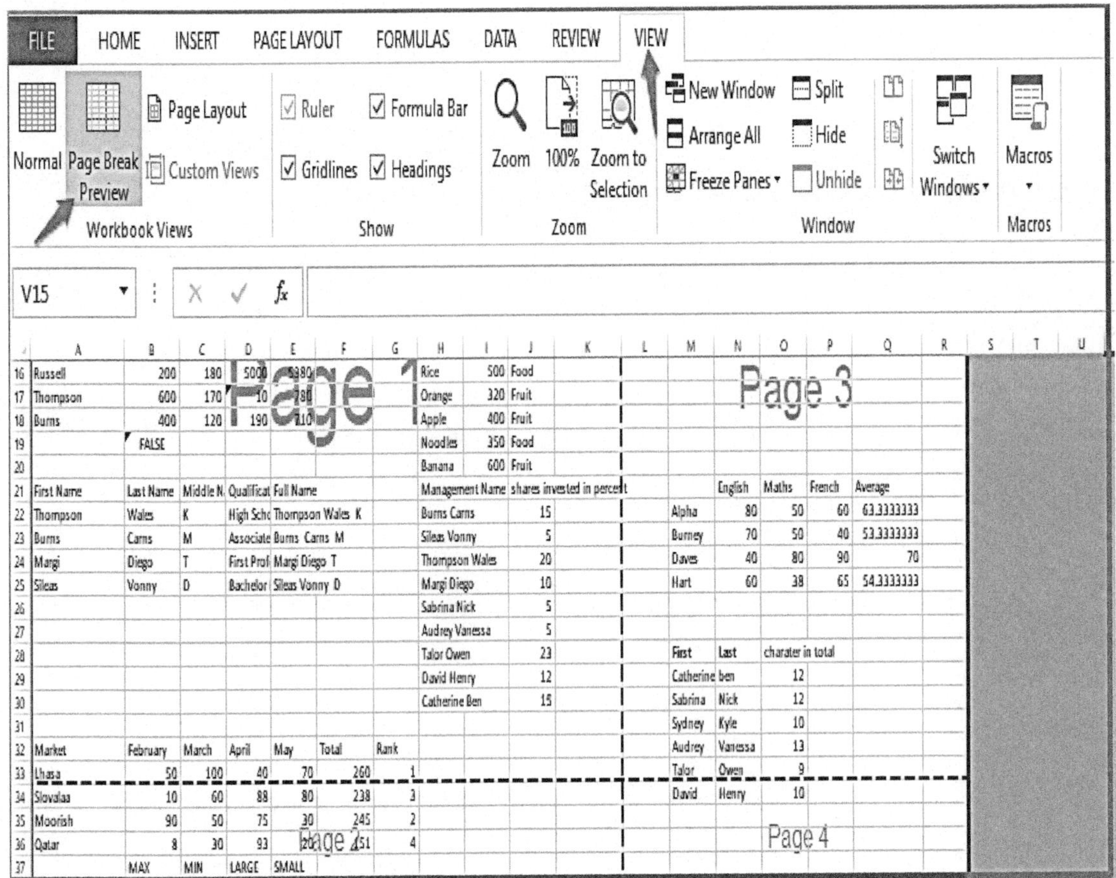

2. **Adjusting the position of the page break:**

a. Inside the "page break preview view", double-click to drag the dashed line to adjust the page break position. Immediately you succeed in moving the page break, the previous dashed line will not be there anymore, but that point will be replaced with a solid line, and as a result, the page will not beak at that point anymore but on the new page break page position that you have just created. Be careful not to adjust the page break too much so that your contents worksheet will not be shortened.

3. **Inserting a page break:**

a. Select the cell below the point where you want the horizontal break to take place and right to where you want the vertical break to set in.

b. Move to the **Page Layout tab** and click the **Break** button.

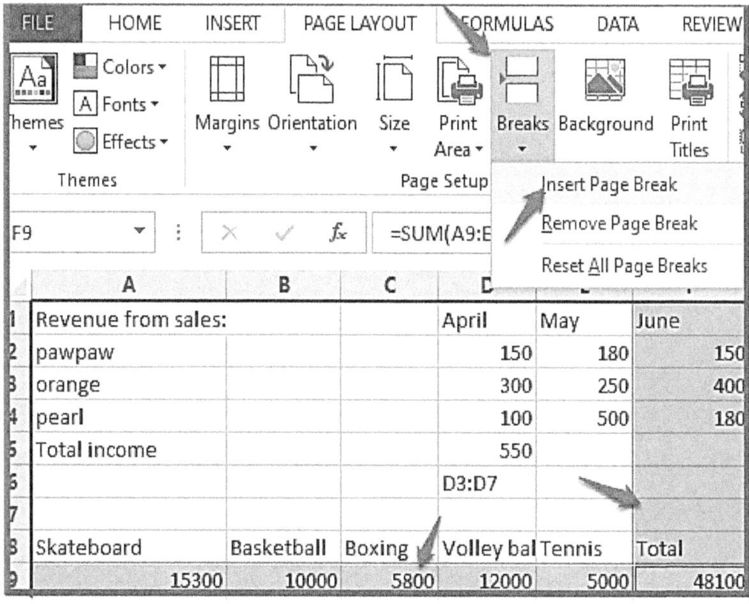

c. Select the **Insert Page Break** from the break button drop-down list and then drag the page break to adjust its location.

	A	B	C	D	E	F
1	Revenue from sales:			April	May	June
2	pawpaw			150	180	150
3	orange			300	250	400
4	pearl	Page 1		100	500	180
5	Total income			550		
6				D3:D7		
7						
8	Skateboard	Basketball	Boxing	Volley bal	Tennis	Total
9	15300	10000	5800	12000	5000	48100
10	18500	15400	8000	6000	14000	61900

4. **Removing a page break**:
a. Select **the cell** below and to the right of the page break and navigate the **Page Layout** tab to click the break button.
b. Choose **"Remove Page Break"** from the Break button drop-down menu.

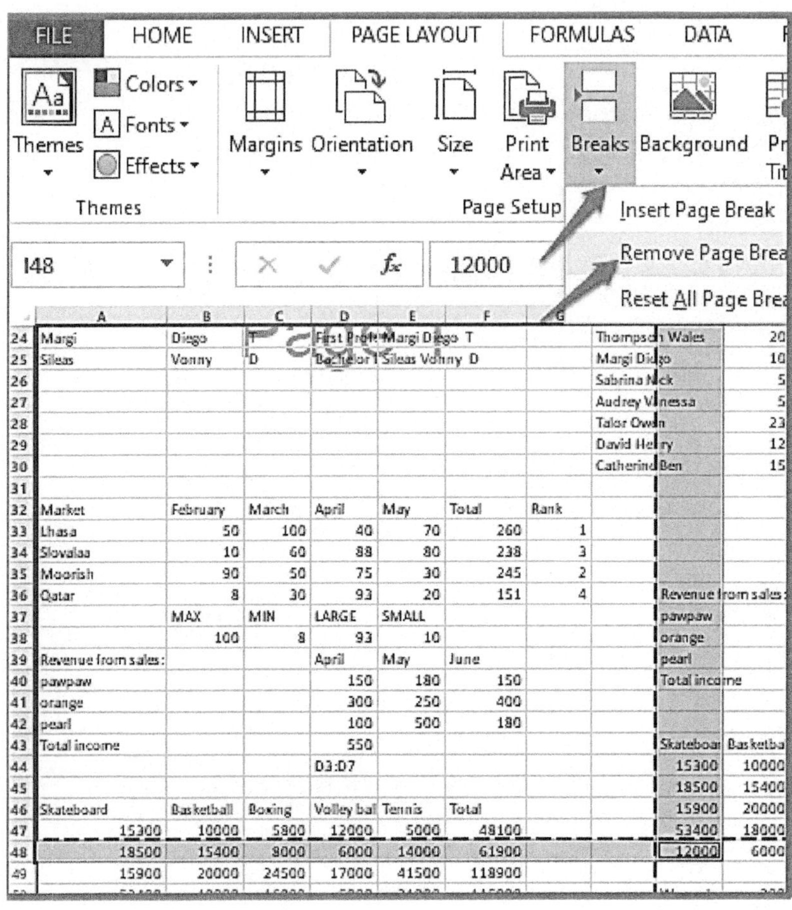

5. **Removing all the solid page breaks (the initial page break you shifted):** move to the **Page Layout Tab** and tap on the **Break** button, then choose "Reset all the page breaks".

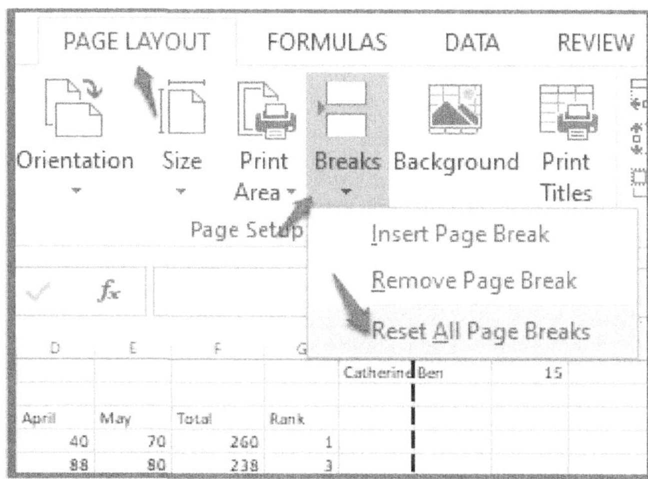

Present A Worksheet in An Attractive Manner

Your ultimate objective is how the work you want to print will get the attention of those people who will read it. You can adjust your worksheet more to make it the best one out there by navigating to the page-set up box. To access the page-set up box, move to the **Page Layout Tab** in the Page set-up group and click on the drop-down arrow.

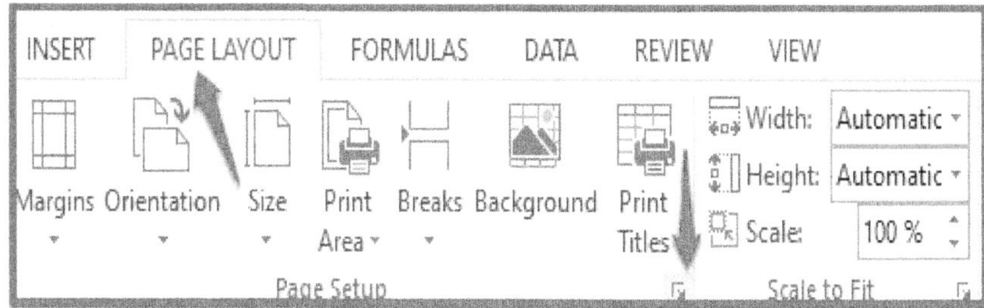

What can I do with the page set-up box? The following are certain things you can adjust inside the page set-up box:

a. **Numbering your worksheet page:** to number your page,

- Maneuver to the **Page** tab inside the page set-up box and insert **1** into the "First-page number text box".

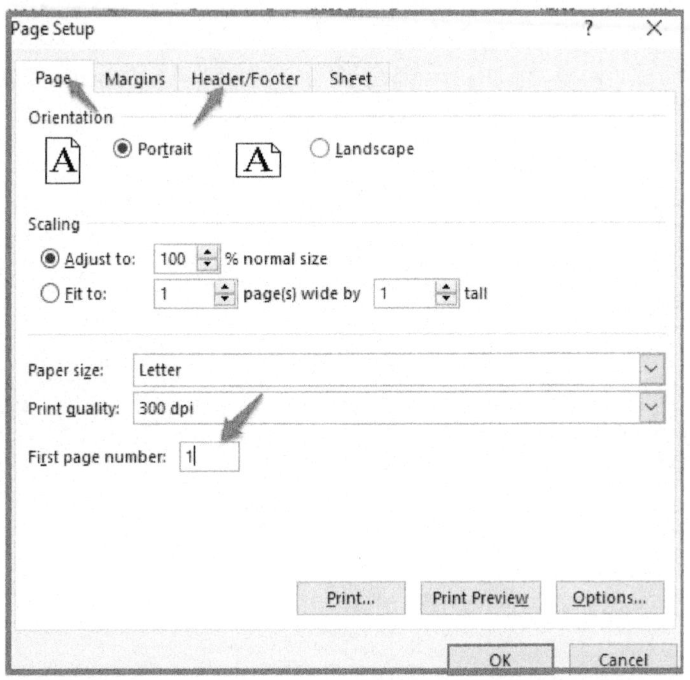

- then move to the header and footer tab and tap on either **footer or header** and pick **"page 1 of?"** from the drop-down list, that is page 1 of (?) the total worksheet pages. You will enter the number of the page number and the total number you are having in your worksheet to the header or footer.

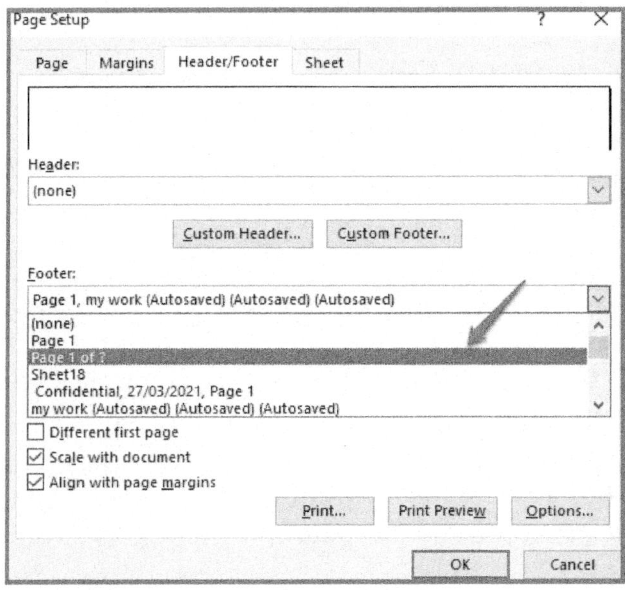

b. **Including headers and footers on page:** tap on the **header and footer** tab on the page set-up dialog box and then click on the "**Custom Header or Custom Footer"** option which will open you up to enter some actions such as, format text, sheet name, page numbers, file name, date, and your name.

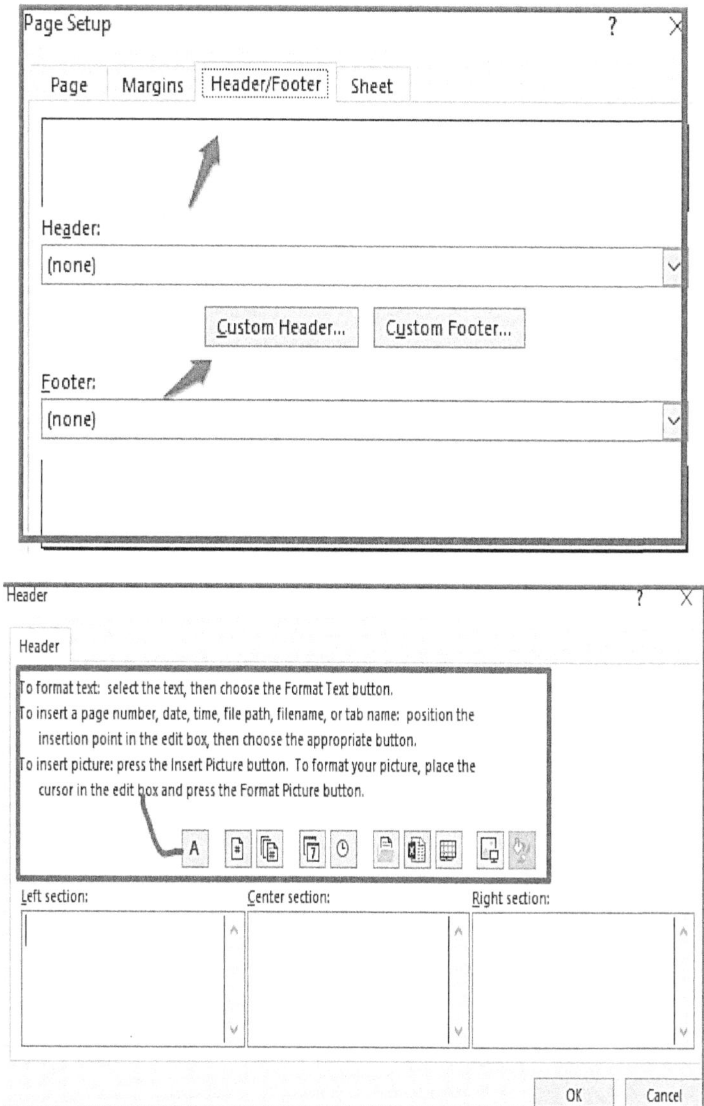

c. **Aligning worksheet page to the center:** click on the **Margin** tab inside the page set-up dialog, where you can either pick horizontal or vertical or both to center the page of the worksheet so as to center it accurately at the center of the sheet.

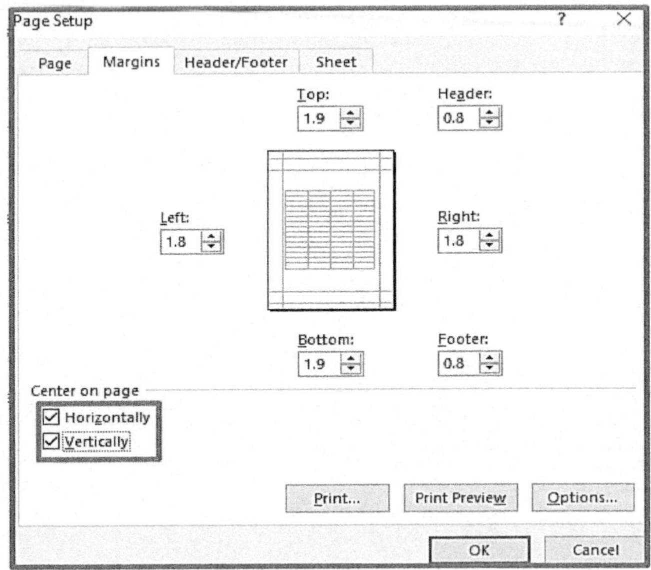

d. **Adjustment for cell gridline, column letters, and row numbers:** Excel neither print the gridline nor columns letters and row numbers by default, the features that give your worksheet an arrangement, but if you choose to print them, you can do that by clicking the **Sheet** tab inside the page set-up dialog box and select whatever feature you desire in the check box.

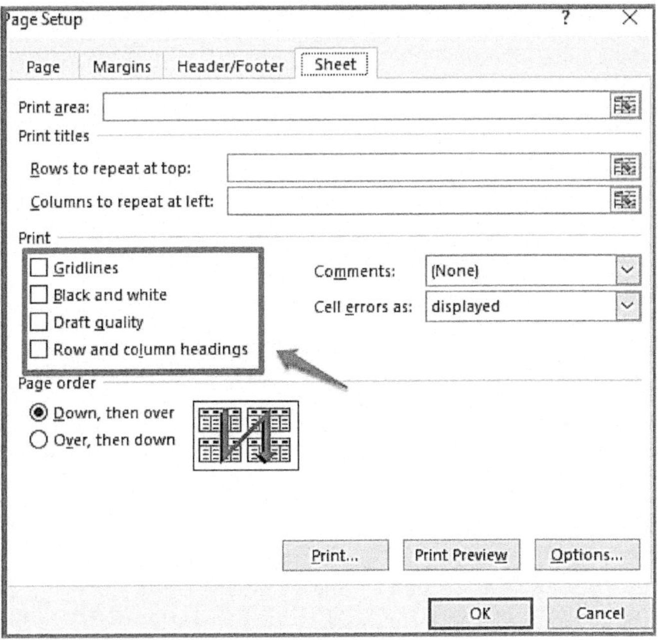

Repeat Rows and Columns Heading on Every Page

Perhaps your worksheet has multiple pages, and Excel does not print title page to every other page by default, and thus if you do not want your worksheet to look absurd because of missing heading on subsequent rows and columns because if the reader finds it difficult to see the title heading, they will as well find it difficult to get the main contents, then you are obliged to set the repeat row and column headings for document that has more than one page. To activate the repeated row and column headings on every page, you have to:

a. Move to the **Page Layout** tab and tap on the **Print Titles** icon, in a jiffy, you will see the page setup dialog box open.
b. Tap on the **Sheet** tab in the page setup dialog box.
c. Locate **row and column references** under the print title.
d. Click the reference selector button that relates to the type you set to be repeated. For example, "Row to repeat at the top" and for column "Column to repeat at the left" in the box provided for each heading.

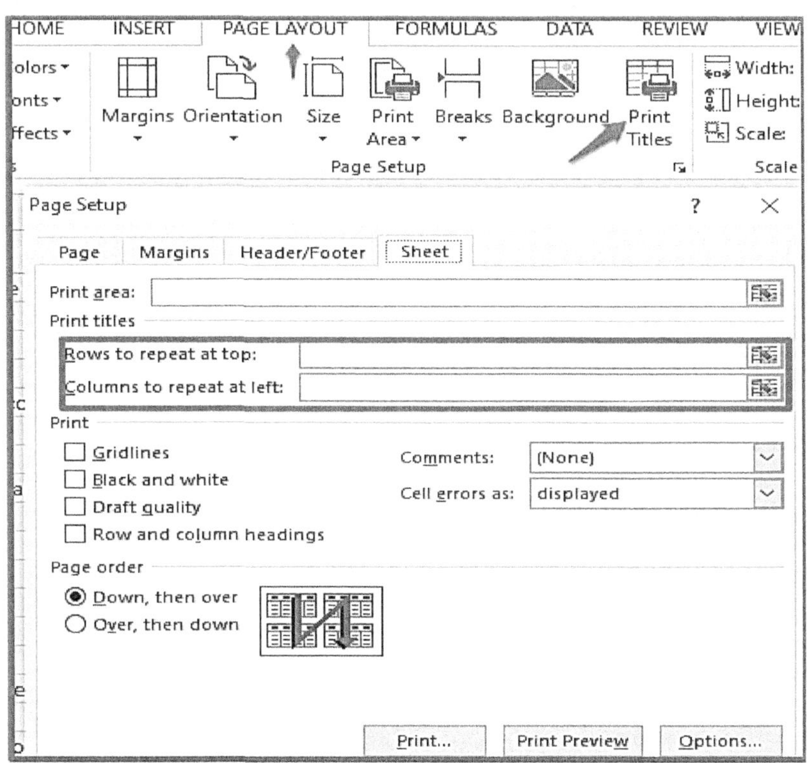

e. Select the rows and columns with the references or addresses you need either by typing their address or by dragging over them if they next are to each other.
f. By now, the respective headings you selected as the cell range must have been listed in the print title section under respective headings.

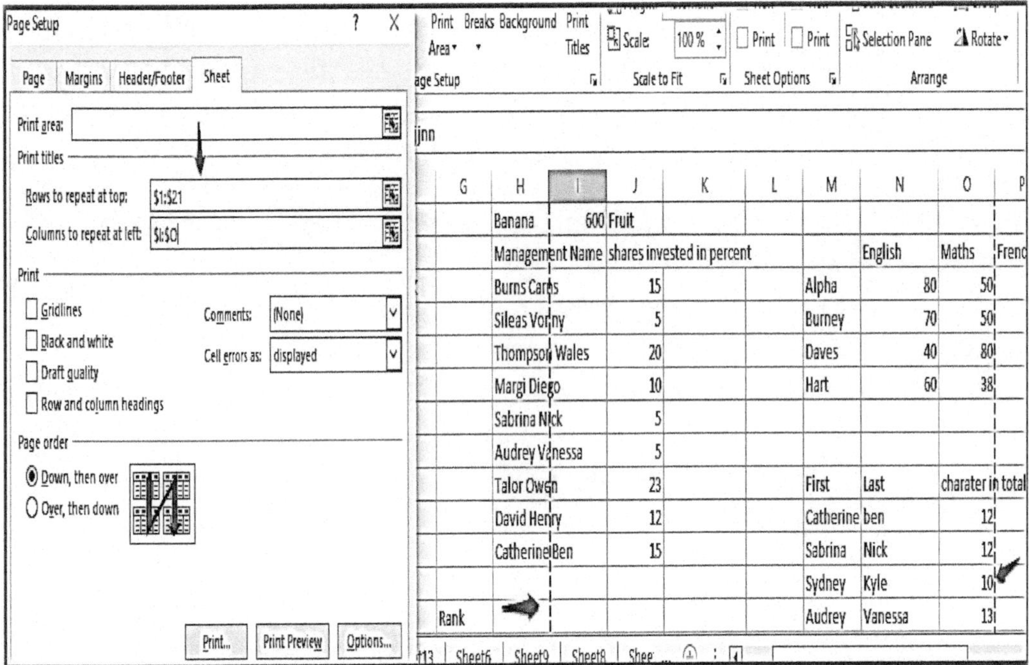

g. This is the pattern you will be repeating if you want to set up repeating row and column heading from step (d) – (f).
h. Tap **Ok** as soon as you are done with the page setup dialog box.

Tips: Before printing a document, check the print preview button in the page setup dialog box to confirm, if the row and column heading repeat themselves on the pages you selected.

Removing Row and Column Headings

To remove row and column headings, do well to:

a. Click on the **sheet** tab in the page setup dialog box.
b. Clear all the cell addresses in the rows to repeat at the top and column to repeat at the left in their respective box.

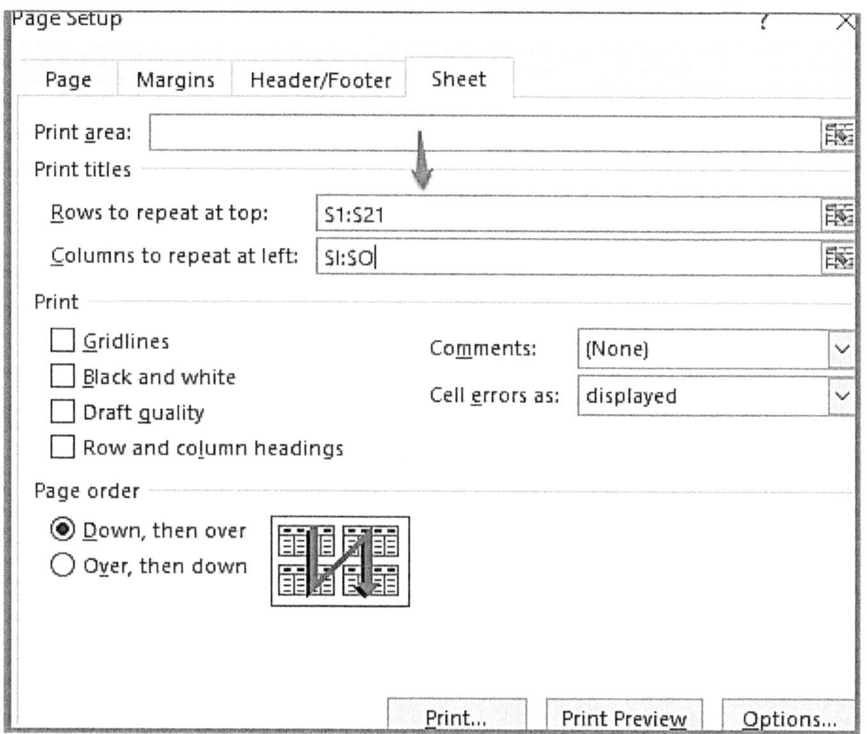
Page Setup
Page
Margins
Header/Footer
Sheet
Print area:
Print titles
Rows to repeat at top:
$1:$21
Columns to repeat at left:
$I:$O
Print
Gridlines
Black and white
Draft quality
Row and column headings
Comments:
(None)
Cell errors as:
displayed
Page order
Down, then over
Over, then down
Print...
Print Preview
Options...

CHAPTER SIX

TOOLS AND TECHNIQUES FOR DATA ANALYSIS

What Are the Sparklines?

Sparklines are the tiny lines that live inside a cell; they show the variation in the dataset. Sparklines are of three types; line, column, and Win/Loss, compares to Excel graph. Sparklines are not graphs; they reside in the cell as a cell background. Let us quickly create one sparklines chart:

a. Select the **exact cell** where you want the chart to show up.
b. Click on the **Line, Column, or Win/loss icon** to open up "create sparklines" dialog box from the insert bar.

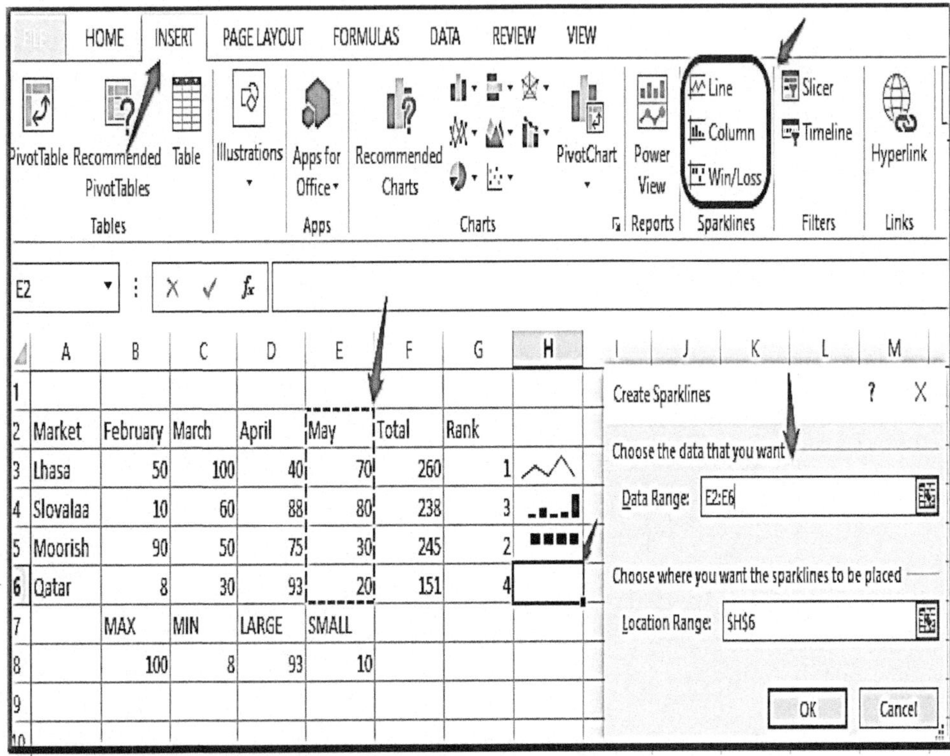

c. Input the range of cells name or drag over a row or column in your worksheet to select the cells from which the data is to be analyzed.

d. Tap on **Ok** to create the sparklines inside the Create Sparklines dialog box.

	A	B	C	D	E	F	G	H
1								
2	Market	February	March	April	May	Total	Rank	
3	Lhasa	50	100	40	70	260	1	F3:F6
4	Slovalaa	10	60	88	80	238	3	B3:F6
5	Moorish	90	50	75	30	245	2	C3:C6
6	Qatar	8	30	93	20	151	4	E3:E6
7		MAX	MIN	LARGE	SMALL			
8		100	8	93	10			

To remove the sparklines, click on the **Sparkline** and tap on the **Clear** button.

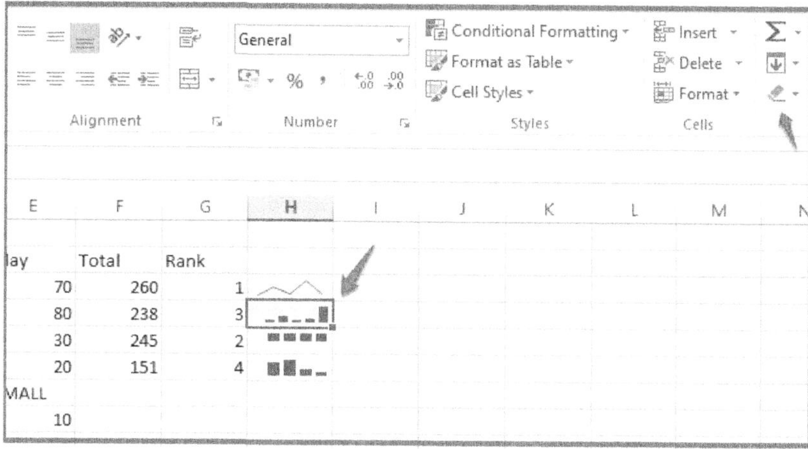

The sparklines' appearance can be improved by moving to the **Design tab** to locate the **sparklines tool** where you can pick some features to change the sparkline's appearance such as bar color, line color, and other various types of sparklines that you can pick as well.

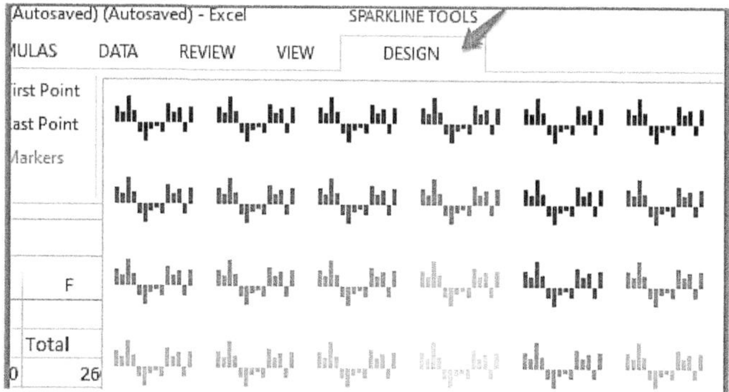

Conditional Format Application for Certain Data That Need Important Attention

The major aim of conditional formatting is to apply a conditional format to data and check if they will meet specific condition or criteria and call attention to it on meeting such condition setup, such as risk-tasks and budget item, it will then tell Excel to highlight those data. For instance, select blue for meeting positive criteria and red or black for meeting negative criteria. Conditional formats give you more understanding of the data. To understand the application of conditional formatting, follow this step-by-step guide listed below:

1. Select the **range values or cells** you want to apply conditional formatting to.
2. Move to the **Home** tab and click on the **"Conditional Formatting"** button.
3. Pick **Highlight cells rule or Top/bottom rules** from conditional formatting button drop-down list:

a. **Picking highlight cells rules:** this is a rule that is demanding attention from a data that is lesser or greater than a certain value or that falls to a specific range of data or numbers. For example, you may decide to highlight a product that has less than 150 in any quantity.

b. **Picking Top/bottom rules:** request for attention from any data that falls within a specific number or percentage within the range of the selected cells.

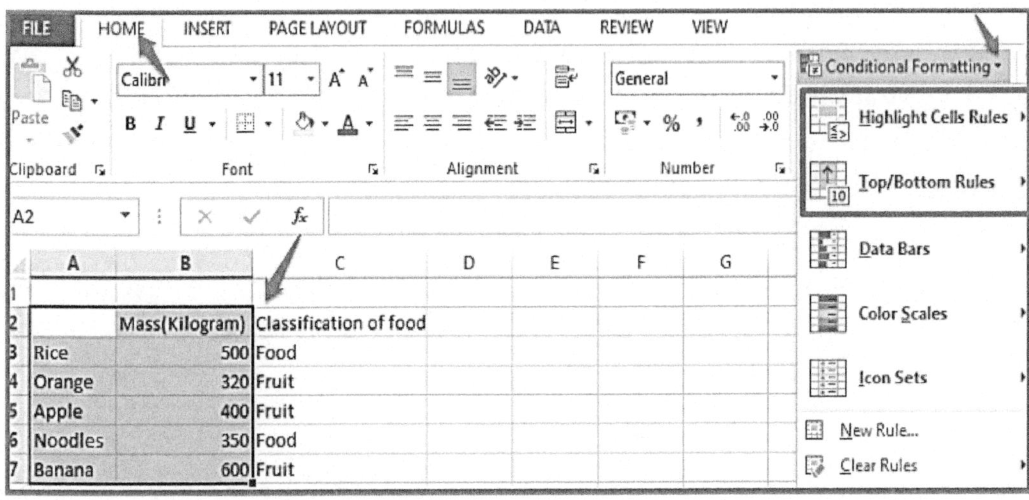

4. Pick an option for the headings you choose above in (3).

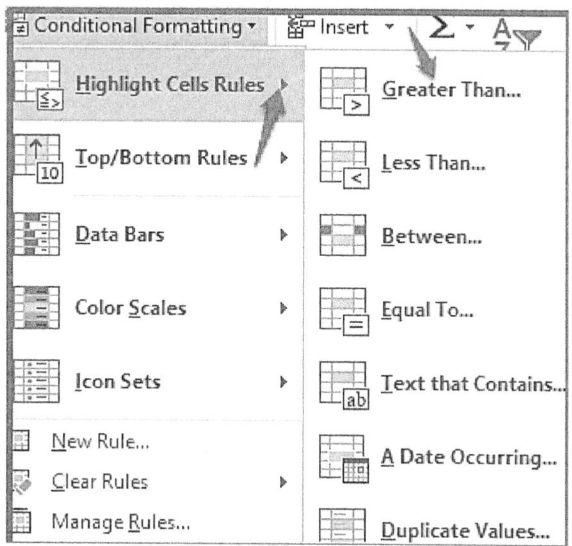

5. Set specific data rules for the cells you selected on the left side of the dialog box. For instance, greater than or less than, texts that contain a specific word or figure, and so on.
6. Select the specific attention you want each data that meet up with the condition to show. For instance, showing blue or red for meeting up with positive criteria or showing red or yellow, for meeting up negative criteria for easy identification, and you may as well refuse to use color at all.

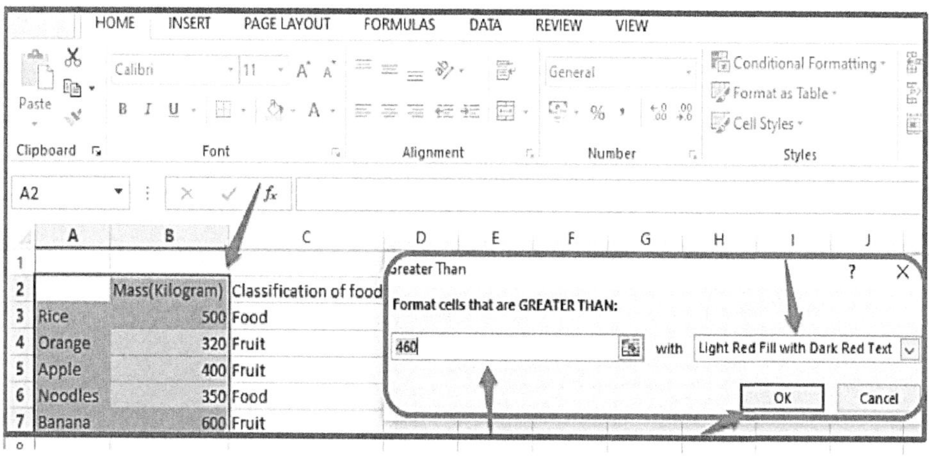

7. Tap on **Ok** to authenticate the process.

How do I remove conditional formats? It is not difficult, kindly:

a. Select **the cells** that have conditional format and move to the **Home** tab to click the **Conditional Formatting** button.

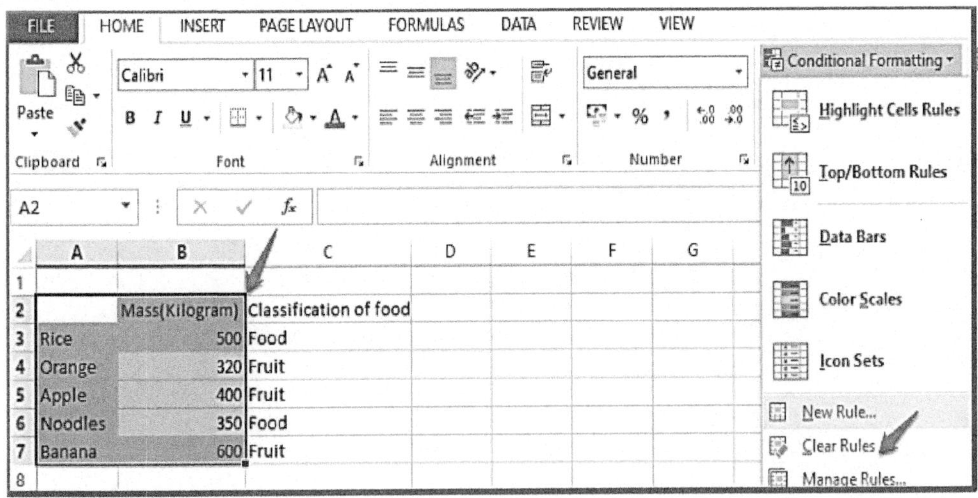

b. Pick the **Clear rules** option, then select "**clear rule from selected cells"** from the clear rule drop-down list.

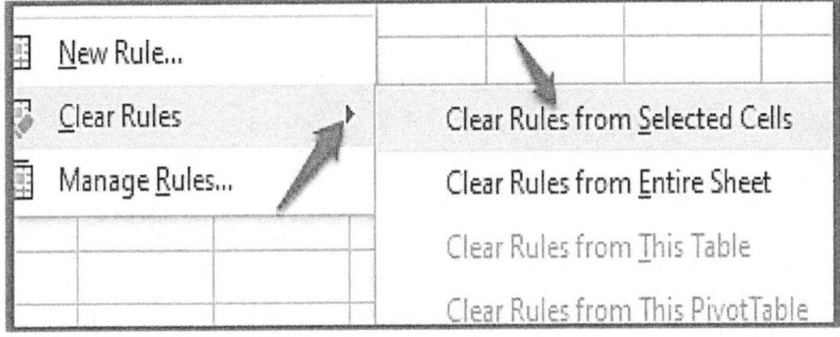

Taking Care of The Information List

Excel is not all about preparing a document for office use alone, at times you have to use Excel to prepare a document for your consumption, even if it is for office use, such document may be prepared on occasion for a later use and such has to be arranged very well so that it will not be confusing next time you are to check it and thus, sorting has to come up for arranging document such as customer information and sort them maybe in numerical or alphabetical order. Filtering is also used to separate essential documents to the safer side, that is, selecting the necessary information by hiding other data and keeping the information required available.

Sorting List of a Data

Sorting data means to organize a full detailed worksheet row based on the data in the column, take for instance, you may logically organize a list by the first name. Data may be sorted numerically, alphabetically and in various other means to meet your need. When sorting, you can choose to sort a column or multiple columns.

To sort a column: if you want to sort a single column, kindly ensure you attach a header to each column for perfect identification and an effective function of Sorting;

- Select **any cell** which will represent other cells in that same column for sorting. Select the cell that has the data type you want to sort, and Excel will update it with other cells in the column.
- Move to the **Data** tab and tap on **Sort & Filter** group, then pick the **Sort type**, probably A-Z(ascending to descending) or Z-A(descending to ascending).

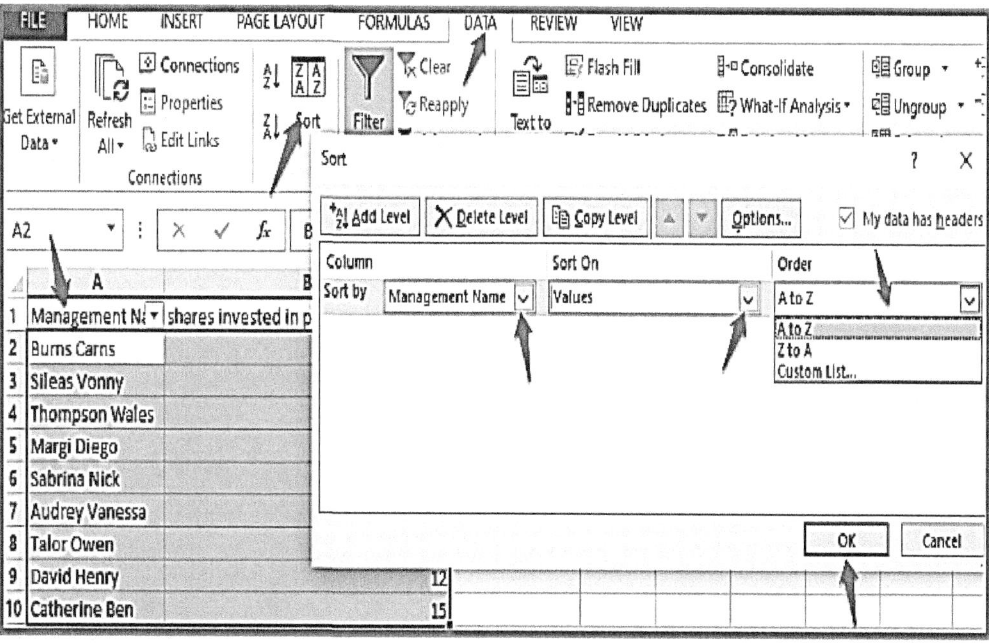

- Tap on a **column heading** and pick "**sort by**" perhaps by the headings and the order you prefer, from top to bottom or bottom to top.

	A	B
1	Management Na	Management Name
2	Audrey Vanessa	5
3	Burns Carns	15
4	Catherine Ben	15
5	David Henry	12
6	Margi Diego	10
7	Sabrina Nick	5
8	Sileas Vonny	5
9	Talor Owen	23
10	Thompson Wales	20
11		

To sort multiple columns: if you want to sort more than one column, kindly:

a. Select the **first cell** in the first column
b. Maneuver to the **Data** tab to open the "**Sort**" dialog box.
c. Inside the Sort dialog box, indicate the column you want to sort under the column for the first column and keep on tapping on **"Add level"** to keep on getting as many as the number of the column you want to sort, and then select the **Sorting order** you will prefer for all the column you have selected.

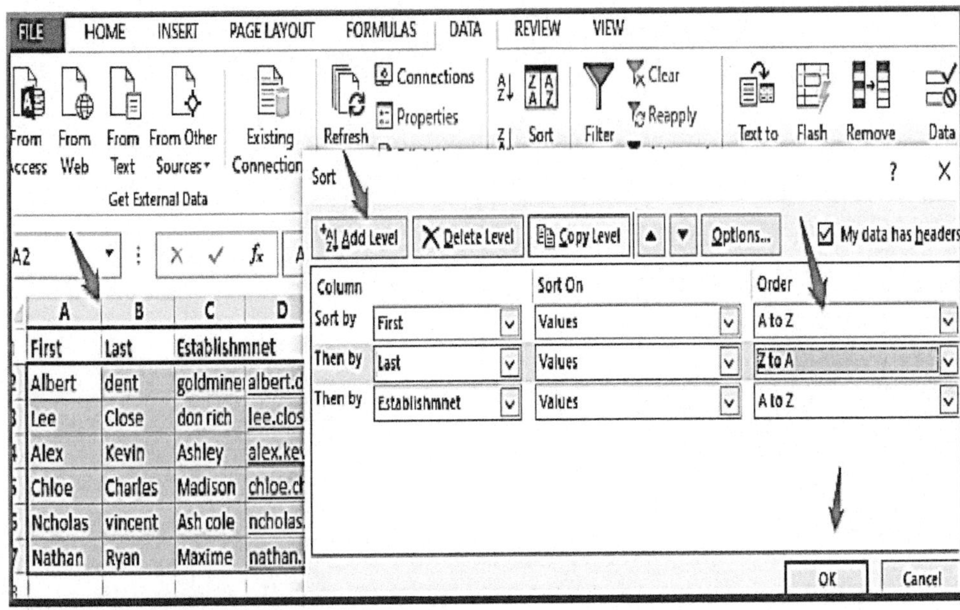

d. Tap **Ok** for authentication.

Filtering List of Data

Filtering list of data is used to analyze data and pick out only the rows that meet the filter condition and thus hide all the other data, provided the data that satisfy the criteria for the filter is established. Filtering will clean up the list of data except for the types of rows of data you demand and at the end of the filtering criteria, the list would have shortened down the worksheet data, so, you can view only the information you desire to see. To filter a list of data, endeavor to the following:

- Ensure you attach a header row for each column to make filtering work effectively.
- Select the data you want to filter, move to the **Data** tab, click on **Filter** under the Sort & Filter group.

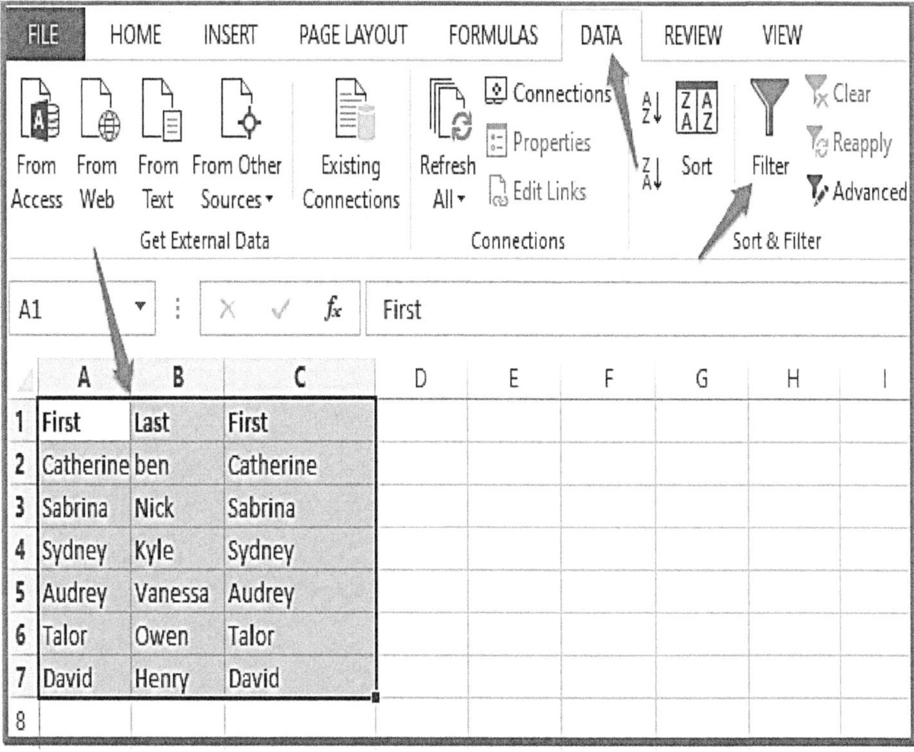

- Tap on each Filter arrow you want to filter and navigate to **Text Filters** to open the options that are available under filter.

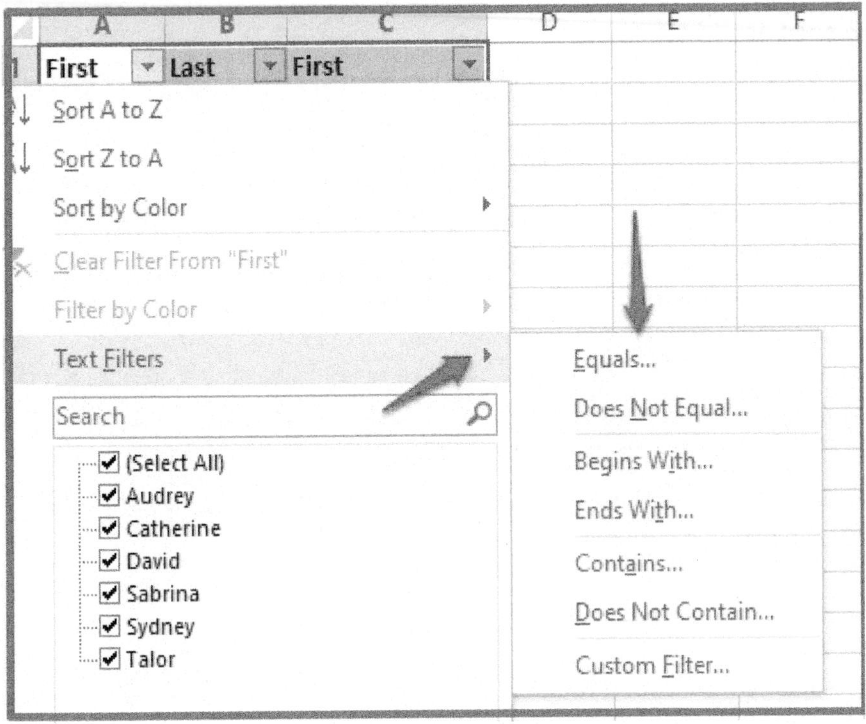

- Tap on the option you want and the Auto filter dialog box will open, supply the condition of the data you are looking for, and tap **Ok**.

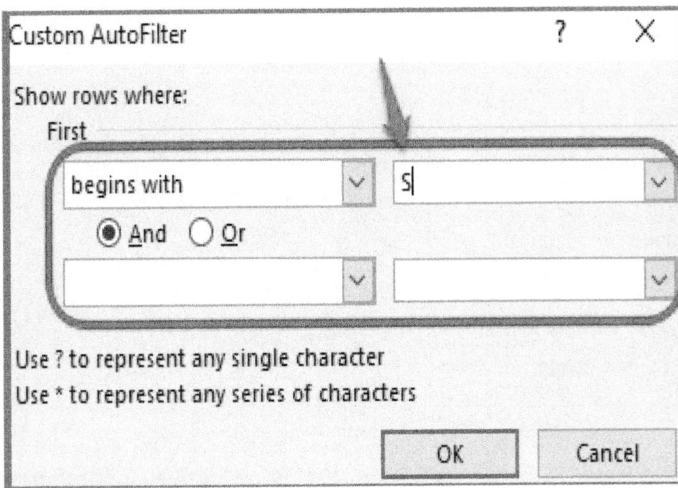

- As soon as you click **Ok**, the filtering will show only the row that meets the criteria with the cells that have that data.

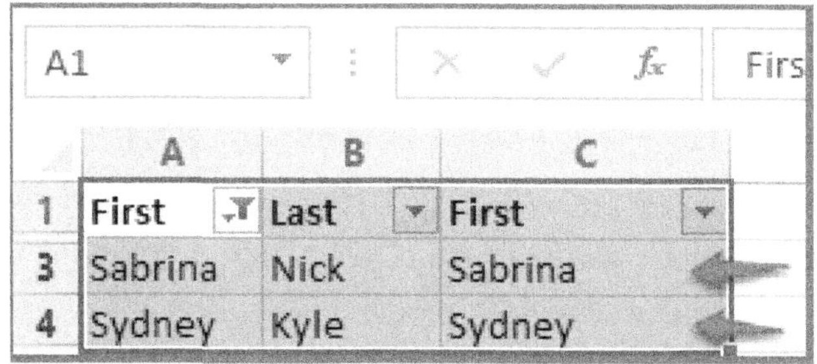

How can I clear all the filters from the worksheet, and get the total information back?

Move to the **Data** tab and click on the **Clear** button from Sort & Filter group.

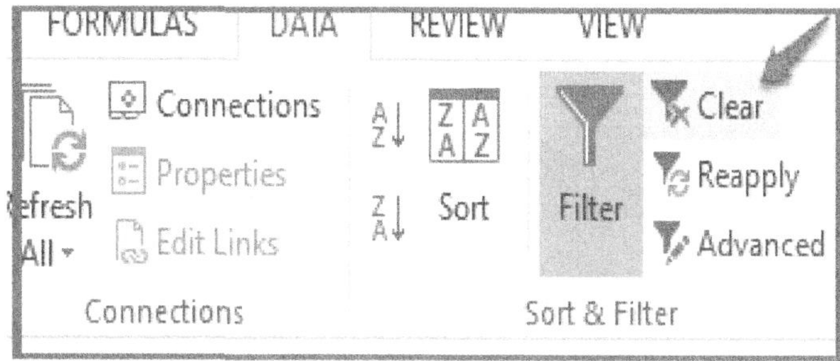

Exploiting Goal Seek Command

Goal seek command is simply a technique of data analysis that focuses more on the result by using the result to formulate an analysis that will help in getting the raw data which will give one the actual result one wants to achieve. Goal seek command is an order you give Excel to experiment result to get the raw data based on the result you desire to achieve coupled with necessary Excel argument.

Goal seek analysis input value in the place of raw data, for instance, you want to borrow money, you know how much to borrow and you have the ability to pay off the loan, and also know the period you will use to pay off the whole loan, but you do not know the exact rate of interest that you will pay in acquiring such loan, Goal seek command will help you in that area. Let us do the computation of interest rate to pay in acquiring a loan with the PMT function with the following guideline:

1. Enter the respective elements into the worksheet, for instance:

- B1= Loan amount, B2= period of the payment monthly, B3= Rate of interest, B4= month payment.

2. Enter the **respective value** for each element above in (1), for instance,

- Cell C1= $120000, that is the amount you prefer to borrow.
- Cell C2= 180, the number of times to pay off the loan if paid monthly.
- Cell C3= the interest rate we are about to calculate for the loan amount.
- Cell C4= the amount of payment every month, but you are not going to insert it here, it will be used in the Goal seek computation because it is the data result.

	A	B	C
1		Amount of loan	120000
2		Number of payment (Monthly)	180
3		Interest rate	
4		Payment	

3. Insert the formula into **Cell C4** by putting in **Cell 4=PMT(C3/12, C2, C1**), this will give you the formula result for the monthly payment value. In this scenario, you wish to be paying $1200 each month, but you will not enter it, it will be using in Goal seek dialog box for interest rate computation. The formula breakdown:

- **C1** is the loan amount
- **C2** is the period it will take for paying off the loan.
- **C3** is the Interest rate that "Goal seek" seeks to find, and the 12 is 12 months, PMT calculates on yearly basis, and thus you have to divide it by 12 to convert it to a monthly basis. But, because cell B3 does not have anything inside, Excel will assume it to be Zero (0).

C4 =PMT(C3/12,C2,C1)

	A	B	C
1		Amount of loan	120000
2		Number of payment (Monthly)	180
3		Interest rate	
4		Payment	-$667

4. Move to the **Data** tab and tap on **What-if Analysis** and then choose the "**Goal Seek"** button from the What-if Analysis drop-down list.

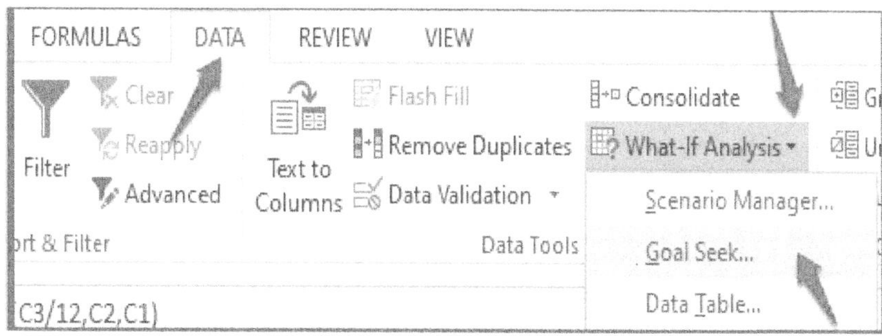

5. Once the "Goal Seeks" dialog box opens, insert the **cell reference** that comprises the formula you are looking at, in this case, it is C4.
6. Then type the formula result into the "**To Value box**", this is representing -1200 because it is the outflow.
7. Insert the **cell address** that comprises the value you want to change inside the **"Changing cell box"**; in this case, it is cell C3.

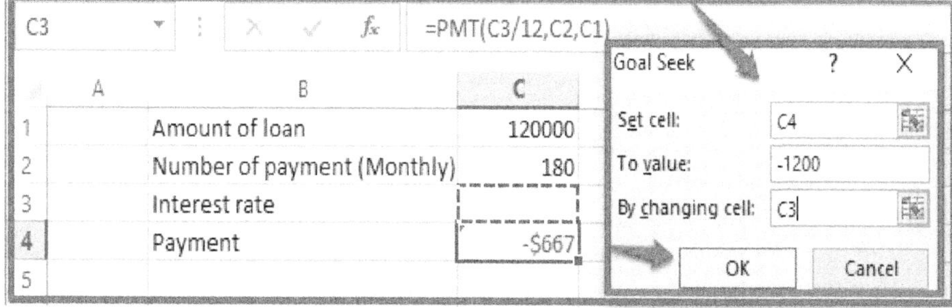

8. Tap **Ok** and Goal seek will run the check for you and provide you with the result.

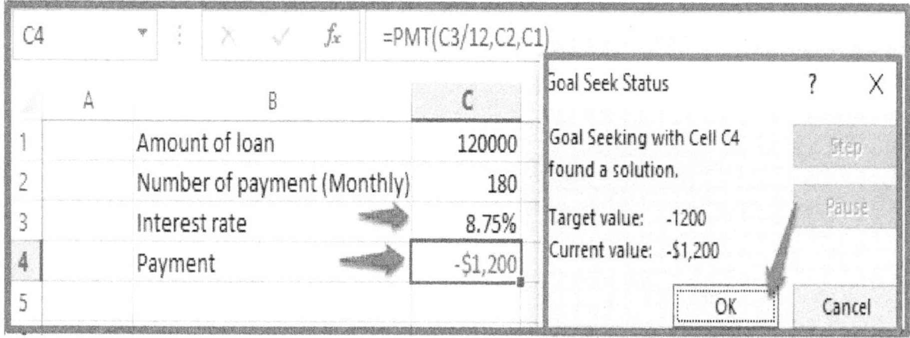

9. Then format the cells to display the actual face value by navigating to the **Home** tab, then, click on the **"Number"** group, then move to currency to format it.

	A	B	C
1		Amount of loan	$120,000
2		Number of payment (Monthly)	180
3		Interest rate	8.75%
4		Payment	-$1,200
5			

Analysing Data with Data Table and What If Analysis

Data tables with What-if analysis are combined to address a complex computation. This technique helps to alter the range of data on a single table and extract the cause of adjusting such on the formula results. Goal seeks and data table are almost the same thing except for multiple variables of data that data table uses in carrying out its process and experiment at once.

Using A One Input Data Table for Analysis

One input data table structures its experiment in a single table and provides the results of each formula to be per the change on the input cell in the formula. To get it right at this level, let us use the rate of interest for this scenario by making use of the following set of data below.

	A	B	C
1		Amount of loan	$120,000
2		Number of payment (Monthly)	180
3		Interest rate	8.75%
4		Payment	-$1,200
5			

In the above information, we are having:

- The amount of the loan, interest rate on the loan, number of payments every month. The monthly payment value is calculated on the other three (3) elements (it is in red), because it is cash outflow or payment.

- The amount of the loan in cell C1 is $120000, the number of payments every month in cell C2 is 180 times, the rate of interest in cell C3 is 8.75%, and the payment value (monthly) in C4 is calculated based on the first three (3) elements; it has to be in red because it is the cash outflow or payment. It is calculated based on: =PMT(C3/12, C2, C1).

  We will be using the above information and analysis to check the number of the monthly payment that will befit you. If your monthly payment capacity will not exceed $1000 compared to $1200 you have been paying before by making use of the data in the above table to formulate different number of payment per month and select the numbers of payment that will give us below $1000.

  Let us forge ahead to check what we have to do to formulate different number of payment (monthly) and monthly payment, kindly:

1. Insert different number payment (monthly) to column E from above the 180 we are having above because you are paying lesser than $1200, enter the number to column E2 down to column E12.
2. Insert, = C4 in cell F1, because it is one row above the value to the column we want to test and thus, it gives reference to cell C4. In referencing, cell C4 you have to refer it, not by inserting the value so that the formula can work but kindly type "=" in F1 and click on C4 to refer it.

F1 =C4

	A	B	C	D	E	F
1		Amount of loan	$120,000			-$1,200
2		Number of payment (Monthly)	180		185	
3		Interest rate	8.75%		193	
4		Payment	-$1,200		207	
5					220	
6					250	
7					280	
8					300	
9					330	
10					350	
11					380	
12					400	

3. Now, select the cell in E1 to F12 and move to the **Data** tab, and tap on **What-if analysis**, then click on **Data table** from What-if analysis drop-down to open Data table dialog box.

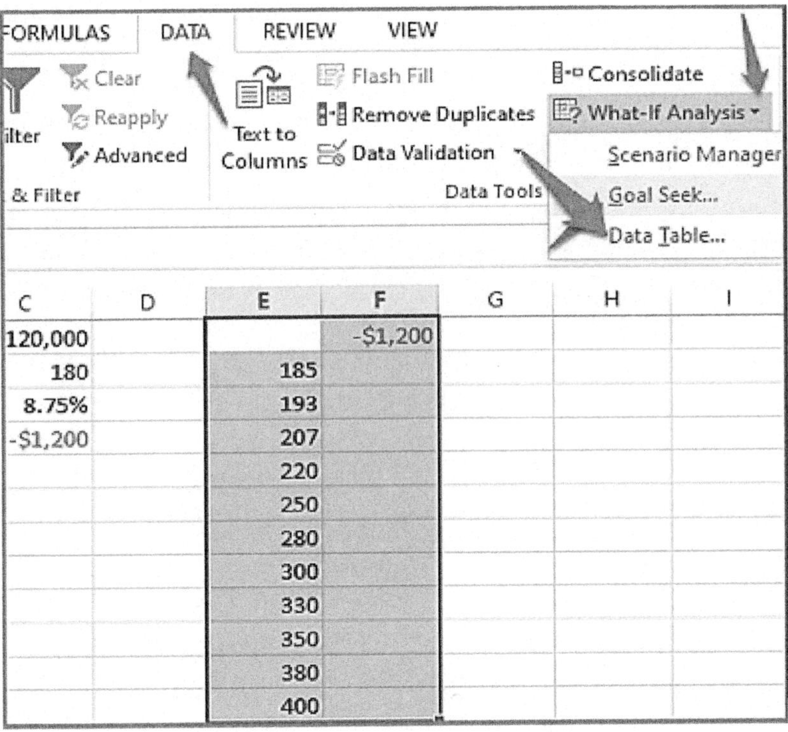

4. Inside the **"Data Table"**, give reference to cell C2 in "Column input cell field"; we will be using the column cell field alone because we are calculating with one input data table.

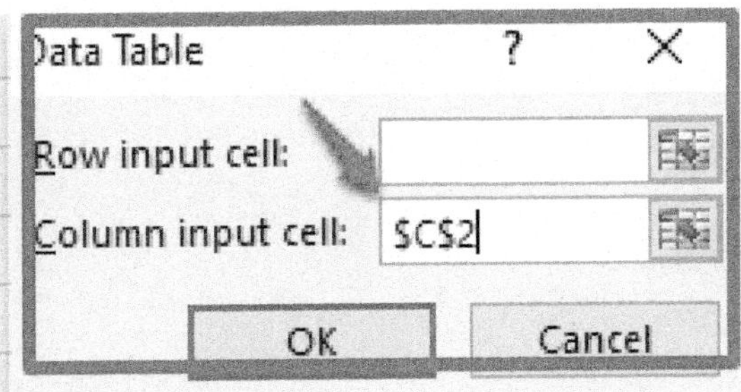

5. Tap **Ok**, and the Data table will process the result and insert the data process into their respective cells.

	A	B	C	D	E	F
1		Amount of loan	$120,000			-$1,200
2		Number of payment (Monthly)	180		185	-1184.01
3		Interest rate	8.75%		193	-1160.89
4		Payment	-$1,200		207	-1125.39
5					220	-1097.14
6					250	-1045.28
7					280	-1007
8					300	-986.937
9					330	-962.911
10					350	-950.068
11					380	-934.462
12					400	-926.016

Note: One Input Data table is done with the calculation, by following the calculation, you can pick E8 which gives you 300 of a monthly payment with monthly payment lesser than &1000 ($986).

Clear the Data table you created by:

- Selecting the whole **Data Table** and tap on the **Delete** button. Note that you cannot delete part of the table, that's why you have to select the whole Data Table.

Using A Two Input Data Table for Analysis

As the name indicates, two input data table permits you to test two input elements rather than one input table, taking for instance the above One input unit that we used in calculating the number of the monthly payment in the column, you can as well add another variable such as loan amount to the row so that the computation will cover both sides and be more detailed by combining loan amount and number of monthly payments to meet a specific need. For instance, you may want to combine loan amount and the number of payments that will give you less than $700, it is that computation that will give you the actual loan amount with the period of time that will give you such. Without much ado, let us analyze the data with two input data table by observing this one-on-one process:

1. Let us get a diverse number of monthly payments to the column and different levels of the loan amount to the row located above the column one cell above to the right.

	A	B	C	D	E	F	G	H	I	J	K
1		Amount of loan	$120,000			$50,000	60000	70000	90000	105000	120000
2		Number of payment (Monthly)	180		185						
3		Interest rate	8.75%		193						
4		Payment	-$1,200		207						
5					220						
6					250						
7					300						
8					350						
9					400						
10					420						
11					500						
12					550						
13											

2. Insert: = **C4 in cell E1** as it represents row above the values in the column. Remember we are working with two input variables and thus, E1 is dependent on both variables (number of monthly payment and amount of the loan), you will not insert C4 directly, you have to reference it, so that the formula can work effectively. Reference it by typing "=" into cell E1 and then move to click on cell C4.
3. Then select **cell (E1:K12)**, and navigate to the **Data** tab to click on the **What-if analysis,** then tap on the **Data Table** from the What-if analysis drop-down, to open the Data table dialog box.

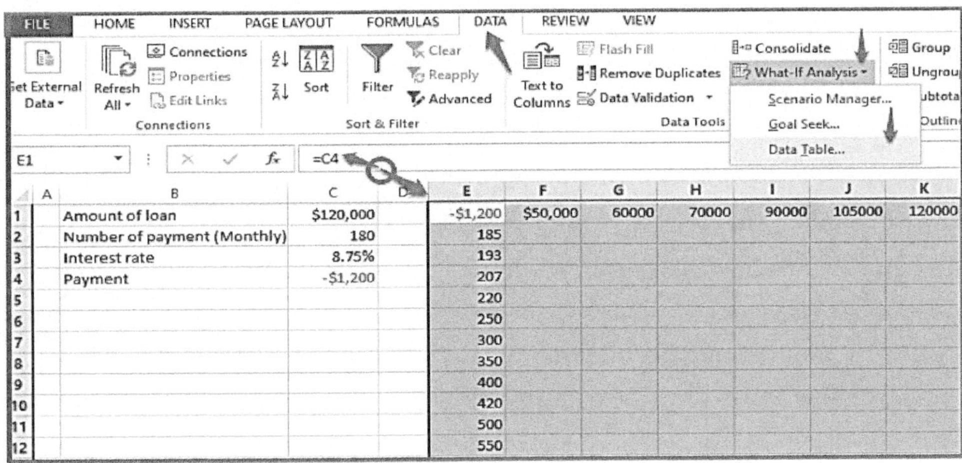

4. Right inside the Data table dialog box, insert into the:
   i. **Row input cell, $C$1**
   ii. **Column input cell, $C$2**

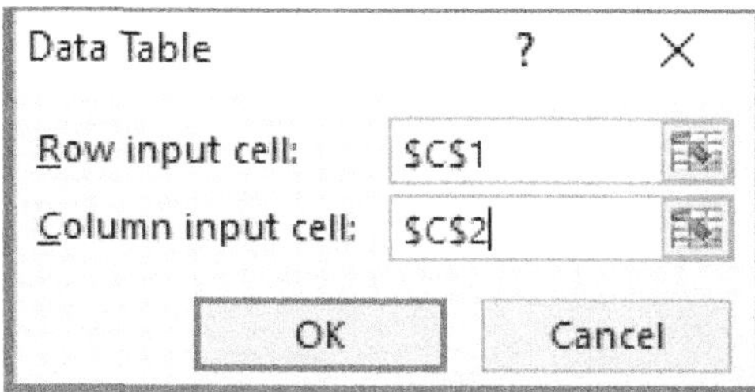

5. Tap **Ok** and Excel will quickly run the check and fill the selected range which you can check carefully to select the combination of the loan amount and number of the monthly payment that best suits you.

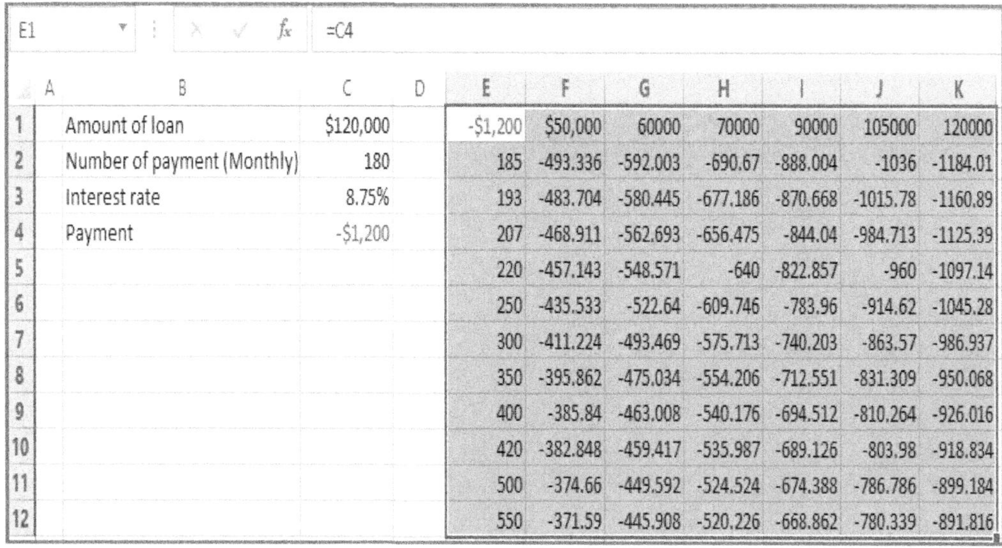

E1 =C4

	A	B	C	D	E	F	G	H	I	J	K
1		Amount of loan	$120,000		-$1,200	$50,000	60000	70000	90000	105000	120000
2		Number of payment (Monthly)	180		185	-493.336	-592.003	-690.67	-888.004	-1036	-1184.01
3		Interest rate	8.75%		193	-483.704	-580.445	-677.186	-870.668	-1015.78	-1160.89
4		Payment	-$1,200		207	-468.911	-562.693	-656.475	-844.04	-984.713	-1125.39
5					220	-457.143	-548.571	-640	-822.857	-960	-1097.14
6					250	-435.533	-522.64	-609.746	-783.96	-914.62	-1045.28
7					300	-411.224	-493.469	-575.713	-740.203	-863.57	-986.937
8					350	-395.862	-475.034	-554.206	-712.551	-831.309	-950.068
9					400	-385.84	-463.008	-540.176	-694.512	-810.264	-926.016
10					420	-382.848	-459.417	-535.987	-689.126	-803.98	-918.834
11					500	-374.66	-449.592	-524.524	-674.388	-786.786	-899.184
12					550	-371.59	-445.908	-520.226	-668.862	-780.339	-891.816

The above worksheet vividly shows how much you can borrow with respective numbers of payment from which you can extract monthly payment that is below $600.

Clear the Data table created by:

- Selecting the whole **Data Table** and tap on the **Delete** button. You cannot delete part of the table and that is why you need to select the whole table.

Using Pivot Table for Data Analysis

Pivot table is one of Excel's indispensable features that grants you the privilege of arranging a large set of data in a worksheet and rationally analyze them. The pivot table works soundly by changing the column to row and also changing the row to column.

Note: Pivot table works perfectly with a set of data that has a column heading label which Excel will use to identify each column.

USING RECOMMENDED PIVOT TABLE

Excel provides a means of generating automatic pivot table; there are many recommended pivot table options that are available for Excel users.

To explore and make use of a readymade pivot table, observe the followings steps:

1. Select **any cell** that contains data inside it in the worksheet.
2. Move to the **Insert** tab and tap on the **Recommended Pivot Table** option

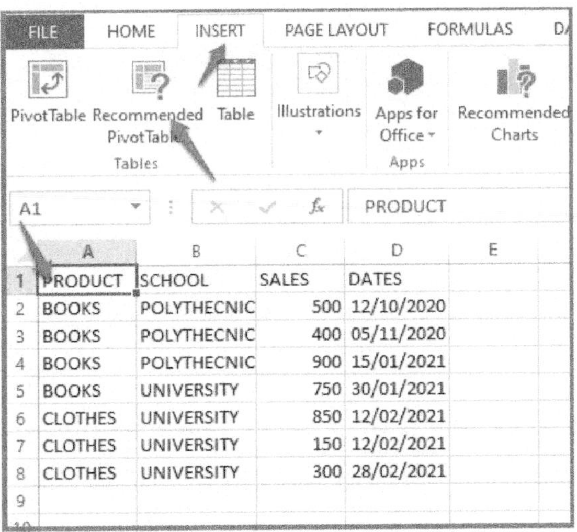

	A	B	C	D	E
1	PRODUCT	SCHOOL	SALES	DATES	
2	BOOKS	POLYTHECNIC	500	12/10/2020	
3	BOOKS	POLYTHECNIC	400	05/11/2020	
4	BOOKS	POLYTHECNIC	900	15/01/2021	
5	BOOKS	UNIVERSITY	750	30/01/2021	
6	CLOTHES	UNIVERSITY	850	12/02/2021	
7	CLOTHES	UNIVERSITY	150	12/02/2021	
8	CLOTHES	UNIVERSITY	300	28/02/2021	
9					

3. And you will be provided with a recommended table dialog box for your worksheet data. Pick any format of the recommended pivot table that suits your needs. For this illustration, we will be choosing the **"Sum of SALES by PRODUCTS and SCHOOL.**

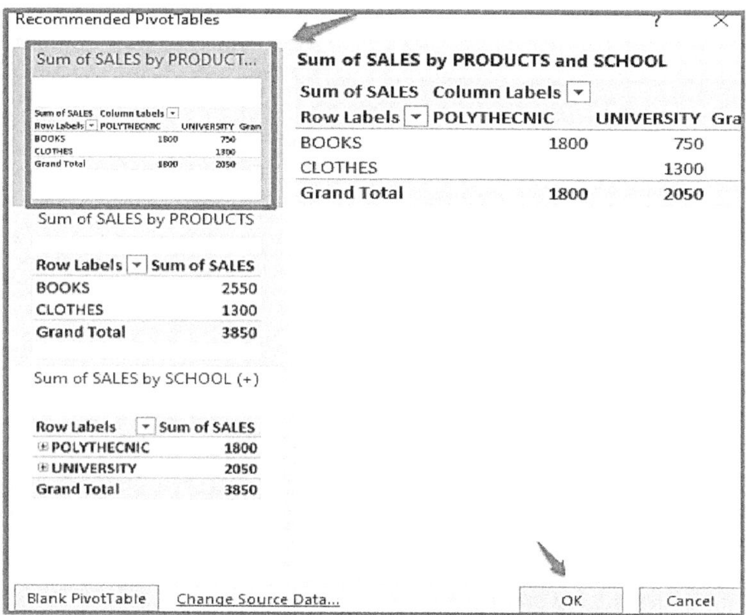

4. Then tap **Ok** and you will see the generated Pivot table.

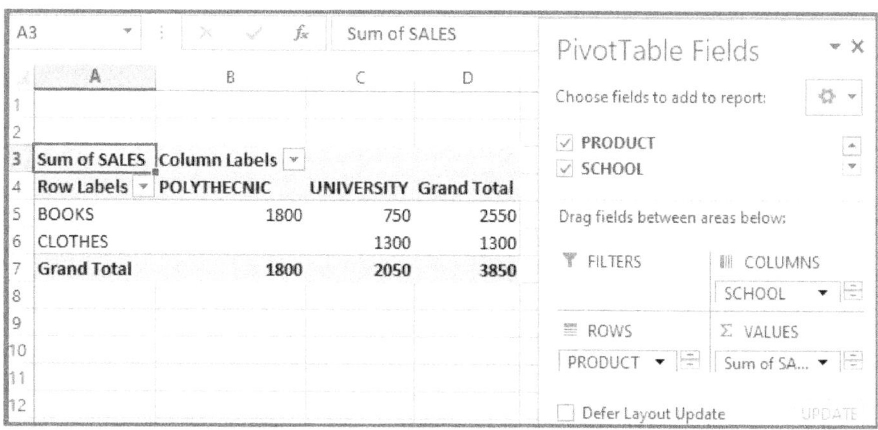

Creating A New Pivot Table

You can create your Pivot table. If the structure of the recommended Pivot table does not correlate with your information, creating a pivot table by yourself will help you to organize list around any of the command label, such as ordering by date to indicate the highest and lowest date order, arrange the price of the product to check the best and least sales and many more. Check the below guide to create a new Pivot table of your choice:

1. Select **a cell** that contains data anywhere in the list.
2. Go to the **Insert** tab and click on the **Pivot Table** button; Excel will select the entire list in your worksheet and use it to open a Created Pivot Table Dialog box.

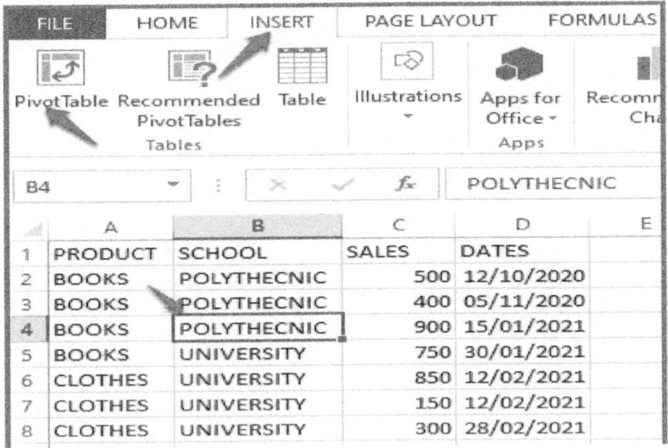

3. Pick **"select a table or range"** button, while the new worksheet will be there on default mode which is the best option. You will edit in the new worksheet and later transfer it to the existing worksheet.

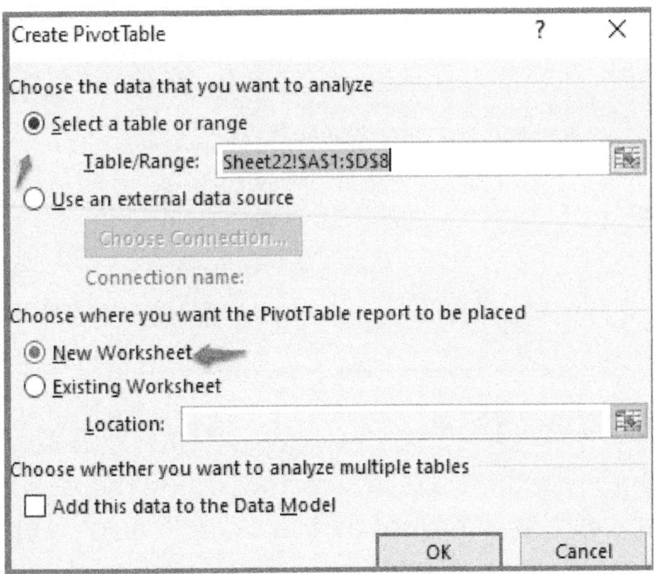

4. Tap on **Ok** and you will be provided with a PivotTable field, select each field you want and drag them to any of the four areas of the Pivot table which are: Rows, Columns, Filters, and Values.

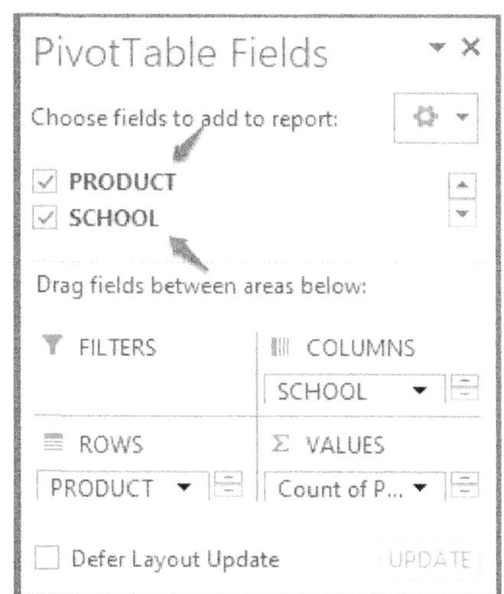

5. In this case, **PRODUCT is added to Value while SCHOOL is added to Column.**

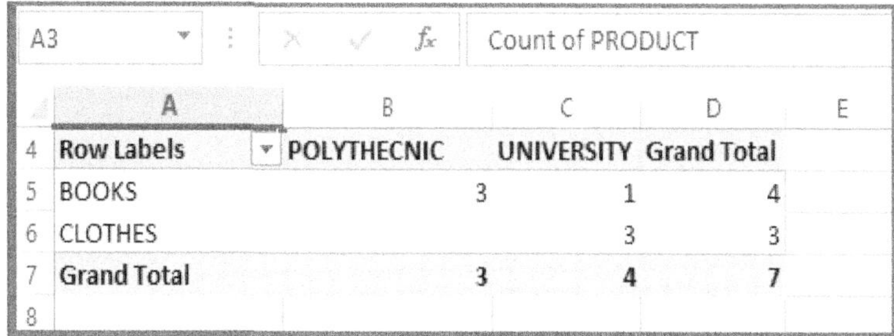

A3 — Count of PRODUCT

	A	B	C	D	E
4	**Row Labels**	**POLYTHECNIC**	**UNIVERSITY**	**Grand Total**	
5	BOOKS	3	1	4	
6	CLOTHES		3	3	
7	**Grand Total**	**3**	**4**	**7**	
8					

Note: you can choose the field with the mouse by placing your mouse on the field, then click and drag it to any of the four areas as you desire, immediately, the Pivot table will compute the selected field and the summation of the amount of products sold in each field.

You may as well sort and filter the Pivot table with the “Sort & Filter” button situated at the upper right side of the **Home** tab.

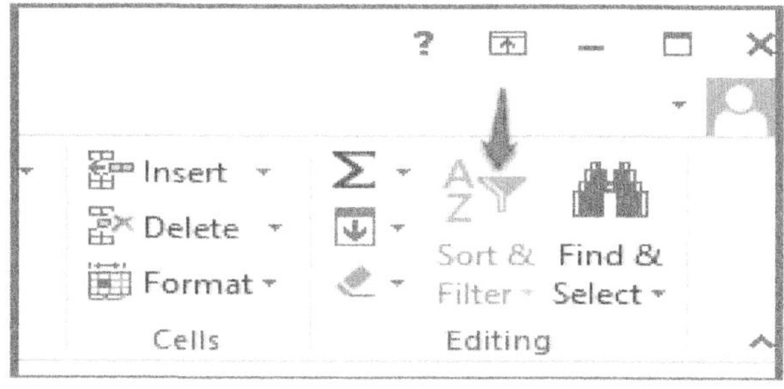

ADDING FINAL TOUCHES TO THE PIVOT TABLE

You are permitted to touch or restructure the default pattern of your Pivot table with Grand total, Report layout, and pivot table styles. Let us check this one by one.

1. **Grand total:** Grand total is the addition of total value. Excel estimates the total value of the column and row by default, but if you are not pleased with it, navigate to the **Pivot Table** design and click on **Grand Total**, and then you can choose **"Remove either column or row or both"**.

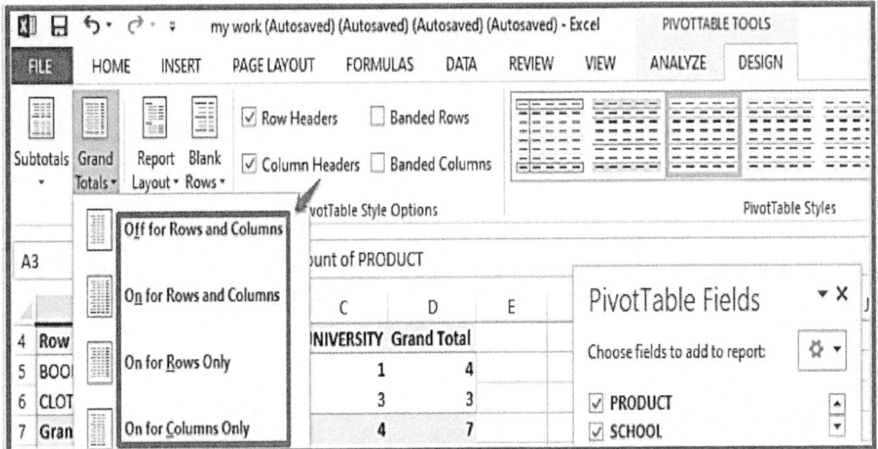

2. **Report layout:** Layout shows how your Pivot table is presented. From the **Pivot table design**, click on **Report layout** to choose diverse layout from various alternatives.

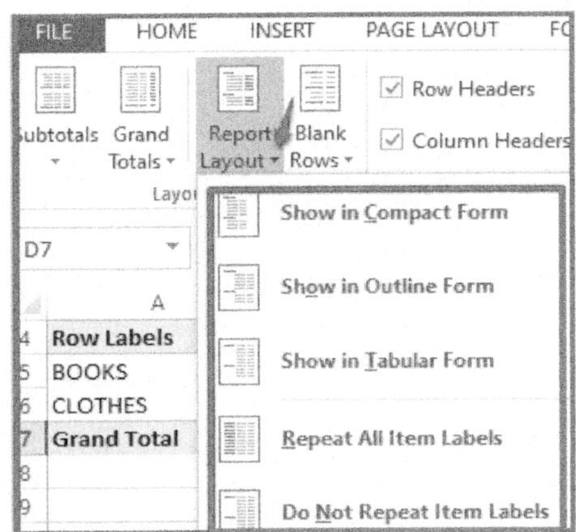

3. **Pivot table style:** Pivot table style breathes some color and design to your pivot table. Once you draw a pivot table, the pivot table style will be there by default, to change it, simply click on the drop-down arrow to see all the pivot table styles; the table style is there by default.

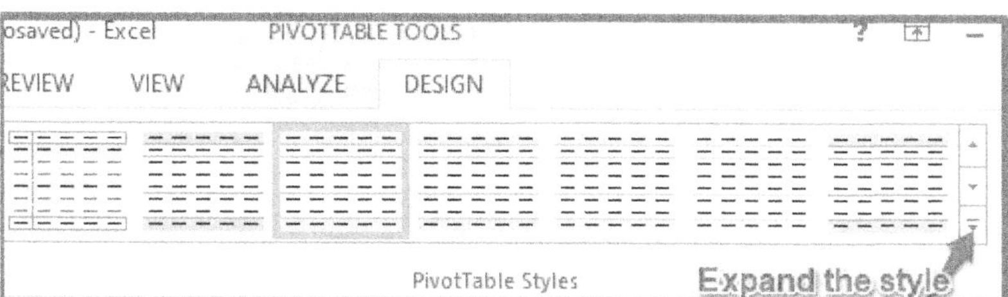

CHAPTER SEVEN

EXCEL 365 SHORTCUTS, TIPS AND TRICKS

Useful Shortcuts

When you find yourself making an exploit through keyboard shortcuts, that is the time you can gain speed in whatever you are doing in Excel. The following shortcuts are amazing shortcuts that you will find useful and necessary as you begin to use the Excel program:

Formula Shortcuts

SHORTCUTS CODE	USES
= Equal to	Start a formula.
Ctrl + '	Switch between formula and cell value.
Shift + F3	Enter a function.
Alt-=	Entering an AutoSum function.
Ctrl + `	From the cell above into the current one.
Ctrl + Shift + U	Expand or collapse the formula bar.
Alt + F8	Create, run and edit a macro.
Ctrl + shift + End	Select all texts from the cursor to the end in the formula bar
Ctrl + End	Inside the formula bar, move the cursor to the end of the text formula.

General Excel Shortcuts

SHORTCUTS CODE	USES
Ctrl + N	Open new workbook

Ctrl + O	Open exiting workbook
Ctrl + W	Close a workbook
Ctrl + F	Open the Find and Replace dialog box
Ctrl + 9	Hide the selected rows
Ctrl + O	Hide the selected columns
Ctrl + shift+ (	Unhide hidden row in a selection
Ctrl + shift +)	Unhide hidden column in a selection
Ctrl + '	Switch between displaying formula and cell value
Ctrl + shift + U	Expand or collapse the formula bar.
Ctrl + shift + %	Percentage formatting without decimal
Ctrl + shift + #	Date formatting with date, month, and year pattern.
Ctrl + shift + @	Time formatting with 12 hours pattern.
Ctrl + Q	Open the Quick analysis tools for selected cells with data.
Ctrl + 1	Open the Format cell dialog box.
Alt + `	Open the style dialog box.

Ctrl + shift + &	Apply a border-box.
Ctrl + shift + _	Remove a border from a cell or selection.
Ctrl + C	Copy cell's item into the clipboard.
Ctrl + X	Cut cell's item into the clipboard.
Ctrl + V	Paste from the clipboard into a cell.
Ctrl + Alt + V	Open paste special dialog box.
Enter	Moving to the next cell down
Shift + Enter	Moving to the next cell up
(Ctrl + A or Ctrl) + (shift + space bar)	Select the whole worksheet
Ctrl + Home	Navigating the selection to the beginning of the selected rows
Ctrl + Shift + Home	Navigating the selection to the beginning of the selected worksheet
Ctrl + space bar	Selecting a column.
Shift + spacebar	Selecting a column.

F5	Open "Go To" dialog box
Ctrl + left arrow	Move to the left end while you are still in a cell
Ctrl + right arrow	Move to the right while you are still in a cell
Esc	Erase your cell entry
Ctrl + ;	Enter the current date.
Ctrl + Shift + ;	Enter the current time.
Ctrl + T	Open the create table dialog box.
Tab	Move to the next cell to the right.
Up / down arrow key	Move the cell one up / down.
Home	Move to the beginning of a row.
Ctrl + Home	Move to the beginning of a worksheet.
Shift + tab	Move to the next cell to the left.
Ctrl + End	Move to the last cell that has contents inside.

Indispensable Tips and Trick for Quick Command

The following tricks and tips will not just help you to analyze or simplify an issue, but also save your time by simplifying things and aid you to crunch long data item. With these simple tools, do not worry, because you will move at a faster pace with Excel.

Absolute and Relative Reference

Excel references cells using an absolute or relative reference, or both. For instance,

a. = **C4*D1**, is referred to a relative referencing because it refers to a certain location by one cell to the left or three cells up the row.

D4 =C4*D1

	A	B	C	D	E	F
1			Rate	5%		
2						
3		Detail	Price	Rate	Total	
4		chair	300	15		
5		desk	230			
6		book	400			
7		pen	150			
8		bag	1000			

b. And thus, if you decide to copy down the formula using Autofill, you will be getting an error notice, because each cell you copy will still be referring to one cell to the left and three cells up the row. In this case, it is either it will give you the wrong answer or give you an error because that D1 should apply to all formulas in that column. For instance, three cells above the row; in this case, it's a text (Rate), in the case of cell D6 =C6*D3, D3 is a text and it is because the formula is relative referencing.

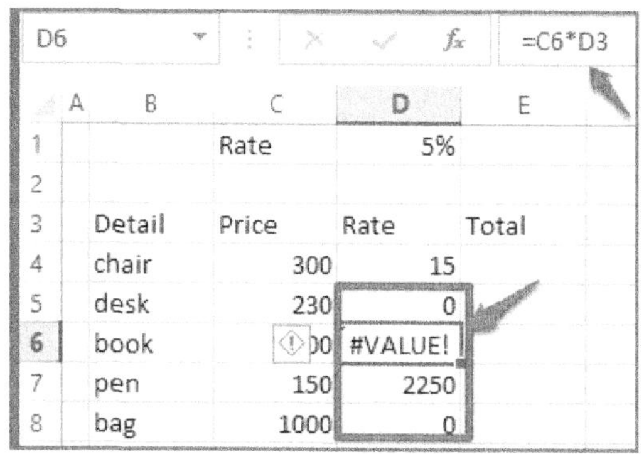

c. In such a scenario like this, we will make use of absolute referencing by making D1 fixed to this location for all the rows, do this simply by highlighting it and press **F4** to switch between relative and absolute cell referencing.

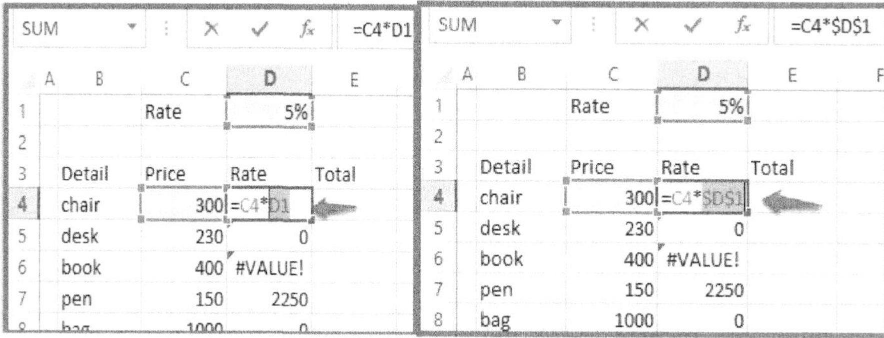

d. Then, you can lock the column, row, and both; but in this scenario, we will keep cell D1 locked, then, if you copy it down now, it will copy the right formulas for each cell.

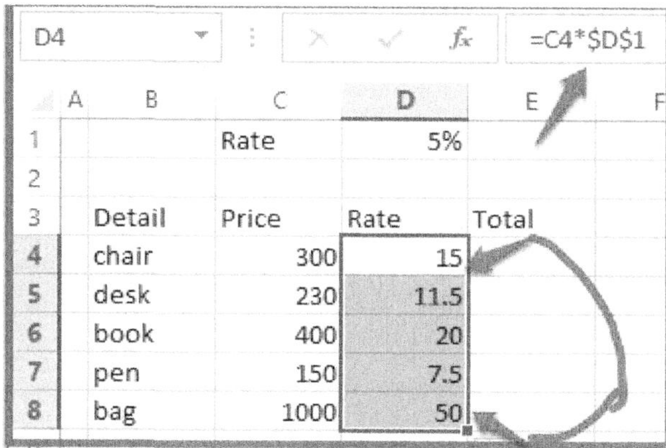

Note: Anytime you copy a formula, make sure you set the relative or absolute referencing appropriately in respect of how the formula will be applied to the data.

Quick Analysis Tool

Quick analysis is used to perform numerous quick actions on the list of data in the worksheet, check this case:

a. When you highlight the list of data and click on the "Quick Analysis" tool icon, it will show up a group of information.

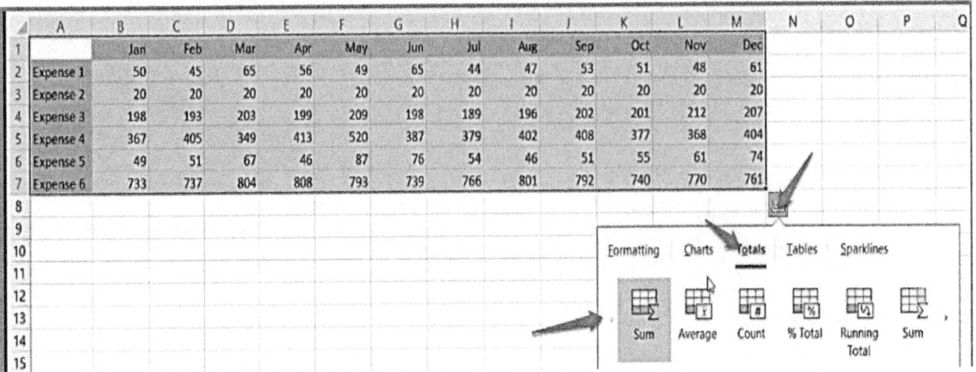

	Jan	Feb	Mar	Apr	May	Jun	Jul	Aug	Sep	Oct	Nov	Dec
Expense 1	50	45	65	56	49	65	44	47	53	51	48	61
Expense 2	20	20	20	20	20	20	20	20	20	20	20	20
Expense 3	198	193	203	199	209	198	189	196	202	201	212	207
Expense 4	367	405	349	413	520	387	379	402	408	377	368	404
Expense 5	49	51	67	46	87	76	54	46	51	55	61	74
Expense 6	733	737	804	808	793	739	766	801	792	740	770	761

b. Click on the **Total** tab where you will be able to select **SUM, AVERAGE,** and others. When you pick from SUM, there is also row sum, column sum, or Running total or percentage.

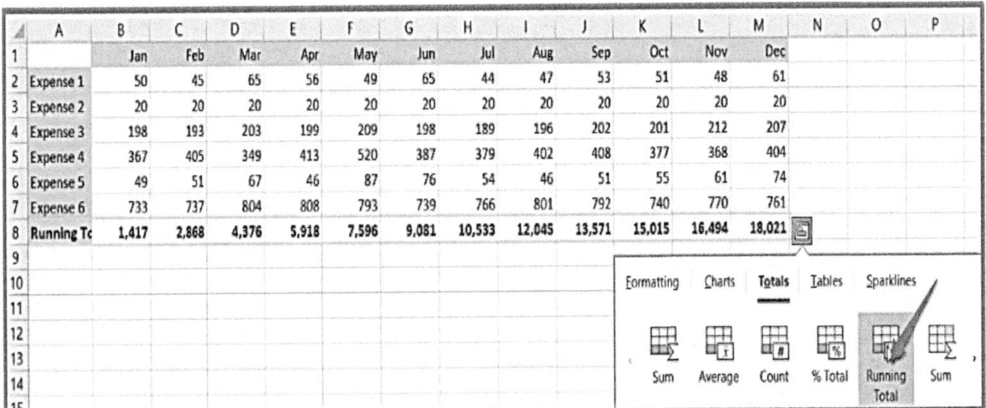

	Jan	Feb	Mar	Apr	May	Jun	Jul	Aug	Sep	Oct	Nov	Dec
Expense 1	50	45	65	56	49	65	44	47	53	51	48	61
Expense 2	20	20	20	20	20	20	20	20	20	20	20	20
Expense 3	198	193	203	199	209	198	189	196	202	201	212	207
Expense 4	367	405	349	413	520	387	379	402	408	377	368	404
Expense 5	49	51	67	46	87	76	54	46	51	55	61	74
Expense 6	733	737	804	808	793	739	766	801	792	740	770	761
Running Tc	**1,417**	**2,868**	**4,376**	**5,918**	**7,596**	**9,081**	**10,533**	**12,045**	**13,571**	**15,015**	**16,494**	**18,021**

c. Click on the **Chart** option, and you will be given a line, clustered area, and so on.

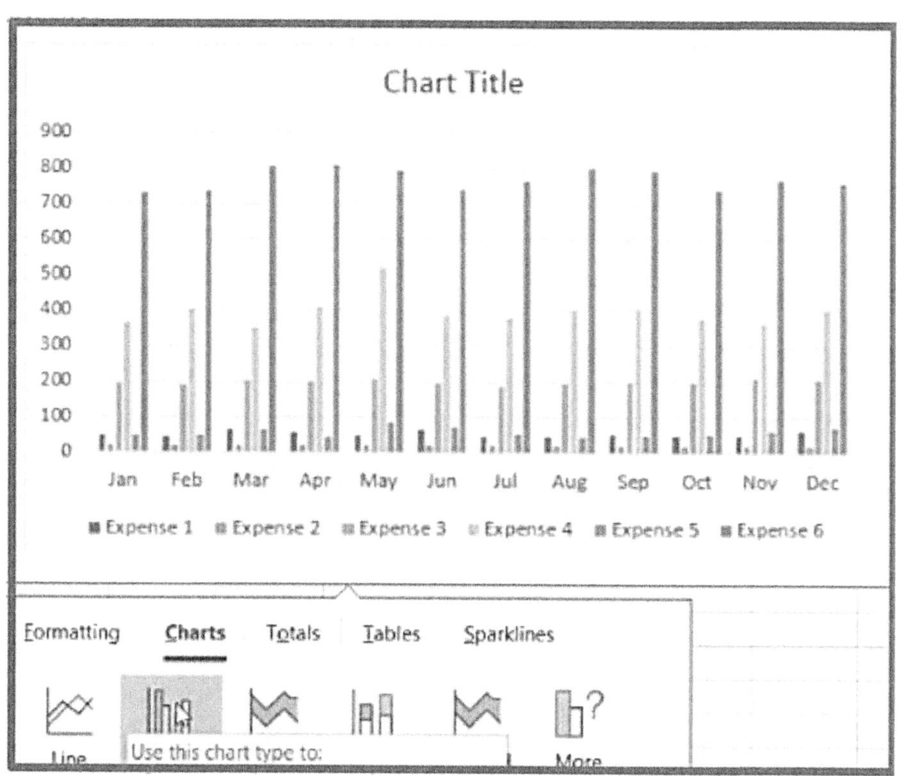

d. Click on **formatting** and you will be given Data bar, color scale, icon set, mark 10%, and others. With the Data tab, all your cells will be represented with a graph in respect of the value they have inside.

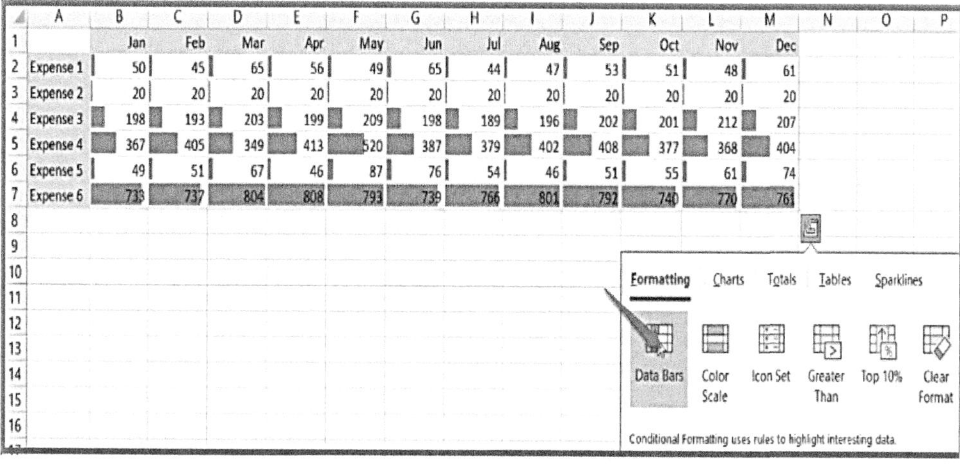

	A	B	C	D	E	F	G	H	I	J	K	L	M
1		Jan	Feb	Mar	Apr	May	Jun	Jul	Aug	Sep	Oct	Nov	Dec
2	Expense 1	50	45	65	56	49	65	44	47	53	51	48	61
3	Expense 2	20	20	20	20	20	20	20	20	20	20	20	20
4	Expense 3	198	193	203	199	209	198	189	196	202	201	212	207
5	Expense 4	367	405	349	413	520	387	379	402	408	377	368	404
6	Expense 5	49	51	67	46	87	76	54	46	51	55	61	74
7	Expense 6	733	737	804	808	793	739	766	801	792	740	770	761

The color scale helps you to adjust the color.

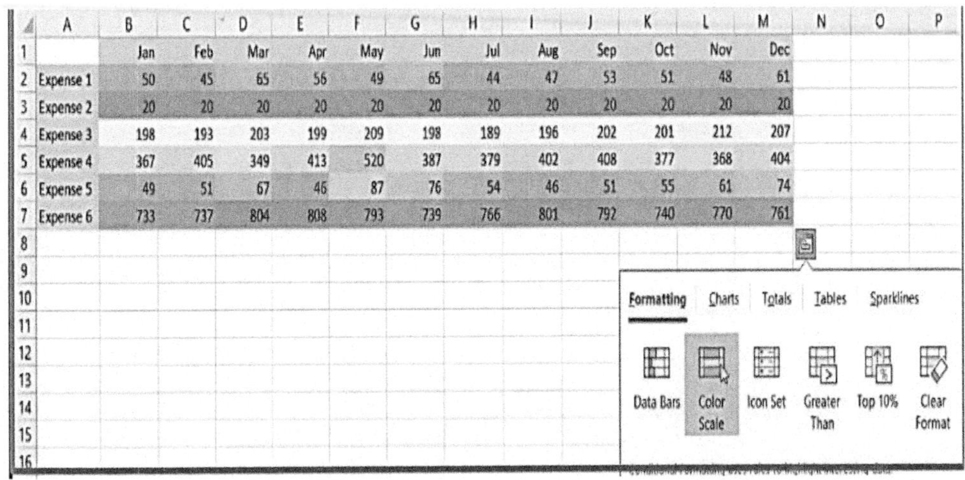

While icon set gives you a pictorial illustration of each data in the list and mark the top, 10% will mark top ten in the list. When you click on the Sparklines, it shows you the small chart of your data.

Autofit Column Width

The Autofit command is the quickest way of adjusting column, to use it;

a. Move to a **boundary between any columns** until you see the cursor change to a black-headed arrow.

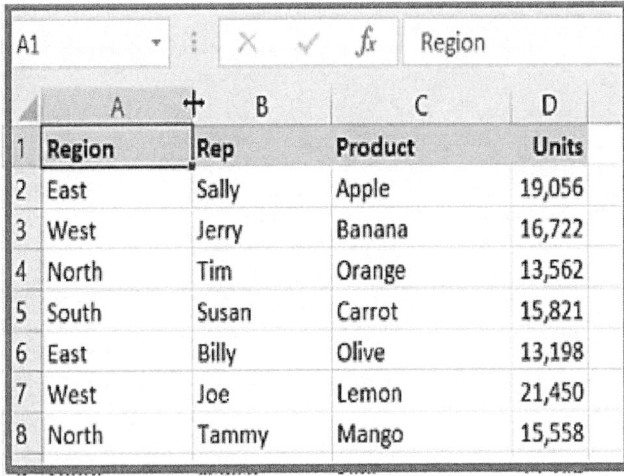

b. Then double-click it, immediately it will readjust the size of the column width to fit the data inside the cell in the column selected perfectly.

	A	B	C	D
1	Region	Rep	Product	Units
2	East	Sally	Apple	19,056
3	West	Jerry	Banana	16,722
4	North	Tim	Orange	13,562
5	South	Susan	Carrot	15,821
6	East	Billy	Olive	13,198
7	West	Joe	Lemon	21,450
8	North	Tammy	Mango	15,558
9	South	Nancy	Kiwi	17,146

c. You can as well highlight **multiple columns** and double-click any of them and all the column width in the column will be adjusted.

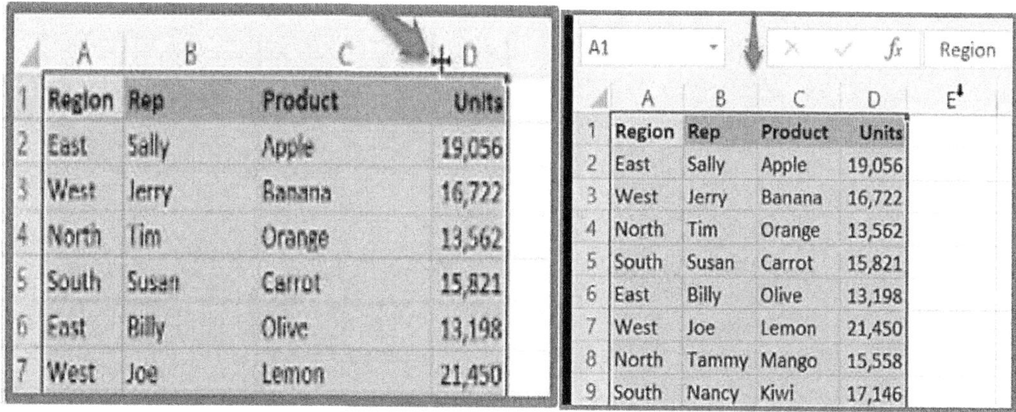

	A	B	C	D
1	Region	Rep	Product	Units
2	East	Sally	Apple	19,056
3	West	Jerry	Banana	16,722
4	North	Tim	Orange	13,562
5	South	Susan	Carrot	15,821
6	East	Billy	Olive	13,198
7	West	Joe	Lemon	21,450

	A	B	C	D
1	Region	Rep	Product	Units
2	East	Sally	Apple	19,056
3	West	Jerry	Banana	16,722
4	North	Tim	Orange	13,562
5	South	Susan	Carrot	15,821
6	East	Billy	Olive	13,198
7	West	Joe	Lemon	21,450
8	North	Tammy	Mango	15,558
9	South	Nancy	Kiwi	17,146

XLOOKUP Function

XLOOKUP is a powerful new function design to replace HLOOKUP and VLOOKUP. Take for instance:

a. We want to look up the name of John in this table and return a value from the February column.
b. You can quickly use **XLOOKUP** and the first element in this LOOKUP value is **John,** the array through which we are going to look up John's name in this area is the John row and we want to return the value from the February column.

=XLOOKUP(A2,A5:A12,E5:E12

	A	B	C	D	E	F	G
1	Name	Month	Amount				
2	John	Feb	=XLOOKUP(A2,A5:A12,E5:E12				
3			XLOOKUP(lookup_value, lookup_array, **return_array**, [if_not_found], [match_mo				
4	Name	Region	Discount	Jan	Feb	Mar	Apr
5	Jim	Region 1	55%	34,533	36,998	31,097	33,439
6	Karen	Region 2	60%	16,588	17,834	19,832	17,309
7	Sally	Region 3	45%	22,793	28,391	22,454	26,749
8	John	Region 4	65%	17,498	17,232	18,767	19,200
9	Jim	Region 5	45%	22,007	21,233	23,984	24,943
10	Sally	Region 6	40%	36,558	35,890	34,210	36,722
11	Karen	Region 7	55%	29,823	29,432	29,656	28,997

c. You will see the result it returns is **17232**, which is the meeting point of **John and February.**

C3

	A	B	C	D	E	F	G	H	I
1	Name	Month	Amount						
2	John	Feb	17,232						
3									
4	Name	Region	Discount	Jan	Feb	Mar	Apr	May	Jun
5	Jim	Region 1	55%	34,533	36,998	31,097	33,439	37,876	29,57
6	Karen	Region 2	60%	16,588	17,834	19,832	17,309	18,085	19,13
7	Sally	Region 3	45%	22,793	28,391	22,454	26,749	28,845	26,99
8	John	Region 4	65%	17,498	17,232	18,767	19,200	20,921	19,63
9	Jim	Region 5	45%	22,007	21,233	23,984	24,943	23,278	22,79
10	Sally	Region 6	40%	36,558	35,890	34,210	36,722	37,646	35,21
11	Karen	Region 7	55%	29,823	29,432	29,656	28,997	29,041	28,87
12	Jim	Region 8	50%	30,678	30,943	31,298	31,884	32,190	32,39

Note: XLOOKUP has one merit and that merit is that it can perform horizontal XLOOKUP as well, let's say we want to lookup February in this list, we are going to return the value from John and it will be the same number **17232**, in the February column next to John.

D8 =XLOOKUP(B2,D4:I4,D8:I8

	A	B	C	D	E	F	G	H	I
1	Name	Month	Amount						
2	John	Feb	=XLOOKUP(B2,D4:I4,D8:I8						
3			XLOOKUP(lookup_value, lookup_array, **return_array**, [if_not_found], [match_mode], [search_mode])						
4	Name	Region	Discount	Jan	Feb	Mar	Apr	May	Jun
5	Jim	Region 1	55%	34,533	36,998	31,097	33,439	37,876	29,578
6	Karen	Region 2	60%	16,588	17,834	19,832	17,309	18,085	19,138
7	Sally	Region 3	45%	22,793	28,391	22,454	26,749	28,845	26,992
8	John	Region 4	65%	17,498	17,232	18,767	19,200	20,921	19,630
9	Jim	Region 5	45%	22,007	21,233	23,984	24,943	23,278	22,790
10	Sally	Region 6	40%	36,558	35,890	34,210	36,722	37,646	35,212
11	Karen	Region 7	55%	29,823	29,432	29,656	28,997	29,041	28,871
12	[illegible]	[illegible]	[illegible]	[illegible]	[illegible]	[illegible]	[illegible]	[illegible]	[illegible]

Remove BLANK

You may have multiple blank cells in a list of a given data; it will not be wise to remove them one by one. To remove multiple blank cells, kindly:

a. Highlight the **total list** of the data.
b. Navigate to the **Home** tab and select the **Find & Select** option from the home tab, then select "**Go to special"** from the drop-down list to open the "Go to special" dialog box.

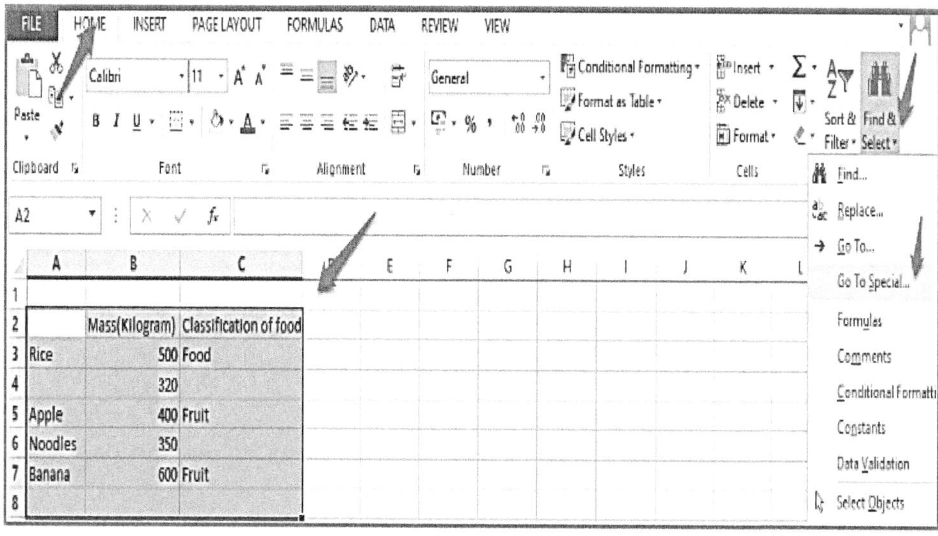

c. Pick **Blank** from the box and tap **ok,** immediately, Excel will highlight all the blank cells in the list.

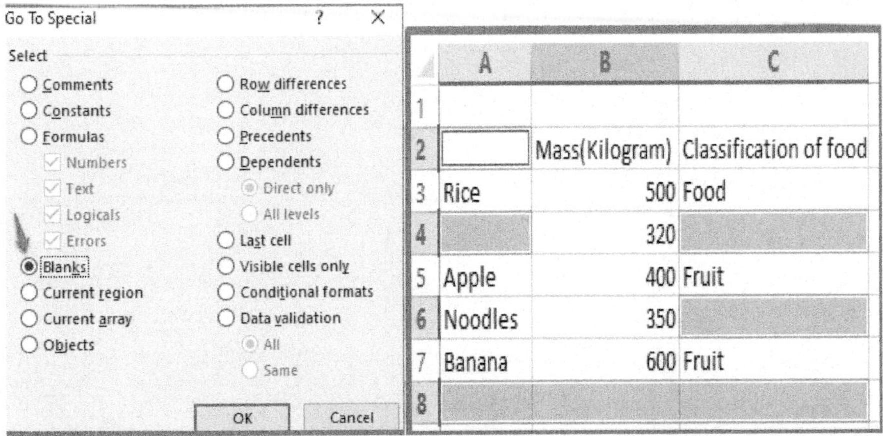

d. Simply right-click on any of the blank cells highlighted, then select **delete** from the drop-down list.

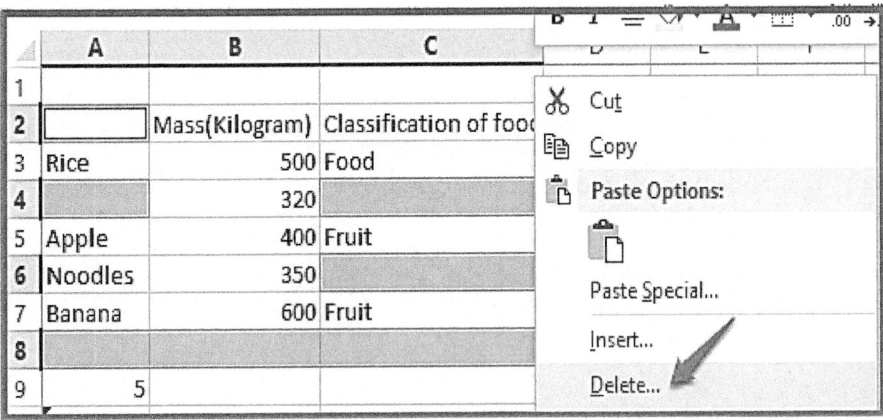

e. You can now pick the **"Shift cells left"** option from the dialog box and tap **Ok**, instantly, all the blank cells will be cleaned up.

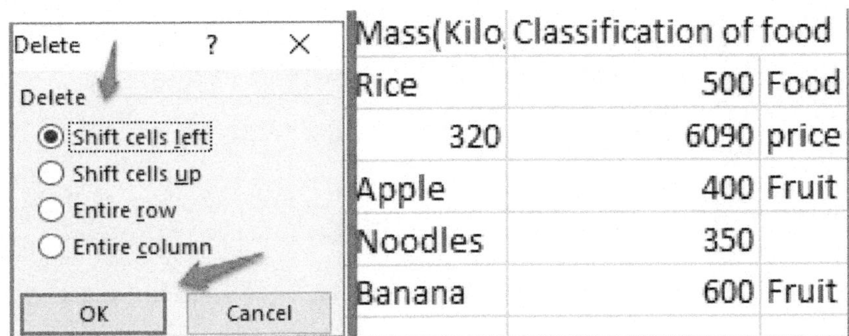

CONCLUSION

Excel 365 has been the talk of the whole world, not because Excel is just a spreadsheet program employed in recording and analyzing various data, but it has also been tested to be beneficial with its new features and updates for everyday business activities.

The idea of Excel 365 is to make Excel an essential part of business enterprises, and as a result of its best techniques used in analyzing various business issues, Excel has been the most used program in every office.

At this point, you will agree with me, that the method and technique analyses used inside this user guide as Excel 365 is capable of managing and analyzing every data and brings it under control, even if it is so large.

I so much believe you must have familiarized yourself with the formulation of formulas and functions that are necessary for executing data, including the techniques for coordinating and regulating data. I hope those techniques will give you a better chance of managing your lists of data and even extract the basic and most important information from the list of data within a given shortest period.

I must confess to you, that the major aim of the user guide is to give you an overview of Excel tools and functions which as improved over time in running our day-to-day Excel operation.

I hereby, wish you the very best of luck as you journey through the era of Excel 365, an online-based version.

INDEX

D

E

F

G

H

I

J

K

L

M

N

O

P

Q

R

S

T

U

V

W

Z

Was this book helpful to you?
Are you pleased with the contents of this book?

We would love to hear from you, please kindly leave a review after buying/reading this book. Thanks

Printed in Great Britain
by Amazon